INTRODUCTION TO QUALITATIVE METHODS
IN PSYCHOLOGY

INTRODUCTION TO QUALITATIVE METHODS IN PSYCHOLOGY

Third Edition

Dennis Howitt

Loughborough University

PEARSON

Harlow, England • London • New York • Boston • San Francisco • Toronto • Sydney • Auckland • Singapore • Hong Kong
Tokyo • Seoul • Taipei • New Delhi • Cape Town • São Paulo • Mexico City • Madrid • Amsterdam • Munich • Paris • Milan

Pearson Education Limited
Edinburgh Gate
Harlow CM20 2JE
United Kingdom
Tel: +44 (0)1279 623623
www.pearson.com/uk

First published 2010 (print)
Second edition published 2013 (print and electronic)
Third edition published 2016 (print and electronic)

© Pearson Education Limited 2010 (print)
© Pearson Education Limited 2013 (print and electronic)
© Pearson Education Limited 2016 (print and electronic)

ISBN: 978-1-292-08299-8 (print)
        978-1-292-08303-2 (PDF)
        978-1-292-13333-1 (ePub)

British Library Cataloguing-in-Publication Data
A catalogue record for the print edition is available from the British Library

Library of Congress Cataloging-in-Publication Data
A catalog record for the print edition is available from the Library of Congress

10 9 8 7 6 5 4 3 2
20 19 18 17

Cover: Cover image © Andy Ryan/Getty Images

Print edition typeset in 10/12.5 pt Sabon by Lumina Datamatics
Print edition printed in Malaysia (CTP-PJB)

NOTE THAT ANY PAGE CROSS REFERENCES REFER TO THE PRINT EDITION

BRIEF CONTENTS

CONTENTS

PREFACE

Before the 1980s mainstream psychology was a quantitative monolith smothering all other approaches to psychology, or so the story goes. Around this time, qualitative methods began to emerge in force and they have grown in strength. This is not entirely a fiction but it is a creation myth rather than a precise and historically accurate account of the dark days before qualitative psychology. Probably my experience is a little different from that of most psychologists. At the end of my first year as a psychology student I was sent for six months to the factory floor (and eventually the personnel offices) of Morganite Carbon which was then in Battersea, London. The reason? Essentially to experience life as a factory worker and to write a project on my experiences. In other words, *participant observation* or *ethnography* – and the experience of real life. At the end of every couple of terms we were sent to other locations. I spent six months at the prison in Wakefield and another six months at St George's Hospital, London. At Wakefield, I did my first study of sex offenders (possibly the first ever study by a psychologist of sex offenders in the United Kingdom). This was an interest which was to resurface years later with my studies of sexual abuse and paedophiles. At St George's Hospital my colleagues included Fay Fransella, an important figure in the field of George Kelly's *personal construct theory* – an early precursor of social constructionist approaches in qualitative psychology. Indeed, I attended the first conference on personal construct theory while at Brunel University and, I am assured though cannot vouchsafe it, was in the presence of George Kelly himself. Actually we got rather a lot of personal construct theory.

At Brunel, I remember being fascinated by the sessions on psychoanalysis given to us by Professor Elliot Jacques. Not only was Jacques famous at the time as an organisational psychologist bringing psychoanalytic ideas to industry but he was the originator of the concept of the midlife crisis! However, the key influence on any psychology student who studied at Brunel University at that time was Marie Jahoda. Ideas and questions were what counted for Marie Jahoda. She had worked with or knew anyone who was important in the social sciences at large. Sigmund Freud was a friend of her family. She would speak of 'Robert' in lectures – this was Robert Merton, the great theorist of sociology. She had worked with and had been married to Paul Lazarsfeld, the great methodologist of sociology. And she had been involved in some of the most innovatory research in psychology – the Marienthal unemployment study. The 'problem' – meaning the intellectual task – was key to doing research. The ways of collecting data merely followed, they did not lead; analysis was a way of life. I have a recollection of Ernest Dichter, who figures in the discussion of market research, talking to us about apples – what else. I followed Marie Jahoda to The University of Sussex and remember the visit of the methodologist of psychology Donald Campbell. My seat was the one next to him. Exciting times.

I have never worked in an environment with just a single academic discipline – always there have been sociologists, psychologists and a smattering of others. My first academic job was at the Centre for Mass Communications Research at the University of Leicester. Now it is remarkable just how important the field of mass communications research has been in the development of qualitative research methods. For example, the focus group, participant observation, audience studies, narrative/life histories and so forth either began in that field or were substantially advanced by it. More than anything, it was a field where psychologists and sociologists collectively contributed. Of course, the styles of research varied from the deeply quantitative to the equally deeply qualitative. Different problems called for different methods. I also remember some radical figures visiting, such as Aaron Cicourel, a cognitive sociologist influenced by Erving Goffman and Harold Garfinkel. Cicourel was a pioneer in the use of video in his research. During a seminar in which he agonised over the issues of coding and categorisation I remember asking Cicourel why he did not simply publish his videotapes. There was a several seconds' delay but eventually the reply came. But it still seems to me an interesting issue – that ethnographic methods are the methods of ordinary people so why bother with the researcher?

Paradoxically, I have always been involved in teaching quantitative methods – I was paid to do so as a postgraduate and from then on. Nevertheless, in academic life you are what you teach for some curious reason. The opposition of qualitative and quantitative is not inevitable; many researchers do both. Aaron Cicourel went along a similar route:

> I am NOT opposed to quantification or formalization or modeling, but do not want to pursue quantitative methods that are not commensurate with the research phenomena addressed. (Cicourel interviewed by Andreas Witzel and Günter Mey, 2004, p. 1)

He spent a lot of time as a postgraduate student learning mathematics and quantitative methods:

> . . . if I criticized such methods, I would have to show that my concern about their use was not based on an inability to know and use them, but was due to a genuine interest in finding methods that were congruent or in correspondence with the phenomena we call social interaction and the ethnographic conditions associated with routine language use in informal and formal everyday life settings. (Witzel and Mey, 2004, p. 1)

There is another reason which Cicourel overlooks. Quantitative methods can have a compelling effect on government and general social policy. Being able to speak and write on equal terms with quantitative researchers is important in the type of policy areas upon which my research was based.

By concentrating on the problem, rather than the method, a researcher makes choices which are more to do with getting the best possible answer to the question than getting a particular sort of answer to the question. For that reason, qualitative approaches are just part of my research. However, where the question demands contextualised, detailed data then the method became little more than me, my participants and my recording machine. Some of my favourites among my own research involved just these.

Qualitative methods in psychology are becoming diverse. Nevertheless, there is not quite the spread of different styles of research or *epistemologies* for research that one finds in other disciplines. Ethnographic methods, for example, have not been common in the history of psychology – a situation which persists to date. But discourse analytic approaches, in contrast, have become relatively common. This is not to encourage the adoption of either of these methods (or any other for that matter) unless they help address one's research question. This may not please all qualitative researchers but any *hegemony* in terms of method in psychology to my mind has to be a retrograde step. So this book takes a broad-brush approach to qualitative methods in psychology. First of all, it invites readers to understand better how to gather qualitative data. These are seriously difficult ways of collecting data if properly considered and there is little excuse ever for sloppy and inappropriate data collection methods. They are simply counterproductive. It is all too easy to take the view that an in-depth interview or a focus group is an easy approach to data collection simply because they might appear to involve little other than conversational skills. But one has only to look at some of the transcripts of such data published in journal articles to realise that the researcher has not put on a skilled performance. It needs time, practice, discussion and training to do qualitative data collection well. Secondly, I have covered some very different forms of qualitative data analysis methods in this book. These are not all mutually compatible approaches in every respect. Their roots lie in very different spheres. *Grounded theory* derives from the sociology of the 1960s as does *conversation analysis*. *Discourse analysis* not only has its roots in the ideas of the French philosopher Michel Foucault but also in the sociology of science of the 1970s. *Interpretative phenomenological analysis* is dependent on phenomenology with its roots in philosophy and psychology. *Narrative analysis* has a multitude of roots but primarily in the *narrative psychology* of the 1990s. And *thematic analysis*? Well – it all depends what you mean by thematic analysis as we shall see.

There is an important issue to raise. Perhaps it is best raised by quoting from Kenneth J. Gergen, one of the key original figures in the move towards qualitative methods in psychology. In the following he describes his early experience as a psychological researcher:

> My early training was in scientific psychology, that is, a psychology based on the promise that through the application of empirical methods, sound measures, and statistical analysis we would begin to approach the truth of mental functioning . . . I learned my lessons well, how to produce from the messy confines of laboratory life the kinds of clear and compelling 'facts' acceptable to the professional journals. A few tricks of the trade: pre-test the experimental manipulations so to ensure that the desired effects are obtained; use multiple measures so to ensure that at least one will demonstrate the effects; if the first statistical test doesn't yield a reliable difference, try others that will; if there are subjects who dramatically contradict the desired effect, even the smallest effect can reach significance; be sure to cite early research to express historical depth; cite recent research to demonstrate 'up-to-date' knowledge; do not cite Freud, Jung or any other 'pre-scientific' psychologist; cite the research of scientists who are supported by the findings as they are likely to be asked for evaluations by the journal. Nor was it simply that mastering the craft of research management allowed me to 'generate facts' in the scientific journals; success also meant research grants, reputation, and higher status jobs. (Gergen, 1999, p. 58)

Quite what Gergen hoped to achieve by this 'confession' is difficult to fathom. As a joking pastiche of mainstream psychology it fails to amuse. In writing this book, I hope to share some of the very positive things that qualitative psychologists can achieve and important ideas which can inform the research of all psychologists irrespective of their point of balance on the qualitative – quantitative dimension. Making research better, then, is an important objective of this book – deriding the work of researchers struggling, as we all do, to understand the world they live in is not on my agenda. Research is about knowing in the best way possible – which is not an issue of the general superiority of one method over others.

This book has a modular structure. It is not designed to be read cover to cover but, instead, it can be used as a resource and read in any order as need demands. To this end, the following pedagogic features should be noted:

- There is a glossary covering both the key terms in qualitative analysis in this book and the field of qualitative research in general.
- Most of the chapters have a common structure wherever possible. So the chapters on data collection methods have a common structure and the data analysis chapters have a common structure.
- Material is carefully organised in sections permitting unwanted sections to be ignored, perhaps to be read some time later.
- Each chapter includes a variety of boxes in which key concepts are discussed, examples of relevant studies described, and special topics introduced.
- Each chapter begins with a summary of the major points in the chapter.
- Each chapter ends with recommended resources for further study including books, journal articles and web pages as appropriate.

This third edition provides a welcome opportunity to provide separate chapters for each of the main types of discourse analysis – social constructionist and Foucauldian discourse analysis. Furthermore, examples showing how to write up qualitative research have been provided in the final chapter. These are annotated with comments concerning each of the reports. You should be able to find more problems and issues than have been identified in the text and, of course, your ideas may well be better than mine.

Dennis Howitt

Companion Website

For open-access **student resources** specifically written to complement this textbook and support your learning, please visit **www.pearsoned.co.uk/howitt**

Lecturer Resources

For password-protected online resources tailored to support the use of this textbook in teaching, please visit **www.pearsoned.co.uk/howitt**

ACKNOWLEDGEMENTS

Author's acknowledgements

A lot of people have contributed their talents and skills to turning my manuscript into this highly polished product. My debt to them is enormous and I would like to mention at least some of them:

Lina, Aboujieb (Editor): Lina's stay at Pearson was short but working with her on projects was a pleasure. She contributed a fresh perspective on things.
Kevin Ancient (Design Manager): Kevin did the text design which makes the book so attractively structured.
Kelly Miller (Senior Designer) did the excellent cover design.
Carole Drummond (Senior Project Editor): Carole did amazing work overseeing the progress of the book from manuscript to book.
Jen Hinchcliffe (Proof reader): Jen is a formidable proof reader but helpful in so many ways.
Phyllis Van Reenen (Indexer): A book without an index is hard to use. Phyllis has skilfully produced first class indexes.
Ros Woodward (Copy editor): It is always a joy to work on a manuscript with Ros. She is so good at spotting problems and keeping me on my toes.

The advice of academic colleagues is always welcome. Their advice greatly improved the contents of the book. So I am extremely grateful to the following for their constructive and supportive comments:

Dr Darren Ellis, University of East London
Dr Naomi Ellis, Staffordshire University
Dr Alexandra Lamont, Keele University
Dr Jane Montague, University of Derby
Dr Dennis Nigbur, Canterbury Christ Church University

Finally, the most special of thanks in appreciation of their very special support at a difficult time for me to Carole Drummond, Dr Jane Montague and Janey Webb (Publisher).

Dennis Howitt

Publisher's acknowledgements

We are grateful to the following for permission to reproduce copyright material:

Text

Sage Journals for extract (on page 145) from 'Mothers, single women and sluts: gender, morality and membership', Feminism and Psychology, 13(3), 326 (Stokoe, E.H., 2003.

Figure

Routledge/Taylor & Francis (for Figure 8.3) Strandmark and Hallberg's model of the process of rejection and expulsion from the workplace from 'Being rejected and expelled from the workplace: experiences of bullying in the public service sector', Qualitative Research in Psychology, 4(1-2), 1-14 (Strandmark, M. and Hallberg, L.R-M., 2007).

PART 1

Background to qualitative methods in psychology

Qualitative methods have gained ground in psychology in recent years. It is common to suggest that, for the most part, the growth of qualitative psychology began in the 1980s at the earliest. This means that qualitative methods fared poorly in the early years of psychology. Qualitative methods had found popularity in the field of marketing psychology somewhat earlier (Bailey, 2014). Nevertheless, for social psychology, health psychology, psychotherapy and counselling psychology, among others, the 1980s marked the start of the period of growth. At this time, theoretically based and philosophical approaches to qualitative psychology began to be developed in some force. They were also practicable and applicable. Despite this, there is a much longer qualitative tradition which needs to be acknowledged. Without doubt, though, mainstream psychology overall has been a predominantly quantitative discipline for much of its history and is likely to remain so into the foreseeable future. Mainstream psychology justifies the description 'quantitative' in just about every respect. Throughout the history of psychology, numbers and counting have been paramount. Despite this, from time to time, qualitative approaches have made a significant impact on psychology. Indeed, qualitative methods hark back to the dawn of modern psychology in the late nineteenth century. Qualitative research was generally somewhat fragmentary and scarcely amounted to a qualitative tradition in psychology.

Surprisingly, qualitative methods in psychology have involved such major figures as Frederic Bartlett, Alfred Binet, John Dollard, Leon Festinger, Anna Freud, Sigmund Freud, Carol Gilligan, Karen Horney, William James, Carl Jung, Laurence Kohlberg, Kurt Lewin, Abraham Maslow, Jean Piaget, David Rosenhan, Stanley Schacter, Wilhelm Stern, E.B. Titchener, Lev Vygotsky, John Watson, Max Wertheimer and Philip Zimbardo according to Wertz (2014). And there are more. Some are primarily regarded as quantitative researchers but nevertheless included qualitative approaches in their research output. A notable feature of the list is the number of psychologists of European origin given America's traditional dominance in psychology. There are good reasons for this as we shall see. Furthermore, again according to Wertz, it is notable that two psychologists have been awarded Nobel prizes (in Economics) for their work. These are Herbert Simon and Daniel Kahneman. Their prize-winning research was based on verbal descriptions and qualitative analyses of everyday problem solving. From this they developed mathematical models.

So there is nothing incompatible between the adoption of qualitative methods in psychology and research success in psychology.

The usual explanation of the dominance of quantitative methods in psychology is that the discipline sought to emulate the achievements of the natural sciences – particularly physics. What is perhaps a little more difficult to explain is why psychology resisted the move to qualitative research so steadfastly despite changes in closely related disciplines such as sociology and anthropology. Just why psychology has been perversely antagonistic to qualitative methods in its past needs explanation. The two chapters which constitute Part 1 of this book have the following major objectives:

- To provide a broad understanding of how qualitative psychology differs from quantitative psychology.
- To provide a review of the history of psychology which explains just why qualitative methods emerged so slowly in most of psychology compared to related disciplines.
- To provide a picture of the development of qualitative psychology from within the discipline, under the influence of related disciplines such as sociology and, as a consequence, of some disillusionment with the methods of mainstream psychology.

The philosophical (epistemological) foundations of qualitative psychology are very different from those of quantitative psychology. Psychology has been so resolutely quantitative that many psychologists may experience something of a culture shock when first exposed to qualitative methods. In that sense qualitative and quantitative research can be seen as two different cultures. Some newcomers may well find their appetites whetted for new research challenges. Qualitative psychology rejects, questions and even turns on its head much which is held sacrosanct by mainstream psychologists.

To date, histories of qualitative research in psychology tend to be fragmentary and, at best, incomplete. They are partial histories – partial in both meanings of the word. Histories of psychology usually take a broad sweep approach so that undervalued research is lost to future scholars. Re-examining the vast backlog of psychological research and theory seeking qualitative work is a major undertaking. Different histories have different starting and end points. For American historians of psychology the starting point is often the work of William James – a likely starting point of virtually any American history of modern psychology (Howitt, 1991). For some qualitative psychologists the story barely pre-dates the 1980s. Each of these is discussed in more detail later. Histories, like most accounts, tend to be self-serving in some way. Furthermore, it has to be remembered that even within the field of qualitative psychology different interest groups vie for dominance. Qualitative methods are not necessarily any more compatible with each other than they are with mainstream psychology.

Just what are the characteristics of mainstream psychology? Qualitative psychologists often allude to the idea that mainstream psychology smothered qualitative psychology due to its foundations in *positivism*. Positivism is essentially a description of the assumptions and characteristics of the natural sciences such as physics and chemistry. For example, these sciences are characterised by the search for universal laws, quantification and empirical investigation. It is often argued by qualitative researchers that psychology rushed to adopt the model of science offered by physics to the detriment of psychology. Through numerous repetitions this sort of claim has become accepted as the truth. However, it is questionable, as we shall see, whether qualitative approaches to psychology are truly anathema to positivism. So use of the term positivism should be somewhat guarded. What does seem clear though is that the majority of psychologists for most of the history of modern psychology adopted research practices based on quantification.

There are good reasons why psychologists emulated an idiosyncratic version of the natural science approach. It hardly has to be said that science had achieved remarkable success in the nineteenth century, especially physics. Similar successes would ensure the future of the fledgling discipline of psychology. So psychology stole from the natural sciences things like experimentation, universalism, measurement and *reductionist* thinking and clung to them even when the natural sciences did not. What psychology failed to take on board were the more observational methods characteristic of other scientific disciplines such as biology and astronomy. Some closely related disciplines such as sociology were in the long term less handicapped by the strictures of positivism, although not entirely so. Sociology, however, turned to qualitative methods rather sooner. Nevertheless, only in the 1950s and 1960s did qualitative methods develop sufficiently in sociology to effectively challenge the supremacy of quantitative methods. So the positivistic orientation that dominated psychology cannot alone account for the late emergence of qualitative methods in that discipline. It took psychology at least three decades to catch up with the qualitative upsurge in sociology from which it adopted several qualitative approaches from the 1980s onwards. In other words, psychology was in the grip of positivism for longer than related disciplines. The explanation is probably simple – positivistic psychology was able to service many of the areas which the State was responsible for as well as commercial interests. We only have to consider clinical psychology, educational psychology, forensic psychology, prison psychology, marketing psychology and industrial psychology to see this. Positivism helped psychology to expand in universities and elsewhere in a way that simply did not happen for closely related disciplines (with the possible exception of criminology within sociology).

So a form of positivism did dominate for a long time in the history of modern psychology but not entirely to the exclusion of everything else. The idea of qualitative psychology being repressed by but eventually overcoming the dragon of positivism is a heroic view of the history of qualitative psychology but not entirely correct. One only has to consider how familiar the work of psychologists such as Piaget, Kohlberg and Maslow has been to generations of psychologists to realise that the story is somewhat more complex. Attributing the late emergence of qualitative psychology to the stifling influence of positivism amounts to a 'creation myth' of qualitative psychology rather than a totally convincing explanation. But numbers and measurement have dominated and still do dominate psychology for most of its modern history. Critics have frequently pointed to the failings of mainstream psychology but have never effectively delivered a knockout blow. Some psychologists freed themselves from the straitjacket of mainstream psychology often with great effect. They never, however, managed to effect a major and permanent change. There would be changes in the hot topics of psychology and some measuring instruments replaced others as dish of the day but, in the end, if one got the measurements and numbers right then science and psychology was being done. But we have now reached a stage where it is freely questioned whether mainstream psychology's way of doing things is the only way or the right way. This is important as it ensures that more attention is being paid to the philosophical/epistemological basis of the parent discipline. Method rather than detailed procedures have to be justified in qualitative research in a way that they rarely, if ever, were in quantitative psychology. Quantitative researchers had no such need for self-justification. The positivist philosophy underlying their work is built into the discipline, adopted usually unquestioningly, and to all intents and purposes is largely still taught as if it were the natural and unchallengeable way of doing psychology. Few outside qualitative psychology question the importance of reliability and validity checks for example. All of these things and more are questioned when it comes to qualitative psychology. Any textbook on qualitative methods has to go into detail about the epistemological foundations of the method employed. Still, after qualitative methods have become increasingly accepted in journals, qualitative journal articles frequently enter some form of philosophical discussion about the methods employed.

One problem for newcomers to qualitative research is that qualitative research methods vary enormously among themselves. Most have complex epistemological foundations whereas some, especially thematic analysis, lack any substantial epistemological roots. Therefore, although qualitative research is clearly different from quantitative research, so too are many of the qualitative methods different from or even alien to each other. A practical implication of this is that qualitative researchers need to understand these matters to carry out their work.

Merely dismissing mainstream quantitative psychology because of its weaknesses is no way forward since, like it or not, quantitative research has provided an effective and rewarding model for doing at least some kinds of psychology. It is a very bad way of answering some sorts of research questions and makes other research questions just about impossible to address. Nevertheless, mainstream psychology has achieved an influential position in the institutions of the State because it is seen as doing some things right. This proven track record is undeniable in fields such as mental health, medicine, education, work, consumer behaviour, sport, training and so forth even if one wishes to challenge the nature of these achievements. But psychology could be better and qualitative psychologists have identified many of its weaknesses and vulnerabilities. Histories of psychology are written with hind-sight and read with hindsight. It is impossible – albeit desirable – to understand historical events as they were experienced. So the story of qualitative psychology that can be written at this time suffers from our incomplete perspective on what psychology was like in the past – as a discipline and institution as well as a corpus of knowledge. Neither are we sure where qualitative research is heading so the end points of our histories is unclear.

We should, then, not simply overlook non-intellectual reasons why qualitative psychology emerged any more than we should overlook them in terms of the mainstream discipline. For example, the numbers of psychology students graduating today are massive compared with the early days of the discipline or even 30 years ago. Furthermore, psychological research was once almost entirely based in university departments. Over the decades, research by practitioners in non-university settings has greatly increased as the practical fields of psychology have increasingly adopted a knowledge-based approach. Academic research would need to be more socially contextualised and probing if it were to be of immediate use to practitioners. It may well have been easy to patrol psychology to promote quantitative approaches when modern psychology was in its infancy. With the expansion in the numbers of psychologists which increased enormously following the Second World War, this sort of control inevitably, if gradually, weakened. The permeation of qualitative methods into health psychology is perhaps an example of these processes at work. Health psychology simply needed the sorts of answers to research questions which qualitative methods provide. Histories of qualitative psychology have not yet begun to seriously address the broader context of psychological research as a stimulus to qualitative research in psychology. Increases in the number of psychological personnel, especially given the growth in practitioner research, may have allowed the changes which fuelled the expansion of qualitative methods in psychology. Other fields of psychology, besides qualitative methods, began to flourish in the 1980s and 1990s – these include largely non-qualitative sub-fields of psychology such as forensic psychology. Forensic psychology had lain largely dormant from the early 1900s only to begin to prosper in the 1980s – exactly the same time that some researchers see qualitative methods emerging with some force in psychology. The point is, of course, that as psychology approached a critical mass and developed an increasingly diverse organisational structure, it gained greater potential to embrace a wider variety of interests. Indeed, some might say that the critical mass encouraged these changes.

Chapter 1 concentrates on two things:

- Describing the essential characteristics of qualitative methods in psychology.
- Discussing the origins of quantification in psychology, including statistical thinking.

The chapter demonstrates something of the subtlety of the philosophical underpin-nings of the quantitative–qualitative debate.

Chapter 2 looks at the varied contributions of an essentially qualitative nature that psychologists have made throughout the discipline's history. At the same time, the chapter tries to explain the roots of these approaches in psychology and related disciplines. The following seem clear:

- Qualitative approaches have been part of psychology throughout its modern history though numerically in a minor way.
- Many of the early examples of qualitative research in psychology have become 'classics' but it is hard to find a clear legacy of many of them in the history of modern psychology.
- Most of the early examples of qualitative research in psychology involve distinctly qualitative data collection methods although distinct and frequently used methods of qualitative data analysis did not really emerge until the 1950s and 1960s in related disciplines and, probably, not until the 1980s in psychology.
- Qualitative psychology has developed a basis in the institutions of psychology (learned societies, conferences, specialised journals, etc.) which largely eluded it in its early history.

CHAPTER 1

What is qualitative research in psychology and was it really hidden?

Overview

- The evidence is that qualitative research in psychology has emerged as an important but minority focus in psychology during the last 30 or 40 years. This progress has not been spread evenly geographically or in terms of the sub-fields of psychology. Although there is a long history of qualitative methods in psychology, it is mainly since the 1980s that qualitative methods are generally acknowledged to have made significant inroads. However, the story is not the same in every sub-field of psychology.

- Among the distinguishing features of most qualitative research is the preference for data rich in description, the belief that reality is constructed socially, and that research is about interpretation and not about hypothesis testing, for example.

- Psychology has historically constructed itself as a science but, then, largely identified the characteristics of science in terms of numbers and quantification which, arguably, are not essential features of science.

- Positivism (the way physical science is/was seen to be done) has frequently been blamed for the distorted nature of psychology's conception of science. This, however, tends to overlook that both Comte's positivism and logical positivism were more conducive to qualitative methods than mainstream practitioners of psychology ever permitted.

- The dominant psychologies since the 'birth' of psychology in the 1870s have been introspectionism, behaviourism and cognitivism.

- The 'quantitative imperative' in psychology has ancient roots in psychology and first emerges in the work of Pythagoras. The imperative involves the belief that science is about quantification. Early psychologists, with their eyes cast firmly in the direction of physics as the best model to follow, imbued modern psychology with the spirit of quantification from the start.

- Statistical methods, although part of the ethos of quantification, were largely fairly late introductions into psychology. That is, psychology was dominated by quantification long before statistical analysis became central to much research.

- Quantification in psychology, including statistical methods, provided part of a highly successful 'shop front' for psychology which served it particularly well in the market for research monies that developed in the United States especially in the second half of the twentieth century.

What is qualitative research?

According to Smith (2008), 'We are witnessing an explosion of interest in qualitative psychology. This is a significant shift in a discipline which has hitherto emphasized the importance of quantitative psychology' (p. 1). More extravagantly it has been written: 'qualitative inquiry has now been seated at the table of the discipline, representing perhaps a paradigm shift – or at least a pendular swing – within psychology' (Josselson, 2014, p. 1). Augoustinos and Tileaga (2012) are in no doubt that the introduction of the qualitative method of discourse analysis into social psychology in the 1980s amounted to a paradigm shift, though they do not explain precisely what they mean by this. A discipline may incorporate new paradigms without older paradigms being toppled. The history of qualitative research in psychology is somewhat enigmatic but there is a history nonetheless. Even since the first edition of this book, it has become clear that various forms of qualitative psychology have gained rather more than a toe-hold in the discipline of psychology. The situation varies geographically but education and training in qualitative methods is at last seemingly common among psychology programmes in some parts. In the UK, for example, few psychology students fail to achieve such training (Parker, 2014) and doubtless fewer will in future. It is no longer possible to ignore qualitative methods in psychology. This does not signal the imminent or eventual demise of mainstream psychology. Mainstream psychology has achieved a great deal of worth despite its flaws. Qualitative research is not the best answer in every case to every sort of research question any more than quantitative research is. Of course, psychology can benefit by incorporating new ways of doing research but mainstream psychology has prospered and no doubt will continue to prosper into the foreseeable future. Psychological research in general has greatly expanded over time and this is likely to continue with the expansion of the knowledge-based society. Researchers need to be increasingly sophisticated as new demands are placed on the discipline for research to guide practice and to inform change. Qualitative methods are decidedly part of the future of psychology and they may become increasingly integrated with other forms of methodology. The customers for psychological research have become increasingly sophisticated about research and more inclined to demand innovation in the methodologies employed. Developments may seem slower in some countries than others but the impression is that it is only a matter of time before they will catch up. We may expect that the research careers of many psychologists in the future will show movement to and from qualitative and quantitative research as well as mixed research. Some may doggedly remain quantitative researchers and others, equally, tie themselves solely to qualitative approaches.

Definitions are never easy in psychology. Even granted this, identifying precisely what constitutes qualitative research in psychology is difficult. One reason for this is the heterogeneous nature of qualitative methods. They are not a single method, they do not all share the same objectives, they have different epistemological foundations, they differ in terms of what is considered important, and they have different roots in psychology and other social sciences. These are complex issues but they need to be understood. Of course, for some students, at least, things can be put simply – qualitative research equates to freedom from the tyranny of numbers and statistics which they feel mars their psychology studies. Unfortunately, qualitative research defined as the absence of numbers does not get us very far, though it may be what attracts some to qualitative research. Qualitative research is impossible to define by a single characteristic like this. Qualitative methods tend to draw from a similar set of assumptions and characteristics, although the same ones are not always equally important to every qualitative method. Sometimes a method may reject key features of other qualitative methods. That is, there is a pool of qualitative characteristics which do not apply always to every qualitative method but there is a substantial degree of overlap across methods. There are studies which may lack numbers but in all other respects are no different from the typical positivistic mainstream psychology study. For example, if the study assumes that its findings are universally applicable or presupposes the analytic categories to be employed then this study is quantitative in nature rather than qualitative – no matter how much the absence of numbers may please students, the fundamental assumptions of qualitative methodology have been violated. So the idea of qualitative research being entirely a statistics-free zone does not effectively distinguish qualitative from quantitative research. Similarly, there are clearly qualitative studies which include at least some numbers and counting or even statistics.

No one characteristic invariably, unassailably and essentially distinguishes qualitative from quantitative methods. Nevertheless, there is a range of things which typify qualitative methods. By no means are all of them characteristic of every type of qualitative research method. The following are the five features which Denzin and Lincoln (2000) list as major defining characteristics of qualitative research:

1. ***Concern with the richness of description*** Qualitative researchers value data which is rich in its descriptive attributes. So they tend to favour data collection methods which obtain detailed, descriptive data such as that produced by using in-depth interviewing methods, focus groups and the taking of detailed field notes. This sort of data is often referred to as thick description. In contrast, perhaps a little stereotypically, quantitative researchers obtain much more restricted and structured information from their research participants. This is inevitably the case when simple rating scales or multiple choice questionnaire methods are used. Concern with the richness of description may be a characteristic of a qualitative method such as interpretative phenomenological analysis (see Chapter 12) but it is difficult to apply as a characteristic of conversation analysis (see Chapter 10). Nevertheless, it is clear that the typical mainstream psychological study fails to collect rich data for analysis preferring to employ rather cryptic questionnaires instead.

2. ***Capturing the individual's perspective*** Qualitative methods emphasise the perspective of the individual and their individuality. The use of rich data-gathering methods such as the in-depth interview and focus groups encourages this emphasis on the individual's perspective. Quantitative researchers, to the extent that they deal with individuals, will tend to focus on comparisons of people on some sort of abstract dimension such as a personality dimension. Again this is not typically a feature of conversation analysis as a qualitative method.

3. *The rejection of positivism and the use of postmodern perspectives* Qualitative researchers tend to reject *positivist* approaches (i.e. those based on a conventional view of what science is – or *scientism*) though qualitative and quantitative researchers both rely on gathering empirical evidence which is an important feature of positivism. Quantitative researchers tend to retain the view that reality can be known despite the problems involved in knowing it. For example, the quantitative researcher mostly uses language data as if such data directly represent reality (i.e. the data refer to some sort of reality) whereas most modern qualitative researchers take the view that language may be a window onto reality but cannot represent reality. The post-positivist view argues that, irrespective of whether or not there is truly a real world, a researcher's knowledge of that reality can only be approximate and that there are multiple versions of reality. In qualitative research, relatively few researchers believe that the purpose of research is the creation of generalisable knowledge. This is a major objective of quantitative research, of course, and quantitative researchers are inclined to make generalisations on the basis of limited data – sometimes as if universally applicable principles have been identified. Positivism is discussed in detail in Box 1.1 and pages 8–9 of this chapter.

4. *Adherence to the postmodern sensibility* The *postmodern* sensibility, for example, reveals itself in the way that qualitative researchers are much more likely to use methods which get them close to the real-life experiences of people (in-depth interviews are an instance of this). Quantitative researchers are often content with a degree of artificiality such as that arising from the use of laboratory studies. Verisimilitude seems much more important to qualitative researchers as a whole and less so to many quantitative researchers in psychology. Qualitative researchers are often portrayed as having a caring ethic in their research and they may undertake 'political' action

Box 1.1

KEY CONCEPT

Auguste Comte's positivism

Perhaps more important than the notion of science in critiques of mainstream psychology are the numerous references to 'positivism'. Indeed, the terms positivism and positivist appear to be pejorative terms when used by qualitative researchers. Better to use a four-letter word than either of these. Given that positivism is not easily defined and that it is used as an 'emotive term' (Silverman, 1997, p. 12), its popularity as an abusive epithet may reveal a lack of understanding rather than an insightful analysis. Nevertheless, the term positivism refers to a major epistemological position in psychology and other related disciplines. Epistemology means the study of knowledge and is concerned with (a) how we can go about knowing things and (b) the validation of

knowledge (the value of what we know). Positivism is a philosophy of science which had its historical beginnings in the Enlightenment. This is the important historical period which dominated the eighteenth century in European thinking. The idea of positivism was systematised in the work of Auguste Comte (1798–1857) in France – he is also credited with coining the term *sociologie* or sociology (it was previously social physics!).

In his writings, Comte proposed a social progression which he referred to as the *law of three phases* to describe the process of social evolution. The phases are the theological, the metaphysical and the scientific (Figure 1.1). Importantly, the scientific phase was also named by Comte the positive phase – hence the close

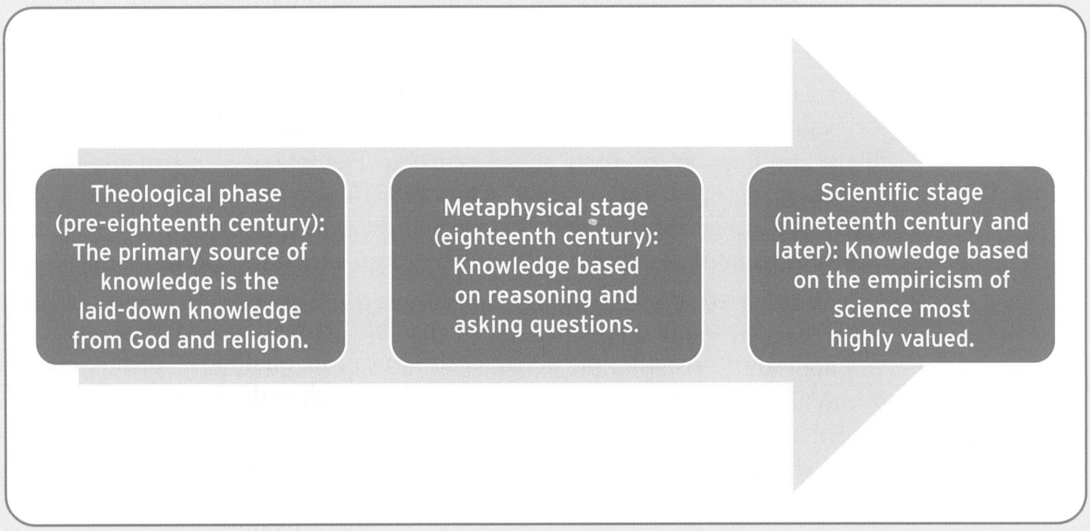

FIGURE 1.1 Comte's stages of social evolution

link to this day between the terms science and positivism. The theological phase is the earliest and in which, essentially, knowledge about society was achieved through reference to God and religion. Religion is a major factor in the continuity of people's beliefs so that people's beliefs in the theological phase are the ones that their ancestors previously held. The metaphysical phase is also known as the stage of investigation as it involved reasoning and the asking of questions rather than the reference to established theological given-knowledge. This phase is based on the idea that there are human rights beyond ones which could be countermanded by any human. The scientific phase involved ways of bringing change to society which are not based on theological arguments or human rights. Science was capable of answering the questions which society needed answers to. Historically, it is easy to see theism (belief in God as a source of knowledge in this context) as characterising Western societies such as France for most of their existence and the metaphysical stage as reflecting the period of the Enlightenment. Since then, society has been in the scientific period.

In Auguste Comte's writings, observable and observed facts have an important role in the accumulation of valid knowledge. So it is easy to see how 'positivistic' describes the mainstream of psychological research. Nevertheless, this orientation is also shared by qualitative researchers for the most part. So observable and observed 'facts' do not differentiate qualitative from quantitative research. Despite everything, Comte did not believe that quantification, if by quantification we mean mathematical analysis, was a realistic possibility beyond the physical sciences. We should be 'abstaining from introducing

considerations of quantities, and mathematical laws, which is beyond our power to apply' (Comte, 1975, p. 112). This quite clearly indicates that Comte's positivism was not antagonistic to qualitative research. Quite the reverse – he was against what qualitative researchers also rail against. Beyond the physical sciences such as physics and chemistry, quantification simply had no place and its relevance not assumed. In other words, mainstream psychology adopted a version of science which was not what Comte would have approved for a non-physical science discipline.

The problem with positivism is that it is best seen as a description or model of Victorian physics and chemistry rather than a definition of what should be meant by science. The characteristics which define science rather than the physical sciences alone may then be somewhat different. Josselson (2014), admittedly an advocate of qualitative methods in psychology, offers the following comment:

> science, in its broadest definition and practice, is a sense-making activity. In accord with contemporary philosophy of science, scientific activity – that is, research – is a means of organizing, sifting, and making sense in relation to a phenomenon of interest. In qualitative psychology, our science is a collective effort to understand people in the contexts in which they live and function. Our hope is that the results of our shared work will promote people's well-being. (p. 1)

Such an approach brings together both quantitative and qualitative psychology under the umbrella of scientific psychology.

conjointly with their participants as well as engaging in extensive dialogue with them. The sense of personal responsibility in their interactions with their research participants is often promoted as a feature of qualitative research. Some of these features are particularly evident in feminist (action) research where the objectives of the researcher, for example, are not merely to identify women's experiences but to change the way things are done on the basis of this research. For instance, in feminist research on pornography (e.g. Ciclitira, 2004; Itzin, 1993) researchers and activists have often been indistinguishable (i.e. they are one and the same person). Other good examples of this in feminist research are child abuse, rape, domestic violence and so forth.

5. *Examination of the constraints of everyday life* Some argue that quantitative researchers overlook characteristics of the everyday social world which may have an important bearing on the experiences of their research participants. Qualitative researchers tend to have their feet more firmly planted in this social world, it is argued. So, for instance, in qualitative research reports much greater detail is often found about the lives of individual research participants than would be characteristic of quantitative research reports.

Based even on these criteria, it is readily understood why a simple, definitive acid test is impracticable. Traditional mainstream psychology, though, would struggle to fit any of the headings. Nevertheless, this in itself would justify the view that the above criteria get us somewhere towards understanding just what we mean by qualitative methods. Perhaps we should not be surprised to find that other authorities list different but overlapping characteristics descriptive of qualitative research. Denzin and Lincoln's (2000) list given above has relatively little in common with those of Bryman (1988). Nevertheless, most researchers would feel that the following list from Bryman also does a lot to capture the essence of qualitative and quantitative research methods:

- Quantitative data are regarded as hard and reliable whereas qualitative data are regarded as rich and deep. Traditionally, mainstream psychologists often spoke of hard data as opposed to the more subjective soft data.

- Research strategies in quantitative research tend to be highly structured whereas those of qualitative research are relatively unstructured.

- The social relationship between the researcher and participant is distant in quantitative research but close in qualitative research.

- Quantitative researchers tend to see themselves as outsiders whereas qualitative researchers tend to see themselves as insiders. That is, there is relatively little 'distance' between researcher and participant in qualitative research.

- Quantitative research tends to be about the confirmation of theoretical notions and concepts (as in hypothesis testing) whereas qualitative research is about emerging theory and concepts.

- Research findings in quantitative research tend to be *nomothetic* whereas they tend to be *idiographic* in qualitative research. Nomothetic refers to studying groups or classes of individuals, which leads to generalised explanations, whereas idiographic refers to the study of an individual as an individual.

- In quantitative research, social reality is seen as static and external to the individual whereas in qualitative research social reality is constructed by the individual.

Once again, some approaches to qualitative psychology, however, lack some of these 'defining' characteristics. That is, researchers sometimes mix-and-match the different features of qualitative and quantitative research. Figure 1.2 summarises the major characteristics of qualitative research.

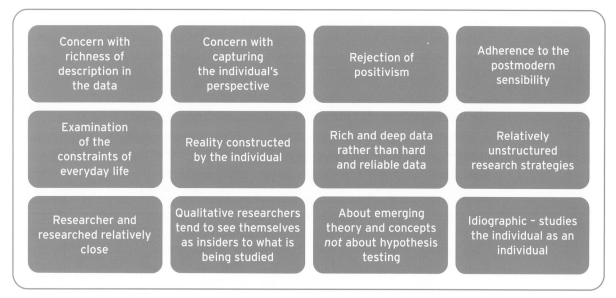

FIGURE 1.2 The major characteristics of qualitative research

Science as normal practice in qualitative and quantitative research

Mainstream psychology usually defines itself as being scientific. The word science has its roots in the Latin *scire*, which means 'to know'. However, science has come to mean a particular way of knowing – what we call the scientific method. Psychology textbooks are replete with claims that psychology is a science. The professional bodies controlling psychology seem to have no qualms about identifying psychology as a science. For example, the British Psychological Society, on its website, announces that 'Psychology is the scientific study of people, the mind and behaviour' (www.bps.org.uk/, accessed 9 February 2015). Similarly the American Psychological Association asserts that 'APA aspires to excel as a valuable, effective and influential organization advancing psychology as a science' (www.apa.org/about/, accessed 9 February 2015). Precisely what this means, in practice, is far harder to pin down. Just how do psychologists construe science? Just what psychology means by science is not clarified anywhere on these websites.

A common accusation is that psychology actually employs an idiosyncratic (if not peculiar) 'received view' of the nature of science. This received view of science can more or less be effectively summarised as follows (Woolgar, 1996, p. 13):

- Objects in the natural world are regarded as objective and real, and they enjoy an existence independent of human beings. Human agency is basically incidental to the objective character of the world 'out there'.

- It follows from this that scientific knowledge is determined by the actual character of the physical world.

- Science comprises a unitary set of methods and procedures, concerning which there is, by and large, a consensus.

- Science is an activity that is individualistic and mentalistic. The latter is sometimes expressed as 'cognitive'.

Woolgar argues that none of the above has survived critical examination by researchers studying the scientific process. That is, psychology's conception of science is flawed – a point which has been echoed repeatedly by qualitative researchers as well as quantitative researchers themselves. Each has been overturned and appears in reverse form as principles in qualitative psychology. The alternative argument is that science is *socially constructed* by human beings:

- who can never directly observe the 'real' world;
- who impose a view of the nature of the world through science;
- who show relatively little consensus as to the appropriate methods and procedures; and
- who act collectively and socially as part of the enterprise of science.

Qualitative researchers commonly refer to the constructivist nature of science as if it is a justification for the qualitative approach to psychological research. Maybe so, but it is questionable whether modern mainstream quantitative researchers, in general, would disagree with this either. Hammersley (1996) paints a picture of the typical researcher as being involved in both qualitative and quantitative research though his viewpoint was from sociology rather than psychology. They make a rational choice between methods to employ in light of the research task in hand. A lot of research cannot readily be classified as one or another of qualitative or quantitative. According to Hammersley:

> It is certainly not the case that there are just two kinds of researcher, one who uses only numbers and another who uses only words. It *is* true that there are research reports that provide only numerical data and others that provide only verbal data, but there is a large proportion of studies that use both. (Hammersley, 1996, p. 161)

Possibly a picture of multitasking qualitative and quantitative researchers is not yet quite so true of psychology as other disciplines. But a glance at a range of psychology journals will show that the use of both within a given study is not unknown.

Nevertheless, the image of researchers able to flit between qualitative and quantitative research methods is a reassuring one. It suggests that the two approaches are, after all, not so far apart. However, one should be careful to consider the implication of this claim. This use of mixed methods (e.g. qualitative and quantitative in the same study) is regarded by some as having substantial benefits. For example, they might use both questionnaires and in-depth interviews in a study. It is less likely, though, that researchers flit between experimental methodology and discourse analysis or conversation analysis. Possibly the gulf is too wide as yet. But it is also the case that researchers are unlikely to incorporate different qualitative data analysis methods into their work as in the case of, say, discourse analysis and interpretative phenomenological analysis (IPA). To clarify, qualitative approaches in psychology include a substantial range of different research activities with very different epistemological foundations. This range includes conversation analysis, discourse analysis, ethnographic studies, focus groups, grounded theory, in-depth interviewing, IPA, narrative analysis, participant observation, phenomenology, and so forth. Their origins and foundations are often very different and so their mutual compatibility simply cannot be assumed.

Importantly, this list includes both qualitative data collection methods (e.g. focus groups) and qualitative data analysis methods (e.g. grounded theory). Distinguishing between the two (data collection and data analysis) is important since qualitative data collection methods are not necessarily followed by qualitative data analysis. In-depth interviews may be analysed qualitatively or quantitatively, for example. This is a mundane but crucial distinction and one which is frequently overlooked. What seems to distinguish recent qualitative research in psychology from the qualitative research

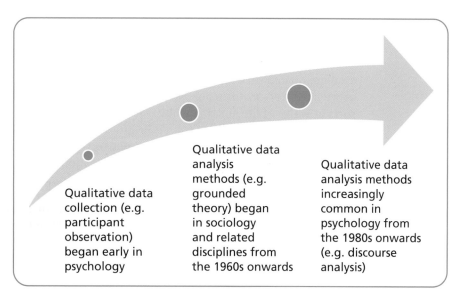

FIGURE 1.3 The relation between the origins of qualitative data collection methods and qualitative data analysis methods

to be found in psychology's historical past is the formulisation of qualitative *analysis* procedures. This is evident in the ready availability of step-by-step instructions in how to go about, say, a discourse analysis to be found in qualitative methods textbooks. Qualitative *data collection* methods such as in-depth interviewing have a long history in psychology; in contrast, qualitative data *analysis* methods are a comparatively recent feature (see Figure 1.3).

According to Hammersley (1996), there is a view among qualitative researchers that qualitative and quantitative research can be regarded as two separate and distinct paradigms for research. The idea of scientific paradigms originated in Thomas Kuhn's book *The structure of scientific revolutions* (1962). Kuhn (1922–1996) argued that science does not progress gradually through a steady accumulation of knowledge. Instead, the process involves revolutionary shifts in the way science looks at its subject matter. A paradigm shift describes when one view becomes untenable and is replaced by something radically different. A paradigm is a sort of worldview – a comprehensive way of looking at things which is more extensive than, say, a theory is. It is a sort of overarching theory which holds together vast swathes of a discipline or the entire discipline itself. So a paradigm shift is a fundamental change in the ways in which scientists view their subject matter. As scientists become aware of anomalies thrown up by the current paradigm then this eventually leads to a crisis in the discipline. Consequently, the development of new ways of understanding becomes crucial. Arguably, perhaps, the move from behaviourism to cognitivism in psychology was a paradigm shift. Kuhn's book was a milestone and particularly notable for promoting the idea that science is socially constructed. Again this is an important view of science for qualitative researchers (not least because some see the replacement of quantitative with qualitative methods in terms of paradigm shift). But be very careful since Kuhn did not write about the social sciences, let alone psychology, in his book. A paradigm shift requires a radical change in the way we go about understanding the world. Simply choosing to study a different aspect of the world does not imply a paradigm shift. So, for example, studying people's responses to painful stimuli under various laboratory conditions (i.e. the mainstream approach) may be perfectly compatible with also studying how people talk about their experience of pain (the qualitative approach). Since both approaches may viably coexist, then one cannot speak of a paradigm shift in this case.

It seems unlikely that we are on the cusp of a paradigm shift in psychology in which a failing quantitative paradigm is being replaced by a newer qualitative one. For one, as we have seen, mainstream psychology is a demonstrably successful enterprise in all sorts of walks of life and in a whole variety of research areas. That could not be taken away overnight. Psychology has never at any point in its modern history been monolithically quantitative in nature – alternative voices have regularly been heard both criticising and offering alternatives to quantification as well as qualitative data-based findings. Although qualitative research was never dominant in the history of psychology, nevertheless qualitative and quantitative research have coexisted and this can be illustrated in various significant research studies throughout psychology's history. The authors of some of this work we have listed earlier. Whether this coexistence has always been one of happy bedfellows is quite a different question.

The beginnings of modern psychology: introspectionism and the founding fathers of psychology

The notion of a founding father of a discipline sits uncomfortably in the pages of a modern textbook. Not only are there the gender implications but it raises questions about what a parent is. Nevertheless, disciplines often identify individuals seen as especially influential in determining the future and shape of the fledgling field. This is most certainly the case with psychology. Two figures, William James (1842–1910) and Wilhelm Wundt (1832–1920), are held in high esteem as initiating defining moments in psychology. It may come as no surprise that their lauded crucial contributions were the setting up of the first psychology laboratory. It is a matter of preference whether one chooses 1876 or 1879 as the symbolic origin of modern psychology. If one opts for 1876 then this is the date when William James set up a small laboratory at Harvard University for *teaching* physiological psychology. Opt for 1879 then this is the date when the first psychology laboratory for *research* purposes was established by Wilhelm Wundt in Leipzig, Germany. Of course, one can find much psychology written before this time but either 1876 or 1879 can be regarded as a particularly iconic, if not defining, moment in the history of psychology. The history of modern psychology pans out fairly smoothly from that time on and, more importantly, either date entwines the origins of psychology as lying in the psychology laboratory. Jones and Elcock (2001) describe this as an origin myth (i.e. creation myth) which involves a self-serving element whereby the beginnings of modern psychology are identified as being in the founding of the laboratory tradition in the discipline. It needs hardly be said that for much of the twentieth century the laboratory experiment (along with the multiple-choice questionnaire) was a major mainstay of psychology and one of its most endemic and characteristic features. This probably gives the impression that psychology and statistical quantification went hand-in-hand from that time onwards. Not quite so as we shall see.

The irony in all of this is that, in their writings, James and Wundt expressed views about how psychology should be done which were compatible with its developing both as a strongly qualitative and a strongly quantitative discipline. Wundt believed that there were different types of topics and issues in psychology and that the appropriate research method depended on the type of psychology involved. Some aspects of psychology, he believed, could be studied effectively within the constraints of the laboratory. However, other aspects of psychology required entirely different (more qualitative) approaches. Of course, mainstream psychology scarcely heeded this simple distinction during its development.

As for William James, recent American scholarship has drawn careful attention to the roots of qualitative methods in his writings. In the very first issue of the journal *Qualitative Psychology*, Leary (2014) sees much of significance to qualitative psychological research in the contribution of William James. Using a process of self-reflection on his own personal experience led James to identify new or undervalued aspects of psychological phenomena. William James's *The varieties of religious experience* (1902/1985), for Leary, is not only a classic but it is still a relevant repository of ideas and insights. That James's writings can be heard across the chasm of time Leary believes is the consequence of the way that he employs first-person narratives, rejects preconceptions from psychology and elsewhere, draws similarities between different psychological phenomena, and develops novel conceptual distinctions. The text is enhanced by examples which improve as well as transform understanding. James's writings avoid shutting future exploration of his subject matter. For some, *Varieties of religious experience* is a founding stone of phenomenology. The qualitative descriptions which James supplied positively influenced psychology in the long term. Indeed, Leary goes so far as to suggest that neuropsychology, not the most obvious contender for the involvement of qualitative methods, would benefit from its input. He argues that qualitative methods are essential to progress of psychology and not just one more kind of research in psychology. Qualitative methods contribute essential ways of dealing with the 'blindness' that we have when new aspects of human experience reveal themselves. This blindness means that no single person can fully appreciate the nature of the phenomenon in question. By joining together or collaborating, some of the consequences of this blindness can be mitigated. What happens after this could be more qualitative investigations though alternative methods may be recruited in order to further our understanding. Included in these could be quantitative methods and experimentation. Even when considering what we would describe as neurological issues, James did not see his qualitative methods as being the servant of neurology. Quite the reverse:

> James placed priority on the qualitative description and assessment of conscious experience, which provided, for him, the best clues to which neurological possibilities, among those currently conceivable, were more likely to be confirmed by subsequent research. It is psychology, largely through qualitative research, that should give direction and meaning to neurology, not the other way around. (Leary, 2014, p. 30)

Probably no recent qualitative researcher has gone quite so far in staking the claim for qualitative research so centrally to mainstream psychology.

Just what would it have been like to study psychology at the time of the founding of James and Wundt's laboratories? According to Adams (2000) and others, introspectionism was a major force in German and then American psychology around the time when modern psychology 'was born'. Introspectionism is the doctrine that valid psychological knowledge should be based on the researcher 'looking inward' at their own conscious sensations, perceptions, thoughts and so forth. The purpose of introspection was the identification of the elements of the mind – much as chemists produced tables of the elements of the physical world. The interrelationships between the different elements were also an aspect of introspectionist study. They had few philosophical concerns and were essentially empiricists cataloguing their observations. The method of introspection was to turn thinking 'inwards' in order to scrutinise the researcher's own experiences. In other words, introspection is internal self-observation.

As a research methodology, introspection is a distinctly first-person approach and very different from the third-person study which characterises the vast outpourings of psychological research over the last 150 years or so. It is interesting then that not only has Wilhelm Wundt been lofted on high as the founding father of psychology because he set up the first psychology research laboratory but he has also been dubbed the founder of introspectionism. In other words, the first scientific psychology was introspectionism which held sway between 1860 and 1927, by which time behaviourism was beginning to dominate the discipline. However, it is wrong to characterise Wundt as an introspectionist if this term is intended to imply an exclusive commitment to introspectionist methods.

According to Baars (1986), the typical account of Wundt in modern psychology is a caricature of the man himself, originally misformulated by introspectionism's leading American advocate Edward Titchener (1867–1927), who had been a student of Wundt's. The term structuralism was used in place of introspectionism by Titchener since introspectionists studied the structure of human thought. The truth is that Wundt did see a place for the systematic self-observation of introspectionism but felt that it was useless for more complex mental processes such as the higher mental functions and emotions. Equally he did not feel that social and cultural psychology could be advanced using the experimental methods of the introspectionists. Wundt, nevertheless, did produce a popular account of self-observation in 1912/1973. This provides a good illustration of how the introspectionist would go about research. Basically the research is carried out on oneself and, in the following, one is being directed to listen to a series of beats of a metronome:

> Now let us proceed in the opposite direction by making the metronome beats follow each other after intervals of ½ to ¼ of a second, and we notice that the feelings of strain and relaxation disappear. In their place appears an excitement that increases with the rapidity of the impressions, and along with this we have generally a more or less lively feeling of displeasure . . . (Wundt, 1912, p. 57)

Titchener and another of Wundt's students, Oswald Külpe (1862–1915), were responsible for the method of trained observation which characterised introspectionism. The behaviourist psychology which displaced introspectionism was fiercely critical of the product of these trained observations.

Control and replicability were part of the intellectual armoury of introspectionism. It should be added that among the general principles of introspection, according to Titchener (1898), was one of impartiality. This meant that the researcher should not approach the investigation with preconceived ideas or expectations of what they are likely to find. Another principle was that of attentiveness, which meant that the researcher should not speculate about the research activity and why the research is being done during the introspection phase. The study is to be taken seriously in its own right. These principles resonate with some aspects of modern qualitative research – for example, bracketing (or epoché) in IPA (Chapter 13) calls for the analyst to abandon outside influences. However, this concept came into modern IPA (Chapter 13) from phenomenology, not directly from introspectionism. After Titchener's death, few psychologists practised internal observation of the sort employed by introspectionists. Instead, the observations turned to third parties such as rats.

It is important also to distinguish between introspectionism and phenomenology, which has had an important influence on qualitative psychology, especially in the form of IPA. Phenomenology is not a sub-field of introspectionism but a reaction against introspectionism and much else. The important name in phenomenology is that of the Austrian-born philosopher Edmund Husserl (1859–1938). In the following, Husserl's name and phenomenology are used interchangeably but the message is clear – introspectionism and phenomenology are distinct and incompatible intellectual traditions:

> Husserl's tendency is in a different direction. If anything, his philosophy is 'extrospective,' moving toward phenomena as objects, in the broadest sense, of perceptual acts. The 'glance' – to use Husserl's language – of the phenomenologist is directed toward what is represented in experience, not toward a repository of mixed sensations within the psyche. The only way to account for the persistence of the accusation of introspectionism in connection with phenomenology is that the term itself has been abused, turned first into an epithet and then into an anachronism. (Natanson, 1973, p. 43)

Husserl's phenomenology went on to have a major influence on philosophy in continental Europe – and on sociology, which partly led to the recent growth of qualitative methods in psychology. However, the real battle against introspectionism in psychology was won long ago by behaviourism which dominated the psychology of the United States and much of the rest of the world for the greater part of the twentieth century. The behaviourist's fight was led by ideas drawn from *logical positivism*. So behaviourism replaced introspectionism as the dominant form of psychology early in the twentieth century.

The logical positivists, behaviourism and psychology

The word positivism has its origins in the work of Auguste Comte (Box 1.1). Positivism is another of those concepts which is used somewhat imprecisely but also can be used as an epithet with pejorative connotations to describe mainstream, non-qualitative, psychology. Positivism became the dominant view in the philosophy of science during the first part of the twentieth century – especially *logical positivism* which had a profound impact on behaviourism in terms of how science was construed. The defining features of logical positivism were its dependency on empiricism together with the use of logical deductions from mathematical and other concepts. The logical positivist movement first emerged in Vienna prior to the First World War, though only became widely established in the rest of Europe and America in the 1920s and 1930s. Migration of important members of the movement was largely responsible for its spread when leading figures in logical positivism moved to the United States. Nevertheless, it was not until 1931 that the American philosopher A. E. Blumberg (1906–1997) first used the term logical positivism to describe the philosophy of the Vienna School. The Austrian philosopher Herbert Feigl (1902–1988) and the German philosopher Rudolf Carnap (1891–1970), important members of the school, moved to the United States and were highly influential on a key player in the methodology of behaviourist psychology, S. S. Stevens (1906–1973). One might be forgiven for not knowing who Feigl or Carnap were; however, Stevens' legacy impacts to this day on every student who has struggled with the concepts of nominal, ordinal, interval and ratio levels of measurement in statistics classes. He was also primarily responsible for the idea of operational definitions entering psychology in the mid-1930s – which he got from the logical positivists although it was the physicist Percy Bridgeman's (1882–1961) idea. Operationism is the idea that concepts in science (including psychology) are defined by the processes used to measure them.

Logical positivism was a philosophy of science and also selectively defined what science was for *behaviourism*'s adherents. Behaviourism developed in the United States under the influence of the psychologist John Watson (1878–1958) though behaviourism in psychology took a number of directions. Watson's behaviourism saw psychology as (a) part of natural science and (b) an objective experimental approach to the prediction and control of behaviour – following Comte's view that the purpose of science lay in prediction. The behaviourist school of psychology embodied key positivist principles in a search for the laws of human behaviour. Sometimes these laws were formulated in mathematical terms, as in the work of Clark Hull (1884–1952).

Logical positivists argued that, scientifically, knowledge came from one's direct observations based on experience and from the application of tight logical reasoning (i.e. logical tautologies – the operational definition is a good example of a logical tautology since it has to be correct no matter what). Among the characteristics of science according to the logical positivist view, and hence behaviourism, were the following:

- Science is a cumulative process.
- Sciences are reducible ultimately to a single science of the real world.
- Science is independent of the characteristics of the investigator.

Most qualitative researchers would reject most if not all of these.

Watson saw that replacing introspectionism by his vision of a behaviourist psychology brought with it the possibility of making psychology like other sciences:

> This suggested elimination of states of consciousness as proper objects of investigation in themselves will remove the barrier from psychology which exists between it and the other sciences. The findings of psychology become the functional correlates of structure and lend themselves to explanation in physico-chemical terms. (Watson, 1913, p. 175)

In other words, psychology would eventually be reducible to physiology in keeping with the reductionist principle in logical positivism. For Watson, psychology was a natural science which would eventually be reducible to a science like physics and chemistry. The influence and dominance of behaviourism on psychology were most apparent between the 1920s and 1960s after which it was in decline and cognitive psychology was in its ascendency. Important behaviourist psychologists included Edward Thorndike (1874–1949), Edward Tolman (1886–1959) and, for the very early part of his career, Albert Bandura (1925–) who later had a major impact on cognitive psychology. Particular mention should be made of the radical behaviourism of B. F. Skinner (1904–1990). Perhaps because of its tight logical foundation, which is a characteristic inherited from the logical positivists, radical behaviourism can be seen as the epitome of logical positivism in psychology.

Logical positivism, it should be noted, gave to psychology through its influence on behaviourism the principle of verification. This means that ideas (maybe theories or hypotheses) are only meaningful to the extent that empirical research allows them to be tested to see whether they remain viable or whether they should be rejected. This principle is shared by modern quantitative as well as some qualitative psychology though in a slightly modified form.

The Australian philosopher John Passmore (1914–2004) famously signalled the ultimate demise of logical positivism in the following words:

> Logical positivism, then, is dead, or as dead as a philosophical movement ever becomes. But it has left a legacy behind. In the German-speaking countries, indeed, it wholly failed; German philosophy, as exhibited in the works of Heidegger and his disciples, represents everything to which the positivists were most bitterly opposed . . .
> But insofar as it is widely agreed that . . . philosophers ought to set an example of precision and clarity, that philosophy should make use of technical devices, derived

from logic, in order to solve problems relating to the philosophy of science, that philosophy is not about 'the world' but about the language through which men speak about the world, we can detect in contemporary philosophy, at least, the persistence of the spirit which inspired the Vienna circle. (Passmore, 1967, p. 55)

Once again, in this we can see in logical positivism traces of ideas which are endemic in qualitative psychology. For example, the phrase 'the language through which men speak about the world' is almost a sentiment straight from discourse analysis (Chapter 9). Nevertheless, as Passmore explains in his reference to Martin Heidegger (1889–1976), logical positivism lost the intellectual battle to philosophies which played a central role in the development of postmodernism, deconstruction and hermeneutics, all of which are key aspects of some forms of qualitative psychology.

Given the response of psychology to logical positivism, it is noteworthy that the logical positivists in general did not write about the possibility of a qualitative psychology (Michell, 2003). However, an exception to this was Rudolf Carnap, who was mentioned earlier. Michell summarises the relationship between positivism and qualitative psychology based on Carnap's writings as follows:

Positivism does not dismiss the possibility of non-quantitative methods in psychology. It was actually a much more subtle, complex and tolerant philosophical position than many detractors now recognize. At heart, it involved a romantic view of science, and it anticipated post-positivist relativism, but the fact that positivists valued science meant that they were sensitive to the dangers of applying quantitative methods in inappropriate contexts. (Michell, 2003, pp. 24–5)

Unfortunately, even if logical positivism was not entirely antagonistic to qualitative psychology, this was probably lost to the mainstream behaviourist psychologist. A careful reading of logical positivist writings might have served the working psychologist well but, if we accept Michell's analysis, the signs are that few went back to logical positivist philosophers in order to understand what they actually intended by their writings.

Possibly the reasons underlying the model of science used by behaviourist psychologists may not reside primarily in positivism. For example, Noam Chomsky (1928–), a linguist and philosopher but highly influential on the demise of behaviourism and the rise of cognitive science, raised a quite distinct level of explanation when asked about behaviourist psychology's impact:

Well, now you've raised the question of why behaviorist psychology has such an enormous vogue, particularly in the United States. And I'm not sure what the answer to that is. I think, in part, it had to do with the very erroneous idea that by keeping close to observation of data, to manipulation, it was somehow being scientific. That belief is a grotesque caricature and distortion of science but there's no doubt that many people did have that belief. I suppose, if you want to go deeper into the question, one would have to give a sociological analysis of the use of American psychology for manipulation, for advertising, for control. A large part of the vogue for behaviorist psychology has to do with its ideological role. (Chomsky, from an interview with Cohen, 1977).

One way of interpreting Chomsky's comments is to suggest that there was big money for universities selling the technology of behavioural control. Whatever the accoutrements of such a discipline then they would be reinforced by this economic success.

The quantitative dominance of mainstream psychology

A full understanding of the position of qualitative methods in psychology requires an appreciation of the nature and extent of the ethos of quantification which has pervaded psychology for much of its history. Histories of psychology, almost without exception, simply have not included qualitative approaches. Try as one may, it seems impossible to identify precisely when the distinction between quantitative and qualitative research emerged in psychology (or other disciplines for that matter). Much the same distinction has a long history in psychology but using different terminology such as objective–subjective or hard–soft research. Each has its own particular, though highly questionable, overtones. Of course, it was not solely soft psychology which was critiqued, quantitatively-based psychology has had its share of critics too. The earliest psychological writing contrasting quantitative and qualitative approaches that I have found (after a great deal of hard and frustrating searching) is by Gordon Allport (1897–1967) way back in 1940:

> If we rejoice, for example, that present-day psychology is . . . increasingly *empirical, mechanistic, quantitative, nomothetic, analytic,* and *operational*, we should also beware of demanding slavish subservience to these pre-suppositions. Why not allow psychology as a science – for science is a broad and beneficent term – to be also *rational, teleological, qualitative, idiographic, synoptic*, and even *non-operational*? I mention these antitheses of virtue with deliberation, for the simple reason that great insights of psychology in the past – for example, those of Aristotle, Locke, Fechner, James, Freud – have stemmed from one or more of these unfashionable presuppositions. (Allport, 1940, p. 25)

Shortly after this, Allport (1942) produced an extensive review of qualitative research (not the name he used) in psychology – the focus was on the use of personal documents providing accounts of the experiences of individuals and their actions in social life. Allport had volunteered to carry out the review for the Committee on Appraisal of Research of the US Social Science Research Council. In his review, Allport made a strong claim about the legitimacy of qualitative research methods in psychology. His view was that qualitative methods were essentially no more problematic in scientific terms than, for example, the experimental method. Among the roles that he saw for qualitative methods were (a) contributing 'reality' to the artificiality of much of psychology's methods and (b) validating quantitatively established knowledge.

The role of qualitative research he saw as being a great deal more than merely illustrating knowledge obtained through psychology's 'scientific' methods and providing hypotheses to be tested.

Allport, of course, was not alone in his criticisms of the then psychology mainstream. A good later example is to be found in Brower (1949). Reading his criticism, it is evident that a vision of what quantification's alternative might be is missing. Furthermore, no mention of the word qualitative is to be found in Brower's paper – he merely writes about 'non-quantitative' as if the only possible alternative was the absence of quantification. It is interesting to read Brower's account of quantification in psychology as being 'insistently demanded', a 'natural accompaniment' of an age of engineering and physical science, and emulating physics as the prototypical science:

> Quantitative methods have found an extraordinary degree of application in psychology and have been insistently demanded on the American scene for a number of reasons. First of all, they represent a natural accompaniment of our mechanical age and the emphasis on engineering and physical science. Secondly, we have unwittingly attempted to emulate physics as the prototype of science without elab-

orating the intrinsic differences between psychology and physics. The methodology of physics makes possible a degree of detachment of subject-matter from observer which can, thus far, be obtained in psychology only by doing damage to the phenomenon through artificialization. In the history of modern physics, astronomy, chemistry, etc., the recognition of the 'personal equation' certainly was a boon to the development of those fields. While the facts of individual differences in perception were derived from psychology, physical scientists did not find it necessary to incorporate psychological methods, e.g. introspection, along with their factual data. As psychology grew on the substrate of natural science, however, not only were the facts of physics incorporated into psychology but the principal method as well: quantification. (Brower, 1949, pp. 325–6)

In other words, one does not need to dig too deeply into the philosophical basis of psychology in order to understand why quantification is so deeply embedded in its collective psyche. The way in which psychologists go about the practice of psychological research is the consequence of their understanding of what that practice consists of. There is no doubt, and examples will be provided later, that there has been a qualitative ethos in psychology which has manifested itself in some classic studies. Nevertheless, as we have seen, it is clear that quantitative approaches have tended to dominate the ways that psychologists believed that psychology should be carried out. It was almost as if quantification was seen as the natural way of doing psychology. Box 1.2 discusses a radically different conceptualisation of the nature of science.

Box 1.2
KEY CONCEPT
Social constructionism

Social constructionism is a broad church and the beliefs of social constructionist thinkers are difficult to define. That is, there is a range of intellectual foundations of social constructionism and none is shared by every social constructionist thinker. Burr (2003) suggests that to be described as a social constructionist, one of the following assumptions derived from Gergen (1985a) has to be met at a minimum (see Figure 1.4):

- *Knowledge sustained by social processes* Social constructionists argue that knowledge is constructed by people through their interactions. Our version of knowledge is therefore substantially the product of language in the form of conversation, etc. in our everyday lives.

- *Historical and cultural specificity of language* The way that we think about any aspect of the world will vary in different cultures and in the same culture at different time periods. For example, once suicide

was regarded as a crime and the body of a person committing suicide punished as if they were alive (Ssasz, 1986). Within living memory, attempted suicide was a crime in the United Kingdom.

- *Critical position on 'taken-for-granted' knowledge* The usual view of mainstream psychology, it is argued, is that the researcher can observe the world objectively. This sort of assumption as well as other assumptions of mainstream psychology would be questioned from the social constructionist perspective which holds that the ways in which people perceive the world do not correspond to a reality.

- *Knowledge and social action are integrated* The different constructions that we have about the world each have their implications for different sorts of social action. So the idea that illegal drug users are 'medically sick' has implications for their treatment which are different from the implications of regarding them as criminals.

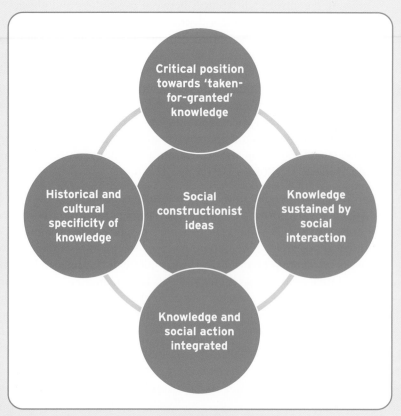

FIGURE 1.4 Characteristics of social constructionist thought

The origins of social constructionist thinking dig deep into the history of postmodernism itself which has its background in the arts such as cultural studies and literature. Postmodernism rejects modernistic ideas which even in art included basic rules such as the 'rule of thirds' putatively underlying good composition. The postmodern position is one of a multiplicity of different perspectives on the world which are incompatible with the idea that there can be grand theories which explain what underlies the world and existence. Berger and Luckmann (1966) produced a crucial book *The social construction of reality* (discussed in Chapter 2) which was a decisive moment in sociology, as well as establishing the constructionist perspective in the social sciences as a whole – and eventually psychology. In general, in psychology the constructionist position served as a radical critique of the work of mainstream psychologists. However, more importantly, it became a focus of styles of research – many of them discussed in this text – which can broadly be divided into two sorts:

- *Interactionally focused* This is what Burr (2003) calls micro-social constructionism and Danziger (1997) called light social constructionism. This is essentially the idea that the world as experienced by people is created or constructed through the regular everyday social interactions such as conversations between people (one aspect of discourse). This is a continual, regular process of everyday life. Although this is part of the work of discourse analysts and, to a lesser extent, conversation analysts, this approach can be attributed to the work of Kenneth Gergen (e.g. 1999) and John Shotter (e.g. 1995a).

- *Societally focused* Burr (2003) calls it macro-social constructionism and Danziger (1997) calls it dark social constructionism. This form of social constructionist thinking regards social power as being central and a crucial aspect of what is constructed through discourse. Michel Foucault was particularly influential on this form of social constructionism. It concentrates on such things as institutional practices and social structures.

The distinction between these two types of social construction is more or less in terms of the idea of agency (Burr, 2003). The type of social interaction which is involved in the interactionally focused form of social constructionism involves an active participant in a conversation contributing to the process of construction.

In the societally focused form of social constructionism the idea is created that the participant in conversation is relatively powerless to produce social change – that is, change in the power structure of society.

The differences between social constructionist approaches to psychology and the quantitative approaches which tend to dominate the field are clearly major. They are not entirely incompatible but they are opposites on a major continuum. Related, but not identical, dimensions of the differences between social constructionist and quantitative approaches include the following:

● *Realism–relativism* That is the difference between the quantitative assumption that there is a physical reality which can be assessed through research and the social constructionist view that there are a multitude of different perspectives or views on reality, none of which corresponds to reality.

● *Agency–determinism* This is the difference between the quantitative assumption that human behaviour is determined by external forces and the social constructionist view that people determine their own actions.

Most of the characteristics of qualitative research are related to this basic assumption of the social construction of knowledge. Of course, it is a powerful idea but it does have a number of limitations. One of the most important of these is that it can appear a relatively weak theory in that researchers often fail to specify just exactly what is being socially constructed and just where a particular social construction will prevail and why.

If positivism does not entirely account for the dominance of quantitative methods in psychology, then what does? Michell (2003) argued that the 'quantitative imperative' best describes psychology's orientation rather than any philosophical considerations. The quantitative imperative is the idea that the scientific study of anything involves measuring that thing. Science and measurement go together according to this and, as a consequence, non-quantitative methods are held to be pre-scientific. But where does this 'quantitative imperative' originate? According to Michell, it is an ancient, still deeply ingrained idea. The notion that quantification and science are inseparable has its roots in the Ancient Greek pre-Socratic Pythagoreans (some 500 years BCE). (BCE is Before the Common Era and is a replacement for BC or Before Christ which is acceptable to all faiths.) Of course, Pythagoras was an important figure in mathematics who believed that mathematics underlay the principles governing phenomena observed in the world. Such a belief is understandable given some of Pythagoras's achievements. For instance, Pythagoras discovered mathematical ratios in things so apparently different as geometry, astronomy and music. So Pythagoras found that, in music, a note an octave above another in pitch has twice the frequency of vibration. Nevertheless, Aristotle (384–322 BCE) questioned how attributes such as colours and tastes could be numbers.

The idea that mathematics underlies all that we experience has had an unchequered presence in ideas about science from Pythagorian times until the present. A closely linked idea is that mathematics would replace other sciences. Physics, especially, among the sciences has had spectacular success in terms of expressing its findings mathematically from Isaac Newton's (1643–1727) discoveries onward and this accelerated in light of the scientific successes in the first part of the twentieth century. Consequently:

> It dominated scientific thinking in the physical sciences, and this meant that it cast an irresistible shadow over aspiring sciences, such as psychology, that were modeled upon quantitative natural science. (Michell, 2003, p. 12)

The belief in the success of the science of physics buttressed the quantitative imperative in psychology which, as a developing discipline, sought to emulate the science of physics above all others (Michell, 2003, p. 12). Not surprisingly, early experimental work in psychology was sometimes distinctly quantitative in nature. A good illustration lies in psychophysics which involved studying things such as the way in which we perceive loudness or brightness or weight. Important researchers including Gustav Fechner (1801–1887) developed mathematical models to link experience with the physical reality underlying such sensations.

Statistics and the quantitative ethos in psychology

In the 1930s and then following the Second World War, there was a growing methodological consensus in psychology which involved various elements thought to be necessary for scientific rigour. These include null hypothesis testing and Fisher's work on experimental design which gave rise to the analysis of variance (ANOVA). For Michell (2003), as with Chomsky (1973), this methodological consensus 'owed more to the values of window-dressing than to any values implicit in logical positivism' (p. 16). Michell shares the view of others that the methodological consensus served psychology well in terms of the economics of research funding and was responsible for the resistance to qualitative methods. That is to say, the sophisticated quantitative methodologies used by psychologists resulted in high status for their research and, hence, attracted funding. Current dominant psychological research has remained substantially determinedly quantitative in style.

Although statistical techniques were first developed in late Victorian times, they were not generally and routinely incorporated into psychological research until just before the mid-twentieth century. Although it is important to differentiate between quantification in psychology and the use of statistics in psychology (i.e. it is possible to have a quantitative psychology without statistics), there is little doubt that statistics played a powerful role in shaping much of modern psychology.

Concepts which seem to be fundamentally psychological in nature frequently have their origins in statistics. In particular, the concept of the variable is so wedded to psychological thinking that it vies to be one of the discipline's core concepts. But variables did not enter psychological thinking until towards the middle of the twentieth century – long after the first psychology laboratory. We will return to this later. Statistical methods have influenced many aspects of psychological theory. For example, statistical techniques such as factor analysis have had important impacts on the study of personality and intelligence. In modern times, to give a rather different example, smallest space analysis has had a major impact on quantitative approaches to profiling crime from the characteristics of the crime scene. In brief, smallest space analysis allows a researcher to find the underlying dimensions along which different crime scenes differ. This simplifies the way in which different crime scenes may be compared. Without dwelling on the point too long, the intimate relationship between psychological research and statistics verges on the indecent. That is, the influence of statistics on psychology has sometimes left the discipline exposed as concentrating on trivial matters such as significance testing and neglecting substantial questions about the nature of psychology itself. Nevertheless, it is impossible to know how differently psychology would have developed without the influence of statistics. As we have seen, psychology has had a powerful impetus towards quantification for all of its modern history.

The relationship between statistical thinking and mainstream psychology is, historically, somewhat confusing. A small number of psychologists have contributed to the development of statistical techniques which are now part of psychology and other disciplines. Good examples of these are Charles Spearman (1863–1945), who is known for a version of the correlation coefficient known as the Spearman rank correlation coefficient but who, more importantly, developed the earliest, most basic form of factor analysis as part of his studies on the structure of intelligence; Louis Thurstone

(1887–1955), who extended this work in ways that led to one of the most useful, early techniques of factor analysis, thereby playing an enormous role in the development of psychological tests and measurements; and Louis Guttman (1916–1987), who could be described as much as being a sociologist as a psychologist, and who contributed statistical methods such as multidimensional scaling to the statistical repertoire. No doubt there are others, but generally psychologists have been major users of statistical techniques rather than innovators.

So like their philosophy, psychologists usually borrow their statistical techniques. Many of the statistical innovations which have been utilised by psychologists were imported from other fields. The origins of regression and the correlation coefficient, for example, were outside psychology. Regression is a biological concept and the statistical analysis of regression was introduced by Francis Galton (1822–1911). Galton was interested in the inheritance of characteristics. His ideas eventually led to what we now know as the correlation coefficient – the standard deviation was one of Galton's ideas too. The form of the correlation coefficient which is known to all psychologists worldwide was developed by Karl Pearson (1857–1936) – the Pearson (product–moment) correlation coefficient. Pearson was not a psychologist and is probably best described as a mathematical statistician. He eventually became a professor of eugenics. His son, Egon Pearson (1895–1980), was also a statistician and he, along with Jerzy Neyman (1894–1981), was responsible for one of the most important statistical influences on psychology which also vies for the title of the most destructive – hypothesis testing and statistical significance. This process of testing the null hypothesis to see whether it can be rejected has almost been drummed into every psychology student since the middle of the twentieth century. Worse still, it is presented as the process by which good research proceeds! That is, statistical significance becomes the primary criterion of worthwhile research to the exclusion of every other indicator of quality in research. Finally, one should not overlook the dominance of the ideas of Ronald Fisher (1890–1962) on the design of experiments and the all-important statistical method of analysis of variance. Virtually all of these statistical techniques will be familiar in name if not in more detail to practically any psychologist, no matter where in the world. They have grown to be the common currency of the discipline.

However, as we have already mentioned, statistical techniques were not important in psychology during the 50 years after the first psychological laboratory had been set up. According to Danziger and Dzinas (1997), psychologists, in general, were becoming familiar with statistical ideas from about the 1930s onwards. As previously noted, the 1930s marked the introduction of the term 'variable' into psychology. While the 'variable' is embedded in psychology talk nowadays (it was another concept originating in the work of Karl Pearson), its absorption into psychology was initially fairly slow. However, it was the cognitive-behavioural psychologist Edward Tolman (1886–1959) who made significant impact on psychology when he introduced the terms independent and dependent variables. Whether or not we regard the term variable as a piece of jargon, its use in psychology has resulted in a view of the world as being made up of variables. Seen as conceptual conveniences, variables constitute another way by which mainstream psychologists tend to distance themselves from what they study. The attraction of using the terms independent and dependent variables, according to Danziger and Dzinas (1997), was that they effectively replace the terms stimulus and response, which were the legacy of behaviourism. The growth in the use of the term variables cannot be accounted for by the growth in the use of statistics in research. The increased use of statistics in the 1940s and 1950s followed after the term variable had been virtually universally adopted by psychologists. Robert Woodworth's (1869–1962) highly influential psychology textbook of that time incorporated the independent–dependent variable terminology so this may have been an important factor in its acceptance. Whatever the reason, with a few rare exceptions such as Guttman's facet theory (Canter, 1983; Shye & Elizur, 1994), mainstream psychologists have lived comfortably in a world constructed from variables. Variable, despite being a common term throughout psychology, is rarely found in qualitative research reports and stands out like a sore thumb when it occurs in that context.

It is worth noting that there have been claims that the quantitative psychologist is a disappearing breed with few keen to take their place (Clay, 2005). This is not a suggestion that mainstream quantitative psychology is declining but signals a shortage of psychologists with specialist training in statistics, measurement and methodology rather than those who routinely use quantification in their research work:

> Psychologists of the 1960s . . . saw themselves as leaders in statistical, measurement and design issues. Psychology departments often had quantitative specialists, and graduate students were well equipped to handle the quantitative aspects of their research. By 1990, that legacy had faded along with the number of students aware of, interested in and able to enter the field. (Clay, 2005, p. 26 print version)

This could be another way of saying that the forces which shaped behaviourist psychology are no longer so potent. Nevertheless, there are still a lot of psychologists with more than a passing interest in quantitative research.

The trouble with history is that the imagination includes the now. So, without really ever thinking it, our picture of the psychology of the past is seen through the psychology of today. And it is difficult to imagine this earlier psychology free from the methodological and statistical baggage that has dominated psychology for substantially more than half a century. But such a psychology can be found in some of the classic papers in psychology. A good example comes from the work of Edward Tolman who was responsible for the introduction of the concept of cognitive maps – which is still a current concept in research. The most sophisticated 'statistical' method in his 'Cognitive maps in rats and men' (Tolman, 1948) was graphs. This is readily available on the Web at Classics in the History of Psychology (http://psychclassics.yorku.ca/Tolman/Maps/maps.htm). Other papers in this archive will give you a feel of the nature of early psychological writings.

CONCLUSION

The story so far has taken us through the philosophical changes in psychology that shaped the discipline since Victorian times until the 1960s. Our quest was to find just why psychology as a whole took a quantitative route over this period. Although positivism is often held to be responsible for this, this philosophy either in Comte's version or as logical positivism does not reject qualitative methods in psychology. However, perhaps it is wrong to assume that psychologists' philosophical knowledge was typically sophisticated enough to appreciate this. The great emphasis of psychology on experimentation for much of its history is very evident and the best model for how to do experiments was the highly successful, and quantitative, science of physics. Of course, historically psychology as a discipline was closer to the sciences in terms of what it studied and consequently how it should be studied than were the social sciences in general. In other words, the bias to quantification was a matter of psychological practices rather than philosophy. Quantification was seen as the way forward and fundamental to psychological science. Quantification created a blindness in psychology which continues still. But this merely is to describe the situation in psychology. It remains difficult to explain quite why psychology resolutely followed the route of quantification when there were clear examples of alternatives. Only by sticking with an antiquated view of what science (especially physics) was could this trajectory be maintained. Hypothesis testing gradually emerged as the one way of doing psychology despite there being good examples of alternative ways of doing research.

The dominance of behaviourist psychology in the first half of the twentieth century brought with it the stimulus and response taken from the physiological work of Ivan Pavlov (1849–1936) on the conditioned reflex. Psychology was reduced to seeking the stimulus which led to the response which, in itself, pushes the researcher towards quantification – there is not a lot more to do but count. All of this happened long before psychologists in general included statistics into the psychology toolkit. Indeed, it is important to distinguish between quantification in psychology and statistical applications in psychology. They are very different. Quantification in psychology is about the idea that psychological systems are fundamentally mathematical in nature. Statistics is built on top of this principle; nevertheless statistics is not the reason for the principle. Of course, statistics is the most obvious interface for most psychologists with quantification in psychology so inevitably the ideas of quantification and statistics tend to meld together. Statistical thinking had not fully integrated into the work of psychologists until the 1950s. It can be seen as the consequence of the quantitative imperative in psychology rather than its cause. In a phrase, psychology was a quantitative discipline long before it was a statistical one.

There had been many voices of dissent against positivism and quantification in psychology. As we will see in Chapter 2, the vocal tide for change strengthened throughout the twentieth century. However, Henwood and Pidgeon (1994) identify Wilhelm Dilthey (1833–1911) as possibly the earliest proponent of the view that psychology should seek understanding rather than identify causal mechanisms. Prus commented:

> Dilthey clearly articulated his disenchantments not only with the positivistic notions of determinism, causation, and reductionism that were already rampant in psychology at the time, but also with what he felt was the misplaced irrelevancy of their inquiry to human lived experience . . . He was particularly troubled by the failure of psychology to recognise the culturally mediated (intersubjective) nature of human experience. (Prus, 1996, p. 38)

Although still a major force, the behaviourism project was on the brink of its decline in the 1950s. Withering criticisms were part of it but it increasingly could not deliver what psychologists needed it to deliver. The emergence of behaviourism had caused psychology 'to lose its mind'. Its predecessor introspection was all in the researcher's mind. Psychologists were becoming dissatisfied with the hard-science project of behaviourism but researchers in fields such as sociology were also examining their disciplines critically. In sociology, wanton empiricism and theory so grand that it did not join up with research data brought about a major reorientation to qualitative research which, mostly, lacked esteem up to this point. A general shift to qualitative research was underway in the discipline at this time – a shift which was to have its impact on qualitative psychology some years later (and other disciplines on the way). In psychology, the shift was in a different direction and towards cognition or cognitivism in which psychology got back its senses. Cognitive science began to be a big player in the 1960s. It was interdisciplinary in scope and cognition in various guises has dominated psychology ever since.

Finally, it is worth asking the question of what those most directly involved in psychological research (students and academics) think about qualitative methods. In an Australian study, for example, Povee and Roberts (2014) interviewed various groups of students and staff in a university psychology department about qualitative methods. Thematic analysis (Chapter 7) was used to analyse the transcripts of the interviews. One core or overarching theme pervaded the analysis – that one's choice of research method should be driven by the research question addressed. The three different types of research method (qualitative, quantitative and mixed) each had its own areas of value and should be appreciated as such. Various other themes were identified:

- *Lack of exposure and confidence* Participants would complain that they had not received sufficient exposure to qualitative research methods in their studies. This led to the feeling that qualitative research is daunting and confusing. There was also a feeling that the lack of staff familiar with qualitative methods to give them support was a good reason for avoiding qualitative research.

- *Time and resource intensive* This theme is partly illustrated by the idea that the qualitative researcher cannot simply stick a questionnaire in front of people, unlike in quantitative research. The demands of qualitative research would deter some from engaging in it. Perceived problems in getting qualitative research papers published also put some off following the qualitative route in their academic career.

- *Inherent to psychology* There were parallels drawn between the conduct of a qualitative study and practice as a psychologist in terms of close interpersonal relationships and good communications. The in-depth interview and the clinical or psychotherapy session both encourage the rich description of subjective experience, for example. That is, the practices of professional psychology are not dissimilar from those of qualitative research.

- *Capturing the lived experience* The ability of qualitative research to capture the lived experience of participants was seen as a major strength of qualitative approaches.

- *Power and the participant–researcher relationship* The reduced power differential between researcher and researched compared to traditional quantitative psychological research was noted by some. Amongst the views expressed was that the influence of the researcher is reduced when the participant feels empowered to honestly and openly share their experiences.

- *Respect and legitimacy* Many felt that qualitative research lacked the respect afforded quantitative research by the profession. This included the idea that qualitative research does not get published so readily thus producing career progression problems. Quantitative methods are taught in ways which suggested anything else is not really important or does not exist. For some, qualitative research is the easy or soft option just involving asking questions without any need to understand methodological issues or epistemology.

- *Subjectivity and rigour* Qualitative research consisted of personal opinion and was susceptible to research bias according to some participants. It is not so rigorous, reliable or valid as quantitative research. Within this theme, however, some participants made comments indicating that they were less than convinced of the putative objectivity of quantitative research. For example, qualitative methods have the virtue of honesty but quantitative methods may fool people with statistics.

- *Limited generalisability and worth* Doubts about the generalisability of qualitative research included the lack of inferential statistics which may prevent generalisation.

- *Characteristics of qualitative researchers* Being a qualitative researcher was identified with being a person – the qualitative researcher who does not like talking with people would be in deep trouble. Some saw qualitative-orientated individuals as lacking in statistical skills and achievement in quantitative methods.

Broadly speaking these themes tend to suggest that qualitative methods are not generally subject to the antagonism that they would have experienced in the past. The bigger problem is the low level of training and support in qualitative research compared to quantitative research methods. There is a perception of qualitative methods as being demanding in terms of effort and time which also may work against the individual adopting qualitative methods in their research.

In the next chapter, we will unpick the story of qualitative methods in psychology and the influence of the broader social sciences on this process.

KEY POINTS

- Many characteristic features have been suggested to differentiate qualitative research from quantitative research. While none of these definitely separates the two in every circumstance, it is clear that the ethos of qualitative psychology is different from the ethos of quantitative research in psychology. Qualitative psychology and quantitative psychology often appear to have very different conceptions of the nature of science.

- Positivism has been argued to have been the philosophical force behind behaviourism which dominated academic psychology for much of the first half of the twentieth century. There is some question about this since logical positivism and Comte's positivism do not, in themselves, dismiss the possibility of a qualitative approach to psychology.

- The quantitative ethos in psychology is part of the long-term view that the world, ultimately, can be reduced to mathematical relationships. This view emerged from the work of Pythagoras and was reinforced by the mathematical successes of physics as the dominant discipline in science.

- Statistics was a relatively late introduction to psychology and so is best seen as the product of the quantitative imperative in psychology rather than its cause.

ADDITIONAL RESOURCES

Brown, S. D., & Lock, A. (2008). Social psychology. In C. Willig & W. Stainton-Rogers (Eds.), *The SAGE handbook of qualitative research in psychology* (pp. 373–389). London: Sage.

Burr, V. (2015). *Social constructionism* (3rd ed.) London: Routledge.

Gergen, K. J. (2015). *An invitation to social construction* (3rd ed.). London: Sage.

Michell, J. (2003). The quantitative imperative: positivism, naïve realism and the place of qualitative methods in psychology. *Theory & Psychology, 13*(1), 5–31.

Parker, I. (2005). *Qualitative psychology: Introducing radical research.* Buckingham: Open University Press.

Potter, J. (1996). *Representing reality: Discourse, rhetoric and social construction.* London: Sage.

Vidich, A. J., & Lyman, S. M. (2000). Qualitative methods: Their history in sociology and anthropology. In N. L. Denzin & Y. S. Lincoln (Eds.), *Handbook of qualitative research* (2nd ed., pp. 37–84). Thousand Oaks, CA: Sage.

CHAPTER 2

How qualitative methods developed in psychology: the qualitative revolution

Overview

- The most significant period of growth in qualitative methods in psychology occurred from the 1990s onward. Studies of the major database in psychology, PsycINFO, which provides a historical record of virtually all of psychology's output, clearly demonstrate this. Much of the growth in qualitative research output has been in the least central journals and in books. Cross-disciplinary journals have a more impressive record of publishing qualitative research than psychology journals.

- This move towards qualitative psychology has not occurred at the same time or the same pace in all sub-fields of psychology; marketing and consumer psychology being a case in point. The acceptance of qualitative methods in these areas was firm by the 1970s.

- The publication of new journals devoted to qualitative psychology (e.g. *Qualitative Research in Psychology*) and the creation of professional organisations devoted to qualitative psychology are evidence of the recognition and newfound status of qualitative psychology.

- Case studies might be considered one of the earliest qualitative methods in psychology, although there are problems with this. Originally case studies were for the purposes of education and training. They illustrated what was known through other research methods. There are also questions about the extent to which Freud's case studies can be regarded as qualitative in nature. There are many recent examples of single-case studies in qualitative research. Case studies can be qualitative or quantitative in nature.

● Participant observation studies in psychology followed on the heels of their introduction into social anthropology and sociology of the Chicago School where the term ethnology was used. The motivation of the researchers involved was essentially a profound concern with particular social problems (such as unemployment and racism) with which they were faced and the inadequacy of mainstream methods at tackling the issue appropriately.

● Sociology, linguistics and philosophy had their role in developing key ideas basic to discourse analysis amongst other qualitative approaches.

● For the most part, the innovations of the 1950s and 1960s took place within sociology rather than psychology. However, the rise in psychology of person-centred approaches in relation to mental health, etc. can be seen as encouraging the need for new ways of doing psychological research.

● Changes in society contributed to the incorporation of qualitative ideas into psychology. In particular, feminism required a constructivist approach and one which was capable of giving women a voice through feminist psychology research. Feminism's rejection of positivistic principles, for example, made it an ally of some forms of qualitative research.

The growth of qualitative methods in psychology

The challenge of documenting the growth of qualitative methods in psychology

Although it is hard to explain why, quantitative methods have dominated psychology for most of its history. Otherwise highly influential voices in the history of psychology frequently failed to encourage a swerve from quantitative to qualitative approaches. This generally has the status of a self-evident truth. It would take a remarkable revisionist historian of psychology to argue otherwise – and there is no sign of contenders for that particular role. On the other hand, it is often claimed now that qualitative methods have finally made the breakthrough in psychology. Progress has been rapid in the last 30 or so years. Qualitative methods now provide a viable and highly visible alternative to quantitative methods. Nevertheless, our knowledge of the development of qualitative methods in psychology is, at best, sketchy and, at worst, inaccurate.

Problems of definition (just what counts as qualitative) add to the difficulties in writing a worthwhile history of qualitative psychology. We have already seen that not everything that is non-quantitative is imbued with the qualitative ethos. Some of the published histories of qualitative psychology should be read with caution. Too frequently it is casually assumed that approaches largely devoid of statistics and numbers are thereby qualitative in nature. Freud's work, for example, is often denoted in these histories as qualitative. But this fails to understand the roots of his work in positivism and its lack of a truly qualitative ethos. The distinction between a qualitative data collection method and a qualitative data analysis method was made in Chapter 1 and should not be underplayed. One reason for this is that the qualitative upsurgence beginning in the 1980s and accelerating in the 1990s seems to have heralded the development of qualitative data *analysis* methods of a sort which were previously unavailable in psychology. The histories of qualitative data collection and qualitative data analysis do not overlap perfectly. Overlapping terminology also adds to the confusion. For example, although what we refer to as discourse analysis was developed into a method for qualitative psychology in the 1980s, one can find references to discourse analysis much earlier – but referring to quantitative approaches. Although databases can help us to track psychological publications back to the 1800s, terminology changes over time. So, earlier publications may use the same words, but not in the modern sense.

Qualitative research as a concept seems to be relatively recent, though no one seems to know quite when it first emerged – perhaps it was imported into psychology. Of course, it would be next to impossible to review the vast output of psychology in the last hundred years or so in the hope of identifying just what is qualitative in nature – there are well over three million psychology research articles in print right now! And the number is rising.

Tracking qualitative methods using PsycINFO and other indicators

Despite this, the most effective way of documenting the rise of qualitative psychology is to use the massive digital databases available to psychologists. Superficially, the task of doing research using these is simple:

- Make a list of key words or search terms which are likely to find qualitative research.
- Use the appropriate research database to search for publications which use any of these search terms.
- Examine these publications (e.g. using the summary provided by the database) to make sure that they are truly qualitative in nature.

Two important studies have attempted to track the emergence of qualitative methods in psychology in this way – both used the American Psychological Association's PsycINFO database. This consists of abstracts (short summaries) of published works, bibliographic citations and so forth. By November 2010 the three millionth record had been entered into the database (American Psychological Association, 2011). The paper in question was resoundingly quantitative with the tile 'Rehabilitating patients with left spatial neglect by prism exposure during a visuomotor activity'. The current rate of expansion of the PsycINFO database is 130,000 additional publications each year. By 2015 PsycInfo was claiming to have over 3,700,000 records (www.apa.org/pubs/databases/psycinfo/index.aspx?tab=2). PsycINFO incorporates a vast range of scholarly journal publications in the behavioural and social sciences starting as early as 1894 and books go back to 1840 and much earlier. Book chapters are also listed, as are PhD dissertations. It is a truly international compendium and almost 30 different languages and 50 different countries are included (American Psychological Association, 2009). About 2500 journals are abstracted, of which the vast majority are peer reviewed – that is, assessed for satisfactory quality by two or three eminent researchers in that field. The entire contents of 300 journals are automatically abstracted and the rest are surveyed for articles which are relevant to psychology. In other words, PsycINFO is the result of a massive cataloguing operation and provides the best source for tracing what has been published in psychology for most of its modern history. Although it would be foolish to regard PsycINFO as the perfect tool for historical research in psychology, it has great potential as part of a broad-brush research approach.

So what are the general trends in qualitative research for the twentieth century? Rennie, Watson and Monteiro (2002) used PsycINFO to identify the qualitative research publications for each decade between 1900 and 1999. They tried various possible search terms and came up with the following as their final list: qualitative research, grounded theory, empirical phenomenological, phenomenological psychology and discourse analy* (the wild card format of this meant that discourse analysis, discourse analytic and other similar terms would be found). Of course, it could be debated whether additional search terms should have been used – for example, there is no mention of thematic analysis, conversation analysis or narrative analysis. Over 3000 records were identified as potential instances of qualitative studies. However, the sifting or weeding-out process eliminated some false hits, leaving about 2500 records dealing with qualitative research. Phenomenological psychology was the only search term which appeared in the database fairly commonly prior to 1970. The remaining terms really only appeared from the 1980s onwards. Qualitative research, grounded theory, and discourse analysis and related terms began to appear much more frequently in the 1990s.

Qualitative publications tended not to be located in mainstream or prime psychology journals but more likely in non-psychology publications. This perhaps indicates a greater interest in qualitative methods outside of mainstream psychology – or some might say the antipathy of mainstream psychology journals to qualitative research. Rennie et al. (2002) concluded:

> Overall, the rise in qualitative research as reflected by three of our search terms, at least, has been dramatic, especially in the last 10 years or so . . . the growth of publications has been heavily swayed by the production of just a few journals that were created for qualitative research . . . (Rennie et al., 2002, p. 188)

This study provides evidence for what we have seen is commonly claimed – that is, the accelerated growth of qualitative methods started in psychology in or about the 1980s but more emphatically so from the 1990s onwards.

The other study using PsycINFO used a shorter historical period but perhaps a slightly more sophisticated analysis. Marchel and Owens (2007) chose to classify each journal as one of three tiers in the following way:

- Tier 1: Journals owned by the American Psychological Association.
- Tier 2: Journals published by but not owned by the American Psychological Association.
- Tier 3: Journals associated with particular divisions of the American Psychological Association.

In other words, an additional criterion was involved in this study – not only had the publications to be in PsycINFO but they had to be associated with the American Psychological Association in some way. This is a much more stringent criterion than that used by Rennie et al. (2002) and so likely to produce fewer 'hits'. This second study covered each of the decades from the 1950s onwards until the 1990s. They also brought things more up to date by including later years up until 2002 since the researchers had noted that the rate of increase in numbers of qualitative publications seemed to be accelerating. In this study, the following key words or search terms were chosen: *action research, autoethnology, case study, discourse analysis, ethnography, ethnomethodology, grounded theory, life history, participant observation, phenomenology* and *qualitative*. The list then overlaps but does not replicate that used by Rennie et al. (2002). For each of the publications found using any of these key words, two raters were used to check the content in more detail. About half of the articles generated by the computer search could not be meaningfully described as qualitative in nature – many more than in Rennie et al.'s study. This left about 600 abstracts containing qualitative research from the 33 American Psychological Association journals studied.

This clearly suggests that the amount of qualitative research in American Psychological Association journals was small overall. The journal with the largest percentage of qualitative studies was *Humanistic Psychologist* which had 22 per cent of qualitative research followed by *The Journal of Theoretical and Philosophical Psychology* which contained about 7 per cent of qualitative research. Taken as a whole, the American Psychological Association journals included few qualitative articles relative to the total number of articles published. The proportion is probably in the region of 1 per cent of all articles published.

According to Marchel and Owens (2007), a qualitative researcher would be well advised to bear in mind the following:

● The most acclaimed or top journals (Tier 1) tend to publish very little qualitative research. Assuming that this is the result of selection preferences (as opposed to authors self-choosing not to submit), these journals should be avoided by qualitative researchers. There is an exception to this in that theoretical qualitative articles seem to be well received by these top journals. This is possibly because the most prestigious journals hold theory at a premium.

● Some newly established journals and those affiliated to specific divisions of the American Psychological Association are more likely to publish qualitative research. This may reflect a gradual process by which qualitative research is entering psychology through more peripheral journals where there is greater variety and flexibility of approaches.

● Cross-disciplinary journals (that is, those not publishing psychological research exclusively) have the best record of publishing qualitative research. Thus the qualitative researcher might well consider publishing in such journals if the subject matter of the research falls into the ambit of a particular journal. For example, if the article is in the field of education then a cross-disciplinary education journal is a good choice for publishing a qualitative research paper.

These findings paint a somewhat pessimistic picture of the penetration of qualitative research into the mainstream of psychology. The overall pattern shows some inroads but qualitative research seems marginal to mainstream psychology. Of course, this rather negative view may be a function of the choice made by Marchel and Owens to concentrate solely on American Psychological Association-related publications. Mainstream psychology journals tend to cater for the particular needs of long-term specialisms within psychology. Many of these specialisms may be almost exclusively quantitative in nature. The enthusiasm in the American Psychological Association for qualitative work at this time may have been quite low. It is, therefore, worth noting that as late as 2008 the American Psychological Association rejected the call to establish a Division of Qualitative Psychology. Instead, Division 5 of the APA (which is devoted to evaluation, measurement and statistics) encouraged qualitative psychologists to join it in a section of that division called 'The Society for Qualitative Inquiry in Psychology'. This is now in operation and the American Psychological Association currently publishes a specialist journal – *Qualitative Psychology* – which first went into print in 2014. If one accepts that Europe has been a more productive home for qualitative psychology, one might regard a search of American Psychological Association journals for qualitative work a biased or inappropriate starting point unlikely to identify new trends readily.

Another reason why these data show only a low level of representation of qualitative research in psychology may reflect that journals publish less qualitative research than books. Rennie et al. (2002) themselves point out that their hit rate for qualitative research is less than 0.5 per cent of PsycINFO records. However, this ignores the superior hit rates found for books and book chapters. Books and chapters in books were as responsible for the increase in qualitative research, as were journal articles. The authors identified Sage books as a key player in this expansion; they point out that these alternative forms of publication are a good way of sidestepping the prejudices against qualitative research which might be found in the journal publication system. This sort of reliance on a single publisher is not entirely unprecedented in qualitative research. For example, the Sociology Press has as its objective the keeping of important grounded theory publications in print.

Publications are not the only indicator of the successful development of an academic specialism. There are other factors within the discipline which are indicative that a specialism has made inroads into the discipline. In what ways have learned and professional associations actively incorporated a new area of research into the structure of the profession? The best news on this front is that the British Psychological Society established a section devoted to Qualitative Methods in Psychology in 2006. This claims to be the 'newest and largest' section of the Society with over 1000 members, though it should be quickly added that the major parts of the Society are called Divisions, several of which in themselves are larger than the Qualitative Methods section. The apparent steady growth in the number of journals devoted to qualitative methods in psychology or willing to accept qualitatively-based papers is a healthy sign. The list of journals specialising in or prepared to accept qualitative research was well in excess of 100 a few years ago (St Louis University, 2009), though relatively few of these were exclusively aimed at psychology.

Virtually any history of the growth of qualitative psychology suggests that it emerged as a significant form of data *analysis* during the 1980s. Nevertheless, the history of qualitative methods in psychology needs more detail and it is rather longer than this seems to imply. This story, as yet, is far from completely documented. The position is somewhat better now than when this text was first published. Some have provided general histories of qualitative methods in psychology (Wertz, 2014) while others have restricted their coverage to particular specialism such as psychotherapy (Levitt, 2015), marketing and consumer psychology (Bailey, 2014), and discourse analysis/conversation analysis (Potter, 2012).

It is not possible to argue that the rise in qualitative research reflects a decline in quantitative methods in psychology. There have been some inroads, especially in specialisms such as social psychology. Apart from these special cases, there is no evidence of a decline in mainstream quantitative psychology as a consequence of the success of qualitative methods. The discipline of psychology is richer for the qualitative input but mainstream psychology shows no sign of suffering a significant body-blow. The dramatic growth in the numbers of psychologists over the last century or so probably is enough to allow for the diversification of psychology without significant cutbacks or slowdowns within most of mainstream psychology. For example, the British Psychological Society had 1900 members in 1950, 2700 members in 1960, 10,000 members in the 1980s, and 33,000 plus members in recent years. Fundamentally, we seem to be witnessing a growth of mainstream psychology and qualitative psychology. Things may not stay the same forever, of course. With more and more psychology students being trained in both qualitative and quantitative methods the balance may change. This could be an increase in multi-method research or more qualitative research.

Box 2.1 discusses critical realism – a key concept in qualitative research.

Box 2.1

KEY CONCEPT

Critical realism

One of the critiques of quantitative research is that it adopts a realist position. The term *realism* is applicable to positivism and psychology in general. Unlike the broadly constructivist approaches to qualitative research, realism assumes that there is a reality outside of ourselves – a physical world – which scientists can get to know and understand directly. Subjectivism, on the other hand, is the view that there is no outside reality beyond ourselves that can be studied directly. A faith that we live in a quantifiable world encouraged the belief that there are laws of science. Physical sciences have generally been successful in the quest for quantification which makes the realist position more tenable. However, this was shattered when modern physics discovered how the act of measurement had a reactive effect on whatever is being measured. Measurement changes reality. So if the science of physics cannot achieve an unfettered view of reality then what chance psychology? Qualitative researchers generally believe that there are many different views of reality but no direct view on reality. They stress that the scientific search for a constant and knowable reality is a pointless task as a consequence.

Critical realism is one philosophical view important to understanding some qualitative approaches to psychological research. The critical realist does not deny that there is a real physical world but does question the extent to which social scientific data can truly or fully reflect such a real world. It is common for qualitative researchers to acknowledge that we view reality through numerous windows or lenses (e.g. different informants or different data collection methods) so we only glimpse reality at best as it is always obstructed in some way. Each window or lens distorts reality in its own way. There will be different perspectives on reality depending on the window being used. There is no way of knowing just what degree of distortion there is. Furthermore, research in psychology, as much as that in the other social sciences, greatly depends on language data. Language can never be reality; at best it is merely a window on reality. Hence, qualitative researchers value the diversity of views of reality. One cannot combine these different views to know what the nature of reality is – they are merely different views of that reality. (In the same way,

it is not possible to combine the paintings of a scene by different artists to give a photograph of the scene.) Nevertheless, the most extreme anti-realist in qualitative psychology is unlikely to ignore a warning that a car is coming! What varies is the assumption of what exactly can be known about the real world on the basis of the data we collect.

There is a view that every method of measuring reality is fundamentally flawed. If different views of reality tend to concur then maybe this means that we are getting somewhere towards understanding reality without revealing reality itself. In other words, all observers bring to research expectations and other 'baggage' which influence the outcome of the research. This baggage includes our culture, our particular interests and our personal perspectives on life. Furthermore, qualitative researchers tend to recognise that the instrumentation (techniques of psychological measurement) have their own built-in theories and assumptions which also affect how reality is viewed. Given this, and it is likely that all psychologists accept it, then how can it be dealt with? One approach taken by qualitative researchers is to provide our observations to others in order to obtain their critical responses as part of the analysis of our data.

Critical realism is an approach to the philosophy of science associated with the work of Roy Bhaskar (1944–2014). It is at odds with the positivist view that the social world can be understood using a natural science approach but, equally, it rejects the view that the purpose of social research is to elucidate the meanings imposed on the world by people and society (which is broadly the position of some qualitative researchers but by no means all). Critical realism defines something as real if it has a causal effect. It does not matter if this is an aspect of the natural or physical world (electricity – which, say, can drive a motor) or the social world. Thus unemployment is real because it can be established that it has effects. Scientific investigation involves the requirement that what is being studied involves mechanisms which can lead to outcomes. This is different from the positivist notion of cause-and-effect in which a constant relationship is expected between events. This does not mean that social scientific methods are identical to those of the natural sciences since social structures are in a more constant state of change than are physical structures. Social structures come before individuals historically, yet the state of flux of social structures is a result of the actions of individuals. So, in this sense, human activity is transformational.

Roberts (2014) stresses the importance of critical realism in providing a qualitative theory of causality. Quantitative researchers claim causality as the province of their methodology and suggest that the domain of the qualitative researcher is the subjective. Critical realism rejects this and indicates that causality is problematic for both the quantitative (empiricist) and the qualitative domains. There are qualitative researchers who believe in an objective world which exists beyond the language, conversation, texts, talk and other constructed features of human life and through which the real physical world is talked about, etc. The crucial difference is that quantitative researchers act as if they believe that data concerning

the real world is merely given to us whereas qualitative researchers reject this. They say that we can have only 'qualified objectivity' in our knowledge of the real world. Roberts explains it this way. In critical realist theory the world is seen as being made up of different layers or domains of reality. The empirical domain can be seen in the work of quantitative researchers in their laboratories who may investigate the relationship between different variables and find causal relationships between them. Other researchers (qualitative researchers) do not operate in this closed domain but work with open systems where causal variables and the like are not self-evident. This is the real domain. In the real domain, causal mechanisms interact with each other in complex ways. In critical realism, knowledge is assumed to be fallible and so is always questionable and to be questioned. To deal with the fallibility of knowledge the social researcher needs to explore causal mechanisms in a variety of research settings.

The main qualitative methods in psychology up to the 1950s

Just where does one look for examples of qualitative research methods in the early history of psychology? In the argot of psychologists the distinction between soft and hard data/science is an important one, though somewhat passé in recent psychology, where quantitative–qualitative seems to be the preferred choice. The hard–soft distinction would lead us to look for early examples of qualitative work in psychology in the 'soft' types of research. Paramount among these would be Freudian psychoanalysis and its commonest method – the case study. Another place to look is where psychology might be or has been influenced by developments in research disciplines related to psychology. An excellent example of this would be participant observation which had its origins in social anthropology and has sometimes been adopted by psychologists. However, the question is whether either of these is genuinely a precursor of recent qualitative methods in psychology.

Case studies

There is little doubt that case studies have been a regular feature of psychology almost since the beginning of modern psychology in the late nineteenth century. Nevertheless, is it a safe assumption to characterise all case studies as qualitative in nature? Routinely, if superficially, the case study is simply accepted as a qualitative method by writers (e.g. Vidich & Lyman, 2000). Consisting as it does of verbal description, it is easy to see the temptation to regard case studies as a qualitative method. Nevertheless, the extent to which all case studies represent a qualitative research approach is questionable. Case studies were adopted into psychology from medicine where they are common. Their original function was to illustrate, pedagogically, what was known about a particular medical condition through an example. It is, therefore, fairly evident that this form of case study does not really amount to research. Substantial numbers of case studies can be found in PsycINFO. From its beginnings in the nineteenth century until 2009, about 21,000 entries refer to case studies (i.e. case study is mentioned in the abstract) and the vast majority of these are after 1960.

A case study is an intensive investigation of a single case – this may be a person, an organisation, a community, an event and so forth. It may feature an extreme case, a typical case or a deviant case. Usually, in psychology, case studies have involved individuals in keeping with the discipline's largely individualistic nature. There are advocates of the use of the case study as a research method (e.g. Yin, 2003) though their research use is seen as very different from their use in illustrative and teaching settings. The phrase 'case study' in the literature covers the difficult circumstance for the quantitative researcher where there is no sample or, in other words, where the sample size equals one (see Barlow & Hersen, 1984, for a discussion of experimental research where the sample size is 1).

Modern qualitative research has quite a different view of sampling from that endemic in quantitative research as we shall see elsewhere in this book (e.g. Chapter 8 on grounded theory). There are many examples of case study approaches in modern qualitative research. Good examples include the following, but there are many more also: MacMillan and Edwards (1999), Potter and Edwards (1990), Locke and Edwards (2003), Voutilainen, Peräkylä and Ruusuvuori (2011) and Ellis and Cromby (2012). These examples do not focus on individuals but events which have been extensively covered in the media. And they are not usually identified as case studies by their authors. There is little reluctance, it would seem, for qualitative researchers to adopt a single case study approach. Almost invariably, for example, a qualitative research study involving conversation analysis will focus on just a small section of a conversation. This is not unusual in any way and is very typical of some sorts of qualitative research. In contrast, the quantitative researcher would be uneasy if a single case study was all that there was despite there being a tradition of such research in quantitative psychology (the work of the behaviourist Skinner being just one example).

Cowles (1888) reported a very early psychological case study. He describes a 28-year-old woman who had extreme fixed ideas as a consequence of a paranoid mental condition. Cowles wrote:

> The problem of this case was to discover the genesis, the growth and the fixation of the central idea, which in this instance had the peculiarity of being unusually complicated. In the first place, there was probably no special hereditary influence in its origin; the paranoiac element is excluded; certainly the right to infer it must be questioned. If it be said to have been 'acquired' because of the typhoid fever at the pubertic period, etc., a neurasthenia must be admitted. But if acquired organic defect be admitted also – while inquiry is excited as to the consistency of this inference – it remains that the 'fixed idea' was conceived some years before, disappeared, and was revived and developed when the supposable new factor of paranoiac defect came in. (Cowles, 1888, p. 262)

Quite clearly, Cowles's study does not involve a qualitative approach. Instead it draws a comparison between this woman's case and what happened with other people. Furthermore, the reference to the 'laws of habit' reveals, perhaps, the writer's positivistic stance. It seems very close in style to the original meaning of the term case study in medicine. Cowles's case study involves imposing pre-existing categories on his observations in a way which generally would be alien to qualitative researchers.

Of course, the reason why case studies are sometimes described as early forms of qualitative research in psychology is that often they lack any manifest quantification. Often they include extensive amounts of descriptive material of the sort which conventional quantitative studies on samples of people generally do not include. So, in the sense that they lack numbers and contain fairly rich descriptive material, the temptation is to regard some case studies as qualitative in nature. On the other hand, it is very difficult to recognise any elements in recent qualitative analysis methods of the sort discussed later in this book. These typically involve analyses which are led by the data and not by what is already known. Qualitative methods characteristically are exploratory and theory generating – the very reverse of what happens in many case studies.

So it is an open question whether the classic case studies in the history of psychology can truly be described as early forms of qualitative study as opposed to a variant of quantitative research. Probably different answers will be given depending on what features of the case study in question are concentrated on. The psychoanalytic case studies of Sigmund Freud (1856–1939) are a case in point. Freud brought a different sort of intellectual tradition from that of psychology's mainstream, though one which was positivist in nature rather than qualitative. He had been, after all, a doctor and a physiological researcher. Several of his case studies are extremely well known even beyond psychology. However, Freud's total output of case studies was very small.

Among the most famous case studies in the history of psychology is that of Little Hans (Freud, 1909) which involved the analysis of a phobia in a 5-year-old boy. The Little Hans study came about when Freud asked people he knew to supply him with observations about the sexual life of children in an attempt to understand infantile sexuality. As a 4-year-old, Little Hans had been a witness to awful events in which a horse pulled its cart over during a fit. A passer-by was killed in the incident. The boy became scared of leaving home and was particularly afraid of horses and over-laden transport. Little Hans's parents were among these informants and, eventually, at the age of 5 Little Hans became a patient of Freud. The fact is that Freud only saw Little Hans once since the boy's father actually carried out the boy's psychoanalysis under Freud's supervision. Despite the obvious source of the fear, Freud and the father chose to explain the fear in psychosexual terms, though Freud much more subtly than the father. One could describe the data as rich, detailed and complex since accounts of the boy's dreams, behaviour and answers to various questions were included. Such richness and depth of data are characteristic of the work of current qualitative researchers. But, unlike many recent qualitative psychologists, Freud was somewhat detached from the process of data collection (as it was largely collected by the boy's father). The Little Hans case study did not really serve to generate ideas. Instead, primarily it was a vehicle to enable Freud to illustrate his theories of infantile sexuality. Furthermore, many of the psychological concepts used by Freud (e.g. id, ego and superego) refer to internal mental processes which qualitative psychologists tend to reject. Freud's ideas, themselves, sit uncomfortably with those of present-day qualitative researchers. Briefly, then, Freud's case studies neglect crucial aspects of qualitative research methodology.

There are other classic examples of case studies in the history of psychology. One particularly important one was Luria and Bruner's (1987) *The mind of a mnemonist: A little book about a vast memory*. This concerned the real-life problems of a man with a prodigious memory capacity. In this book, the reader is provided with a detailed account of how a man with neurological problems dealt with his profound memory and perceptual difficulties. *The mind of a mnemonist* is clearly essentially quantitative in nature and contains relatively little purely descriptive material about the man's everyday experience of memory. In fact, the book includes descriptions of many little experiments carried out on the man's memory. At the other end of what would seem to be a continuum, *The man who mistook his wife for a hat* by Oliver W. Sacks (1985) ought to be mentioned since it concerns a man with no proper memory. *The man who mistook his wife for a hat* is much more descriptive and might, in its own way, be said to be a qualitative study.

Despite its relatively early appearance in the psychological literature, the case study in psychology is not readily classified as an early form of qualitative research. This is despite the fact that they are frequently descriptive in nature and often contain no obvious characteristics of quantitative research such as numbers and statistics. But this lack of obvious quantification should not be taken to indicate that most case studies are qualitative in nature. What other of the characteristics of qualitative methods do case studies incorporate? Look back at Figure 1.2 which describes many of the features of qualitative research and then ask yourself the question of just how many of these actually describe the case studies of early psychologists. Some do, some do not. So there can be no automatic presumption that a case study will be qualitative in nature. Dividing research simply into qualitative versus quantitative seems inadequate when considering case studies. One might argue for a third category – non-quantitative may be a possibility – to cover the situation where a study seems to have emerged from a quantitative orientation but does not involve quantification as such. A good discussion of case studies in their many guises and how they should be conceptualised can be found in Flyvbjerg (2006).

Participant observation and ethnography

Participant observation is part of ethnography and is rarely discussed separately from it nowadays. It would seldom be carried out without other ethnographic methods. So we can speak of participant observation and ethnography as one, although ethnography is the more up-to-date term. Participant observation and ethnography are unquestionably qualitative in nature. Some such studies may include some elements of quantification but this is not a defining feature and generally they don't. They also happen to be the longest-established qualitative data collecting method with the possible exception of in-depth interviewing. So the history of participant observation/ethnography in psychology is particularly important in terms of qualitative research. Ethnography is the discipline which generates descriptive studies of different human societies through the use of fieldwork (as opposed to, say, secondary sources). It involves a holistic methodology in which all aspects of a social system are viewed as interacting rather than acting independently. It remains at the core of cultural anthropology and is important within modern sociology. Interestingly, ethnography is presented as the most important method in Vidich and Lyman's (2000) history of qualitative methods in sociology and anthropology. However, this dominance is not repeated in the history of qualitative methods in psychology at all forcefully. In participant observation, the researcher is, to varying degrees, immersed in the activities of a community over an extended period of time, collecting extensive and valuable information. The methods employed for obtaining data within this broad approach include active participation in the activities of the group, collecting life histories from members of the group, direct observation, group discussions and self-analysis by the researcher. The descriptive data collected in an ethnographic study are rich and detailed, as demanded by qualitative researchers in general.

The earliest ethnographers, who were largely missionaries and travellers, saw 'primitive peoples' as constituting part of a chain of development which had led to Western culture. Thus by studying other cultures, the early stages of the development of Western cultures could be better understood. However, the sheer diversity of societies throughout the world, according to Vidich and Lyman (2000), made it very difficult to explain how different the moral values of these societies were compared with modern Western values. This revelation sat very uncomfortably with the view that Christianity had a monopoly on legitimacy and truth. Furthermore, the work of early ethnographers often served to provide justifications for the extremes of colonialism and imperialism.

In the late nineteenth century, the cultural diversity of immigrants and others in American cities drew researchers' attention to the need to find out more. W. E. B. Du Bois (1868–1963), an African-American himself, carried out the first study of an American community which was published in 1899 as *The Philadelphia Negro*. It included 5000 interviews and simply described the Black population of Philadelphia. It also was intended by the local Quaker community, which financed it, as a way of uplifting the Black community. But really this is the start of qualitative research in American sociology and influenced the Chicago School of Sociology in the 1920s and 1930s. The first professor of sociology at Chicago was Robert Park (1864–1944) who, significantly, had been a journalist, but also trained in psychology. He saw in sociology a means to social reform. He famously told his students in 1927 'gentlemen, go get the seat of your pants dirty in real research' (cited in Bulmer, 1984, p. 97). Members of the Chicago School in the 1920s and 1930s employed participant observation in very much the anthropological style. The big development was that the Chicago School applied the method to then contemporary Western communities under the name of ethnography. The church sponsored a good proportion of these early investigations. Robert Lynd (1892–1970) and Helen Lynd (1896–1982) wrote the book *Middletown: A study in contemporary American culture* (Lynd & Lynd, 1929) which was another example of this influence on qualitative research. Their later *Middletown in transition: A study in cultural conflicts* (Lynd & Lynd, 1937) shed the church influence in favour of a much more Marxist stance.

In early but crucial anthropological research, Bronislaw Malinowski (1884–1942) travelled to the Trobriand Islands in Papua New Guinea in 1914. His intention was to carry out the fieldwork for his PhD at the London School of Economics over there. Stranded there by the advent of the First World War, he eventually overcame his initial reluctance and began to live life much more as one of the Trobriand Islanders – that is, as a participant observer. There is an interesting link to early psychology. Malinowski had previously spent time at the University of Leipzig where he came under the influence of the psychologist Wilhelm Wundt. Despite being often seen as the founding figure of experimental psychology (as we saw in Chapter 1), Wundt actually saw limitations in this approach (which he called *Physiologischen* – psychology) and argued for a different form of psychology (*Volkerpsychologie* – sometimes translated as folk-psychology) to deal with the role which social and community living played on the human mind. Malinowski laid down the principles of participant observation, though the influence of Wundt on him has largely been overlooked by psychologists. Later, Frank Boas (1858–1942) and his student Margaret Mead (1901–1978) promoted similar approaches to fieldwork in American cultural anthropology.

Participant observation is common in the PsycINFO records from the 1930s on and the abstracts of nearly 3000 records included the phrase up to 2009. One very early mention of participant observation to be found in psychology journals lies in a book review by Dearborn (1920) of an anthropological study in Northern Rhodesia (now Zambia). An excerpt in which Dearborn comments is illustrative:

> To them, the union of the sexes is on the same plane as eating and drinking, to be indulged in without stint on every possible occasion. One would like to know as to the relative number of neurones in their (inhibitory) neopalliuni compared with those in a restrained man cultured and virile with habitual self control; would Sigmund Freud expect to find the number equal? (Dearborn, 1920, p. 284)

So in addition to the routine scientific racism of the first sentence (Howitt & Owusu-Bempah, 1994), Dearborn's consideration of the anthropological study basically becomes translated as a matter of physiology – that is, essentially a quantitative approach to what he actually regards as a rich anthropological study! Dearborn is wondering whether the brain structures of civilised people are different from those of what he regarded as primitive people. Dearborn, thus, offers a somewhat racist biological reductionist perspective from psychology about the complex social system of the people of the then Northern Rhodesia. In the reference to Freud, there is a reminder that Freud made extensive use of anthropology in some of his writings – especially in his book *Totem and taboo* (1918; published in Germany in 1913 *Totem und tabu: Einige Übereinstimmungen im Seelenleben der Wilden und der Neurotiker*). Freud, of course, like others at this time, did not carry out original anthropological research himself. His work based on anthropological studies is probably best described by the phrase non-quantitative rather than qualitative. Remember, Freud had trained in medicine and his psychoanalytic work was essentially a version of positivism highly influenced by the physiological research of the time. However, the inference of internal mental states such as the id, ego and superego not only was alien to behaviourism but, interestingly, alien also to most current qualitative approaches which reject the search for internal mental states. Discourse analysis and conversation analysis are examples of this opposition.

We have noted already that the coverage of the PsycINFO database goes beyond quintessentially psychological publications to include those which, although coming from other disciplines, are of psychological interest. So to some extent, the first appearance of particular qualitative methods in the major psychological research database may merely signal the possible interest of psychologists in the method rather than their actual adoption of the method. Nevertheless, there is clear evidence that at least a few psychologists adopted participant observation for their research in the 1930s and 1940s.

One of the earliest and most significant examples of participant observation studies in psychology was the Marienthal study by the psychologist Marie Jahoda (1907–2001), the psychologist to become sociologist Paul Lazarsfeld (1901–1976) and the sociologist Hans Zeisel (1905–1992). This was the first study of unemployment and was first published in Austria in the 1930s (Jahoda, Lazarsfeld, & Zeisel, 1933) and reprinted most recently nearly 70 years later (Jahoda, Lazarsfeld, & Zeisel, 2002). Marienthal, itself, was an Austrian town devastated when dreadful economic circumstances led to the closure of the local factory which had been the major source of jobs. High levels of unemployment were the result of this. Some details of the Marienthal study are given in Chapter 5 (Box 5.1). Jahoda et al. describe their study in the following terms:

> It was the aim of the study to draw an image of the psychological situation of a community suffering from unemployment, using cutting edge methods of research. From the outset we focused our attention on two objectives. One with regard to substance: contributing material concerning the problem of unemployment – and a methodological one: trying to give a comprehensive and objective account of the socio-psychological facts. (Jahoda et al., 2002, p. v)

In other words, the Marienthal study was essentially ethnographic in nature, using participant observation and interviews, for example, together with some quantification too. Furthermore, the cross-disciplinary nature of the study was unusual at this time.

So different is the Marienthal study from the typical behaviourist laboratory experiment of the period that it is worthwhile noting that the ethos (and ethic) underlying

Marienthal was more concerned with 'the problem' which motivated the research than any abstract philosophical notion:

> In a speech in 1994, Marie Jahoda announced her 'testament': a relevant social psychology draws its themes from the problems of the social present, not from abstract theories; does not look for answers independent of their time, but recognises that social events and human behaviour take place in a context; does not want to prove but to discover? ... Because things count which cannot be counted, qualitative methods have their place in it as well as quantitative ones. And with all the difficulties that this brings, the unfashionableness and the lack, in some scientific circles, of prestige, it also brings the deep satisfaction of making it possible to master the problems of the day. (Klein, 2001)

There were elements of action research in the study but more so the concern that the researchers had for the participants in their study is refreshingly modern and a typical sentiment of recent qualitative researchers. The Marienthal study married both qualitative and quantitative data in addressing the researchers' research question.

A few years after Jahoda et al.'s study, John Dollard (1900–80) travelled from Yale University to the deep south American town he called Southerntown. Racial segregation was endemic at the time. The original intention was to study the personality of Black people using interviews, but he rapidly realised that whiteness and White people were an essential part of their personality. So the study changed to that of the study of the community. Kidder and Fine (1997) discuss Dollard's study in terms of what they call the 'qualitative stance' which 'enables researchers to carve open territory about which they have vague hunches rather than clear predictions' (p. 37). What Dollard has to say about his own research makes fascinating reading as he wrestles with the strictures of his chosen discipline, psychology:

> Many times during the conduct of the research and the arrangement of the materials I have had a bad conscience on the score of method. Should the researcher expect to be believed if he cannot lock his findings into the number system and present them in the manner conventional in the physical sciences? So far I have managed to stave off this pressure by such consolations as these: the first loyalty of a scientist is to his material; he must seek where it can be found and grasp it as it permits. (Dollard, 1937, pp. 16–17)

Dollard's method in *Southerntown* was purely participant observation. He spent months as a member of a community just knowing and interacting with different people. He rejected using interviews as a method of studying community members because of the risks that this would create in such an intensely racial context.

The book *When prophecy fails: A social and psychological study of a modern group that predicted the destruction of the world* (Festinger, Riecken, & Schachter, 1956) was a novel participant observation study which led to a great deal of experimentation on the topic of cognitive dissonance – one of the most famous concepts in the history of psychology and which is primarily associated with the name of Leon Festinger (1919–89). The researchers were intrigued by a prophecy reported in the local newspaper that there would be a great flood which would bring about the end of the world. Marion Keech, through automatic-writing in which the movements of one's hand seem to be under external and not personal control, claimed to have received messages from a planet known as Clarion to that effect. The flood would occur on 21 December. A group of believers led by Mrs Keech had given up the jobs and studies, given away their money and possessions, and left their families. They believed that a flying saucer would rescue 'believers'. Festinger and his co-workers decided to infiltrate this group in order to understand what would happen when the world did not come to an end at the appointed time. In the hours prior to the time of the predicted cataclysm, the group actively avoided publicity and only true believers had access. However, on the 20 December no flying saucer arrived to rescue the true believers. A few hours later Mrs Keech, through automatic-writing, received a message that the God of the Earth had stopped the cataclysm. Finally, in the afternoon of the day of the predicted cataclysm the group sought the attention of the news media, thus reversing its previous shunning of publicity, and the group urgently campaigned to broadcast its message to a wide audience. In other words, when the belief about doomsday was threatened, cognitions changed in ways which allowed the belief to survive. The impact of this essentially qualitative study was in terms of the generation of numerous studies using laboratory methods – the typical psychology of the time – rather than a rush to using participant observation in psychology.

Although both participant observation and case studies have been seen by modern qualitative researchers as early examples of qualitative research in psychology, they do not typify current qualitative psychology. Recent textbooks on qualitative methods in psychology do not cover case studies in any significant detail compared with other data collection methods. Similarly, participant observation or ethnology is sometimes covered but it is not at the core of qualitative methods as it would be in other disciplines. Case studies can be presented from a range of perspectives – the quantitative, the qualitative, the psychoanalytic, the pedagogic and so forth. Participant observation/ethnographic studies may also straddle the quantitative and the qualitative. Generally speaking, the impact of case studies and participant observation/ethnology on the substance of psychology has been very modest indeed. Within psychology they appear more to be admired for their novelty appeal than providing a core of psychological knowledge. Few appear in psychology textbooks, for example. Related social sciences disciplines have embraced these methods and the comparison between psychology and these disciplines is quite dramatic in this respect.

The radical innovations of 1950–1970

Historically, qualitative psychology has been fed by other disciplines – principally sociology and philosophy, both of which relate to sociolinguistics, which is a third major input. Sociology was changing in the 1950s and 1960s and these changes would eventually come to have a big impact on qualitative psychology, albeit after a rather substantial delay of three decades or so. Changes within psychology also played a role in paving the way for recent qualitative psychology and these should not be overlooked by anyone seeking a comprehensive understanding of qualitative research in psychology. We have seen that positivism and behaviourism did not completely monopolise psychology in the first half of the twentieth century. It is probably true to suggest that clinical and similar areas of psychology were less enamoured with behaviourist approaches than much of the rest of psychology. Not surprisingly then, these fields also generated fresh ways of looking at their subject matter which differed significantly and necessarily from those of mainstream psychology. So, in the next section, we shall describe important developments which moved psychology towards qualitative methods in the 1950s and 1960s as well as developments in other disciplines.

The constructed nature of reality

Qualitative researchers generally believe that there are many different views of reality but no direct view on reality. They stress that the scientific search for a constant and knowable reality is a pointless task as a consequence. The work of the clinician Carl Rogers (1902–87) was both based on humanism and phenomenology – probably the idea of client-centred therapy is the key enduring Rogerian innovation. This demanded the sort of intensive study of the individual which characterises some qualitative research. But more important in this context was the work of George Kelly (1905–67) who published in 1955 the two-volume book *The psychology of personal constructs* (Kelly, 1955a, b). Personal construct theory involves the fundamental view that an individual constructs their own world and the job of psychology is to understand this constructed version of reality.

Underlying personal construct psychology are the processes by which individuals create a meaningful understanding of their lives while being free to change these understandings in light of the experience. Kelly's influence is probably greatest on psychotherapy, clinical psychology and counselling psychology, though this does not represent the full breadth of his influence. One of his important metaphors was that of individuals as (incipient) scientists who created, tested and recreated their self and the world. Among the consequences of this is that people's theories allowed them to deal with future events. Psychological problems occured when a person's personal constructions of the world did not effectively incorporate new events or did not articulate with those of people around them. This process of construct formation and change is ongoing and lacks fixedness – which fits well with postmodern ideas in qualitative psychology. The therapist (or researcher) may identify an individual's personal constructions using the repertory grid methods. In the repertory grid method, the individual is asked to differentiate between three important persons in their lives by saying which two are similar (and how) and which one is different (and how). They then apply this similarity–difference 'dimension' to other people in their world. This process is repeated for different sets of three individuals. By comparing the patterns of descriptions across different people the psychologist begins to see beyond the descriptions used and into the nature of the underlying constructs used by the individual.

It could be argued that George Kelly comes close to being an early influential qualitative psychologist. The influences on his work – particularly phenomenology – are fairly obvious and the broadly qualitative orientation clear. Some basic assumptions of qualitative research are evident in his theory. For example, although he believed in a 'reality' he accepted that individuals have their own version of or perspective on reality – that is, accessing reality is not possible and how people experience it should be the focus of research. This brings Kelly's work in line with Husserl's philosophy discussed later in this book. It also has to be said that George Kelly, his repertory grid method and his personal construct theory were enormously influential in the 1960s and 1970s in various countries and the United Kingdom, perhaps, in particular. In other words, there were elements of a qualitative revolution in George Kelly's work and this pre-dated by two decades the arrival of discourse analysis, interpretative phenomenological analysis and narrative analysis from the 1980s onwards. At the time, personal construct theory was a vibrant alternative to mainstream psychology which was only just emerging from the straitjacket of behaviourism. It was centred on the individual as an individual who actively constructs his or her version of the outside world. To be sure, the repertory grid technique was rudimentary but it did not lend itself to mainstream investigation.

Perhaps the constructivist nature of Kelly's work helps establish his work as an important precursor to recent qualitative psychology. According to Potter (1996a), there is a wide variety of qualitative methods which are essentially constructionist. These include conversation analysis, discourse analysis, ethnomethodology and rhetoric. If this is Kelly's legacy, then it can be seen as part of the thin thread of qualitative methods in psychology which we have identified throughout the history of modern psychology. But Kelly's work and the way in which it developed was not entirely immune from quantification, which tends to suggest that its roots in qualitative methods were not quite so strong as some suggest. Also, the sort of data gathered using Kelly's repertory grid is generally not the rich, detailed, 'thick' description which is the lifeblood of much recent qualitative research. Nevertheless, it was this grid method which held prominence in the research of psychologists. It would be reasonable to suggest that George Kelly's work was a significant challenge to mainstream psychology, particularly in those parts of the world where qualitative methods grew effectively just a couple of decades or so later.

Personal construct theory is seen as an early precursor to more recent social constructionist approaches. It should not be regarded as an example of social constructionism, however (Ashworth, 2008). Personal constructs are cognitive in nature and, as a consequence, not entirely compatible with some recent approaches to qualitative psychology (e.g. discourse analysis) which have theoretical disagreements with cognitivism (see Chapter 9 on discourse analysis). Nevertheless, in some ways Kelly came frustratingly close to an even more profound breakthrough which occurred in the work of two European sociologists, Peter L. Berger (1929–) and Thomas Luckmann (1927–). They were the first to use the term social construction, although their basic idea did have earlier roots. Their book *The social construction of reality* (1966) is a major classic in the social sciences and is best regarded as a theory of knowledge. Their idea was that people and groups of people interact together as a social system. Within this system, they begin to generate ways of understanding the actions of members of the system. These ways of understanding (or concepts or representations) become consolidated in the relationships within the system. Eventually conceptions of reality become institutionalised into social structures and become, in this sense, the reality. In other words, although ideas and activities can appear to have a natural or built-in character, they are best considered to be created by members of that society. So ideas which seem to be common sense are the product of social interactions in which the actors believe that they share an understanding of the world and this understanding effectively becomes reality as a consequence. The process of social construction is a continuous one and the product of the dynamics of interaction.

A major figure in the promotion of social constructionist ideas in psychology is Kenneth J. Gergen (1935–). On the way to this, Gergen wrote in the 1970s an article conceptualising social psychology as history (Gergen, 1973). His basic argument in this was that psychological truths are transient and changing partly because of the interaction between the institution of psychology and the people that it studies. Psychological knowledge is therefore subject to revision in the process of interaction. For example, he points out that certain generally accepted concepts in psychology may be affected:

> . . . psychological principles pose a potential threat to all those for whom they are germane. Investments in freedom may thus potentiate behavior designed to invalidate the theory. We are satisfied with principles of attitude change until we find them being used in information campaigns dedicated to changing our behavior. At this point, we may feel resentful and react recalcitrantly. The more potent the theory is in predicting behavior, the broader its public dissemination and the more prevalent and resounding the reaction. Thus, strong theories may be subject to more rapid invalidation than weak ones. (Gergen, 1973, p. 314)

Essentially we can see in this a version of a key assumption of social constructionist psychology (Gergen, 1985b) and modern qualitative analysis as a consequence – that knowledge is historically and culturally specific. Another feature shared with much recent qualitative psychology is that social constructionist psychology is critical of 'taken-for-granted' and common-sense assumptions about the way we explain and describe people. But, ultimately, this leads to a more critical and complex understanding which includes the political:

> Social constructionists are concerned with examining the words that people use and the ways in which people understand the world, the social and political processes that influence how people define words and explain events, and the implications of these definitions and explanations – who benefits and who loses because of how we describe and understand the world? … From this perspective, a single, uncontested, universal, or true definition of any concept does not exist. Definitions of terms depend on who gets to define them; thus, definitions reflect the interests of people with power. (Muehlenhard & Kimes, 1999, p. 234)

The need for the discovery of grounded theory

As crucial as any other event in the development of qualitative methods in psychology was the introduction of grounded theory by the sociologists Barney Glaser (1930–) and Anselm Strauss (1916–1996). This is probably still the commonest method of qualitative data analysis and several qualitative data analysis methods in psychology use at least some of its principles. The name 'grounded theory' is indicative of the close relationship between the data being used and the theoretical ideas derived from the data. So there is a sense in which the theory is closely tied to the data. This is a better way of putting it than suggesting that grounded theory is embedded or emerges out of the data. It does not mean that the theory is merely waiting to be found in the data. It is not – it is created by the hard analytic work of the researcher. Grounded theory stands in distinct contrast to the idea common in mainstream psychology that the data are there to test a pre-established theory. The ideas were published in Glaser and Strauss's (1967) book *The discovery of grounded theory*. Grounded theory does not allow the use of hypotheses derived prior to the analysis of the data. So a grounded theory analyst may choose to avoid the adverse influences of things such as literature reviews in order to escape predetermining their ideas. Fundamental to the approach is that the researcher should be generating new categories based on the data with the proviso that these categories should demonstrate a good fit with the data. Grounded theory involves constant repetition of aspects of the analysis in order to obtain ultimately the best possible fit of the analysis with the data. This sort of fine-grained, close to the data analysis is the bedrock of almost all recent qualitative methods in psychology.

Famously, Glaser and Strauss later went in different directions in terms of grounded theory. Glaser continued with the general tack of *The discovery of grounded theory* with the publication of his book *Theoretical sensitivity* in 1978. Strauss and Corbin (1990) presented a version of grounded theory which left Glaser so unhappy that he wrote a book-length refutation of their work (Glaser, 1992). The core issue between them was the extent to which the theory should be left to emerge primarily from what can be seen in the data rather than forcing the data into a partially preconceived structure or framework. Glaser took the view that theory should emerge out of the data so to speak, Strauss preferred preconceived frameworks. Despite the influence of grounded theory on many modern qualitative methods, there is a degree of selectivity concerning what aspects (and versions) of grounded theory are used. For example, grounded theory according to Glaser eschews recording and transcribing interviews as essentially counterproductive with no benefits. This is because the grounded theory analysis can be much speedier when the researcher produces field notes (a written account) which are completed as soon as possible after the interview. In so doing the researcher begins to identify concepts which have a good fit with the field note data early on. In other words, the detailed transcription of recorded data which characterises conversation analysis and some forms of discourse analysis is not central in Glaser's version of grounded theory. The links of grounded theory to ethnography which relied on field notes rather than recordings are evident in this. However, Glaser's view is very much a minority one and researchers adopting Strauss's perspective typically make use of recordings. Of course, that methods change in detail over time is not at all surprising whether they are quantitative or qualitative in nature. Grounded theory is discussed later (Chapter 8).

Phenomenology in sociology

Phenomenology has a long history in psychology as we saw in Chapter 1. Its influence can also be seen in the writings of George Kelly discussed earlier in this chapter. However, the more direct route of phenomenology into recent qualitative psychology was through sociology and the ethnomethological approach developed by the sociologist Harold Garfinkel (1917–2011) in the 1950s and 1960s. The term ethnomethodology literally refers to the methods or ways that people use to understand their day-to-day worlds. It does not simply apply to individuals but also to groups of individuals such as in the case of organisations. Ethnomethodology's basic idea is that the way in which a person understands their everyday world constitutes a social fact. Individuals and groups in society create these social facts. Understanding these social facts is the role of the researcher. The nature of individuals' accounts of social situations and how they make sense of the world are important aspects of the theory. Thus explaining to one's boss why one has to have the next day off is an account. But the method by which these accounts are made meaningful to another person is more important. Many accounts used in explaining one's behaviour or understanding social behaviour do not normally have to be given in any detail because of their 'taken-for-granted' character. In order to elucidate such taken-for-granted accounts, ethnomethodologists have sometimes employed procedures which violate the expectations based on these. For example, imagine a scenario in which guests were invited to dinner but no food was provided. One likelihood is that the guests would formulate accounts for the host's behaviour. People are highly able to account for social order where it fails and, in so doing, maintain that social order.

The influence of ethnomethodology on conversation analysis (Chapter 10) is readily seen. Conversation analysis essentially deals with what superficially may seem like a disorganised aspect of social interaction – conversation – but shows that it has an underlying order and that those who take part in a conversation are aware of the 'rules' which govern conversation. It was developed in the 1960s by Harvey Sacks (1935–75), though his early death in a motor accident led to Gail Jefferson (1938–2008) and Emanuel Schegloff (1937–) subsequently promoting and developing his ideas. For example, recordings of lectures by Sacks had been transcribed by Jefferson and eventually published as a book after his death as he was not a prolific writer of academic papers for publication. Many aspects of conversation came within Sacks's purview – the selection of the next speaker in conversation, conversational turn-taking, the openings of conversations and the repairs of 'errors' made during conversation.

Phenomenology in psychology

Phenomenology has historically had adherents in psychology. However, as a historical enterprise, tracing the development of phenomenology in psychology is somewhat problematic. To be sure it is possible to identify individual psychologists who were influenced by phenomenology. For example, Cloonan (1995) examined the work of a number of (almost exclusively North American) psychologists who took their inspiration from phenomenol-ogy. These were Donald Snygg (1904–67), Robert B. McCleod (1907–72), the Dutch psy-chologist Adrian L. van Kaam (1920–2007) and Amedeo Giorgi (1931–). The work of each of these is thoroughly reviewed by Cloonan in terms of its phenomenological credentials. Giorgi's approach is singled out as by far the most coherent, phenomenologically-based work. To be able to name psychologists influenced by phenomenology in itself does not establish a growing phenomenological movement in any meaningful sense. So, perhaps to overstate this, phenomenology has been a somewhat gossamer-thin thread in most of the history of psychology – the sort of growth that can happen within academic disciplines which is hard to detect.

The exception to this – again tentatively – is the work of Amedeo Giorgi and others of the so-called Duquesne School. Duquesne University had a good tradition of phe-nomenology beginning in the 1950s but in the philosophy department. The psychology department there had begun to go down a similar radical route by the 1960s when Giorgi joined the teaching staff. Giorgi had received conventional training in psychol-ogy but had grown dissatisfied with the way that psychology was done. This prompted him to explore some of the radical approaches to research, especially phenomenology. This led to what is regarded as the first successful method of carrying out phenomeno-logical research in psychology. It is strongly based on the phenomenological philosophy of Edmund Husserl whose intellectual task was to describe how people experienced 'reality' in their consciousness. Conscious experience was the only valid knowledge according to Husserl. Giorgi's method can be described as rampantly descriptive and his work involved largely cataloguing the characteristics of phenomena as experienced by people generally. It was not about individual experiences as such since these were the basis for developing a description of how, in general, the phenomenon was expe-rienced. Giorgi had a long career using his style of phenomenological research and substantial amounts of research were carried out. But the question is whether this led to a significant influx of phenomenology into psychology. Certainly Giorgi achieved the important step of establishing a journal devoted to phenomenological psychology (*The Journal of Phenomenological Psychology*) which provides a vehicle for this sort of research. However, whether it paved the way for the recent growth in qualitative psychological methods (with the exception of interpretative phenomenological analysis) is also a moot point. Giorgi's work is discussed in greater detail in Chapters 12 and 13. Certainly, the phenomenologically-based movements in sociology discussed above can be seen as having a massive impact widely on qualitative psychology in comparison.

Radical linguistics

In the 1950s, it was the general view in linguistics that speech and language are representational – a way of communicating what is inside the mind to the outside world. The word was an essential unit in understanding speech. Ludwig Wittgenstein's (1889–1951) idea that language is essentially a toolkit to do things was reflected in developments in linguistic theory in the 1950s and 1960s. John Austin (1911–60) importantly contributed speech act theory which essentially involved the idea that speech is social action and does things rather than represents things. Paul Grice (1913–18) with his maxims of good conversation established the rule-driven nature of conversation. These, and many others, were important in revising the subject matter of linguistics and the eventual development of discourse analysis in social psychology. In passing, it might be noted that Wittgenstein was influential on the logical positivists though they may not always have interpreted him in the way he would have liked. Table 2.1 presents a timeline of qualitative methods in psychology.

TABLE 2.1 Timeline of qualitative methods in psychology

Decade	Key events	Impact
Eighteenth century	The Age of Enlightenment in Western Europe	Led to the ideas of positivism which dominated much of the early history of modern psychology.
1860s		Introspectionism was the first major school of scientific psychology and lasted until the 1920s. It aimed to quantify and is not generally regarded as a qualitative approach. It should not be confused with phenomenology which is a qualitative method.
1870s	William James founded the first laboratory to teach physiological psychology in 1876.	Both of these have been seen as seminal moments in the development of modern psychology.
	Wilhelm Wundt founded the first psychological research laboratory at the University of Leipzig in 1879.	Symbolically they mark the beginning of the dominance of laboratory research in psychology which lasted throughout most of the twentieth century.
1880s	First published psychology case study by Edward Cowles.	This method is imported from medicine. It tends to be illustrative rather than analytic and thus is not an early qualitative method. Famous examples by Sigmund Freud came later. Similar questions can be asked about these.
1890s	About this time and later some of the most well-known statistical techniques, common today, were developed.	Statistics has been a major force in psychology since the 1930s onwards and, in many ways, has very much defined the discipline.
1900s	The American Psychological Association was founded in 1892 and the British Psychological Society in 1901.	The importance of professional bodies in the development of psychology cannot be stressed too much. The APA has about 150 000 members. The growth of trained psychologists has increased dramatically since the Second World War. The dominance of quantitative approaches in these organisations probably held back the development of qualitative research in psychology.
1910s	Logical positivism developed by the Vienna School but not so-named until 1930s.	Highly influential on behaviourism as it developed in the first half of the twentieth century.
	The anthropologist Malinowski began studying other cultures through a process of immersion and involvement.	This was the beginning of participant observation which is now commonly described as ethnography. Participant observation common in psychological publications from 1930s onwards. Earlier writers on anthropology often took the observations of others such as missionaries as the source of their data.
1920s	The Chicago School of Ethnography.	Brought anthropological methods to studying American city life.
1930s	In this decade, most psychologists had knowledge of statistical techniques though these started to be developed in the late nineteenth century.	Statistics generally is seen as a prime feature of quantification and partly responsible for the inadequacies of quantitative research.
	Jahoda et al. (1933) conducted the Marienthal study of the experience of unemployment in Austria. It was essentially a psychological ethnographic study and included participant observation among a mixture of innovative qualitative and quantitative data collection methods.	This study would have been impossible had a pure behavioural psychological approach been taken. It is a still-relevant, major exposition of qualitative psychology with its emphasis on the context of experience and radically different research ethic.

TABLE 2.1 (*continued*)

Decade	Key events	Impact
1940s	Content analysis was developed during this period by media researchers such as Paul Lazarsfeld. However, this work was essentially quantitative in nature although more qualitative approaches emerged later.	Content analysis was an early method of dealing with textual material such as media content. It tended to be quantitative in nature.
	The first publications of research involving focus groups were written by Paul Lazarsfeld.	Slowly developed through marketing research to blossom in the social sciences in the 1990s.
1950s	The emergence of cognitive psychology.	Cognitive psychology and its derivatives now dominate psychology.
	George Kelly publishes *The psychology of personal constructs* in 1955.	Personal construct psychology was widely influential in the 1960s as an alternative to mainstream behaviourist psychology. It is regarded by some as a precursor to social constructionist approaches.
	Harold Garfinkel begins to establish ethnomethodology as an approach in sociology.	Probably most important as an influence on conversation analysis.
1960s	Berger and Luckman publish *The social construction of reality* in 1966.	Led to social constructionist ideas which began to enter psychology in the 1970s and 1980s.
	Glaser and Strauss publish *The discovery of grounded theory* in 1967.	Provided the archetypal analytic method in qualitative research – grounded theory – which underpins much qualitative analysis.
	Harvey Sacks establishes basic concepts of conversation analysis and Schegloff publishes the first conversation analysis paper in 1968.	Conversation analysis has some adherents in psychological qualitative methods. Increasingly allied with discourse analysis
	Amedeo Giorgi and others of the Duquesne School develop a psychological methodology for phenomenological research.	Although Giorgi provided an alternative way for doing psychology, his methods did not challenge the mainstream effectively but did provide a counterpoint.
1970s	Feminism begins to emerge as a significant force in psychology.	Feminist psychology needed constructionist explanations of gender as a way of countering the dominant, negative view of women promoted by mainstream quantitative psychology and the opportunity to give women a voice.
	Gilbert and Mulkay's studies of the way in which scientists write in journals about science and the way it is presented, for example, in conversation.	This was an important step in the development of discourse analysis as it demonstrated the way in which accounts vary in different contexts.
1980s	Julian Henriques, Wendy Hollway, Cathy Urwin, Couze Venn and Valerie Walkerdine publish *Changing the subject: Psychology, social regulation, and subjectivity* (1984).	This book marks a major, early attempt to introduce Foucauldian ideas into psychology.
	Jonathan Potter and Margaret Wetherell publish *Discourse and social psychology* in 1987.	This book had a big impact and has since been cited by over 800 publications in PsycINFO.
1990s	Ian Parker and co-workers publish important work on Foucauldian discourse analysis and major fields of psychology in *Deconstructing psychopathology* (Parker, Georgaca, Harper, McLaughlin, & Stowell-Smith, 1995) and *Deconstructing psychotherapy* (Parker, 1999a).	Parker established a research focus for Foucauldian discourse analysis.
	Jonathan Smith publishes first paper on interpretative phenomenological analysis (IPA) in 1996.	IPA has had an important influence on the way in which health psychology, in particular, approaches qualitative research. This is the first attempt at a systematic qualitative method with its roots based almost exclusively in psychology.

TABLE 2.1 (*continued*)

Decade	Key events	Impact
2000s	The qualitative methods section of the British Psychological Society established in 2006 and has about 1000 members. An attempt to establish a division for qualitative inquiry for the American Psychological Association failed in 2008.	The progress of new areas of psychology is substantially determined by building a professional infrastructure. To have a section of a professional society devoted to an area of interest is part of the way that this can be achieved.
	Funding bodies such as the Economic and Social Research Council (ESRC) require that doctoral students in psychology (and other disciplines) are trained in both quantitative and qualitative methods.	Increasingly, academically trained psychologists are aware of qualitative methods.
	Specialist qualitative methods-based journals such as *Qualitative Research in Psychology* established.	A similar outcome is achieved by the setting up of specialised publications in particular areas of research. By having a qualitative research journal for psychological publications it may be possible to encourage distinctly psychological approaches to qualitative methods.

The recent history of qualitative psychology

The rise in qualitative methods in psychology has been to some degree accompanied by a reduced allegiance among quantitative researchers for many of the trappings of science and positivism. It is like two graphs going in opposite directions. For example, few psychologists, if any, today would take the view that the aim of their research is to develop universal scientific laws applying to their subject matter. Although psychology, as a whole, remains resolutely empirical, just what characterises the research mindset of the typical psychologist currently? Silverman (1997) argues that the quest of the typical modern researcher is to achieve 'cumulative, theoretically defined generalisations deriving from the critical sifting of data' (p. 12). To call this positivism would be to wring most of the meaning out of the term. Nevertheless, mainstream psychologists are still prone to prefer decontextualised understanding in which generalisations are made from data but with little or no attention to culture or other contextual matters. However, some believe that psychology is rendered virtually useless beyond the Western population on which it was based as a consequence (Owusu-Bempah & Howitt, 2000).

Willig and Stainton-Rogers (2008) argue that 'qualitative approaches have been part and parcel of psychology from its very beginnings. While marginalized and muted for about the first 80 years of the 20th century, they never completely went away' (p. 3). However, Billig (2008) claims that the reaction against modernism in psychology is much older than this. He suggests qualitative psychologists '. . . have tended to accept somewhat shallow histories of their own ideas' (p. 186) while claiming that the Earl of Shaftesbury (1671–1713) was 'almost a pre-post-modern figure' (p. 123)! Nevertheless, a psychologist time-warped from any point in the history of psychology (whenever we want that to begin) would be utterly confused by the array of different approaches to qualitative research in current psychology. It, then, would also be true to say that over the past 30 years much of the resistance to qualitative methods has melted away – especially those parts of the world where the grip of behaviourism and positivism was not so tight. It is tempting but misleading to suggest that the

TABLE 2.2 Where the detailed development of qualitative methods in psychology can be found in this book

Qualitative data collection methods	Qualitative data analysis methods
● Interviewing, Chapter 3	● Thematic analysis, Chapter 7
● Focus groups, Chapter 4	● Grounded theory, Chapter 8
● Ethnography, Chapter 5	● Social constructionist discourse analysis, Chapter 9
	● Conversation analysis, Chapter 10
	● Foucauldian discourse analysis, Chapter 11
	● IPA, Chapter 13
	● Narrative analysis, Chapter 14

epicentre of research has shifted in the sense that qualitative research is much more in the European intellectual tradition than the American. Evidence of this is in the backgrounds of the key figures discussed throughout this book. Nevertheless, we should not overlook the fact that origins of statistics and positivism were also in Europe.

The recent history of qualitative methods in psychology has been less about new data collection methods and more about new methods of data analysis. This is a key distinction but largely overlooked. Recent textbooks on qualitative methods in psychology tend to dwell on data analysis methods but neglect data collection. This trend precisely identifies what has been happening in qualitative methods for the most part in the past 20 or 30 years.

One can explain recent developments in many different ways but understanding something of the origins of different aspects of qualitative psychology is important. So in later chapters you will find an account of how each of the approaches originated – so the origins of qualitative data collection methods (e.g. focus groups and in-depth interviews) as well as qualitative data analysis methods (e.g. conversation analysis and interpretative phenomenological analysis) are presented in detail in later chapters. Table 2.2 indicates where the origins of individual methods are discussed. Of course, this does not account for why some approaches begin to be adopted more widely whereas other contenders for glory are stillborn and largely forgotten. Broad changes within a discipline are helpful when trying to unravel this puzzle but broader changes beyond the discipline can also be crucial. Political changes and other social forces may be involved.

A good instance of this is the development of feminist psychology which has had enormous impact on qualitative methods in psychology. Feminism has been a major impetus to qualitative research in psychology since the 'second wave of feminism' started in the 1960s but showed substantial expansion in the 1980s and onwards. The politics of feminism had a great deal to say about how research was typically conducted in psychology at the time. The available research tended to be advantageous to male power and disadvantageous to women. Wilkinson (1997) is just one psychologist who has provided an account of what she calls the 'patriarchal control of women' (p. 253) that is aided by mainstream psychology. But, perhaps more importantly, the relationship between the researcher and his/her subject matter – women – was different in feminist research. Instead of being neutral, feminist researchers were political and involved professionally with the women they studied. The mainstream psychology of 30 or 40 years ago would tend to regard itself as value neutral and objective about issues which feminists felt passionately about. Also feminists saw that part of their task was 'giving voice' to women in all sorts of contexts. So giving a voice to victims of sexual violence and domestic violence was an important aim and the very sort of topic at which qualitative research excels. Similarly, women's bodies became a major area for study in relation to pornography, objectification of the body, eating disorders, menopause and so forth. Of course, mainstream positivist psychology in the 1960s and 1970s was the place where feminist psychology of that time had to begin and some, at least, chose quantitative research as their basic research orientation (Gergen, 2008). However, at a time when definitions of gender and related matters were in a state of flux, something different was needed – something which did not regard matters as fixed and determined but something which allowed for change. Inevitably, constructionist approaches provided part of the answer to this. And, since Berger and Luckmann's (1966) *The social construction of reality* such an alternative was available. Many of the current qualitative psychology research methods which are at their roots constructionist in nature have increasingly been recruited by feminist researchers for their research. These would include conversation analysis and discourse analysis, of course. Equally, qualitative data collection methods have the potential for just 'giving voice' to women of all sorts. Research methods such as focus groups have a particular role here since they do not cut off a woman from other women in the same way as in-depth interviews can do.

Furthermore, feminist psychology was one of the first areas of psychology to involve specialist journals more than amenable to publishing qualitative research in psychology. *Feminism & Psychology*, founded in 1991, had a major impact and, although not totally excluding quantification, has an agenda which is archetypically qualitative in ethos.

CONCLUSION

We have seen that even during the years when positivism and behaviourism were at their most potent and powerful, psychologists were sometimes drawn to qualitative investigations. Generally this was because their interest in a topic could not be addressed effectively through laboratory experiments or even questionnaires. These psychologists cannot be described as isolated renegades since they were usually more than capable of operating both within and outside the psychological mainstream. Several ways of linking qualitative and quantitative research exist. There is the classic view that the qualitative approach provides information to the researcher who then verifies ideas quantitatively. In many respects, this describes the study by Festinger et al. (1956) into the failed doomsday prophecy. The number of laboratory and related studies which stemmed from this was countless. There is a second view

that the qualitative and the quantitative can both usefully inform the same research question. Jahoda et al.'s (1933) study of unemployment is a good example of this. As will be seen in later chapters, Paul Lazarsfeld, who also worked on this project, made various important contributions to methodology in sociology (and related disciplines) including both qualitative and quantitative ones. And there is the third view which was inherent in Dollard's (1937) study in Southerntown where he abandoned his original research plan when he realised that it failed to deal with the compelling nature of the situation. Despite his quantitative socialisation, he saw that his intellectual needs in terms of his research could not be fulfilled without putting quantification on hold.

There is another example of the lost opportunities of psychology which perhaps helps to explain the slow emergence of qualitative methods in psychology. Roger Barker (1903–90) and Herbert Wright (1907–90) were innovatory ecological psychologists. For example, they published a book in which they observed and described the activities of a particular boy over a particular day (Barker & Wright, 1951). Unusually, the famous sociologist Aaron Cicourel when interviewed suggested that this book was influential on his own ethnographic style of research (Witzel & Mey, 2004). In 1947, the same authors set up the Midwest Field Station at a town they called 'Midwest' in Kansas. This operated for 25 years, studying people in their ecological setting and gave rise to one form of ecological psychology:

Psychology knows how people behave under the conditions of experiments and clinical procedures, but it knows little about the distribution of these and other conditions, and of their behavior resultants, outside of laboratories and clinics. (Barker, 1968, p. 2)

This does not apply to scientific disciplines such as chemistry (e.g. chemists know the distribution of oxygen, hydrogen and other elements in nature) and entomology (e.g. entomologists know about, say, how malaria is distributed in the real world). Psychologists know no more than ordinary people, in general, about the real-world occurrence of their concepts such as punishment, fear and social pressure. In this book, Barker puts forward an important statement of his behavioural settings theory. A behavioural setting is a substantial and natural environmental unit which normal people recognise as a part of their everyday lives. A behavioural setting has specific time, place and object features but, more importantly, it has a shared expectation about behaviour within that setting. The environmental setting is a powerful determinant of what people do. Despite some enthusiasm for the theory, it has not grown to be a significant part of modern psychology. In part, Scott (2005) asks the question why this innovatory approach faded rather than prospered. Among his reasons are:

• Psychology was (is) dominated by individualistic approaches which made it difficult

for a form of psychology based largely on non-individualistic concepts to prosper.

• The practice of psychology was generally the laboratory experiment which has core assumptions which are not favourable to naturalistic methods of data collection.

• Field methods are frequently extremely labour intensive.

• Those who succeeded Barker in the field did not find themselves working in institutions and funding environments of the sort which allowed the Midwest Field Station to be set up.

• Scott believes that there is a 'critical' mass in terms of doctoral students in a particular field which helps to spread the field more widely. For example, training programmes in ecological psychology had not been created. Other fields of psychology have suffered similarly – i.e. in the case of Gestalt psychology because its advocates were migrants from Europe who had to work in smaller departments with less chance of developing this critical mass.

• Ecological psychology was not about psychology as most psychologists considered it to be. How, then, could ecological psychology attach itself to mainstream psychology at the time?

We have to remember that Barker's ecological psychology was an active field at much the same time as psychology was resisting a qualitative turn – and at precisely the same period in the 1950s and 1960s when other disciplines including sociology took that turn. What is interesting is that we know that in some ways psychology began to be responsive to a wider variety of approaches from the 1970s onwards. Some of these changes probably made it much easier for certain sorts of qualitative methods to emerge. Most of the qualitative analysis methods in this book do not rely on any of the large-scale ecological methods advocated by Barker. Indeed, it is clear that ethnographic methods have not been attractive to many psychologists and few truly ethnographic studies have been carried out in psychology. The data for modern qualitative analyses are relatively straightforward to collect and can be carried out with relatively small amounts of data if those data are sufficiently analytically rich.

Gilbert and Mulkay (1984, p. iii) reproduce the following at the start of their important book on the discourse of scientists. There might be a more general lesson to be learnt from it – no matter what, it is a fitting end to this chapter as it says so much about qualitative methods:

The physicist Leo Szilard once announced to his friend Hans Bethe that he was thinking of keeping a diary: 'I don't intend to publish it; I am merely going to record the facts for the information of God.' 'Don't you think God knows the facts?' Bethe asked. 'Yes', said Szilard. 'He knows the facts, but he does not know *this version of the facts*.' Freeman Dyson, *Disturbing the Universe* (Preface)

KEY POINTS

- The evidence, based on publications' databases, is clear that qualitative methods began to grow in psychology in the 1980s and have generally expanded fairly quickly since the 1990s. However, in real terms, qualitative research publications are a small percentage of the total numbers of publications.

- There are fascinating examples of qualitative research in the history of psychology. In some cases, these are seminal studies in psychology which have been reprinted on several occasions. Nevertheless, caution is in order when evaluating the credibility of some of these methods as exemplars of qualitative methods in psychology. For example, case studies are not intrinsically quantitative or qualitative in nature. Indeed, the original function of case studies was for educational/illustrative purposes rather than research purposes.

- Qualitative data collection methods have a far longer history in psychology than qualitative analysis methods which are much more recent.

- Psychology lagged behind other disciplines in the turn to qualitative methods which first started in sociology, for example, in the 1950s and 1960s. Many of the most important qualitative analysis methods had their origins at this time. Grounded theory and conversation analysis are cases in point.

ADDITIONAL RESOURCES

Ashworth, P. (2008). Conceptual foundations of qualitative psychology. In J. A. Smith (Ed.), *Qualitative psychology: A practical guide to research methods* (pp. 4–25). London: Sage.

Hill, C. E. (2011) Qualitative research in counseling and psychotherapy. *Psychotherapy Research, 21* (6), 736–738, DOI: 10.1080/10503307.2011.620642.

Levitt, H. M. (2015). Qualitative psychotherapy research: The journey so far and future directions. *Psychotherapy, 52* (1), 31–37.

Vidich, A. J., & Lyman, S. M. (2000). Qualitative methods: Their history in sociology and anthropology. In N. L. Denzin & Y. S. Lincoln (Eds.), *Handbook of qualitative research* (2nd ed., pp. 37–84). Thousand Oaks, CA: Sage.

Wertz, F. J. (2014). Qualitative inquiry in the history of psychology. *Qualitative Psychology, 1* (1), 4–16.

PART 2

Qualitative data collection

There are many, very different sources of qualitative data. Qualitative data include new data collected using qualitative research methods such as interviewing, focus groups and participant observation (ethnography) and already existing data obtained from sources such as the Internet, the media or recordings of therapeutic interviews, for example. The main requirement is that the qualitative data must be extensive and rich in deep detail. Apart from that, there are few, if any, limits to the types and origins of data which can be used in a qualitative analysis. The mass media are a very rich source of material for qualitative analyses – reports in newspapers, interviews in magazines and newspapers, recordings of interviews broadcast on television or radio and so forth are all potentially rich data sources for the qualitative researcher. So some researchers find autobiographical material from books, magazines and newspapers relevant to their research interest in identity. For researchers interested in conversation, the Internet is a rewarding source in the form of emails, for example, which despite being written down have many conversation-like features. Facebook and Twitter are also potential sources of conversation-like data. Text messaging on mobile telephones similarly has its own conversational aspect which might be utilised in qualitative research. The following may be helpful to anyone wishing to use Internet-based data in their research:

Evans, A., Elford, J., & Wiggins, D. (2008). Using the Internet for qualitative research. In C. Willig & W. Stainton-Rogers (Eds.), *The SAGE handbook of qualitative research in psychology* (pp. 315–333). London: Sage.

Kazmer, M. M., & Xie, B. (2008). Qualitative interviewing in Internet studies: Playing with the media, playing with the method. *Information, Communication & Society, 11 (*2), 257–278.

Hookway, N. (2008). 'Entering the blogosphere': Some strategies for using blogs in social research. *Qualitative Research, 8*, 91–113.

Kaun, A. (2010). Open-ended online diaries: Capturing life as it is narrated. *International Journal of Qualitative Methods, 9* (2), 36–48.

Mann, C., & Stewart, F. (2000). *Internet communication and qualitative research: A handbook for researching online*. London: Sage Publications.

In the next three chapters we deal with what are probably the most demanding data collection methods for qualitative research. These are qualitative interviewing (Chapter 3), focus group interviewing (Chapter 4) and participant observation/ ethnography (Chapter 5). These are somewhat traditional data collection techniques in the social sciences in general, including psychology. Each requires considerable interpersonal skills, which some people have in copious quantities but others struggle to muster, as well as the professional skills of the well-rounded qualitative researcher. Appropriate training in interviewing is often in short supply in the education of psychologists and interviewing is rarely dealt with in sufficient depth as part of psychology methods training. The apparent conversational nature of interviews is somewhat misleading as it suggests that good interviewing is a matter of good conversational skills. This helps but there is a great deal more to be learnt besides. It should be mentioned, however, that some researchers deliberately adopt a conversational style in interviews in order to allow them to be analysed as if they were conversation. While this may be all-well-and-good for the discourse analyst, it is not so good for narrative analysis where the important thing is not how people talk about things together but how people experience and describe significant episodes in their lives. This requires a more reflective stance. In these circumstances, a rapid exchange of speech turns between the interviewer and interviewee, for example, would most likely be counterproductive. Like most matters in research, these are issues of both judgement and clarity about the purpose of one's research.

There is another important matter which is addressed in the next three chapters. It is no good merely learning narrowly defined skills of interviewing, focus group moderation and participant observation. A few tips on how to conduct face-to-face interviews do not constitute the skills of a qualitative researcher. Data collection needs to be treated as a process involving a range of activities before and after data collection. For example, where can the researcher go for help with their ideas, how can the researcher go about recruiting volunteers to take part in their study, and how does the researcher go about making sure that those who agree to take part in research actually do so? These aspects of managing research effectively make all the difference but are rarely taught to students. So for this reason you will find in Chapters 3 to 5 a lot of advice on all aspects of data collection including the sort of stuff that research methodology textbooks frequently overlook:

- Chapter 3 deals with qualitative research interviewing.
- Chapter 4 explains what a focus group is and how it should be conducted.
- Chapter 5 introduces participant observation (ethnography) – an important qualitative method but one which is too frequently neglected in modern qualitative research in psychology.

CHAPTER 3

Qualitative interviewing

Overview

- Interviews of all sorts are ubiquitous in all aspects of modern society.

- The qualitative interview is a common tool in psychology and social sciences research. It has potential for most forms of qualitative data analysis, though it may not yield the natural conversation that researchers in some fields of qualitative research would seek.

- Typically a distinction is drawn between the open and the closed interview or the structured and the semi-/unstructured interview or the quantitative and the qualitative interview. Open-ended, semi-structured interviewing characterises qualitative data collection.

- Early examples of interviewing can be seen in Thucydides' history of the Peloponnesian War (about 400 BCE). However, interviewing as a social sciences research tool emerged with the work of the Victorian philanthropist Charles Booth in the late 1800s, when he began his research on poverty among Londoners. Freud, Piaget and Dichter are among the influential psychologists whose work was founded on interviewing.

- The use of sound recordings of interviews was accepted and fairly common by the mid-1950s.

- During qualitative interviewing the researcher needs to take the stance of an active listener, aware of the detail of what is said while steering the research along the pathways demanded by the research question.

- An interview guide is prepared to provide clarity as to the areas or questions to be covered. The 'guide' is an aid rather than something to be read out verbatim during the interview.

- It is important to consider the qualitative interview as a process which begins prior to the interviews and continues into the interview and beyond. A great deal of preparation goes into planning an interview and a great deal of skill goes into the successful execution of an interview. Aspects of the research need active management by the researcher if the interview is to proceed to its maximum effect.

- It is possible to discern the use of more conversational styles of interviewing in some forms of qualitative research where the interactional nature of the interview is evident. This may be appropriate where the interview is to be analysed more or less as if it is conversation but less appropriate where, for example, the researcher is seeking to obtain a narrative life history. Views differ as to the suitability of interviews as the preferred kind of data as opposed to recordings of real-life conversation – discourse analysts have debated this issue, for example.

- Qualitative interviewing is a key aspect of much phenomenological analysis and interpretative phenomenological analysis. However, other analysis methods such as thematic analysis and grounded theory may be used to effectively analyse qualitative interview data.

- Narrative analysis has its own preferred protocol (see Chapter 14) for interviewing but general advice about interviewing applies here too.

What is qualitative interviewing?

Interviews feature in many parts of our lives. Job interviews, psychiatric interviews, university application interviews, market research interviews, magazine and television interviews, and police interviews are just a few examples. No unitary set of principles covers how to conduct all of these since each differs in its context, purpose, objectives, format and structure. Qualitative research interviews superficially have much in common with these other forms of interview but they have their own distinctive features and their own requirements. Qualitative interviewing characteristically involves questions and probes by the interviewer designed to encourage the interviewee to talk freely and extensively about the topic(s) defined by the researcher. Success is not guaranteed as factors such as the skills of the interviewer, the topic and interviewee's potential to provide good qualitative data also have a part to play. The objectives of the research interview are not the same as, say, those of a journalistic interview and the contexts are very different. For example, (a) the qualitative researcher is bound to adhere to the values and ethics of research and (b) the researcher has a responsibility to help develop theory out of the interview data – things which other forms of interviewing lack. Of course, it is perfectly possible to carry out qualitative analyses of journalistic interviews if the research question allows this. Qualitative research is very flexible in terms of the data it uses.

Interviews are often described as varying between the structured and the unstructured. Most of us have, at some stage, taken part in a market research interview in the street or over the telephone. Such interviews typify structured interviews. The questions asked are often simply read from a list and the interviewee chooses from another list of possible answers for each question. There is little opportunity for the interviewer to depart from the prepared 'script'. In other words, as much as possible is planned and predetermined. Almost always the market research interviewer is a casual 'employee' rather than the researcher – that is, the actual interviewer is a hired-hand. In general, structured interviewing achieves the following:

- The interviewer ensures that participants are chosen for the study who have the required characteristics to fulfil sampling requirements (this sort of sampling, known as quota sampling, is almost universal in this context). Furthermore, since the interviewer actively recruits research participants at the time of the interview, reasonably large samples can be obtained and speedily since the interviewer generally stands in a busy street where many potential recruits pass by. Such interviews can be fairly alienating for the participants. The interviewer usually offers a very limited number of choices and the participant, as a consequence, may feel it impossible to effectively communicate their actual views. However, the multiple-choice pre-coded answer format allows the data to be quickly transferred to a computer for analysis. Qualitative researchers see such methods as alienating for the researcher, too, since the researcher is effectively distanced from the participants in the research.

- Speed in the research process. Provided that the necessary infrastructure is in place, the structured interview may be implemented as soon as the questionnaire design and general research plan are completed. The infrastructure would include a team of interviewers and data entry assistants as well as responsible researchers. A research report can be delivered to commissioning clients in a matter of a few weeks or even days.

Academic quantitative researchers use variations on the theme of structured interviewing in their research. The strengths and weaknesses of the approach remain much the same. If structured interviewing meets the needs of one's research, then data can be collected fairly economically in terms of both time and financial costs. (Another version of the structured approach is the self-completion (tick-box) questionnaire.)

In contrast, few of us are likely to have been participants in qualitative interviewing. Qualitative interviews are time-consuming for everyone involved and are more complex in terms of planning and recruiting suitable participants than structured interviews. Often qualitative interviews are referred to as semi-structured. In theory there is also the unstructured interview which lacks any pre-planned structure. It is not usual for qualitative researchers to choose to collect their data using unstructured interviews as they are something of an oxymoron. Is it really possible to conduct an interview with no pre-planning? However, the semi-structured interview can vary enormously in terms of the amount of pre-structuring. The whole point of the qualitative interview is that it generally generates extensive and rich data from participants in the study. Such reasons for using qualitative interviewing touch on the ethos of qualitative research, just as much as structured interviewing reflects the quantitative ethos. Unlike everyday conversation, the qualitative interview is built on the principle that the interviewee does most of the talking – the researcher merely steers and guides the interviewee, probes for more information and interjects in other ways when necessary. It is not generally expected that the interviewer will answer questions – that is the role of the interviewee. Equally, the interviewee does not ask the interviewer personal questions of the sort that the interviewer is free to pose. That is not in the 'rules' of the interview. The interviewee can be asked to talk at some length about matters that are difficult for them – perhaps because they have not thought about the issue, perhaps because the topic of the interview is embarrassing, and so forth. The task of the interviewer is also a demanding one. The interviewer has to conduct the business of the interview while at the same time dealing with a great deal of information that bombards them during the interview. This information has to be absorbed and retained so that probes using this new information can be inserted wherever necessary. Although a sound recorder is important to most qualitative interviewers, this does not lighten the burden of absorbing, understanding and reflecting upon what the interviewee has to say during the course of the interview. The interviewer needs to be on top of what has gone before in the interview in order to explore issues further and clarify what is unclear.

In this chapter, we refer to qualitative interviews rather than unstructured or semi-structured interviews since it is a misconception to think that qualitative interviews lack structure – they simply do not follow a prescribed structure. This freedom is not achieved with a haphazard approach to the interview since the successful interview requires preparation of both the interview content and setting. A good qualitative interviewer needs highly developed listening skills, on-the-spot analytic skills, satisfactory interpersonal skills and experience. Qualitative interviewing skills take time to develop.

The contrast between the highly structured quantitative interview and the qualitative interview is mostly to do with the amount of freedom available to the researcher and interviewee in the qualitative interview compared with the structured interview. It is useful to contrast qualitative interviews with structured interviews and, consequently, the similar but self-completed (tick-box) questionnaires. Table 3.1 provides an extended comparison of structured interviewing and qualitative interviewing (drawing partially on Bryman & Bell, 2003; Howitt & Cramer, 2011).

TABLE 3.1 A comparison of structured versus qualitative interviewing

Structured interview	Qualitative interview
1. The interview uses a pre-written list of 'closed' questions which is not usually departed from and the questions are asked in a standard fashion.	1. Although the researcher usually has a list of 'areas' to explore through questioning, there is no rigid structure and flexibility is vital.
2. Answers are usually selected from a pre-specified list given to the participant or, alternatively, the interviewer classifies the answer according to a pre-specified scheme.	2. The researcher wishes to encourage 'open' answers in which the interviewee provides elaborate and detailed answers.
3. The structured interview facilitates a quantitative analysis.	3. The qualitative interview normally does not lend itself to quantitative analysis methods.
4. Structured interviews are relatively short as well as being fairly predictable in duration.	4. Qualitative interviewers encourage 'rich' detailed replies leading to lengthy interviews of a somewhat unpredictable duration.
5. Structured interviews are not normally recorded.	5. A recording is virtually essential for most qualitative interviews.
6. The high degree of structuring facilitates reliability, validity and similar assessments.	6. The assessment of the reliability and validity of a qualitative interview is a complex issue and not easily addressed. However, see Box 3.1.
7. The interviewer in the structured interview is basically a question asker and answer recorder.	7. The qualitative interview requires the interviewer to be an active listener concentrating on what the interviewee says while formulating questions to help the interviewee expand on and clarify what has already been said.
8. The structured interview is driven by the researcher's agenda and is based on prior knowledge and theory. That is, the structured interview is not generally exploratory.	8. The qualitative interview is largely steered by the responses of the interviewee which the interviewer may explore further with the use of careful questioning. The qualitative interview seeks to explore the thinking of the interviewee.
9. Interviewees have little choice other than to keep to the agenda as set by the researcher. There is limited or no scope for idiosyncratic responses to be made. There may be a somewhat token opportunity for the interviewee to ask the interviewer questions or to express additional thoughts.	9. Sometimes it is suggested that qualitative interviewing encourages 'rambling' answers which may provide a wider perspective on the subject matter of the interview.
10. Standardisation of the questions asked and the possible answers is a characteristic of structured interviewing.	10. A lack of standardisation is inevitable in qualitative interviews and the interviewer expects to rephrase questions, generate new questions in response to the interviewee's answers, probe the meaning of what the interviewee says, and so forth.
11. Inflexible.	11. Flexible.

TABLE 3.1 (*continued*)

Structured interview	Qualitative interview
12. The interviewer is often a 'hired assistant' rather than someone involved in the planning of the research.	12. In many cases it is ideal if the qualitative interview is conducted by the researcher. This allows the researcher to respond quickly to matters emerging in the interviews and make changes if necessary.
13. Some would suggest that structured interviews can best be used for hypothesis testing purposes.	13. Some would suggest that qualitative interviews are exploratory and more to do with hypothesis generation than hypothesis testing.
14. Repeat interviewing is uncommon in structured interviews except for longitudinal studies.	14. Additional or repeat interviewing is appropriate in qualitative interviewing as it provides the researcher with an opportunity to reformulate their ideas or 'regroup'. Repeat interviewing allows the researcher to check their analysis against the perceptions of the participants in their research.

Structured questionnaires (and their frustrations and inadequacies) are familiar to everyone – it is difficult to be in a job without having to complete them at some stage, for example. Structured interviews and questionnaires have the enormous advantage of being quick and easy to process – which is their *raison d'être*. Both involve a list of pre-specified questions which are administered in a standard form with as little variation as possible. In other words, the questions and answers are determined by the researcher in the planning stage of the research. Of course, structured interviews (and questionnaires) are strongly associated with quantification in psychology and, hence, clash with the general qualitative research ethos. But the emphasis of quantitative questionnaires on 'identifying' dimensions of differences between people (as in psychological scales) rather than understanding individuals as individuals is another bone of contention. The qualitative researcher rejects all of this and the accompanying ease of data analysis by adopting an approach to interviewing which allows interviewees far greater opportunity to control and structure the data provided by them. Thus, in contrast to structured interviewing, qualitative interviewers hand a great deal of control, albeit temporarily, to the interviewee.

The ubiquity of the interview in much qualitative research might encourage the idea that qualitative interviewing is easy. Furthermore, their relative lack of predetermined structure should not be taken to indicate that they are casual ways of collecting data. The qualitative interview, like all forms of research methods, requires the researcher to develop understanding of the method, experience of using the method, and familiarity with analysing the data gathered using the method. Some researchers have remarked on the conversational nature of the qualitative interview. Burgess (1984, p. 102) referred to them as 'conversations with a purpose'. This, although a common view, is questionable. It is wrong to imagine that qualitative interviewing is easy in the sense that conversations are easy.

Furthermore, qualitative interviews are not subject to the same conversational principles as a typical everyday conversation. There are many differences between an interview and what modern research has taught us about conversation. Conversations do not normally consist of one person asking another a series of questions, for example. So what is the advantage of conceiving qualitative interviews as conversations? There is a debate in discourse analysis about the usefulness of qualitative interviews for discourse analytic purposes. Research interviews simply are not natural conversation and are less informative about the social use of language than more naturalistic conversation would be. Nevertheless, some discourse analysts are happy to use qualitative interviews on the grounds that interviews are a form of conversation which occurs in everyday life, albeit a highly specialised form of conversation in the case of the research interview. Quite often, discourse analysis researchers who wish to use interviews in discourse analysis carry out a very conversational form of interaction which is very interactive in character compared with the usual qualitative interview. However, this conversational style often produces data which are as revealing about the interviewer as they are about the interviewee. For an interpretative phenomenological analysis or a narrative analysis this 'conversational' style of interviewing might be too glib to produce the needed sort of data for these approaches. Qualitative interviewing calls on many skills which are not those involved in ordinary conversation. In addition, the effective use of qualitative interviewing involves much more than the interaction between researcher and participant during data collection. Box 3.1 explores important issues about the role of qualitative interviews in qualitative research.

The development of qualitative interviewing

The interview has a long history (Kvale, 2007). Among early examples was Thucydides (460–395 BCE) who wrote an eight-volume history of the 27-year Peloponnesian War between Athens and Sparta based on interviews with those involved. It is known that the ancient Egyptians carried out population censuses (Fontana & Frey, 2000) and, of course, Jesus Christ was born in Bethlehem where Joseph and Mary had travelled for the Roman tax census – a sort of interview. Perhaps more importantly in terms of qualitative interviewing, the earliest journalistic interview was with Brigham Young, the leader of the Mormon religion, which appeared in the *New York Herald Tribune*. The interview had been conducted by the newspaper editor and politician Horace Greeley (1811–1872) in Salt Lake City, Utah, on 13 July 1859. Among other things, the Mormon leader described slavery as 'of Divine institution'!

More directly, the use of interviewing in the social sciences was a development out of the work of Charles Booth (1840–1916), a Victorian philanthropist, who in 1886 surveyed the social and economic circumstances of Londoners (Fontana & Frey, 2000). This was eventually published as *Life and labour of the people of London* in various editions from 1889 onwards. Interestingly, Booth was dismissive of the quality of the information gathered in census returns which led to his studies of poverty (pauperism) among London's East Enders. The findings from these interviews led Booth to argue in favour of the introduction of pensions for the elderly. Methodologically it was an early instance of triangulation (see Chapter 16) since Booth used the data from both interviews and from ethnographic observations in reaching his conclusions.

Kvale (2007) claims that there have been instances of qualitative interviews 'throughout the history of psychology' which were 'a key method' in the creation of 'scientific and professional knowledge' (p. 5). He associates qualitative interviews with some of the most significant contributions to psychology:

- Sigmund Freud (1856–1939) is discussed because of his extensive therapeutic interviews – including the client's free associations during the interview. The method of free association encourages the client to talk about things as they come to their mind without restraint. Free association requires the avoidance of self-censorship which, in its turn, requires the interviewer to be accepting of what is said and to avoid exhibiting any signs of being judgemental. There is no orderly basis to the free association and the therapist interviewer does not know in advance just where the interview will lead. In this sense, the Freudian interview is clearly one of the more unstructured forms of qualitative interviewing. Of course, generally the objective of this sort of interviewing is to unveil new personal insights and understandings rather than, say, to collect information for future analysis.

- The work of Jean Piaget (1896–1980) was based on interviewing children, at length, in a natural setting. He commonly introduced tasks for the child to carry out as part of the interview. Because Piaget had trained in psychoanalysis, his approach to interviewing had parallels with those of Freud. Through the use of these methods, Piaget began to understand the meaning of ideas such as number, size and weight which were central aspects of his work.

- Another important use of qualitative interviews was developed by Ernest Dichter (1907–91), a market research psychologist who founded motivational research. Dichter described the influence of psychoanalytic methods on his use of qualitative interviewing in his studies of consumer motivation. His whole approach to marketing was based on ideas about motivation stemming from psychoanalytic principles.

It is of some interest that all the psychologists identified by Kvale as central to the history of qualitative interviewing in psychology were of European origin, though Dichter spent most of his working life in the United States. In this context, it is also worth mentioning that Kvale describes how the famous, although largely discredited, Hawthorne Study was seminal research involving qualitative interviews (Mayo, 1949). In this, thousands of employees working at the Hawthorne Electrical Plant were interviewed in depth as well as being studied in other ways. Although Kvale attributes this work to Fritz Jules Roethlisberger (1898–1974) and William J. Dixon, the prime mover in these studies was the European psychologist and sociologist Elton Mayo (1880–1949). Quite clearly, the influence of European researchers, philosophers and social thinkers on the use of interviewing as a 'qualitative' research method is noteworthy. However, these historically important users of qualitative interviewing would employ other data collection methods in addition to the interview – this is evident in the work of Piaget and Mayo in particular.

Seemingly simple factors have encouraged the development of qualitative interviewing in psychology as well as other disciplines. It is too easy to ignore the role of technological advances in enabling and simplifying qualitative data collection methods. One important factor was the increasing availability of accessible methods of recording long interviews in their totality. Sound recording only became generally available in the period after the Second World War with the introduction of magnetic tape sound recording. This meant that an hour or two of interview could be recorded without interruption, thus eliminating the need for note-taking during and after interviews. Of course, note-taking during the course of an interview can interfere with the smooth flow of the interview and detract the interviewer. McBain (1956) published an early paper on the use of sound recording in psychological laboratories in which he mentions that their use was common by that time in communication, personality and clinical research and that it had advantages in terms of transcription. However, even earlier, Bevis (1949) was recommending the use of recording as a method of reducing 'bias' in interview research. The ability to record interviews was a major contribution in that it provides far greater opportunities for both checking and transcribing the contents of interviews. Transcription recorders can speed up the process of transcribing by allowing re-tracking back to a particular point in the recording. The advent of computers and high-quality digital recording equipment was a further impetus to qualitative interviewing. Not only is it now possible to study the sound patterns in detail but word processing allows the rapid cutting and pasting of data files. Furthermore, computer programs allow the easy movement back and forwards in a digital sound file in order to facilitate editing its contents.

By the 1970s and 1980s, the interview had become a common research tool in other disciplines, especially sociology, thus further encouraging its use among the somewhat more reluctant psychology community. References to semi-structured interviewing in psychological journals are fairly rare up to 1980 at about 100 and structured interviews are referred to about 400 times during the same period. However, there was a massive increase between 1980 and 2010 when the figures were approximately 6000 publications using semi-structured interviews and 11,000 using structured interviews. The main point of these figures is that they reveal a major increase in the use of interview methods of all sorts and, especially important here, clear evidence of the growing role of qualitative interviewing in psychological research.

How to conduct qualitative interviews

Generally speaking, it is regarded as important that researchers carry out their own qualitative interviews since it promotes familiarity with the detail of one's data. Fundamentally, the qualitative interview needs to be understood as a product of a special social situation with its own very distinctive characteristics which make it different from other social situations. There has been a lot of research into interviewing in various branches of psychology and it is worthwhile bearing in mind findings from this research in connection with qualitative interviewing – for example, achieving good rapport with participants in one's research. The need to avoid leading the interviewee overly is a feature of most forms of interviewing. So by studying interviewing in general it is possible to avoid many of the basic errors that novices make. Good interviewing skills together with careful preparation are the major aspects of success in qualitative interviewing. It is one of the crucial features of qualitative research that the researcher uses extensive, rich, dense and detailed data no matter its source. Consequently, the efforts of the interviewer have to focus on encouraging this descriptive richness. While training and experience are needed in order to carry out an interview well, success involves many different features of the data collection process other than just the interview itself. The researcher needs to be in command of all stages of the research process which include recruitment and retaining of participants.

The qualitative interview is very flexible and it can be carried out in a variety of ways to meet the demands of a particular research study. The following indicate some of the dimensions on which qualitative interviews vary:

- Traditionally interviews are seen as a dyad – the interviewee plus the interviewer. Qualitative researchers are much more flexible than this in terms of the format of interviews. For example, the focus group is a sort of group interview which may involve more than one interviewer and two or more interviewees (see Chapter 4 which discusses focus groups in detail). Equally, qualitative interviews may be carried out with more than one interviewee at the same time such as when partners (e.g. married couples) are the subject of the research. The interviewer–interviewee dyad may not always be the best in all circumstances. Indeed, it may not be possible always to adopt the traditional structure – for example, other family members may wish to join in.

- Interviews do not have to be carried out on a face-to-face basis. The telephone interview is a feasible substitute in some circumstances. It has the big advantage of being economical in terms of time and money. There is no travelling between interviews, for example, which can be very time consuming and not every person who agrees to be interviewed can be relied on to make the appointment. Some researchers claim that the telephone interview may be useful where a highly sensitive topic is being discussed but, equally, it may be the case that the telephone interview seems a little casual and superficial when very sensitive topics are being raised. So, for example, the telephone interview may be appropriate when sexual matters are being discussed but inappropriate, say, where a recent bereavement is the focus of the discussion. Each circumstance is different and the researcher needs to consider many factors when reaching a decision about the style of interviewing to employ. One important and major criticism of telephone interviews – poor response rates – actually has little or no relevance to qualitative research since sampling in qualitative research is usually for theoretical purposes rather than in order to represent the characteristics of the population from which a sample is taken. Of course, the other major drawback of the telephone interview is the loss of non-verbal features of communication, which, in some circumstances, can be informative. There are also possibilities for carrying out qualitative interviews over the Internet. The likelihood is that these are written text not involving the spoken word.

- For some researchers, especially those who approach research from a mixed method strategy (i.e. being willing to combine qualitative and quantitative methods in a creative fusion), there may be advantages in using both fairly structured questions in combination with relatively unstructured ones. In this way, fairly simple data (e.g. demographic and other background details) may be quickly collected while at the same time providing the opportunity to allow the participant to discuss their feelings, experiences, life histories and so forth in detail.

The qualitative interview, as we have seen, falls more towards the unstructured than the structured end of the dimension. But this can be misleading since structure here refers largely to the pre-planning of the interview. It should not be taken to imply that qualitative interviews are somewhat haphazard or shambolic events. The fact that the questions asked during the course of a qualitative interview cannot be entirely known prior to that interview does not mean that the interview is chaotic. And it does not mean that the interviewer has not worked hard in preparation for the interview. Not having a detailed list of questions means that the interviewer has to work hard all through in order to make the interview as structurally coherent as possible. As we have seen, the difference between the quantitative and the qualitative interview is largely to do with the lack of constraints placed on the replies of the participants and the freedom of the researcher to create appropriate questions within the qualitative interview. The totally unstructured interview is rarely if ever found in qualitative research and it is wrong to imagine there are successful interviews where the researcher has no particular agenda in mind. The qualitative or semi-structured interview, because of its very nature, demands that the researcher has good question-asking skills together with well-developed listening skills. Asking good questions is impossible without having absorbed and understood what has gone before in the interview.

Preparatory stage for the qualitative interview

The qualitative interview requires careful planning if it is to be fully effective. Although the constraints on student work may be somewhat different from those on professional research, the newcomer needs to be familiar with all of these preparatory stages. Since the qualitative interview is *not* normally a freewheeling conversation but a planned process,

TABLE 3.2 Stages in the qualitative interview process

Prior to the interview	During the interview	What happens after the interview?
1. Research conceptualisation and development	1. Recording the interview	1. Support for the interviewer
2. Preparation of the interview guide (interview schedule)	2. Orientation stage of the interview	2. Data protection and management
3. Suitability of the sample for in-depth interviewing	3. What qualitative interviewers 'do' when interviewing	3. Data transcription
4. Interview trialling (piloting)	4. Bringing the interview to a conclusion	
5. Inter-interview comparison		
6. Communication between interviewers		
7. Sample recruitment and selection		
8. Participant management		
9. The preparation/selection of the interview location		

a number of factors have to be taken into account early on. In many cases, some of the preparatory stages will involve relatively little work as they are fairly straightforward but these same stages can be exacting in other circumstances. For example, participants may be difficult to obtain if they are a highly specialised sample but, if just members of the public or fellow-students will suffice, then there may be little difficulty in obtaining suitable people for interview.

Like all research, qualitative interviewing needs to be focused. It is rare for qualitative interviews to be carried out over a lengthy period of time with limitless opportunities to ask further questions. (Such research would only be practicable with just a single participant or a small number of participants.) Just what length of time then is available for a typical qualitative interview? Normally, qualitative interviews should take no longer than about two hours or so. Within this constraint, it is obvious that there must be considerable selectivity in the coverage of most qualitative interviews. Indeed, without some focus to the interview, participants might find the range of questions asked somewhat perplexing and, possibly, intrusive. Participants need to understand the interview's purpose not least because they have an important part to play in ensuring that the interview meets its objectives. Without the cooperation of the participants then qualitative interviews are destined to fail.

The following are the major stages in preparation for the qualitative interview – see Table 3.2 for an overview.

Step 1   Research conceptualisation and development It is difficult to generalise about how research ideas develop. However, it is always important to develop clarity about the objectives and purposes of one's research as soon as possible in the research process. Now this is not to suggest that the researcher has to have complete clarity about the research topic under consideration. There are many circumstances in which the researcher needs to gather data simply to understand a phenomenon better: that is, the extant research in the field may be poorly developed and the interviews are needed to shed light on the topic in question. The qualitative researcher needs, at this stage, to develop a clear understanding of why qualitative interviews are required to meet the objectives of the study. Now this justification does not need to be elaborate but a choice has been made and the researcher should be able to articulate the basis of their decision.

Step 2   **Preparation of the interview guide** Standard practice in the use of qualitative interviewing dictates that a skeletal outline of the interview should be prepared prior to beginning the main data collection phase. Such an outline structure is referred to as the *interview guide*. This may be as simple as a list of areas or topics to be covered or it may list the questions. Of course, topics may be covered and questions answered during the course of the interview without any direct prompt from the researcher which means that the interviewer needs to be flexible as to whether each question on the interview guide needs to be asked directly. Asking a question when the participant has already answered it in response to earlier questioning can be perceived by the interviewee as lack of interest on the part of the interviewer rather than their inexperience. The guide may be adapted in light of the experience – perhaps an important but unanticipated issue seems to be emerging in the interviews, which is felt should be systematically included in subsequent interviews. While this is a reparative action, it is characteristic of the flexibility of qualitative research interviewing. Structured interviews, in contrast, cannot be responsive in this way. The interview guide is not the focus of the interview in the same way as the questionnaire is in the structured interview. It is not necessarily consulted throughout the interview but the interviewer may take time-out towards the end of the interview to check that everything has been covered. Don't worry, the interviewee will understand why this is necessary. The guide is usually quite short and so easily memorised. After a few interviews, the interviewer may only make cursory reference to it.

For inexperienced interviewers, there is a danger that the interview guide becomes overly the focus of the researcher's attention to the detriment of the interview's quality. The interview guide is employed in the background of the interview rather than being the lynchpin of the interaction as the structured interview questionnaire is. The primary focus of the qualitative interview is on what the interviewee has to say and ensuring that sufficient supplementary questions/probes are introduced to fully explore the issue from the participant's perspective. In other words, the qualitative interviewer is an *active listener*. The active listener needs to (a) absorb as much of what is being said as possible and (b) formulate further questions to 'fill the gaps' in the interviewee's replies where their account is unclear, contradictory or too short, for example. The interview guide provides the structure through which the richness of the participant's replies is maximised. The purpose of the qualitative interview and its success lie in the richness of the data which emerges. In summary:

- The interview guide should structure the questions or topics to be covered in a natural, sensible and helpful sequence. This, of course, may need to be varied in each interview as, for example, it is pointless and counterproductive to ask a question when the required information has already been mentioned by the participant. Furthermore, a disorganised sequence of questioning makes the interview difficult for both the interviewer and interviewee. There is a considerable amount of memory work during an interview and a logical and natural structure can help both parties in an interview.

- Even if one is conducting a qualitative interview it may be desirable to collect simple basic and routine information using direct and structured questioning. Basic demographic information such as age, gender, educational qualifications, occupation and so forth may be effectively collected using such structured methods. This is not a recommendation but merely a possible resource for the researcher. There are dangers in that it may set up an atmosphere of short questions and answers. Furthermore, in some contexts, the researcher might wish to explore in-depth matters such as education which, in other contexts, would be regarded as relatively unimportant.

- The interview guide is not a list of all of the obvious questions or topics which might be of interest. Research is carried out for a purpose and the interview needs to be informed by the questions and ideas guiding the research. It is simply impossible to include every question that might be thought up about a topic. There are practical limits to the length of any interview and two hours or so is the likely maximum length tolerable. Much longer than that and considerable strain is placed on both interviewer and interviewee.

Step 3   **Suitability of the sample for in-depth interviewing** It is difficult, but not impossible, to carry out an effective qualitative interview with certain types of individuals – for example, young children – but the use of language appropriate for the group in question can certainly help. However, the richness of response required in the qualitative interview may simply not emerge with such groups no matter what adjustments the researcher makes. The qualitative approach, in this case, may not be appropriate. The advice of knowledgeable informants about such groups together with pilot interviews may be helpful in planning such difficult research.

Step 4   **Interview trialling (piloting)** One cannot guarantee that the early interviews in a series will produce data of the quality expected. There are many reasons for this, including the skill of the interviewer as well as the adequacy of the interview guide. For this reason, it is a wise step to try out one's interviewing style and procedures in advance of the main data collection phase. This is the pilot study stage. Such an early trial can involve either:

- a number of practice interviews as part of gaining experience and identifying problems; or
- beginning the main data collection but recognising that the early interviews may have problems, which may need to be addressed by modifying one's procedures.

The choice between these two depends very much on the scarcity of suitable participants. Where participants of the right type are hard to obtain then even inadequate interviews might be of value. Of course, trialling interviews is best done by obtaining the comments of both the interviewees and others such as members of the research team or a research supervisor.

Step 5   **Inter-interview comparison** Interviews are usually part of a series of interviews rather than one-off events in research. As a consequence, the interviewer will have completed other interviews or be aware of interviews that colleagues have done. Issues which have emerged in these earlier interviews must impinge on the current interview. The interviewer may have already incorporated these topics into the new interview but sometimes things which have emerged before may not emerge in the current interview. The researcher needs to consider this and possibly seek the reasons why this is the case by carefully questioning. This across-the-board view of a series of interviews adds to the complexity of the interviewer's task.

Step 6   **Communication between interviewers** Just how many different researchers will be conducting the interviews? Using two or more different interviewers produces problems in terms of ensuring similarity and evenness of coverage across interviews. How are developments to be communicated between the interviewers? It is possibly worth considering the use of much more structured interviews if the logistics of using several interviewers become too complex. However, this may well be problematic and there may not be any enthusiasm for, or advantage in, a structured approach.

Step 7   **Sample recruitment and selection** Although conventional random sampling is very unusual in qualitative research, nevertheless the researcher needs to employ a strategy to recruit appropriate sorts of participants. Sometimes this strategy may be relatively simple where selection is not restricted to a special group of participants. Where a specialised group of individuals is required then more care and ingenuity have to be exercised. For example, a health psychologist may be interested in people with a particular type of medical condition (cancer, chronic pain, carers of persons with dementia and so forth) for which no publicly available list of names exists. That is, in conventional research terms, there is no accessible sampling frame such as the electoral list from which participants may be selected. Of course, it would be a long, difficult and, ultimately, pointless task to contact people from the electoral list to find out whether they fit the required characteristics for inclusion in the study. The alternative approach involves drawing up a list of individuals or organisations who may be able to help recruit suitable people for the study. For example, if the researcher wishes to interview chronic pain sufferers then among the possible 'contacts' are:

- hospital departments dealing with chronic pain sufferers – perhaps a 'flyer' may be left around to publicise the research and obtain recruits, though hospitals may have suitable contact lists;
- GPs who may be able to identify a number of their patients who fall into this category;
- self-help groups for chronic pain sufferers;
- a snowball sample in which a few known sufferers are identified and asked to nominate others that they know in the same circumstances;
- advertising in a local newspaper.

The researcher should ask themselves why a particular individual or organisation should be prepared to help in this way. There are many reasons why individuals and organisations will not cooperate with researchers and, of course, the researcher may need to work hard in order to prevent these reasons from prevailing. Generally, researchers need to try to establish a good relationship with key members of organisations with the aim of securing their trust and eventually cooperation. Interpersonal contacts (e.g. who do you know who might be helpful?), in these circumstances, are more likely to be fruitful than formal letters requesting cooperation. Once cooperation has been obtained, the organisation may still impose conditions and requirements. It might be insisted, for example, that the initial contacts with potential research participants are made by a member of the organisation rather than the researcher.

Establishing credibility and cooperation can be a time-consuming process – and it may, of course, end in failure. A contact may appear enthusiastic to help but turn out to be in no position to ensure the organisation's cooperation. Organisations are unlikely to cooperate with researchers who are not broadly sympathetic with the aims of that organisation. All of this might be seen as risking compromising the research. Sometimes one's primary sample recruitment method may fail. It would appear to be difficult, for example, to do research on burglars if one fails to obtain the cooperation of prisons or the probation service. In these circumstances, alternative methods of sample recruitment may have to be resorted to. For example, organisations dealing with ex-offenders might be a source of recruits or, conceivably, a snowball sample of burglars might be obtained if one could make initial contacts with a few members of the burglar fraternity.

Step 8

Participant management One of the frustrating aspects of qualitative interviewing is the extent to which the researcher is dependent on the participant being at a certain place at a certain time and happy to be interviewed. It is very easy to waste time and effort setting up interview appointments only to find that the interviewee fails to turn up. Now this may be because of all sorts of reasons. It is not appropriate to assume that such no-shows indicate that the would-be participant is not really interested in taking part. Sometimes they may simply forget. So it is important to 'keep the participant on-board' during the period before the appointment for the interview. This involves such things as:

- writing letters thanking the participant for agreeing to take part while at the same time reminding them of the date, time and place of the interview;
- using courtesy telephone calls the day before or the morning of the interview to remind the participant of the interview and to check whether any problems or issues have arisen;
- providing the participants with some background details about the research and its purpose together with a description of the ethical arrangements involved in the research. Participants who lack such information may get the wrong idea about the nature of the research and back-out for the wrong reasons.

Step 9

The preparation/selection of the interview location There are many potential locations for research interviews, each with its advantages and risks. Precisely what the possibilities are depends somewhat on the individuals being studied and judgements as to what is appropriate. The lengthy nature of the qualitative interview means that one would rarely interview participants in the street or on the doorstep, as commonly occurs in market research interviews. One obvious choice is for the interviewee to travel to the researcher's workplace. Among the problems with this is that the researcher is relying on the participant to do all of the work in meeting the appointment. There may be some complex logistics involved which result in the loss of some interviews. There are other difficulties such as:

- the need to find a suitable uninterrupted, quiet place;
- the communication problems which might be involved in ensuring that all relevant colleagues are informed that the interview is taking place – they need to know where to direct the interviewee when they arrive, for example;
- some offices may appear to be cold and sterile places in which to conduct interviews on sensitive topics;
- offices tend to be available during the working day which may be when the interviewee is not available because of their job.

An obvious alternative is to visit the interviewee at home. An advantage is that interviewees may be more relaxed on home ground. However, the home may not be a suitable location for a number of reasons:

- There may be too many distractions from children, animals, etc. There may be other people around in front of whom the interviewee might not wish to discuss certain problems – or, alternatively, the other people might want to contribute to the interview.

- It is more difficult to set up recording equipment in someone's home since setting up has to be done on the spot – or there may be a canary singing in the background, making it harder to transcribe the recording.

Of course, there are many other locations which may be considered. The main point is that location needs to be actively considered in order to best serve the interests of the research. Also remember that there may not be a single best interview location for all research participants.

There may be safety issues involved in the use of certain locations. Visiting interviewees at home is not without its dangers and arrangements may need to be made concerning the interviewer's safety. Similarly, some research locations may be intrinsically more dangerous than others (e.g. prison) and again appropriate consideration may need to be given to interviewer safety. Boxes 3.2 and 3.3 at the end of this chapter give details of two studies in which qualitative interviewing was involved.

The qualitative interview stage

Although a good interview involves the interviewee seemingly doing most of the work, in reality the interviewer has to maintain a great deal of involvement in what is happening during the interview. In particular, the qualitative interview is highly dependent on the researcher's quick absorption of the detail of what is being said. Kvale describes the good interviewer in the following terms:

> The interviewer must continually make quick choices about what to ask and how; which aspects of a subject's answer to follow up – and which not; which answers to interpret – and which not. Interviewers should be knowledgeable in the topics investigated, master conversational skills, and be proficient in language with an ear for their subject's linguistic style. The interviewer should have a sense for good stories and be able to assist the subjects in the unfolding of their narratives. (Kvale, 1996, p. 147)

The following are some important considerations for the interview stage.

Step 1

Recording the interview Few authorities dispute that qualitative interviews should be recorded in their entirety. Recordings of interviews are critical to producing good quality transcriptions. The following are key considerations:

- Do *not* assume that it is sufficient to speak into a voice recorder to check the quality of the recorder. A recorder which is adequate for individuals to use to make memos, etc. may not be suitable to record an interview which is a much more complex recording situation. Always try out the equipment in a situation as close as possible to the research setting.

- Use the best quality recorder available since high-quality recordings both save time in the long run and help maximise transcript quality.

- If one is transcribing large amounts of interview material, then a recorder which facilitates back-and-forward movement through the recording is a big advantage. However, there are computer programs which can help with this when used with a foot control.

- It is useful to be able to monitor the sound quality during the course of the interview which means that a recorder capable of simultaneous recording and playback through headphones/earphones is a boon. It also means that the risk of nothing being recorded because of operator error is minimal.

- Digital recordings are generally to be preferred.

- Take precautions to make sure that you have the capacity to record a lengthy interview on your recorder.
- The quality of the microphone used will affect the quality of the recording. The use of an external microphone is usually to be preferred as it ensures a better quality recording of conversation. There are some microphones which are particularly good at recording more than one individual.
- The quality of the recording will be affected by how close participants are to the microphone so try to ensure that all participants are seated near to it. Generally, faced with a choice, it is better to maximise the quality of the recording of the interviewee than the interviewer.
- Extraneous noise in the environment affects the clarity of the recording. Directional microphones may help if this is a problem.
- Try to avoid setting up the microphone in such a way that it picks up sounds caused by the movements of the interviewer or interviewee. Moving papers on the desk on which the microphone is placed may result in parts of the recording being impossible to transcribe.
- Stereo recordings are usually easier to transcribe.
- Video recording is more difficult and also more intrusive on the interview situation than sound recording. The interviewee may be reluctant to be recorded on video because they feel uncomfortable or embarrassed. This suggests that you should think very carefully before using video (and perhaps try out video as a preliminary measure before carrying out the research) when investigating highly sensitive research topics since videoing may exacerbate the situation. If your research does not really require video, it is probably best avoided. However, if your analysis is to involve the transcription of gesture and gaze then the use of video is essential.

Step 2   **Orientation stage of the interview** The major spoken contribution of the researcher in a qualitative interview is the introductory stage of the interview. In this, the interviewer begins the process of engaging with the interviewee by:

- introducing themselves;
- explaining the purpose of the interview and what it is hoped to achieve during the session;
- indicating the typical amount of time the interview will take;
- explaining the ethical basis of the research in general and in particular explaining that they, the interviewee, are free to withdraw at any stage and ask for their data to be destroyed;
- allowing an opportunity for the interviewee to ask any questions before the interview starts;
- throughout this process encouraging the interviewee to speak and respond extensively; explaining that it is the interviewee's views, perceptions, responses, etc. that the researcher is interested in and that time is not constrained in terms of giving answers.

Step 3   **What qualitative researchers 'do' when interviewing** The role of the interviewer in qualitative research can be best understood by considering what the researcher does and does not do during an interview:

- The interviewer does *not* normally take detailed notes. The detail often required for many types of qualitative analysis can only be achieved using a sound recording together with careful transcription. Generally speaking, the most detailed notes are inadequate for this purpose. Some researchers may prefer to take notes as an aid to their memory but this is not a requisite. Some, however, would question whether note-taking is appropriate during the qualitative interview. The case against note-taking is that it takes up some of the interviewer's attention during the interview and that for the interviewee it may be distracting. For example, it may appear to signal that the interviewee has just said something particularly 'noteworthy'. In contrast, it might be thought that note-taking is part of the interviewer's active synthesis of what is being said during the interview. For the novice researcher, taking notes complicates an already difficult task and, perhaps, should be avoided until the other skills involved in qualitative interviewing have been mastered. If notes are to be taken, the question arises about what these should consist of. If the notes are seen as purely an aide-memoire then it becomes obvious that things such as names and dates should be noted down as one may refer to particular family members by name or sort out the chronological order of events.

- The qualitative interviewer normally does *not* do a lot of talking during the course of the interview itself. Doing so can be a sign of problems in the interview or inexperience.

- The qualitative interviewer does not interrupt the interviewee's replies. Of course, accidental interruptions can happen but generally the interviewer should defer to the interviewee in these circumstances.

- During a qualitative interview, once the scene has been set and the arrangements clarified, the researcher is largely listening to the replies to the questions and issues raised by the interviewer. The direction of the interview is largely in the control of the interviewee though the interviewer may have to intervene when there is too much drift – the researcher's primary role is to steer the interview when it needs to be focused or expanded.

- During the qualitative interview, the researcher is actively building a mental picture and understanding of what the interviewee is saying. It is essential that the researcher engages with the replies of the interviewee as it may be necessary to consider extending the questioning, insert probes, seek clarification or identify problems in the account. Sometimes this may involve very minor but crucial points of clarification (for example, just who is the participant talking about at this time?). Sometimes the structure of the narrative might be questioned (e.g. 'So just when did this happen? Was it before you left the children's home?'). The researcher needs to ask themselves questions about whether what is being said by the interviewee makes sense in terms of what has been said before. The interviewer's objective is to ensure that the detail in the participant's answers is sufficient and to interrogate the information as it is being collected if necessary. This is very much in keeping with the view that qualitative data analysis starts at the stage of data collection. It also reflects the qualitative ideal that progress in research depends on the early and repeated processing of the data. The qualitative interview, because it requires active listening, absorption of what is being said and asking appropriate supplementary questions, places considerable demands on the interviewer. Consider the structured interview in contrast where recording the interviewee's answers precisely is the most important task. There is no need in the structured interview to do much more than get brief answers from the respondent in order to 'tick the right boxes'. This can be achieved without the level of involvement required by the qualitative interviewer whose work is likely to be ineffective without their full engagement with what is being said.

- The qualitative interviewer needs to be able to use silence effectively. One of the biggest faults of novice interviewers is not allowing the interviewee the necessary 'space' in which to both think and talk. A gap of silence does not indicate that a qualitative interview is going badly. Neither does it indicate a lack of skill on the part of the interviewer. Quite the contrary: being comfortable with silences is indicative of a good interviewer. This is quite different from normal conversation in which gaps in conversation tend to be avoided. By using silences effectively, not only does the researcher avoid shutting up the interviewee prematurely but the interviewee is encouraged into a more thoughtful and considered way of responding. From the viewpoint of the interviewee, if the researcher quickly fills silences then the impression may be created that the interviewer wants to proceed more quickly and that the interviewee is giving answers that are too long. Clearly this is an undesirable situation in light of the objectives of some qualitative interviews.

- Question asking: Unlike the structured interview, question asking in the qualitative interview should not be regarded as primarily for the purpose of presenting a standardised stimulus for the interviewee to respond to. Generally, in structured interviewing, the interviewer is encouraged to ask exactly the same question in exactly the same way. Only where it is apparent that the interviewee does not understand or asks for clarification is the standard interview 'script' departed from. In qualitative interviewing, the objective is to get the interviewee talking freely and extensively about the topic of the questioning. This means that the way questions are put will vary from interview to interview since the needs of the interviewees will vary. Furthermore, because it is vitally important in the qualitative interview that the interviewer understands what is being said then the questioning needs to reflect this. Thus reading the question out word-for-word may be inappropriate since it may be better to engage the eye of the interviewee to establish the person-to-person nature of the interview than to keep one's head down in the list of questions. Questions in the qualitative interview are structured in ways which encourage extensive responses and inhibit simple yes or no replies. So, for example, a question such as 'Do you have a good relationship with your parents?' may be an excellent question for a structured interview but inadequate for a qualitative interview, where a question like 'Can you describe to me your relationship with your parents?' may be more productive.

Step 4   Bringing the interview to a conclusion The end of a qualitative interview is not signalled simply by the final topic on the interview guide being reached. The satisfaction of the researcher and the interviewee is an additional important criterion. So there needs to be some consideration of the interview experience as part of the process of concluding the interview. It is always wise, at this stage, to leave the voice recorder running given that important information often emerges at this stage. The following are some of the steps which may be associated with the finishing of the interview:

- The interviewer may wish to take a short 'time-out' break to review the interview guide in light of how the interview proceeded. Topics not adequately covered may be returned to at this stage.

- The interviewee may be given the opportunity to discuss things that they think are of some relevance but which have not emerged thus far in the interview.

- The interviewer should thank the interviewee formally.

- The interviewer should enter a debriefing stage in which the interviewee's experience of the interview is discussed. This may involve (a) allowing the interviewee to ask any questions they wish about the research; (b) checking that the interviewee remains happy that the recording can be part of the research; (c) providing names and contact details of organisations, etc. which might be able to deal with issues of a counselling or therapeutic nature arising from the interview (a psychologist must be qualified in order to offer such support and researchers are not in that position); and (d) obtaining feedback about the interview content and interviewing methods employed.

Box 3.1 explains how quality can be achieved in qualitative interviews.

Box 3.1
KEY CONCEPT
Ensuring quality in qualitative interviewing

Just how does a researcher know whether their qualitative interviews have achieved a satisfactory quality? Of course, not all interviews with all participants have a potential to achieve the highest standards. Some interviewees will provide less than optimum data no matter who the interviewer is. This is a built-in inevitability with qualitative interviewing. But the participant is not the only source of variability in interview quality. The approach of the interviewer has a lot to contribute. However, it is important for the interviewer to get a feeling for how well the interview process is going. If things appear to be less than optimal then there may be an opportunity to revise one's approach. Kvale (1996) has a number of criteria which may be indicative of the interview quality:

- Are the interviewer's questions comparatively much shorter than the replies of the interviewee?

- Are the interviewee's replies to the point of the interview and extensive? Kvale (1996) uses the terms spontaneous, rich, specific and relevant (p. 145) to describe good quality answers.

- Does the interviewer follow up the relevant parts of the interview and seek clarification of what is being said?

- Is the interview complete in itself? That is, is the story that it contains self-contained and requires little by way of extra explanation or description for it to make sense?

- Are important features of the interviewee's answers summarised and/or interpreted by the interviewer during the course of the interview?

- Does the interviewer validate or verify their interpretations of the answers during the interview itself?

- Is the interviewer knowledgeable about the topic of the interview? The more generally informed the interviewer is concerning the research topic, the easier the interview will be. Of course, this also allows the interviewer to be frank about aspects of the interview that they do not understand.

- Does the interviewer ask questions in a straightforward, clear and simple fashion? Is the interviewer understood easily? Does the interviewer avoid using jargon which is unknown to the interviewee?

- Does the interviewer impose a clear structure to the interview and provide useful summaries at appropriate points of the interview?

- Is the interviewer sensitive to what the interviewee is saying? Does the interviewer seek to clarify any nuances of meaning that a reply may have? Is the interviewer sensitive to emotionality in replies and does he or she deal with this effectively?

- Does the interviewer have a gentle approach to the interview which allows the interviewee to respond at their own pace and in their own time? This includes being accepting of pauses and thinking time by not interrupting these. Does the interviewer avoid interrupting what the interviewee is saying?

- Does the interviewer exhibit openness to what the interviewee is saying? For example, does he or she allow the introduction of new aspects of the topic by the interviewee?

- Does the interviewer appear to remember what the interviewee has said previously? A poor interviewer may appear not to have registered what the interviewee has already said and so, for example, may pose questions which the interviewee has essentially already answered.

- Is the interviewer prepared to be critical or questioning of what has been said? Does he or she question the interviewee in ways which might help establish the validity of what has been said? Matters of logical consistency might be raised.

- Does the interviewer show evidence that they are steering the interview in ways which are relevant to the purpose of the research? That is, does the interviewer seem to have a firm grasp on what the research is about? For example, the interviewer may need to ensure that the interviewee does not digress too much from the topic of the interview.

Obviously, the more of the indicators met by the interviewer the better, in general, the interview will be.

What happens following the qualitative interview?

There are a number of post-interview considerations to bear in mind:

- *Support for the interviewer* While not all qualitative interviews involve sensitive and perhaps distressing material, some of them do. Interviews with victims of sexual abuse, sexual abusers, domestic abusers, those suffering bereavements and so forth all have potential for distressing the interviewer as well as the interviewee. Of course, during the interview, the interviewer avoids demonstrating their feelings and emotions. However, these will remain as baggage after the interview is over. How are they best dealt with? One approach is for the interviewer to have a confidant with whom he/she may work through the interview experience. This may be little other than just someone to talk to. Having 'buddies' who have experience of similar interviews or are currently involved in the same sort of interview has its advantages. These are not therapeutic sessions in any formal sense but involve social and emotional support where necessary. This said, such discussions are not necessarily emotionally heavy but may, instead, be emotionally relieving in other ways. For example, while outsiders might think that discussions of interviews with child molesters induce strong negative emotions, post-interview sessions of this sort may be riddled with laughter. This is common in any work group dealing with distressing situations.

- *Data protection and management* Usually as part of the ethical considerations for qualitative research, plans are presented or requirements imposed about matters such as the safe storage of the interview recording and its eventual disposal. These should be followed at the appropriate time.

- *Data transcription* Issues surrounding the transcription of recorded data and methods of transcription are discussed later (Chapter 6).

How to analyse a qualitative interview

There are circumstances in which qualitative interviews conducted by, for example, therapists and counsellors can be regarded as 'natural' for the purposes of research. This is standard practice, for example, in conversation analysis. Numerous examples of qualitative researchers using interviews in this way exist, such as, the interviews conducted by police officers with suspects (e.g. Benneworth, 2006) and the interviews of therapists with their clients (e.g. Antaki, 2007). In these cases, the interviews were initially for professional purposes and their eventual research use secondary and even fortuitous. The ethics of using such resources in research needs to be considered (Chapter 16). Participants, for example, may not know or expect that the recordings would be used for research purposes. Is it appropriate, then, to use their data?

The choice of analysis methods for qualitative interview data is constrained by whether such data are natural conversation or not. If it can be regarded as natural conversation then qualitative analysis methods such as conversation analysis and discourse analysis are not ruled out. Therapeutic interviews are regarded as suitable for analysis – they are not produced for research purposes. Opinions seem to vary considerably on the issue of whether research interviews can be regarded as natural conversational data.

One example of where research interviews have been used in this way is given by Rapley (2001). In this he raises the question of the role of the interviewer as a key player in the production of interview talk. The argument is that since interviews can be conceived of as being social interactions, then potentially they may be analysed in ways appropriate to any other social interactions. In Rapley's paper, he explains how both the interviewer and the interviewee construct themselves through talk as particular types of people. The local detail of the production of interview data within a particular interview is important in analysing interview data irrespective of the analytic method adopted, he argues. Whether one would wish to carry out research interviews solely for such analyses to take place is somewhat unlikely – Rapley uses published interviews to make his points, for instance. Furthermore, judging from the extracts he reports, these interviews were very conversational in nature since the contributions or turns of the interviewer and the interviewee were relatively short. It might be much more difficult to apply such an analysis to more typical qualitative interviewing.

This reflects the distinction that Seale (1998) makes between (a) using interview data as a research topic and (b) using interview data as a resource for obtaining information which has some bearing on the reality of the interviewee's life outside of the interview context. If one wishes to use research interviews as the object of study as Rapley (2001) does then this is a clear focus, but one which is very different from using the research interview as a means of gaining a perspective on the life and experiences of the interviewee. Although these constitute clear choices for the researcher, they are both appropriate methods of qualitative data analysis using research interview data. Box 3.2 describes an interview study in which a perspective very different from that of Rapley is represented.

According to Potter (2003) among the disadvantages of the research interview for discourse analysis is that interviewees tend to take the role of theorists and experts since they are abstracted from the social context they normally inhabit. Furthermore, the relative value of an interview about a particular topic may be low compared with naturalistic talk if this can be obtained. One strategy that can be adopted is to base the interview on a more everyday conversation style in which the interviewer is a more active participant than in the more formal qualitative interview. If TV interviews are legitimate sources of data for analysis, what makes the research interview any different?

Irrespective of all this, there are a number of analytic procedures which could be used, appropriately, in order to analyse the data from qualitative interviews (Figure 3.1):

- Grounded theory (Chapter 8) can be construed as a somewhat generic approach to qualitative data analysis which is not constrained by a particular interest in language in action, for example, unlike conversation analysis and certain forms of discourse analysis.

- Thematic analysis (Chapter 7) could be used since this merely seeks the dominant themes which underlie the content of the conversation.

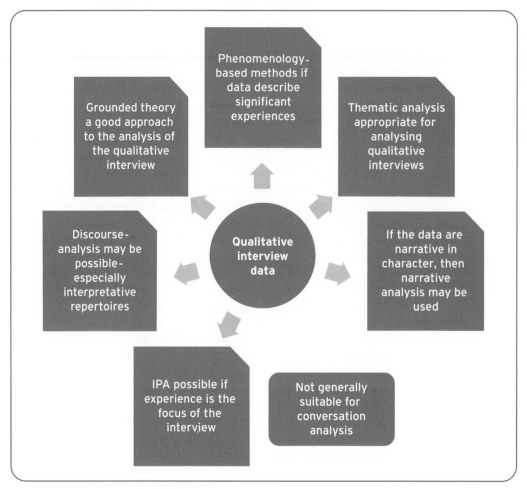

FIGURE 3.1 How to analyse qualitative interview data

- Phenomenological analysis (Chapter 12) or interpretative phenomenological analysis (Chapter 13) might be an appropriate approach if the interviews concentrate on how individuals experience phenomena such as health matters.
- Narrative analysis might be appropriate if the interviews took a substantial life-history/narrative form. However, some narrative analysts prefer to construct their qualitative interviews following McAdams' (1993) scheme and those of others (see Chapter 14).

Finally, in some circumstances a formal method of data analysis may not be necessary. This is most clearly the case where the researcher is using interviews as a way of obtaining basic knowledge and understanding before planning, say, a more focused research study.

When to use qualitative interviews

To summarize, qualitative interviewing is a potential data collection method for a range of styles of qualitative research. It is probably least useful to the researcher whose primary objective is the study of naturally occurring conversation. Despite numerous advantages, there is no sense in which the research interview can be construed as naturally occurring conversation though it may share some features with it. We have seen that it is important to distinguish between the research interview and other forms of interviews by professionals and their clients which are commonplace. The job selection interview, interviews between doctors and patients, and police interviews can be conceived as naturally occurring conversation and, as such, analysed using methods designed for application to everyday conversations. Against the general rule, narrative analysis (Chapter 14) tends to use McAdams' (1993) approach to qualitative interviews. However, this does not prevent the use of any other form of qualitative interview for narrative analysis if it elicits appropriate narrative material from the interviewee.

A researcher's position in the realism–relativism debate also has a bearing on appropriate methods of data analysis. Researchers who adopt, say, a realist approach may find in the qualitative interview content which provides them with a viable perspective on a person's life. That is, if the researcher accepts that what people say maps onto social reality though, perhaps, not with complete fidelity then the qualitative interview can provide narrative information which contributes substantially to a particular field of research. At the same time, it is obvious that the qualitative interview sheds no light onto how groups of individuals talk together about a particular topic. Focus groups (Chapter 4), because of their interactive nature, are much better at doing this.

Careful thought must go into the decision to use qualitative interviews in a particular study. While, in some cases, it is difficult to conceive of any other method, there are frequently alternatives to be considered. There is no question that such interviews are expensive in terms of time and resources. Consequently, they may be out of the question if, for whatever reason, the researcher needs a large sample. Now large samples are not typical of qualitative research, anyway, since the purpose of qualitative research is interpretation and not estimates of population characteristics. So the need for a large sample should set warning bells ringing, questioning the status of the research as qualitative research. Of course, the general question of whether the research is truly qualitative in nature should always be asked. For example, if a relatively simple research question is involved then a quantitative approach might be more appropriate given that structured questionnaires are cost minimal compared with qualitative interviews. This may appear to be a little patronising but experience indicates that sometimes student researchers, especially, reject a quantitative approach simply because they wish to avoid the problems associated with using statistics. However, if their research question is one which implies quantification or is expressed in quantitative terms, then a detour through qualitative methods is not only wasteful but it is also unproductive. So once the research question has been clarified (usually it helps to write this down) then its position on the quantitative–qualitative dimension needs to be assessed. As a simple example, how many women have depression after childbirth is clearly a quantitative question but how do women experience depression after childbirth is most probably qualitative.

The qualitative interview can take a variety of forms, of course. Normally, we think of it as a one-on-one, face-to-face situation in which there is an interviewer and an interviewee. But this is far from the only possibility. There may be two or more interviewers and two or more interviewees. These have their own dynamics and their own requirements in terms of ethics (see Chapter 17) among other things. The reasons for these variations are numerous. For example, an interview at home with a sex offender may require more than one interviewer for safety reasons. A researcher may arrive at someone's home expecting to interview one person but the entire family wants to be involved. Furthermore, the face-to-face situation may be replaced with telephone interviews or lengthy exchanges over the Internet. These, for some research, may have advantages though their impersonal nature may impact on the research in a variety of ways.

Evaluation of qualitative interviewing

The ideal circumstances in which to use a qualitative interview are where the experiences, thoughts, life histories and feelings of an individual (as opposed to individuals as part of a group) are the researcher's primary focus. The interview may, of course, be part of a series of interviews with different people allowing for comparisons between different participants or different types of participants. The qualitative interview might be regarded as one of the archetypal data collection methods in qualitative research in general. Nevertheless, the qualitative interview is not always the preferred source of qualitative data for all qualitative analyses. So, although the qualitative interview would be the data collection method of preference for interpretative phenomenological analysis because of its capacity to provide detailed accounts of experiences, it would not normally be the preferred method for conversation analysis given that research interviews are not the ordinary conversations of ordinary people. There is no set way of analysing the qualitative interview, which makes a simple evaluation of such interviews impossible and one is almost always faced with a choice of qualitative analysis methods. The method chosen will depend partly on what research questions the researcher is addressing. Of course, the actual quality of the interview is determined by rather different factors from the ones which determine that it is relevant and appropriate for a particular research study. The qualitative interview requires careful preparation if it is to achieve its full potential as a way of collecting pertinent data.

The following may be helpful in putting the method into context:

- The apparent subjectivity of the qualitative interview is not a particular problem in qualitative research terms – indeed it is an advantage. The ethos of quantitative research may be to seek to capture an objective reality but this is not the case for qualitative research. The qualitative researcher may, instead, wish to explore the different viewpoints of participants in the research or the ways in which participants talk about the research topic. Subjectivity issues, of course, do arise where the researcher seeks to regard interview data as representing reality rather than different viewpoints on reality. In a sentence, ultimately interviews are about what the participants say about what they think and do rather than about what they actually think and do. Participant observation/ethnography (Chapter 5) might be more appropriate where it is important to document what people do rather than what they say about what they do.

- The qualitative interview has advantages over focus groups (Chapter 4) in that it allows the researcher substantial control over the data collected. In contrast, the focus group hands even more control to the group under the researcher's guidance. A group of individuals may develop an agenda for discussion which is quite distinct from those of the individual members. This does not make it invalid, it merely is different. Focus group researchers have far less time to devote to the individual than to individual interviews. But, then, the focus group is not intended to serve the same purpose as the individual qualitative interview.

- Like most other qualitative data collection methods, the qualitative interview is extremely flexible and is not necessarily constrained by a conventional structure. For example, the researcher might wish to use family photographs and get the participant to talk about these as part of a study of families.

- In qualitative research, qualitative interviews may be combined with other data collection methods. An obvious example of this is their use in the context of ethnographic or participant observation approaches (Chapter 5).

- The qualitative interview can be used in a variety of ways in relation to research. For instance, many researchers have used the interview as part of a preliminary, exploratory, stage for their research especially when the topic is a relatively new one and the researcher cannot rely on the inspiration of the previous research literature on which to build their ideas. Quite simply, there may be a lack of knowledge on a particular topic and the obvious initial stage of research would be to talk to those people who may have experiences, thoughts and ideas which are relevant to the research topic. Out of these interviews, the researcher hopes to generate ideas for research which are grounded in people's experiences.

- However, it is wrong to think of the qualitative interview as merely an idea-generating technique. It may be useful used in this way but this use tends to undermine the qualitative interview since it implies that there are better methods of doing the 'real' research. The qualitative interview can provide information which is, in itself, sufficient for the purposes of the research.

- The resource-intensive nature of qualitative interviewing should always be a consideration. This, in the end, may lead to the view that the qualitative interview is the only practicable choice to achieve the researcher's aims. On the other hand, the researcher should question why it is that they need to use the qualitative interview. What is it about the research question which cannot be addressed in different ways? Indeed, has the researcher done sufficient preparatory work (e.g. the literature review) to be sure that the research question could not be addressed in other ways more effectively?

- There are many circumstances in which there are no feasible alternative ways of data collection. For example, it is not possible to do observation-based studies of contraception use.

CONCLUSION

The qualitative interview has enormous attractions as a qualitative data collection method. Indeed, it is difficult to imagine research questions which could not be, in part, informed by interviews with relevant participants. A great deal of research would benefit from giving a 'voice' to the participants in the research. The qualitative interview is an excellent way of doing this. As a stand-alone data collection method it has few challengers. Properly carried out, it supplies rich data that other methods can only serve to supplement. Nevertheless, the limitations of qualitative interviewing especially in terms of the heavy drain on resources are important. Furthermore, the practicalities of research ensure that most interviews are carried out on a one-to-one basis.

The qualitative interview is an archetypal approach to data collection both in qualitative research and research in general. For the qualitative researcher, though, it may not be appropriate for every research purpose. For example, it is a somewhat 'unnatural' form of conversation and, consequently, may not be ideal when the researcher wishes to study natural, real-life conversation. Like all data collection methods, its value depends on how precisely it maps to the researcher's purpose.

This chapter has stressed that qualitative interviewing is quite a sophisticated research skill despite its apparently, but superficially, conversational nature. Doing a good qualitative interview draws on all aspects of a researcher's skills – including analytic and theoretical ones. Of course, there are everyday conversational skills which are helpful in developing good qualitative interviewing ability – for example, they may help develop a good rapport. Nevertheless, the qualitative interviewer is carrying out a particular sort of performance which is different from those normally involved in being a good conversationalist. For example, the listening skills of the researcher are essential to a good interview as is their ability to remember what has been said so far in the interview. Normal conversation may be effective without this. A transcript of an interview is very one-sided compared with everyday conversation – typically the researcher says little at most stages of an interview and the interviewee appears to be contributing disproportionately.

KEY POINTS

- The qualitative interview in its various forms is the bedrock of qualitative research. It supplies a means of gathering extensive and detailed data on virtually any topic. Of course, the focus group is a variant of this. Nevertheless, it does not always supply appropriate data for every research purpose and so is the data collection method of choice for only some qualitative research.

- A researcher planning to use qualitative interviews needs to appreciate that they involve a planning/preparatory stage, the interview itself and post-interview considerations. A researcher who fails to plan properly for the interview may waste their time in any number of ways. For example, the interviewee may fail to make the appointment, the researcher may badly structure the interview and dominate the exchanges through lack of planning, or the interview is inaudible on the recording and so cannot be used. These are just some of the possible problems.

- A distinction should be made between the quality of an interview and its suitability for particular research purposes. Ideally, the researcher should be technically proficient in interviewing but also clear in terms of the overall strategy of the research.

- There is potential to analyse qualitative interview data using a variety of different analysis methods. Of course, it is better where the researcher matches the content of the interview to the requirements of the method. Each of the different methods of analysis will provide a different form of analysis according to the theoretical basis of the method.

Box 3.2

ILLUSTRATIVE RESEARCH STUDY

Interviewing sex offenders about pornography

One of the notable features about a lot of psychological research is that it concentrates on relationships among aspects of the data rather than describing the psychological phenomenon being researched. But there are times in research when the topic that the researcher is studying is little known about. In these circumstances, it would seem important that the researcher seeks to familiarise themselves in whatever way they can. If there is no substantial research literature then interviews and other methods might be called upon to fill in the picture. When

Howitt (1995) began work interviewing paedophiles he was motivated by a desire to explore the topic of fantasy. Now fantasy is a word which means something to most of us but usually not quite the same thing. For some of us it may be a 'pipe dream' like winning the National Lottery, for others it may be unrealistic ideas about what is going on around us. From trying to interview ordinary people about their fantasies it was clear that what they had to say did not stimulate the researchers in their understanding of fantasy.

As happens in research, serendipity then took a hand. Howitt and Cumberbatch (1990) had published a detailed review of the research literature on pornography for a government department. As you can imagine, this sort of task is a political hot-potato. Everyone, including politicians, has their own views on such a topic. Happenchance, Howitt heard Ray Wyre (1951–2008), an expert on counselling sex offending, criticise Howitt and Cumberbatch's report in a radio interview. It then dawned on him that this was the context in which to begin to study fantasy – that is, fantasy and sex offenders. Fortunately, Ray Wyre was more than helpful in providing Howitt with access to sex offenders at the then famous Gracewell Institute. It also became rapidly apparent that relatively little published research was available on paedophiles at that time. There has been a massive escalation since then but things can move very fast in new research fields.

In the previous few sentences is hidden a lot that is relevant to this chapter. In particular, virtually all of the preliminary requirements for planning the research were dealt with or defined by the choice to base the research on sex offenders at a sex offender treatment clinic. The sample was clearly defined by this, the location was determined by this, managing the participants was essentially done by the clinic, and so forth. Even issues such as the suitability of the men for qualitative interviewing were also predetermined since the men had been selected for therapy based on cognitive methods in which they needed to be able to reflect but also discuss their offending with others. Similarly, the clinical environment was not a distraction for the simple reason that the men's days were spent in this environment.

Of course, the researcher needed to plan the interviews. The interview guide was simply a list of the areas which the researcher wanted to explore in the interview – things like the men's childhoods, their offending behaviour in detail, pornography, fantasy, parents, adult relationships and so forth. No true piloting was carried out. The first interview or two were somewhat tentative and explorative of the methodology but it rapidly became apparent that the interviews worked in the sense that they produced copious in-depth data. The men seemed to benefit from the process – perhaps as a way of trying to make-good the harm that they had caused, perhaps because they were receiving relatively benign contact compared with the somewhat hostile and challenging group therapy work that they were engaged in, or perhaps because they began to understand themselves better. Of course, there was the occasional minor crisis to deal with – the man might become emotional or cry, areas of the interview might result in the man refusing to give information (e.g. it was too emotional to discuss their mother or their violent crimes). These were not predictable. No notes were taken during the interviews but the material committed itself readily to memory because of its emotive nature. The recording was made on professional quality equipment and monitored during the interview for quality.

Interviews with such men which included graphic detail are a challenge to the interviewer. Not only are they physically and mentally tiring but they are emotionally draining. This is partly because of the nature of the interviews' contents but also because these men often had fairly distressing childhoods and sad lives in general. This meant that the interviewer needed to find the opportunity to talk with sympathetic others in order to share the experiences which, in a way, was a contribution to formulating an analysis of the data. The interviews were transcribed in a verbatim form. However, what was apparent quite early on in the interview series was that analytic ideas came to the researcher out of those interviews. In other words, not only was the analysis beginning to be formulated during the interviews but this analysis could feed back into the later interviews in terms of ensuring relevant areas were covered. For example, it became clear very early in the interview series that there was a connection between abuse experienced by the man in his own childhood and early sexual experiences with other children with the abuse that he perpetrated on children in his adult years. Howitt describes this as homology. So, for example, the offender tended to offend against a child of a similar age to his own when he had the sexual experience in childhood. In all of this is a hint that the more vivid interview material is, the easier it is for this detailed familiarity with the data to translate into analytic ideas. At the more descriptive level, it became clear that pornography in relation to paedophiles can be a rather complex thing. The research was conducted before the widespread use of the Internet so the use of Internet child pornography was not an issue. However, what was significant was that the offenders tended to use otherwise innocuous films and television programmes as part of their sexual fantasy about children. So a Walt Disney film featuring children could be used to feed fantasy without any need for the material to be sexually explicit.

Ultimately, there is no other way than the qualitative interview of collecting data for research such as this. With care, a detailed narrative can be collected which not only explores the research issue in detail but allows the researcher to contextualise this in the lives of the interviewees.

Box 3.3

ILLUSTRATIVE RESEARCH STUDY

Distressing 'unfeminine' medical symptoms

Polycystic ovarian syndrome (PCOS) is a medical condition in which both ovaries are impaired by cysts. The condition results in dysfunction in the reproductive system together with physically more apparent characteristics such as obesity and excessive hair growth as well as hair loss which follows the characteristic pattern of men. Since its identification in the 1930s, polycystic ovarian syndrome has been covered in the medical literature from a medical perspective. Kitzinger and Willmott (2002) suggest that the condition has received little general discussion, apart from this, and what references there are to it tend to be to 'bearded ladies' and other 'deviations' from 'true' femininity. Women with PCOS, according to research, experience stress associated with the symptoms of their condition and the attendant distress though probably not psychopathology. Quite obviously, PCOS can cause identity problems in women and Kitzinger and Willmott adopted a feminist perspective towards trying to understand how sufferers manage their female identities. The researchers describe their key finding being the way in which such women experience themselves as 'freaks' (a term used by many of the women) who fail to conform to 'the norms of "proper" womanhood'. Body and facial hair were the most disturbing symptoms that the women experienced in relation to the condition. Proper women, in the women's view, are free from hair on their bodies and faces, have regular menstrual periods, and are capable of childbearing.

In this context, we are more interested in the method of interviewing adopted by Kitzinger and Willmott (2002) who describe their methodology in some detail. They interviewed 32 women of whom nearly all were volunteers recruited through a 'flyer' distributed by a PCOS self-help group. Although more women volunteered, the researchers restricted their interviews to those volunteers who were geographically convenient, relatively inexpensive to visit at home for the purposes of the study, and could be seen within the timescale of the study. The typical volunteer to the study was white, heterosexual

and aged between 25 and 34 years. Interviews lasted between 45 and 90 minutes and were based on a broad and wide-ranging interview guide (schedule). The intention of the guide was for the women to tell their stories rather than provide a fixed structure. Open-ended questions were used together with prompts, if necessary, and follow-up questions. According to Kitzinger and Willmott, the final interview structure explored the following areas:

- how the woman came to be diagnosed with PCOS;
- and how they dealt with these symptoms;
- how the woman felt about suffering PCOS.

All of the interviews were transcribed using an orthographic procedure and the analysis was based on organising the data into 'recurrent themes'. Kitzinger and Willmott describe this as 'thematic analysis' though it is unclear whether they involved all of the procedures described later (see Chapter 7). The authors felt that it was inappropriate to use any form of quantification because the interviews were 'loosely structured'. They suggest that a checklist of symptoms might be appropriate if it was desired to quantify just how many women experienced each symptom. They illustrate each theme in their analysis in their research report by verbatim quotations from the interviews. They clearly locate their analysis of the data closer to the 'realist' approach rather than to relativist positions:

> We differ in our analysis from some discourse analysts in that we take what women say as evidence for what they experience, i.e. we treat their talk as 'interpretative autobiography' rather than as locally specific 'action'. (p. 351)

So Kitzinger and Willmott describe a number of decisions that they took as researchers which reflect some of the points made in this chapter. In particular, the use of a self-help group greatly facilitates this sort of sample gathering. Some of the women involved did not know other women with the same complaint so methods such as snowball sampling simply would not work as a consequence. The choice to interview the women in their homes was a sensitive one given that the condition discourages the women from venturing into some contexts. Given that so little is known about the experience of the syndrome, the need to explore using open-ended interview methods is virtually self-evident. Most importantly of all, the researchers precisely define how they intend to analyse the data as textual evidence about the experiences of the women in their sample. Kitzinger and Willmott were well aware of the debate in qualitative research about qualitative interview data so theirs was a thought-out decision and not evidence of any naivety about the qualitative ethos.

ADDITIONAL RESOURCES

Arksey, H., & Knight, P. T. (1999). *Interviewing for social scientists: An introductory resource with examples.* London: Sage.

Busher, H., & James, N. (2009). *Online interviewing.* London: Sage.

Higher Education Academy. (n.d.). TQRMUL Dataset Teaching Resources: Shazia's Interview. https://www.heacademy.ac.uk/resources/detail/subjects/psychology/tqrml/interviews/ (accessed 23 February 2015).

Fontana, A., & Frey, J. H. (2000). The interview: From structured questions to negotiated text. In N. K. Denzin and Y. S. Lincoln (Eds.), *Handbook of qualitative research* (2nd ed., pp. 645–672). Thousand Oaks, CA: Sage Publications.

Kvale, S. (1996). *Interviews.* Thousand Oaks, CA: Sage.

Kvale, S. (2007). *Doing interviews.* Los Angeles, CA: Sage.

Morris, A. (2015). *A practical introduction to in-depth interviewing.* London: Sage.

Opdenakker, R. (2006). Advantages and disadvantages of four interview techniques in qualitative research. *Forum Qualitative Social Research, 7* (4), Article 11. http://www.qualitative-research.net/index.php/fqs/article/viewArticle/175/391 (accessed 23 February 2015).

Truesdell, B. (n.d.). Oral history techniques: How to organise and conduct oral history interviews. http://www.indiana.edu/~cshm/oral_history_techniques.pdf (accessed 23 February 2015).

CHAPTER 4

Focus groups

Overview

- A focus group is a sort of collective interview, directed by the researcher (moderator), which exploits the interactive potential of the situation in order to generate rich data.

- There is no single use for focus groups since they can be used as a preliminary exploration of a topic for the guidance of the research or a way of evaluating a project when it is completed, for example.

- Although currently a somewhat ubiquitous data-gathering approach, its origins were in the work of Robert Merton on the focused interview in the 1940s. The approach was fairly rapidly adopted by market researchers but relatively ignored by academic researchers until the 1970s and afterwards when it became increasingly accepted in academic research.

- Focus groups basically consist of a moderator plus six to ten group members. It is usual to have about four separate focus groups for every category of group being studied.

- The planning stage is crucial if the best quality data are to be obtained. In particular, a plan needs to be drawn up specifying the sorts of participants that each group should contain. Groups should be chosen with the quality of discussion in mind. For example, one should avoid groups in which status differentials might encourage some members to defer to their formal superiors. Planning can also include decisions about what sorts of people would provide the richest data on the topic in question.

- Focus groups have a structure and unfold in an orderly questioning sequence in order to facilitate the quality of the discussion.

- Moderators (group leaders) need to be socially skilled in order to ensure that the focus groups are not dominated by a few individuals.

- The analysis of focus group data is a matter of choice but several qualitative data analysis methods can be used. It has recently been proposed that the discussions of focus groups can be analysed using discourse analysis approaches.

What are focus groups?

Like many other qualitative data collection methods, it is difficult to say precisely what a focus group is. Gibbs (1997) summarises the variety of available definitions by identifying what appear to be the key features of a focus group. These, she suggests, are:

- organised discussion;
- collective activity;
- social events;
- interaction.

From these, it is clear that a focus group involves interaction. But so do other research methodologies. So, for example, how does a focus group differ from a normal interview? Well, a focus group does involve a researcher asking questions – though the interviewer is called a 'moderator' in focus group research. There can be more than one moderator – one an expert in focus group methodology and the other an expert in the subject matter of the research, for instance. However, a focus group involves not a single interviewee but typically six to ten 'members' (the recommended range varies). But even these two features do not fully define a focus group since the key to focus groups is the opportunities for interaction between members of the group when responding to the questions posed by the moderator. This dynamic interaction between people in the focus group is the remaining major distinctive feature of focus groups though it could be claimed to characterise participant observation and ethnography too. So, obviously, focus groups have some of the elements of an interview – that is, the researcher guides the discussion by posing questions. Nevertheless, it would be incorrect to describe focus groups as multi-respondent interviews because this fails to recognise the centrality of group interaction in focus groups. Furthermore, it cannot be described as a group discussion because the focus group discussion is planned, steered and controlled by the group moderator rather than members of the group.

Figure 4.1 illustrates this schematically. In the interview, the interviewer has the strongest control on events with, normally, the interviewee being less influential. Typically in a focus group, the moderator has considerable control but this is impacted by the relatively greater influence of the group and the interaction between group members. The point of a focus group is to take advantage of the interaction between group members which may produce information different in certain respects from that produced by a separate interview with each group member. Considerable effort is taken when planning a focus group study to optimise the contribution of these group dynamics. This is why, for example, the size of a focus group is usually stipulated to be in the six to ten member range. This is not so big that participants feel swamped by the number of other people trying to have their say and not so small that the group dynamic fails to generate good discussion. Similarly, focus groups try to avoid other features which might adversely affect interaction. So, for example, the members of any particular focus group are chosen so that they are similar in status. Sitting in a focus group with, say, your line manager and the top boss would not only inhibit most of us from participating but would also influence what we have to say. This is one reason why members of focus groups are often (but not always) chosen because they are strangers and unlikely to be in contact with each other in the future. Just a caution – focus group practice is extremely varied and there are always exceptions to every rule, seemingly. The advice given in this chapter does not constitute a set of rules but some rules of thumb plus a little insight which will help you plan a focus group.

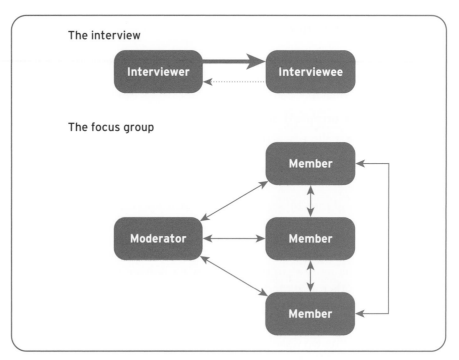

FIGURE 4.1 Relationships in interviews and focus groups

So focus groups have their dynamic quality as a defining feature. It should be pointed out that other data-gathering methods have their own dynamics. However, the focus group relies on the self-stimulating power of the group to generate data which might not be available through other means. It has to be remembered that focus groups generate data which are partly a product of the focus group dynamic. Consequently it may be a mistake to think that what is said in a focus group reflects motivating factors in other situations. This ability to generate ideas through discussion is one of the advantages of the focus group method promoted by its advocates. In effect, the members of the focus group are given the task of making sense of the issue. This is achieved through group dynamics – that is, through the relatively normal processes of discussion and debate among ordinary people. This is very hard to emulate using conventional interviewing techniques with a single interviewee.

Focus groups may be used in at least three different ways:

- As an early stage of research in order to explore and identify what the significant issues are.

- To generate broadly conversational data on a topic to be analysed in its own right.

- To evaluate the findings of research in the eyes of the people that the research is about: that is, in discussions of research conclusions.

For the researcher, the focus group has other advantages: that is, most of the resources come from the participants. The researcher generally 'facilitates' the group processes in order to ensure that a pre-planned range of issues is covered but, at the same time, allowing unexpected material to enter the discussion. So, ideally, the researcher does not dominate the proceedings. If necessary, the researcher steers the discussion along more productive lines if the group seems to be 'running out of steam'. For this reason, the researcher conducting the focus group is known as the moderator or the facilitator.

It is probably misleading, if not wrong, to regard focus groups as an alternative to ordinary interviews. They simply are not the same thing and cannot meet the same functions. In much the same way, it is clear that focus groups do not aspire to the same representative sampling that surveys do. Indeed focus group methodology adopts a radically different approach to participant selection and recruitment. The focus group method needs to be understood in its own right and not regarded as a 'cheap and cheerful' substitute for 'better' ways of conducting research.

The development of focus groups

Many of the early developments in social psychology (and the social sciences in general) were the consequence of considerable research interest in the new mass media of radio, cinema and eventually television in the 1920s, 1930s and 1940s. More than any other research at the time, research into the mass media demanded approaches which were grounded in social reality and, consequently, research methods capable of tapping into real life. The funding of the research was often from commercial organisations – not the usual source of academic funding (Morrison, 1998). Paul Lazarsfeld (1901–76) and Robert Merton (1910–2003) were two major figures in this field who made significant methodological innovations in a number of areas. For example, the panel study was developed to study how voting intentions changed during the course of an American election campaign. This needed samples of people to be assessed at several different stages in the election campaign. In other words, the panel study was developed to study the effects of the election campaign.

Much the same sort of background was responsible for the development of focus group methodology. It had become clear from research in the early part of the twentieth century that the mass media were not as powerful at changing the behaviour and attitudes of the audience as many had feared. Out of this realisation came a new emphasis in mass media research, known as 'uses and gratifications', which stressed the importance of understanding how the audience made use of the media and what, psychologically and sociologically, the media provided. This clearly demanded new research methods. Even more pressing was the Second World War and its need to mobilise all resources including social sciences research. Merton developed the focused interview (the focus group) as a method of understanding audience responses to wartime propaganda (Merton & Kendall, 1946). Merton and others:

> . . . were assigned by several war agencies to study the social and psychological effects of specific efforts to build morale. (Merton, Fiske, & Kendall, 1956, p. 5)

In these early days, the members of the focus group often 'focused' on pamphlets, radio programmes, films and the like. In other words, the early focus group was more than a guided group discussion and had specific materials to focus on. Certainly it is the general consensus that Robert Merton was the direct originator of the focus group. It has to be said that others had previously carried out group interviews, notably Emory Bogardus (1882–1973) (Bogardus, 1926) but these were dominated by the researcher posing questions to individuals in the group – that is, the key dynamic aspect of the focus group was missing. While Merton was to argue that the focus group was in some ways different from the focused interview (Merton, 1987), there is sufficient overlap for the focused interview to be generally regarded as the precursor of the focus group. Among Merton's complaints was that the modern use of focus groups is in the absence of related quantitative studies. Reading early accounts of the method (Merton et al., 1956), it is clear how soon some features of the focus group were established. For example, the optimum size of a group was held to be about ten to twelve people (which is slightly higher than the modern recommended range), homogeneity (similarity) of group membership was considered important to ensuring a good group dynamic, and attention was paid to the spatial arrangements whereby classroom-style seating was replaced by a circular pattern. Of course, modern focus group practice sometimes ignores these basic requirements – especially homogeneity.

So in the academic field of mass communications research, the divide between the commercial interests of market researchers and the academic interests of university people was blurred. Some academics such as Paul Lazarsfeld would cross-fund their academic work by taking on market research projects with little academic potential. It was in advertising and marketing that the focus group first took a fresh hold. Academic researchers were slow to adopt it. According to Morrison (1998), following the early promise of focus groups in the 1940s, focus groups were 'lost sight of' by academic researchers until the 1970s when they were rediscovered as an 'exploratory tool' and eventually gained respectability in the 1980s – and this process of adoption occurred later in psychology. So for the three decades from 1950 onwards, focus groups were largely in the domain of the market researchers. Academics were keener to use large sample surveys to collect data on public opinion and the focus group is the antithesis of these. In the minds of academics, focus groups were 'tainted' by their association with commercial interests – and commerce was anathema and a distortion of academic values to them. The term focus group only begins to make the occasional appearance in the psychological databases in the 1970s and then in connection with marketing-focused research. Calder (1977), whose background is in social psychology, discusses focus groups with reference to qualitative marketing research. As if to illustrate the gradual emergence of focus groups out of marketing, Festervand (1984–85) discussed the potential application of focus group research to the healthcare services. Suddenly interest in focus groups grew markedly in psychology in the 1990s over a range of psychological research areas. Now the method is common, with scores of studies using the method in psychology being published every year. Puchta and Potter (2004) point out the focus group research of Lunt and Livingstone (1996) as being among the earliest in psychology. In this, Lunt and Livingstone examine how the audience understands political messages – thus essentially bringing focus groups back firmly to their origins in mass communication research.

Ultimately, like some other methods in the social sciences, focus groups are now highly familiar to members of the public. We are all well aware of their ubiquity in modern politics, for example their use by modern political parties. There are claims that it is the most commonly used research methodology on Earth. Such familiarity should not, however, lead to the view that focus groups are easy data-gathering methods or that they can be conducted with very little training or skill. Like other qualitative methods, focus groups may appear easy but this is illusory. Of course, it takes little effort to gather together a group of people to discuss a topic but it is another thing to ensure that the best quality, focused discussion results.

How to conduct focus groups

One could typify the focus group as a group interview with about six to ten similar people, conducted by a skilled moderator, and lasting up to about one and a half to two hours. The focus group is dynamic in the sense that the moderator encourages interaction between participants but controls the situation so that all participants get an opportunity to contribute. A lot of hard work goes into the planning, organisation and analysis of focus groups in order to produce good quality data. For example, the size of a focus group – usually, but not invariably, between six and ten people – is important. As has been mentioned, the consequence of having too many group members is that it is harder to get a turn at speaking and some may not like speaking to a large group of people. If there are too few members in a group then the focus group may lack stimulation, thus stultifying proceedings.

The work of the researcher can be divided into a number of components:

- planning
- recruitment of participants
- running the focus group
- analysis of the focus group data.

One must appreciate that focus group methodology has no single purpose and that focus groups can be used for several, quite distinct purposes. According to Calder (1977), there are three different approaches to the use of focus groups:

- *The exploratory* This describes attempts to generate information and knowledge in a field which has previously been largely under-researched. So it is a trawling approach which seeks basic knowledge and ideas in a new field.
- *The clinical* This describes attempts to understand why people do what they do using the skills of a trained analyst or expert.
- *The phenomenological* This is the use of focus groups by researchers to understand things from the point of view of other groups in society. The researcher will learn how different sorts of people feel about something.

This list is, perhaps, less than complete since the focus group can be used for purposes which are not listed. So the trialling of new consumer products in focus groups in order to consider improvements prior to production would, at best, only loosely fit into the first category. But we can see something of the flexibility of the focus group in Calder's scheme.

Although it is usual to speak of focus group methodology, it would be only in exceptional cases that a researcher conducts just one focus group. Normally, the researcher plans to compare several focus groups on a topic using different categories of members for different focus groups. However, advice on how to conduct a focus group can vary. The following summarises the broad strategy (Figure 4.2).

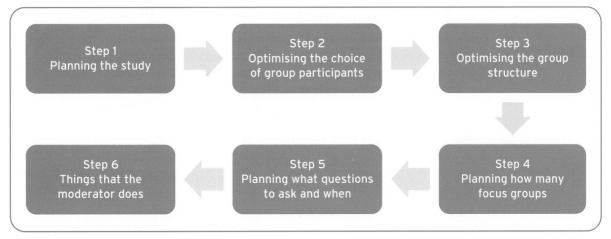

FIGURE 4.2 The steps in a focus group study

Step 1

Planning the study The origins of a study may be at the initiative of the researcher or may be instigated by other people such as organisations commissioning research. In either case, it is important to develop a (shared) understanding of what the study is about. So there should be clarity about the following (according to Krueger & Casey, 2000):

- The research problem that the study will attempt to illuminate.
- The factors which led to the study being commissioned. Often, for student work, these factors will be a class exercise, a dissertation or research project as part of one's degree, or similar. Each of these will place different demands on the study planned.
- The specific purpose of the study.
- The types of information which it is hoped the study will obtain.
- What types of information are the priority for the data collection.
- The person or persons who want the information that the study will collect.
- What will be done with the information.

Each of these is relevant to the planning of the research in detail. Of course, some may seem irrelevant to student research. But that may be illusory. For a student, their supervisor is an important 'client'. Has a clear understanding been reached between you and your supervisor on these matters? Even if there is no obvious 'client' for your research, can you address these questions?

Also remember to have an appropriate degree of humility as a researcher and do not be afraid to seek the help and advice of other people. The job of the researcher is to find out, not to know. So you may wish to talk over issues to do with the research with key informants.

Step 2

Optimising the choice of group participants Just what are the important characteristics of the participants in your focus groups? This is a matter not of defining sampling characteristics but of maximising the richness of the data. What sorts of participants will yield the most satisfactory information relevant to your research question? These, of course, may not be the most readily available potential participants since we are not talking 'convenience sampling' here but purposive sampling aimed at optimising data quality and relevance. A good example of this is the customers who send for a holiday brochure but never purchase any of the holidays. This would be a particularly good group of participants for a focus group study trying to understand the factors which are influential on holiday purchases. One approach is to provide such non-buyers with a free holiday with the only cost being taking part in a focus group for a couple of hours.

Of course, without having details of a proposed study it is difficult to suggest groups of potentially data-rich participants. The only rule-of-thumb would be that there is likely to be a variety of particularly significant types of group members and that the more effort put into their inclusion the better.

One consequence of such a strategy is that people in the optimum categories are likely to be at a premium since they have particular characteristics. So it is important to do as much as possible to ensure that those approached actually turn up to the focus group:

- Ask yourself why people would be prepared to take part in your study. What is the best way of making your request to ensure that they will take part? What are the gains for them as individuals or as members of society?

- Consider appropriate inducements though in light of the ethical considerations (see Chapter 17).

- Contact potential group members at least two weeks before the intended date of the focus group. This gives them time to plan their attendance by putting it in their diary and rescheduling their activities if necessary. The closer to the day of the focus group the more likely that you find that participants have other things scheduled.

- Follow up an agreement to participate with a 'courtesy' thank you letter or e-mail.

- Remember to give participants a 'courtesy' telephone call on the day of the group meeting (or the day before perhaps) to check whether any problems have arisen. The main point of this is that is serves as a reminder.

- Consider the convenience of your study for potential participants rather than yourself. Make it easy for people to take part. There is little point in scheduling your focus groups at times which make it difficult for your ideal participants to attend because, say, they have to be at work. Similarly, where would it be most convenient to hold the focus groups from the point of view of the participants? They may be deterred by lengthy journeys to the research site and so forth.

- Choose the best person to make the invitations. Although it may feel natural that the researcher should invite people to participate, there are circumstances in which someone else might do a better job at recruitment. Personal contacts are often the most effective. So a local person with lots of contacts may obtain more recruits than yourself. For one reason, they help establish your bona fides as a researcher.

Put thought into the question of how you are going to recruit people with the characteristics you desire in your study. So you may wish to consider the following possibilities:

- Are there any key individuals who may have access to the sorts of people that you need? For example, if you wish to study people who have survived cancer are there organisations to support cancer survivors?

- Can the organisation commissioning the research help provide access to suitable groups of participants?

- Would it be possible to contact a few suitable group members and then ask them to nominate others similar to themselves – as in snowball sampling?

Focus groups do not include representative samples and the choice of participants is largely to optimise the productivity of the discussion. At best participants in a focus group typify the sort of person with the characteristics specified by the researcher. If a variety of different sorts of participant are selected for a particular focus group, they should be chosen in a way which would be expected to maximise the productivity of the group discussion – some mixes of participants could inhibit discussion or make the focus group unmanageable. Of course, experience in running focus groups will lead to better and more refined judgements about group membership.

Finally, in this step, you need to think carefully about what you tell your recruits concerning the focus group before the group meets. Gibbs (1997) offers the following practical advice. Only provide focus group members with sufficient detail to allow them to decide whether or not to participate. They should not be given any indications of the questions that will be asked in advance of the meeting otherwise they may work out their own views which may be fixed and not responsive to spontaneous group processes at the meeting.

Step 3

Optimising the group structure The point of a focus group lies in the directed discussion produced by the focus group members. It follows from this that a focus group should involve all of the group members reasonably equally. If one or two members dominate the focus group then this defeats the purpose. Although it is the responsibility of the moderator to prevent individuals from dominating the proceedings, problems may be built into a focus group if the choice of members was not optimal. In particular, it is generally the case that a focus group with similar people of equivalent status is condu- cive to quality data in focus group research. On the other hand, a focus group consist- ing of people of different social statuses or superiors and subordinates have a built-in imbalance which may result in some people dominating the group. The moderator can limit this to a certain extent by inviting individuals to talk in various ways or limiting the length of contributions to a minute or two. However, groups whose dynamics are likely to inhibit some members from full participation are to be avoided. As already hinted, two obvious factors can contribute to this:

- If the group is too homogeneous so that everyone shares much the same perspective on the subject matter then discussion is likely to be curtailed. For that reason, it is sometimes suggested that focus groups should be heterogeneous in terms of their membership, though there are limits to this.

- If the group contains people of an apparently superior status then the group may defer to them. This may simply be that certain group members appear to be more knowledgeable than the others who accept what they say unquestioningly.

Ultimately, experience is the basis for anticipating such problems. A focus group which fails to generate discussion warrants careful attention in order to assess why this was the case. Plans may have to be revised.

It is not a part of focus group methodology to simply use a single focus group. No matter how productive a single group may be in terms of ideas and interesting responses, the researcher needs to plan to run several different groups. At a minimum, three or four groups are needed when there is no attempt to use a variety of differ- ent categories of groups. Krueger and Casey (2000) refer to this as a single-category design. It is the simplest structure for focus group research. In addition to single- category designs, they list the following:

- *Multiple-category design* This is where the focus groups are organised into several particular types of respondents. For example, in a study of the experience of can- cer the multiple-categories might be (a) cancer patients, (b) cancer survivors and (c) carers of cancer patients.

- *Double-layered design* This is where the groups employed are distinguishable on two dimensions. These dimensions might be age (young and old) and cancer sufferer versus cancer survivor. This would give us four groups: (1) young cancer sufferers, (2) old cancer sufferers, (3) young cancer survivors and (4) old cancer survivors. The researcher would probably study three or four groups in each of these four categories.

- *Broad-involvement design* This acknowledges that there are some areas of research in which a broad range of groups might feel they have a relevant voice. As a consequence, a variety of groups are identified to represent this range of interest groups. For example, the researcher may be studying neighbour disputes. Groups which might have an interest in taking part in focus groups might include: (a) mediators employed by local authorities, (b) the police, (c) people with difficult neighbours, (d) neighbours who have been taken to court by the authorities and (e) officers of the local authority. Of course, by including such a wide range of groups, the research.

Step 4

Planning how many focus groups Although one rule of thumb would be to have three or four groups for every category of group studied, this is not a definitive statement of numbers of groups. There are problems in stipulating the number of focus groups to run even with some knowledge about the purpose of the study in question. The 'saturation' criterion might be appropriate. This suggests that the researcher collects data until it appears that no new things are emerging out of the study. It could be argued that this is a subjective criterion. Nevertheless, it is one which is of some practical value within the ethos of qualitative research. In grounded theory it is known as theoretical saturation (see Chapter 8).

Step 5

Planning what questions to ask and when It is generally accepted that relatively few questions are required for a focus group compared with the equivalent structured interview. A researcher who finds that they have to ask a great many questions to keep the discussion going might suspect that the focus group is not going particularly well. Possibly it implies that the group dynamic is just not working or, equally, it could be a sign that the questions are in some way faulty.

There are two main issues with questions for focus groups: (1) 'what are the characteristics of a good question?' and (2) 'ideally how should questions be organised or sequenced during the course of the focus group?' The first is the easiest to address. A good question is posed in a way which communicates well and avoids causing confusion – so the basic question-framing skills that you may have from in-depth interviewing would be appropriate here. Among other things, the questions should be phrased in a style suitable for a conversation rather than writing-down. The acid test is whether the question slips off the tongue readily without clumsiness, errors or stumbling over one's words. The questions should be pitched at a level appropriate for the sorts of people participating in your focus group; long questions are to be avoided as should complex ones (i.e. compound questions). Complex questions really contain more than one question. This can be inadvertently the outcome of using two words instead of one. So asking whether the participants had found the focus group 'interesting and useful' is really to ask two separate questions and the hearer may be confused as to how to answer the question. They may have found the group interesting but not very useful. As a consequence, they may find it hard to answer a question which the researcher believes to be simple and straightforward.

The sequencing of questions is not so easily dealt with. Krueger and Casey (2000) present a model of the sequencing of questions for focus groups which can be summarised as shown in Figure 4.3. It is a useful way of illustrating the flow of a focus group session. Without appropriate sequencing of questions, the focus group can become problematic. According to Krueger and Casey, the sequence consists of (1) opening questions, (2) introductory questions, (3) transition questions, (4) key questions and (5) ending questions. Jump in too soon with a key question, for example, and the participants may be inhibited by the complexity of giving an adequate response. Shy group members will not have been eased into the group dynamic and the focus group may fail to provide the quality of contributions that the researcher is seeking. The flow of the questions in Figure 4.3 can readily be seen as facilitating group processes. There are other helpful sequencing rules which can be incorporated. Krueger and Casey argue that (a) general questions should come before specific questions; (b) questions asking about positive features of something should precede questions soliciting the negative aspects; and (c) uncued questions should precede cued questions – that is, one would ask the group about their experiences of hospital before asking for their experiences of specific aspects of the hospital such as food, information, medical care and so forth. This describes one version of the process of funnelling questions.

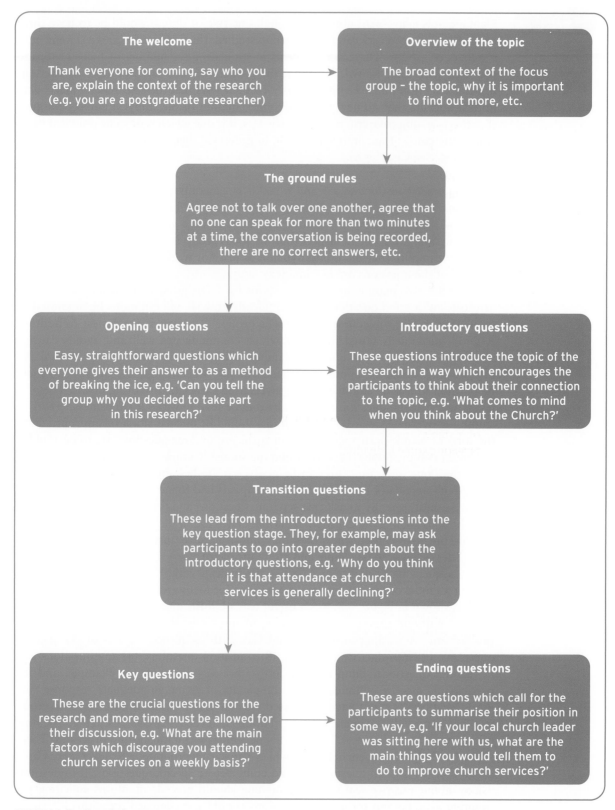

FIGURE 4.3 The flow of a focus group

Step 6 Things that the moderator does There are a number of characteristics which researchers see as important in a moderator (Gibbs, 1997):

- avoids expressing personal opinions;
- avoids appearing judgemental.

The moderator is responsible for the efficient and successful running of each focus group whether or not they are the main investigator. It is clearly a skilled and complex role which places considerable demands on the moderator in terms of interpersonal skills but also the discipline of remaining essentially detached from the discussion. Moderators, for example, do not involve themselves in the debates. The focus group moderator has many tasks (Gibbs, 1997), though it should be appreciated that things vary more in practice. For example, there are circumstances in which the moderator allows much freer debate and does little steering (Flick, 2002). This would depend very much on the purpose of the research. The moderator's tasks include the following:

- At the start of the meeting, describing and explaining the purpose and objectives of the session.
- Ensuring that members of the focus group feel relaxed and comfortable in the situation and feel, ultimately, that this was a positive experience.
- Posing clear questions for discussion.
- Controlling the discussion by asking supplementary questions designed to open up the debate or to encourage the participants to focus more precisely on the issues which are fundamental to the research.
- Ensuring that all members of the group participate and preventing the dominance of a small number of individuals. There are various ways to achieve this, including targeting some individuals with questions aimed at encouraging them to participate.
- Highlighting differences in perspectives which emerge in the focus group discussion in order that the group might engage with the nature of the differences.
- Stopping conversational drifts which steer the conversation away from the topic of the focus group.
- The moderator is responsible for recording the focus group session (either just the conversation or video) but it is usually the case that the moderator also takes notes during the course of the session.
- In circumstances where the moderator has an assistant then that assistant might take much more comprehensive notes than the moderator is in a position to, take responsibility for recording the session, and deal with logistic issues such as refreshments. The assistant can be involved more actively such as asking supplementary questions (Krueger & Casey, 2000).

Boxes 4.1 and 4.2 later in the chapter describe studies relying on focus groups for the collection of data.

How to analyse data from focus groups

There are numerous approaches to the analysis of focus group data. However, it needs to be appreciated that focus groups have a long history and that modern qualitative research is just a small fraction of their use. The role of focus groups in marketing has meant that the analysis of focus group data has been built on rather different intellectual traditions from those which form the basis of modern qualitative psychology. In particular, market

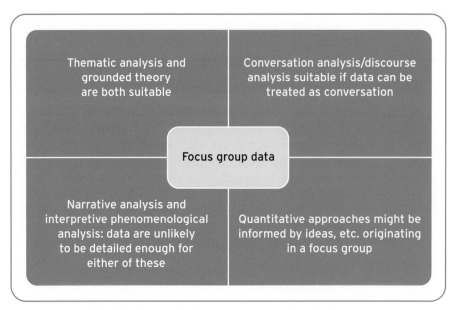

FIGURE 4.4 Ways of analysing focus group data

researchers tended to regard their subject matter from the point of view of Freudian psychoanalysis with its emphasis on hidden motivations. So, many focus group researchers have looked to focus groups as a way of revealing why people make the choices that they do. In other words, beware the fact that focus groups have been analysed from a range of perspectives which may not share the approaches favoured in qualitative psychology. At the most basic level, some merely present their impressions of what the groups had to say, perhaps picking out particular quotations to illustrate a point. This, of course, hardly warrants the description 'analysis' though it may be sufficient for the sponsors of the research. Remember that much focus group research is carried out for market research purposes and the sponsor's needs in terms of analysis may not be very sophisticated. Ultimately, the chosen analysis route for focus group data will largely be dependent on the particular reasons why a focus group was the preferred method to collect data (see Figure 4.4):

- Perhaps the focus group study was carried out to generate research ideas to be pursued in some depth at a later stage in the research. In these circumstances, the needs of the researcher may be met by listing the major and most significant themes emerging out of the focus groups and identifying any research questions that these might suggest.

- On the other hand, the researcher may have collected the focus group data to better understand how people experience the topic being discussed by the focus group. So, the researcher may wish to understand people's experience of chronic pain. The content of what is said in the focus groups on this forms the basis of the analysis. In these circumstances, the researcher may wish to conduct a thematic analysis (Chapter 7) on a transcript of the data.

- Another researcher may be interested in the focus group discussion as conversation and may study the way in which conversation is governed during the course of focus groups. The data, in this case, may need to be transcribed using the Jefferson transcription system (Chapter 6).

- Transcribed focus group data usually will be suitable for grounded theory analysis (Chapter 8) but its use in discourse analysis (Chapter 9) would depend very much on the researcher's purpose and, perhaps, whether focus group data are sufficiently conversational.

Puchta and Potter (2004) adopt an approach in which the interaction in a focus group is regarded as data for understanding the discursive processes involved in the running of a focus group. This is described in Box 4.2.

When to use focus groups

Focus groups are a means of obtaining data which would be difficult to obtain using other forms of data collection method. People's opinions, beliefs, feelings and experiences are highlighted in focus groups in a way which other forms of interviewing simply cannot match. Furthermore, the focus group allows the researcher to capture responses of the group to the expressed opinions, beliefs, feelings and experiences of other group members. Other data collection methods such as observation and interviewing simply cannot capture such things. Because the participants have an active role in the focus group, it becomes apparent what they regard as the priorities in relation to a particular topic. Other data collection methods tend to impose the researcher's priorities onto the situation. The focus group is seen to be particularly good at eliciting clear understandings of the members' feelings, attitudes and beliefs. Of course, we need to be careful when suggesting that focus groups can identify people's attitudes. As Puchta and Potter (2004) argue, there are two conceptions of attitudes. One regards attitudes as pre-formed – already built into the individual before the research. The other conception regards attitudes as performed – meaning that the attitude emerges from the research situation. Examples of both of these things can probably be found in most focus groups. However, performed attitudes are of very limited use if one wishes to use attitudes to understand why people do things.

Focus groups can be used in a variety of ways. Especially for multi-method studies, they can be exploratory in the sense that they stimulate discussion on a topic and ideas are thrown up by the group. If the researcher has no knowledge base on which to build then this is a vital function. For example, it may help the researcher plan questions for a survey or even suggest hypotheses to quantitative researchers. On the other hand, a focus group can be used to evaluate people's reactions to a study just completed by the researcher. It can be a way of providing feedback on the main research's findings.

Focus groups have a rationale which is not always shared with other data collection methods, especially in terms of sampling. They do not attempt to estimate the distribution of characteristics in the population which is possible, to some extent, using interviews with formal sampling methods. Populations are not sampled in focus group methodology which, instead, selects group members intentionally in order to gain the maximum richness in the data. It thus employs a purposeful selection strategy rather than a random procedure. Focus groups, nevertheless, do allow contrasts and comparisons to be drawn in terms of different categories of group members. It is nonsensical to evaluate focus group methodology as an alternative to the individual interview since a focus group is not a cheap alternative to the individual interview and the two are not in competition essentially. It is unlikely that focus groups can be used successfully to gather extensive life-history or narrative accounts from individuals (Barbour, 2007). The interview may be a better approach. Consequently, focus groups may not be useful, in general, to interpretative mostly used phenomenological analysis or narrative analysis.

There is a sense in which participation in focus groups can be empowering. They provide a collective means of addressing issues which are otherwise the province of decision makers. The participant takes part in a decision-making process in which their voice is important. Partly as a consequence of this, focus groups have been popular in feminist research.

Examples of the use of focus groups

Boxes 4.1 and 4.2 demonstrate the use of focus group methodology in research.

Box 4.1

ILLUSTRATIVE RESEARCH STUDY

The experience of womanhood

How do Black women and White women perceive womanhood? What are the similarities and what are the differences? Settles, Pratt-Hyatt and Buchanan (2008) expected that, on the basis of the existing research literature, both to be concerned about their roles as (a) mothers, (b) partners and (c) workers. The groups were likely to differ in terms of (a) the amount of role flexibility they had in terms of managing work–family responsibilities, (b) the types of sexism and sexual harassment they experienced and (c) the sexual mistreatment they report may differ along the lines of different stereotypes of the groups. According to the researchers, 'there is little or no empirical research that focuses simultaneously on Black and White women's thoughts and feelings about their experiences as women and how those perceptions shape their sense of self and the world' (p. 456). This led them to the view that the best way to examine their research question was to use qualitative focus groups in which women were encouraged to discuss their 'lived experiences' rather than adopt a methodology which essentially imposed the researchers' preconceptions onto the research and data collection.

The researchers used a total of 14 Black women and 17 White women as participants of one or other of the six focus groups that they ran. For four of the focus groups, newspaper advertisements and flyers were used to recruit the participants together with suggestions about other possible participants from the women (i.e. snowball sampling). For the remaining two focus groups, the participants were recruited from the 'subject pool' of psychology undergraduates at an American university. For what it is worth, there were no significant differences between the Black and White groups of participants in terms of socio-demographic factors such as age (which spread from 18 years to 84 years), education, being parents, number of offspring and sexual orientation though, as

the researchers suggest, the sample sizes may have been too small to show differences. On the other hand, Black women were significantly more likely to be single whereas White women had greater likelihood of being unemployed.

The focus groups were limited to a maximum of ten participants though the maximum in practice was seven participants. The size of groups varied according to the availability of suitable participants. Although the groups were designed to be heterogeneous in terms of factors such as age, each group was homogeneous in terms of race. So there were three Black focus groups and three White focus groups in total. In their groups, the women were asked about 'their positive and negative gender- and race-related experiences' (p. 456). Interestingly, their participants were deliberately selected to be varied in terms of their ages and socio-economic backgrounds in order to maximise the diversity of the women's 'experiences and responses' (p. 456). The facilitator and her assistant were of the same race (and gender) as the members of the group in question. This was done, according to the researchers, to 'increase group comfort and cohesion' (p. 457). Before each focus group began, the women participating in the research signed consent forms agreeing to participate and that the session could be recorded and completed a short demographic questionnaire. The focus group facilitator had the task of asking the group the questions for discussion whereas her assistant was responsible for managing the audio-visual equipment and taking notes about the inter-action. The focus groups lasted for about two hours each.

At the start of the session, the facilitator outlined the general purpose of the focus group and informed the participants of their (ethical) rights. She also listed the ground rules governing discussions within the focus group which included the idea that there were no right or wrong answers to the questions, that participants should regard themselves as free to speak, and that all participants should be respectful of any differences in terms of points of view that manifested themselves. As an 'icebreaker' to the group discussion, each session began with an opportunity for each participant to talk about something important relevant to their sense of self. This, for example, might be their role as a mother or partner. The focus group interview was carefully structured and followed a guide or protocol in order to 'ensure consistency across groups' (p. 457). The initial questions were very open ended or broad such as:

- 'How has being a woman positively (negatively) influenced your life?'
- 'What are some of the advantages (disadvantages) of being a woman?'
- 'Does being a woman help you to know more about who you are or give your life a sense of purpose?'
- 'Are there things that you find special or valuable about being a woman, even if they make your life harder?'

Questions about positive aspects of womanhood were posed before those about the negative aspects. Rather more specific questions were used as the follow-up questions in order to stimulate the group discussion or to encourage participants to elaborate what they have already said. Examples of such questions included:

- 'Do you have home or care-giving responsibilities? If so, what types?'
- 'Are there unique, different or special things about being a woman? If so, what are they?'

The focus group ended with the participants being debriefed, compensated for their time and thanked. The women recruited from the community received a small cash payment plus a meal whereas the university students were rewarded by being given course credit. Of course, there may be ethical concerns about the involvement of students in research by their professors for credits of this sort (see Chapter 17).

The researchers argue that the appropriate method of analysing their data was grounded theory since no convincing existing theory was available to guide the analysis. (See Chapter 8 for a detailed discussion of grounded theory.) The analysis was carried out using eight trained coders who were either university students or faculty. The analysis proceeded on a line-by-line analysis of verbatim transcripts of the recordings of the focus group sessions. The analysts were seeking 'salient' categories in the data. They applied 'conceptual ordering analysis' which involves ordering the categories developed from the most concrete to the most abstract (Strauss & Corbin, 1998). The analysts met on a weekly basis to reach a consensus about the themes generated during the analysis. A simple quantitative analysis was then applied to the data in order to identify the group participants who mentioned each of the themes developed during the analysis. This had nearly 90 per cent inter-rater agreement.

The researchers identified a number of primary themes during the analysis which represented the views of women of both races. They are as follows together with the component sub-themes:

- Theme 1: Gender-based mistreatment
  - Gender discrimination
  - Sexual harassment
  - Concerns for safety
  - Sexism
- Theme 2: Perceived advantages
  - Ability to express emotions
  - Leniency from men in power
  - Equality with men
- Theme 3: Friendships and community
  - Women value and form deep friendships
  - Friendships offer social support
  - Difficulty forming friendships with women
  - Negative aspects of friendships with women
- Theme 4: Caretaking
  - Positive aspects of caretaking
  - Caretaker role is meaningful
  - Mother role is important to future self
  - Difficulties associated with caretaking, overall
- Theme 5: Work and family options
  - Value having options/have more options than men
  - Difficulty making work–family balance choices
  - Challenges integrating work and family

A secondary theme, which applied only to Black women, was:

- Theme 6: Inner strength
  - Strength learnt from other Black women
  - Characteristics of inner strength

Each of the themes is carefully discussed with illustrative quotations. The researchers indicate that these have minor edits such as the removal of material which detracts from clarity in their view.

Box 4.2

ILLUSTRATIVE RESEARCH STUDY

The practice of focus groups

While researchers have typically concentrated on the content of the group interaction in focus groups, other approaches are possible. In their book *Focus group practice*, Puchta and Potter (2004) explore another aspect of the focus group – the interaction between the group moderator and the group members. They concentrate on such things as how opinions are produced in the group and how the moderator encourages informality in the group. We will concentrate on the latter. Informality does not just happen – it has to be worked on if it is to be achieved. Putting people 'at their ease' is an important skill in focus group moderation. Puchta and Potter (2004) point out that research with nominal groups and Delphi groups may be different from their focus groups since in these group members are asked to contribute in turn thus the group dynamic is reduced.

Puchta and Potter give detailed examples of how interaction is generated so as to maintain informality while at the same time managing things in order to achieve the researcher's ends. Their main findings can be summarised as follows:

- The moderator construes the interaction as talking and chatting rather than something more formal such as a classroom.

- The moderator's talk does not appear as if it were scripted or highly planned. Instead, pauses and hesitancies help reinforce the impression of informality while the use of idiomatic language works to the same end.

- The physical environment of the focus group is more suggestive of a domestic rather than an office setting.

- The moderator claims to be seeking 'gut feelings' which suggests that contributions can be thrown in spontaneously without the need for rational explanations.

Thus the moderator may work to reduce any perceptions of him- or herself as being aloof in the eyes of the group members. Another way in which this is achieved is by using language devices which characterise everyday language but are rarely to be found in formal situations. They describe how in a focus group on hair shampoo one participant mistakes a reference to roots (as in hair roots) for roots as a reference to roots music (i.e. world music, African music, etc.). The moderator uses the word 'oh' when she finally realises the speaker's mistake. Oh is commonly used in everyday language to indicate a revision of understanding or a 'change in knowledge state' (Puchta & Potter, 2004, p. 43). Puchta and Potter argue that the focus group moderator will only use 'oh' when to do so has no potential impact on the moderator's perceived neutrality as in this case. Had the participant said something like 'this shampoo is aimed at selling to pensioners' then to respond to this with 'oh' would imply that the moderator does not share the same view as the speaker. In the same 'roots' episode, the moderator laughs about the speaker's misunderstanding when it becomes apparent. To laugh in the focus group context may risk creating the impression of the moderator's aloofness if it in some way signals the assumed superiority of the moderator because it is essentially judgemental. However, in the 'roots' exchange, Puchta and Potter suggest that the laughter is akin to the laughter of friends when there is a similar misunderstanding. In other words, in very precise circumstances 'oh' and laughter can be used non-judgementally to produce the informality which otherwise would be seen as aloofness and counter to the informality that the focus group moderator is there to achieve.

Evaluation of focus groups

A focus group provides a dynamic way of researching the beliefs, ideas, opinions and experiences of group participants engaged interactively. Because of the researcher's degree of control through the moderator of the broad discussion, it can be an effective and efficient way of obtaining a variety of perspectives. Out of the data is likely to emerge some understanding of why participants think in particular ways. No other data collection method achieves this degree of control with a dynamic and interactive approach. Interviews allow greater control but involve no group processes; participant observation allows group processes but leaves the researcher with little control over the moment-to-moment interaction. So focus group methodology stands as a distinct data-gathering resource for researchers. Consequently, one should be cautious about regarding focus groups as a way of understanding 'social reality' or even real-life social interaction because of their degree of artificiality. The discussions that are held in a focus group may have little bearing on what happens in everyday conversations.

Of course, focus group methodology should not be judged against criteria that it is not designed to meet. In particular, focus groups are not miniature sample surveys which allow one to estimate distributions of ideas, opinions, beliefs and so forth in the general population – or any other population for that matter. One would not expect to be able to map the results of a focus group-based investigation onto the results of a sample survey. The focus group cannot achieve representativeness in the same sense and the sample survey cannot provide the dynamic account that focus group data can.

Sloppy focus group research may not be very demanding but good quality, well-prepared focus group studies place a big drain on a researcher's resources. They take time, are not easy to organise and produce data which, often, cannot be effectively dealt with in a routine fashion. To run a focus group requires good interpersonal skills, a well-honed understanding of the research question, and an ability to focus on the needs of the research within the focus group context. While just about anyone could run a focus group of sorts, it requires great skill to generate data which are relevant to the research question. One has only to look at television discussions to understand something of the things that can go wrong – people merely expressing entrenched positions, people talking over each other, people not addressing the issue at hand and so forth are common.

The focus group presents particular ethical issues which are not characteristic of other data collection methods. In particular, it is not possible to ensure anonymity and confidentiality for things said in an open setting. The researcher may be in a position to guarantee anonymity and confidentiality in publications but the data have been collected in a public setting. It is worthwhile discussing this problem with the group in order to solicit an agreement of confidentiality concerning the group discussion but this cannot be policed and, as a consequence, may not be regarded as perfectly satisfactory.

Finally, focus group methodology is an approach to qualitative data collection. In itself, the methodology does not have specific analytical procedures associated with it. As a result, one should not judge the method on the basis of what may appear to be examples of poor data analysis. Sometimes a report of a focus group study may simply highlight a few somewhat unexpected things for discussion. Such selected highlights may not be regarded as a careful and thorough analysis of the data. But this is not to be blamed on the data collection method since it is a consequence of the lack of rigour in the analysis applied.

CONCLUSION

The focus group is a commonplace data collection method in the modern world. It would, therefore, seem almost inevitable that its use in academic psychological research will also expand further. No doubt distinctive academic styles of focus group will emerge to meet the specific requirements of qualitative psychology. This is certainly the case with the analysis of focus group data but it also may apply to the conduct of the focus group. We have seen that mainstream market research focus groups may be built on theoretical (interpretative) frameworks which are not shared by academic qualitative researchers. In particular, the rise of focus group methodology in market research paralleled the rise in psychodynamic (psychoanalytic) theories about consumer motivation in commerce. Rarely does academic qualitative research show any theoretical allegiance to psychoanalysis – quite the reverse. This means that the caucus of market research focus group studies may have very little to say of relevance to the analysis of this form of qualitative data. Thus, qualitative researchers may feel that qualitative data analysis methods such as grounded theory, thematic analysis, conversation analysis and discourse analysis are the preferred approaches. Of course, this opens up a whole variety of research questions which market research focus groups simply are not intended to address. For example, the focus group could be modified to enhance its potential to generate naturalistic conversation. In academic focus groups some of the conventions of the market research focus group could be eschewed. In particular, the role of the moderator in controlling the focus of the group discussion might be lessened in favour of letting the conversation take a more 'natural course'.

KEY POINTS

- A focus group usually consists of a group of six to ten dynamically interacting individuals discussing a topic in response to questioning by the researcher (moderator). In order to facilitate discussion, the focus group is relatively informal and the researcher plans the groups in a way which will maximise the interactive nature of the discussion. For this reason, focus group members are often selected to be strangers to each other and obvious status differentials which might inhibit some group members from participation or encourage others to dominate the situation are avoided. There are normally at least three or four groups in a study for each type of group included in the researcher's design.

- The organisation of a focus group can be a complex matter since it is the researcher's responsibility to select groups in a way which will ensure effective collection of data relevant to the research question. A strategy for obtaining appropriate participants by using, say, existing interest groups or key informants is important. There is no attempt in focus group methodology to draw statistically representative samples. The organisation of the focus group meeting should be cognisant of the needs of the group members in order to maximise their likelihood of participation. The moderator of the focus group needs considerable social and research skills to ensure good quality data are collected.

- The analysis of focus group data can employ a variety of methods. Traditionally, the analysis of market research focus groups has tended to be guided by a psychodynamic theory of consumer motivation. This is inappropriate for the work of most qualitative researchers, for example. But, of course, the appropriate form of qualitative analysis for focus group data depends on the research purposes of the researcher. Some of the common qualitative data analysis methods discussed in this book – grounded theory, discourse analysis, etc. – could be used if they match the purposes of the researcher.

ADDITIONAL RESOURCES

Barbour, R. (2007). *Doing focus groups.* Los Angeles: Sage.

Iowa State University. (2004). Focus group fundamentals. https://store.extension.iastate.edu/Product/pm1969b-pdf (accessed 23 February 2015).

Krueger, R. A., & Casey, M. A. (2015). *Focus groups* (4th ed.) Thousand Oaks, CA: Sage.

Morrison, D. E. (1998). *The search for a method: Focus groups and the development of mass communication research.* Luton: University of Luton Press.

Stewart, D. W., & Shamdasani, P. N. (2015). *Focus groups: Theory and practice.* Thousand Oaks, CA: Sage.

Wilkinson, S. (2008). Focus groups. In J. A. Smith (Ed.), *Qualitative psychology: A practical guide to research methods* (2nd ed., pp. 186–206). London: Sage.

CHAPTER 5

Ethnography/ participant observation

Overview

- Participant observation refers to a wider set of methods including intensive observation which are also known as ethnographic methods. Ethnography is the better term to use as it is in keeping with other disciplines.

- Participant observation specifically refers to observational techniques in which researchers involve themselves extensively and in depth with a group or community.

- There are different forms of participant observation which vary in the extent to which the researcher is integrated into the group concerned and how apparent the researcher's actual role is.

- Field notes are the basis of ethnography/participant observation and are made after the observation has been completed. They are detailed and may be structured in terms of separate observations and interpretations sections.

- Ethnography/participant observation is one of the most complex research methods and places both intellectual and interpersonal demands on the researcher. The intellectual demands include formulating the research questions, questioning whether the particular research question can benefit from participant observation, deciding what issues to address in the observation process, and writing effective field notes. Among the interpersonal demands are defining the researcher's role, gaining and maintaining entry to the research context, and effectively using key informants.

- Ethnography/participant observation is primarily a data collection method. It, in itself, is not a method of analysis though it does focus on culture. Given the age of the method, there are a variety of ways of analysing the data but the grounded theory approach (Chapter 8) is typically used in recent research.

- The problems for a researcher using ethnography/participant observation include (a) the labour- and time-intensive nature of the process, (b) the complexity of the data collected and the need to integrate different aspects of the data, and (c) the possibility of subjectivity in the procedure and accusations of subjectivity.

- Although ethnography/participant observation has not been commonly used in psychology, the potential of the method warrants its consideration by qualitative researchers.

What is ethnography/participant observation?

Participant observation is best regarded as a data collection method rather than a data analysis method. There is no standard way of carrying out the analysis of field notes and the other data collected though grounded theory (Chapter 8) is a commonly used and systematic approach. Participant observation originated in the work of anthropologists working in non-Western cultures but is frequently employed in modern Western settings. Confusingly, participant observation refers to two distinct things:

- A very specific methodology, named participant observation, which involves the recording and analysing of the researcher's observations when closely immersed in a group or culture. Its most significant feature is the close involvement of the researcher in the research setting through participation or engaging with a group or community over a protracted period of time.

- A general methodology or broad strategy, for collecting data in a field setting. This sometimes is called participant observation and it includes the more specific approach described above. So a formal definition of participant observation would also identify it as a broad strategy for collecting data in a field setting. It involves collecting a variety of different sorts of data pertinent to answering the research question.

There is another term or concept, ethnography, which is essentially the study of cultures. For the purposes of this chapter, it is possible to regard both ethnography and participant observation as similar, if not identical, where we are referring to a complex simultaneous method of data collection in field settings. The overlap seems often to be almost complete as rarely is participant observation (the specific technique) used on its own without the involvement of other methods. Ethnography seems to have emerged as the preferred term in the 1970s (Bryman, 2004). Furthermore, the term ethnography also refers to the product of ethnographic research – the published account based on the research – and care needs to be taken to distinguish these two meanings.

So ethnography/participant observation is a blanket term covering a range of related methods. There are a number of dimensions along which ethnographic/participant observation studies vary. Among the more important of these dimensions are the following (Dereshiwsky, 1999; also based on Patton, 1986):

- *The observer's role in the setting* The observer's involvement may vary from that of a complete outsider uninvolved in the group dynamics to full membership of the group.

- *The group's knowledge of observation process* If the participants know that they are being studied then this is known as overt observation. Covert observation involves the participants not knowing that they are part of a study.

- *Explication of the study's purpose* This can range from full explication to even misleading explanations.
- *Length* The observation may be a relatively short single session of just one hour or there may be multiple observations which continue for weeks or even years.
- *Focus* The focus of the researcher may be on a relatively narrow aspect of the situation or it may be more holistic in which rich data are collected through the observation of a number of aspects of the situation in depth.

Participant observation literally implies that the researcher does not simply observe events in particular social or cultural contexts but also has 'hands on' experience. Although the extent to which the participant observer is a full participant in the community (living life completely as a member of the community) rather than as a guest in the community varies, the expectation is of a substantial term of engagement with the community. (There are other methods of observation which do not require such involvement. For example, a study of whether drivers of new cars jump traffic lights more frequently than drivers of older cars could probably be carried out using a simple checklist identifying the age of the car – e.g. from its number plate – and ratings of whether the driver crosses the lights legally or illegally.) Part of the ethos of participant observation is that the perspective of members of the group or community studied is regarded as a major focus. These perspectives will vary widely as different group members or members of the community will differ in terms of their roles, their activities and in many other ways. Thus participant observation can be seen as diametrically opposite to *surveillance* which demands no participation and might be possible through purely technological resources such as CCTV cameras.

There are, of course, also instances of researchers observing communities without those who are being observed being aware of the fact. This would be rare in modern research for ethical reasons. The term 'immersion' is frequently used to describe this process. 'Immersion' can involve living with the group being studied (as in the early anthropological studies of other cultures) but, equally, the immersion may be confined to the working day or some other more limited arrangement. The latter is more typical of participant observation in one's own culture as practised by sociologists and other modern users of ethnographic approaches. A participant observer cannot be expected to be equivalent to any other member of that community since he or she often comes from a very different social background. However, the expectation is that participant observers come closer to the experiences of regular members of the community than is typical in research. In this way, hopefully, the careful and conscientious observer obtains a reasonably full understanding of the way that the society functions.

Traditionally, data are collected primarily in the form of field notes written-up by the observer as soon after the events as possible. This would normally take place in 'private time' away from the community. There is no reason why, in appropriate circumstances, the data collection should not use technological aids such as voice recordings of field observations, computers or even video, though these can be intrusive. Using computers for writing field notes is advantageous as these can be fed directly into computer-aided qualitative data analysis programs such as NVivo. As we have seen, there is every reason why the researcher should not be confined solely to the observations recorded in the field notes as sources of data. It is possible to incorporate the following and more (see Figure 5.1):

- semi-structured interviews
- group discussions
- life histories of members of the community

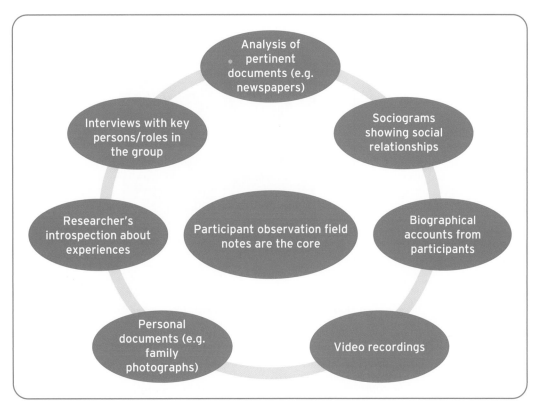

FIGURE 5.1 Possible elements of a participant observation/ethnographic study

- personal documents including photographs;
- relevant media coverage;
- other documentation.

   These are familiar methods in their own right but in the context of ethnography/ participant observation they can be seen as a resource which can be compared with the researcher's direct experiences. There is a sense in which participant observation can be regarded as too narrow a phrase to capture what is actually done in such studies and ethnography might be seen as the more appropriate broader term. Even quantification is not unknown in participant observation-based studies. The field notes which are made should be recorded in a relatively pure form – that is, the observations and the interpretations of the observations kept separate. In other words, the 'experiences' of the observer are the primary form of data in participant observation but these 'experiences' should be distinguished from more analytic statements in the field notes. This is a common requirement in qualitative research of all sorts. One way of doing this is to keep the 'pure' observations on one side of a notebook and analytic comments relevant to them on the other side – the two separated by a margin, for example.

   Participant observation can provide the researcher with an initial fairly detailed picture on which to base a major research initiative. Although there are other ways of doing this, the knowledge from participant observation may provide the researcher with a better understanding of what to include in their interview schedules, questionnaires or further observational studies. Thus participant observation can help ensure that the researcher is sufficiently knowledgeable to proceed with later stages of their research on an informed basis.

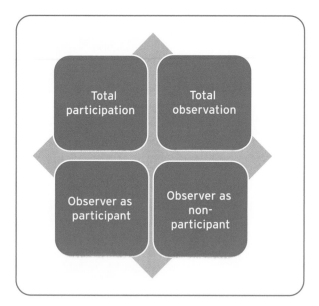

FIGURE 5.2 Participation and observation in ethnographic research

The role of the observer in this sort of field research varies in terms of the extent to which the observation and participation are manifest (see also Figure 5.2):

- *Total or complete participation* The researcher assumes entirely the role of a member of the group or organisation being studied without revealing their additional role as researcher to the other group members. For example, the researcher obtains work in a factory in order to understand aspects of the experience of work.

- *Total or complete observation* In this, personal involvement in the community is minimised and the researcher remains detached. There is no doubt as to the observer's role. So, for example, the researcher may spend time on a factory floor making observations or taking notes while at the same time making no efforts to engage with the workers there.

- *Participant as an observer* The researcher's identity as a researcher is made known to the group being studied. For example, the researcher spends time in a youth club and may engage in the activities of the club members who are aware of the observer's status as both a club member and a researcher. Of course with this status, the observer need not necessarily fully participate in the group's activities.

- *Observer as non-participant* This is not a form of participant observation since there is no direct engagement with the group in its day-to-day activities. Sometimes the term 'ethology' is used in psychology, for this, but this really refers to the study of animal behaviour.

Of course, which variant of participant observation that is used is not entirely in the researcher's hands. Some may be excluded by the particular circumstances or the particular research question which the researcher is pursuing. Some of the dimensions along which participant observation/ethnographic studies differ are illustrated in Figure 5.3.

The development of ethnography/participant observation

The origins of participant observation lie in anthropology initially and then in the Chicago School of Sociology where it was applied to modern urban settings. The roots of anthropology go deep into history since, after all, travellers to other cultures who wrote an account

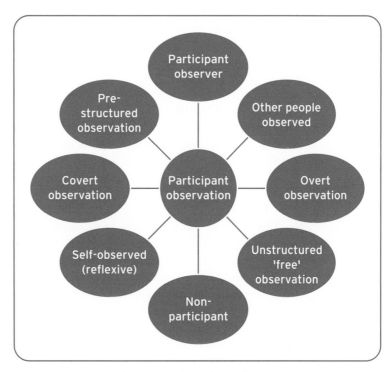

FIGURE 5.3 Dimensions of participant observation studies

of their experiences can be regarded as anthropologists of sorts. The era of Western colo-
nisation starting in the fifteenth century provided an impetus to anthropology and scholars
during the Age of Enlightenment (nineteenth century) began to study other cultures much
more analytically though they drew heavily on the information provided by colonisers
and travellers. Here is not the place to dig into the detail of the history of anthropology,
of course. Suffice it to say to say that even until the beginning of the twentieth century,
cultural anthropologists relied heavily on secondary sources such as travellers' writings. So
their basic data were collected secondarily through informants rather than directly through
observation and experience. The first identifiable user of participant observation was the
American researcher Frank Hamilton Cushing (1857–1900) who joined an anthropological expedition to New Mexico. He lived there with native American people (Zuni Pueblo)
for five years beginning in 1879. Cushing eventually became accepted into the Zuni community and took part in their activities.

   More influential though, were the crucial changes which occurred as a result of
Bronislaw Malinowski (1884–1942) being stranded in the Trobriand Islands in the
area we now refer to as New Guinea. Malinowski was born in Krakow, Poland, where
he studied for a doctorate in philosophy. He became interested in anthropology and
studied at Leipzig University (he was somewhat influenced by Wilhelm Wundt there).
He then moved to the London School of Economics since many of the most eminent
anthropologists at the time were British. In 1914, while working towards his doctorate
in anthropology, Malinowski travelled to Papua and then to the Trobriand Islands.
The First World War broke out, but he was a citizen in the Austrian–Hungarian Empire
in a British-protected region of the world. He chose to be exiled in the Trobriand
Islands as an alternative to being interned for the rest of the war. At first, Malinowski
played the part of the aloof colonial anthropologist relying on formal interviews with
informants and avoiding direct contact with the indigenous Trobriand people whom
he initially construed as 'savages'. The long months of exile and the concomitant bore-
dom and loneliness led him to interact with them more and more and, in so doing, he

learnt their language and made friends. His long period of exile provided him with the opportunity to develop his ideas about participant observation and the importance of day-to-day experience of the community in achieving a finely tuned understanding of how the community works.

A second important stream in the development of participant observation was the urban sociology of the first Chicago School in the USA. This approach to sociology was concerned with understanding urban environments and the earliest of this research was carried out in Chicago itself, though urban sociology became a general approach in American sociology. However, in addition to this, the anthropologist Lloyd Warner (1898–1970) was also a graduate student there between 1929 and 1935 and taught there between 1935 and 1959. William Foote Whyte (1914–2000) explained how he went to the University of Chicago specifically to study with Lloyd Warner (Whyte, 1984). This is important because Whyte was the author of probably the best known example of participant observation research in American sociology – *Street corner society* (Whyte, 1943). This study was of an Italian immigrant community in Boston where Whyte lived for 18 months.

Lloyd Warner was involved in one of the most famous studies in the history of psychology – the Hawthorne Experiments, which gave birth to the phrase 'the Hawthorne effect'. He began working with the psychologist Elton Mayo (1880–1949) on a series of integrated studies of factory life and the effect of introduction of various sorts of changes on the dynamics of the work groups within those factories; for example, changes in the lighting conditions and payment levels within the factory. Warner's influence was principally on the 'Bank Wiring Room' experiment in which he recommended the use of anthropological methods to observe the natural work group behaviours of workers. The researchers made records of all that they could observe of the behaviour of the groups just as an anthropologist would a different culture. This led to the construction of 'sociograms' which are diagrams indicating the levels of interpersonal involvement of members of the work group based on these observations.

Despite a number of notable exceptions, such as those described in Boxes 5.1 and 5.2 participant observation/ethnography has not been a major data collection method in psychology and has not featured greatly in the recent rise of interest in qualitative methods despite numerous references to it in the writings of qualitative researchers. Another major exception to the rule is the study by Larsson and Holmberg summarised in Box 5.3 later in the chapter. Miller, Hengst and Wang (2003) explain that Wilhelm Wundt (1832–1920), the parent of modern psychology, wrote extensively in the field of cultural psychology and pursued his interest in ethnographic material determinedly. Nevertheless, ethnographic methods have generally been marginalised in psychology. However, the upsurge of interest in cultural psychology and especially cultural child development has stimulated more interest in ethnographic methods.

How to conduct ethnography/participant observation

We have already seen how, typically, participant observation is part of a web of various methods, several of which are used in any one study. Thus it is hard to describe how to carry out a participant observation without reference to the other methods of data collection used at the same time. Nevertheless, the core of the method and the thing which makes it different is the use of an observer to collect data. So this needs to be the focus of our description of participant observation though it should be patently obvious that

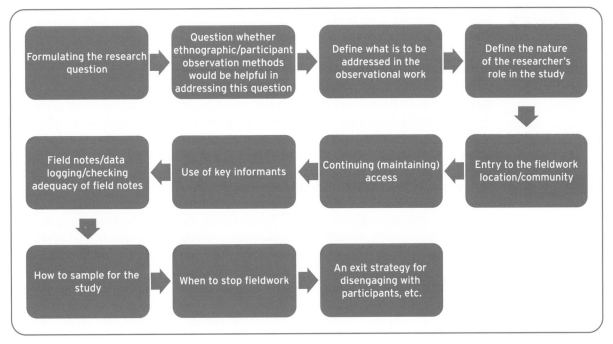

FIGURE 5.4 Important aspects of a participant observation study

participant observation requires researchers with a very broad range of skills both in terms of experience of research methods as well as the interpersonal skills to function effectively in the field context as an observer and a participant.

The following are some of the important stages in participant observation – see Figure 5.4 for an overview.

Step 1   **Formulating the research question** Participant observation will be employed where the researcher has a broad area of study to address, though it is unlikely that at the initial stages they will have a focused research question in mind. The normal expectation is that the researcher will begin to understand the specific aspects that need to be focused on. In other words, the researcher will start to re-formulate or otherwise develop their ideas during the course of the participant observation. This sort of process is not unusual in qualitative research and is not especially problematic in terms of participant observation. This does not give the researcher *carte blanche* since it is essential that if participant observation is to be used the research question is one which can be effectively addressed by participant observation. Whyte put it this way:

> The planning process is begun but not completed before the researcher enters the field. I am not proposing that we enter with blank minds, leaving it to subsequent observations and experience to shape research plans. Striving for such a state of unconsciousness would be folly, but it is important to avoid the other extreme of becoming so fixated on a previously prepared and detailed research design as to miss opportunities to gather data about problems that may turn out to be more important. (Whyte, 1984, p. 35)

One of the important skills which any researcher has to learn is the selection of appropriate research methods to address particular issues. This needs knowledge and experience to do well.

Step 2

Question whether a particular area of interest lends itself to participant observation There are many activities which are regarded as essentially private and these are unlikely to be amenable to investigation using participant observation or any other sort of observation. Obvious examples of this are the activities which we regard as private – sexual activity, toileting and consultations with a doctor, for example. There may be areas of these activities where the researcher might gain access but generally these are things for which one would need to consider alternative data collection methods. Or, of course, where the ethical risks of covert observation are substantial despite its feasibility then a rethink of approach will be necessary.

Step 3

Define what is to be addressed in the observation process The clear definition of the research question will be of use here since it will help identify the aspects of the situation that the researcher will study. There will be a degree of selectivity in what is observed purposefully, though, of course, one cannot be totally sure just what will be relevant especially in types of situations with which one has little or no familiarity.

Step 4

Defining the researcher's role A major consideration in participant observation/ethnography is for the researcher to define a viable role which permits him or her to participate in a setting or to be sufficiently at its periphery to enable the observation to take place. There is no single approach to this which will work for all circumstances. There are many reasons for this, including the characteristics of the researcher – adult researchers cannot be full participant observers in a class of schoolchildren for obvious physical reasons. On the other hand, they might be able to function as an adult assistant in the classroom. Social characteristics may also hinder entry into a research setting. Public field settings with a lack of structure are probably the easiest to participate in. So it is easy to be a participant observer of music concerts as a member of the audience.

Step 5

Entry to the research location/entry to the community The research locations for participant observation/ethnography vary in the extent to which they are formal settings such as a factory or informal settings in the community such as, say, a football match. The means of entry will differ between the two. The formal organisation usually requires a formal request for entry to carry out research – so, for example, the researcher may need to approach senior managers. The informal organisation, however, is not one without a social structure. There may be key individuals – often called gatekeepers – who may facilitate the entry of the participant observer into the group. Of course, somewhat informal ways will be needed to contact such individuals. Care is needed to match the entry method to the community in question. For example, in his classic study of the Italian–American slum district in the North End of Boston, Whyte (1943) initially attempted to gain entry to this working-class community by approaching social workers in a settlement house. Whyte identifies himself as middle class and eventually realised that it was incongruous to approach middle-class gatekeepers in trying to achieve his ends. He likens this to trying to gain entry to, say, Ghanaian communities by contacting the American Embassy for help! So what would be a more appropriate means of entry? Well, Whyte heard from a social worker about a particular member of the community, Doc, who was eventually contacted. Doc helped Whyte's passage into the community. Of course, this is a complex matter and one which is difficult to discuss without reference to a particular example. It is also important to remember that modern researchers are likely to require permission from research committees in order to enter organisations for research purposes. For example, research in hospitals will require such ethical clearance. This adds stages of complexity to the process of gaining entry to research sites. There is a distinction to be made between overt and covert observation. Covert observation occurs when the researcher does not identify herself or himself to the community as a researcher making observations. The researcher does not need to contact others for help and there is no process by which the researcher needs to explain or justify their activities to those about to be observed. But, then, of course, considerable ethical problems may arise (Chapter 17).

Step 6

Continuing access Participant observation/ethnography involves maintaining relations with the group studied and not just the entry process to the research location. Considerable thought and skill are needed in terms of interpersonal relations since those being studied may have concerns about the nature of the researcher's activity. The completely covert research study does not entirely avoid this risk as there may be difficulties over matters such as credibility. For example, a researcher who gains access to a factory floor by obtaining employment there may, nevertheless, appear different from others working there. For example, their accent may not match that of the group members and so might arouse interest or they may not be able to engage in simple conversations such as 'What did you do at the weekend?' or 'Where do you live?' without risking revealing their identity. Researchers who have indicated their status as a researcher may come under suspicion as to their 'true' identity – the researcher may be seen as being from social security, a management spy and so forth. The outcome of all of this is unlikely to be a direct confrontation such as a demand that the researcher stops his or her activities or some form of abuse. Instead, the resistance may take the form of providing misinformation deliberately to sabotage the research. Of course, the extent of these suspicions may vary according to the individuals involved – some of those being observed may be relaxed about it whereas others may be more inherently suspicious. The researcher has to be sensitive to such issues and deal with them to the best of their ability. This will vary according to circumstances but it would generally be wise to avoid situations which are likely to promote suspicion. For example, a researcher who seems unnecessarily friendly to members of management is more likely to come under suspicion since they may be seen as more likely to, say, inadvertently let slip information to them. Equally important is the possibility of providing written information about issues such as data confidentiality, data security, anonymity of individuals in any reports and so forth. This would need to be specifically tailored to the particular research situation. But there is a further aspect to this. The preceding comments perhaps imply that any hostility or suspicions of the researcher reflect on the competence of the researcher. This may be the case but, equally, it may reflect pre-existing tensions or relationships in the group into which the researcher inadvertently stumbles. In this sense, the response of those being observed constitutes valuable data which provides insight into the group. No matter what, this should be recorded in the field notes. It is not something to be quietly ignored.

Step 7

The use of key informants In any social environment, some individuals take on more important roles in our lives than others. Similarly, in ethnography/participant observation, some individuals tend to have a more important role in relation to the researcher. There can be several reasons for this. In particular, the key informant (a) may play a more central role in most aspects of the group's activities than others, (b) may have an interest in the research which is greater than that of the others, or (c) may have a special rapport with the researcher and so forth. Key informants can play a role in smoothing out the research process and may act as a source of social support at difficult times. In some contexts, the key informants may choose to provide information of what the group is planning to do in the future – for example, it might be helpful for the researcher who is studying a delinquent gang to know that they are planning a seaside trip at the weekend.

Step 8   **Field notes/data logging** The making of field notes is probably the only defining characteristic of the data for participant observation. The objective of taking field notes is to have a comprehensive database of one's observations in the field setting. Thus, the more complete the notes the better. But this is an unrealistic requirement in many ways since it begs the question just how much detail is enough? Furthermore, are there no restrictions on the observations which are recorded? This is not to imply that the participant observer should record everything since this would be a limitless and impossible task. Completeness in terms of the field notes is relative to the particular study in question and the theoretical and conceptual issues that the researcher brings to the field. Also, since these theoretical and conceptual issues will be modified in light of the experience, then what is a sufficiently complete set of field notes will also change. These are difficult matters to address in the abstract but the following ought to be taken into account:

- One important function of field notes is to help the researcher familiarise themselves with the social context of the research setting including the people within that setting and the interrelations between the two. Good field notes will contain such information in order to build up a picture of these important social relationships as well as helping to identify key figures in understanding what happens in the group.

- Memory will adversely affect the quality of the field notes if there is too much delay between the observation and the making of the field notes. It will also be affected by the nature of the intervening events, so the general advice is to make the field notes as soon as possible after the observation. The normal advice is to do it the same day without fail. Of course, in some circumstances, it would be helpful to make some brief notes immediately after the observation if it is not possible to do the full version until later. This can be done in a number of ways such as using a voice recorder, although this may increase the labour rather than ease it. Handwritten or computer-written notes are probably better in most circumstances.

- It may be helpful to carefully plan the periods of observation in a way that allows the making of notes easier. For example, one can plan the observation periods so as to give sufficient time for lengthy field note-making periods immediately afterwards. This could be something as simple as using lunch breaks for field note-making rather than more observation. The longer the periods of observation the more difficult it is to make field notes effectively.

- Note-making must not be rushed since these are the records that you will use for your analysis later on and if you don't understand what you wrote then the notes are not useful. So you need to write with a high degree of clarity and to make the notes as detailed and graphic as possible in order to achieve this.

It is incorrect to assume that the observations will be at the same level throughout the period of the study. Spradley (1980) suggests three distinct phases: (a) descriptive observation – the initial stage where the researcher is struggling to understand the complexity of the research situation; (b) focused observation which is narrower and focuses on aspects which are most relevant to the research question; and (c) selective observation which occurs near the end of the study when the researcher is seeking further evidence about something that has emerged in the focused observation stage.

Some pointers to the adequacy of one's field notes lie in: (a) greater variety in terms of the researcher being able to interact and relate to the group being studied will improve field notes, e.g. by involving people of a wide variety of different roles and statuses as well as a wide variety of group activities; (b) the greater the involvement of the observer with the group the more likely they are to understand the meanings of what is said and the nature of what is done; and (c) the more that the observer and those they are researching understand each other then the better the interpretation of events as included in the field notes.

What should be observed? This is another matter which is very difficult to address in general terms without specifying more precisely the purpose or research aims of the project. Few psychologists are likely to be in the open-ended situation of travelling to a totally different culture to try to understand that culture. Instead, they will be working in a specific location to understand a particular issue. For example, they may wish to understand the activities of work-groups within a hospital context. In these circumstances, the research will be rather more focused and precise. Although ethnography/participant observation studies usually progress from rather general to rather more specific observations on the basis of the experiences of the researchers, the starting points for different studies can vary widely. Ethnography/participant observation is very flexible – one of the strengths of the method. Flexibility does not indicate vacillation but a process of reflection throughout the timescale of the research project. By thinking about what has been observed, the key features of the situation will begin to be more apparent. Once this is achieved, then alteration is appropriate and not to accommodate developing ideas in the research would be to miss the point of ethnography/participant observation.

Step 9

How to sample In ethnography/participant observation, the objective of the researcher is to understand better the community or group under observation. Rarely, if ever, is the task to obtain estimates of the rates of occurrence of different sorts of characteristic such as the average age of the members of the community, for example. Consequently, the probability sampling used by some quantitative researchers is simply inappropriate for ethnography/participant observation which tries to find explanations of key aspects of the workings of the group or community. To achieve this aim, it is clearly more important to seek out situations and individuals who have the most to contribute in order to develop this understanding. By way of illustration, imagine research taking place on the factory floor. Random sampling of informants has a good chance of omitting the one or two individuals who are the most crucial in the activities on the factory floor. The participant observer would be looking for these individuals actively by obtaining information, for example, from key providers of information as to whom they may be.

Step 10

When to stop fieldwork Most research is constrained by resources. This applies as much to research by students as research financed by, say, the Government. These constraints may determine how much fieldwork can be done. However, sometimes another strategy is used. The term 'theoretical saturation' is used to describe the situation where additional data collection produces nothing additional relevant to the concepts, ideas and theories which are guiding the research. When this occurs, the researcher has established a pattern of strong relationships between his or her analytic categories. Furthermore, the categories developing in the analysis will be well understood when the point of saturation is reached. That is, the researcher is clear about the properties or characteristics of the category and additional data collection is doing nothing to encourage a reassessment of the characteristics of that analytic category (Strauss & Corbin, 1998). Or, another way of conceiving this is to simply discontinue the observation when it is clear that new entries in one's field notes seem very familiar in terms of what was written in earlier field notes.

Step 11   Leaving the research site It is probably self-evident that ethnographic/participant observation research involves a continual process of negotiation and involvement from the very earliest stages of the research. We have seen that this involves negotiating entry and maintaining involvement in a way which allows the fieldwork to continue. But very little is usually written about the process of exiting from the fieldwork situation. The research process may have come to an end possibly because the fieldwork is complete or possibly because the research has run out of time or funds. It is not unusual for the fieldwork to be brought to an end because of interpersonal problems in the research setting such as when the participants become non-cooperative because of developing suspicions about the motivations of the researcher. But in the smoothest fieldwork process the research has to come to an end. Participants have trusted the researcher with information, for example, so how does one provide reassurances about the future actions of the researcher? Friendships may have been formed and attachments made. How are they to be brought to an end? Should they be brought to an end?

These are difficult questions if the researcher is to avoid possible feelings of being exploited or used by the participants. This is an area where there is little established protocol but a clear need for sensitive actions and clear decisions about the process of separation of the researcher from the research site. Reeves (2010) provides a detailed account of her experiences in this regard. She writes, insightfully, if not from bitter experience:

> Although the emotional relationships that develop due to the negotiation of access and the establishing of rapport can support the researcher in the fieldwork and may, in themselves, be data, they become ever-more challenging when it is time to leave the study site and/or population. The issues relating to access, which researchers are much more aware of and tend to plan in greater detail, are just as important in these latter stages of the fieldwork. The same ethical principles that informed the design and conduct of the work to this stage are necessarily part of the withdrawal. However, to complicate matters, decisions or events within the fieldwork phase may only now reveal themselves as important. It is the nature of relationships that they are at their most challenging when there is a significant event. Thus, the ethnographic researcher needs to be aware that the trajectory of fieldwork is shaped by the manner in which relationships with formal and informal gatekeepers are developed and played out. (Reeves, 2010, p. 329)

How to analyse ethnography/participant observation

According to Robert Burgess, researchers often comment that participant observation and ethnographic data simply fails to 'speak for itself' (Burgess, 1982, p. 236). Furthermore, field research does not neatly divide into the stages which usually are claimed to typify quantitative research – literature review, research question formulation, data collection, data analysis, etc. The analysis of a participant observation/ethnography study must start with the realisation that it is primarily about understanding culture, social structures and organisations by the immersion of the researcher in relevant contexts (Figure 5.5). A number of things follow from this, the most important of which is the broad nature of the data collection methods that may be involved. This means that the researcher's skills are at a premium stretched simply because so many different types of data have been employed are involved. Of course, the task is less complex if the study involves only participation observation, though this would rarely be the case.

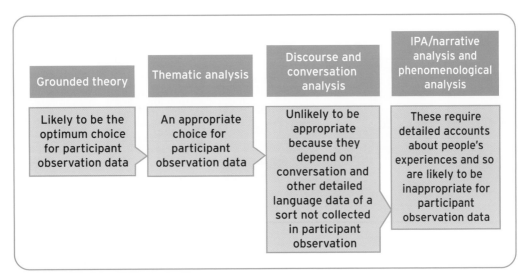

FIGURE 5.5   Evaluation of possible ways to analyse participant observation data

From reading this chapter, the following should be clear:

- There is no 'cookbook' approach to the analysis of participant observation/ethnography taken in its widest sense. Although this may feel like a deterrent against such studies, it should be seen as a positive aspect rather than a negative one. There are many forms of research which are easier than participant observation/ethnography.

- There may be very different approaches to data collection involved in participant observation/ethnography so the linking of different analyses is an inevitable component of the process. That is, just how do you link the outcomes of a participant observation study with the outcomes of the related in-depth interview study?

- Participant observation/ethnography is typical of qualitative research, in general, since its objective is the collection of extended in-depth or rich data. Thus, it would be expected that such data may be amenable to certain forms of qualitative analysis – grounded theory being the obvious candidate. Equally clearly, some forms of qualitative analysis are ruled out – discourse analysis and conversation analysis, for example – since they are dependent on an exact and detailed transcription of texts. The field notes for participant observation/ethnography simply do not attempt to record conversation in this manner.

The analysis of participant observation/ethnography has largely been in ways which are highly redolent of grounded theory (see Chapter 8). This is not to say that grounded theory has always been formally involved in the analysis – however, there are distinct similarities:

- The analysis is seen as starting with the initial data-gathering phase rather than being a distinct and separate processing.

- The analysis works by a process of formulating largely descriptive field notes to which the researcher adds interpretative (or analytic) notes. This is not dissimilar to the process of coding data in thematic analysis, grounded theory, discourse analysis and so forth.

- The analytic process proceeds through the stages of data examination, tentative analytic ideas, re-examination of the data in light of this tentative analysis, the reformation of the analytic ideas and so forth.

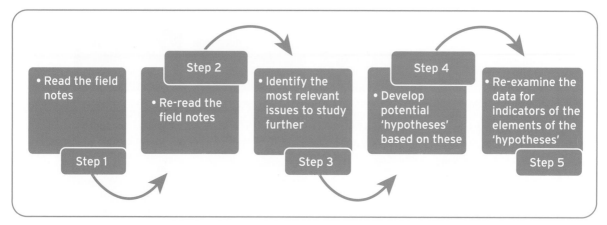

FIGURE 5.6 One approach to fieldwork analysis

Burgess (1982) describes one approach to the analysis of fieldwork which translates into the process presented in Figure 5.6. The similarities to grounded theory are clear.

Examples of the use of ethnography/participant observation

Boxes 5.1 to 5.3 provide examples of the use of ethnography and participant observation in research.

Box 5.1

ILLUSTRATIVE RESEARCH STUDY

A crucial participant observation study: Marienthal

Otto Bauer (1891–1938), who was a leading figure of the left-wing Social Democrat Party in Austria in the late 1920s, suggested to the Austrian research community that it would be an important venture to study unemployment. Researchers from the Austrian Research Unit for Economic Psychology worked under the direction of the famous psychologist/sociologist Paul Lazarsfeld (1901–1976). The research planning began in 1930 at exactly the time Marienthal's textile factory closed down. Marienthal is a town close to Vienna. The fieldwork for the research was carried out largely by a researcher Lotte Schenk-Danzinger

(1905–1992) who was working as the supervisor of a relief group which distributed second-hand clothing. Apparently a total of 24 working weeks were spent on the fieldwork and the weight of the research materials collected was about 30 kilograms (*An Unemployed Community: Marienthal*, agso.uni-graz. at/marienthal/e/study/00.htm, accessed 23 February 2015).

A book based on the study, mostly written by Marie Jahoda, was published in 1933 although the authors' obviously Jewish names did not appear on the front of the book as a concession to the National Socialist government at the time. The authors, Jahoda, Lazarsfeld and Zeisel, wrote:

> It was the aim of the study to draw an image of the psychological situation of a community suffering from unemployment, using cutting-edge methods of research. From the outset we focused our attention on two objectives. One with regard to substance: contributing material concerning the problem of unemployment – and a methodological one: trying to give a comprehensive and objective account of the socio-psychological facts. (Jahoda et al., 2002, p. v)

Not only was this the first psychological study of unemployment, but it was also notable for its varied approach to methodology and data collection. These included the analysis of documents, observation techniques, participant observation, surveys and so forth. The book is exceptionally vivid in terms of its descriptive material. The scientifically dry material is presented using verbal portraits of unemployed individuals and even materials taken from children's school essays. The involvement of researchers in Marienthal was also guided by the principle that they should fit naturally into the community by participating in activities of use to the community. The flavour of the relationship between the researchers and the unemployed families can be assessed from the following:

> Our investigations in Marienthal began with visits to the homes of about one hundred families. The ostensible occasion was to ask them about their particular needs in connection with our proposed distribution of clothing. The observations and interviews recorded during these visits taught us much about the basic posture of the families. Whichever member of the family eventually came to collect the clothes was

asked to tell us his life history which was usually done willingly. These people were then observed in a variety of surroundings: at our courses and at political meetings we talked about them and with them, taking notes of everything as we went along. From these notes and from the special information obtained from meal records, time sheets, etc., detailed descriptions of each family emerged. (Jahoda et al., 2002, p. 45)

Of course, such an approach would be familiar to cultural anthropologists of the time as well as sociologists of the Chicago School. The extent of the involvement and interaction between researchers and participants is not surprising in this context. Some modern qualitative research exhibits similar features but, of course, this extensive interaction would equally not characterise recent developments in qualitative psychology analysis.

At the end of the book, biographies of some of the unemployed in Marienthal were presented, though many more were collected which could not be included. This would not be unusual in some reports of modern qualitative research. What might surprise modern qualitative researchers is the extent to which the researchers systematically incorporated quantitative data with the qualitative. This included data on the diet of the families and data on the walking speed of those living in this community dominated by unemployment. Such diverse information allowed the researchers to study the experience and structure of time for the unemployed. Paul Lazarsfeld, who became a highly influential sociologist in the United States, is probably mainly regarded for his quantitative methodological work. Rigid separation between qualitative and quantitative research may not always be desirable. Quite the reverse is probably closer to the truth.

Box 5.2

ILLUSTRATIVE RESEARCH STUDY

Ethnography: violent football supporters

Suggestions that ethnographic approaches and participant observation hold promise in psychology are far more common than studies actually using them. One exceptionally important ethnographic study was Marsh,

Rosser and Harré's (1978) study of a football crowd. One could say that the book was an investigation of football hooliganism – it was in a sense but it also totally reformulated ideas about how to understand such behaviour. Football violence is presented in the book as a social construction by 'moral entrepreneurs' (such as media and politicians) rather than representing an accurate picture about what happens at matches:

> Vandalism, for example, might be thought of as a collection of clearly identifiable acts requiring sanctions for the simple reason that they offend against the property, both individual and collective, of members of society. But contrast the reaction to football fans who run through a town creating damage as they go with the reaction to university students during rag week creating similar damage. The former damage will be viewed as the result of 'destructive hooliganism' and dealt with accordingly, whilst the latter will be seen as arising from an excess of good-natured high spirits and over-enthusiasm. Although the damaging acts are very similar, football fans are 'deviants' whilst students, for reasons not made explicit, are somehow excused. (Marsh et al., 1978, p. 10)

The research is described by its authors as being ethogenic in nature which means that it is essentially about the speech which makes intelligible the action which accompanies that speech. That is, ethogenic is about the speech which accounts for one's actions. Nevertheless, the methodology employed by Marsh et al. is decidedly ethnographic in nature. (At the time of the research the idea of ethnography was the conceptual new kid on the block.) The research involved a mixture of data collection methods including observation, interviewing, descriptions of incidents and the collection of cultural artefacts such as threatening and offensive chants against the opposing team and its fans. The observation utilised existing surveillance cameras which were spread liberally around the football ground. The participants in the study were a relatively small number of the local fans of the football club in question. What this means is that the observation part of the ethnographic study was covert and, therefore, cannot be described as participant observation.

At the time when the study was carried out, football grounds had a mixture of seating and standing places which allowed more movement than the all-seater stadiums which characterise modern football. Special areas were fenced in, typically where the young visiting team fans would congregate. The police would send fans as appropriate to these fenced areas – a process known to all concerned as 'penning'. Thus the police essentially separated different groups of fans in the most effective way possible. This segregation was a cooperative activity between the police and the fans – both of which repulsed or ejected marauding fans from the 'other side'

when they entered the 'wrong' area. When the videos of the 'standing' fans were analysed it emerged that there was an essentially stable pattern of groups which the fans themselves recognised when they were interviewed. Not only that, the different groups had important behavioural and social characteristics which could be attributed to them.

For example, Group A consisted essentially of young males in the 12–17-year-old age group. They had a pattern of dress which could be described as the 'aggro outfit' together with 'emblems of allegiance' such as flags and banners. They were the noisiest group of fans. This group had several different social roles including a system of chant leaders who were responsible for organising the chanting as well as writing some chants when needed; aggro leaders who were always at the forefront of hostilities with the opposition team's fans; nutters who engaged in some of the more outrageous incidents; heavy drinkers with a reputation for excessive drunkenness who were regularly ejected from the ground; the fighters who were a small group renowned for being violent (they are different from the aggro leaders who only engage in ritual conflict with the other team supporters); and the organiser who would organise the coaches to transport the fans to other football grounds for away matches. In contrast, Group C exhibited no particular style of dress from that worn by young men of their age group in general. They were older and up to the age of 25 years. Distinguishing clothing, flags and banners were not part of the make-up of this group and they would not have been identifiable as football fans outside the football ground. Generally speaking, membership of Group C was of higher status than membership of other groups and it was an aspiration to join Group C from other groups.

The organised nature of the football crowd even extended to the coaches taking the fans to and from the match. There was a natural order of who was allowed to sit where on the coach. Failure to comply with the 'natural' order would result in the offender being told to move and where. The researchers carried out extensive qualitative interviews with members of the various groups of fans. Interestingly, the fans were generally well aware of the different groups in this football ground culture. The researchers had videotapes of various incidents which had happened at football matches. The important thing was how the fans accounted for these events irrespective of whether these accounts reflected the contents of the tapes precisely. For example, there was a basic observation on the part of the researchers that fans talk about fights being extremely violent while injury was fairly uncommon. The researchers would stop their tape-recorded interviews and play them back to the fans for their comments. This often brought about some reflection on the part of the fans about what they had said. So Wayne, a fan, in the first part of the interview expressed the following view:

> Kids go charging in – there's boots flying all over – real mad sometimes. With teams like Sunderland – they're mad – just lash out. So now we try to get the boot in first – as they arrive and before they can get together. You can get the boot in first and maybe scare them off a bit. We got a couple as they were coming up from their coach and they didn't know what hit them. It makes them think, don't it? (pp. 93–94)

After hearing the tape played back, he said:

> You goes in there – sort of going in to nut people, or give them a kicking or something like that. But, normally, anyway, the kids don't all get beaten up. You can tell when somebody's had enough – really you're trying to stop them giving you a lot of mouth. You get mad at them but you know when to stop. (p. 95)

These may be seen as two somewhat contradictory accounts – the first very violent whereas the second seemingly describing rule-bound activities. It is a picture of conflict but control is an important element of it. The violent view is very much the dominant view of the football fan which could be found in newspapers, etc. as out of control and extreme. The evidence from this ethnographic study was that where a fight actually occurred then the fans could provide justifications for this happening as opposed to the usual situation where the 'aggro' between groups of fans was largely ritualistic in nature – that is, threatening displays in the form of offensive and threatening chants but no real threat of violence for the most part because 'aggro' is governed by rules which usually prevent extreme violence taking place.

According to Marsh et al., the rules can be seen in the accounts that the fans gave in explanation of their actions and the justifications they see for some acts. This does not mean that the fans had a comprehensive understanding of the 'rules' which governed their actions at football matches. The researchers tried a simple device of changing aspects of real events on the basis that this might help them understand better the rule-driven nature of the activities of the fans. The fans realised that there were things wrong with these 'incorrect' sequences of events and suggested what 'should' have happened in reality. Similarly, they were given examples of events which 'went wrong' because someone was hurt and the fans could explain the reasons for this. In other words, the rule-driven nature of the behaviour of fans at football matches could be identified from circumstances in which the 'rules' had failed. Ethnomethodologists have taken similar approaches when they immersed people in essentially chaotic situations and found that people treated the chaotic situation as meaningful (see Chapter 10 on conversation analysis for a discussion of this type of research). These studies are known as *breaching* studies.

This study by Marsh et al. (1978) demonstrates the potential of ethnographic style research in psychology. They essentially took a notorious problem – violence at football matches – and generated an analysis which substantially revised many of the 'common-sense' views of the problem which could be found throughout the media and among the general public at large. None of this would have been possible simply by interviewing the football fans since many of their initial comments seemed to reflect the views of people on the outside. It was only when the fans were asked to account for actual events at matches that a new picture emerged of the rule-driven nature of the interactions among different groups of fans. One might suggest that because the researchers were outsiders to the fans' culture then they saw events and heard discussions through new eyes and ears. Without the careful observation of the crowds at the football ground, they may have been left with the impression of the violence of an undifferentiated mass of people. Instead they were able to see the intricate structure which helped them identify very different patterns of conduct associated with these various groups within the crowd of fans.

When to use ethnography/participant observation

Ethnography/participant observation is at its most useful:

- When one wishes to understand the operation of a naturally occurring group, community or culture. The assumption is that if the researcher engages with the group skilfully and at length, they will see the group acting in a natural way without being affected significantly by being involved in a research study.

Box 5.3

ILLUSTRATIVE RESEARCH STUDY

Ethnographic research: a modern example from organisational psychology

Within psychology, ethnography has only gained a substantial foothold in cultural psychology and research on children's development (Miller, Hengst, & Wang, 2003). Outside of these, it is difficult to find instances of the systematic use of ethnography within the discipline. The work that we are considering here is a little different since it involves the work of organisational psychologists. Holmberg and Larsson (2006) express considerable enthusiasm about the use of ethnographic methods in organisational research. They see potential in ethnography to provide a richness of understanding to organisational psychology. The research involved participation by them as observers in various of the organisation's settings, the shadowing of important people in the organisation, and research interviews, both formal and informal, with individuals in the organisation.

The research involved the introduction of a system of cognitive-behavioural treatment to the Swedish correction (prison) system. The study concentrates on the use of a standardised manual for the cognitive behavioural treatment of offenders. There is a concept in forensic psychology referred to as 'manualisation'. Research into therapy had frequently noted that there is considerable variation in how therapists implement cognitive-behavioural therapy. Some depart markedly from the basic theory and practice of the approach. These variations are strongly associated with variations in the success of the treatment. Those therapists who stick most closely to the theoretical and practical basics of treatment are likely to experience greater success in their therapy. Manualisation involves the provision of detail of how to conduct cognitive-behavioural therapy in the most effective ways in order to maximise the effectiveness of treatment (see Howitt, 2012, for a fuller discussion). The purpose of the study was to understand the underlying reasons why therapists vary in the extent to which they precisely implement treatment procedures. Data were collected from treatment and other staff of the organisation and consisted of:

- formal and informal interviews;
- questionnaires;
- observation of training sessions, meetings and facilitation meetings;
- official documents.

The research took place over two years and at different sites belonging to the correction services which were employing the manualisation approach. The researchers had frequent contact with members of staff. The researchers were actively involved with the organisation and presented some of their research findings including to the participants in the study.

It was clear that manual-based treatments were an aspect of a wider attempt to reform the correctional service. So other changes were being made by top management at the same time including managerial methods and procedures, the logistics of the organisation, quality control management, and the diagnosis of clients. Many of the decision makers at head office saw manualisation as part of the wider attempt to reform the service. The new approach was seen by them as more cost-efficient, more rational, more standardised and more scientifically based than what had gone before. The previous management of the correction services was seen as very traditional in its approach, highly variable in the ways that management was done, and sometimes verged on the dysfunctional. In the context of all of this, the process of manualisation was seen as providing a service more based on research evidence as well as being more appropriate to the new management system which was concurrently being implemented. Top managers saw all of these changes as matters involving implementation and control.

While that was the way top management saw things, things were not quite the same in the bottom-up view of the workers carrying out the therapy. In interviews with the researchers, the treatment staff in the corrections service revealed what the researchers term a 'complex mix of attitudes and feelings' about their work. The manual-based treatment programme was seen as being challenging. However, when the treatment programme went really well they found the experience highly satisfying and rewarding. Measurable progress was therefore at the root of this. For example, one said: 'To complete a whole series (a programme), felt really good, like reaching the summit of Mount Everest. Having an overview of the whole programme makes me feel more secure in my role and I think I do a better job . . .' (p. 4) But many of those working on the therapeutic programme found that the manualised methods were slow to learn and be proficient with. Most experienced problems when trying to find time to give their full attention to the treatment programme. They had other regular work tasks to complete in addition to their work on the programme so one complained at the endless Sunday evenings at home preparing for the programme in their spare time and the feelings of guilt when they could not help cooperative committed clients as much as they would like. These are examples of how the personnel working on the programme had issues which were very different from that of the top management's 'implementation' process.

The observations made by the researchers during facilitation meetings and training sessions provided a rather different understanding of the issues. Treatment staff at these meetings had questions covering just about every aspect of the new programme imaginable. In contrast with the interviews, not all of the staff revealed themselves as secure or as experienced as they had communicated to the researchers in the face-to-face interviews. They discussed a great deal the problems of just how to deal with the circumstances of a particular treatment involving a real client but using the treatment manual as the basis of what they did – that is, to what extent could they adapt the manual's procedures to particular circumstances. Thus the meetings involved a 'negotiation' around the degree of standardisation and how particular situations should be responded to. The facilitation meeting was also used as a vehicle for discussing issues to do with supporting the treatment work. Issues such as resource allocation, work routine changes, practical matters of the use of rooms and the like were involved. Advice and support were part of these meetings. But there were other things in the observations which failed to emerge in the interviews:

> The facilitation meeting could be seen as an arena where manuals, rules and directives were drawn into a process of sense making and interpretation where the participants' different experiences of clients, difficulties and their own individual tactics were made public. A consequence of these discursive activities seemed to be that it was possible to make sense of both the bureaucratic context (manuals, rules, etc.) and individual experience in a way that allowed the staff to establish a standard or a reasonable (and possible) way of performing this task. In the organisational units that did not have these kind of meetings the personnel expressed uncertainty, loneliness and a need for clearer direction from their immediate superior. (p. 5)

What is the advantage of the fuller ethnographic approach? Larsson and Holmberg suggest that interviews and documents provide a basic picture of both the intentions of management and the way in which staff perceive the changes in work practices. In contrast, observations provided insights and interpretations which were rather different in nature from those obtained in interviews. Observations allowed the research to go beyond the superficial label of, say, facilitation meeting to find other things going on at such meetings which were matters that participants did not/could not talk about spontaneously in the interviews. This would include learning processes, social support processes, sense making of the situation, and so forth. It would seem that the facilitation meeting studied in depth provides information about where the real work of the organisation is done. That is, things do not filter down from top management but appear in interaction between different levels of the organisation.

- When broad observations are appropriate rather than narrowly focused ones. Thus, ethnography/participant observation is quite different from the fine-grained approaches which, for example, conversation analysis and discourse analysis deal with. It does not operate at the same level of detail. Ethnography/participant observation is about studying social interaction and cultures in as full and natural a way as possible.

Ethnography/participant observation can be regarded as a method in its own right capable of generating a rich variety of data which are unobtainable in any other way. However, it is a resource-hungry approach compared with most other methods of qualitative research. As a method, it has a lot to commend it to qualitative psychologists though the concentration of much qualitative psychology almost purely on language is probably a limitation on its usefulness. However, what else can compete with it as a way of studying groups in their social environment?

While it is reasonable to suggest that participant observation/ethnology is not a frequently used method in psychological research, it has a somewhat wider role in psychology than research. You will find that observation is used in a variety of professional contexts in psychology such as in business, counselling and education, so taking the method seriously as a research tool would add to the general practical skills of any psychologist.

Evaluation of ethnography/participant observation

Any evaluation of ethnography/participant observation needs to take into account the range of things which can be included in such a study. Observation, alone, would be rare and this is not the place to evaluate every method used. This said, among the criticisms that may be attached to ethnography/participant observation are the following:

- Ethnography/participant observation, being primarily a qualitative data *collection* method, is not clearly associated with particular methods of data analysis. This means that once having collected the data, the researcher may be left with important questions about how to analyse the data. To some extent, this is always the case in research.

- Ethnography/participant observation is resource-intensive. It takes a lot of time and consequently money to do properly. The traditional anthropologist or ethnographer had the luxury of time. Of course, not every researcher has a year or two to devote to fieldwork but, then, not every piece of research involving ethnography/participant observation needs that much time. Early anthropologists, for example, might familiarise themselves with the local language and engage with the culture before beginning their main fieldwork. Furthermore, they may have seen their work as much more exploratory and less built on previous research and theory than modern researchers. Researchers with a predefined or more limited focus than traditional anthropologists may require substantially less time in the field.

- Mainstream psychologists may question the objectivity of ethnography/participant observation methods. Consequently the first task of the participant observer is to make notes about what was actually seen and heard. It is incumbent on the participant observer that they try to keep description separate from interpretation. Keeping these separate when writing up field notes is inevitably difficult at times but nevertheless essential. Of course, some styles of recording events are intrinsically better than others. For example, it may be objective to write that 'when Debby approached she was not smiling' than to write 'Debby approached hostilely'. Although she might have been hostile, this cannot be assessed from the fact that she was not smiling.

- Field note-taking can be problematic. While the methodology of ethnography/participant observation may appear simple, practical things are rather more complex since the researcher is often unable to make field notes immediately after observing the group, though this would, perhaps, be the ideal. Given the nature of ethnography/participant observation, it is not so easy to use technological help such as digital recordings as it would be, say, for an interview.

- Not only do delays in writing-down fieldwork observations risk producing distortions due to memory, they mean that the participant observer needs to be extremely well disciplined about making the notes each day on a regular basis.

- Ethnography/participant observation, because of its very nature and its resource intensiveness, realistically cannot be employed for representative work on major organisations or even national issues – that is to say, ethnography/participant observation might not be feasible when representative samples of a large organisation are to be studied. Other methods would be more appropriate such as surveys, although ethnography/participant observation might be employed as a means of exploring issues prior to the full-scale study.

- Often ethnography/participant observation is used in conjunction with other methods. This means that analytic methods have to be developed which integrate the several different aspects of the research.

- Pole and Lampard write of ethnography/participant observation:

> Observation is a research method which perhaps more than any other relies on the capacity of the researcher to interpret a situation as it unfolds around him/her . . . Moreover, where participation is emphasised, the researcher may also be directly responsible for some of the social action which he/she is observing. Taking all of this into account, observation is perhaps the most demanding of research methods, necessitating a great deal of thought and practice. The problem here, of course, is that practice can only effectively occur in real research situations. (Pole & Lampard, 2002, p. 71)

If we add to this the additional range of research and interpersonal skills required by the method, then it is evident that ethnography/participant observation is a demanding form of research, probably unsuited to the complete novice other than as a training exercise.

CONCLUSION

Becker and Geer (1982) suggest that techniques such as ethnography/participant observation and unstructured interviews are the prime ways that data can be collected in which 'surprises' can be found. Pre-structured questionnaires are only capable of generating 'findings' about pre-specified and thus partially 'known' things. There are, of course, many other ways of collecting data which meet these requirements since the crucial factor is the lack of pre-structuring of the data collected rather than a particular method.

Unfortunately, ethnography/participant observation has been a relatively uncommon form of research in psychology despite being mentioned frequently. Perhaps it is a little too unlike the conventional laboratory experiment to be readily accepted by researchers with a psychology background. Subjectivity is not regarded as a virtue in mainstream psychology and it is notable that the currently popular methods of qualitative psychology tend to use approaches which can be construed as objective. (Again conversation analysis and discourse analysis are the best examples.) Its data do not consist of precisely recorded spoken language or text that tends to characterise much of the data central to modern qualitative psychology. But there are other factors in the neglect of ethnography/participant observation such as its labour-intensive nature which work against it. All of this is a pity because it means that psychologists underuse a method aimed at understanding social systems and processes. Although other qualitative approaches in psychology may have some relevance, they simply lack the broad, in-depth treatment that ethnography/participant observation affords.

KEY POINTS

- Ethnography/participant observation cannot be described as a major qualitative technique in psychology but it has been influential in the form of a few seminal studies. Naturally, this is most common in social psychology.

- Although ethnography/participant observation refers to a specific style of research, in reality participant observation and ethnography use participant observation in a wider research context which might include interviews, diaries, general documents and participant observation, among other things. Such a broad study is expensive in resources and relatively uncommon as a consequence.

- Ethnography/participant observation puts considerable demands on the interpersonal resources of the researcher as well as on their powers to memorise and record data for analysis. Clearly there is a big disparity between the sorts of data generated by these methods and the sorts of data needed for those qualitative data analysis methods which concentrate on language in action such as discourse analysis and conversation analysis. The same is true for narrative analysis and interpretative phenomenological analysis which concentrate on detailed accounts of individuals' experiences.

ADDITIONAL RESOURCES

Genzuk, M. (2003). A synthesis of ethnographic research. http://www-rcf.usc.edu/~genzuk/Ethnographic_Research.pdf (accessed 23 February 2015).

Miller, P. J., Hengst, J. A., & Wang, S.-H. (2003). Ethnographic methods: Applications from developmental cultural psychology. In P. M. Camic, J. E. Rhodes & L. Yardley (Eds.), *Qualitative research in psychology: Expanding methods in methodology and design* (pp. 219–233) Washington, DC: American Psychological Association.

O'Reilly, K. (2009). *Key concepts in ethnography*. London: Sage.

Rapport, N. (2014). *Social and cultural anthropology: The key concepts*, 3rd ed. Abingdon: Routledge.

PART 3

Qualitative data analysis

Mostly qualitative methods produce data in the form of words. There are qualitative analyses carried out on visual data but this is relatively uncommon as yet in psychology. So when we think of qualitative psychology we are largely thinking words. There are numerous different ways of conceptualising language and, characteristically, there are different methods of analysis in qualitative psychology depending on how the researcher wishes to use these words. Of course, a newcomer to qualitative psychology may initially find it difficult to know what each of the various qualitative analytic methods achieves. So in this introduction to Part 3 the focus will be on how to select an appropriate analytic method for your data. The eight different analytic methods discussed in the next few chapters are based on very different epistemological and historical roots – something which is not usually an issue when choosing different quantitative methods but is important in relation to qualitative research. These different epistemological roots are summarised in Table P3.1. Furthermore, the different names given to the different methods can cover quite a range of different forms of analysis. So, for example, there are a variety of different techniques which use the same overall title of discourse analysis. Within psychology, the range is slightly smaller, yet ranges from social constructionist discourse analysis to Foucauldian discourse analysis. A reader unaware of this might struggle to understand exactly what the nature of discourse analysis is. These are not fully compatible approaches and they can have very different concerns. This is a problem built into the field and newcomers to discourse analysis cannot be blamed for the confusion that this may cause. So it is perhaps a case that being forewarned is forearmed. It does raise the question of whether to deal with the methods separately. For this edition, the two major approaches to discourse analysis have been given separate chapters.

In this book, eight different approaches to qualitative data analysis in psychology are discussed in detail. It so happens that they fall fairly naturally into three major groupings. This is not to suggest that they are treated this way in the research literature but that understanding what these three groupings are helps unravel what the field of qualitative data analysis involves. Of course, judgements of similarity are bound to be contentious so this scheme may not be accepted by all. Researchers sometimes claim to be using a variety of analytic methods in a study – which may be from more than one grouping. This is probably because many of the analytic methods have overlapping procedures. Indeed,

TABLE P3.1 Backgrounds and epistemological basis of qualitative analysis methods

Thematic analysis	The epistemological basis of thematic analysis is relatively unspecific other than it follows the broad general features of qualitative approaches.
Grounded theory	Grounded theory is a reaction to the large-scale social theory of sociology prior to the 1960s. It provided rigorous methodological procedures for theory building.
Discourse analysis (two types)	The roots of discourse analysis are in the idea of speech as action as well as Foucault's approach to social systems. Social Constructionist and Foucauldian Discourse Analysis are distinct strands of research and theory.
Conversation analysis	Conversation analysis adopts a strongly ethnomethodological approach to language in its attempt to understand conversation as a skilled performance.
Interpretative phenomenological analysis	Interpretative phenomenological analysis is strongly based on phenomenology and a number of related approaches. It concentrates on experiences as experienced by the individual.
Narrative psychology	Narrative psychology concentrates on life-story data which it interprets from a critical realist perspective. In many respects it shares many of the perspectives of interpretative phenomenological analysis.
Phenomenology	Phenomenology is the philosophical system of Edmund Husserl which has found expression in psychology as phenomenological psychology. This involves a variety of methods which adhere, to differing extents, to Husserl's philosophy. It concentrates on how things are experienced in consciousness.

despite the different epistemologies, often very similar analytic processes are involved. So where a researcher claims to be carrying out a discourse analysis and grounded theory analysis, they are probably indicating that their method of discourse analysis has many overlapping features with grounded theory. Nevertheless, Figure P3.1 should be useful. It is important to note the following:

- Many qualitative analytic methods tend to be dependent on transcribing the data from, usually, an aural to a written form. Thus the figure starts with transcription. This is dealt with in Chapter 6. Of course, if the data are already in written form, it will not be necessary to involve transcription. For the most part, just a word-by-word transcript is sufficient for many of the qualitative data analysis methods discussed in this book. However, for conversation analysis and some versions of discourse analysis the use of the Jefferson transcription system is universal. This method transcribes additional features of language such as overlapping speakers and gaps in the conversation.

- Thematic analysis and grounded theory are fairly generic qualitative data analysis methods. Thematic analysis basically consists of various methods for categorising the data into a number of major themes or descriptive categories. Grounded theory does this and more. It is better conceived as a strategy for data collection and data analysis since, for example, it has procedures for sampling to maximise the relevance of the data to theory as well as ways of coding the data to produce themes. Then it goes further and involves ways of generating more general theories. Both of these approaches are less constrained by epistemological factors than any of the other methods described in the next few chapters.

- Conversation analysis is a coherent approach to the structure of conversation as an orderly aspect of social interaction. In contrast, the term discourse analysis is far wider and includes activities, at one pole, very similar to those of conversation analysis but, then, involves aspects of the work of the French academic Michel Foucault who provided a critical approach to social institutions at the other pole. Both of these can legitimately be called discourse analysis but to assume that they overlap greatly is a mistake and can lead to confusion.

- Narrative analysis, phenomenological analysis and interpretative phenomenological analysis are in many ways similar. All three rely strongly on qualitative data and, usually, in-depth interview data. They can be seen as versions of critical realism since, although

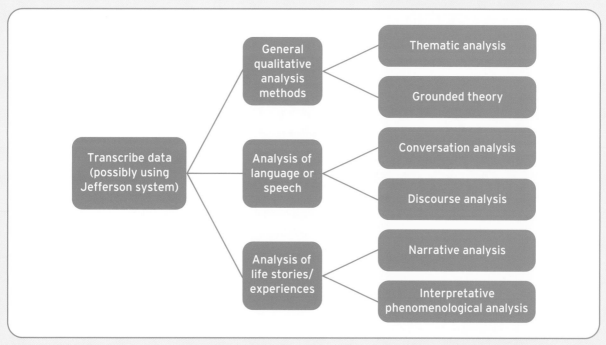

FIGURE P3.1 Pathways through Part 3 of the book

they are sensitive to the qualitative idea of relativism (i.e. we can never know reality exactly – it is always perceived through a mirror), they take the view that what people say has something substantial to say about their lives and experiences – that is, what people say is more than ephemeral chatter. All three can be seen as being based on phenomenology though narrative analysis is probably more dependent on the developments in personality theory known as narrative psychology.

To what extent can these different analytic procedures be regarded as fundamentally incompatible? In some ways they are but researchers often have careers in which they use a variety of fundamentally irreconcilable methods in their research. For example, questionnaire studies and experiments have very different epistemological foundations but many quantitative researchers will use both. With exceptions, this happens unproblematically. Difficulties and issues can occur among researchers using methods which have very similar if not identical names. For example, discourse analysis stretches from social constructionist orientated approaches to a very different, Foucauldian pole. Narrative analysis also tends to be used to refer to very different procedures. Such confusions and their disentanglement are part of the meat of academic life. Having a wide variety of different analytic methods may be confusing to newcomers but they should be regarded as part of the way in which disciplines develop rather than damaging schisms.

Another way of looking at all of this involves understanding that the different approaches to qualitative analysis tend to be associated with different subdivisions of psychology. So, for example, a qualitative researcher in the field of health psychology would naturally be more likely to turn to interpretative phenomenological analysis since it originated in that field and is more tailored to the needs of researchers in that field. Similarly, narrative analysis is more tailored to personality and clinical psychology. Social psychologists have tended to be the most involved with conversation analysis and discourse analysis to the extent that these deal with social interaction through language. Other fields of psychology tend to pick and choose their approach. For example, educational psychology has involved interpretative phenomenological analysis. Doubtless other subfields of psychology will generate their own chosen qualitative analysis methods.

CHAPTER 6

Data transcription methods

Overview

- Transcription is the process of turning sound (and video) recordings into written text prior to the further analysis of the material. Orthographic (or secretarial or playscript) transcription simply attempts to note down the words spoken. This is not as simple as it first appears as there are numerous decisions to be made by the transcriber about what to include and what to exclude.

- Other forms of transcription describe more precisely the characteristics of the way that people speak by indicating just how the words are said and where overlaps occur between speakers, for example.

- There are a number of transcription systems but largely they have made no inroads into psychology. The exception is the Jefferson transcription system which is important in conversation analysis (Chapter 10) and the social constructionist version of discourse analysis (Chapter 9).

- The Jefferson transcription system was devised by Gail Jefferson, an important figure in the development of conversation analysis. It tries to give a clearer indication of how words are said but it does not include all relevant features such as the facial expressions or gestures accompanying the words. That is, transcription inevitably loses information from the original speech, though precisely what is lost depends on how the transcription is done.

- There is no requirement that Jefferson transcription must be used for all qualitative data analysis though it is especially important when one is treating language as an activity which does things rather than simply communicating information. Transcription techniques are much better developed for auditory than for visual recordings.

- Transcription is a time-consuming process which is prone to errors. A researcher should always choose a method of transcription which matches the purpose of their research. Many researchers argue that the transcriber should avoid putting more into the transcription than their analysis calls for though this is not adhered to in many published studies.

- Jefferson transcription uses keyboard strokes which are universal on keyboards but uses them to indicate different aspects of the way in which the words spoken are said.

- Jefferson's method can be seen as a lower-level coding system since it highlights certain aspects of the data, so deeming them important, but ignores others. This is easily seen as the original conversation is richer than the recording of that event which is richer than the transcription of the event.

- It is anticipated that digital files of transcripts, recordings and mixed audio-transcript material will be made available by researchers via the Internet more frequently than at present.

What is transcription?

Data for qualitative researchers take many different forms. However, among the commonest forms of data is the spoken word. Transcription is the process by which a sound (or video) recording of the spoken word is turned into written language for subsequent analysis. It is important to note that the spoken word and the written word are not the same thing since the spoken word has features which normally the written word lacks. Simple examples of the difference are pitch, volume and pace characteristics, along with other variations which the spoken word exhibits in profusion but which the same words written down usually lack. Although it is perfectly possible for summaries of language data to be used for some research purposes, it is virtually universal in modern qualitative research that one works with a written transcript which is a *verbatim* (word-for-word) record of the spoken word or, in some cases, sections of spoken word particularly relevant to the research question. The basic choices of transcription methods which are commonly used in qualitative psychology are as follows:

- The orthographic/secretarial/playscript transcription which concentrates solely on the words which are said, not how they are said. This is the form of transcription that most types of qualitative research use.

- Jefferson transcription which uses common keyboard symbols to provide additional information over and above what is available in the secretarial transcription. The additions are things like the way in which the words are said, where speakers overlap, and so forth. This system of transcription is used mainly in conversation analysis (Chapter 10) and in the type of social constructionist discourse analysis associated with Potter and Wetherell (1987) (Chapter 9).

Research imposes limitations on the data which are collected. For example, the decision to audio-record a focus group discussion imposes its own parameters and a decision to video-record changes the situation too. Should the researcher choose to take notes during an interview then this also has its influence. For example, the note-taking researcher might appear to be rather more formal. Whatever choices are made in research, they will have a bearing on the nature of the data and, as a consequence, what can be done with the data. Much the same is true of transcription: once a choice is made about who transcribes, what is transcribed and how it is transcribed then these choices have consequences. For example, Potter and Hepburn (2009) suggest:

Crucially, advocates of a straightforward orthographic or 'play-script' version of transcript . . . often fail to appreciate that they are not a more neutral or simple record. Rather they are highly consequential transformations. For example, orthographic transcript imposes the conventions of written language which are designed to be broadly independent of specific readers. Such a transformation systematically wipes out evidence of intricate coordination and recipient design. It encourages the analyst to interpret talk by reference to an individual speaker or focus on abstract relations between word and world. (p. 1)

The point is that by *not* indicating how words are being said, the analysis is steered to interpreting the words just in the way they would be in formal written language. In consequence, many of the features of language as it is used in interaction to achieve certain ends are lost. So if the researcher's emphasis is on what language does then the secretarial, orthographic or playscript transcription is inappropriate. Ultimately, however, no transcription is the same as the original spoken words on which it is based.

Is a transcript necessary?

Not all forms of qualitative research necessitate the use of transcripts. For example, the classic work of Michel Foucault, which is the basis of critical discourse analysis, did not employ transcripts of any description and this would typify those working in the Foucauldian tradition (Fairclough, 1993). For the critical discourse analyst, interviews and transcripts amount to methodological tools to enable these discourses to be identified – their concern is not with the detail of how talk is constructed. Critical discourse analysts are interested in the ideological dimensions of power embedded in text. On the other hand, the use of transcripts is virtually universal in the work of conversation analysts and social constructionist discourse analysts. They are much more interested in the mechanics of how talk and other texts are constructed.

In just what ways do transcriptions differ in terms of spoken words being written down? These differences should identify some of the limitations of the orthographic/secretarial/playscript transcription. Among the additional non-verbal communications that occur during an interview or focus group are the following:

- *Proxemic communication* The use of the physical space between persons in a conversation. For example, think of the way in which ordinary women on television reality shows will physically move their chairs apart to indicate their loathing for an ex-partner who refuses to believe that her baby is his.
- *Kinesic communication* The range of body movements and postures which may reveal more than the spoken word does. For example, the individual who folds their arms during a conversation might be perceived and interpreted in a particular way.
- *Paralinguistic communication* This includes the changes in volume, pitch and other characteristics of the voice. For example, it is known from research that many people's voices rise in pitch when they lie.
- *Chronemic communication* The variations in the pace of speech and the silences which are introduced into speech. For example, people may speak faster when they are in an emotional state.

None of these appears in a word-for-word orthographic/secretarial/playscript transcription. Other methods of transcription, such as the Jefferson transcription method, partly include these 'missing' elements. However, no transcription method is available which includes all of the above. There are some aspects of human interaction for which transcription procedures are being developed. For example, Hepburn (2004) seeks to provide methods by which crying during the course of interaction may be described and transcribed by the researcher.

Discussions of the role of transcription in qualitative research identify a range of different considerations and there is no simple view that one transcription method is better than another for the entire field of qualitative research. Although, as we shall see, things have been standardised for conversation analysis and constructivist discourse analysis where the Jefferson transcription system is required to be used, this does not apply for all transcripts. What transcription method one uses depends on the purpose and nature of one's research. Hammersley (2010) suggests that there are numerous decisions that have to be taken in relation to how a transcription should be carried out for any study. These include the following:

- Do I need to translate any part of a particular recording and, if so, how much? Since it is not an absolute requirement of qualitative research that a transcription is produced then some qualitative research may not involve a transcript. And even if a transcript is produced, the researcher may decide to transcribe only part of the recording. So selective transcription is a possibility although the researcher needs clarity about why they chose to be selective in a particular way.

- How will the contents of the recording be represented? The choice, at its extremes, are between presenting the sounds actually made, including pitch, pace and intonation (as in Jefferson transcription) as well as accents/dialect or to present the words used in a conventional textual form like writing. In the latter, errors in the use of a word may be 'corrected' such as where the wrong word is used.

- Where there are many speakers, will the researcher try to indicate to which individuals a speaker is mainly addressing where the talk does not indicate this? It is possible, for example, that in a focus group discussion two speakers actually talk to each other but try to avoid the others hearing. Clearly such indications are easier where the recording is a video recording in which it can be seen who is addressing whom by indicating the direction of their gaze, for example.

- Should non-word vocalisations be included (e.g. uhuh), coughs, intakes and outtakes of breath, laughs and so forth? Some of these may not be intended to communicate anything but equally they may be important to the analysis. Sneezing seems to have no alternative meaning but coughing can indicate all sorts of things apart from the physical response.

- What should be done about pauses and silences? A decision needs to be made about whether they are timed and, if so, just how they should be timed. Is their precise length important down to a fraction of a second or is it sufficient to note that they are long or short in terms of how the listener is likely to perceive them. Is the absence of talk to be treated differently from what is a notable silence in the conversation? That is, silence may have various meanings. Who decides on the significance of pauses and silences?

- Should physical gestures which accompany words be included if they have been recorded on the video, say?

- Just how should a page of transcript be laid out? Often it is done like a script for a play but then overlapping utterances may need to be identified.

- How should the speakers be identified? Giving a name is indicative of gender, giving a category such as parent and child suggests that these roles may be the important way of understanding what is happening in the transcript.

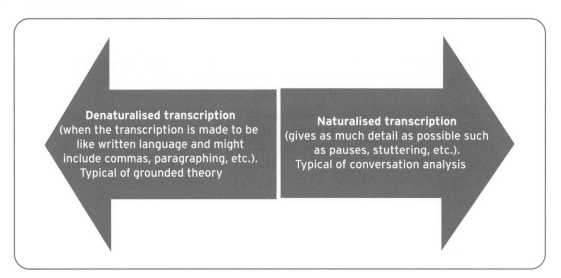

FIGURE 6.1 The naturalised-denaturalised dimension in transcription

- When selecting parts of transcripts for inclusion in a research report what aspects should be chosen? Should the interviewer's question be given? Should the transcript in the report follow exactly the style of the researcher's transcript or should it be tailored especially for the report?

So the general assumption across qualitative research is that 'Transcripts are produced for particular analytic purposes' (Nikander, 2008, p. 225). In other words, the purpose of the analysis determines how the transcript is carried out. Alongside this goes the idea that transcripts do not have to be 'perfect' to be useful. Indeed, it is difficult to define perfection in this context. Qualitative researchers are aware of the limitations of the transcription methods that they use. They frequently note that their recordings and transcripts are valuable and in-depth representations of the thing they are studying – they are not that thing.

Bucholtz (2000) argues that transcription can be seen as a continuum. The extremes represent what she calls naturalised versus denaturalised transcription (Figure 6.1). These are the main types of transcription but transcripts may be anywhere on the dimension between these two extremes:

- Naturalism describes transcripts in which every nuance is captured if possible – detail is important in these transcripts.
- Denaturalism describes transcripts where, for example, grammar is corrected and 'noise' such as stuttering, pausing and accents are eliminated. That is, idiosyncratic elements are not included.

For some types of qualitative research, the choice is already made by convention. Conversation analysis uses naturalistic transcripts of the sort developed by Jefferson. But there are decisions to be made for other forms of qualitative analysis. Oliver, Serovich and Mason (2005) suggest that the researcher should reflect on the needs of their research and make decisions in keeping with these. Transcription decisions have an important bearing and an impact on the outcomes of the research. This is not only in terms of what can be achieved – conversation analysis without naturalistic transcripts just would not work; on the other hand, thematic analysis, grounded theory and critical discourse analysis could be effective using denaturalised transcripts. The transcription decisions can also have a bearing on how the participants in the research are perceived and understood by anyone reading the research. If the transcript includes vernacular speech full of pauses then this may say something about the participant involved. Some have suggested that there should be a naturalised and a denaturalised version of the transcript. The latter might be particularly useful for 'member checking' – having the transcript checked by members of the group involved.

This partly explains why transcription is seen as 'a powerful act of representation' (Oliver et al., 2005, p. 1273). If you like, the transcription is constructed by the researcher. This reflects a highly influential argument made three decades ago by Ochs (1979). She basically claimed that transcription can be regarded as a selective process which involves the theoretical goals and conceptualisations of the researcher/ transcriber. By way of illustrating one aspect of what Ochs argued, the qualitative research literature reveals many definitions of the term transcription which fit with the primary theoretical concerns of the research tradition in question. Conversation analysts tend to define it as situated practice whereas the linguistic anthropology sees transcription as a cultural practice – which makes transcripts 'artefacts', demonstrating time and historical aspects. So transcription is held to reflect theory as well as helping formulate the nature of the theory. Hammersley (2010) suggests, however, the need for a middle ground since the idea that transcripts are constructed can be taken too far. The question, according to Hammersley, is whether the transcript more or less adequately reflects what was going on at the time of recording. He suggests that it is a slippery slope from the assumption that a transcript is constructed to the idea that the data are purely the creation of the transcriber.

It is imperative for researchers to think about their transcription needs before beginning the transcription process. The researcher's task is to optimise their transcription procedure in light of what they want their research to address. To give a simple example, what is suitable for transcribing an audio recording may not be suitable for transcribing a video. For instance, Norris (2002) suggests that her system for transcribing videos places the emphasis on action rather than on language as audio transcription methods do. Furthermore, transcriptions of interviews, place fewer demands on the transcription system than would transcriptions of classroom interactions with many participants.

As students will recognise, transcription is a 'behind the scenes' activity which is very often not discussed in research publications. That is to say, although not a closely guarded secret, transcription processes are not always apparent in the qualitative research literature. Although it is wrong to suggest that authors ignore issues to do with transcription, they could do more to explicate their decisions and processes in relation to it. The consequence is that students are sometimes confused about transcription – they aim too high and assume that a transcript has to be perfect to be useful. However, no criteria of perfection are available. As a result, students may feel inadequate or skill-less when they have choices to make or difficulties in the process of transcription. Unknown to them, their discomfort may well be shared by highly skilled researchers faced with the same recording. No two researchers will transcribe the same data to produce absolutely identical versions.

O'Connell and Kowal (1995) carried out a systematic evaluation of a variety of different transcription methods including that of Jefferson. All of the methods did a good job of simply recording the actual words said. Where they differed was in the other aspects of speech which were captured. Some transcription systems were good at indicating paralinguistic features (such as when words are accompanied by laughter, sighs or even groans – the Jefferson system does this to some extent), others were good at including prosodic features such as how loud or soft some words were and which parts of words were emphasised (the Jefferson system is also a good example of this), and others were good at recording extra-linguistic features such as accompanying facial expressions or hand gestures (the Jefferson system is poor at this). No single system was good at doing all of these things. Ultimately, in O'Connell and Kowal's (1995) phrase, there is no sense in which a transcription can be regarded as 'a genuine photograph of the spoken word' (p. 105).

In much the same vein, Coates and Thornborrow argue that there is no such thing:

> as the perfect transcript, the 'true' version of a recording (audio or video) of spoken interaction. A transcript of the speech recorded on audio- or videotape is always a partial affair. Different researchers focus on different aspects of language: a phonetician will make a fine-grained phonetic transcript; a linguist interested in collaborative talk will use a stave to capture the interaction of different voices; a narrative analyst may transcribe stories in 'idea units'. . . the decision about how to transcribe is always a theoretical one. In other words, the same chunk of data can be transcribed in many different ways: each method of transcription will represent the data in a particular way and will illuminate certain features of talk but will almost certainly obscure others. (Coates & Thornborrow, 1999, pp. 595–596)

So it has to be recognised that the notion of complete fidelity between a recorded source and a transcript is unrealistic and misleading. But even more mundane considerations come into play. Nikander suggests that:

> Practical compromises are typically made between the ideals of faithfulness to the original, the readability and accessibility of the final transcript, as well as time and space issues. (Nikander, 2008, p. 226)

Such compromises are a matter of judgement which will be easier for the seasoned qualitative researcher than the newcomer to qualitative research.

Ashmore and Reed (2000) systematically address the issue of the differences between, among other things, the event which occurred, the recording of the event, and the transcription of the event. Each of these is different in substantial ways. One of the crucial things they point out is that transcriptions of different recordings of otherwise exactly the same event can differ. That is, a recording with the microphone nearer the first speaker produces a different transcript from a recording made with the microphone nearer another speaker. This is not a matter of transcriber errors but reflects that different things can be heard at different locations. So even the recording is something of a reconstruction imposed on the original event just as the transcription is a reconstruction built on the recording.

Issues in transcription

Just as interviewers in an interview, the transcriber is an actor positioned socially and culturally in relation to the participants in the research. It is important to make this relationship clear in qualitative research. The reasons for this can be illustrated by a study by Witcher (2010). His research was based on semi-structured interviews with older Canadians living in rural parts. Witcher observed that he positions himself as a 'relative insider' since he had been brought up in that same community – participants in his research included members of his own extended family. He was no longer a complete insider because of his relatively youthful age and his status as an academic living outside the community.

The insider–outsider dimension is an important one in qualitative research and should be reflected upon by the researcher. It has a bearing on the process of transcription. Transcriptions of unfamiliar dialects full of colloquialisms are common in qualitative research and present their own difficulties (MacLean, Meyer, & Estable, 2004). So, for example, inaccuracies occur in transcriptions because of the difference between what the participants intend to communicate and the meaning that researchers incorporate in the transcript. For example, there are words which can easily be misrepresented or misinterpreted because they are not used as they would be in standard English. Take the following: 'We couldn't get out fishin, we were waitin to see (pause) they go out in the store, and they (pause) you know, make little things' (Witcher, 2010, p. 127). In this, the store is a building or room where supplies and equipment were stored – not a shop. As a relative insider, Witcher knew the dialect and the meaning of unique words such as this. In other words, the distinction between the emic (insider) perspective and the etic (outsider) perspective. Oliver et al. (2005) put it a different way – that transcribers can be naïve about the language they are transcribing. They provide the example of a prisoner who claimed that among his repertoire of sexual activities was 'tossin' the salad'. This phrase was meaningless to the transcriber who was somewhat thrown by the phrase. In this case, its meaning became clear later in the interview. It was prison slang for oral–anal contact. An interviewer may ask for clarification, of course, but not all qualitative data consist of interviews so the meaning of such phrases may never become clear.

The transcriber can also create problems of meaning for whoever reads the transcript or excerpts from it. The following from Oliver et al. (2005) is a good example of this. On the recording the interviewee is sniffling and the transcriber marks the transcript with (sniffs). Just what should the reader of the transcript interpret this to mean? Is the interviewee crying, have they got a runny nose, or are they on drugs?

What sort of transcription is appropriate, then, depends on the researcher's objectives for the research. This decision requires a reflective pause as no form of transcription automatically deals with every possibility. You need to ask yourself carefully what you are asking of your research and how this will be realised by your methodology. What is the best method of transcription to address your needs? Colloquial English may be recorded as such but this might offend any participant who reads the transcript as it can appear quite insensitive. Some researchers use participants to validate the transcript, which increases this risk. A more denaturalised approach, however, being somewhat tidied up might lose valuable data. Quite different but nevertheless important is that naturalistic transcripts may influence the research team since Oliver et al. (2005) found that assumptions were made about the educational level of African American speakers in these.

Another problem is mispronounced words. One example is the participant who said that he practised 'annual' sex. This, the researchers took to mean anal sex, but should it or should it not be recorded as annual in the transcript? This might risk embarrassing or offending the participant should they read the transcript. It is sometimes the practice to use 'member checking' in which members of the group involved read the denaturalised version to see if it has lost any meaning from the original recording and the naturalised version of the transcript. This has clear advantages but, at the same time, offers these very opportunities to cause embarrassment or offence.

Again, should one include involuntary vocalisations such as burping, sniffing and coughing? If there is a lot of laughter then how should this be understood? What if the laughter was nervous laughter – this would change the meaning given to it. The interviewer might know but not necessarily the transcriber.

The way in which the transcription is recorded on the page can affect its impact (Nikander, 2008). Much of the transcription carried out by psychologists uses the drama type of organisation in which the contributions of speakers are organised in rows.

However, it is perfectly possible to use columns for some forms of transcription whereby each speaker is allotted a separate column. Some claim that the column layout helps to identify patterns of asymmetry in terms of the contributions of different speakers.

Increasingly, qualitative research operates in an international context both in terms of carrying out the research and, especially, disseminating the product of research. This, inevitably, involves translation in some cases. Berman's (2011) article critiques positivist models of translation in relation to feminist and community-based research. She argues that translators and interpreters ought to be considered to be co-researchers rather than as a problematic mechanical aspect of research. Back translation is recommended in the positivist model (translating from language A to language B and then translating translation B back to language A to see whether the two versions of A are the same). The task of the researcher is to eliminate errors. Others have called for translators to be seen as active producers of knowledge. So the researcher needs to know a lot about their translator's background and competencies. They are often mediators between the researcher and the participants in the research study. The translator should be present throughout each step of the research, Berman argues.

It is important to stress that transcription methods vary substantially in qualitative research. The method of transcription employed by a researcher is not an arbitrary matter but should be based on a consideration of the nature of the research and what the researcher hopes to learn about. This is not to suggest that a researcher needs to develop a new transcription method for every new study. That would be pointless and futile. It is always sensible to look at the methods employed by researchers doing similar work to oneself. In psychology, the Jefferson transcription method is quite often used by researchers interested in constructionist discourse analysis and conversation analysis. It would be rarely, if ever, used by researchers using thematic analysis, grounded theory, narrative analysis based on narrative theory, or interpretive phenomenological analysis. But it is the best documented approach to transcription and makes a good starting point to introduce the practicalities of transcription.

The Jefferson approach to transcription

Despite its initially appearing somewhat daunting, the Jefferson transcription system uses many symbols and conventions which make intuitive sense. For example, the use of underlining in this system denotes emphasis and capitals are used to indicate that some words are being said LOUDLY. There is nothing complicated in any of this – the difficulty is more to do with the number of conventions in the Jefferson system rather than any of the individual elements, each of which is simple in itself. Furthermore, the Jefferson transcription system is built up, almost exclusively, from characters universally available on standard computer and typewriter keyboards. This means that Jefferson transcription is readily implemented by any researcher prepared to spend some time learning its basics. Of course, the keystrokes used in the Jefferson system do not have the same meaning as they would normally. Actually, it would be more correct to say that some symbols have both their normal and an additional meaning in the Jefferson system. Thus capital letters have their conventional meaning but, as we have already mentioned, words in capitals are spoken louder than the other words around them. The use of (brackets) is indicative of a word not identified with complete certainty from the recording. Overall, these additional keystroke symbols basically tell the reader how the words in the transcript are actually being said. The Jefferson system includes methods of indicating pitch, speech volume, speech speed, emphasis within words, pauses or their lack of, overlapping speaking, laughter and other non-words, and extra information from the transcriber. The main Jefferson conventions are given in Table 6.1. Refer back to this table whenever necessary to understand what is happening in a transcript. You may also spot that there are slight differences between transcribers on certain matters of detail. The Jefferson system evolved gradually and will probably continue to do so. Not surprisingly then, new symbols were added at different stages in the development of this method of transcription. In addition, sometimes transcription symbols were replaced by others. This occasionally adds some-what to the problems involved in using Jefferson transcriptions. In particular, it may be

TABLE 6.1 The Jefferson transcription system (as described in Jefferson, 2004)

Jefferson symbol	Example	Usage
Pitch indicators		
↑	absol↑utely	Pitch rise symbol. Bearing in mind that there are continuous variations in the pitch of speech, ↑ indicates that the following has an 'unexpectedly' markedly higher pitch than the previous speech. Multiple arrows may be used to indicate greater extents of this.
↓	Absolutel↓y	Again considering the normal variations in the pitch of speech, ↓ indicates that the following is spoken at a markedly lower pitch than the previous speech.
*	I'm sor*ry	What follows the asterisk is spoken in a squeaky or creaky voice.
.	sure.	The word before is spoken with a falling intonation possibly indicative of stopping though it does not have to be followed by a pause.
Speech volume indicators		
CAPITALS	for GOODNESS sake	CAPITALS mark speech that is noticeably spoken at a louder volume than the speech around it. This is assessed in terms of that speaker's general volume. It is incorrect to put a loud speaker's talk in capitals throughout.
underlining	For goodness sake	This indicates speech spoken louder than the surrounding text though underlining does not indicate things are quite so loud as the use of capitals does.
º º	And when I discovered that she had °died°	The superscript ° or degree sign is used to mark the start and end of noticeably quieter speech.
Speech speed indicators		
›‹	Then I said›we'd better hurry home‹	The speech between these signs is faster than surrounding speech.
‹›	On reflection, I think things are ‹best left alone›	The speech between these signs is slower than surrounding words.
Emphasis indicators within words		
:	de::licious	The colons show the elongation of the previous sound. Multiple colons can be used to indicate the extent of the elongation.
?	right?	The? indicates that there is a questioning (rising) tone whether or not the speaker is grammatically asking a question.
underlining	kerumbs	The use of underlining shows emphasis made in a word. It indicates both where the emphasis is and the strength of the emphasis. The emphasis can be in pitch or loudness.

TABLE 6.1 (*continued*)

Jefferson symbol	Example	Usage
Pauses or lack of		
(0.1)	Let me think (3.1) no I don't remember	The numbers enclosed by round brackets (3.1) indicate the length of a pause in speech expressed in tenths of a second. So (3.1) indicates a pause of three and three-tenths of a second. This is a long pause and they are more typically 0.3, 0.5 and so forth. If they are clearly a part of a particular speaker's speaking then they are included in their speech. If they do not involve a particular speaker then they are put on another line of transcript. A new line is used where there is any uncertainty about this.
(.)	I was thinking (.) would you like a break	The stop in brackets (.) can be described as a micropause which is apparent but too brief to measure precisely.
-	r-r-really	The preceding sound is cut off by the hyphen.
[]	I [think the] job [No if you]	The square brackets [] show where one section of talk is immediately followed by successive talk with no interval between. It can happen when the speaker changes but also within the talk of a single individual.
Overlapping speaking		
==	I =think the=job =No if you =	Sometimes equals = signs are used instead of square brackets to indicate the same thing.*
Laughter and other non-words		
hhh	hhh I'm sorry that it has come to this	The h indicates an audible breathing out – several can be used to indicate its length.
.hhh	so to recapitulate.hhh the committee has voted against	The .h indicates audible breathing in. The h gives an indication of the length of the breath.
heh heh	heh heh HEH	This is voiced laughter much as in ha ha ha. Since it is equivalent to a word one can add other symbols.
h	Do(h)n't tick(h)le m(h)e	The (h) indicates that laughter is occurring within speech.
Extra information from the researcher		
((note))	((Clare speaks in a mock Scottish accent))	Double round brackets enclose comments made by the transcriber which indicate things such as the characteristics of the delivery or something to do with the context of the speech, for example.
()	the treasure is buried under the () and it is all mine	Round brackets with just space inside indicate that something has been said which the transcriber cannot recognise. The amount of space indicates the approximate length of the 'missing' word.
(word)	she had a (bunion) operation	Round brackets with a word inside mean that the subscriber is not absolutely certain what word has been said but believes that it is the word in brackets.
(word)/(word)	(nights)/(likes)	Indicates two equally possible hearings of what was said
→	John: →	The use of the side arrow indicates that a particular line of transcript is of special importance in terms of the analytic points being made by the analyst.
Gaze (for video transcription)		
_____	62 _____ ...... 62 if you would just	Some transcribers use an unbroken line to indicate that a person is gazing directly at another person while speaking and then a dotted line to indicate the gaze has broken. Essentially it involves adding an extra line (with the same number as the text) to indicate gaze.

*See the text of this chapter for details of how overlaps appear in transcriptions.

a problem when it comes to studying research which used slightly earlier versions of the Jefferson transcription method. Hutchby and Wooffitt (1998) also go into more detail about Jefferson transcription.

Reading a Jefferson transcription is not too difficult, especially if you use Table 6.1 to check the meaning of the transcription symbols. For illustration, consider the following study of neighbour dispute mediation. The transcript is of a section of a recording of a meeting between two couples and a dispute mediator. The couples are Graham and Louise (G and L) and Bob and Ellen (B and E). Bob does not appear in this segment of transcript. In case you have any difficulties, you can find an annotated version of the transcript later. This contains examples of each of the different features in the transcript. The transcript is not as complex as some and it does not include every transcription notation symbol but it makes a very clear starting point.

```
 1G:    y'know it's getting – it's getting real serious this is (.) ↑but the
 2      lad keeps getting away with it (.) unfortunately (.) his mother hasn't
 3      got a bloke there (.) so she is talking in [front of the children
 4L:                                              [she's not living there half
 5      the time is she=
 6G:    =no she's out at night and they are using it as a- a rendezvous for the
 7      gang
[…]
 8G:    that's the whole top [and bottom of it
 9L:                         [it's like the dustbin left out for a week (?) on
10     [the pavement
11G:   [IT'S ALL TO DO with this one lad (.) right (.) we've had report- we've
12     got connections at the school (.) they said 'what's the point of him
13     coming to school he knows nothing (.) he only causes trouble' (0.5) so
14     [they never bothered about him
15L:   [it's like they've had words with this woman and can't get through to
16     her from school you know [course (.) he's left now so
17G:                            [(?)
[…]
18G:   (?) °no no° I mean the funny thing about this is that (.) in actual
19     fact (.) I mean the lady's got to be responsible (.) she's got to
20     be responsible [at the end of the day because [she's never there [she
21E:                   [well she's never there is she
22L:                                                  [() she's effing and
23G:   can't control him
24E:   yeah
```
(from Stokoe, 2003, p. 326)

It is important to understand the intellectual origins of Jefferson's approach to transcription. In terms of research, her focus was on the fine detail of interaction between people. In particular, she was not so much interested in the broad patterns of conversation but on the ways that aspects of conversation are shaped in a continuous fashion by what has happened earlier in the conversation. In other words, speech is endlessly contingent on itself. Just as a flavour, on one famous occasion the then British Prime Minister, Gordon Brown, performed a slip of the tongue in which instead of saying that he 'saved the banks' he actually came out with the words 'saved the world' when answering questions in Parliament. Of course, one way of looking at this is to suggest that it was a Freudian slip which revealed truly what the Prime Minister was thinking. However, Atkinson (2008) was reminded of Gail Jefferson's (1996) paper 'On the poetics of ordinary talk' in which she discusses how the choice of a wrong word was the consequence of the words which immediately preceded it. So Atkinson checked what the Prime Minister had actually said:

> GORDON BROWN: 'The first point of recapitalisation was to save banks that would otherwise have collapsed and we've not only saved the world – erh – saved the banks.'

Notice that the extract contains a sequence of 'w' sounds – was, would, otherwise and we've. Thus Gordon Brown's error can be seen as an unfortunate recapitulation of the 'w' sound rather than any manifestation of his personal psychology. Jefferson was adamant that such speech-induced errors are not the consequence of hidden psychological motivations as is the case with Freudian slips.

Potter (2003) makes the point of Jefferson transcription clear using the following excerpt from a telephone call inviting someone over (Davidson, 1984, p. 105):

> A: C'mon down he:re, = it's oka:y,
>
>   (0.2 sec)
>
> A: got lotta stuff, = I got be:er en stuff

Potter writes:

> Note the way the speaker upgrades the invitation. Why might this be? The likely reason is that the pause of 0.2 of a second is a cue to an impending refusal. Conversational actions such as invitation refusals are typically prefaced by some delay, and research has shown that speakers modify their actions on the basis of such predictions . . . (Potter, 2003, p. 82)

In other words, without the indication of a delay the interpretation of this short snippet is less clear. The situation would not be rectified by later refusals or acceptances from the other person since the upgraded invitation may or may not be effective.

Remarkably, there appear to be no 'rules' governing the orthographic/secretarial/playscript approaches to transcription. Just what should go into the transcript and just what can be left out? For example, does the transcriber identify things which cannot be heard clearly or do they insert their best attempt, when is it appropriate to transcribe the accent of the speaker, and what does one do about overlaps in speaking? For this reason, it would be appropriate to use Jefferson transcription conventions about these basic matters even when the additional linguistic codings which Jefferson transcription adds are not used.

What the transcription symbols mean

Graham is the speaker for the first three lines

There is a brief, unmeasured, pause in the speech

Graham says 'but' at a markedly higher pitch

Graham and Louise are speaking together

Graham takes over conversation from Louise without pause

Graham talks loudly

A pause timed at half a second

Transcriber cannot hear

Some text omitted

no no is spoken noticeably quietly

Ellen begins talking at the same time as Graham then Louise overlaps with Graham

```
1 G:   y'know it's getting – it's getting real serious this is (.) ↑but the
2      lad keeps getting away with it (.) unfortunately (.) his mother hasn't
3      got a bloke there (.) so she is talking in [front of the children
4 L:                                             [she's not living there half
5      the time is she=
6 G:   =no she's out at night and they are using it as a- a rendezvous for
       the
7      gang [...]
8 G:   that's the whole top [and bottom of it
9 L:                        [it's like the dustbin left out for a week (?) on
10     [the pavement
11:    [IT'S ALL TO DO with this one lad (.) right (.) we've had report- we've
12     got connections at the school (.) they said 'what's the point of him
13     coming to school he knows nothing (.) he only causes trouble' (0.5) so
14     [they never bothered about him
15 L:  [it's like they've had words with this woman and can't get through to
16     her from school you know [course (.) he's left now so
17 G:                          [(?)
[...]
18 G:  (?) °no no° I mean the funny thing about this is that (.) in actual
19     fact (.) I mean the lady's got to be responsible (.) she's got to
20     be responsible [at the end of the day because [she's never there [she
21 E:                 [well she's never there is she
22 L:                                                [( ) she's effing and
23 G:  can't control him
24 E:  yeah
```

The development of transcription

Just who the first person was to instigate an orthographic/secretarial/playscript transcription of social scientific data is unknown. Perhaps it is not such a big step from having a typist transcribe from the boss's dictation recording to having another typist transcribe research interviews and other data. Phonetic transcriptions of language began in the twentieth century with systems such as the *International Phonetic Alphabet.*

Gail Jefferson (1938–2008) has been an influential figure in many disciplines including sociology and anthropology – and more recently psychology. The questions which guided her research cross the boundaries of different disciplines. Fortune led her to conversation analysis (Chapter 10) as it was being developed by Harvey Sacks (1935–1975). She took one of his courses to complete a requirement of the degree in dancing that she was taking. It so happened that Jefferson had previous experience of doing orthographic/secretarial/playscript transcriptions from when she had been a typist. Jefferson began transcribing some of the lectures by Sacks that had been recorded. Sacks was not the most prolific of writers and Jefferson's transcriptions of his recorded lectures are an important part of his legacy (e.g. Sacks, 1992). Eventually Jefferson began her PhD under the supervision of Sacks. It was at this time that her methods of tracing the really fine detail of interaction began to develop and evolve. Her method was an attempt to combine both a precise record of what was said with the way in which it was said. As a consequence, rather than simply note that the speaker laughs she tried to indicate more of the detail of how that person's laughter was combined into the speech. Jefferson's is not the only language transcription system, of course. One which competes in many respects was developed by the linguist John Du Bois (Du Bois, Schuetze-Coburn, Cumming, & Paolino, 1993). This does much the same as the Jefferson system. Indeed his system shares a lot of notation conventions with the Jefferson system but differs in detail. But there are others, such as HIAT or heuristic interpretative auditory transcriptions (Ehlich, 1993), John Gumperz's transcription notation (Gumperz & Berenz, 1993) and CHAT (codes for the human analysis of transcripts) (MacWhinney, 1995). These seldom, if ever, appear in qualitative psychology.

As in so many areas of research, the advent of the personal computer has eased the task of transcribing interactions considerably. The Jefferson system, for example, involves the transcription of silences, gaps and pauses in speech fairly accurately. Computer programs such as Audacity and Adobe Audition (formerly Cool Edit) allow the transcriber to assess these with a greater degree of accuracy by allowing the measurements to be made against a wave trace of the sounds. See the Additional Resources at the end of this chapter for more details.

Transcription in the future may be affected by the availability of digital voice recognition software. If a computer can turn digital recordings into words then this might facilitate the making of the verbatim transcription. There is software that can do this, though it is not readily available. However, the big problem is that the software needs to be able to distinguish between two or more speakers given the nature of much qualitative data. Matheson (2008) discusses her system for doing so and the general problems of voice recognition software in qualitative research. Of course, this is a long way away from software that can transcribe using the Jefferson system. The advantages of using software to turn a recording into text may not be as great as might first appear. Johnson (2011) studied the speed and accuracy of software-assisted transcription and compared these with the 'traditional' listen-and-type method. He transcribed an interview twice, firstly using voice recognition software and secondly using traditional listen-and-type methods with a week's delay between the two. The computer method employed was to listen to the recording through headphones and repeat what was said directly into the computer's microphone. This was because the voice recognition software available could not cope with the original recording. It took 14 per cent more time to transcribe the interview using voice recognition software. Furthermore, there were more errors using this method than using the traditional approach. This meant that the voice recognition version of the transcript required more checking. Some parts of the transcript produced using the computer voice recognition software were nonsense since the program recognised the word 'drainage' as train itch and 'mosquitoes' as business vetoes puke.

Gail Jefferson's story is closely connected to conversation analysis and much more detail about the background to this can be found in Chapter 10.

How to do Jefferson transcription

Jefferson transcription was initially developed using manual typewriters before technological advances in the form of computers made transcription much easier (Potter, 2004). This is important since anywhere from 10 to 24 hours of work may be required to transcribe 1 hour of recording. (The figure varies according to who is making the estimate.) It also means that one should be careful to match one's transcription needs to the purpose for which the data are being transcribed. Thus the essential and central assumption is that the choice of transcription method should match the needs of your particular analysis. This is no time to routinely devote so much labour to an unnecessary task. For example, you may decide that Jefferson transcription suits your purposes because of its fine-grained perspective on language data but feel that the bulk of what is on the recording is irrelevant for your purposes. So long as you have a basic set of principles to help you determine what is relevant and what is irrelevant and these principles are consistently applied then there is nothing against such a partial analysis. Almost certainly, the use of the Jefferson transcription system is *de rigueur* for conversation analysis, though researchers have questioned its ubiquity in other forms of qualitative research including discourse analysis.

Given that there are so many different varieties of qualitative research, a one-size-fits-all approach to transcription may not be adequate. One suggestion is that novices use the Jefferson system in order to establish whether or not it works for their style of analysis. There is little point in using the elaborate system if just a transcript of the words said would suffice. One might initially be guided by the approach taken by other researchers who study in areas similar to yours. They, after all, may have had more experience in the use of transcription and probably have a more considered approach to what is essential for this particular type of research. The researcher who is interested in the processes which occur in conversation may well need an elaborate transcription procedure than a researcher who is more interested in the substance of what is said rather than how it is said. For the researcher interested in conversation, the literal words used may be inadequate for understanding the processes of conversation. A researcher who is interested in regional accents in conversation may find both the literal transcription and the Jefferson transcription inadequate because neither adequately deals with this aspect of how words sound. Phonetic transcription would be more appropriate in this case though this is virtually unknown in psychological research. A transcription method needs to be carefully considered to see whether what it does will meet the purposes of your research (Potter, 1997).

Irrespective of the transcription method chosen, there are some basic principles which constitute valuable advice for those planning the transcription of spoken language (O'Connell & Kowal, 1995):

- *The principle of parsimony* This suggests that a researcher should not transcribe features of speech which are not intended to be part of the analysis. In other words, only do in transcription that which will be helpful.

- *Keep transcriptions in reports as simple as possible* This means that transcriptions provided in reports of your research should only include features which are important in making your analysis intelligible to the reader. Thus, a Jefferson transcript may not be appropriate even though it has been carried out by the researcher.

- *Avoid creating a spurious impression of accuracy in your report* O'Connell and Kowal (1995) found that transcribers working on radio interviews actually ignored the vast majority of short pauses when transcribing the interviews. About a fifth of short pauses were included but the basis for their inclusion was not at all clear. Similarly, if the researcher assesses the lengths of pauses subjectively then it is misleading to use the convention (0.9) which implies a greater degree of accuracy in measurement than was the case. This does not apply to all research, of course, and computer-assisted methods employed by transcribers may increase the accuracy of such judgements.

- *Checking transcriptions* One would not expect transcriptions to be error-free and transcriber errors are common. Things such as verbal omissions and additions, translocations and word substitutions may all occur in transcriptions. Consequently there is a case for using an independent checker to look for such errors.

Like most aspects of research methods, transcription is best learnt if one has a basic understanding of how it is used and presented in research publications. So general reading of qualitative papers featuring transcription is recommended as a preliminary stage before beginning transcription yourself. You have already had the opportunity of using the neighbour disputes transcript presented earlier. But transcripts can be rather more detailed than that one, especially where the transcript contains a lot of laughter or where the speaker breaks up a lot of words as they speak. By reading papers using transcription you will encounter the work of different transcribers, which can look extremely complicated at first. Experience with a variety of transcripts will help you better understand what is expected. When reading transcripts, pay attention to (a) understanding what has been said and (b) understanding how it is said. Right from the start, you will probably find that parts of many transcriptions are meaningful since some of the transcription symbols are, to a degree, self-evident: for example, capital letters for loudly spoken words, up and down arrows for rising or falling pitch respectively, a? for a questioning tone, and so forth. In context, you might be able to have a stab at some of the less obvious conventions such as how to indicate a quietly spoken passage. You can check the main conventions by consulting Table 6.1 which lists the Jefferson transcription methods, explains them and provides illustrations. They have been organised into different aspects of spoken language for convenience. Of course, to begin with you will consult this table regularly but gradually it will become second nature to use the notation method.

It is not recommended that you attempt any major transcription of data until you have practised on a manageable segment of your recording and begun to gain

TABLE 6.2 Steps in transcription

Step 1: tuning into the recorded interaction	Step 2: rough transcription	Step 3: adding Jefferson symbols and transcribing sequencing accurately
Listen to the recording several times	Names of speakers for each segment of conversation	Add the fine detail of the transcription symbols taking special care with overlaps, etc.
Decide whether all of the material needs transcribing	The words said written down as pronounced typically	Make sure that the transcription is in its clearest form for readers
If not, decide what parts need to be transcribed	Put any non-transcribable features in brackets, e.g. ((gun fired))	
	Only use continuous capitals for loud passages and nowhere else	
	Indicate pauses, etc. for later more precise measurement	

confidence. Of course, you will also have queries which you may need to resolve by checking Table 6.1 for details of the Jefferson system or by consulting with people more experienced in transcription than yourself if necessary. There are a number of websites which help with learning transcription, some of which provide recordings to transcribe.

The following are the main stages in carrying out a Jefferson transcription, based on the approaches of Atkinson and Heritage (1984), Gumperz and Berenz (1993), Langford (1994) and Roberts (2007). The procedures described are not absolutely fixed and eventually you will develop your own working methods. However, the following may be reassuring to a novice transcriber (see also Table 6.2).

Step 1 Tuning into the recorded interaction Transcription is a focused activity rather than a completely routine process. For this reason, you need to listen a number of times to the recorded interaction that you are to transcribe. By listening to the recording repeatedly you should be able to reach the following decisions:

- Am I going to transcribe all of the recording? While this seems to be an obvious choice to make, it does have its consequences. In particular, transcription takes a considerable amount of time, effort and similar resources. Consequently, complete transcription risks being a little rough or inaccurate. If a section of the recording is unlikely to be analysed then what is the point in straining resources by transcribing it?

- If not, what aspects of the recording am I going to transcribe? In this case you need to have a means of identifying the parts of the recordings you will transcribe. So, for example, you may be studying how children of migrants construe their national identity. In this case, you are looking for material on the recording which refers to this topic. The boundaries may be determined, for example, by a relevant question from an interviewer or a focus group leader. But content is not the only possible criterion. For example, the researcher may be interested in how adult family members bring children into family conversations, in which case, the boundaries will be around the entry of a child into the family conversation. Boundaries may sometimes be very clear but sometimes not so.

The segment of recording should be listened to several times in order to reach a general understanding of what is going on in that sequence of interaction. Effort should be made to identify each of the speakers. This may not be easy, especially in circumstances in which the transcriber was not the data collector. Also, the number of overlapping sequences has a considerable bearing on speaker identification. This process can be difficult so it should be carried out independently of or separately from capturing the words said and the way they are said. This is also where the value of a stereo-recording becomes most self-evident.

Step 2   **Rough transcription** Take a look at Box 6.1 which gives some advice on how a transcription should be laid out and also at the transcription provided earlier. The important thing to remember is that these are guides as to style and that some things are probably better left until last. Inserting line numbers is one such late job to be done. This is because the precise layout of a transcription is a matter of judgement, not simply the application of rules. Line length in transcription is affected by the need to be able to insert overlapping speech clearly. This may involve trial-and-error until the ideal is achieved. Although in some transcription systems the line number refers to an individual speaker's turn, in Jefferson transcription the line lengths are arbitrary. As a rule they are kept to a moderate number of words. One way of doing this is to use the natural groupings that occur in speech such as the words which are said before a breath is taken or the words which amount to one or two specific information inputs into the interaction. But, clearly, there is room for variation in terms

Box 6.1

PRACTICAL ADVICE
How to lay out a transcription

According to Potter and Hepburn (2009), the following is the best way of laying out a Jefferson transcription:

- *Font* It is important to use a proportional font otherwise the spacing of overlapping conversation, for example, is very difficult. Their recommended font is Courier in 10pt size.

- *Line numbers* Each line of a Jefferson transcription includes a line number. Although these can be typed in manually, they can also be inserted automatically by Word. The important steps are (a) end each line of transcript by pressing the Enter key to force a line break; (b) select all of the lines which you want numbered using your mouse; and (c) you will find numbering in the options for paragraphing. Remember that line lengths are arbitrary so you can force line breaks where you feel that it is convenient. The line numbering convention helps you identify an excerpt from a transcript since the line numbers will be part way through the

sequence. The line numbering is fairly arbitrary and the same recording transcribed by a different researcher may have lines of different length and perhaps more or fewer lines for the same amount of the original recording. This arbitrariness is important in that it gives the flexibility needed to be able to indicate overlapping speech.

- *Layout* (a) Use 25 mm (1 inch) margins at top, bottom, left and right of the page and (b) use a code number for the extract and ideally include some indicator of the source of the extract.

- *Speaker's/contributor's name* Have the speaker's/contributor's name in **bold** and try to clearly separate this from what they say with some space.

- *Blank space* Because you may wish to make notes on the transcript, it is important to include a copious amount of blank space to the right of the text. Judicious use of the Enter key will help you with that.

of how things appear on the transcript. This, normally, is of little or no consequence.

At the end of the rough transcription then the transcriber should have recorded the following:

- The names of the speakers for each turn in the conversation or interaction.
- All of the words spoken, usually attempting to use the word sounds as spoken by the speaker rather than how they would appear in standard English. For example, 'summat' for 'something' or 'yer' for 'you' or 'your'. But this is not an area where standardisation among transcribers is apparent. Of course, a great many features of accents can be represented reasonably accurately using conventional orthography (methods of writing down words). One could, also, use phonetic spelling systems but this requires a degree of sophistication on the part of the reader which may not be met. Alternatively, some transcribers use 'pseudo-phonetic' forms as used in comic books (e.g. b'cuz I luv ya). In the end, all of these things make a transcription more difficult to read and, as such, may not be desirable. On the other hand, there are circumstances where the precise pronunciation of words may be very important, for example, where a speaker mocks another speaker by speaking in an exaggerated version of their accent.
- Any non-transcribable features such as when the speaker coughs or clears their throat. These will be put in double brackets ((clears throat)).
- Remember that capitals are not used in Jefferson transcription other than for proper names which will start with a capital letter. Capitals are used in the system to indicate things spoken distinctly loudly.
- Points where there are any pauses. You will probably find it easier to mark these with brackets enclosing x's (e.g. (xx)) as an indication that the fine timing should be entered in the next phase.

It has to be remembered that this is the rough transcription phase and the rough transcription may not meet all of these criteria. This is not particularly important since the final phase of transcription provides plenty of opportunity to correct any inadequacies left over. Two important things to consider throughout this stage are issues concerning effective communications with the reader and how the transcript contributes to this.

Technology for transcription has improved rapidly since the era of the typewriter and the reel-to-reel magnetic tape recorder. Digital recording equipment (and video recorders) mean that digital files are readily available for computer processing. These, generally, are of a very high quality. Computer software is available which make for easy copying and editing of these files together with easy search facilities. Faces and voices may be disguised and names edited out of the recording for ethical reasons. According to Potter:

> The simplest way to transcribe is to work with two windows on a computer screen, one running the audio file, the other running the word processor. Audio programs are available that allow a stepwise movement through the file using a physical representation of the wave form that is ideal for timing pauses and noting overlaps. (Potter, 2003, p. 82)

Step 3   Adding Jefferson symbols and transcribing sequencing accurately This final stage is the one in which the transcript is finally transformed by adding the detailed Jefferson transcription symbols where they apply. Up to this point you have done most of the straightforward work, including adding some of the Jefferson notation. But that is not necessarily the fine detail or the best arrangement for the reader to understand. This stage concentrates on the detailed sequencing of the conversation and not merely the words said. These symbols are the square brackets to indicate overlapping or simultaneous utterances by two or more people. Examples are to be found in the Stokoe (2003) excerpt (on page 145) but they are so important in Jefferson transcription that they bear repeating. So look at the following, which uses square brackets []:

11 Gary:	where do you think that we ought to [go out tonight?]	
12 Sarah:		[is there anything] on the television?

Square brackets are used to show when Sarah and Gary are speaking together at the same time. Single brackets are used to indicate when two people start talking at the same time:

17 Sarah:	I wouldn't mind watching something
18 Gary:	[well
19 Sarah:	[like a documentary

Equals signs (=) are used to indicate latching, which is where another speaker takes over the conversation from another speaker without a pause:

28 Sarah:	you always want what you want on=
29 Gary:	=what m↑e?

Things can be more complex in conversation and more than one speaker can latch at the same time in which case square brackets ([) might be needed to indicate this. For example:

28 Sarah:	you always want what you want on=
29 Gary:	= [what m↑e?]
30 Shane:	= [too right]

Of course, there are other speech characteristics which could be included – those which indicate how individual words are said in the recording. These are common in Jefferson transcriptions and explained in Table 6.1. Refer to this for clarification whenever necessary but it can also serve as a memory aid to ensure that you have considered all of the different transcription possibilities. As with most things, experience is essential in order to ensure quality transcriptions which are useful both to the researcher but also to the reader.

Pauses in conversation are common. Largely in Jefferson transcription they are signalled using (.) or (0.5) to indicate different lengths of pause (see Table 6.1). However, look at the following:

38 Sarah:	you choose
39	(.)
40 Gary:	i'm not bothered
41	(.)
42 Sarah:	are you sulking?

In this exchange the pauses are not attributed to either Sarah or Gary since they are given a separate line. They are pauses in the conversation and *not* pauses in what either Sarah or Gary are saying individually. If the pause was clearly attributable to, say, Sarah, then it would appear in a line indicated as being said by Sarah.

Remember that there are limitations to any transcribing system and the features of speech that you wish to include are not part of the system. If you need to add additional transcription features, which may not be part of the Jefferson system, then this is a choice open to you. Of course, you need to carefully describe and explain any such additional coding.

Certain computer programs are often recommended to students to help them with the process of analysis. A complete novice to transcription may prefer to leave this aside until they have built up basic transcription skills. It also has to be said that many transcriptions are made without their benefits and that they are not adopted by all qualitative researchers. They do have various advantages such as enabling a degree of 'noise reduction' to improve the sound quality of the digital recording. They also permit other forms of editing of sound excerpts. Perhaps more importantly, they also display the waveforms of the sound in the recording. In this way it is possible to measure pauses in conversation very precisely and to note where sounds are exceptionally loud or exceptionally soft. The main programs to consider are Audacity and Adobe Audition. The former is a free download and the latter has a free trial download option. See the Additional Resources section at the end of this chapter for more details.

When to use Jefferson transcription

The decision to use Jefferson transcription rather than an orthographic, secretarial or playscript word-for-word record should be a serious consideration (Table 6.3). If the research takes a conversation analysis perspective then it would not be credible not to use the Jefferson transcription system – this is true also for some forms of discourse analysis. This might be expected because of the intimate association of Gail Jefferson's work with the development of conversation analysis. But not all researchers, by any means, are interested in the approach to conversation taken by Jefferson and her colleagues. Some qualitative researchers may be interested in other aspects of the contents of conversations, interviews and the like, not because they are interested in the way participants structure these things but because of what the participants in the conversations have to say about topics relevant to their research question. For example, if the researcher is interested in the

TABLE 6.3 When to use Jefferson transcription

Definitely use Jefferson transcription	Possibly use Jefferson transcription	No advantage in using Jefferson transcription so use orthographic transcription
• Conversation analysis	• Discourse analysis (especially Potter and Wetherell version)	• Narrative analysis
		• Interpretative phenomenological analysis
		• Thematic analysis
		• Grounded theory phenomenological analysis

life histories of sex offenders it is the substantive material about each offender's life history which can be found on the recording which is important to that researcher. Issues such as how the offender 'recovers' from errors made in telling his life history are not likely to be a particular interest of the researcher in this case. So it is questionable whether there would be any benefit to using Jefferson transcription in this instance. It is clear that there would be considerable resource costs accruing from choosing to do Jefferson transcriptions, the question is whether there would be any research gains from doing so. The resources spent on the Jefferson transcriptions could be used for other things.

It is mainly where speech is being researched as social action that Jefferson transcription comes into its own. Clearly, researchers employing conversation analysis and discourse analytic perspectives view research in these terms and it would benefit from the use of Jefferson transcription in many cases. This does not mean that such a researcher would *always* gain from using such a fine-grained transcription method as Jefferson's. There is, in research, always a question of the level of analysis which needs to be employed. For example, in general, it is very difficult to see the advantages of using Jefferson transcription when the likely sort of data analysis method to be employed is a thematic analysis. Such an analysis is based on developing relatively broad categories which describe the contents of interviews, focus groups and so forth. This does not require the fine-grained transcription method provided by Jefferson. A secretarial or playscript transcription will be almost certainly all that is required in these circumstances. Similarly, it should be noted that some analytic methods tend not to employ the Jefferson transcription system. For example, research in the interpretative phenomenological analysis tradition (see Chapter 13) typically does not use the Jefferson system. This is true also for narrative analysis (Chapter 14), grounded theory (Chapter 8) and thematic analysis (Chapter 7).

Given that transcriptions are often available for further analysis by other qualitative researchers, there is a case for fully transcribing the data using the Jefferson system. This is simply because the Jefferson transcription maximises the additional information accessible to the secondary analyst. Without it, the value of the transcript is reduced. It is also an argument against using 'stripped down' (less complex) versions of Jefferson transcription such as Jefferson 'Lite' which is recommended by some (e.g. Parker, 2005). But these are issues of some controversy in qualitative psychology for which no definitive answer is available.

Evaluation of Jefferson transcription

It needs to be remembered what the Jefferson system does. The words said are recorded in ways which suggest something of the way that they sound, though this does not amount to a fully phonetic rendition. So you will see some words written down as they sound in

TABLE 6.4 Advantages and disadvantages of the Jefferson transcription system

Advantages of Jefferson system	Problems with the Jefferson system
1. It records talk as experienced by participants in the conversation and so keeps the analysis focused on this rather than merely the words used.	1. While the Jefferson symbols can sometimes be used very precisely such as times in tenths of a second, other symbols such as : are less carefully defined.
2. Analysis of conversational interaction is facilitated by the system compared with a secretarial transcript.	2. It is restricted in terms of what aspects of interaction it deals with. For example, it is not good for coding emotion.
3. Even if the words are the focus of their analysis, it allows other researchers to more adequately check the original analysis as the transcript is closer to what is on the recording.	3. Although the system may be modified, it tends to set the format of and the parameters for what is transcribed.
4. It has gained dominance over other methods so can be regarded as the standard system of notation.	4. Its origins in the days of typewriters mean that it does not capitalise on the potential of computers to use colour and a range of characters, fonts and sizes.
5. By forcing the researcher to spend time in transcribing, it encourages a more thorough approach to analysis.	5. It is very time consuming for the researcher to use.
6. It requires skilled transcribers and cannot be carried out by, say, secretarial assistants.	6. There is disagreement about the value of Jefferson transcription even among discourse analysts.
7. One can use the line numbers to rapidly refer to a particular part of the transcript.	

dialect, for example. This, of course, adds to the difficulty of reading some transcripts. Table 6.4 provides an evaluation of the advantages and disadvantages of the Jefferson transcription system.

O'Connell and Kowal (1999) are somewhat critical of some aspects of transcription that appear in the psychological literature. They go so far as referring to some of the 'standardisation practices' in transcriptions as pseudo-scientific:

- They point to instances of elaborate Jefferson transcriptions which contribute nothing to the author's interpretation of their data and which, often, are not referred to in the publication. The question then becomes one of why include something that seems to add no value.

- They question the breaking up of words when the transcript is intended to be read by others. Thus indications of the prolongation (e.g. wa::s), pitch movement and so forth which occur within words or within syllables interfere greatly with the lexical integrity of the transcript. This occurs frequently in transcriptions using the Jefferson method and its value is difficult to appreciate in circumstances in which these things are not referred to in the analysis of the discourse. They may be useful for the researcher, but are they useful to the reader?

- They dislike the use of the same notation symbol to mean different things. For example, this has occurred in the Jefferson system during its evolution when a – was used to indicate a cut-off word but also a brief, unmeasured pause.

- Measurement of such things as variations in pitch are not objective in general. Even the recording of pauses in speech is problematic since Jefferson transcription usually involves measured pauses in terms of tenths of seconds. The problem with this is that the objective and the subjective are very different. Half a second of pause when someone is speaking very fast may subjectively appear to be much longer than the same length of pause when someone is speaking slowly. So some researchers prefer to count the pause in terms of the 'beats' of the speech (the speed of the speech).

Probably the most vexed issue to do with transcription is that of whether it is necessary at all. Not all qualitative researchers use transcription and the use of coded transcription in the style of Jefferson is not always employed even where literal transcription itself is. While Jefferson transcription is *de rigueur* in conversation analysis and some forms of discourse analysis, it is not regarded as so important or it is even regarded as unimportant by other qualitative researchers including Foucauldian, phenomenological and narrative analysts. A good example of the criticisms of transcription can be found in Hollway (2005):

> Once the face-to-face situation is reduced to a visual and especially an audio record, much is lost. But the audio record is still a far richer record than a Jeffersonian transcript. For me, the interruption of flow that is involved when I read such a transcript, even if I am familiar with all the symbols, means that I lose much more meaning than I gain. When analysing interview data I regularly go back to the audio record to check my progressive sense-making. (p. 314)

Hollway's reluctance to employ transcription may not be too surprising given that she broadly works in the Foucauldian tradition (Chapter 11) where the detail of ordinary conversation is not so important. She also hints at the problem of using Jeffersonian transcriptions – once the transcript has produced the detail that it does then just how can it be used in order to understand the richness of the data? Given that she argues that a Jefferson transcription is less rich than the audio tape recording then the consequences of transcription are likely to be somewhat negative in her view. However, just how her own method works is also unclear. No matter, many qualitative researchers do find transcription invaluable. Furthermore, you will struggle with some qualitative studies if you do not have the basics of Jefferson's method whether or not you are enamoured of it.

CONCLUSION

The process of transcribing recorded speech is regarded by many qualitative researchers as having beneficial spin-off effects. The close familiarity with the data which many forms of qualitative analysis require means that transcription is necessary to help achieve this intimate knowledge. For this reason, transcription is not something that the analyst should generally delegate to assistants. Transcription is:

> an integral part of the analytic process. This, then, precludes 'farming out' the transcription (i.e., having it done by a professional transcriber or clerical help). Time-consuming and tedious, it nonetheless provides the analyst with an intimate acquaintance with his/her data. (Psathas & Anderson, 1990, p. 77)

Of course, this applies to the novice qualitative researcher even more strongly since they will learn little by getting a friend or partner to do their data transcription for them. So there is little choice but for most qualitative researchers to spend considerable numbers of hours on the, at times, rather mundane task of transcription. But, in qualitative research terms, this is good for the soul.

The use of a speech transcription system is more or less essential in research using language data. Methods of using recordings in an untranscribed form are not really available although it has been controversially suggested that the analysis of the data does not necessarily require the transcription stage (see Chapter 8 on grounded theory). It is self-evident that the transcription is a very resource-intensive process. Jefferson's system of transcription operates at a finer level of detail than literal transcriptions of the same recording and so is even more time consuming. As a consequence, a researcher needs to question just what they are trying to achieve by using transcription. Simple questions such as why an orthographic/secretarial/playscript transcription will not suffice need to be addressed. Even if a method of transcription such as Jefferson's is used it is appropriate to ask whether there are additional aspects of interaction which should be used in the transcript. The Jefferson transcription system evolved largely to serve the requirements of conversation analysis which imposes its own intellectual ethos on its subject matter, so why is the system needed for research which does not share this ethos?

Researchers need to appreciate that their data are not actually speech as such but transcriptions based on recordings (or video) of speech. The recording is less than or a reduction of the original interaction and the transcription is less than that recording. Although the Jefferson system is correctly described as a system of spoken language transcription, this tends to hide the fact that it can also be regarded as a low-level coding or categorisation system. By this is meant that the use of the Jefferson system imposes a degree of structuring on the data in terms of what is included and what is not included. Although researchers tend to focus primarily on the things which the system includes, it is evident that what it excludes is also important. For example, in the Jefferson system there is scant attention given to things such as regional accents which we know from research can have a bearing on how speech is received. Similarly, the emotional aspects of speech are not systematically included in the Jefferson transcript – things such as anger or irritation might be heard in the recording but are not transcribed.

Of course, if a researcher wants a complete transcription of the recorded speech then it is difficult to better the sound recording itself. What the transcription supplies (Jefferson or otherwise) is a somewhat simplified version of events which systematically omits certain aspects of the original. Unfortunately, the original recording is not particularly conducive to analysis using any of the major qualitative analysis methods.

It is almost inevitable that coded or categorised material (including transcriptions which can be seen as a low level of coding) misses out whatever the coding system is not designed to address and highlights those features which the system is designed to address. So conversational difficulties, for example, become very clear from a transcription using the Jefferson system since these are part of conversation analysis which sired the Jefferson system. On the other hand, interpersonal difficulties which may be apparent to members of the conversation are not fully highlighted in the Jefferson system. This is not surprising when one considers that the Jefferson system does little to include such revealing factors as the facial expressions, sidelong glances and the like through which interpersonal factors may be expressed in a group of people conversing. In defence of Jefferson transcription, if one is needed, things can appear on the transcript which indicate bad relations between people. For example, lengthy and awkward pauses (silences), interrupting another person consistently and rudely, and not allowing a person to speak when it is their turn to talk are all indicative of animosity. Furthermore, further details such as the emotional tone of the speaker (e.g. sarcasm) may be given in brackets if the transcriber considers this pertinent.

A researcher may feel that it is important to include additional features into the transcription system that they use. If the system does not address the aspects of interaction which the researcher believes to be important then there is every reason to develop or modify an existing system if not create one anew. For example, Butler (2008), while sticking with conventional conversation analysis transcription symbols adds / to indicate syllables spoken in the same staccato voice as in Good mor:ning ev'/ry/o:ne/ (p. 202).

The transcript is a very portable form of data and easily handled in a research context. It provides a primary focus for the analysis, a means of communicating with other researchers about your data, and a means of including the data in publications. It does have the drawback, however, that it is lengthy compared with a typical publication in a psychological journal. Partly for that reason, it might be anticipated that the Internet will be increasingly used because of the ease and cheapness of circulating substantial amounts of transcript data, its potential for circulating audio and video files within ethical constraints, and its potential for combining audio and transcript material together. All of this will mean that more substantial data extracts can be circulated among researchers than is possible within the confines of a journal article.

KEY POINTS

- Transcription is not a neutral activity but one in which the transcriber makes numerous choices. While this may be a subtle process, different transcribers transcribing the same segment of a recording may not completely agree in terms of what is in the transcription. This, generally, is not a question of one transcription being better than the other but simply reflects the nature of communication between people and the difficulty of defining transcription systems with perfect accuracy.

- While for some purposes a straightforward literal transcription of the words which are spoken in conversation may be sufficient, some analyses need to pay attention to how things are said and not to what things are said. Conversation analysis is exacting in terms of its transcription requirements and uses the Jefferson transcription system to indicate how words are being spoken. Discourse analysts also tend to use this system. However, it is pointless doing all of the work involved in a Jefferson transcription where the analysis does not call for it.

- Transcription should never be regarded as a tedious but necessary chore. It is hard work but the point of this hard work is that not only does the transcription get done but the transcriber (usually the researcher) begins to be increasingly familiar with the data. As a data familiarisation process, transcription generates the intimate knowledge of the data which begins to stimulate the researcher into generating ideas about what is going on in the data. Without this familiarity, analysis is impossible.

- Since transcription will lose aspects of the original recording, it is always important to check the transcript against the recording. This, of course, can be done by the researcher themselves. Nevertheless, there are advantages in seeking the opinion of experienced colleagues about the veracity of the transcript to the recording. This is especially important with novice researchers.

ADDITIONAL RESOURCES

Adobe Audition. www.creative.adobe.com/products/audition/ (accessed 26 February 2015).

This is a professional quality digital editing program which may be used to improve the sound quality, disguise voices and variously change a digital sound recording. It also displays a graphical trace of the sound as a graph or wave trace. This can be used to assess the length of pauses very accurately as well as helping you make judgements as to the relative loudness or quietness of words or syllables. There is a free trial download available at the web address above. However, as the program Audacity does much the same but for free then the choice is, as they say, a no-brainer. Audacity is listed below.

Antaki, C. (2002). An introductory tutorial in Conversation Analysis. www-staff.lboro.ac.uk/~ssca1/sitemenu.htm (accessed 23 February 2015).

Audacity. audacity.sourceforge.net/ (accessed 23 February 2015).

This is a sound editing program which can be used for free. It allows digital enhancements of all sorts to a digital sound file. Furthermore, it displays a sound wave trace which allows the precise measurement of pauses and 'loudness' and 'softness'.

Bucholtz, M., & Du Bois, J. (n.d.). The Transcription in Action Project. www.linguistics.ucsb.edu/projects/transcription/index.html (accessed 23 February 2015).

This is devoted to the transcription system by John Du Bois.

Edwards, J. A. (n.d.). The transcription of discourse. www.cs.columbia.edu/~sbenus/Teaching/APTD/Edwards_transcription_Handbook_of_DA.pdf (accessed 23 February 2015).

This discusses issues in and methods of transcribing language.

Jefferson, G. (2004). Glossary of transcript symbols with an introduction. In G. H. Lerner (Ed.), *Conversation analysis: Studies from the first generation* (pp. 13–31). Amsterdam: John Benjamins.

Liddicoat, A. J. (2007). *An introduction to conversation analysis*. London: Continuum, Chapter 2.

Schegloff, E. Transcription symbols for conversation analysis. www.sscnet.ucla.edu/soc/faculty/schegloff/TranscriptionProject/page1.html (accessed 23 February 2015).

CHAPTER 7

Thematic analysis

Overview

- Thematic analysis is an important and relatively straightforward form of qualitative analysis. It is an excellent starting point to begin qualitative research as it makes only modest demands in terms of basic ideas.

- Thematic analysis has been criticised for lacking a consistent and transparent formulation of how it is carried out. This chapter seeks to rectify this by outlining a more rigorous approach to thematic analysis. As a consequence of its lack of a commonly accepted protocol, studies using thematic analysis should always include detailed information about how the analysis was carried out.

- Thematic analysis is just what it says – an analysis of the major themes to be found in interview and other qualitative data. It is much less dependent on theory than are, say, discourse analysis (Chapter 9), conversation analysis (Chapter 10) and narrative analysis (Chapter 14). This makes thematic analysis a more accessible introduction to qualitative data analysis for students and other newcomers to qualitative methods.

- The history of thematic analysis goes back to the 1950s and the development of quantitative content analysis. Calls for a qualitative approach to content analysis emerged at that time. Thematic analysis shares a lot in common with qualitative content analysis though the latter has been more systematically developed especially in Europe.

- Thematic analysis requires the researcher to identify a limited number of themes to adequately describe what is happening in textual data such as interviews. This is easy to do superficially but a set of themes which describe in depth what is to be found in the data is more demanding to achieve.

- Thematic analysis requires that the analyst has an intimate knowledge of their data which can be achieved by collecting the data oneself, transcribing the data oneself, and reading and re-reading the data a number of times. Then the researcher begins to code the data – perhaps line by line or every two or three lines – to indicate the contents of small quantities of the data. Codings are brief descriptions of small chunks of data. There are no 'rules' to say precisely how this is done but the more 'conceptual' the codings are the better.

- The codings are a level of abstraction away from the data. From these codings the researcher tries to develop or identify the themes which describe the major features of the data. This process can involve the sorting of cards on a table, each bearing the name of a coding or a theme.

In this way, it may become more evident just which codings go closely together and, consequently, what the themes might be. Each theme needs to be carefully defined and differentiated from other themes.

- As the analytic ideas develop, the researcher may re-check the data or the codings in order to maximise the fit between the data, the codings and the themes.

- Thematic analysis is a descriptive method rather than a theory building approach to qualitative research (in contrast to grounded theory). Among its advantages is that it tends to generate research findings which are readily understood by the general public and policy makers.

What is thematic analysis?

Thematic analysis is the analysis of what is said rather than how it is said. Generally it can be recommended as an introduction to qualitative research because of its relative lack of complexity. Quite simply, the data are examined in order to identify relatively broad themes which summarise the content of the data, hopefully fairly completely. Recently there have been attempts to provide systematic guidelines about how to do thematic analysis in order to correct some of the perceived weaknesses of the method. Braun and Clarke (2006) proposed a more stringent version of thematic analysis though they do write a little disparagingly about the previous state of affairs with thematic analysis. They state: 'Thematic analysis is a poorly demarcated, rarely acknowledged, yet widely used qualitative analytic method within psychology' (Braun & Clarke, 2006, p. 77). One has to have some sympathy with this since it is relatively easy to find thematic analysis studies which appear to have adopted a somewhat basic and unsystematic approach to analysis. Details of how a particular thematic analysis was carried out have been traditionally missing from reports though, of course, this is a situation which is easily rectified once researchers become aware of the problem: 'It can be seen as a very poorly "branded" method, in that it does not appear to exist as a "named" analysis in the same way that other methods do . . .' (Braun & Clarke, 2006, pp. 79–80).

The analysis which is presented in thematic analysis consists of broad categories or themes describing significant features of the data. Thematic analyses often refer to the themes 'emerging' from the data as if it were something that themes did on their own without the active involvement of the researcher. The impression is thereby created that the researcher simply reads through transcripts of interviews or some other form of data a few times and then 'sees' five or six (or even fewer) themes which reoccur commonly in the transcripts. These themes are laced together in a report with illustrative quotes or excerpts from the transcripts for each theme. One major problem with this is that the researcher appears not to be doing a great deal of analytic work in order to develop the themes. The task seems too easy – so long as a few themes are suggested and a few illustrative quotes found, then the job of analysis is done. What this means is that the researcher fails to present the argument justifying their particular analysis. The intellectual demands on the researcher seem to be minimal but, more importantly, the fit of the themes with the bulk of the data is unknown.

In Potter's (1998) terms, this amounts to the researcher thinking up a few plausible themes and then trawling through the transcripts to find extracts that illustrate these themes. The problem is that this gross disrespect for and injustice to the data misses the point of qualitative research. Basically it is little different from the way in which quantitative data collection forces data into predetermined categories. Since there are no criteria to decide on the themes, who can say that there is anything wrong with this analysis? So there is a basic, underlying lack of transparency in many thematic analyses. Just what did the researcher do with their data in order to develop the themes? To what extent do the themes encompass all of the data? It may be that key features of the data are ignored along with key analytical insights. The lack of clear, consistent and extensive effort going into the analysis means that the value of the analysis is difficult to assess. This is hardly a satisfactory situation. Hence the need for a more systematic and transparent approach to thematic analysis. Such approaches have been formulated recently (Braun & Clarke, 2006; Howitt & Cramer, 2014). Thematic analysis as discussed in this chapter is based on these.

Thematic analysis, even in its recent more structured forms, is a useful technique which is fairly accessible to novice researchers. As a form of qualitative data analysis it is less demanding than the other methods of qualitative analysis discussed in the next few chapters. The main reason for this is that the process of data analysis is not intimately linked to particular areas of theory as it is with other methods. In some respects, thematic analysis is most similar to grounded theory, though it does not involve the same level of sophistication in data collection and theory building. However, properly done, thematic analysis has quite a lot in common with these other analytic methods. Certainly, the practical skills of data analysis learnt through thematic analysis will help a researcher when they move on to these other approaches. None of this is a criticism of thematic analysis – merely a recognition of its more limited horizons.

Bringing these and other points together, thematic analysis is a useful analytic approach in circumstances in which:

- the data collection is finished;
- there are no strong theoretical perspectives to drive the analysis – though Braun and Clarke (2006) suggest that there are two forms of thematic analysis whereby some are driven by pre-existing theoretical concerns and others are driven by the data;
- the data consist of detailed textual material such as interviews, focus groups, newspaper articles and the like;
- the data are rich in the sense of being full of detail and information such as will occur in in-depth interviews and materials taken from the media, etc.

Quite clearly these are fairly minimal demands for a qualitative study. Since no particular theoretical orientation is associated with thematic analysis and because it is flexible in terms of how and why it is carried out, it is probably the most accessible qualitative analysis procedure for researchers most familiar with quantitative methods. Even laboratory researchers, the archetypal quantitative demon for qualitative researchers, often interview their research participants in some depth. Thematic analysis could provide them with a way of organising and analysing these data. Similarly, researchers planning to develop a structured questionnaire may wish to explore the topic first of all by interviewing informants about the research topic. Thematic analysis may provide them with a suitable way of dealing with these data.

In some ways, thematic analysis occupies the middle ground between quantitative and qualitative analysis. Thematic analysis does not carry the theoretical 'baggage' that many other qualitative analysis methods do (and quantitative ones too for that matter). For example, the researcher may have a realist position in relation to what the participants say in their interviews. (Generally such a position is problematic in qualitative data analysis where a subjectivist or relativist position is often regarded as *de rigueur*.) This is not to say that anything goes in thematic analysis.

Thematic analysis, despite its currency in research publications, rarely gains more than a perfunctory mention in psychological research textbooks. There are exceptions to this, such as Howitt and Cramer (2014). As we have seen, there have been other signs of a revival of interest in thematic analysis where a systematic approach is involved. Although it is not possible to provide a completely standard or universal set of guidelines on how to do thematic analysis, it is important to establish it as a method and not just a loose label to attach to simple studies involving codifying data.

According to Howitt and Cramer (2014), the central processes involved in thematic analysis are transcription, analytic effort and theme identification. While conceptually these are three separate processes, in reality they do not follow this rigid order and the processes overlap considerably. Just as in grounded theory (Chapter 8) and many other forms of qualitative analysis, the researcher may feel it necessary to go back and forward between stages in order to check and refine the themes that are being developed (see Figure 7.1):

- *Transcribing textual material* Any form of textual material can be used ranging from, say, material from the Internet to transcriptions of in-depth interviews or focus groups. The transcription method used in most published thematic analyses is a secretarial/playscript one (see Chapter 6) and, in general, there is no reason to use a more detailed Jefferson transcription. Of course, if you can think of a reason for doing Jefferson transcription for a thematic analysis then there is no reason not to do so, though who can say what these circumstances might be? Transcription, in qualitative research, is not to be seen as a tedious chore since, in the hands of a good researcher, transcription familiarises the researcher with the data and is an early push or stimulus towards trying to understand and, hence, analyse the data. The familiarity that transcription brings with the data is very closely focused and systematic because of the nature of transcription. The analysis might begin much earlier during the data collection phase for the in-depth interview or focus group, for example.

- *Analytic effort* This is crucial in all forms of qualitative analysis and short cuts to a successful analysis are rarely to be found. Analytic effort is the work or processing that the researcher does on the text in order to generate the final themes – that is the thematic analysis. The analytic effort includes the following components: (a) familiarisation with the data so that it is known in detail to the researcher; (b) the detailed

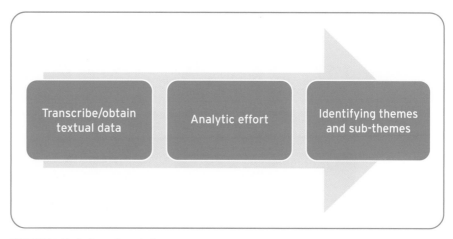

FIGURE 7.1 Basic thematic analysis

codings and conceptualisations which the researcher applies to their data such as line-by-line coding or much broader-brush approaches to identifying the overall themes; (c) the extent to which the researcher is prepared to process and reprocess the data analysis to ensure that the analysis fits the data as closely as possible; (d) the extent to which the researcher is presented with difficulties during the course of the analysis and what effort is put into resolving these difficulties; and (e) the frequency and thoroughness of the researcher's checks between the analysis of the data and the data.

- *Identifying themes and sub-themes* While the naming of themes and sub-themes is the end point of thematic analysis, there is considerable variation in the extent to which researchers refine the themes for presentation in reports, etc. A researcher might decide that five or six themes effectively describe what they have identified as the key features of the data. Other researchers might well be dissatisfied with the same themes since they feel that they less than completely describe what is happening in the data. All of this continues with the analytic work through to the end product of the final thematic analysis. Since the identification of themes is partly dependent on the amount and quality of analytic effort the researcher has put into their analysis, it is likely that different researchers looking at the same data will end up with rather more or rather less sophisticated findings from their analyses. This underlines the importance of understanding precisely what the researcher has done to generate the themes discussed in the report. Of course, in qualitative research it is accepted that different researchers will have different readings of the same data. These can be equally meretricious. This is not at all the same as different analysts producing different analyses simply because they differ in terms of how diligent their analyses have been or how closely they have stuck to the principles of good thematic analysis.

Figure 7.2 presents some of the key elements of thematic analysis which help to differentiate it from other forms of qualitative data analysis.

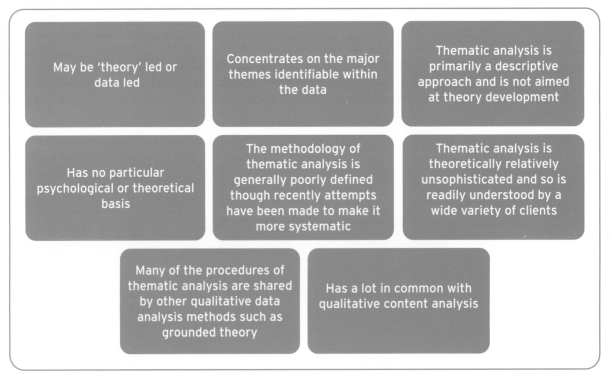

FIGURE 7.2 The key elements of thematic analysis

The development of thematic analysis

The phrase thematic analysis first appeared in psychological journals in 1943 though it is substantially more common now. For instance, in the years between 1998 and 2008 there were nearly 1000 publications which included thematic analysis in their summaries. Despite this, one has to accept the 'poor relative' status of thematic analysis in the field of qualitative research (Howitt & Cramer, 2014). Hopefully this is changing. Interestingly, thematic analysis has lacked the high-profile advocates that characterise some other forms of qualitative analysis. Researchers who used thematic analysis typically provided little or no detail about how they carried out their analyses other than a phrase such as 'we conducted a thematic analysis of . . . ' . Some researchers, although they essentially identify themes, made no reference to thematic analysis as their method. For example, Gee, Ward and Eccleston (2003) suggested different types of cognitive distortions among sex offenders by using what they describe as a 'Data-driven approach to model development (grounded theory) . . . to analyse the interview transcripts' (p. 44) though their research appears to be thematic analysis since it lacks crucial features of grounded theory.

Is thematic analysis just a simple version of grounded theory? Although anyone carrying out a thematic analysis may learn a lot from considering the grounded theory approach, there is no indication that thematic analysis is in any sense a derivative of grounded theory. Indeed, thematic analysis seems to pre-date grounded theory very substantially. And why should this not be the case? The basic idea of thematic analysis is a simple one – that complex qualitative data might be effectively summarised by identifying the major themes which re-occur within it. This is hardly a rocket-science breakthrough given that themes are little other than categories and that the process of categorisation is a basic attribute of human thinking. It also has to be acknowledged that thematic analysis is a relatively common form of qualitative data analysis in psychology so it must resonate with the needs of substantial numbers of researchers more than some other qualitative analysis methods.

While the full history of thematic analysis will probably never be written, it is possible that thematic analysis did not emerge initially out of qualitative research but out of quantitative research. Content analysis is the generic name given to various approaches to the analysis of the media such as news articles, television programmes and so forth which had its origins in mass communications research in the first half of the twentieth century. The first book on content analysis was Bernard Berelson's (1912–79) *Content analysis in communication research* published in 1952. However, content analysis had been developing in mass communications research during the 1920s and onwards. Important figures in this early history were Paul Lazarsfeld (1901–76) and Harold Lasswell (1902–78). Content analysis was central to the analysis of propaganda demanded by the US Government during the Second World War. Basically this form of content analysis sought to find coding categories which effectively described substantial aspects of the data – once these had been developed then the frequencies of occurrence of each of these categories could be quantified. It would also be possible to cross-tabulate one category against another in a typical, quantitative manner. There is a famous sentence in mass communications research which goes 'Who says what to whom in what channel with what effect'. In the form of who, what, whom, what channel and to what effect, this phrase appears as the nub of many content analyses.

However, the publication of Berelson's book in 1952 led to the immediate demand that a qualitative form of content analysis was also needed. Siegfried Kracauer (1889–1966) responded to its publication with the claim that qualitative aspects of the text were being ignored in favour of counting and measuring (Kracauer, 1952), which must count as a fairly early rehearsal of the qualitative/quantitative debate. The response to this was far from swift, though Kohlbacher (2006) sees the legacy of this early debate in the work of Altheide (1996) and others. There is also the possibility that qualitative content analysis had a major emergence in continental Europe with the work of Philip Mayring in the 1980s and beyond though the impact elsewhere was not great. However, the methodologies employed are more than a little redolent of major principles of qualitative analysis. Bryman suggests that qualitative content analysis 'comprises a searching-out of underlying themes in the materials being analysed' (Bryman, 2004, p. 392). This seems very close to being a definition of thematic analysis.

The interplay between qualitative content analysis and thematic analysis, however, is not really evident in the literature in general, so all of this is speculative. One lesson from all of this may be that qualitative researchers sometimes need broader-brush approaches to qualitative analysis than methods such as discourse and conversation analysis achieve in general.

How to do thematic analysis

If one is looking for an up-to-date account of thematic analysis methodology written by psychologists then the guidelines that Braun and Clarke (2006) provide are the best available systematic approach to thematic analysis. Theirs is a toughened-up description of how to do thematic analysis which draws heavily on their familiarity and involvement with other forms of qualitative analysis. Their approach imposes high standards on thematic analysis and the work of the analyst with the aim of improving the end product. According to Braun and Clarke (2006), the process of carrying out a thematic analysis may be broken down into six separate stages though, as with most qualitative analysis, there is a great deal of unbridled going backwards and forwards between the different stages of the analysis. The process of thematic analysis may be visualised as being much as in Figure 7.3. The six steps of the analysis are clearly listed in sequential order but the overlap of the stages is patently obvious. While doing a thematic analysis the researcher may move backwards and forwards between stages with the purposes of checking one aspect of the analysis against one or more of the other steps in the analysis. Obviously checking is more frequent between steps which are close together but this does not preclude checking, say, what is written in the report against the original data. The distinction between different stages of the analysis is conceptual for the most part since the different stages may not be totally distinct in practice and are often concurrent. Looping backwards and forwards are ways of improving the analysis – they are not signs that the analysis is proceeding badly. Without this looping backwards and forwards, the analytic effort going into the process is probably insufficient. You might wish to read Box 7.1, later in the chapter, next as it describes the practical process of carrying out a thematic analysis.

Step 1   Data familiarisation In this early stage, the researcher becomes familiar with the close detail of the transcript or whatever other text is to be used. Quite when data familiarisation occurs will differ according to the details of the study concerned. If the researcher had conducted interviews and focus groups then they are likely to be actively processing these while the data are being collected. Data familiarisation will also take place during the process of transcription – if the researcher is transcribing their own data. Otherwise and additionally, playing a recording through repeatedly or reading a transcript through several times are important steps in data familiarisation. Although someone else may do the interviews or make the transcripts, no one but the

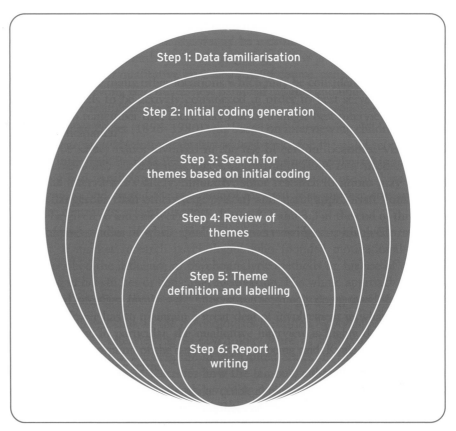

FIGURE 7.3 Braun and Clarke's model of thematic analysis: all steps may refer backwards and forwards to other steps

researcher can do data familiarisation since this is a key stage in developing the analysis. During the data familiarisation stage, the researcher will begin to think about what is happening in the data – this is inevitable but the qualitative researcher should plan to put substantial time into doing this. The more data from the more participants there are, the easier it is to begin to formulate patterns which cohere. These early thoughts about what is happening in the data may suggest ways in which the data might be coded or, indeed, ideas about the themes apparent in the data.

Thematic analysis normally uses a literal transcription after the style of a secretary. Although it is not impossible to use the Jefferson transcription (Chapter 6), it is difficult to see what function Jefferson transcription will achieve in thematic analysis since it is largely about expressing how things are said rather than what is said. Thematic analysis concentrates on what is being said and so has no way of coping with this additional detail. Transcription is not a mindless chore in qualitative research but a positive and important aspect of data analysis. It is, therefore, sound advice to a novice researcher that they should do all of the data collection and transcription themselves. Many professional researchers would not want to do any different.

Step 2 **Initial coding generation** On the principle that higher levels of analytic effort lead to better research, the initial, formal analysis step in thematic analysis is the line-by-line coding of the data. These codings are not the themes that the research will generate, but a stage in the process of working towards those themes. By coding each line, the researcher is working with the detail of the data rather than the broad sweep of the data. A coding is little other than a label to describe the contents of a line (or two) of transcript or textual data. The lines are basically arbitrary as the text or transcript is usually surrounded by white space on the paper on which the researcher makes his or her notes. Since the themes are abstractions from the data, the initial codings are usually best if they are based on an abstraction rather than something more concrete. In other words, the more conceptual the researcher's codings the better the final themes are likely to be. The researcher's coding should indicate something that is interesting or important about that snippet of the data. Initial codings involve the researcher systematically working through the entirety of the data – or a subset of the data selected because it deals with a particular topic or matter of interest to the researcher. Coding does not have to be done line-by-line – if every line is not possible then every two or three lines would probably be all right. It really does depend on circumstances. There is no requirement even that the numbers of lines to be coded have to be equal every time. Furthermore, the researcher may choose a unit of analysis other than the line of text. There is nothing wrong with coding sentences in their entirety if the researcher feels that this might be advantageous. Initial codings seek to capture a segment of text's essence; it is not the intention at this stage to identify broader themes though, of course, ideas as to what the themes might be may occur at any stage in the analysis. Initial codings are not sophisticated analyses of the data – sometimes they may appear to be nothing other than jottings or notes which summarise bits of the text.

Do not forget that the researcher, at this stage, already has a broad picture of the data rather than simply the brief initial codings. This means that the initial codings are likely to be guided by this fuller picture and not simply a line or two of text. Initial coding development (and the later development of themes) is not something that simply happens when a researcher looks at their data. Codings do *not* emerge from the data according to Braun and Clarke (2006) but are actively created by the researcher trying out ideas in relation to their data. Codings and themes are not located in the data as such but created in the interplay between the data and the work that the researcher is investing in the data analysis.

There may be two different approaches depending on whether the data are data-led or theory-led according to Braun and Clarke (2006):

- *The data-led approach* This is dominated by the characteristics of the data and the codings are primarily guided by a careful analysis of what is in the data. This is the approach taken in the example in Box 7.1.
- *The theory-led approach* The structure for the initial codings is suggested by the key elements of the theory being applied by the researcher. Feminist theory, for example, stresses that relationships between men and women are dominated by the power and dominance of the male gender over the female gender in a wide variety of aspects of the social world including employment, domestic life and the law. Thus a thematic analysis based on feminist theory would be orientated to the expression of power relationships in any textual material.

Of course, there is something of a dilemma here since it is unclear just how a researcher can avoid applying elements of a theoretical perspective during the analysis process. How would it be possible to differentiate between a theory-led coding and a data-led coding unless the researcher makes this explicit in their writings?

Initial codings are not usually reported by researchers using thematic analysis but Clarke, Burns and Burgoyne (2008) do describe some of their initial codings for a number of lines of text. It is useful to look at these since they show that initial codings are often nothing particularly sophisticated and that there is nothing magical in them given that they are quite mundane. The codings are for the piece of text on the left as a whole, not line by line:

it's too much like hard work I mean how much paper have you got to sign	1. Talked about with partner
to change a flippin' name no I I mean no I no we we have thought about it	2. Too much hassle to change name
((inaudible)) half heartedly and thought no no I jus- I can't be bothered,	
it's too much like hard work.	

It would be difficult to argue that these codings required a great deal of insight, creativity or any sort of special powers. They are little other than a succinct way of putting things in this example. It is not difficult to see that hard work is a dominant aspect of this snippet and that the discussion ('we have thought about it') is the second aspect. Of course, the researchers might equally have coded the contents as 'paperwork is a deterrent' and 'partners have considered name change'. Notice that there are other aspects of the excerpt that different researchers with different research aims might have coded if they wished. For example, the codings might be 1. Rhetorical question ('it's too much like hard work I mean how much paper have you got to sign to change a flippin 'name') and 2. Change of personal pronoun from 'I' to 'we' and back. In other words, the codings are partially guided by the researcher's perspective on the research and not just the contents of the interview.

Of course, the researcher will notice that they have initial codings which are very similar to each other despite differences in wording. So it may be appropriate to re-name these with the same coding – provided, of course, that the researcher is convinced that the different codings mean the same thing. Otherwise, things may be left alone until the following has been done.

At the point at which the initial-coding stage has been completed, the researcher will naturally need to understand better the material which Coding A includes compared with, say, the material which Coding C includes. In other words, the researcher should put together all of the transcript or text which has received Coding A, likewise for Coding B, Coding C and so forth. One way of doing this is simply to copy-and-paste the material from a word processor file under these different headings. On examining the material which has received Coding C, for example, it may become clear to the researcher that:

- the coding's label is not quite accurate or precise enough and needs to be changed;
- some of the material which has received that coding is different in important ways and so a new coding may be identified for the parts of the data which do not really match with the other material;
- the material which has received Coding C is not really different from the material which has received Coding F, for example. So the researcher may decide to combine these codings.

Obviously it is far better that you practise the process of coding on a small piece of text rather than for the first time once your data have been collected. You may find it helpful to copy some text from the Internet, say from chatrooms, etc. which have a lot of potentially usable material. Try coding some of this.

Step 3   Search for themes based on the initial coding The sequence is close reading of text, producing codings for each line or group of lines of text, and then turning these codings into themes. The question is just how codings can be turned into themes. The answer is more hard work: more analytic effort on the part of the researcher. At this point the researcher will probably notice that although the list of initial codings that has been developed seems to be useful in that the data and the codings given to the data make sense and distinguish one sort of material from another sort of material, nevertheless some of the codings on the list have more to do with each other than they do with other codings on the list. In other words, what are the patterns among the codings? To take a silly example, if the codings were dog, lettuce, cat, carrot, apple, rabbit, aardvark then one might be inclined to suggest that these different codings are related to two categories – (1) animals and (2) vegetables. Actually, one might suggest that the second group is fruit and vegetables – or a group and a sub-group perhaps. These groups are pretty much what a theme is. So themes are basically the result of categorising the codings into meaningful groups of codings. Of course, it is possible to develop themes which are relatively mundane if the analysis is somewhat concrete. The researcher needs to use their powers of abstract thought if the analysis is to be of a good quality, but that is what research is all about anyway. Themes identify major patterns in the initial codings and so can be thought of as a secondary level of interpreting the text. Of course, it may be that the initial coding process has identified aspects of the data of considerable importance which warrant that coding itself be described as a theme. Like all aspects of qualitative data analysis, it is practically impossible to completely separate the coding phase from the theme-generation phase. There is an interplay which no description of the process can quite capture.

What can be done to encourage the researcher to conceptualise themes from the codings? Well, in many ways this is to ask how one can encourage the processes of categorisation and reasoning which characterise human thinking in general. That is, anything which facilitates or encourages abstract thinking is to be recommended. In some circumstances the themes may well be fairly obvious from the codings which have been developed. But there may be a need to work harder and more effectively to develop themes. For example, simple methods of sorting might help. Each coding might be written on a small card or slip of paper. This allows the codings to be sorted and re-sorted into piles on the basis of similarity. Placing the piles in approximate relative positions is a good idea as this tentatively indicates the relationships between the different themes. In the course of this, the researcher may decide that there are some piles of codings which do not constitute a single theme but are close together. These may be thought of as sub-themes within a more general theme.

In some analyses, it may become obvious that certain codings are the reverse of other codings. This is quite a different situation from codings being thematically different. In this case, the codings belong to the same theme but indicate opposing aspects of the same theme. It would be quite wrong and misleading to treat these 'polar opposites' as if they were different themes.

'No pain no gain' is not quite the way to describe the process of theme development but it does get close. Although pain is not essential, hard work is key to ensuring that themes are as well developed and useful in the data interpretation as possible. Computers may help with the data management for a thematic analysis and ease the pressures due to large amounts of material to analyse. Word processing programs have the facility to allow limitless cutting-and-pasting. However, there are some specialist computer programs (especially NVivo) which can help achieve the same ends and more but in a different way.

Step 4

Review of themes So far we have gone through the process of developing a set of tentative themes which help to understand the data. Depending on circumstances, it is possible that these themes are not fully defined or even particularly refined at this stage. It is essential, then, to examine these themes against the original data. Once again, the researcher needs to organise the data around the themes just as previously the data have been organised around the codings. This is simply a matter of cutting-and-pasting the material which had previously been organised around the different codings so that it is now organised around the different themes. In other words, all of the evidence in support of a particular theme has been drawn together. Like all qualitative analyses, any analysis can be regarded as tentative and so the researcher may decide to review the themes or even the codings in light of what is to be found associated with these developing themes. The more systematic the analysis is, the greater becomes the task of data management during this process of theme development. With larger data sets, the researcher might prefer to analyse half the data first, then refine this analysis on the basis of how well it deals with the second half of the data set.

There are a number of possibilities:

- You may find that there is very little in the data to support a theme that you have identified, so the theme may have to be abandoned or modified in light of this.
- You may find that a theme needs to be divided or subdivided since the data which are supposed to link together into the one theme imply two different themes or sub-themes.
- You may feel that the theme works by and large but does not fit some of the data which initially you believed were part of that theme so you may have to find a new theme to deal with the non-fitting data. You may need to check the applicability of your themes to selected extracts as well as to the entire data set.

Step 5

Theme definition and labelling Accuracy and precision are the watchwords of any academic research. It is unlikely that a researcher can define and label the themes emerging in their research without being prepared to reconsider and refine the analysis at all stages. While it may appear easy to give a label to a theme, it may prove more troublesome to define precisely what the theme is. Most important is the extent to which a particular theme that has been identified by the researcher can be distinguished conceptually from all of the other themes. That is, for each theme, can the researcher say just what it is and just what it is not? Of course, an analysis which attempts to deal with all of the data will be more exacting than one which deals only with particular aspects of the data. The process of developing sub-themes is likely to continue at this stage. As the themes become clearer, data which previously were hard to code just might become understandable in light of conceptual developments during the analysis.

Up to this point, thematic analysis has been described in ways which suggest that it is all in the head (and on the desk) of the researcher. This is a somewhat solitary process. Going 'public' with your analysis is probably a good idea at any stage but, especially, in the step in which the analysis is being refined. Simply talking with other people about your ideas, in itself, will help you to identify problems in your ideas or your own understanding of your ideas. It helps you see the wood for the trees but also continues the process of clarification in a different modality. But, additionally, talking with others may allow them to question you about your ideas and, possibly, throw in analytic ideas of their own.

Step 6

Report writing The report – which might be a student dissertation or an article for a prestigious research journal – is a sufficiently detailed description of the stages of the research (see Chapter 15). It tends not to be a 'warts and all' account in the sense that the write-up is usually more orderly than the research had actually ever been. Qualitative writing tends to include more description of the problems of analysis than other forms of research report. It is notable that many, if not most, reports involving thematic analysis fail to include much detail about the analytic process. It is almost as if the analysis emerges fully from the data with little happening in the middle. This is an erroneous picture of qualitative analysis and good practice would insist on some detail of the process of analysis being included. Difficulties in the analysis should be highlighted – it is no use to other researchers if problems are swept under the carpet.

Report writing can be construed as the final stage of data analysis – that is, it is the stage at which the researcher may have to refine and alter the analysis in light of problems which emerge during the process of writing-up. All stages of the analysis process relate back to each other and the strength of the research question which initiated the research study is part of the success of the study. Indeed, the research question may well be reformulated a number of times during the course of the analysis – even at the stage of writing the report. So report writing is not merely telling the essence of the 'mechanics' of the research project – the steps in the research – but a further opportunity to reflect on one's data, one's analysis and the adequacy of the data in relation to the analysis and vice versa. The story told in the report reflects the researcher's final thinking. Report writing is not to be regarded as a chore but part of the data analysis process which involves the final synthesis. Nevertheless, it is understandable why report writing can feel something of an uphill struggle.

The explanation and description of the themes in the final report involve, in thematic analysis, appropriate illustrations taken from the material which is associated with the theme. Among the criteria that might be applied to this selection are the following:

- How typical the material is of the data which 'belong' to a particular theme.

- How apposite the material is in relation to the theme. Some excerpts might illustrate particular features of the theme better than others.

- How 'eye-catching' the excerpt is. Some data may be rather more vivid than other data and so may be chosen in preference to other excerpts.

- You may prefer to illustrate the various themes using excerpts from, say, just one of the participants in the research. In this way it may be possible to get into a little more depth about a particular case – to put the analysis in the context of an individual's life.

Each of the above implies a somewhat different selection strategy. It is clearly helpful to indicate in your report the basis for your excerpt selection.

The final report will provide a discussion of the relevant research literature. Typically in thematic analysis the researcher will have little, if any, reluctance about informing the developing analysis using previous research findings, although this is a choice that the researcher always has to make. This may be either (a) the previous research literature that helps justify why you have posed your particular research question or (b) the research literature which relates to your analysis once it has been formulated – that is, how does your analysis relate to other analyses of similar material? Of course, it could be both. It might be pointed out that the previous research may primarily be quantitative in nature. In this case, it might be appropriate to review this literature as part of the explanation why a qualitative approach is needed in addition. Since there are no previous qualitative analyses, the new qualitative analysis will not be so affected by these findings. The study reported in Box 7.2 is one in which the literature review is largely quantitative and so has reduced relevance to the development of themes. Whatever the approach taken to the literature review in relation to the data analysis, the final report must include your attempt at synthesis and integration of the previous research literature with your new analysis. The development of this synthesis is part of understanding the nature of the themes that you have identified. Quantification is also an issue in the study described in Box 7.3.

Irrespective of the steps described above, at its heart thematic analysis involves the data, the coding of data and the identification of themes. This is not a linear process in the sense that the researcher may frequently go backwards and forwards between all three, creating extra loops in the analysis process. This helps check and also refine the analysis which is being carried out. The data and the analysis of the data are constantly juxtaposed to both check the adequacy of the analysis but also to encourage its refinement.

When to use thematic analysis

Thematic analysis is what it is and probably has little to offer the researcher whose perspective is in, say, conversation analysis and discourse analysis. It does not have the level of sophisticated theory associated with it that these do. On the other hand, this 'theory' may not really be the researcher's interest and it may not be found useful. The following points may help determine whether thematic analysis is appropriate:

- Thematic analysis is best seen as a descriptive method in that it attempts to come up with a limited number of themes or categories to describe what is going on in the data.

- Thematic analysis, unlike grounded theory, is not aimed at theory generation although it may be helpful in this regard. For example, the themes developed in thematic analysis are not expected to be related or inter-connected in some way, whereas the categories identified from a grounded theory analysis do need to be explored in terms of their relationships with each other.

- Similarly, thematic analysis is not primarily aimed at providing a detailed interpretation of the data as opposed to describing its broad features. While interpretation and description do overlap, thematic analysis can serve its purpose by simply describing what is going on in the data.

- Thematic analysis provides a rather broad-brush approach to data analysis as opposed to the fine-grained approaches which characterise some qualitative research methods.

- Thematic analysis does not have a strong voice on the data which are collected and the process by which they are collected. So, unlike grounded theory, thematic analysis may be used on a completed data set and there is no requirement that the data being collected are reviewed part-way through the analysis and new approaches to sampling, etc. instigated if necessary.

- Thematic analysis, generally, is not steeped in the intriguing but sometimes frustrating epistemological debates that other qualitative methods are. Indeed, thematic analysis fits comfortably with some of the assumptions of quantitative research. Hence it may be a way for quantitative researchers to feel comfortable with qualitative data.

- Thematic analysis may, in some cases, be amenable to simple quantification since a theme may be coded as present or absent in, say, a percentage of the interviews.

Quite clearly, the closest method to thematic analysis is grounded theory. However, despite the fact that many of the stages in thematic analysis have their parallels in grounded theory, the two approaches are substantially different, as can be seen from the above bullet points. So it would not be fair to suggest that thematic analysis is a simplified or 'lite' version of grounded theory. However, it is probably true to suggest that there are some grounded theory analyses which produce outcomes which are indistinguishable from those of thematic analysis.

Examples of the use of thematic analysis

Boxes 7.1 to 7.3 give examples of the use of thematic analysis in research.

Box 7.1

ILLUSTRATIVE RESEARCH STUDY

Thematic analysis: functions of pornography

Just what does a researcher do when faced with a substantial number of transcripts of interviews which need analysing? Thematic analysis is an obvious choice. Internet sex offenders – basically men who use and download child pornography in this case – are a key group to understand if sex offending research itself is to develop (Sheldon & Howitt, 2007). Just how are these men different from traditional contact paedophiles? Just what does the Internet offender get out of using child pornography on the Internet? The primary source of information about Internet sex offenders, given the relative paucity of previous research in this area, has to be interviews with the offenders themselves. What are the functions of Internet child abuse images in the lives of such offenders? The answer to this question, of course, lies in the 51 interviews conducted with Internet sex offenders and contact offenders that the authors carried out. The transcripts of such a large number of in-depth interviews produce a great deal of information which needs to be effectively summarised. The analysis by Sheldon and Howitt (2007) produced perhaps some predictable outcomes but, also, some 'surprises'. Internet sex offenders clearly have a strong sexual proclivity towards children since, for example, they are sexually aroused by children. So it might be expected that sexual arousal might be the main function that child pornography serves for these men. The research confirmed this expectation but added other functions which were not so predictable.

During the course of lengthy interviews, the Internet sex offenders were asked about their use of child pornography images. All of the interviews for this study were

conducted by Kerry Sheldon who carried out the analysis. In terms of the data analysis, she had (a) interviewed all of the participants in the study and (b) transcribed in full all of the interviews using direct literal (secretarial) methods. There was no reason to carry out a Jefferson-style transcription (Chapter 6) since the objective was to understand how the offenders accounted for their offending. Because of the close involvement of one researcher with the interviewing and transcriptions, the data were very familiar before the analysis stage of the research began.

Of course, the interviews and transcripts contained much data irrelevant to the question of the functions of Internet child pornography, consequently relevant material to this topic needed to be identified. Since only certain aspects of the questioning were pertinent to this, it is relatively easy to identify the relevant material. This was done by cutting-and-pasting the relevant material from the computer files of the transcripts into a new file. However, an equally viable approach would be to highlight the relevant text on the transcript with a highlighter pen or change the font colour on the computer. In this case, the substantial quantities of data meant that it was best to use a computer to store the relevant material ready for perusal when coding the data.

The phases of the thematic analysis employed were similar to those used in other forms of qualitative analysis. The coding process began with a descriptive level of coding which involved the minimum of interpretation or abstraction. The codings were applied, as was appropriate, to 'chunks' of data or transcript. So it could be just a word, a phrase, a sentence or a paragraph. For example, the avoidance of negative feelings/moods was described by some offenders as their reason for using child pornography and so the code 'negavoidance' was given each time this occurred in the transcripts. Coding was a complex, interconnected process so the initial codings would be revised in light of the things which appeared later in the transcript and so forth. Some codes would be subdivided or revised if the initial codes seemed to be an inadequate fit to the data or codes would be combined if they overlapped too much in terms of meaning. Jotting down ideas and codes was an integral part of this early stage – somewhat similar to the 'memo' in grounded theory (see Chapter 8).

The next stage of data analysis (theme development) involved more interpretation and inductive reasoning. That is to say, constructs which embraced a number of the initial codes were identified. These captured the overall meaning of some of the initial descriptive coding. Throughout the analysis, the analyst would move backwards and forwards between the data (interview extracts) and the codes, as well as between the developing themes and the codes. In order to facilitate theme development, the individual codings were written onto different cards together with a brief clarifying description. These cards could then be moved and shuffled around and organised into 'theme piles' where they seemed to have a great deal in common. This allowed the analyst to establish whether the themes 'worked' in relation to the codings (and the extracts).

Although the initial stages of this particular thematic analysis were led by the data, in the final stage the researcher drew from psychological theory and research as an aid to interpreting the codings into overarching themes. Engagement with the literature was considered very important in that it led to better understanding of the meaning and implications of the patterns in the codings (i.e. the themes). The researcher simultaneously sought to generate clear definitions of each theme and a clear name. Overall, only a few themes were created during this thematic analysis but these themes were general concepts which subsumed the lower levels of coding.

Of course, if themes are very clearly defined it becomes possible to quantify their occurrence in the data. There are different ways in which this could be done:

- How prevalent is a theme? That is, how many (or what percentage) of interviews included each theme.
- What is the incidence of a particular theme? That is, how often a particular theme occurs throughout the data or how often it is mentioned by each participant. The former is generally the easier.

After the thematic analysis was completed, the interviews were scrutinised again and the number of interviews which mentioned a particular theme was counted. The importance of a theme is not a function of the number of times it appears. There will be certain themes which are more important than others because they are particularly pertinent to the research question.

There were four themes identified in what the offenders told the researchers about the functions of child pornography in their lives. These were: (a) Sexual arousal, (b) Emotional avoidance, (c) Collecting and (d) Facilitating social relationships. These are very different themes and they could not have been anticipated in their entirety prior to the data collection and analysis. The themes identified through the thematic analysis were illustrated by excerpts, examples of which are given below:

- Theme 1: Sexual arousal. 'Girls got dressed up in school uniforms at University [disco revivals] which was a turn-on so I started to look for school uniforms, school girls on the Internet.' This was the overwhelming theme in terms of frequency of occurrence.
- Theme 2: Emotional avoidance. 'But when I was online it was a completely discreet and isolated world.'
- Theme 3: Collecting. 'Particularly when the images were getting younger and I noticed . . . you would get sets of images as well and that played quite a big part as well . . . to get complete sets of things.'
- Theme 4: Facilitating social relationships. 'I was more interested in the conversations I was getting, the friendship I was getting . . . the images . . . provided me with a form of communication . . . that was my pleasure . . . I was very lonely . . . to prove that they were genuine they sent me the indecent stuff . . . I had to prove myself that I were genuine by doing the same to them.'

Of course, this amounts to a classification system for men's reasons for using child pornography. Although the sexual arousal function was extremely common (75 per cent of Internet-only sex offenders), there is clearly potential to use the system in order to further develop research and theory in this field. For example, could it be that certain types of use are more associated with eventual contact offences against children than others? The fit of the excerpts to the names of the themes seems good. Also, certainly in terms of the examples cited though this is more generally true, the themes are conceptually very different. Of course, there are some offenders who mentioned things which corresponded to more than one theme but these different themes were clearly distinguishable from each other. If the illustrative excerpts do not fit the themes very well then this may be a signal that the analysis is not complete and more work needs to be done. It is a common error in student work and the mismatch of excerpt to theme is a sign that all is not well with the analysis process.

Box 7.2

ILLUSTRATIVE RESEARCH STUDY

Thematic analysis: a website for women paedophiles

Female sex offenders have only the sparsest of coverage in the psychological literature (Howitt, 1995) for any number of reasons – that they are rare in the criminal justice system being the most important one. Lambert and O'Halloran (2008) carried out a deductive thematic analysis, which they attributed to Braun and Clarke (2006), concerning female sex offenders. My overall impression is that Lambert and O'Halloran's paper is more quantitative than qualitative in ethos. In their paper, Lambert and O'Halloran describe their analysis of the 'personal stories' of six women and the 'frequently asked questions' (FAQs) that they found on a website for women with a sexual interest in children. They describe the data as being written by women with a sexual interest in children for other women with a similar sexual interest. There are claims that in terms of the Internet perhaps up to one-third of 'offenders' are female (Finkelhor, Mitchell, & Wolak, 2000).

Lambert and O'Halloran give no indication of the amount of material involved but describe the stages of the analysis in some detail:

- Stage 1: The material on the website was read several times and the material for the analysis identified and copied onto a document. A more detailed examination of this data set was initiated and any thoughts about the data were put inside the left-hand margin. 'These notes related to concepts and phrases that the researcher considered interesting or significant' (p. 287).

- Stage 2: The data set was re-read a number of times more and the notes made at Stage 1 were converted into themes. They define a theme as 'something important that relates to the research interest, and represents some level of patterned response or meaning within the data set' (p. 287). Interestingly, and in keeping with the general 'quantitative' aura of this 'qualitative' report, a second researcher also carried out an analysis of the data set and developed her own set of themes. The final set of themes was a result of a negotiation between the two researchers

'until agreement was reached as to the validity and appropriateness of each theme' (p. 288).

- Stage 3: The data were re-read and the themes formed into 'specific clusters' of themes by drawing on known psychological concepts. Nine themes (e.g. 'child as seducer', 'sex with children is natural' and 'child sexuality oppressed in society') which relate to the concept of cognitive distortions were categorised into the broad theme of cognitive distortions.

- Stage 4: 'The clusters were categorized based on their relationships to a specific psychological concept' (p. 288). In addition to cognitive distortions, the themes of sexual motivation, recognition barriers, personal factors and role of the Internet were also created.

- Stage 5: The researchers identified statements from the data to illustrate each of the themes in each of the categories. Actually, the researchers say that they were to 'provide evidence of the existence of each theme within the various categories' (p. 288). These illustrative extracts were further examined in order to relate them back to the research question ('to investigate how women with a sexual interest in children engage with the Internet', p. 284) and the relevant research literature in order to produce a 'scholarly report'.

An example of a text excerpt used to support a theme is the following which is used to clarify the theme 'child as seducer':

B: 'an hour later I had really had my first lesbian experience with a 10 yr old and I was truly ashamed of myself as I had let her do what she wanted with me and I had responded to her requests and I had become a victim. I hadn't touched her but she had done things to me like I could not believe, even down to a very good session of oral sex and I was 12 years older than her.' (p. 291)

Despite the researchers identifying this theme and despite their penchant for quantification, there are no indications in the report of how common the theme of 'child as seducer' was identified in the data.

It is very clear from the report that this thematic analysis was guided not particularly by the data but by existing psychological theories and concepts related to male sex offenders – but applied to women with a sexual interest in children. In other words, this analysis was led by the literature review rather than by the data. Now this may be a useful way of analysing data but it is questionable whether it constitutes a qualitative data analysis in the fullest meaning of the phrase. Indeed, it might be regarded by some qualitative researchers as an elaborate way of trawling for examples to illustrate well-known themes. In other words, this thematic analysis seems largely to confirm what we know already from research on male sex offenders. Quite clearly it is useful to know that there is such a correspondence but whether one should regard this as thematic analysis is open to debate. Interestingly, since the themes were ostensibly developed from the data, rarely does the analysis question what has previously emerged from studies of male offenders. There are occasions when the researchers raise some slight criticisms of what is already known and its relevance to female offenders: 'Maternal incest is seen as particularly rare but the stories posted on the website show this to be untrue and it is argued that this form of abuse is much more prevalent than many assume. . .' (p. 293).

Box 7.3

ILLUSTRATIVE RESEARCH STUDY

Thematic analysis: dressing and body concerns

Body image is a staple topic for psychological investigation. However, in contrast, the everyday, ordinary grooming that we all do and its role in the maintenance and regulation of body image has been largely ignored (Frith & Gleeson, 2008). Researchers have tended to concentrate on negative aspects of body image whereas positive body image has been generally overlooked. Body image can be seen as being multidimensional involving attitudes, perceptions and evaluations of physical appearance. Psychological research generally has placed emphasis on social learning and cognitive factors in body image. One's appearance and associated beliefs and assumptions are intimately involved in the sense of self. There is a process of self-regulatory activity by which people govern and deal with issues to do with their body image.

Frith and Gleeson (2008) sought to shed light on how women 'create, manage, and negotiate, their body image' (p. 249). They focused on normal daily grooming practices involving dressing one's body. In particular, the researchers wanted to know: (a) whether women perceived that there was a relationship between the clothing they wear and the way they evaluated their body and (b) how women used clothing to conceal parts of their body which they felt to be unsatisfactory in order to assess the extent that this can be regarded as a self-regulatory practice. The researchers hoped to use the exploratory potential of qualitative methods to generate ideas for further research questions and theory development. Their methodology involved something they describe as the 'little used method of qualitative questionnaires'. This allowed them the opportunity of dealing with a larger sample than face-to-face interviews would have allowed. The qualitative questionnaire is an open-ended questionnaire which allows women the opportunity to make clear their key issues in relation to the research topic. Unlike closed-ended quantitative questionnaires, the qualitative questionnaire shows the subtlety, incompatibilities and ambiguities experienced by an individual in relation to their body image. A volunteer opportunity sampling method was used in which students contacted the participants on behalf of the researchers. Eighty-two women took part. Overwhelmingly they described themselves as White (88 per cent) and the second largest category was the 6 per cent who refused to answer this question.

Questions included on the questionnaire were:

- 'How much does the way you feel about your body influence the kinds of clothing you buy or wear?' (This assessed the participant's belief that there is a relationship between body image and dress.)
- 'Do you dress in a way that hides aspects of your body'?
- 'Do you dress in a way that emphasizes aspects of your body'?

The instructions asked the participants to write as much as possible, give examples wherever possible of clothing items they had bought, would like to buy, and wish they had not purchased. Data analysis used inductive thematic analysis as described by Hayes (2000). This is summarised in Figure 7.4. As can be seen, their approach was more or less similar to the methods described in this chapter. Thematic analysis is an inductive process in that general themes are derived from the instances available (or the data in other words). The researchers chose it for their data because it does not involve using a ready-made theoretical framework.

Unusually, and so noteworthy in qualitative research, the researchers used a second rater in order to assess the reliability of the themes developed in the analysis. Figure 7.5 shows the themes and sub-themes developed during the analysis.

Most women were bothered in some way about aspects of their body and mostly they felt that their feelings about their body influenced their dressing habits. Over 40 per cent wrote on their questionnaire that their feelings about their body had a big influence on what they wore. They report being conscious or insecure about features of their own bodies that they don't like or even hate. Phrases such as 'stick out too much' or 'out of proportion' were used. Then they would do things such as hide bulges by choosing new clothes to do just that. Or they wrote about big jumpers as being nice to hide in. About a third hid their bottoms, a third hid their legs/thighs, a quarter hid their stomach and a tenth hid their breasts in this way. But at the same time, participants reported using clothing to emphasise aspects of their body which they were happy with – half mentioned emphasising their breasts, a third mentioned

Step 1	Step 2	Step 3	Step 4
The questionnaires were carefully read through. Sentences (meaningful units) relevant to the research topic are identified. For example 'I do not like the size of my bust' is a meaningful unit of text and sentence.	The parts of the text (sentences) which were about the same issue were put together into grouping or analytic categories. These were then given a provisional definition. The same text could go into more than one catagory if appropriate. For example 'I dislike *** about my body' would be an analytic category	The questionnaires were systematically examined. The researchers wished to make sure that each of the categories of the analysis were given appropriate names, were clearly defined, and were represented in the data.	Categories were brought together as appropriate into a number of broader themes inclusive of a number of categories. For example 'Women use clothing to hide aspects of their body that they dislike' would be a theme based on the categories

FIGURE 7.4 How Frith and Gleeson analysed their data

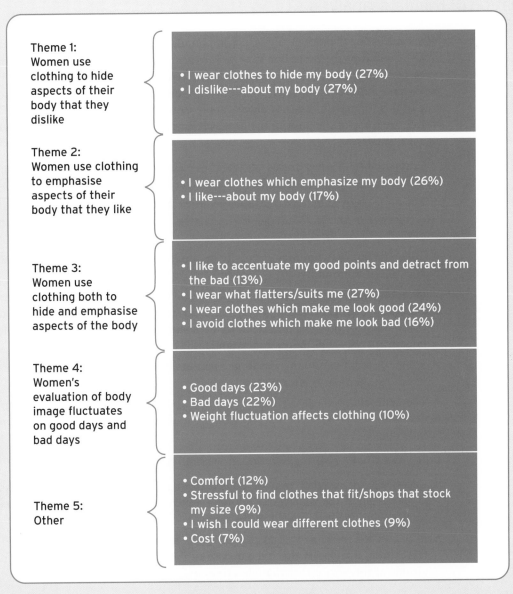

Theme 1:
Women use clothing to hide aspects of their body that they dislike

- I wear clothes to hide my body (27%)
- I dislike---about my body (27%)

Theme 2:
Women use clothing to emphasise aspects of their body that they like

- I wear clothes which emphasize my body (26%)
- I like---about my body (17%)

Theme 3:
Women use clothing both to hide and emphasise aspects of the body

- I like to accentuate my good points and detract from the bad (13%)
- I wear what flatters/suits me (27%)
- I wear clothes which make me look good (24%)
- I avoid clothes which make me look bad (16%)

Theme 4:
Women's evaluation of body image fluctuates on good days and bad days

- Good days (23%)
- Bad days (22%)
- Weight fluctuation affects clothing (10%)

Theme 5:
Other

- Comfort (12%)
- Stressful to find clothes that fit/shops that stock my size (9%)
- I wish I could wear different clothes (9%)
- Cost (7%)

FIGURE 7.5 The themes and sub-themes identified by Frith and Gleeson

emphasising their legs/height, and a sixth mentioned emphasising their waist/stomach. These things are not static but fluctuate over time and across circumstances.

Frith and Gleeson's study is interesting at a number of levels. From the point of view of methodology they clearly document numerically the extent to which certain themes, etc. are to be found in the data. So there is an element of quantification. What makes it different from a quantitative study is the use of the research participants to generate the data from their own resources – the researcher does not use pre-specified categories in the research but uses the participant's writings to generate categories and, eventually, themes. Furthermore, they do

not characterise individuals as having a fixed characteristic but, instead, see things as being in a state of variability, flux, fluctuation and so forth. So a woman does not feel consistently or permanently good or bad about her body but these feelings may occur at certain times or they may vary sometimes unexpectedly. Much the same is true of the clothing strategies that a woman adopts – variability in strategies is a more accurate description than stability. Perhaps most important of all, body image is not a fixed characteristic of women but something that also changes. All of this is very different in tone from the typical quantitative study. That is to say, despite the numbers this study clearly is steeped in the qualitative ethos.

Evaluation of thematic analysis

When evaluating thematic analysis, it is important to remember that the Braun and Clarke (2006) version of the procedure may be substantially better than those adopted by other researchers claiming to use thematic analysis. That is, thematic analysis covers a range of procedures and not all of them would meet Braun and Clarke's ideals. So what may be true of their approach may not always apply to what has happened in practice. The following are some of the positive things which Braun and Clarke say can be claimed about thematic analysis:

- Compared with other forms of qualitative analysis, thematic analysis makes fewer demands in terms of data collection and fewer constraints in terms of data analysis.
- Thematic analysis is relatively easy to learn and understand compared with other qualitative methods. Consequently it may be used by a novice researcher with little difficulty.
- Thematic analysis findings are easily understood by intelligent and educated members of the community.
- Its accessibility to the general public means that it can be used for participatory studies involving particular groups and the researcher. For example, it is unlikely that a thematic analysis of interviews with staff in a casualty unit will produce findings which they will fail to understand.
- Thematic analysis summarises large amounts of data by offering descriptive themes which can be rich in information.
- Thematic analysis can be useful in qualitative research which may inform policy development because of its accessibility and use of data produced by involved individuals.

Braun and Clarke also suggest, though without any systematic evidence, that:

- 'unanticipated insights' may be gained through thematic analysis – this, however, is only likely if the procedures adopted are centred on the data and the researcher revises their analysis in light of the data;
- it 'allows for social as well as psychological interpretations of data' (p. 97) – while this is true, it suggests that the purpose of thematic analysis is to provide interpretations of this sort rather than descriptions.

On the other hand, experience suggests that thematic analysis is such a catch-all term that some research described as thematic analysis fails to live up to Braun and Clarke's expectation or the expectations of qualitative researchers in general. In my experience, there are any number of student dissertations, for example, which seem to pluck a few quotations out of the data, label them with a theme, and basically fail to meet the ideals of a thematic analysis or qualitative analysis in general. But, as we have seen, it is easy to do far better than this. Figure 7.6 summarises some of the quality criteria which can be applied to a thematic analysis.

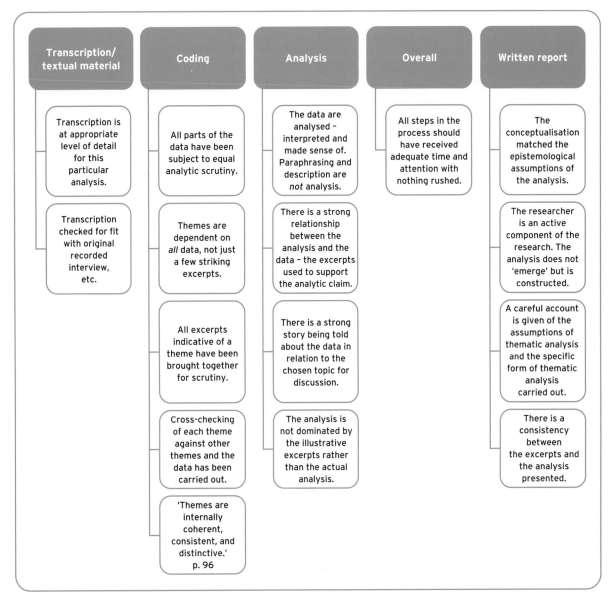

FIGURE 7.6   The quality criteria for a thematic analysis (after Braun & Clarke, 2006)

CONCLUSION

The label thematic analysis says more or less what is involved in this sort of analysis. Thematic analysis is a research procedure in which textual material (newspapers, interviews and so forth) is analysed in order to indicate the major themes to be found in that text. *The Concise Oxford Dictionary* defines a theme as 'a subject or topic on which a person speaks, writes, or thinks'. While this is not quite the sense of the word 'theme' as used in thematic analysis, it is a common-sense meaning which gets sufficiently close. Those new to qualitative analysis are probably right to be considering thematic analysis as their first steps in qualitative research. Its lack of a theoretical infrastructure as well as the limited demands it places on the researcher are good enough reasons in themselves to try out thematic analysis. Its user-friendly reputation is a boon but it is capable of generating useful, if limited, summary descriptions of the data in the form of themes. Adopting a superficial approach to thematic analysis will show in the very limited scope of the analysis generated. Ideally the researcher will not be satisfied with the mundane and superficial. The approach described in this chapter should allow researchers to avoid the trap. The simplicity of thematic analysis disguises the fact that it is the hard work of the analyst which is decisive in generating the themes. The more the researcher is prepared to challenge the analysis at each stage the better the final outcome is likely to be. No matter how tempting it is to suggest a few themes which then become 'the analysis', this does disservice to the idea of thematic analysis.

KEY POINTS

- Historically, thematic analysis has existed as a method virtually without any well-known advocates. As a consequence, its development as a methodology has been delayed until very recently. It is notable, then, how readily the method can be brought into line with the major objectives of most qualitative analysis. Ultimately, because it is a descriptive method rather than a theory-directed approach, thematic analysis cannot substitute effectively for the theoretically stronger methods discussed in the next few chapters.

- A good thematic analysis is built on a great deal of analytic work on the part of the researcher. The processes involved are generally very familiar to qualitative researchers and are based on the intense, detailed and hard work of the analyst. The major processes are data familiarisation, data coding, date recoding and theme development. A researcher unwilling to devote the required amount of intense effort will tend to produce weaker and less-convincing analyses. They have only superficially analysed their data so produce less insightful and comprehensive themes.

- In order to ensure the future development of thematic analysis as a sophisticated procedure, researchers should report in some great detail the way in which they went about the thematic analysis. The analysis does not simply 'emerge' from the data but is the consequence of a lot of good practices and a lot of hard work employed by the researcher which should be described in the report.

- Almost without exception, a good thematic analysis may be amenable to quantification. If themes can be properly defined then it should be unproblematic to count, for example, the number of times a particular theme emerges in different interviews. Prevalence is the number of participants who say things relevant to a particular theme and incidence is the frequency of occurrence of the theme throughout the data set or the average number of times it occurs in each participant's data.

ADDITIONAL RESOURCES

Boyatzis, R. E. (1998). *Transforming qualitative information.* Thousand Oaks, CA: Sage.

Braun, V., & Clarke, V. (2006). Using thematic analysis in psychology. *Qualitative Research in Psychology, 3,* 77–101.

Howitt, D., & Cramer, D. (2014). *Introduction to research methods in psychology* (4th ed.). Harlow: Pearson.

This also contains a simpler approach to thematic analysis.

Miles, M., & Huberman, M. (1994). *Qualitative data analysis: An expanded sourcebook.* London: Sage.

CHAPTER 8

Qualitative data analysis: grounded theory development

Overview

- Grounded theory was seminal in defining qualitative research as a systematic form of research. It grew out of the work of Barney Glaser and Anselm Strauss in the 1960s, although subsequently Glaser and Strauss developed somewhat different emphases in terms of how grounded theory research is carried out.

- Grounded theory is theory which develops out of a close interaction between the data and the developing understanding of the data. The fit between the theory and the data should be close in grounded theory. The process of theory building involves constant checking backwards and forwards between different aspects of the analysis process.

- Typically, grounded theory proceeds from the initial data collection and analysis stage to the collection of further new data guided by the initial analysis (theoretical sampling). The process is typically one of line-by-line coding of transcribed texts such as interviews or focus groups. These codings are then sorted into categories from which the basic theoretical ideas and relationships can be identified. The process may proceed to other stages including the collection of fresh data to help 'validate' the study's emerging theoretical ideas and to also examine whether the theory is more generally applicable.

- The researcher writes ideas, concepts and other analytic notions in a memo as an aid to theory development.

- Grounded theory probably works best where people's common-sense understandings of the world provide appropriate data to help answer the research question.

- There are a number of criticisms of grounded theory. Some question the nature of the 'theory' which emerges, the delay it imposes on the use of theory may be counterproductive where there is relevant theory already available, and its frequent lack of clarity, for example.

- It is notable that a good proportion of grounded theory studies concentrate solely on the initial theory building stages. These generate the categories which largely constitute the theory in many studies. Some researchers are reluctant to go beyond this stage to test out the theory and hypotheses derived from the theory in order to broaden its applicability.

What is grounded theory?

According to Bryman (2004), grounded theory is the most widely used way of analysing qualitative data. Grounded theory was groundbreaking in the sense of providing a relatively formal but vigorous approach to the analysis of qualitative data. It also involved ways of collecting data which had a mutuality and an interrelation with the analysis of the data. It was a development of the 1960s when among the discontent of academics was the gulf between *empirical* research and theory building as well as the general feeling that *qualitative* research lacked the rigour that academic disciplines require. It grew from the work of the sociologists Barney Glaser (1930–) and Anselm Strauss (1916–1996). While nowadays it is commonplace for qualitative researchers to take great pains to establish the validity of their analyses, such concerns were really the contribution of Glaser, Strauss and grounded theory. (See Chapter 16 for a discussion of some of the many quality criteria that have been proposed by qualitative researchers.) One might say that grounded theory is based on two major concepts. Both concepts were heretical in terms of the positivistic social science of the time. *Constant comparison* involves the simultaneous collection and analysis of the data. The data and the analysis are constantly being compared one with the other. This violates the positivist view that data are collected and then analysed, with the analysis having no influence on the data collection process. *Theoretical sampling* is the idea that the theory/categorisation which the researcher is working on should help determine what data is to be collected next.

The first major publication detailing grounded theory was Glaser and Strauss's (1967) *The discovery of grounded theory*. It can be regarded as both innovative and radical as well as being decisive in undermining the dominant sociology of the time. The book determinedly argued for a close relation between empirical research data and theory to replace the highly speculative grand sociological theories of the time which had little grounding in research data and, equally, the barren wastes of atheoretical empiricism which gave much research a bad name then. Like many others they rejected the idea that science depends on an independent external reality (the positivist position). Scientific knowledge is the consequence of the process of observation and the sense-making process engaged in by a community of researchers or observers which leads to a consensus. Thus empirical reality is an ongoing process by which meaning is interpreted in the common project of scientific observation (Suddaby, 2006). Grounded theory essentially assumed that there must be a close link between empirical data and theory building and required that the data analyses which led to the theory and the theory itself were thoroughly tested and convincingly questioned and challenged. Grounded theory provided a way forward in the development of qualitative research – though it was never intended exclusively for qualitative data. There are clearly potential credibility issues in qualitative research methods. A stereotype of qualitative research around the 1950s/1960s would highlight the apparent subjectivity of the analysis process. None of the usual quality checks which pervade quantitative research – issues such as reliability and validity – typified qualitative research at the time. Not that Glaser and Strauss were advocates of reliability and validity in the form that they take in quantitative research. They were uncertain as to whether traditional concepts of reliability and validity were appropriate to grounded theory and felt that they stultify the process of discovery through research. Instead, for example, their approach to validity would include respondent validation – the idea that the theory developed out of research should make sense to those participating in the research. But, of course, there is much more to validation in qualitative research than that (see Chapter 16).

Glaser and Strauss's early work on grounded theory was written at a time when positivism and quantification had the upper hand. Perhaps it then should come as no surprise that Glaser and Strauss wrote of the 'discovery' of theory much as positivist psychologists had sought to 'discover' the laws of psychology. The laws of psychology, somehow, waiting in the real world to be found. A few years later, the growing idea that scientific knowledge is constructed by researchers rather than discovered by them (Gergen & Graumann, 1996) probably made this view contested in grounded theory. This is one example of how grounded theory has changed over time and is part of the explanation why apparently different factions of grounded theory researchers have emerged. Indeed, Glaser and Strauss parted academic company in the 1990s over the matter of how grounded theory should be done. (Remember, grounded theory incorporates quantitative research although it is regarded primarily as a qualitative analysis method.) Hutchinson, Johnston and Breckon (2011) describe the changes in how the production of theory is described in grounded theory over the years:

> The original grounded theory texts (Glaser 1978; Glaser & Strauss 1967) refer to discovering theory as emerging from data separate from the scientific observer or researcher involved. Therefore, despite setting out to counter the dominant positivistic practices of the time, they appeared to still conform to a naïve or scientific realist framework. Strauss and Corbin's (1990, 1998) subsequent revisions of the methodology appeared to move away from this position towards a more interpretative stance by acknowledging the researcher as an active part of the theory generating process. However, in attempts to outline more usable guidelines for conducting grounded theory, they described a number of technical prescriptive procedures, which again communicated a more objective stance. This debate surrounding the role of the researcher in the knowledge construction process led to another notable revision of the methodology proposed by Charmaz (2000, 2006), which acknowledges the constructivist perspective. Charmaz assumes that neither data nor theories are discovered. Rather, she identifies the fact that we are part of the world we study and the data we collect and suggests that grounded theories are constructed through our past and present involvements and interactions with people, perspectives and research practices (Charmaz 2006). More recently, in attempts to reposition grounded theory in light of the current philosophical and epistemological landscape, a distinction has been made between objectivist and constructivist revisions of grounded theory (Bryant 2002; Bryant & Charmaz 2007; Charmaz 2000, 2006). (Hutchinson et al., 2011, p. 248)

The grounded in grounded theory is fairly straightforward since theory in grounded theory is situated in the empirical work involved in data collection. However, the nature of theory in grounded theory might cause some problems. This is not a problem per se for newcomers to grounded theory alone. The word 'theory' itself is hardly the most consistently applied term in psychology and its meaning just about embraces anything which is not just an empirical relationship. Theory can be a very loosely defined phrase referring to things such as broad principles or personal reflections but it can also involve relatively 'hard' definitions. So theory can also include things such as 'a well-developed system of ideas which integrate considerable amounts of knowledge' and, maybe, 'has the potential for allowing prediction'. Fish (1989) rejects the value of the notion of theory since, in his view, it really refers to 'theory talk' which is a way of thinking about things in research which has acquired 'cachet and prestige'. This can be seen quite often in fashionable conceptualisations in psychology which are major talking points but then fade from researchers' radar screen. So don't worry too much if discussions of 'theory' seem to be beyond your grasp.

One frequently reads the phrase 'middle-range' theories to describe grounded theories but this is not a self-evident term either. There is a problem in that many grounded theory analyses do not push the method or its use of data to its limits. Consequently, some of the theory generated by grounded theory analyses fails to represent grounded theory in its fullest meaning as intended in some of the original publications of Glaser and Strauss. It is important to remember that much of the data used in grounded theory analyses consist of 'rich' data from individuals in the form of interviews, focus groups, diaries and so forth. This, then, implies that grounded theory is theory for which these forms of data are pertinent. However the term middle-range theory was put forward by the distinguished American sociologist Robert Merton in his book *Social theory and social structure* in 1949. The middle-range theory occupies the space between the sort of simple, everyday hypotheses or explanations that researchers use when describing their empirical observations and the much more complex, all-inclusive grand theories which are drawn up to explain major areas of life. Actually, it is harder to come up with examples of grand theories in recent psychology than it is to think of middle-ground theories. Most of the best examples of grand theories come from classic fields of psychology such as Freud's psychoanalytic theory, Piaget's theory of cognitive development, symbolic interactionism, Eysenck's personality theory, Cattell's personality theory, Vygotsky's cultural historical school of psychology and so forth. According to Merton, grand theories do little to guide researchers directly in terms of how to collect pertinent empirical evidence. They tend to be rather abstract and, consequently, somewhat difficult to apply directly in empirical research. For one reason, they were major integrations of many aspects of a particular field of psychology and, therefore, fail to meet the highly specific needs of researchers planning research.

Middle range is a description which applies to many theories in psychology which are based in data but synthesise a range of studies and findings. Psychology is replete with examples of simple, empirical generalisations which do little than attempt to explain the relationship between a pair of variables. So, middle-range theory goes beyond the requirements of a highly particular piece of empirical research but falls well short of being all-embracing, all-encompassing theory. Examples of middle-range theory in psychology are then numerous. Theories such as the just-world theory, cognitive dissonance, the pathways model of sexual offending, relative judgement theory might all be considered psychological, middle-range theories. These are examples of middle-ground theory in mainstream psychology *not* middle-ground theory developed from grounded theory. This level of theorizing typifies much of the useful theory in psychology.

Grounded theory is grounded in particular sorts of data pertinent to the research question. Consequently, we should expect that grounded theories are particularly related to the sorts of in-depth data which can be obtained using focus groups, in-depth interviews, diaries, narratives, newspaper stories and the like. So theories about the different ideologies underlying people's thinking, how different sorts of person interact with others, the ways children talk about authority figures in their lives and so forth would be examples of middle-range grounded theories. Middle-range theory is not really a mysterious concept – it is just based on a rather ill-defined idea.

There is another way to theory development in grounded theory – this is known as the 'rewrite' technique. According to Glaser:

> One version of rewriting techniques is simply to omit substantive words, phrases, or adjectives; instead of writing 'temporal aspects of dying as a non-scheduled status passage', one would write 'temporal aspects of non-scheduled status passage.' Substantive theory can also be rewritten up a notch: instead of writing about how doctors and nurses give medical attention to a dying patient according to his social loss, one would talk of how professional services are distributed according to the social value of clients . . . In each version of the rewriting technique, the social scientist writes a one-area formal theory on the basis of his substantive theory; he does not generate the former directly from the data. These techniques produce only an adequate *start* towards theory, *not* an adequate formal theory itself. *The researcher has raised the conceptual level of his work mechanically; he has not raised it through comparative understanding.* (Glaser, 1982, p. 226)

In other words, if theory is generated through re-write techniques then its grounding in the data cannot be taken for granted and needs to be assessed against relevant data.

As we will see in detail later, the process of carrying out a proper grounded theory analysis is demanding. The procedures involved are based on constant referral back and forward between the data and the analysis. There are numerous different ways of doing this but none is easy. Not surprisingly, then, some researchers describe their research as being based on grounded theory despite the fact that the work they present shows few indications that the rigorous procedures of grounded theory have been employed. This sort of lip-service to grounded theory is unfortunate since the newcomer to qualitative research may be confused as to what actually grounded theory is in practice. So be wary of the possibility that a study which claims to be based on grounded theory actually is only minimally so. Like all research and especially qualitative research of a high standard, grounded theory methods are exacting, time-consuming and meticulous. They demand close familiarity with the data and such intimacy itself takes a good deal of time and effort to achieve.

The ultimate aim of grounded theory is to develop theory appropriate to the data and justifiable by a close examination of the data. However, much grounded theory research stops short in the development of theory and concentrates on categorisation of aspects of the data. The process of categorisation is fundamental to grounded theory anyway so such descriptive accounts of the data are valuable even though it is difficult sometimes to describe the product as middle-range theory. Essentially the process involved in grounded theory:

- brings the researcher into close familiarity with their data;
- encourages the researcher to code small elements of the data;
- encourages the researcher to synthesise these various small elements into categories; and
- continually requires the researcher to compare the data with the developing theory (categories) in the analysis.

This process, in the most successful instances, may lead to the development of theory. But it should be noted that the sort of theory that grounded theory generates does not have all of the characteristics which mainstream psychologists, as a whole, regard as the signs of a good theory. In particular, many psychologists assume that a good theory will help them make predictions about what people will do in certain circumstances. This sort of precise prediction is not an aim of grounded theory. The theory developed in a grounded theory analysis may be capable of being applied to new sets of data but it is not usually possible to make causal predictions. According to Charmaz, grounded theory provides the guidelines for the collection and analysis of data which are then used to develop theories which account for and explain that data:

> Throughout the research process, grounded theorists develop analytic interpretations of their data to focus further data collection, which they use in turn to inform and refine their developing theoretical analyses. (Charmaz, 2000, p. 509)

The following are some of the important characteristics of grounded theory:

- *Systematic* The process by which theory is developed is through the careful application of the general principles and methods of grounded theory.
- *Guidelines* Grounded theory is essentially a system of guidelines which guide data collection, data analysis and theory building. The emerging research and theory are closely tied to social reality as far as that is represented in the data.
- *Inductive processes are more important than deductive processes* This is very different from conventional theory building in psychology in which hypotheses are deduced from theory and these hypotheses are subjected to empirical testing. Such an approach to theory building is commonly communicated to psychology students in introductory mainstream psychology textbooks.
- *Theory building is a continuous process* Grounded theory develops theory through a continuous process rather than by critical tests of hypotheses as in conventional

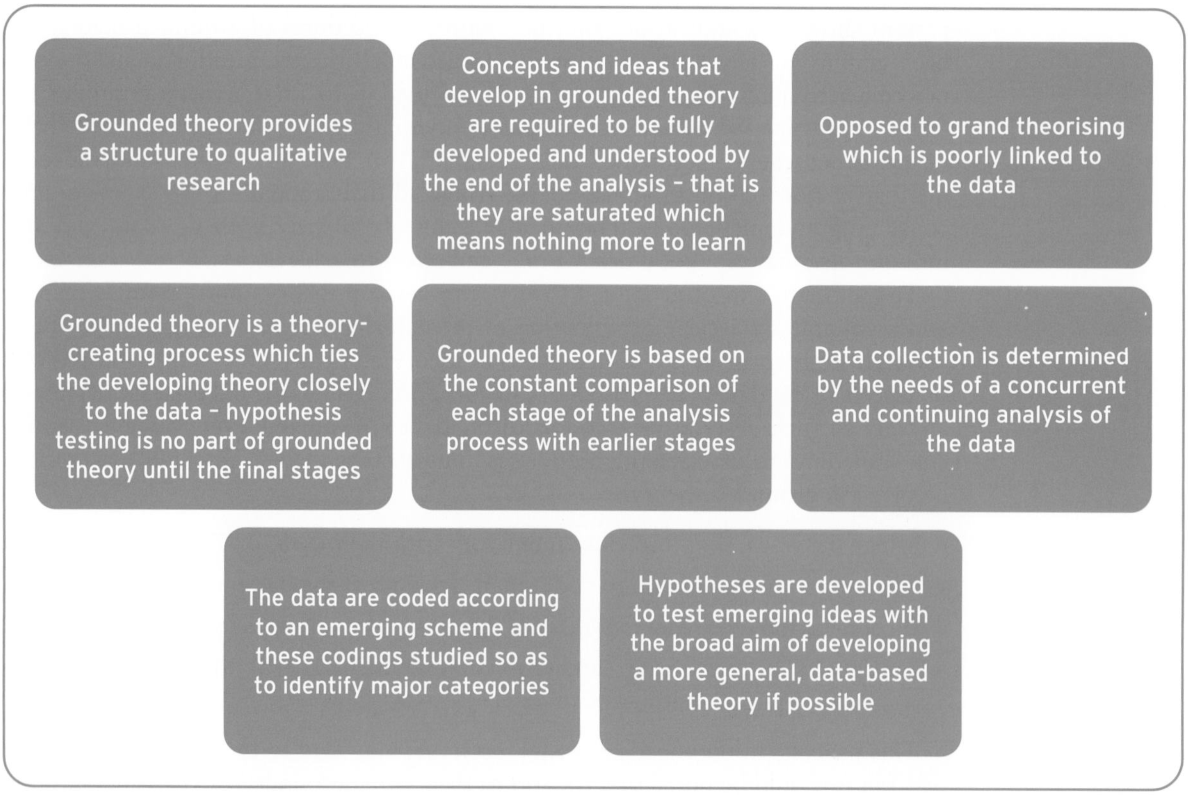

Grounded theory provides a structure to qualitative research	Concepts and ideas that develop in grounded theory are required to be fully developed and understood by the end of the analysis – that is they are saturated which means nothing more to learn	Opposed to grand theorising which is poorly linked to the data
Grounded theory is a theory-creating process which ties the developing theory closely to the data – hypothesis testing is no part of grounded theory until the final stages	Grounded theory is based on the constant comparison of each stage of the analysis process with earlier stages	Data collection is determined by the needs of a concurrent and continuing analysis of the data
The data are coded according to an emerging scheme and these codings studied so as to identify major categories	Hypotheses are developed to test emerging ideas with the broad aim of developing a more general, data-based theory if possible	

FIGURE 8.1 Key elements of grounded theory

theory building. It is impossible to separate grounded theory research into a small number of discrete stages since theory development begins early – even at the data collection stage – and continues to the stage of writing-up.

Some of the main elements of grounded theory are shown in Figure 8.1.

The development of grounded theory

The popularity of grounded theory over the last 50 years is undeniable. But why? According to Thomas and James:

> Grounded theory, and other techniques of analysis in qualitative inquiry are bound to be popular because they meet a need. For while qualitative inquiry is absolutely valid, it is difficult to do . . . it may entail taking part, watching and listening, in schools and other environments. But when all this is done, what comes next? Such ways of doing research can lead to a floating feeling, a lack of direction. What does one do with one's data? Surely one can't just talk about it. Grounded theory offers a solution: a set of procedures, and a means of generating theory. As such, it has become widely used and its reputation as an accessible and thorough explained method in qualitative inquiry has grown and grown. (Thomas & James, 2006, p. 768)

Barney Glaser and Anselm Strauss published their book *Awareness of dying* in 1965. Strauss began to work at the medical school of the University of California at San Francisco and gradually realised that hospitals found dying a difficult subject to deal with. He began fieldwork into the topic and hired Glaser to help. The researchers came to the view that the expectation of death both on the part of the patient and the people around him or her had a big impact on interaction between those involved. They distinguished a number of different classifications of this expectation which ranged from open awareness to closed awareness to suspicion and to mutual deception. Nurses had difficulties where the patient did not know that they were dying since they had to avoid revealing it to the patient. The book attracted a lot of attention and, arguably, can be seen as the first occasion when grounded theory was employed in research. Their later book, *The discovery of grounded theory* (Glaser & Strauss, 1967), was essentially an attempt to describe the method of grounded theory and its limitations. It became one of the classics in sociology and beyond.

Glaser and Strauss were intent on closing the 'embarrassing' (Glaser & Strauss, 1967, p. vii) gap between theory and empirical research in sociology. Interestingly, given this intent, Glaser had been a student of both the arch methodologist of sociology (and certain areas of psychology for that matter), Paul Lazarsfeld, and Robert Merton, the outstanding theorist, at Columbia University. Of course, Lazarsfeld as a methodologist was creative and innovative. He crossed the divide between quantitative and qualitative readily and saw both as important (Bailey, 2014; Morrison, 1998). According to Strauss and Corbin (1994), the book had three distinct purposes:

- To provide a rationale for the grounding of theory in data. That is, a method for developing theory in which the development of theory was part of an interplay with research data.
- To provide a logic for and detail of grounded theory.
- To provide a sound basis for thorough qualitative research in sociology given the low status of qualitative sociology at the time.

Probably out of these three, the final purpose has been the book's most startling achievement and its earliest. As we have seen, grounded theory is often described as being in opposition to the dominant and theoretically highly speculative sociology which emerged and enveloped sociology in the first half of the twentieth century and beyond. More specifically, writers tend to specify the reaction of grounded theory as being to the Chicago School of Sociology. The school developed an ecological approach to the sociology of urban areas. It had a big influence on criminology and contributed some of the earliest approaches to quantification to that discipline. It replaced armchair-theorising with an emphasis on the collection of data and its rigorous analysis. But the theory that developed at the University of Chicago tended to think 'big' in terms of very broad processes which were contributing to social and urban change. In the works of some of the earliest members of the Chicago School were elements which linked sociological change to basic natural science models in ecological research. Human communities were treated as if they consisted of subpopulations which operated in response to similar forces to those in ecological populations. So, for example, a subpopulation would begin to invade a territory and eventually achieve dominance only then to fade when another subpopulation began to succeed in the same territory. But the Chicago School was long-lasting and its influence complex – at the time a massive proportion of graduates in sociology were graduates of the school. One of its influences was in terms of the use of standardised measuring instruments for the collection of data.

Of course, it is possible to see in psychology's quantitative dominance many of the characteristics of the Chicago School. Despite the Chicago School's exploitation of the field setting, the focus was on very broad processes rather than the detail of social interaction. Much the same can be seen in much of the psychology of the twentieth century in the sense that the discipline concentrated on what could be quantified. These tended to be fairly gross abstractions. Charmaz (1995) argues that in sociology the theorist and the researcher were largely distinct roles in early twentieth-century sociology. Something of the same can be seen in the divide between the theorist and the empiricist in much psychology during the same period.

According to Thomas and James (2006), 'grounded theory represented a resolution of different epistemological positions and a solution to a broader problem about perceptions of the status of qualitatively-based knowledge in the social sciences' (pp. 767–768). They suggest that symbolic interactionism was declining as a force in the social sciences but, more importantly, the 'hard' science approaches of statistics and structural functionalism which squeezed other approaches powerfully was also somewhat in decline. Grounded theory reversed many of the features of the dominant sociology of the time in a number of ways:

- It established qualitative research as a legitimate venture in its own right rather than relegating it to a preliminary or preparatory stage of refining one's research instruments in preparation for the 'scientifically credible' quantitative study.
- The distinction between research and theory was removed by insisting that theory development and data collection were integral. Data collection and data analysis in the sense of theory development were virtually inseparable. Grounded theory provided methods by which theory development could be validated against the empirical data.

Grounded theory can be seen as a general qualitative methodology which enables it to be adapted to a variety of areas of research. Furthermore, grounded theory requires no particular sort of data so it can be employed with diaries, biographies, newspaper and magazine articles, interviews and more. This clearly means that the potential spread of grounded theory is substantial and its penetration into disciplines such as anthropology and psychology as well as fields such as social work and education not surprising.

One of the major developments in grounded theory was the consequence of Glaser and Strauss going somewhat separate ways later in their careers. That is, the version of grounded theory expounded in *The discovery of grounded theory* evolved somewhat differently in the writings of the two men. This resulted in two options of how grounded theory analysis should be carried out. The split became most evident by the 1990s when Glaser criticised Strauss's then recent ideas and their differences became part of a more general academic debate. Onions (n.d.) provides a comparison of Glaser's approach and Strauss's approach. For example, Onions suggests that in Glaser's approach the good researcher begins with an empty mind (or 'general wonderment') whereas in Strauss's version the good researcher has a general idea of where to begin the research. For Glaser 'the theory is grounded in the data'; for Strauss 'the theory is interpreted by an observer' (p. 8). For Glaser 'The credibility of the theory, or verification, is derived from its grounding in the data'; for Strauss, 'The credibility of the theory comes from the rigour of the method' (pp. 8–9). For Glaser, 'A basic social process should be identified'; for Strauss, 'Basic social processes need not be identified' (p. 9). There is more to it than this, of course, but the flavour is captured to a degree by these examples. Perhaps the most telling comparison is that which suggests that for Glaser the characteristics of the researcher are passivity and disciplined restraint whereas for Strauss the researcher is a much more active participant. Furthermore, Glaser's strategy for grounded theory is not exclusively qualitative since anything can be data which the researcher comes across during his or her studies. Quantitative data (such as surveys and statistical analyses) can be part of the process of theory development in grounded theory. This is Glaser's perspective. The consequence of all of this is the difficulty in specifying quite what grounded theory procedures are. One solution, of course, is for the researcher to identify which camp they adhere to. The differences may not be so important so long as one explains just what the assumptions underlying one's analysis are.

How to do grounded theory

Grounded theory is a means of data analysis directed towards theory development. It is not a specific means of collecting data and a variety of data can be used though textual data are by far the most typical. No particular type of data is required although, as hinted, it does suit some types of data better than others – interviews and similar materials are well handled by the approach. Grounded theory can be applied to interviews, biographical data, media content, observations, conversations and so forth. It is possible and recommended that the researcher uses a multiplicity of sources in grounded theory. A key characteristic is, of course, that the data should be as richly detailed as possible – that is not simple or simplified. Charmaz (1995, p. 33) suggests that richly detailed data involve 'full' or 'thick' written descriptions. Questionnaires using yes–no and similar response formats do not meet this criterion. As such, data are usually initially transcribed using a notation system – it could be the Jefferson transcription system (Chapter 6) though more typically the transcription is much simpler, such as the orthographic/playscript format.

Grounded theory has been seen as a form of sophisticated filing system (Potter, 1998). In particular, the grounded theory 'filing system' does not simply file items under a range of headings but also provides extensive cross-referencing to other headings or categories in the filing system. So, for example, the grounded theory library catalogue might file the present book under the heading of 'psychology' but it would also be cross-referenced, say, under 'methods' or 'qualitative research'. Potter's analogy is a useful one and serves to remind us that data in grounded theory can be filed under several categories rather than a single one. There are, however, limitations to Potter's analogy:

- The grounded theory 'filing system' may be constantly changed and refined through to the final stages of the research – the theory to be found in the report or publication. Most filing systems remain the same until they cease to be useful – for example, a library cataloguing system might be revised when there are so many books under the heading sociology that it is no longer a useful way of quickly accessing books. At this point, new subcategories of the category 'sociology' may have to be developed such as sociological theory, industrial sociology, urban sociology and so forth. The system in grounded theory is different – the categorisation process will tend to reduce the number of categories, more clearly describe what each category is, and provide a picture of what is going on in the data.

- The grounded theory 'filing system' is developed through a constant process of comparing the data with the filing categories. That is to say, although some of the filing categories may seem to emerge out of inspection of the data, these categories are constantly subject to adjustment, modification and change in light of fresh data and whether or not the categories make sense. Indeed, the categories may become more inclusive or less inclusive depending on the researcher's revised understanding of what the categories are about.

- Perhaps a trifle oddly, the grounded theory 'filing system' developed in one study may well be abandoned for other studies and new and different filing systems created. Indeed, the researcher may deliberately choose to ignore other grounded theory 'filing' systems in order to see the extent to which new studies generate grounded theory 'filing systems' which are similar or different from previous 'filing systems'.

There is a huge literature from different disciplines on grounded theory as well as numerous examples of its use. As one might expect, this results in some variation in how grounded theory is carried out. Indeed, any researcher carrying out grounded theory will probably develop their own idiosyncratic working methods within the broad procedures which characterise grounded theory.

It is not possible to divide a grounded theory analysis into discrete, independent steps. Although explanations of grounded theory have to be sequential, a grounded theory analysis involves going backwards and forwards between analytical stages very flexibly. This is not a random process but purposive in that it is based on the constant need to check and test the fit of one's emerging theoretical ideas with the data, the codings, the categories and new data. Memo-writing is an important tool in this. The memo may be as simple as a notebook in which the researcher records theoretical ideas as they develop in his or her thinking through the process of the grounded theory analysis. These notes do not have to be elaborate theoretical speculation since they may include half-thought-out ideas concerning matters that the researcher needs to think about. At a more conceptual level, they may be suggestions as to how codings, categories and concepts relate or link together. A memo can include diagrams if these are the best way of presenting the ideas. Boxes of text linked by arrows where appropriate (like a flow diagram) might be a typical diagrammatic memo. It is useful to record what aspects of the analysis are interdependent as well as identifying possible relationships. A researcher's categories cannot be understood solely in their own terms – they take their meaning also from what they are not. So to understand a category such as 'male' really needs an understanding of other categories such as 'female' from which it derives part of its meaning. This is known as interdependency.

The memo is not totally independent of the data. The memo needs to include the most important and significant examples of data which are illustrative of the more general run of the data. So the memo should be replete with illustrative instances of data plus problematic aspects of it at the particular stage of the analysis. Of course, the researcher new to grounded theory may struggle to know exactly what to include in the memo. It may be useful to note the following in this regard:

> If you are at a loss about what to write about, look for the codes that you have used repeatedly in your data collection. Then start elaborating on these codes. Keep collecting data, keep coding and keep refining your ideas through writing more and further developed memos. (Charmaz, 1995, p. 43)

Sometimes memo-writing is described as the intermediary step between data and the theory in the final written report or journal article. Sometimes the advice is to start memo-writing as soon as one recognises something of interest in the data, the coding or the categorisation process. This may be a little late in practice. The general consensus is that the researchers should start memo-writing as early as possible – the sooner the better is the dictum to work with. Hence, some researchers prefer to start memo-writing at the stage of developing the research question.

Characteristically, quantitative researchers seek to reduce concepts to a minimum by developing a small number of concepts which explain as much of the features of the data as possible. A famous principle in quantitative research is Occam's razor, which states that the researcher should use no more than the least number of concepts needed to account for the phenomenon in question. Conceptual density (Strauss & Corbin, 1999) is a phrase used to describe the richness of concept development and relationship identification in grounded theory. In other words, this is another indication that theory development in grounded theory is quite different from that in quantitative research. The main stages in the development of a grounded theory are shown in Figure 8.2. You may notice that this figure is rather more complex than any of the equivalent ones in Chapters 7 and 9–14. This simply reflects the characteristics of grounded theory. The key components of the grounded theory method include coding/naming, comparison, categorisation, memo-writing, theoretical sampling and the literature review. The following describes each of these and follows Charmaz's (1995, 2000) procedural recommendations and Bryman's (2004) scheme.

Step 1 **Developing a research question** Deciding upon a research question is a major step in virtually any research. As any student seeking ideas for a project or dissertation knows, the research question is one of the most difficult aspects of planning research of any sort. The sources of research questions can be many – the opportunity to do research with a particular organisation, personal interest based on experience, matters of public concern, the research literature, and so forth. The research described in Box 8.1 later in the chapter on experiencing symptoms of heart attacks is partially based on (a) the previous research literature and (b) the institutional context in which the authors were working (basically the field of public health). Whether the research was stimulated by personal interest is not revealed by the researchers.

The role of the literature review in developing research questions in quantitative research is a very clear and important one – quantitative research ideas are almost invariably justified on the basis of the findings of previous research and theory in the field. The literature review is construed as a preliminary stage in any research and is

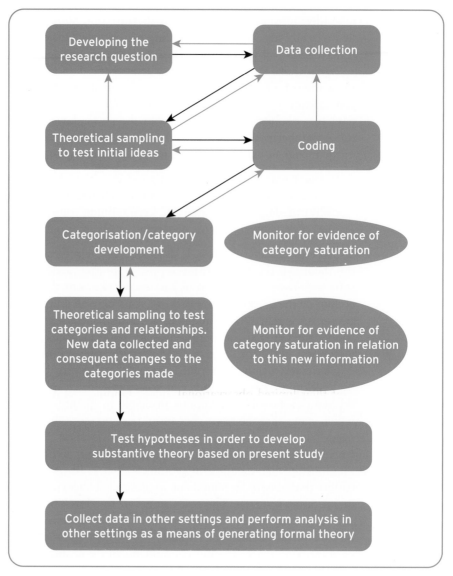

FIGURE 8.2   The process of theory development in grounded theory

carried out largely in advance of the new research's detailed planning. In other words, quantitative research is viewed as a process of building new research on the foundations of previous research. In distinct contrast, the role of the literature review in grounded theory does not occupy a similar clear-cut position. Sometimes it is argued that the literature review in grounded theory research should be carried out at the end of the research process. So, rather than stimulating the new research, the literature review is primarily to allow the comparison of the new analysis with previous analyses in that field. This helps ensure that the grounded theory analysis is grounded in the new data rather than in previous theory. At the other side of the debate, the literature review is seen as part of development of the new research. Strauss and Corbin (1999) suggest that the grounded theory methodology may begin in existing grounded theory so long as they 'seem appropriate to the area of investigation'. Then these grounded theories 'may be elaborated and modified as incoming data are meticulously played against them' (pp. 72–3).

Ideally, the decision to use grounded theory should be taken very early in the planning of the new research. This is because grounded theory includes methods for sampling which depend on the feedback of the analysis of the first few interviews, for example. Although it is possible to make the decision to use grounded theory after all of the data have been collected, this is not ideal for the reason just mentioned. Grounded theory is about theory development, and hypothesis testing of the sort used in mainstream quantitative psychology is not part of the process. One advantage of grounded theory is that it can be used to research areas for which little or no past research is available or where qualitative methods have not been previously used.

Step 2 Theoretical sampling (This may occur prior to starting data collection but alternatively at various stages in the process of data collection.) There are important differences between sampling in quantitative and qualitative methods:

- Qualitative research tends to use small samples for various reasons but especially because data collection and analysis is so demanding that large samples are impracticable. There is generally no assumption that samples in qualitative research are in some way representative.

- The qualitative researcher seldom knows the characteristics of the population so true random sampling is not feasible.

- Not all participants can be regarded as equal in terms of their contribution to understanding social phenomena. Some people make poor sources of information because of their limited observational, understanding and interpretational skills. The quest for 'rich' data would suggest that certain sources are to be preferred over others. This is not an assumption made by quantitative researchers in their sampling. Marshall (1996) likens this to the situation in which one's car has broken down. Who would you prefer? A passer-by selected at random or a car mechanic?

Grounded theory probably has the most different approach to sampling of all. In grounded theory, sampling is usually determined on the basis of the theories one builds up to interpret the data over the period of the grounded theory analysis. This is known as theoretical sampling. Because of the intimate contact of the grounded theorist with their data from the time at which data are first collected, they will be reaching tentative interpretations of their data at various stages before data collection is complete. It is these interpretations which drive the need for further data and further sampling. So the researcher would decide on what further data should be collected on the basis of their evaluation of what additional data would help them in their interpretations. The choices are, of course, between seeking data which might challenge their interpretations but, equally, it might help them elaborate their emerging interpretations (or, in other words, theory).

Put another way, theoretical sampling is about how to validate the ideas developed during the memo-writing process which is continuous through the development of a grounded theory. If the ideas that the researcher has noted in the memo are sound and have validity then one should be able to test them by coming up with suggestions about the sort of circumstances in which they apply and the circumstances in which they don't apply. This might involve selecting a participant(s) for inclusion in the research because they might throw up difficulties for one's developing theory. These difficulties might require the researcher to reformulate their ideas or to limit their range of applicability, for example. The task of the researcher is partly to suggest to which samples the theory applies and where it does not apply. It is not simply new sample members who might be recruited; grounded theorists might use theoretical sampling to guide them to other aspects of their data for consideration in light of the theory. Equally, the researcher may seek new situations to examine whether or not the developing analysis applies there. The point is that such additional sampling of people, situations or data should feed into subsequent memo-writing and theoretical development. In this way, the memos and the ideas therein become ever more closely embedded or grounded in the data.

Although theoretical sampling may apply throughout the range of stages of a grounded theory analysis, it is equally applicable to the initial selection of sources and sites for the initial data collection. Since it is likely that the researcher has some preliminary ideas of what sorts of people or situations will be the most productive in terms of theory development, theoretical sampling applies to the earliest stages of grounded theory research.

Step 3   **Data collection** Grounded theory takes a very generous perspective on what constitutes data. Typically, in grounded theory analysis, the researcher will begin with a quantity of textual material – the data. This may be in the form of documents; material from the newspapers, magazines or the Internet; or, possibly the most likely, transcripts of in-depth interviews, focus groups and the like. Indeed, it can be appropriate to incorporate several different forms of data. Of course, probably most grounded theory research would use primary sources such as the above-mentioned interview and focus groups.

Step 4   **Coding/naming** The data are then subjected to a lengthy, complex and demanding close examination by the researcher. In order to achieve this, the researcher undergoes a line-by-line analysis of the text and essentially scrutinises each line for meaning. Each line is numbered sequentially for convenience and reference purposes. Coding is achieved by giving each line of the analysis a descriptive code or codes. (Although the coding usually goes line-by-line, there is no reason why other units of analysis such as sentences, paragraphs, speaking turns, etc. could not be used.) Basically these codes are at a level of abstraction which essentially describes what is in that line of text/data. Sometimes the code is very closely related to the data but, ideally, since the end product is a theory abstracted from the data, codings should aim at a higher level of abstraction than mere description, as that is where the theory is going. This is referred to as coding the data. While, in terms of reading about coding, one imagines that this calls for some sort of insightful, meaningful and sophisticated description, in reality the researcher will largely use at least some relatively mundane descriptions. Remember that each of these initial codings is based on just a few words of data and so is likely to be fairly close to the data at this stage. There simply is not enough information to go beyond this. It is also important to understand that these codings are likely to be different for different researchers using exactly the same data. The differences may be simply the words used and essentially the researchers are saying the same thing in different ways. Nevertheless, sometimes the differences may be more fundamental than that. Basically, then, each line's coding describes what is happening in that line or, in other words, what is represented by that line. Coding in grounded theory is therefore the creation of codes and not the application of pre-specified codes as it would be in content analysis. Another way of describing coding, according to Potter (1997), is that it is a process of giving labels to the key concepts or ideas which appear in a particular line (or paragraph, etc.). The main point of coding is to keep the researcher's thinking firmly on the ground of the data. According to Charmaz (1995), line-by-line coding helps the researcher to avoid the temptation of over-interpreting the data such as by attributing motives to the speaker in the text.

The end point of coding in grounded theory will leave the researcher with pages of text and each line coded with a description. It is likely that the researcher will emerge from this stage with broader ideas about what is going on in the data – maybe ideas of how the different codings actually fit together, which codings are much the same as each other despite using different labels, and so forth. The researcher would normally make a record of these ideas in the form of a memo. (See the above section on memo-writing.) There is no reason why the researcher cannot revise any of the codings at any stage during this process.

There are several types of coding that are involved in grounded theory. The most important among these is:

- *Open coding* This is the form of coding described above which works as closely to the original data as possible. It is sometimes known as *in vivo* coding because of this.

The next two forms of coding are more about finding relationships among the open codings.

- *Axial coding* This is the process of relating codings (categories and concepts) together. It is, in a sense, the second major reworking of the data, though the emphasis is on the open codings much more than the data. Both *inductive* and *deductive* reasoning may be involved in the creation of axial coding. Axial coding is about relationships between different aspects of the developing theory. It is about organising the initial codes and identifying key concepts. It is a somewhat controversial feature of grounded theory, with experts disagreeing about its relevance and value. It is key to Strauss and Corbin's (1998) methods but rejected as optional by others (e.g. Charmaz, 2006). Axial coding may be facilitated by any method that helps juxtapose the open codings in a way which helps the analysis. So, for example, writing the open codings on pieces of card or paper may facilitate attempts to form groupings of codings which seem to be similar. Shuffling slips of card and paper on the floor or a desk is much easier than shuffling ideas around in one's mind.
- *Selective coding* This is the process by which the researcher identifies a category to be at the core of the analysis and relates every other category to that category. It basically involves the development of a major theme or storyline around which all other aspects of the analysis are integrated.

These two latter forms of coding dominate in the next step.

Step 5   Category development through comparison/constant comparison The line-by-line codings obtained earlier represent the starting point of the conceptual analysis of the data and are best seen as a preliminary process in developing grounded theory. These codings need to be organised into categories incorporating several codings. In this way, a conceptual synthesis of the codings begins to develop. The categories need to stay true to the original codings: there is no sense in which the codings should be forced into categories which they do not fit well and there should be no arbitrariness in the categorisation of codings. In other words, although codings are an early step in developing theory, they are too close to the detail of the data to provide, in themselves, a satisfactory synthesis of what is happening in the data. Codings constitute the smallest formal unit in a grounded theory analysis and by combining them appropriately we may move on to a better perspective about how to understand the data. So the process of building codings into categories or inducing categories from the codings is crucial to theory development.

Of course, the combination of data into broader categories is a common feature of analysis in quantitative research as well as qualitative research. For example, in quantitative research statistical procedures such as factor analysis and cluster analysis are used in order to provide the researcher with ways of grouping variables essentially into broader categories. Such statistical techniques are not generally available to qualitative researchers. Furthermore, this sort of statistical/empirical classification process in quantitative methods concentrates on what the data share rather than considering the data in their entirety. That is, it draws up categories based on correlations and ignores anything not based on correlation. Put another way, category development in quantitative research involves neglecting a great deal of the data which do not correlate across variables. In qualitative research, the aim is to synthesise all aspects of the data into an analysis.

In addition, the categories need to be understood as fully as possible by the researcher whose tasks include labelling the categories effectively so it is clear what the category is about. All of this means that the researcher may need to work tirelessly on their categories since this level of analysis moves the analysis towards theory development. Furthermore, the categories need to be compared to ensure that they do not overlap. It is a possibility that categories given different labels are actually much the same thing. So, for example, the researcher might begin to recognise that their category of 'anti-democratic principles' is redolent of existing ideas and theory such as 'authoritarianism'. Although grounded theory analysis in one of its versions (Glaser's) should not be influenced by the research literature at this stage, it is inevitable that a researcher's knowledge of research and theory may have some impact on category development.

There are two important principles which are essential to understanding category development in grounded theory. They are *constant comparison* and *category saturation*. These will be discussed in turn next.

To take constant comparison first, this is a process of critically checking any aspect of the analysis against other aspects of the analysis. The object is to critically assess the extent to which these different aspects work in relation to each other. By checking to see how well the elements of the analysis fit, gel and articulate together and making changes and adjustments wherever necessary, the analysis begins to develop coherence, leading to refinement in the analysis. If we take the line-by-line codings, constant comparison would involve the researcher checking things such as:

- Do differently coded lines have different content – or have different codings been used for much the same content?
- Do similarly coded lines have similar content – or are the same codings being used for very different things?

Furthermore, the comparison process can be used more widely in assessing theory development. For example:

- Interviews with people occupying similar roles in an organisation could be compared in terms of their experiences of the workplace – how they account for their actions within the workplace, for example.
- Comparisons between one data set and another – or even one study with a further study.
- Comparisons of categories derived from the codes with the original codings.
- Comparisons of any aspect of the grounded theory analysis with the original data.

Unlike quantitative analysis, grounded theory does not condone forcing ill-fitting categories onto data. Instead the categories, etc. of the analysis are reconsidered and modified to allow a better fit with the data. Glaser wrote:

> Comparative analysis can also be used to compare conceptual units of a theory or theories, as well as data, in terms of categories and their properties and hypotheses. Such conceptual comparisons result . . . in generating, densifying and integrating the substantive theories into a formal theory by discovering a more parsimonious set of concepts with greater scope. (Glaser, 1982, p. 228)

So it should be clear that the term 'comparative' is used somewhat differently in grounded theory from the way it is used in psychology and the social sciences in general (Glaser, 1982). In grounded theory, comparison serves the process of theory generation and the comparison processes may include ensuring the accuracy of the evidence, specifying a concept, checking a research hypothesis, etc. Comparison in grounded theory forces the researcher to deal with detail.

We can now turn to the other important concept: saturation. The concept of category saturation is used in grounded theory to indicate the point at which the analysis can go no further. This is the point at which doing further comparisons, etc. fails to necessitate further refinements to the theory. The concept of saturation can be used in relation to decisions about whether or not to terminate data gathering – especially helping the researcher decide whether to interview additional participants. When additional interviews cease to generate anything of substance which is different from what has emerged before, then this is likely to be the appropriate moment to stop recruiting new participants. It is somewhat like searching the Internet. Google for 'grounded theory' and thousands of web pages will be listed. However, in a sort of law of diminishing returns, you will find that you learn everything of importance from the first few websites you visit and that eventually new pages turn up nothing but familiar stuff. That is the time when the web search would be over. Much the same happens in grounded theory analysis.

Saturation as applied to the categories being developed (category saturation) occurs when after many comparison steps the researcher finds that the categories do not change and nothing new is being learnt about the categories. The key thing is that grounded theory is about theory development and when one's analyses (comparisons) cease to develop one's theoretical understanding then there is no point in further analysis. It should be stressed that theoretical saturation applies to *all* of one's categories at the same time – not partial sets of categories.

Step 6   Theoretical sampling, etc. to test categories and relationships During this stage of the analysis, there is still work to be done to check the theory against the data. The principles of theoretical sampling are again employed to seek new data to test the adequacy of the relationships which have been identified during the process of the analysis. One is not merely seeking evidence that will confirm what has emerged but also evidence which may bring about a questioning of the theory and its concepts together with a possible revision of that theory or of some of the concepts.

Step 7   Test hypotheses in order to develop substantive theory based on the present study A theory based on categories and relationships between categories is clearly of value. However, such a theory would be more useful if it allowed us to go beyond the basic theory to develop hypotheses about how the theory relates to other aspects of the thing being researched. For example, when Glaser and Strauss's book *Awareness of dying* was discussed earlier it was pointed out that there were several different categories of awareness possible: open awareness, closed awareness, suspicion and mutual deception. These categories became much more interesting when Glaser and Strauss found that these different categories of awareness of dying affected the ease of interaction between medical staff and patients. The testing of this 'hypothesis' and its confirmation extended the grounded theory towards being a substantive theory.

Step 8   Collect data and perform analysis in other settings as a means of generating formal theory The grounded theory has now been generated in a particular sort of research setting. Does the theory have any potential to be useful in other research settings? Of course, this potential partly depends on the nature of the theory that has developed. But, for example, the theory described in Box 8.1 concerning the perception of symptoms of heart attack might have some relevance to the perception of cancer symptoms, for example, or the way we respond to bad medical news in general. The more that the theory generalises to other situations, the closer it comes towards being a formal theory about a particular phenomenon. Many researchers do not take grounded theory to this stage.

When to use grounded theory

Grounded theory is explicitly a way of developing theory so that it closely fits the data on which it is based. It is not a data collection method as such even though it has a lot to say about what data ought to be collected as the analysis proceeds. Unlike several qualitative analysis methods in this book (e.g. discourse analysis and narrative analysis) it is not associated with a particular sort of content. The grounded theory approach changed the way of carrying out qualitative data analysis forever. It is possible to see elements of grounded theory in most of the methods described in other chapters. What is not so evident is when one would use grounded theory in preference to the other methods described in this book. Grounded theory places considerable intellectual demands on the researcher and proper training in the method is reputed to take quite a number of months. Furthermore, the grounded theory approach of combining data collection with data analysis in a sort of interactive way is not the easiest of things to do either practically or intellectually. It is perhaps unsurprising to find that not every researcher who claims to use a grounded theory approach to data analysis seems to adhere to all aspects of its rather demanding methodology.

What sort of research aims does grounded theory have the most to contribute to? According to Potter (1998), it works best when the issues involved are easily handled from the perspective of 'a relatively common-sense actor'. In other words, where the theory developed is pretty close to the 'everyday notions' of the participants in the theory. Perhaps this is inevitable in any research which gives a 'voice' to the participants in the research. Put another way, grounded theory may simply codify the ways in which ordinary people understand and experience the world. But if Potter is correct, this implies that grounded theory does not amount to much of a method of data analysis at all. This, perhaps, belies some of the complexity of the approach. Possibly Potter is referring to cases of grounded theory analysis which fail to achieve more than a basic level of abstraction.

It is probably not unexpected, then, to find that grounded theory is often used in relation to medical illness and interpersonal relationships. These are topics readily amenable to the common-sense inputs of the participants in the research. But, equally, what is amenable to the common-sense interpretations of research participants may well be the sort of research which policy makers find meaningful. That is, the less abstract the theoretical contribution of the researcher is because it is closely tied to common-sense understandings, the easier it is for the policy maker to make use of the theory. The participants, the theory and the policy maker are all 'on the same wavelength'.

This is a slightly depressing view of grounded theory and one that, perhaps, needs some revision since it implies that grounded theory is rather limited. Grounded theory is not quite so directly tied to particular sorts of data and research as many of the other data analysis methods in this book are. Conversation analysis, discourse analysis, interpretative phenomenological analysis and narrative analysis link analysis with a particular sort of theoretical perspective. This can be seen as a strength but it is also a limitation. Grounded theory is a way of developing theory – it is a theory of data analysis rather than any substantial area of psychology, for example. This makes it very different in scope. So it primarily offers itself to researchers who wish to develop theory without staking a claim as to its pre-eminence in this field. In a sense, its nearest rival for the attentions of the qualitative researchers is thematic analysis which may well generate analyses which can seem very like those of grounded theory. This is not a surprise as they share some of the same procedures. Nevertheless, grounded theory encourages the researcher to go rather further in theory development than does thematic analysis.

Grounded theory offers intellectual stimulation and challenge to researchers rooted in the methodology of mainstream psychology. There is virtually no characteristic of mainstream research in psychology which is not reversed or revised in grounded theory. Not that grounded theory would be antagonistic to using some of the findings of mainstream psychology – relevant information is relevant information in grounded theory – but it would consider that mainstream psychology's approach to theory generation is relatively crude and unproductive.

Examples of grounded theory studies

Two examples of the use of grounded theory are presented in Boxes 8.1 and 8.2.

Box 8.1

ILLUSTRATIVE RESEARCH STUDY

Grounded theory: when a heart attack strikes

Acute myocardial infarction is a heart attack. The blood supply to part of the heart is stopped, causing heart cells to die. Unfortunately, despite the fact that early treatment for heart attacks can be very effective, death can follow. This, of course, depends on whether the victim recognises the symptoms (such as chest pain, nausea and excessive sweating) of the heart attack very quickly – delays of more than two hours are dangerous. Actually, women are less likely to seek medical attention following these symptoms than men. Understanding the meaning of symptoms of a medical condition is a complex process and, naturally, the symptoms of a heart attack may not be properly recognised the first time it happens. All of this and more led Brink, Karlson and Hallberg (2002) to recognise the importance of victim's thoughts, feelings and actions at the time when the symptoms of the heart attack first hit.

The study took place at a Swedish hospital. The participants were a sample of survivors from a consecutive group of victims of acute heart attacks. They were selected to be a fairly varied group in terms of age, education, employment and the severity of their condition. Equal numbers of men and women were chosen. They had agreed to take part in a tape-recorded semi-structured interview which took place in hospital usually between four and six days after entering the hospital. However, no details are provided in the report about the interviews themselves.

The analysis involved the coding of the transcripts of the interviews and began once the first three interviews had been carried out and transcribed. The coding (labelling) process was guided by three questions from Glaser (1978):

- What are these data a study of?
- What category does this incident indicate?
- What is actually happening in the data?

The authors describe how they questioned and compared the phenomena in the data for differences

TABLE 8.1 Brink et al.'s typology of reactions to heart attack symptoms

		Acute reactions	
		Ready to act (Forced by others, dramatic symptom onset, pain reaction)	**Delay** (Take medication, wait and see, practical obstacles)
Health beliefs	**Awareness of risks** (Previous experience, knowledge, common-sense, rational thinking)	Understanding of symptoms	Misinterpretation of symptoms
	Illusions of invulnerability (Can't happen to me, outside imagination, never had such problems, unaware of risks)	Amazement at having symptoms	Disregard of symptoms

Based on Tables 1 and 2 of Brink et al. (2002).

and similarities which helped the researchers to develop concepts. They explain the development of aspects of their analysis as follows:

> An example of an initial category from the present data is 'outside imagination', which mirrored one reaction to receiving the diagnosis 'acute myocardial infarction'. Events that were found to be conceptually similar were grouped under more abstract concepts or categories. Using axial coding, categories and subcategories were linked together at the level of properties and dimensions, e.g. the category 'outside imagination' was placed under the larger category 'illusions of invulnerability'. By answering questions of 'who, when, where, why, how and with what consequences', conceptual relationships among categories were developed . . . Finally, in the selective coding procedure, two core categories were developed, labeled *acute reactions* and *health beliefs*. (p. 536)

Acute reactions ranged in extremes from ready to act to delay with seeking care. Health beliefs ranged from awareness of risks to illusions of invulnerability.

The researchers then began to understand better what was happening in their data which allowed them to focus. That is, the researchers began to realise that the categories of symptom perceptions had a relationship with the two core categories of *acute reactions* and *health beliefs*. These four different perceptual patterns about the onset of symptoms were labelled as follows (Table 8.1):

- Understanding: This is where the victim understood that the situation was serious and that they needed

to do something. Acute reactions = ready to act; health beliefs = aware of the risks involved in the situation.

- Amazement: These individuals felt a sense of amazement that the symptoms were happening to them. Acute reactions = ready to act; health beliefs = illusions of invulnerability.

- Misinterpretation: The victim did not link the symptoms to heart problems – so they thought that the pains, for example, were due to another problem. Acute reactions = tended to delay; health beliefs = aware of the risks.

- Disregard: Some victims just got on with their normal everyday jobs. Acute reactions = tended to delay; health beliefs = illusions of invulnerability.

The grounded theory analysis was validated using 'very short interviews' with different patients who were asked about 'their thoughts, feelings and actions at the onset of the heart attack' (p. 536). However, no details are provided about how this validated the original findings.

So, this is clearly a study based on the principles of grounded theory. That the researchers go beyond the categories that they work up in their analysis to attempt a theoretical understanding can be seen in the typology of symptom perception based on the broad categories of health beliefs and acute reactions. This could be described as a 'model' – or it would be in quantitative research – but equally it constitutes a theory in the sense that it links together different aspects of the analysis.

Box 8.2

ILLUSTRATIVE RESEARCH STUDY

Grounded theory: bullying in the workplace

Workplace bullying has serious effects on its victims. It may seriously affect their ability to maintain social contacts, their reputation, professional status, health and so forth. Strandmark and Hallberg (2007) argued that most research on bullying concentrated on issues such as the prevalence of bullying and the relationships between the bully and victim. They suggest that research largely neglected the experience of being bullied.

The researchers employed grounded theory. They recruited their participants from newspaper advertisements and a website. Participants were selected to be heterogeneous in their characteristics. The open-ended interviews were based on an interview guide which included the following themes:

- Thoughts and feelings related to bullying.
- The psychosocial work environment.
- Working group.
- Perceived health.

The interviewing process involved probes and clarification questions. The first 15 or so open interviews were carried out alongside simultaneous data analysis. This analysis used coding, memo-writing and fairly standard grounded theory procedures:

> The initial coding process, which started as soon as the first interview was transcribed, was carried out close to the data on a line-by-line basis, while the focused coding took place on a more conceptual level. Constant comparisons were made between different parts of the data, different incidents and experiences, and between different emerging concepts to explore similarities and differences in the data. The preliminary categories were saturated in subsequent data collection. Theoretical sampling was conducted to refine each category and to saturate the categories with information. Thus, saturation meant that additional data did not add new information. During the entire process of analysis, conceptual relationships between categories were hypothesized,

sought, and verified in the data. A core category, central to the data, was identified that determined the emerging theoretical framework. (p. 5)

Theoretical sampling was, of course, based on the emerging findings of the data analysis. According to the authors:

> This [theoretical sampling] was carried out either by re-analyzing collected data, going back to informants for additional information, or by interviewing new informants until new data did not add new information. (pp. 4–5)

The analysis of the data led to a core category (central theme) which the researchers labelled 'being rejected and expelled from the workplace'. This basically is the 'story' which emerged from the data – the process by which the victim of the bullying experienced a resolution of the conflict through rejection and expulsion. Of course, other categories were associated with this overriding theme:

- Changing a person's image by means of slander: this refers to the slander and backbiting spread among colleagues in the workplace about the victim of the slander.
- Betraying a person through deceit: this refers to the feeling of being deceived by others in the workplace who appeared to be on their side but who failed to deliver support for them. This included immediate colleagues, union representatives and staff in personnel.
- Devaluing a person through insults: this refers to the negative actions of others which were specifically designed to devalue the victim. The victim felt stigmatised by the bullying and began to feel worthless.
- Legitimising bullying through unjust treatment: this refers to various unfair practices applied against the victim of bullying. For example, one participant complained that she wanted time off to help her prepare her son for a school examination and was

refused. On the other hand, another colleague was given ten days' leave for her 60th birthday party!

And there was another category in which the victim could temporarily gain relief from the social support of their family:

- Mobilising power through support: this was the support that the victim sometimes received from their family and, to a lesser extent, managers and others in the workplace.

The authors bring these elements into a conceptual model which ends in the state of being rejected and forced out of the workplace (see Figure 8.3). The authors do not explain the snaking pattern within the diagram.

In many ways, this study presents a relatively complete grounded theory study. Certainly it shows the interplay between data collection and data analysis which characterises grounded theory. Perhaps where it fails is that once the theoretical model has been presented (that which is summarised in Figure 8.3) then the process does not go on to establishing a more formal model which is applicable to workplace bullying in other types of research setting. The authors are aware of the need to do this but fail to go to this final step in grounded theory. In other words, the grounded theory analysis stops early compared with the process described in this chapter and summarised in Figure 8.1. While this is a common occurrence in reports of grounded theory, it is still not the complete process. However, the paper describes a grounded theory analysis which is substantially complete compared to many.

The researchers actually present a literature review both before the study was carried out and to some extent afterwards. This raises an interesting question since the prior literature review simply identifies that the experience of workplace bullying is under-researched compared with other aspects of bullying. So in a sense, the prior literature review cannot affect the analysis of the data because the prior literature fails to address this issue. Maybe these are circumstances in which the *a priori* literature would be acceptable to all grounded theorists.

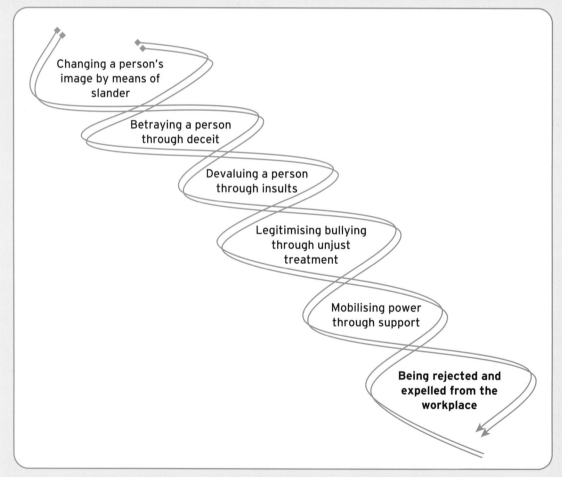

FIGURE 8.3 Strandmark and Hallberg's model of the process of rejection and expulsion from the workplace.
(*Source:* Strandmark & Hallberg, 2007)

Evaluation of grounded theory

Grounded theory, implemented in full, is clearly a demanding process. In its fullest form, the resources that it requires may be beyond a student researcher. Nevertheless, the first few steps of grounded theory are reasonably practicable in terms of student research. The impression is that substantial numbers of self-styled grounded theory analyses tend to adopt this 'lite' version of the procedure. That is, the analysis ceases when a 'theory' based on the initial codings has been developed that the researcher finds satisfactory. Grounded theory demands a thoroughness of approach and analytic work which should help students avoid the familiar qualitative research failing 'of trawling a set of transcripts for quotes to illustrate preconceived ideas' (Potter, 1998, p. 127).

When reading some grounded theory analyses, one may not always be convinced that the analysis emerges from the data rather than from such preconceived ideas. However, this risks evaluating a research method in terms of poor examples of the method rather than its better achievements. The more transparent research publications are about the details of the methods employed the better as this will contribute to maintaining high standards.

The case for grounded theory includes the following:

- Grounded theory provided an alternative to the hypothesis-testing approach in research. The hypothesis-testing model of research was dominant in quantitative psychology in the 1960s when grounded theory was first developed. (Of course, hypothesis testing is still very important in mainstream psychology.) Grounded theory is dismissive of the hypothesis testing approach in social theory development.

- Grounded theory was influential since it helped base qualitative research on systematic research procedures. It actually turned around the fortunes of qualitative research in sociology.

- Because much of the theory generated using grounded theory is closely tied to what research participants say, grounded theory speaks in a voice that is readily understood by people, including policy makers and practitioners in many fields. In other words, grounded theory theories are highly amenable to use in areas of social and public policy.

- Rather than qualitative research being seen as an initial exploratory stage in research, grounded theory showed that qualitative research could be effective in theory development. It encouraged the valuing of detailed qualitative research.

Among the criticisms of grounded theory are the following:

- The potential for collection of data is endless in grounded theory and virtually any textual or spoken material could be subjected to a grounded theory analysis. Because theory development occurs after the data have begun to be collected, theory cannot guide the subject matter for a grounded theory analysis. So there is a sense of any research area will suffice – the theory will emerge.

- Grounded theory almost requires that theory development is delayed until after data collection has begun, which makes it difficult to build theoretical depth rather than a multiplicity of theories.

- Vagueness surrounds some of the procedures of grounded theory. Not surprisingly the theory is relatively vague about the mental processes that are involved in theory development compared with the practical steps that the researcher carries out alongside this. It is much easier to describe the process of coding than to explain how to come up with ideas for coding. At another level, grounded theory is far less clear about the processes involved in testing a theory than about those involved in generating theory. The examples in Boxes 8.1 and 8.2 are either silent about the testing process or somewhat vague – perhaps reflecting this criticism.

- Many of the aims of grounded theory are to be admired but the method risks providing an excuse for an inadequate qualitative analysis of data. There are no guarantees that grounded theory will produce outcomes which are of any value. Of course, this is true of any of the other methods described in this book. In itself, grounded theory primarily provides a means of processing data in a way which promotes abstract conceptualisations by the researcher – which possibly may result in valuable theory. Grounded theory involves a great deal of hard work which is difficult to abandon no matter the outcome of the process since so much time and effort have been involved. The criteria for deciding the value of a theory are not really apparent in grounded theory.

- Grounded theory might be a 'fail-safe' method of data analysis in circumstances where a researcher has data but has failed to develop appropriate research questions. The lack of other options for analysis may mean that grounded theory is adopted but not for positive reasons.

- Grounded theory concentrates on the development of theory and tends to reject prior consideration of theory in the field because these prior theories may 'sully' the analysis. But there are many circumstances where well-developed theory is available. For example, discourse analysis and conversation analysis both have well-developed theory based on qualitative method. Why not employ this theory? Or should grounded theory be reserved for circumstances in which there is no relevant theory? Both the examples in this chapter (Boxes 8.1 and 8.2) use grounded theory when relevant qualitative theory is unavailable.

- Grounded theory methods encourage the analysis of text on a line-by-line basis. These lines are the result of arbitrary divisions too. So they can be fragments and not even complete sentences. This may encourage the researcher to concentrate on rather small units of analysis. This is rather different from the use of larger units of text which are typically used in discourse analysis (Grbich, 2007; Potter, 1998). This limitation of grounded theory makes it a less comfortable 'bedfellow' for other methods of analysis than would be apparent in the literature. Of course, this is a problem created by the process of line-by-line coding and may not necessarily be a big problem in practice since other levels of analysis (e.g. those in the memo) may be employed. Indeed, when one considers Glaser's lack of enthusiasm for audio recording and his view of transcription as being time-wasting (Glaser, 1998), this suggests that the researcher's awareness of the content of an interview and their conceptualisation of this can be important aspects of grounded theory – and it is not based on the finicky close analysis usually found in grounded theory studies.

- It may sometimes be difficult to differentiate between the outcomes of a grounded theory analysis and a thematic analysis (Chapter 7). While a thematic analysis is a categorisation process with no great aspirations to theory development, grounded theory analyses may sometimes come up with much the same sorts of data categorisation scheme. Unless the grounded theory analysis goes beyond this by using theoretical sampling and so forth then an opportunity has been lost. But who can guarantee that there is more in one's data than thematic analysis can elucidate?

Of course, our question here is the relevance of grounded theory for psychological research. Howitt and Cramer (2014) pointed out that some grounded theorists write of it as if it is inimical to certain sorts of theory development in psychology. Strauss and Corbin wrote specifically that:

> grounded theory researchers are interested in patterns of action and interaction between and among various types of social units (i.e., 'actors'). So they are not especially interested in creating theory about individual actors as such (unless perhaps they are psychologists or psychiatrists). (Strauss & Corbin, 1999, p. 81)

If grounded theory is about the social (interactive) then time will tell the extent to which grounded theory can help in the theoretical development of more purely psychological issues.

There is another sort of critique of grounded theory and that is in terms of the research work actually claimed to be examples of the method. From time-to-time when dipping into grounded theory research, one comes across publications which claim to be grounded theory but reflect the method badly. Suddaby (2006) suggests that there are a number of common misconceptions which should be avoided in a grounded theory analysis. His comments are based on papers submitted as grounded theory to academic journals. Thus the comments reflect the characteristics of weak grounded theory studies. As such they constitute a warning about things to avoid:

- *Grounded theory is not an excuse to ignore the literature* Grounded theory is built on the belief that a whole range of sources of information are relevant to the analysis. This includes well-established findings from positivist research as well as qualitative findings emerging in new research, for example. The researcher is not a blank slate – a grounded theorist cannot enter a well-researched area unaffected by existing ideas. Similarly, a grounded theorist does not enter a research field purposelessly without any sort of research agenda or plan. The best research will follow from the best preparation and planning. A totally structureless approach to research will usually result in a structure-less research report according to Suddaby (2006). Glazer and Strauss (1967) differentiate between substantive theory (based on a body of past research) and grounded theory. Substantive theory can contribute to the development of the grounded theory. Many of the grounded theory studies in psychology seem to be launched from substantive theory. This does not mean that the grounded theory sticks to the substantive theory or merely tests it in some way qualitatively. But the quantitative theory is not simply accepted – its characteristics are usually considered carefully as part of the analytic strategy.

- *Grounded theory is not a way merely to present raw data* Grounded theory involves the complex and abstract analysis of the data. It does not advocate minimal data analysis and it most certainly does not advocate trite conclusions. Suddaby (2006) gives as examples of trite conclusions things like 'change is difficult' and that 'political leaders are charismatic'. These are mind-crunchingly obvious conclusions and do not need grounded theory to bring them into the light. There may be a number of reasons for this sort of largely unprocessed presentation. One is the lack of clarity about the nature of the grounded theory – it is not narrative analysis or phenomenology where the 'lived experiences' of the participants in the research are what the analyst is trying to understand and describe in detail. These methods need their own highly concentrated research approaches to obtain the right sort of data. The analysis of such data is not a grounded theory, of course. In narrative and phenomenological analysis, sometimes it is appropriate to present somewhat unprocessed data. The grounded theory interview and the phenomenological interview are not the same thing. Additionally, the failure of the grounded theorist to push the analysis to a more abstract and appropriate conceptual level can lead to this underanalysis. The analysis, for example, may have not properly employed the constant comparison method. The conceptual understanding of the categories, etc. needs to go beyond the obvious. This may well involve an interplay between existing knowledge of all sorts and the developing grounded theory. There is another reason for underanalysis. That is, the researcher may have simply stopped collecting new data too soon. Category saturation means that no new data are being collected which challenge the category structure so far developed. Although authors have the habit of suggesting that data saturation is the criterion for the cessation of data collection, this is not quite the case. The important thing is data saturation in terms of the analysis rather than data collection as such. It is probably rather easy to sit through an interview and think that one has heard it all before in previous interviews. The process of analysis is integral to data collection, don't forget. By not collecting sufficient data then the analysis may not go much beyond the data.

- *Grounded theory is not theory testing, content analysis or word counts* Goulding (2002) referred to *methodological slurring* in which interpretative (qualitative) methods are used to analyse positivistic assumptions. The realist ontology assumes that there is a real world knowable to the researcher in which things happen. So such reports may start with good qualitative credentials but then do something crudely and probably ineffectively quantitative with the data.

- *Grounded theory is not simply routine application of formulaic technique to data analysis* There is nothing mechanical about the process of grounded theory. So theoretical saturation is not a formula which is solved when a certain number of interviews have been carried out. Simply by going from open coding to conceptual or theoretical coding does not guarantee anything but a mundane analysis. The results may look neat and tidy but the original data becomes remote and the purpose of the research may become lost. There is no logico-deductive process involved and data analysis requires considerable inductive reasoning skills.

- *Grounded theory is not an excuse for the absence of a methodology* Grounded theory is an exacting methodology which needs to be reported in some detail in order to achieve credibility. It is far from an anything goes approach and needs rather more than a token citation of Glaser and Strauss's classic book. It is not appropriate to collect a fairly meaningless bunch of data. Instead the write-up needs to be transparent so that it demonstrates the use of the core features of grounded theory such as theoretical sampling and constant comparison. Just how are the data used to generate the analytic categories? Is there an openness to alternative interpretations of the data? Is there skill exhibited in demonstrating the integration of the literature review, the data and experience? All of these things and more are required.

CONCLUSION

So important is grounded theory in the development of qualitative research methods that all serious researchers should be familiar with its basic ideas and procedures. Having said that, it is an approach which often seems poorly understood and full-blown examples, from psychology, of its use are hard to come by. In one sense, grounded theory ticks all of the boxes since it promises a theoretical analysis based on qualitative data without theory being reviewed as a prerequisite. This might seem to be a dream scenario to a student with a dissertation or project to write – or even the researcher who has a pile of interview transcripts but no real idea about analysing them. However, it should be clear that grounded theory is personally demanding for the researcher and abstract thinking abilities are at a premium if the analysis is to be anything but mundane.

An important question is whether the sorts of theory that can be derived from grounded theory meets the needs, intellectual or otherwise, of the researcher. Partly the problem lies in the typical sorts of data used in grounded theory studies rather than grounded theory itself. That is, it is difficult to move to a more abstract level from the common-sense explanations provided by participants in the research. Consequently, it is often the case that grounded theory studies generate categories to describe what is going on in the data but things are not taken much further than that. The formal theory promised by grounded theory materialises too infrequently because the range of data available in a study is too limited. Grounded theory needs a rather broader approach to the data available than a typical research study generates.

KEY POINTS

- Grounded theory basically involves a number of techniques which enable researchers to effectively analyse 'rich' (detailed) qualitative data effectively. However, quantitative research findings may also be involved.

- It reverses the classic hypothesis-testing approach to theory development (favoured by some quantitative researchers) by defining data collection as the primary stage and requiring that theory is closely linked to the entirety of the data.

- The researcher keeps close to the data when developing theoretical analyses – in this way the analysis is 'grounded' in the data rather than being based on speculative theory which is then tested using hypotheses derived from the theory.

- Grounded theory does not mean that there are theoretical concepts just waiting in the data to be discovered. It means that the theory is anchored in the data.

- In grounded theory, categories are developed and refined by the researcher in order to analyse (usually textual) data. The analysis should maximise the fit of the developing theory (categories) to the data and any other relevant information source. Since the theory is closely tied to the data, many researchers using grounded theory do not consider previous theory relevant to developing the analysis.

- The theory which emerges in grounded theory research is often described as 'middle range' and is not intended to be far-reaching or to be an all-encompassing 'grand' theory. However, since theories are often based on common-sense ideas from participants they may not be particularly abstract or elaborately synthesised.

- Grounded theory is principally 'inductive' (that is, does not deduce outcomes from theoretical postulates). It is systematic in that an analysis of some sort will almost always result from adopting the system. It is a continuous process of the development of ideas – it does not depend on a critical test of a hypothesis derived from the theory as is characteristic of mainstream psychological theory development which can be regarded as deductive.

- Comparison is the key process in grounded theory – all elements of the research and the analysis are constantly compared and contrasted.

- Computer programs are available which help the researcher organise the materials for the analysis and effectively alter the codings and categories.

ADDITIONAL RESOURCES

Charmaz, K. (2008). Grounded theory. In J. A. Smith (Ed.), *Qualitative psychology: A practical guide to research methods* (2nd ed., pp. 81–110). London: Sage.

Gibbs, G. R. (2010). Grounded Theory: Core Elements Part 1. https://www.youtube.com/watch?v=4SZDTp3_New&feature=relmfu (accessed 27 February 2015).

The above is just the beginning of a series of short videos on YouTube concerning grounded theory. Get to the end of the above and the others will be displayed.

Hawker, S., & Kurr, C. (2007). Doing grounded theory. In E. Lyons & A. Coyle (Eds.), *Analysing qualitative data in psychology* (pp. 87–97). London: Sage.

Henwood, K., & Pidgeon, N. (2003). Grounded theory in psychological research. In P. M. Camic, J. E. Rhodes & L. Yardley (Eds.), *Qualitative research in psychology: Expanding perspectives in methodology and design* (pp. 131–156). Washington, DC: American Psychological Association.

Payne, S. (2007). Grounded theory. In E. Lyons & A. Coyle (Eds.), *Analysing qualitative data in psychology* (pp. 65–86). London: Sage.

CHAPTER 9

Social constructionist discourse analysis and discursive psychology

Overview

- There are many different things referred to as discourse analysis in the humanities and social sciences in general. However, so far as psychology is concerned discourse analysis largely refers to two discernible threads. This chapter concentrates on social constructionist discourse analysis. This may also be described as Jonathan Potter and Margaret Wetherell's discourse analysis or the Loughborough School of Discourse Analysis. Chapter 11 deals with the other thread – Foucauldian discourse analysis based in the poststructuralist ideas of Michel Foucault.

- Briefly, Potter and Wetherell's approach involves a micro-level of analysis concentrating on the constructivist nature of conversation, interviews and other text which collectively are referred to as discourse. This is referred to as social constructionist discourse analysis. Foucauldian discourse analysis operates at a more macro level and primarily seeks evidence of discourses (systems of knowledge) in text. The nature of the discourse and its relation to other discourses are drawn out in the analysis. Foucauldian discourse analysis tends to be associated with a more 'political' level of analysis. Probably its most important advocate is Ian Parker.

- Discourse analysis involves the analysis of language at a level beyond individual words.

- Social constructionist discourse analysis refers to a variety of ways of studying and understanding talk (or text) as part of social interaction. It sees discourse as being constructed in interaction as well as constructive interaction.

- Social constructionist discourse analysis may be regarded as a body of ideas about the nature of talk and text. As such it can be applied to much of the data collected by psychologists in the form of language. However, it is not the only way of studying language. The same data may be analysed quite differently according to the objectives of the researcher. For example, thematic analysis may simply seek the main broad themes in the same data.

- The intellectual roots of social constructionist discourse analysis are largely in linguistic philosophy of the 1950s onwards. Most influential was speech act theory, which regards language as social action.

- Social constructionist discourse analysis draws widely on theories of language and linguistic concepts established in sociology and linguistics especially. These include rhetoric, voice, footing, discursive repertoires and the dialogical nature of talk.

- The practice of discourse analysis involves a variety of procedures which centre around the processing and reprocessing of the text under consideration. These include transcription and coding/categorisation.

- Social constructionist discourse analysts developed a form of approach to psychology known as discursive psychology which is strongly antagonistic to cognitivism in psychology.

- Increasingly social constructionist discourse analysis has been integrated with conversation analysis (Chapter 10). The consequence of this is that it has adopted a more microscopic approach to the analysis of text than other forms of discourse analysis.

- Discourse analysis is only good for what it was intended. It should not be treated as a 'universal' approach to the analysis of qualitative data. When one's interest is in language as action, it provides both theory and practice to guide the analysis.

What is social constructionist discourse analysis?

There are two major approaches to discourse analysis in psychology:

- The social constructionist account of discourse analysis developed by Jonathan Potter (1956–) and Margaret Wetherell (1954–). As a consequence of its adherence to conversation analysis (see Chapter 10) it might be seen as based in ethnomethodological theory. Sometimes it is identified as the Loughborough (University) School of Discourse Analysis though Potter and Wetherell had already written their key book *Discourse and social psychology* (1987) before Potter joined Loughborough University. Nevertheless, in the years since 1987, Loughborough University's department of social sciences gathered together a substantial group of like-minded researchers under the umbrella of DARG (the Discourse and Rhetoric Group) including both psychologists and sociologists. Edwards (2012, pp. 425–460) portrays the core of the cooperation as follows:

> Common to us all at that time was a concern with how psychology's standard way of dealing with thought and understanding, as products and processes of individual mentality, could be approached in an alternative way through an examination of talk and text, and shown to be intrinsically, and not just peripherally or additionally or derivatively, social. (p. 420)

- The other approach to discourse analysis associated with psychology originated in the adaptation of the work of Michel Foucault (1926–1984) to psychological purposes. This is usually referred to as Foucauldian discourse analysis. The term critical discourse analysis is associated with Foucauldian discourse analysis though far from exclusively so. That is, Foucauldian discourse analysis and critical discourse analysis are not synonymous though in practice they seem often to overlap. Ian Parker (1956–) is a well-known advocate of this approach (Burman & Parker, 1993; Parker, 2002).

Foucauldian discourse analysis will be discussed in more detail later (in Chapter 11). For now, we will concentrate on Potter and Wetherell's social constructionist discourse analysis and explain its method of analysis. Potter and Wetherell provide what is probably the more student-friendly or student-usable of the two methods of discourse analysis discussed in this book. The procedures for carrying out social constructionist discourse analyses are generally clearer and perhaps a little more practical. It substantially outstrips Foucauldian discourse analysis in terms of numbers of publications.

Figure 9.1 is a mind-map using ideas from Potter's (2003) synopsis of many of the major aspects of psychological discourse analysis and its wider intellectual links. The mind-map suggests connections between different traditions in psychology which relate to discourse analysis. All elements of the mind-map should, at some level, interconnect using arrows but for simplicity's sake only major relationships are indicated. Constructionist thinking has a long history in psychology and entered the discipline way before the turn to discourse. Social constructionist thinking (see Box 1.2) is an important precursor to Potter and Wetherell's take on discourse analysis and is a

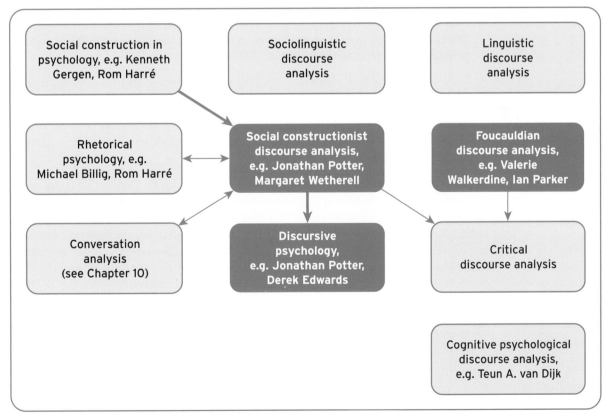

FIGURE 9.1 A mind-map of discourse analysis

continuing influence on most recent qualitative theory. Potter's mind-map gives some support for Coyle's claim:

> The term 'discourse analysis' has been based on different assumptions and has different aims. This makes it difficult to provide an account of the commonalities of discourse analysis except in the broadest terms and any representation of the field will inevitably satisfy some and irritate others. (Coyle, 2007, p. 99)

Initially, even social constructionist discourse analysis can cause newcomers some confusion. Discourse analysts themselves sometimes seem keen to highlight this in their writings. For example, Stubbs wrote this about discourse analysis:

> The term discourse analysis is very ambiguous. I will use it . . . to refer mainly to the linguistic analysis of naturally occurring connected speech or written discourse. Roughly speaking, it refers to attempts to study the organisation of language above the sentence or above the clause, and therefore to study larger linguistic units, such as conversational exchanges or written texts. It follows that discourse analysis is also concerned with language use in social contexts, and in particular with interaction or dialogue between speakers. (Stubbs, 1983, p. 1)

Twenty years later, Jonathan Potter himself provided a crisper, less convoluted definition:

> Discourse analysis is the study of how talk and texts are used to perform actions. (Potter, 2003, p. 5)

But shortly afterwards Potter added that discourse analysis is a very ambiguous term thus portraying it as a somewhat incoherent field:

> in mid 80s it was possible to find different books called Discourse Analysis with almost no overlap in subject matter; the situation at the start of the 00s is, if anything, even more fragmented. (Potter, 2004, p. 607)

There is clearly a hint that the term discourse analysis could become a catch-all description of all sorts of different things:

> there is no simple way of defining discourse analysis. It has become an ever broadening church, an umbrella term for a wide variety of different analytic principles and practices. (Edley, 2001, p. 189)

There are many reasons for this confusion and complexity. Partly, this is the result of discourse analysis featuring in various forms in a range of academic disciplines. One could scarcely expect this to result in a massive consensus of ideas given this eclectic background. The interdisciplinary nature of discourse analysis, the process of change and development which characterises all fields of psychology, personal preference and differences in intellectual traditions all impinge on the question of exactly what discourse analysis is. If we focus primarily on 'discourse analysis' within the confines of psychology things are simpler. Discourse analysis first emerged in psychology about 30 years ago. This is more than enough time for diversity of opinion about its nature to develop.

Given this, it is important to note Taylor's view that discourse analysis is best not regarded as just another method in the methodological armoury of psychologists:

> it is not enough to study what the researcher does (like following a recipe!). We also need to refer back to these epistemological debates and their wider implications. (Taylor, 2001, p. 12)

That is, understanding discourse analysis depends at least as much on understanding its intellectual roots as on knowing how to do technical things, like Jefferson transcription, well or how to perform the mechanics of a discourse analysis. Put this way, the task actually becomes clearer and some of the confusion drops away. In other words, there is a lot of theory to be understood as well as practical skills to be mastered.

Potter and Wetherell's achievement lay in bringing together a rather disparate array of approaches to language in a social context under the rubric of discourse analysis. Then, in addition, they presented their ideas in ways which were relevant to psychology and resonated with the concerns of a good few (especially social) psychologists. They were eclectic in a positive sense and provided coherence to their wide-ranging material. Nevertheless, the result was an amalgam of a variety of approaches to language in a social context which defy succinct summary. Yet it is easy to overcomplicate discourse analysis which, in its original formulations at least, amounted to the disciplined search for particular sorts of language devices within texts of all sorts. Because text is replete with acts which do something (simple examples would be arguing, requesting and demanding) rather than merely describe, then within this framework it is not unreasonable to refer to these texts as discourse.

We can quote Tseliou's (2013) description as a starting point for a fuller explanation. Probably not everything is made clear by the definition but it can be built upon:

> Discourse Analysis is a widely deployed term, which is often used to denote both theoretical and epistemological approaches to discourse, as well as various methods for its analysis. Discursive Psychology is one Discourse Analysis trend closely affiliated with the tradition of Conversation Analysis, with Austin's speech act theory and Wittgenstein's philosophical approach . . . Discursive Psychology emphasizes the performative aspect of language, the importance of context, and the intersubjective construction of any phenomenon. For Discursive Psychology there are no psychological phenomena outside discourse. Language is not a means to express attitudes or feelings. Instead, it is itself the arena in which these concepts are constructed while people engage in everyday discursive transactions. Talk is rhetorically designed so as to strengthen our arguments. Simultaneously, this 'design' also facilitates the management of accountability issues related to our points-of-view. As a consequence, even the same person's account may vary depending on the rhetorical context. For example, Discursive Psychology research has identified a number of rhetorical devices, like 'vivid description'. These are deployed when the speaker wants to construct his/her account as factual, that is, as existing independently of his/her personal view. This construction thus functions as a way to undermine potential accusations that the speaker's account is motivated by interest. Discursive Psychology also emphasizes the role of wider systematic ways of talking about phenomena. These are considered as rooted in cultural, ideological, and social practices. In Discourse Analysis terminology, they are known as interpretative repertoires. (p. 655) [Abbreviations replaced by full phrases and citations omitted for clarity.]

A reading of this extract should quickly tell you that discourse analysis is rooted in older traditions in the humanities and social sciences, that the way it construes language is nothing to do with grammar or similar aspects of language, that it spawned the field of discursive psychology (Edwards & Potter, 1992; Edwards & Middleton (1988), that it rejects traditional social psychological concepts and that the way language is constructed to do things is basic to all of this. So there is a close link between discourse analysis and discursive psychology. Their roots are very similar.

Not too long after Potter and Wetherell published *Discourse and social psychology*, Edwards and Potter published important writings in the field they initially tentatively termed discursive psychology. Especially important in this context is their book *Discursive psychology* (Edwards & Potter, 1992). It is based on discourse analysis and discourse theory but it is not quite the same. Discursive psychology, in a sense, is what is achieved intellectually in terms of knowledge as a consequence of applying discourse analysis to psychology-related topics. Originally, for the most part, these psychology-related topics tended to be the typical fare of cognitively-based social psychology – topics such as attitudes, attribution, cognition, emotion, persuasion and more according to Augoustinos and Tileaga (2012). But discursive psychology redefined these issues so that they were primarily to be seen as discursive matters to be understood through the analysis of talk. Not surprisingly, discursive psychology has little truck with things like memory and attitudes construed in terms of cognitive structures. Memory and attitudes are not like that, the argument goes, since they are actively constructed within social interaction. Give a family a pile of their family photographs and they begin to construct memories of family members and family events in the process (Edwards & Middleton, 1988). Memory is not some sort of fixed structure but actively produced in social interaction. Edwards (2012) actually uses the phrase discursive *social* psychology interchangeably with discursive psychology probably because of discursive psychology's concentration on social psychological issues. According to Billig (2012) (who was there at the start and so should know):

> the category 'discursive psychology' is not simple. The term is used to describe a sub-disciplinary specialism, a topic, a syllabus, etc. Its meaning can be contested. Academics can formulate competing versions of discursive psychology, even proposing sub-species such as 'material discursive psychology' or 'critical discursive psychology'. I do not wish to intervene in these disputes. Academic life is full of turf wars, as close neighbours, who might seem indistinguishable to outsiders, battle heatedly. Whatever their views on psychoanalysis, social psychologists, like other academics, often act as if they are bent on confirming what Freud wrote about 'the narcissism of small differences'. (p. 414)

Others have staked a claim to discursive psychology (e.g. Harré and Gillett, 1994, in *The discursive mind*) their work is of historical interest and not an important influence directly on Edwards and Potter. Lester (2014) in her overview of discursive psychology makes no mention of these alternative stakeholders in discursive psychology other than those associated with Potter and Edwards. She has the following to say by way of defining what discursive psychology is:

> Discursive psychology can be thought of as both a theoretical orientation to the study of language and a methodological approach, wherein the analyst begins with discourse in that discourse is assumed to be the medium of human action (Potter, 2012). Perhaps not surprisingly, then, discursive psychology is focused on naturalistic studies and engages in the analysis of audio and video recordings of people interacting in their everyday and institutional contexts. Discursive psychology emphasizes three principles related to defining discourse. First, discourse is positioned as action-oriented, resulting in an analyst asking: 'What is the discourse functioning to do in this interaction?' Second, discourse is understood as constructed by the words or conversational devices employed within a given interaction. As such, the analyst considers how the language itself functions to create particular versions of the world. Third, the discourse is presumed to be situated within a given interaction. Thus, the analyst considers how the discourse is situated in a particular

conversational sequence (e.g., how does one speaker take up a question posed by another speaker) and whether it may also be institutionally-bound (i.e., medical settings, therapy contexts). (pp. 141–2)

Therefore one can maintain a distinction between discursive psychology as a body of knowledge and discourse analysis as a method of building knowledge relevant to psychology. Nevertheless, the distinction is not always maintained and authors at times use the terms discourse analysis and 'discursive psychology' interchangeably (e.g. Willig, 2008a). However, for the purposes of this book, the focus is on discourse analysis, the methodology. Maintaining the distinction between the two has the important advantage of helping to label more clearly what otherwise goes under the unspecific general label of discourse analysis.

Rhetoric is another fundamental aspect of this sort of discourse analysis and is discussed in Box 9.1.

Box 9.1

KEY CONCEPT

Rhetoric

One frequently sees references to the concept of rhetoric in discussions of discourse analysis. Furthermore, the phrase rhetorical psychology is sometimes mentioned. Now the underlying meaning of the concept of rhetoric is simply that of argument or argumentation. Alternatively, it is the practice of using language persuasively and effectively. As a topic of study, rhetoric has a history which goes back to the Greek philosopher Aristotle (384–322 BCE) who defined rhetoric in terms of an ability to appreciate what is likely to be convincing in all circumstances. Though for Aristotle, rhetoric was part of speech, its modern usage includes all forms of text. The study of rhetoric was revived to a significant level in the twentieth century in various disciplines though it was not particularly associated with psychology. Mainstream social psychology from the 1930s onwards developed its own particular version of persuasive communication especially the Yale group led by Carl Hovland (1912–1961), though this partly focused on attitude change – an unpopular concept with many qualitative researchers studying discourse because of its roots in traditional psychology.

The association between discourse analysis and rhetoric may seem natural since social constructionist discourse analysis and rhetorical analysis share a focus on language as social action and language as doing things. But there is a little more to it than that. The close association between discourse analysis and rhetorical analysis

was also institutional in that Michael Billig was a member of the Department of Social Sciences at Loughborough University in the 1980s as were Jonathan Potter, Derek Edwards and others. Billig (2012) paints a picture of his journey from fairly traditional social psychological research to rhetoric as a lone one with little if any contact with like-minded academics or even dissidents in psychology until the Loughborough University DARG group. Billig gave his lectures but his research time was free from constraints. He portrays the library at a former university as providing the main confines of his academic world. He would sit alone in the library, he says, reading just what he was inclined. This isolation was liberating and he was able to read Aristotle, Plato and old English works on rhetoric. One book that emerged from this academic isolation was *Arguing and thinking* (Billig, 1987). Its basic theme can be summarised as human thought is argumentative in nature which, in itself, is not novel. In comparison to what he saw as the tedium of the mainstream psychology journal, Aristotle's *Rhetorica* was engrossing and he felt spoke to what he calls the official topics of mainstream social psychology from centuries ago.

It is important not to regard rhetoric as something confined to particularly skilled orators. Rhetoric is intrinsic to all forms of discourse and according to Billig (e.g. 1992, 1996) it is part of the process of giving or expressing views in contexts which do not necessarily appear to be argumental in nature. Billig argues that rhetoric and evaluation are inseparable. Although discourse analysts subsume rhetoric under their sphere of interest, those psychologists with a special interest in rhetoric do make a case for its being a distinct research field. Rhetoric and discourse analysis are used interchangeably in some publications (e.g. Billig, 1997). Billig unashamedly refers to himself as an antiquarian and implies that his journey was a meander rather than a trip. Furthermore, he seems little drawn to aspects of discourse analysis such as the elaborate recording of coding conventions frequently employed therein.

His argument against the mainstream cognitive social psychology of the time was that it compounded two mistakes:

> So much cognitive social psychology was making a double mistake. It portrayed thinking as being based upon cognitive models that, at best, were suited for describing the sorts of perceptual processes that we share with animals. This sort of cognitive social psychology either ignored language or treated language as if it were based on categorizing the world. But we do not merely use language to categorize the world, as animals might categorize visual stimuli as 'food' or 'non-food'. In Bartlett's (1932) felicitous term, we can turn around on our categories. We can use language to argue about categories. In short, we are deeply rhetorical and the facility to negate was central to human thinking. It certainly was central to *Arguing and thinking*, which was saying 'no' to conventional psychological assumptions. (Billig, 2012, pp. 416–17)

Rhetorical psychology is not the same as the wider family of discourse analytic methods despite sharing an emphasis of the analysis of text within a broad social constructionist context. Rhetorical psychology specifically focuses on identifying discursive strategies and argumentative material within the text. However, the extent of rhetoric within text is seen as more pervasive than one might at first expect. The rhetorical analysis pays detailed attention to the use of language and the patterns in argumentation. By doing so, argumentation can be seen to relate to the immediate argumentative context and cultural themes beyond this. From this point of view, some standard issues in social psychology such as attitudes, social representations and categorisation may be alternatively construed as being rhetorical in nature. The rhetorical nature of much social action should not be seen to lie in the arguments and disputes but as fundamental to human thought and language. That is, rhetoric is characteristic of social interaction far beyond adversarial contexts. Every assertion (logos), involves the possibility of its refutation (the antilogos). Drawing on the Protagorean 'spirit of contradiction' (490–420 BCE), Billig (1987) suggests that claims to truth,

accounts of happening and statements of viewpoints may well be refuted by another person. This refutation is quite simply built into the way that we construct arguments – their logical basis, their factual basis, their relevance and so forth may be challenged by another.

Time for a more concrete illustration. In an interesting example of the analysis of rhetoric, Gibson (2013, 2014) chose to reanalyse audio tapes from the archives of the Stanley Milgram Obedience experiments (e.g. Milgram, 1974). It is probably impossible to study psychology without learning about the Milgram electric shock experiments which have been discussed from any number of different perspectives since the 1960s. Although the experiments are usually couched in terms of obedience to authority, substantial numbers of participants at some stage showed non-compliance in the studies. In Gibson (2014) the focus is on the dissenters whereas the earlier 2013 paper dwells more on compliance. Just to remind you, the basic set up involved a Learner – an accomplice of the Experimenter – who was coached in the ways to respond. There was also a Teacher who was *not* an accomplice and was actually the one being studied. Finally there was the Experimenter who was involved at various points. The Teacher administered electric shocks to the Learner for failing in the learning task in some way. The voltages delivered or required to be delivered (in reality none actually were) by the Teacher increased incrementally as the experiment progressed. The extent to which many of the participants were prepared to go following the Experimenter's instructions is generally seen as a graphic example of obedience to authority. Milgram's recordings of the majority of the trials of the study and variants of the study are available from the archives. There were exchanges between the Learner, Teacher and Experimenter. The Learners' comments were predetermined as part of the research and some of the comments by the Experimenter were standard prods. The most famous of these is the Experimenter saying to the Teacher 'You have no other choice, you must go on'. The Teachers would engage the Experimenter in a process of negotiations about continuing with the experimental procedure. These negotiations produced radical departures from the standard experimental procedure. The fourth prod was somewhat ineffective. The four prods were, in order:

- 'Please continue' or 'please go on.'
- 'The experiment requires that you continue.'
- 'It is absolutely essential that you continue.'
- 'You have no other choice, you must go on.'

The procedure was that the above would be used in order whenever the Teacher refused to continue. At each refusal the Experimenter would start from the top of the sequence. When they had all been used and the Teacher still remained defiant the research session was discontinued. To answer specific queries from the Teacher, there were two additional prods:

- 'Although the shocks may be painful, there is no permanent tissue damage, so please go on.'
- 'Whether the Learner likes it or not, you must go on until he has learned all the word pairs correctly. So please go on.'

The procedure developed a little over time so there were slight variations as the final definitive version of the study was approached. The maximum shock given and whether or not the Teacher obeyed the Experimenter and delivered the maximum possible shock were the outcome measures used by Milgram. Disobedience could, of course, proceed in a number of different ways. For one thing, the Teacher could merely get up and leave when an unacceptable level of shock was reached. Similarly, the Teacher could simply say something like 'No, I don't accept that' following every probe. However, this is not normally the way that conversation would work, even though these suggestions help us understand something of the nature of rhetoric. So what did happen in the exchanges which led to abandonment of the trial? The following is one extract which Milgram (1974) himself published in which the Teacher is described as a professor of the Old Testament. Here is what happened after the Teacher reached 150 volts on the electric shock generator dial:

EXPERIMENTER: It's absolutely essential to the experiment that we continue.
TEACHER: I understand that statement, but I don't understand why the experiment is placed above this person's life.
EXPERIMENTER: There is no permanent tissue damage.
TEACHER: Well, that's your opinion. If he doesn't want to continue, I'm taking orders from him.

EXPERIMENTER: You have no other choice, sir, you must go on.
TEACHER: If this were Russia maybe, but not in America.

(Milgram, 1974, p. 48, in the original TEACHER is given as SUBJECT)

The session was stopped after this. Milgram, without the benefit of modern understanding of conversation, suggests that, on the basis of this, the Old Testament professor did not assert his disobedience by refusing to go on. Instead Milgram suggests that the professor was asserting the equivalence between the Learner's orders and the Experimenter's orders. That this is a feasible reading of the exchange is unlikely. The Teacher could have responded to the Experimenter's prods with phrases like 'up yours' but this sort of rebuttal is not what one would expect in the circumstances. Instead the professor takes the edge off his point-blank refusal in a slightly less confrontational way. Politeness seems to be a characteristic of exchanges about not continuing (Milgram, 1974). However, politeness does not seem to be a feature of the Experimenter's prods – they generally rather curtly negate what the Learner has to say. What the professor does is to use his wits and suggest circumstances in which he would go on possibly assuming that these requirement would never be met. The professor's rhetoric extracts him from the situation without amounting to a point-blank refusal and without breaking the normal standards of conversation in an academic setting. The professor also alters what the Experimenter expresses as a statement of fact by insisting that it is merely a statement of opinion. The fact, rhetorically, is reversed to be an opinion. The professor's rhetoric, though, may have been pushed in a firmer direction had the experimenter continued with the final prod by repeating it.

We can turn to another example taken from Gibson (2013, p. 299), L refers to the learner, E to the experimenter, and T to the teacher. (16) refers to a 16 second long pause:

59 L: Experimenter! Get me out of here! I won't be in
60   the experiment any more. I refuse to go on, let
61   me out!
62 E: Please continue.
63 T: Not under those conditions. Not with him
64   hollering.
65 E: I just checked on him, and he er, seemed pretty
66   willing to continue so please continue.

```
67 T:    No not unless I think, you see he's hollering in

68       there it's just er

69       (16)

70 E:    It's absolutely essential that you continue.

71 T:    Well I'm not gonna continue with the man

72       hollering that he wants to get out of there I mean

73       er (2) it might be essential to you but it's not that

74       essential for me.

75       (3)

76 E:    I was just in there and he seemed willing enough

77       to continue.

78 T:    Well, that's what he says but you know it's not

79       er

80       (14)

81 E:    ((inaudible))

82 T:    I mean I- I'd be glad to walk in there if he says to

83       me go on I'll go on but I'm not going to go on

84       with the man hollering in there to stop.

85 E:    You have no other choice you must go on.

86 T:    Well I don't say that I mean I'm just not gonna go on

87       unless he says to go on.

88 E:    Well we'll have to discontinue the experiment then.
```

Gibson (2013) suggests that there are several rhetorical strategies exhibited in this particular piece of transcript by the Teacher to bring his participation to an end:

- He draws attention to the hollering by the Learner repeatedly in three separate locations in the transcript in lines 64, 67 and 72.
- The Teacher particularises the Experimenter's third prod by contrasting the importance of the continuation to the Experimenter but not to himself.
- The Teacher imposes the requirement that he can reassure himself that the Learner wishes to continue before the Teacher will continue. This in part deals with the rhetorical claim (which is a departure from the standard script) by the Experimenter that he had just been in there and the Learner seemed willing enough to continue. This seems to be associated with the Teacher being lost for words and not able to complete his argument clearly. Of course, the gap may also have been deliberately left by the Experimenter to tacitly put pressure on the Teacher.
- The Teacher also repeats that the man is hollering but adds that it is for the experiment to stop in contrast with the Experimenter's claim that the man seemed willing to continue. That this is expressed in the past tense seems to work as a concession to the Teacher's claim to have just heard the hollering which is stated in the present tense.

There is reason to think that the final prod 'You have no other choice, you must go on' was ineffective. Maybe it is a rhetorically weak prod. In less than 10% of occasions that it was used did participants press for further shocks. This was two people, only one of which proceeded to full obedience whereas the other delivered only one more shock before successfully stopping the experiment. Perhaps prod 4 provides the Teacher with an easy way of dealing with it by suggesting that they had no choice but to continue. It is very obvious that there was an alternative. Please continue, in contrast, is more complex to deal with rhetorically. For example, the politeness of the request may require more work when formulating an appropriate repost. The anti-logos is possibly too obvious.

The key elements of discourse analysis can be specified fairly strictly. Language is not construed as a means of communicating internal cognitive realities (our beliefs, attitudes and other cognitions as it would in mainstream psychology) to the outside world. Instead, these 'things' are seen as being constructed in language in numerous different ways. Discourse analysis assumes at the most fundamental level that truth and reality are not knowable through language. Potter and Wetherell's discourse analysis, then, draws together a number of radical assumptions about the nature of language. Language is not regarded as mere communication but is seen to be involved in social interaction in a more creative, active and influential way. The dialogue of ordinary conversations is now the main focus of discourse analysis but any form of text may be studied. Interactions between therapist and client, for example, would also be considered appropriate for study. There is a tendency towards preferring to employ 'real conversation', though precisely what makes everyday conversation more real than researcher–participant interviews is not entirely clear – or why a research interview is more unreal than a doctor–patient consultation appointment, for that matter. Potter (2012) distinguishes between the naturalistic language of everyday life and the 'worked-up' language characteristically found in the data of mainstream psychologists. Another way of regarding this is that it identifies a preference for language data which lacks any impact of the researcher conversationally who then need not feature in that aspect of the analysis. The move away from interviews as a basic data collection method in discourse analysis is discussed in Box 9.2. There is also a distinction made between basic and applied discourse analysis. This distinction is hard in discourse analysis since there is a sense in which discourse is always practical – it is about the practice of language. In these circumstances how can one separate out what is basic research since this involves everyday-life practices anyway? Applied discourse analysis seems to be used to refer more to the extension of discourse analysis beyond everyday life to professional or institutional settings – doctor's surgeries, call centres and that sort of thing.

Deeply embedded in discourse analysis is what is known as 'speech act theory' (Austin, 1975). In this, language is seen as being part of a social performance. During these language performances all sorts of things happen. People create their own social identities or have them created by others or they are jointly constructed; power relationships are determined, exercised and maintained; and, generally speaking, a lot of social tasks are performed through language. This is why the model of language as communicating between internal thoughts and the external world is inappropriate for discourse analysis. For discourse analysts, language is a practice, not grammatical and other reductionist linguistic principles.

In the discourse analysis tradition, language is regarded as being socially situated. There have been shifts in dominant opinion but, broadly speaking, discourse analysis can be applied to a wide variety of different sort of texts and not just conversation. In a sense, it is largely irrelevant if that text is natural conversation, say on a bus, Internet chatroom talk, newspaper headlines, in-depth but fairly conversational interviews, or what have you. All of these have featured in discourse analytic studies. Nevertheless, there has been a move away from using interviews as a preferred data source but there is no embargo on such work (see Box 9.2) and earlier studies based on interview data are not devalued. The key characteristic of data suitable for discourse analysis is that they involve the societal and social use of language. As we have seen, discourse analysis shifts the conceptualisation of language from what is represented using language to language as social action – what language can do and how it works to do things. Quite clearly, then, there is more potential in using naturally occurring talk for such studies than, say, instruction manuals for operating household appliances.

What are the major theoretical principles of discourse analysis? According to Potter (2003), the following are its core features (see Figure 9.2):

- **Action orientation** Language is the most important context for the actions and interactions of people and they are embedded in social practices such as making invitations.

- **Situation** Discourse is situated in a number of senses: (a) *institutionally situated* – discourse may take place in an institutional setting (for example, a counselling unit) and is spoken by a person occupying a particular identity within that institution

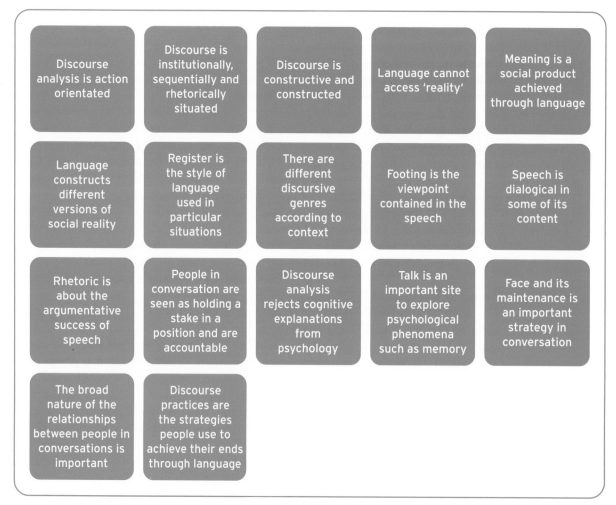

FIGURE 9.2 The various potential ways of seeing research interviews in discourse analysis

(e.g. receptionist), all of which is relevant to what is said; (b) *sequentially situated* – language is situated sequentially in discourse such that what is said at a given time is dependent on but not determined by what went before which, in turn, is relevant to what comes later; and (c) *rhetorically situated* – a segment of discourse may be situated within the context of a rhetorical process and so involve methods of resisting attempts to counter it, such as claims that 'you would say that wouldn't you'. See Box 9.2.

- **Construction** Discourse is both constructed and constructive. It is constructed from substantial building blocks including categories, commonplace ideas and broader explanatory systems as well as words, of course. It is constructive in the sense that it can build accounts of the world and also maintain these.

Much as one would like to present discourse analysis as a series of steps from A to Z, it is more than a system of analytic practices (much as grounded theory is). Discourse analysis is built on a theoretical conceptualisation of what language is but also contributes to the development of this theory. Consequently, the would-be discourse analyst should learn as much as possible about its theoretical ideas before much can be gained from learning the seemingly more practical aspects of doing discourse analysis – otherwise it is a bit like writing poetry never having read a poem. Reading discourse analytic work in books and journal articles is the main route to mastery of the theory. Nevertheless, some of the features of language which inform the work of a discourse analyst can be listed. As such, they constitute a sort of itinerary for discourse analytic work. Understanding the dead-ends in the relevant theory is equally important. So the following list is a theoretical starting point (Wetherell, Taylor, & Yates, 2001) – are any of them recognisable in the text (discourse) that you intend to analyse? It constitutes a lightning fast tour around the perspective of the typical discourse analyst:

- Language does not provide a way of accessing some fixed reality.
- Language is constructive or constitutive of social life. Through language things are done such as building social relations, objects and views of the world.
- Meaning is produced in the context of language exchanges between people. There is no cultural storehouse of agreed definitions or meanings which can be applied. In discourse analysis, researchers refer to the co-production of meaning. In other words, the analyst needs to seek to understand the processes by which meaning is created through language. For example, meaning can be regarded as a 'joint production' of two or more individuals in conversation.
- Language is used to construct versions of social reality. It follows then that a researcher should question the text to establish the characteristics of the particular version of reality being constructed in the text. Furthermore, what is accomplished by using this particular version of reality in the text? Discourse analysts use the term interpretative repertoires (often this is interchangeable with the words 'ideology' and 'discourses') to describe the 'broadly discernible clusters of terms, descriptions, and figures of speech often assembled around metaphors or vivid images' (Potter & Wetherell, 1995, p. 89).
- 'Discursive practice' is a phrase used to describe the things that happen in language which achieve particular outcomes.
- 'Discursive genres' refers to the type of language which is under analytic consideration. Thus the speech associated with 'The News' may have particular features which are very different from the language used by, say, a priest in church. Thus it may be possible to see contextualisation cues in the type of language used.

- Footing refers to whether the person speaking talks as if they are the author of what is being said, the subject of the words being said, or whether they are using the words of someone else. The footing may change at different stages of any piece of text.

- Speech is dialogical – during talking we incorporate or combine into it things from other conversations. Sometimes this takes the form of reporting what 'Ellie said' or what 'Nick replied'. More frequently, though, the dialogical elements are not presented so directly or indicated to be as such. When a child says 'I mustn't talk to strangers' they are reflecting previous conversations with teachers and parents.

The following are in addition to the above and are taken from Potter and Wetherell (1995):

- Rhetoric refers to the interest that discourse analysis has in how talk can be organised to be argumentatively more successful (persuasive).

- Stake and accountability refer to the way in which people regard others as having a vested interest (stake) in what they do. Consequently, they impute motives to the actions of others which may help to dismiss what the other person has said.

- Discourse analysis actively rejects the use of concepts from cognitive psychology such as personality traits, motives, attitudes and memory stores. Instead, it reformulates these to explain how they are constructed through language. So instead of memory being seen to reside somewhere in the minds of people, discourse analysts have emphasised how memory is socially constructed such as when a family looks together at a family photograph album.

- Talk and the other forms of discourse are regarded as the important sites for understanding typical psychological phenomena. So there is no need for suggesting internal psychological mechanisms to account for what is being said. So racism in talk is seen as the means by which racial discrimination is put into practice. Psychological constructs such as authoritarianism or racist attitudes are also unnecessary and misguided from this perspective. Traditional psychological topics such as the nature of individual and collective identity, the nature of mind, the construction of self and others, and so forth are typical areas of discourse analytic reformulation.

- Discourse analysis does not simply involve the social uses of language. It also focuses on discourse practices in the course of talk and writing. Discourse analysts identify the resources which people use to achieve their ends through language. For example, what are the argumentative strategies used in discourse and what categories are being used. Thus, when newspapers and politicians discuss drugs they use language reflecting war and battle. So they speak of 'the war on drugs' for example.

In addition, the following might be considered important enough for inclusion:

- The concept of face refers to the language strategies which serve to protect the statuses of participants in conversations. The notion of face is drawn from the work of Goffman (1959) to indicate the valued persona of the individual. So we speak of 'saving face', for example. Face saving in a conversation is a collective phenomenon to which more than one member of the conversation may contribute – not just the person at risk.

- Register refers to the language style which is employed in a particular situation. So the language style associated with attending church may differ importantly from that used when returning faulty goods to a shop. Register is dependent on the field of activity (e.g. television interview) and the medium in use (e.g. spoken language versus written language).

- The broad tenor of the relationship in question (e.g. lecturer–student, police officer–suspect).

Box 9.2

CONTROVERSY

Interviews in qualitative research

Discourse analysts frequently argue for the use of naturalistic data and can be particularly critical of the value of the research interview. This begs the question of just what is unnatural about research interviews – and just what is problematic about interviews from a discourse analytic perspective. Linguists such as Wittgenstein and Austin often would make up examples of language in order to get over their point. Both social constructionist and Foucauldian approaches to discourse analysis show some reluctance to use the interview. Foucault, for example, did not use interviews in his classic works (Foucault, 1978). Foucault wrote of interviews as the progeny of confession – the confession box is a means of social control. Interviews straitjacket thinking and do not allow for taken-for-granted modes of reproduction to be challenged. This said, it is also true that many discourse analytic studies in the past have used research interviews to obtain their data. Nevertheless, there is a move against using interviews.

Part of the reason for this is that social constructionist discourse analysis has moved ever closer to conversation analysis over the last 30 years or so. Conversation analysis (see Chapter 10) is unimaginable without the use of recordings of everyday conversations. Conversation analysis began with research into telephone conversation and, according to O'Rourke and Pitt (2007), there seems to be an assumption that the 'well shaped ways' of a culture are not materially affected by the technology of the telephone. So naturalistic does not preclude technological means of transmission. One of the contributions of conversation analysis which has been highly influential on discourse analysis is the way it deals with the context of a conversation. Its stance, at least initially, was that context was internal to what was being analysed and not external to it unlike the classic formulations of language would have it. Conversation analysis holds that participants in a conversation are orientated to the context defined by the features of the conversation. These formal features of conversation, according to Sacks, the founder of conversation analysis, do not vary with things like the number of people in the conversation. The numbers may change in the conversation and new personnel may replace others but the features of conversation stay the same; 'I don't know

which features they don't hold across' (Sacks, 1995, p. 34). Whether this applies to the research interview is a different matter.

O'Rourke and Pitt (2007) propose that four quite distinct analytic stances apply to the research interview from a discourse analysis perspective. These are given in Figure 9.3. They are clearly very different and it is difficult to see the final category as being commensurate with the 'no made-up examples' dictum.

Of course, there may be other reasons for the reluctance to use interviews as data. Such a distaste for interview data would have been shared historically by many mainstream quantitative psychologists. One way of presenting the problem is to raise the issue of whether what the research discovers would be unaffected by the researcher who made the discovery. According to O'Rourke and Pitt, the discourse analytic ideal of no researcher involvement is manifest in Potter's (2002, p. 541) 'dead social scientist test'. That is, would the interaction in the interview have been the same if the researcher had died before the interview began? In regular interviews it can be said that the interviewer acts as interpreter twice – at one level the interviewer is the interpreter of the conversation in much the same way as the participant in the research is, but at another level the interviewer is the interpreter of the entire exchange independently of the participant.

In an important if somewhat controversial paper, Potter and Hepburn (2005a) argue that there are many problems with the type of interview frequently used in social research. They should be replaced by naturalistic data for the purposes of discourse analysis. One problem is that too much detail is lost in reports of interviews in research publications. For example, the question asked is omitted and there is no indication of the intonation, etc. used. Understanding of what went on during the interview is therefore unclear. Potter and Hepburn make a distinction between problems with interviews which are fixable to some extent (*contingent problems* in their terms) and intractable problems built into the nature of the interview method (*necessary problems* in their terms). Among the fixable, contingent problems with interviews are:

- the disappearance of the interviewer from the transcripts of the interview and its analysis;

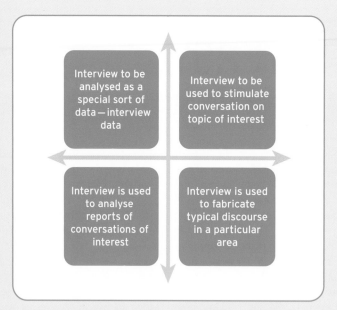

FIGURE 9.3 Some theoretical building blocks of discourse analysis

- transcription conventions are used which lack theoretical bases such that a great deal is lost in terms of the relationship between the interviewer and participant, the collaboration that takes place between the two of them, and the interaction between them;

- often the interview is presented in such a way that the reader cannot readily see the relationship between the analytic claims developed by the researcher and the contents of the interview;

- often too little information is given about the recruitment of the participant and the briefing of the participant prior to the research.

Potter and Hepburn's major solution to these problems is that interviews should be presented in a transcribed form – they recommend the Jefferson transcription method (as discussed in Chapter 6). Not all interview transcriptions, though, need to use the Jefferson system. They suggest that in some contexts some transcription systems are better than others though they do not explain what transcription systems are best for particular sorts of context. Neither do they formulate a detailed method describing how these transcriptions should be used. However, they do say that such a transcription may help reveal the conversational aspects of the interaction in the interview, which in their turn may reveal things about the interview. One could suggest that this is a self-evident truth but it is far from clear just how the Jefferson transcription would radically alter the conclusions drawn from qualitative interview studies. For example, in what ways would an interpretative

phenomenological analysis (IPA) study be improved by the use of, say, Jefferson transcription when generally IPA researchers see no advantage in its use? Perhaps this is the reason why they also propose substantial research into the process of interviewing using the insights to be drawn from discourse and conversation analysis.

In a memorable phrase, Potter and Hepburn (2005a) suggest that research interviews are essentially 'turned into the textual equivalents of speak-your-weight machines'. The interviewer puts the question in and out comes the interviewee's answer. Granted that this is an overstatement, it still does not correspond well to the procedures for doing qualitative interviews described in Chapter 3. Yes, some qualitative interviews are rather like the Potter and Hepburn 'model' but these tend to be bad qualitative interviews. They often appear to be rushed or disorganised judging from the transcripts. Potter and Hepburn (2005a) acknowledge that a lot of interviewing is bad but ultimately they seem to see the solution in abandoning interviews rather than improving them. Bad interviews will be frantically conversational in nature with the interviewer rushing from topic to topic, interrupting and generally over-contributing. A well-conducted interview may have very few conversational characteristics. If the topic of the interview is of importance to the interviewee then the interviewee may well talk at length without giving sway in the conversation to the interviewer or feeling the need to do so. To transcribe such interviews may add something but it is unlikely that, say, conversation analysis will have very much to say about the transcripts since conversation analysis deals with dialogues and not monologues.

The above problems can be fixed to some extent. But the following problems are largely intractable and are difficult to fix according to Potter and Hepburn:

- That the researcher is inevitably using a fixed if poorly defined social scientific ethos in terms of the research categories, the research agenda, and their orientation to the material involved. So you will find social-scientific terminology used by the researcher in questioning the interviewee. Even where it is not, then somewhat abstract language may be used. Though it is difficult to see that the use of technical terms will always be a problem given that, for example, the professional language of teachers overlaps with that of psychologists and other researchers.

- The problem of 'footing' which is broadly that the interviewer and participant will speak from different positions within an interview – so a teacher may be speaking for themselves as a private individual, themselves as a teacher, for teachers at their school, or for teachers in general.

- The very different stakes that the interviewer and interviewee may have in a topic – for example, the stake of the feminist researcher will be very different from that of the abusive partner.

- There is a risk of cognitivism in the research interview. By this they mean the deployment of terminology and ideas which originate in cognitive psychology. So when an interviewer speaks of attitudes, values, personality and so forth they are culling notions from cognitive psychology which is anathema to discourse analysis.

Of course, there is quite a lot of good sense in what Potter and Hepburn argue but whether or not they have identified invariably insuperable problems is not quite so clear. For example, the role of researcher may transcend in the mind of the interviewee any particular stake that the interviewer may have. Researchers, after all, will be seen to be seeking the truth in the eyes of the interviewee. This does not mean that stake and footing will not have a role to play, of course. Neither does it mean that the researcher can ignore them in their analysis. However, the extent to which they are a problem varies and it is unlikely that the best researchers will ignore them.

In his critique of Potter and Hepburn's ideas, Elliot Mishler (2005) recounts the tale of the fabled king of France who ordered his royal mapmakers to make a completely accurate map of France. Nothing was to be omitted, not even the smallest hamlet or farm. The royal map makers did their job well and after a number of years the map had grown bigger and bigger such that it

was a duplicate of the country itself in terms of its size as well as the level of detail. Fables usually have a moral, so what is it in this case? Presumably a map of France as large and detailed as France is of little or no practical use – it is so big and detailed that the manageable picture is lost. In this fable, Mishler identifies problems with the work of Potter and Hepburn. They want to expand the detail that goes into the analysis without explaining just what this extra detail will do for the analysis other than help provide a more accurate picture of what is happening in the interview. But can one have an overkill of transcription detail? More academically, he sees the problem as being a mixture of 'naive' realism and positivism – that is to say, the idea that through research the researcher can identify the reality of the world. So when Potter and Hepburn recommend the use of transcription methods to help understand interviews better it is as if they are suggesting that the researcher can identify what the true meaning of the interview is. But if this is what they mean, then there are important questions about just what this has to do with the qualitative ethos. Put another way, while it is obvious that the analysis of interview data is the researcher's perspective on the interview material from a qualitative perspective, it is not so obvious what Potter and Hepburn are aiming to achieve within the boundaries of the general qualitative ethos. Of course, Potter and Hepburn rebut strongly that their suggestions have any such positivist foundation by arguing that behaviourism and conversation analysis have nothing in common. But they are possibly protesting too much. To be sure, in their writing they recognise the theory-loaded nature of transcription but unless this theory is regarded as in some way definitive, then the problem remains of quite what transcription will do in terms of the interpretation of interview data. When they write phrases such as 'an understanding of precisely what the interviewee is saying' (p. 322) they seem to be making Mishler's point for him.

One of the fundamental assumptions that Potter and Hepburn appear to make is that the researcher can only properly understand what the participant is saying by reference to a transcription of a passage of an interview. Whether or not this is the case may be questioned. While it is a basic assumption that the response to something that has been said tells the researcher a lot about what has been said, this assumption is based on ordinary conversation and not research interviews. Now it may be the case that research interviews are often extremely conversational in nature but they do not have to be so. As mentioned elsewhere, examining research interviews conducted by discourse analysts and other qualitative researchers often reveals them to be simple question and answer structures – a question is asked and a response is made. And this is repeated until the list of questions is exhausted. Now it may be good enough for conversation where a transcription is informative but is it the case for the research interview too? Qualitative interviews are not necessarily conversational and the interviewer may actively seek to understand more clearly what the participant is trying to say at the time that they say it through the use of probes, etc. Further questions may be asked or the participant requested to explain more clearly what they mean or what they are trying to say. If the meaning of what the participant is saying is clarified, then the task which Potter and Hepburn want accomplished through transcription has already been achieved. That is to say, in a good interview, the interactive nature of an interview is employed to clarify and elaborate what the participant is saying. With this in mind, it is difficult to see the extent to which a Jefferson transcription will further the quest of understanding what the interviewee has said. Seeking clarification is an aspect of language which may yield improvements in understanding at least as good as interpreting a segment of Jeffersonned text.

Smith (2005) takes up this argument by suggesting that the better training of student researchers is part of the solution. Potter and Hepburn (2005b) explain that this is true only if that training is based on what is known to happen in interviews. This appears to mean that the training should be based in those disciplines capable of dealing with the type of conversation found in interviews – in other words, some form of discourse analysis or conversation analysis. Unfortunately, Potter and Hepburn do not give any good examples of the successful use of their recommendations in interview research. What they do instead is to create a sort of straw man based on an interview which was part of a discourse analytic study. They edit this transcript in a way which they claim reflects the typical interview study. As a consequence, it is difficult to be precise about just what it is that transcription and the other recommendations will do for interview research. Just how would any of the classic or not-so-classic interview studies be improved by using Jefferson transcription and discourse/conversation analysis insights? What Potter and Hepburn have to say is helpful but it may not justify abandoning interview research. Perhaps it is telling that Potter and Hepburn conclude that 'serious attention to interviews as an interactional event will highlight the virtues of studying naturalistic materials' (p. 324). So possibly this indicates that we do not have the solution to the problems of research interviews after all. For many topics, no naturalistic data are available that could be used in place of interviews.

Potter (2012) reminds us that Potter and Wetherell's (1987) text *Discourse and social psychology* suggested new ways of carrying out open-ended interviews. In particular, they suggested that such interviews might work better if they were rather more engaged in style – possibly even confrontational. This was offered as an alternative to what may be a futile enterprise directed towards neutrality in in-depth interviewing. For one thing, such an approach may encourage the use of more varied interpretative repertoires and other resources by participants in the interview. Potter describes this sort of interview as an arena of ideological engagements. Both the interviewer and the participant would be drawing on their ideological resources when constructing the interview. Potter identifies a number of studies as demonstrating this interviewing approach, including Wetherell and Potter (1992), Billig (1992), and Augoustinos, Tuffin and Rapley (1999). Whether such novel virtues can be detected in every report using discourse analysis with in-depth interviews is a somewhat different matter. It is worthwhile studying the style of interviewing adopted by discourse analysts in light of this. That is, to what extent do the interviews result in an 'ideological arena' either intentionally or unintentionally?

The research interview, unlike other research methods, imposes subjectification on the participant(s). The participant is recruited on the basis of some sampling criteria and then the interviewer makes specific just what is to be talked about in the interview. This imposes an identity on the interviewee and the interviewer which both must recognize as others will:

> Thus, the research interview actively involves a form of subjectification that is not present in other modes of research. (Fadyl & Nicholls, 2013, pp. 26–27).

There is such problem with naturally occurring text since there is no involvement of a researcher. There is a type of power relation in interviews which participates in the production of discourse. So do we address the discourse relevant to what attracted our attention to the subject matter in the first place or the power relationship? We may be merely proliferating discourses at the expense of addressing our original research question. We may be simply privileging interview text over other forms of text.

Perhaps we can leave the final commentary on all of this to Parker (2014):

> A false opposition is often set up between interviews on the one hand and 'naturally occurring' conversation on the other to warrant research on what is then supposed to be ordinary talk (e.g., Edwards and Potter, 1992). In a research interview we still, at least, have the option of attending to how the psychologist structures the interaction (and there have been some

very good conversation analysis studies devoted to this structuring), including them in the phenomenon being studied. The focus on everyday conversation, in contrast, is complicit with the gaze of mainstream psychology on the activity of others supposed to be non-psychologists. Secondly, it reduces phenomena to the level of the individual, and this reduction proceeds both downwards from the level of social processes and upwards from the level of physiological functions. There is an increasing focus nowadays on interpersonal interaction. Even though there is often an explicit attention to the interaction as such rather than a search for cognitive processes inside the heads of participating individuals, this focus on interpersonal interaction is still at the expense of analysis of broader power relations (e.g., Edwards, 1997). (p. 200)

The development of social constructionist discourse analysis

One of the ways of understanding language might be termed traditional linguistics. The major concerns of this are matters such as:

- word sounds (phonetics and phonology);
- units which make up words (morphology);
- meaning (semantics);
- word order within sentences (syntax).

This is a largely reductionist view of language which breaks it down into its elements such as sentences, words or even just sounds. Beaugrande (1996) dismisses this as 'language science' since it serves to disconnect language from real life. This sort of atomistic approach to language was rapidly beginning to be replaced in philosophy, history, anthropology, sociology, communications theory and linguistics itself in the mid-twentieth century with a view of language as social performance. According to Willig:

The assumption that language provides a set of unambiguous signs with which to label internal states and with which to describe external reality began to be challenged. (Willig, 2008a, p. 160)

Language was no longer seen as the means of transmitting internal states to the outside world or describing reality but as doing something in its own right – as constructing any number of versions of reality, for instance. The examples of this are many and include Wittgenstein's philosophy and Austin's speech act theory. Psychology, however, was stuck in the 1950s, 1960s and 1970s with a rather moribund understanding of language which focused on how the outside world was represented in language – social representation was the order of the day in terms of psychological research. The new light began to shine on psychology when in the 1970s: 'social psychologists began to challenge psychology's cognitivism, in the 1980s the 'turn to language' gained a serious foothold in psychology' (Willig, 2008a, p. 161).

So the roots of discourse analysis were firmly in more fertile soil outside the discipline of psychology. *The Oxford companion to the English language* (McArthur, 1992) claims that the origins of discourse analysis were in emerging sub-fields of linguistics which studied language in units bigger than single sentences:

- Zellig Harris's (1909–1992) work in the 1950s on the relationship between language and the social situation in which it creates it might be the earliest example of this.
- The linguistic anthropologist Dell Hymes (1927–2009) investigated forms of address between people – in other words, speech related to the social setting.

- It has been suggested by Potter (2001) that the roots of discourse analysis go back to the first few decades of the twentieth century in the work of the Austrian-British philosopher Ludwig Josef Johann Wittgenstein (1889–1951). Wittgenstein's conception of language as a toolkit to do things has clear links with discourse analysis. That is, language does more than merely represent things.
- Speech act theory was developing in the 1950s and 1960s under the influence of two British linguistic philosophers – John Langshaw Austin (1911–60), especially in the edited book of his work *How to do things with words* (1962), and Herbert Paul Grice (1913–88), especially his maxims for conversation (Grice, 1975). Speech act theory sees language as social action which is an underlying concept in discourse analysis.

The contribution of speech act theory is to be found in the work of John Austin (e.g. 1975). He used the term performatives for utterances which have a particular social effect. All words perform social acts, according to Austin. There are various aspects to this:

- Locution is simply speaking.
- Illocution is what is done by saying these words such as questioning, commanding, promising, warning and so forth.
- Perlocution is the effect or consequence of these words on the hearer – that is, what the speaker has done.

As already indicated, the work of Paul Grice, especially his maxims of cooperative speech, was closely associated with speech act theory. These maxims, above anything else, indicate the way in which exchanges between people are governed by rules which help meet the principle of conversation cooperation. Grice's four maxims are:

- Quality: contributions to conversation should be truthful and sincere.
- Quantity: sufficient information should be provided during conversation.
- Manner: contributions to a conversation should be brief, clear and orderly.
- Relation: contributions should be relevant.

If any of these maxims are violated, so long as the cooperative principle remains operative, the hearer may tend to assume that the maxim is being applied. That is, if the contribution seems irrelevant the hearer will seek to understand it as relevant.

The term discourse analysis was originated by Zellig Harris (1909–92) in a paper published in 1952 – although picked up by PsycINFO at the time, this paper has only very rarely been cited in the psychology literature, indicating the lack of direct influence of Harris's work on psychology. The study of discourse showed rapid growth in the 1960s and 1970s, effectively on a pan-disciplinary basis, but it took until the 1980s before it began making substantial inroads into the discipline of psychology. Its route into psychology was through sociology. Jonathan Potter's initial training was in psychology and sociology and later he carried out research in the sociology department of the University of York in the United Kingdom. In particular, he worked with Michael Mulkay on the sociology of scientists. Mulkay, together with Nigel Gilbert, had published highly influential works on scientific discourse (e.g. Gilbert & Mulkay, 1984). They distinguished between the accounts of work published by scientists in scientific journals and the accounts of work provided by scientists in conversation. Scientific discourse in the two settings was different and used different *interpretative repertoires*. So in the formal setting the empiricist repertoire (formal scientific) was used but in the informal setting a quite different repertoire was used. The latter could be described as a contingent repertoire since it is highly dependent on biographical elements and personalities. The importance of this was that such thinking was best characterised by reference to ideas from discourse analysis. Mulkay ran academic discussion groups on discourse analysis in which Potter and other luminaries of the field participated (University of York, Department of Sociology, n.d.). Jonathan Potter and Margaret Wetherell's *Discourse and social psychology: Beyond attitudes and behaviour* was published in 1987. It is regarded as a classic and was the key vehicle for the introduction of discourse analysis into psychology. For many years Jonathan Potter worked at Loughborough University as part of a influential qualitative researchers studying discourse, conversation and rhetoric. The origins of Potter and Wetherell's constructionist discourse analysis explain why it is sometimes referred to as Anglophone discourse analysis.

How to do social constructionist discourse analysis

Discourse analysis is often presented by practitioners as being a craft or a skill rather than a sequence of things to do from which the analysis emerges. So there are no lists of detailed step-by-step explanations about how to do discourse analysis which, say, the grounded theory literature provides. There is plenty of information about the basic skills involved in data collection (such as interviewing, which is dealt with in detail in Chapter 3) and transcription (which is covered in Chapter 6). The process of analysis in discourse analysis tends to be slightly mystified by practitioners and presented as being difficult. Part of the problem, from the point of view of a newcomer, is that discourse analysis involves disproportionately more theory than most qualitative research methods. Much of what you need to know has been summarised earlier in this chapter. Read in depth on these topics and you will progress quickly towards mastering the field. Discourse analysis has a sophisticated conception of language which is highly distinctive and sets the parameters for any new analysis of data. As a consequence, it is vital to understand the nature of discourse analysis's approach to language in addition to studying the research publications of discourse analysts to see just how discourse analysis is done. This takes time and is a continuous process even for the most expert practitioners in the field.

The different styles of discourse analysis do not have a common universal pattern. This makes it doubly important to familiarise oneself with examples of the major types of discourse analytic studies by reading the pertinent research literature. Such reading provides an understanding of the subtlety of thought behind some discourse analyses. One will quickly begin to realise that doing discourse analysis involves the use of a wide range of theory. All of this is to say that the fledgling discourse analyst can learn a lot simply by employing the basic theory as they read through their transcripts – e.g. the register being employed, how awkwardnesses in the conversation are managed, the nature of the rhetorical devices being employed, the discursive repertoires being used and so forth. This is part of all discourse analyses and is the starting point for achieving some originality in one's research.

It is probably obvious, then, that because discourse analysis has this added dimension of theoretical sophistication, the expectations of the newcomer to discourse analysis in terms of theory should not be too high. No one would expect the novice discourse analyst to produce work which is totally original and theoretically innovative. So there will be, initially, a considerable mismatch between what can be seen in the best research reports and what the student is capable of. Typically, a novice researcher closely follows the model of a discourse analysis study which has impressed them and which is close to their research interest. In quantitative research, this is often called a replication study – the sample is varied, maybe aspects of the methodology change and so forth – but, overall, the new study is built closely to the original. Although this may lack in terms of creativity, such replications perform a useful purpose in themselves. Adopting this sort of approach when new to discourse analysis is a good learning exercise and the student can aim much higher once they have built up this experience.

Clear expositions of how to do discourse analysis are somewhat rare. This is partly because the procedure adopted by a researcher may reflect their particular research interests but also because different researchers can have different styles of doing the same thing. In addition, it is generally held that there is no basic set of procedures which guarantees a satisfactory analysis of data. Potter puts things this way:

> There is no single recipe for doing discourse analysis. Different kinds of studies involve different procedures, sometimes working intensively with a single transcript, other times drawing on a large corpus. Analysis is a craft that can be developed with different degrees of skill. It can be thought of as the development of sensitivity to the occasioned and action-orientated, situated, and constructed nature of discourse. Nevertheless, there are a number of ingredients which, when combined together are likely to produce something satisfying. (Potter, 2004, p. 611)

Perhaps more graphic is an earlier description of the process of discourse analysis from Potter:

> doing discourse analysis is a craft skill, more like bike riding or chicken sexing than following the recipe for a mild chicken rogan josh. (Potter, 1997, p. 95)

Discourse analysis is characterised by its practitioners as an 'open-ended' and circular (iterative) process (Taylor, 2001). The discourse analyst has the task of finding patterns though without any clear conception of what these patterns are likely to look like. Taylor suggests that there is 'blind faith' on the part of the researcher that somewhere in the data is something justifying the researcher's investment in the analysis. The analyst will repeatedly go through their data in terms of what fits and what does not fit the tentative patterns formulated by the analyst. This process of examining and re-examining may involve an investment of time which is problematic for researchers working to conventional timescales and, especially, students working to their own time constraints: 'Data analysis is not accomplished in one or two sessions' (Taylor, 2001, pp. 38–39). Furthermore, it may be difficult to anticipate both the directions in which the analysis will go and the end point of the analysis. With 'rich' qualitative data, new analytic findings may emerge even when the analytic possibilities may appear exhausted.

Despite all of this, there is advice which can be followed. The following is based on Potter's (2003) suggestions about the short sequence of steps to consider when doing a discourse analysis (Figure 9.4). The advice is good but, as with all qualitative research, advice on the analysis only takes seconds to read but putting it into practice is very time consuming indeed:

Step 1   Gathering materials for analysis Naturalistic conversation and interviews (see Box 9.2) are the main types of data that have been subjected to discourse analysis. Nevertheless, data from focus groups, the Internet, newspapers, television and a wide range of other sources may, on occasion, be used. The general characteristic of all of these is that they involve interaction. Where, for example, interviews and focus groups are employed, the primary aim of the researcher is to provide what Potter (2003) describes as a 'conversational environment' (p. 80). The purpose is to create a situation in which

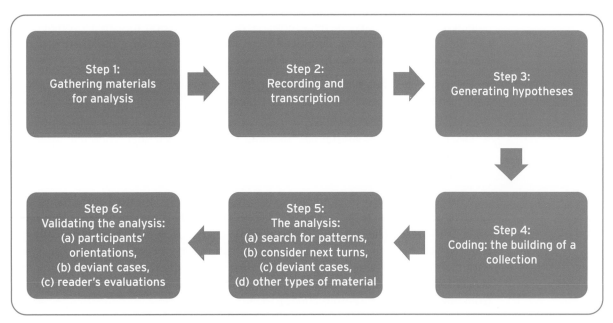

FIGURE 9.4 A summary of Potter's (2003) steps in discourse analysis

discursive practices become evident together with the nature of the resources which participants draw upon in these circumstances. If the researcher's preference is to use naturally occurring conversation, then access to this may be substantially more diffi- cult. Just think of such potential resources – police interviews, social services inter- views, counselling interviews, medical interviews, telephone calls to businesses, and the like – and it becomes apparent why access to them is difficult. Ethical concerns are clearly important but organisations may have any number of other reasons why they do not wish to share such materials with researchers. There is more discussion on aspects of managing research in the form of interviews and focus groups in Chapters 3 and 4.

Step 2

Recording and transcription There is no justification for not audio recording and tran- scribing the data for discourse analysis. Although some grounded theorists (e.g. Glaser, 1998) have argued that this is time consuming and the researcher would be better off collecting new interview data to inform their analysis, there is little support for this view among the vast majority of qualitative researchers. The function of transcription is to facilitate the analysis and communication with other researchers. In addition, using the Jefferson system allows specific detail to be made available for analysis which traditionally would simply be regarded as inconvenient or a nuisance. Harvey Sacks (1992) realised that such specifics in conversation as hesitations, pauses, coughs and so on were attended to by people engaged in interaction. There is much more infor- mation about recording and transcription in Chapters 3 and 6. Generally speaking, the Foucauldian discourse analyst is infinitely less likely to use Jefferson transcription than would a researcher following Potter and Wetherell's constructionist approach to discourse analysis.

Step 3

Generating hypotheses The word 'hypothesis' is not being used in the scientific sense of a testable and refutable relationship. Rather, it indicates that researchers need to develop ideas about what is going on in social interaction in order to stimulate and guide their research ideas. In terms of deciding what topics to address, a number of common possibilities may be relevant to the researcher's work. Researchers often come to collect their data having developed some ideas, questions or a broad set of issues which, hopefully, their research can address:

- The researcher has a general interest in a particular research setting – such as doctor–patient interaction, classroom education, and so forth – and how interaction is carried out in these settings.
- The researcher has substantial amounts of data which they collected for other research purposes but seem under-analysed or even wasted.
- The researcher has received an invitation to carry out research on a particular topic.

Whatever generated the impetus for the research, there is a need for a focus, perspective or overview to be applied by the researcher. This may develop at the initial stage of the research, although Potter (2003) suggests that it is characteristically the transcription stage since this is the stage at which the researcher begins to really work with their data. For whatever reason, 'the first part of discourse research is often the generation of more specific questions or hypotheses or the noticing of intriguing or troubling phenomena' (Potter, 2003, p. 83).

A discourse analyst may make a log of analytic notes to help with this process of idea generation – much as the memo in grounded theory (see Chapter 8). On the other hand, talking through one's data and analysis with like-minded others in formal or informal discussion sessions may also be productive. For example, a group of researchers may meet to discuss a particular data segment, each throwing in his or her own analytic ideas for consideration.

Step 4

Coding Be careful here since in most descriptions of qualitative data analysis, coding is a way of reducing a mass of transcription down into a number of descriptive notes which essentially summarise the original data. The purpose of coding is to encourage line-by-line familiarity with the data but, more importantly, it may be a start to the process of generating analytic ideas. Nevertheless, a closer reading of Potter indicates something rather different about what is done in discourse analysis. He writes:

> The main aim of coding is to make the analysis more straightforward by shifting relevant materials from a larger corpus . . . it is a preliminary that facilitates analysis. Typically it involves searching materials for some phenomena of interest and copying the instances to an archive. This is likely to be a set of extracts from sound files and their associated transcripts. (Potter, 2003, p. 83)

In other words, the process is one in which extracts are selected and put together because, for whatever reason, they seem to have something in common. It is likely that the researcher has developed a description for this – that is a code. This is not a rigid and fixed process since the extracts may be moved to other groupings as the analysis proceeds. There will be rogue extracts which need to be dealt with as best as can be done. The researcher may feel that a particular extract does not fit where it has been grouped or that it is generally problematic. No matter how frustrating such problem cases are initially, in the long run they tend to be productive of new ideas and interpretations.

Step 5

The analysis The process of analysis involves both inductive and deductive aspects. For example, reading through a particular extract may help instil ideas in the mind of the researcher about the processes going on in the extract. This is inductive and, in everyday terms, relatively speculative because it is based on not a great deal of data.

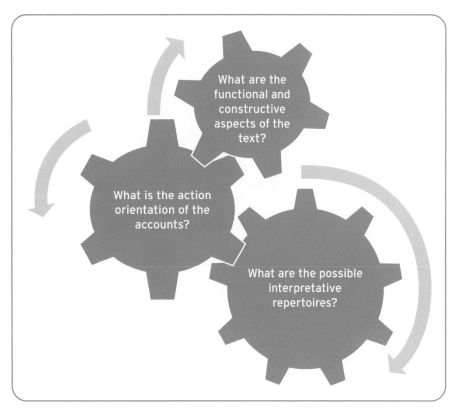

FIGURE 9.5 Willig's (2008a) advice to discourse analysts

Things do not stop at this since this inductive explanation of what is happening in the data can be evaluated against other related extracts. This is a deductive process which helps to establish whether the explanation is viable or whether it works only in some specific circumstances or that it is a totally blind alley, analytically speaking. Willig gives her account as follows (see Figure 9.5 also):

> Analysis of textual data is generated by paying close attention to the constructive and functional dimensions of discourse. To facilitate a systematic and sustained exploration of these dimensions, *context, variability* and *construction* of discursive accounts need to be attended to. The researcher looks at how the text constructs its objects and subjects, how such constructions vary across discursive contexts, and with what consequences they may be deployed. To identify diverse constructions of subjects and objects in the text, we need to pay attention to the terminology, stylistic and grammatical features, preferred metaphors and figures of speech that may be used in their construction [i.e. interpretative repertoires] . . . Different repertoires can be used by one and the same speaker in different discursive contexts in the pursuit of different social objectives. Part of the analysis of discourse is to identify the action orientation of accounts. To be able to do this, the researcher needs to pay careful attention to the discursive contexts within which such accounts are produced and to trace their consequence for the participants in a conversation. This can only be done satisfactorily on the basis of an analysis of *both* the interviewer's and the interviewee's contributions to the conversation. It is important to remember that discourse analysis requires us to examine language *in context*. (Willig, 2008b, pp. 100–1)

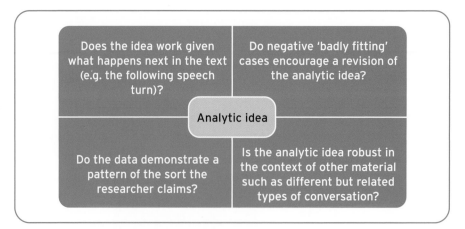

FIGURE 9.6 Things to check during the analysis stage

Potter (2003) discusses four aspects of the analysis (see Figure 9.6):

- *Search for a pattern* The analyst may search through the body of data to establish how regularly a particular pattern occurs. If a pattern is common then this adds strength to the analysis. Of course, the pattern may be specific to given circumstances which would need to be identified.

- *Consider next turns* In discourse analysis the sequencing of interaction has important analytic implications. What happens next in interaction is informative about what went before. As a consequence, we will understand better what is under consideration if we understand what comes next. So understanding the next speaker's conversational turn has strong implications for the analyst's understanding of a segment of text.

- *Focus on deviant cases* Deviant cases are simply parts of the discourse in which very different things seem to be happening compared with the normal pattern that otherwise seems to be emerging in the analysis. Understanding these cases may be analytically much more rewarding than if the usual pattern occurs.

- *Focus on other kinds of material* There is a range of additional materials which could be brought into any particular analysis. If the study is of telephone calls to emergency organisations then the researcher might find it helpful to compare their findings from this study with studies of other telephone calls to organisations. Equally, the researcher might compare the calls to emergency organisations with telephone calls between friends. This is partly a case of what the study is about and what other types of data are available.

Step 6   Validating the analysis According to Potter (2003), there is no firm distinction between the process of analysis and the process of validating the analysis in discourse analytic work. Hence, some of the procedures used in validating the analysis are similar to those used in the analysis itself:

- *Participants' orientations* If a particular excerpt is given a particular interpretation by the analyst, it is important to see whether this interpretation is supported by how the next participant in the discourse responds.

- *Deviant cases* These are used during the analysis but can also be used in the validation stage. Potter (2003) gives the example of news interviews where it has been shown that the interviewer is not held responsible for the views expressed in the interview. But there are deviant cases where the interviewer is blamed or otherwise held responsible. It has been found that these interviews may lead to problematic interaction which has a distracting effect on the interview.

- *Coherence* Do the findings of the new study cohere with those of similar earlier studies? If yes, then this is evidence of validity. Nevertheless, if the findings of the new study do not fit in with those of earlier studies then the research community may be justified in treating the new study with considerable caution.

- *Readers' evaluations* A range of extracts indicative and illustrative of the researcher's data analysis are included in publications. This leaves the reader in a position to check the researcher's analysis in a way which is impossible with other research methods.

At the end of the analytic process, whenever that comes, the researcher is faced with an important but quite difficult question concerning the worth of the analysis. Indeed, the question may be one of whether the researcher has produced an analysis at all. There is a range of circumstances in which something which looks like an analysis is reported. Nevertheless, does it amount to a serious attempt by the researcher at interpreting the data or even developing new theoretical ideas? Antaki, Billig, Edwards and Potter (2003) suggest a number of ways in which data may be under-analysed:

- *Under-analysis due to summary* Simply summarising, say, the main themes which can be seen in a particular segment of transcript does not constitute an analysis. It may claim to be by the researcher but it adds nothing to the transcript other than brevity. The summary does not move the analysis to a greater stage of abstraction than the original data. Indeed, it takes away the detail on which a discourse analysis could be based.

- *Under-analysis due to taking sides* While qualitative researchers will have a position on many of the topics they research, taking sides with the participant's point of view may lead to a concentration on this point of view which ignores much of the rest of what is going on in the data. As a consequence, the data analysis is incomplete. Antaki et al. suggest that by choosing extracts supporting the participant's point of view that the researcher is attempting enlistment rather than analysis.

- *Under-analysis due to over-quotation or isolated quotation* If the researcher resorts to reporting numerous snippets from the text (with little contribution from the analysis themselves) then this does not amount to analysis. For one thing, it separates the text from the context in which it is said. The researcher in this case may contribute brief summaries in his or her own words but these would be descriptive rather than analytic. It is also a problem if the researcher takes a particular extract and leaves it to 'speak for itself', isolated and extracted from context.

- *Analysis failure due to the circular discovery of (a) discourses and (b) mental constructs* For example, the analyst may identify a number of extracts which he or she describes are representing Ideology X or Discourse Y. Then this ideology or discourse is used to 'explain' why a person says particular things. Unfortunately, it is not possible to establish that there is an ideology or discourse underlying language simply on the basis of a series of quotes held to represent that ideology.

- *Under-analysis due to survey* For example, the analyst may notice that a certain form of discourse is used by some participants and seemingly generalise this to all similar participants. Of course, without evidence that such a generalisation is possible, such overgeneralised claims essentially boil down to a failure to completely analyse one's data.

- *Under-analysis due to spotting* Basically this means that the researcher is doing little other than identifying in the data examples of processes which have been identified by discourse analysts as important aspects of language in a social context. It is good that a student does this as part of their development. Nevertheless, such 'spotting' is little different from the activities of a bird-watcher who identifies the 'lesser crested sparrowhawk' or the laboratory technician who identifies someone's DNA. In terms of discourse analysis, this sort of activity does not constitute analysis.

Burman (2004) adds another analytic failing which she feels that Antaki et al. may have overlooked because it is so basic that it was taken for granted – 'underanalysis' through not having a question to ask of the data. She suggests that the weakest examples of discourse analysis founder because they do not give the reasons why the particular analysis was carried out and was considered worth doing.

A degree of self-reflection about your experiences of your analytic processes will help you assess whether your analysis is worthy of the name.

When to use social constructionist discourse analysis

Discourse analysis is probably among the most familiar qualitative data analysis methods to psychologists. Certainly this seems to be the case for countries such as the United Kingdom and Sweden, for example, though it is probably not the case in the United States. This is not to suggest that psychologists in general have a good idea of what discourse analysis is about and how to carry it out. Once it is understood that discourse analysis is primarily a theory-based approach to understanding language in society and the regulative practices of language and their significance for subjectivity then some of the misconceptions that mainstream psychologists have about it as a method of data analysis become apparent. Discourse analysts may have overstated their claim to being an alternative way of understanding psychological phenomena such as when it is recommended as a soundly-based alternative to cognitive approaches to psychology. It is not the answer to every researcher's concerns in psychology. Discourse analysis is not even necessarily an apt choice of research method for addressing qualitative data in general. Discourse analysis is good for what it is good for – that is how language works in social interaction to do things. The nutshell synopsis of all of this is that discourse analysis can, for some research purposes, be counterproductive. Potter put the issue as follows:

> To attempt to ask a question formulated in more traditional terms ('what are the factors that lead to condom use amongst HIV+ gay males') and then use discourse analytic methods to answer it is a recipe for incoherence. (Potter, 2004, p. 607)

So where the researcher is interested in language as social action then discourse analysis has a place. Otherwise, think again. Discourse analysis views things differently from mainstream psychology. Discourse analysis would be a bad choice to use to study the biology of rape but an excellent way to explore how researchers use sociobiological explanations of why men rape or how such sociobiological explanations have been incorporated into everyday understandings of rape.

When Potter asks the question 'Is there a discourse analysis answer to any psychological question?' his answer is no because:

> One of the mistakes that people sometimes make when they are to carry out discourse work is to treat discourse analysis as a method that can simply be plugged into a predefined question: for example, 'I am interested in the factors that cause people to smoke: should I use an observational study, an experimental simulation, or discourse analysis?' What this misses is, first, that discourse analysis is not just a method but a whole perspective on social life and research into it, and, second, that all research methods involve a range of theoretical assumptions. (Potter, 1996a, p. 130)

The answer to the questions of whether discourse analysis is the best way to address the analysis of qualitative data is fairly obvious. If the researcher is buying into the theory of discourse analysis then the method is appropriate, otherwise other methods may be more appropriate. Although every qualitative researcher is operating through the medium of language as the core of his or her data, not all qualitative researchers are interested in or need the fine-grained analysis of how language works in social interaction which characterises discourse analysis. So interpretative phenomenological analysis (IPA) (Chapter 13) is dependent on data in the form of language but what it does with the data is quite different. IPA extracts from language people's experiences of phenomena such as pain. Not much of discourse analysis's theory would have any particular relevance to understanding such experiences. Of course, a discourse analyst could take IPA interviews and analyse these as discourse. However, this would probably address none of the issues which IPA is interested in.

Examples of social constructionist discourse analysis

In order to illustrate some of the variety of social constructionist discourse analysis, three different examples are given in Boxes 9.3, 9.4 and 9.5:

- The first example (Box 9.3) is a very typical example of social constructionist discourse analysis in which interviews about marriage are subjected to analysis. Jefferson transcription is used. Although discourse analysts have turned somewhat against interviews in recent years, it is possible to see how the key analytic concept of interpretative repertoires serves the analysis well.

- The second example (Box 9.4) draws on mass media material for its data. It basically deals with how sports people talk about the 'zone' as it features in their performances. This study draws a little more on conversation analysis than the first. Firstly it uses the Jefferson transcription system which is synonymous with conversation analysis. Secondly it uses the conversation analysis notion of *category entitlement* for the analysis.

- The third example (Box 9.5) involves an analysis of American president's speeches referring to terrorism. No use is made at all of Jefferson transcription although the authors use numerous quotes from the speeches. This study is interesting as the analysis seems to have been largely framed prior to the data being studied. In other words, it has some of the features of the traditional case study where the data is merely a way of illustrating established ideas. There are also signs of a less than complete analysis being carried out in the sense that some of their analytic conclusions can be challenged in terms of the data they present.

Box 9.3

ILLUSTRATIVE RESEARCH STUDY

Example of interpretative repertoire research in discourse analysis: for better or worse

Not surprisingly, over the last two or three decades a variety of styles of discourse analysis have emerged. One which is very common is the search for interpretative repertoires (sometimes similar concepts such as different discourses or different ideologies are used instead) which provide the broad structure for talk on a particular topic. A good and convincing example of this is Lawes (1999) which involves the way people talk about marriage. She points out some of the issues associated with marriage at the start of the twenty-first century – fewer marriages taking place, more marriages failing, more births to unmarried parents, and the like. She concentrates on the group she identifies as 'Generation X' – Western White people born in the 1960s and very early 1970s. The statistical data that Lawes identifies suggest that this entire generation were 'marriage-aversive'.

Lawes indicates that her study employed Potter and Wetherell's (1987) approach to discourse analysis. Her sample of 20 interviews with 12 male and eight female 'Generation X' participants is described by Lawes as a 'rather generous sample' for this sort of analysis. There is no attempt to generalise from this sample, in the tra-ditional manner of quantitative research, but, instead, the generalisation would be from the sample of talk she accumulated to show how marriage is understood. Participants' names and potentially identifying informa-tion were fictionalised for ethical reasons. A flyer was used to recruit participants, though no further details of their location are provided. The interviews generally took place in the interviewee's home and typically lasted for about 90 minutes.

Interviews for the research were open-ended single-respondent interviews. The interaction between the interviewer and the interviewee was included in the anal-ysis. The style of interviewing permitted 'the researcher to participate fully in a relatively informal, conversational exchange' (p. 4). Lawes suggests that because of the nature of the analysis, it is not strictly necessary for the interviewer to remain neutral but may express a point of view. The questions which appeared on the publicity flyer were used to guide the interview. These questions included:

- How is marriage different from other kinds of 'couple' relationships?
- How would you feel about never marrying?
- What is a good enough reason for getting married?
- What is a good enough reason for getting divorced?
- Have you experienced pressure from other people to get married?

The interviews were recorded and eventually transcribed. Just for the record, this amounted to about half a million words! The transcription system adopted is described as being a simplified version of the Jefferson transcription system (Chapter 6) though the precise details are not presented. The illustrative excerpts of transcripts included in the paper contain little indication of Jefferson coding conventions, e.g. such as timings and other symbols. This is a positive feature as such minute detail is not discussed in the paper and the resulting illustrative excerpts are easily read as normal text.

Lawes is very graphic about how she analysed her data and it is worth reproducing what she has to say here:

Analysing discourse is a lengthy process of 'living with' one's data, reading, re-reading and following up hunches until a pattern of language use emerges. This typically involves looking out for repertoires or dis-courses which organize the text, signalled by repet-itive idioms or metaphors, for instance, one of the most important in this body of talk was the leitmotif of 'success' and 'failure' . . . One simultaneously looks for variability which might signal differences between [interpretive] repertoires; here, agentic talk about success and failure was offset by talk of fatalism and passivity. From these differences, informed hypothe-ses can be made about the differing functions which [interpretative] repertoires might serve. (p. 5)

Two interpretative repertoires (discourses or ideologies) were identified by Lawes: (a) the romantic repertoire and (b) the realist repertoire. The romantic repertoire deals with 'marriage-in-theory' which 'is presented, without irony, as a true or factual account of what marriage *is*' (p. 7). Finding the 'right' person is a common and effective way of explaining in the romantic repertoire: 'obviously, if you're going to get married then you're with the right person' (p. 7). Commitment is also part of this repertoire and takes the form of events (e.g. engagement) and a process which is ongoing throughout a marriage which works. This interpretative repertoire can be used to discuss both successful and unsuccessful marriages.

The realist interpretative repertoire deals with marriage in the real world. Marriage can wear out and be affected by things such as infidelity, illness and debt. It also can be used in accounts of both successful and unsuccessful marriages. The permanence of marriage is not held to be realistic: 'a gamble you take, isn't it. I think so. I think getting married is probably one of the biggest risks you ever take.' (p. 12)

The two repertoires identified by Lawes can coexist in the talk of a single individual. They are not alternatives in that sense. There are not two groups of people – the romantic and the realist – but they do amount to rather different ways of accounting for different aspects of marriage.

Box 9.4

ILLUSTRATIVE RESEARCH STUDY

Discourse analysis in sports psychology: the mysterious 'zone'

Sports psychology has become an increasingly important, quantitative sub-field of psychology. The practical and applied nature of the discipline means that research which points directly to solutions to problems or enhancement of performance has taken priority. Qualitative research, perhaps, does not meet this criterion of immediate utility and was rare in sports psychology until around the year 2000. Things appear to be changing now and there is less reluctance about using qualitative methods and their use seems to be increasingly common in sports psychology. Locke (2008) presents a discursive perspective on a concept commonly used in sports psychology – that of 'the zone'. This refers to he exceptional 'psychological' state in outstanding athletic performances which can be described as effortless, automatic and successful. It has been used by talented athletes to account for their the exceptional performances. Her research also allows us to illustrate the way in which discourse analysis may use the mass media as a source of data. Locke's approach was to use excerpts from a television programme about the athletic performances of elite athletes. The programme analysed was called 'Losing It' which was a scientific documentary looking at sports

psychologists working with two elite athletes – including Sally gunnell. One of the problems with media data of this sort is that the extent of the editing of the piece is usually unknown though not entirely unknowable. Editing can make different contributions seem like conversation and may alter the nature of the conversation. These are perhaps more serious issues for conversation analysis than discourse analysis.

The zone refers to 'the zone of optimal functioning', which was an idea first discussed by Hanin (1980) who thought an individual athlete would have a particularly optimal performance state when their anxiety level was within a given range or zone. Nobody knows just how Hanin's theoretical concept became part of the everyday parlance of athletes – especially elite athletes. They use it as if it were a special and distinct mental state – rather different from what the original theory claimed. For athletes, the state involved being relaxed, entirely focused on the performance, and achieving a peak performance effortlessly. In the zone, the athlete is sort of on a roll, in a groove or in a flow in their performance. But, of course, in discourse analytic terms, the zone is part of the way in which athletes account for outstanding or peak performances.

As such, it matters little if the concept of the zone would pass scientific scrutiny. So in discourse analysis terms, the zone is not regarded as something real but a resource used by athletes to achieve particular effect when they are discussing their athletic performance.

In her analysis, Locke uses the concept of *category entitlement* drawn from conversation analysis. Put simply, it refers to who is seen as appropriate to talk about a certain category of content; that is, the person who can command the expert status on any topic. This would apply to expertise on talking about 'the zone' as much as any other topic. So, the athlete Sally Gunnell is presented in the programme as having such a right. Among the discursive themes which emerged in the study were the way that the elite athletes 'invocated' the zone when explaining their exceptional athletic performance but in a way that denies or lessens their own personal agency (actions) in their success. Put in other terms, athletes often present themselves as being 'modest' about their successes. They seem to have to exercise a degree of modesty when they describe their achievements in a competition. Agency appears in the athlete's accounts in a number of ways. It is important to stress that the 'doing of modesty' is an important characteristic of athlete's accounts. For example, they tend to present 'the zone' as something which is not within their control or of their doing (or agency). The events surrounding experience of 'the zone' can be portrayed as difficult to remember or provide information about. While other athletes may not demonstrate these tendencies, Gunnell's accounts are festooned with such references. Read the following extract carefully and try to find where agency is used:

Extract 2 – Equinox: Sally Gunnell

34 SG: but I don't (0.8) ever remember (0.8) coming off (.)

35 the last (1.0) hurdle and and knowing that she was there

36 (.) and this is what happened she was actually right

37 ahead of me and she was ahead of me all the way in but I

38 don't (0.6) remember this and it was only me sort of like

39 fighting and going over the line and (0.8) y'know I

40 stood over the line and it was like (1.0) my life was

41 almost starting again (.) it had almost been on hold for

42 that last (0.4) y'know fifty two (.) seven seconds

Such minimalisations of agency occurred fairly regularly in what Gunnell had to say during the course of the programme. When she uses such words as 'remember' and 'recall' these are not being used in any technical sense but are ways in which she manages her account of things that have happened. So they provide ways of both claiming responsibility and denying responsibility for her achievements. References to limitations of one's memory can be seen as a resource used in the rhetoric of accountability. Despite Gunnell's giving her account of the race she goes on to claim that she does not recall what happened (line 38). The consequence of this is that what happened comes to appear somewhat mystical. The use of the phrase 'life was almost starting again' is interesting since it softens or weakens the implication of what she is saying. By softening her assertions she effectively makes it less likely that what she says will be challenged or questioned by anyone hearing her claims as they are made less extraordinary. The device is used in line 41 twice. Furthermore, if she overstated the extraordinary and mysterious nature of 'the zone' then the risk is that she may appear as 'odd' in some way. Thus it is essential for Gunnell to construct herself as normal and rational. Another way of doing this is to suggest that anyone is capable of having this experience. The interviewer (BM) also uses such 'softening' devices when he suggests that it is almost like a religious experience:

Extract 4 – Equinox: Sally Gunnell

70 BM: and it's almost like a religious experience

71 SG: yeah you feel as though someone's almost (.) helping you

72 I must admit just because it (.) it does feel so alien

73 (.) at times (.) y'know as I said before it

74 doesn't actually (.) particularly feel like (.) me out

75 there and you almost get into its like a tr(a(nce (.) and

76 uh you feel as though someone y'know I always said (.)

77 someone's watching you and just sort of like you know (.)

78 pulling you round (.) the track and and and (0.2) and

79 letting you flow around that track yeah it's a yeah (.)

80 it is (.) an amazing feeling

Box 9.5

ILLUSTRATIVE RESEARCH STUDY

Moral exclusion of terrorists in presidential speeches: a case of category use

This is a rare example of American research using discourse analysis. Pilecki, Muro, Hammack and Clemons (2014) describe the use of US drone strikes in the Yemen in 2011. One led to the death of Anwar al-Awlaki, a US citizen. This amounted to the first execution without trial of a war-time enemy by the US government since the American Civil War. Three other US citizens were also killed by drones, only one of which could possibly be deemed a legitimate target, according to Pilecki et al. If we add in other actions subsumed under the 'war on terrorism' such as indefinite detention for terrorism suspects and advanced interrogation techniques like waterboarding, there is clearly a need to account for such acts. These acts are far removed from the generally accepted ideals of the USA. What can explain such findings as over three-quarters of Americans believe that the torture of terrorists is acceptable in order to obtain information? There has been a substantial amount of research into President George Bush's rhetoric on terrorism, though rather less for President Obama, despite such activities continuing during his presidency. What is the nature of the moral discourse concerning counterterrorism which justifies such extreme measures against terrorism? How did the two presidents 'frame' terrorism as a special category such that they become unworthy of justice and moral treatment? Just how did the presidents render terrorists as so morally abject that they legitimately could be subject to immoral treatment? How was the counterterrorism strategy framed as the normal, rational and proportionate response to the purported threat of terrorism?

Pilecki et al. express the view that language is crucial to our understanding both of concepts and social categories. As a descriptive term, 'terrorist' fails to identify all of the features ascribed to terrorists. According to Pilecki et al., political leaders shape how categories such as terrorist are understood using rhetoric. Who are terrorists, what do they seek to achieve, and what are their reasons for carrying out terrorist acts? The presidents 'framed' terrorists as a special category of violent/dangerous

people who did not warrant the just and moral treatment that a murderer or drunk-driver would attract.

In order to demonstrate this process, the research concentrated on the presidents' speeches and the moral content found therein. From the discourse analysis perspective, the task of the presidents was to particularise terrorists. They had to be distinguished from other groups as people who have violated fundamental moral values. By doing so, terrorists would appear underserving of normal considerations of justice and fairness. In this way, the in-group retains its moral 'authority' despite the commissioning of immoral acts which deny the terrorist the due process of the law. This is a complex discursive accomplishment according to Tileaga (2007). The researchers culled presidential speeches from the White House website and new media websites. To be eligible for study, the transcript of a speech by one of the two presidents and related to the war on terrorism. They were also searched for the word terror and its derivatives such as terrorism and counterterrorism. Twenty such speeches were found with 11 being those of Bush.

The analysis was basically discourse analytic in style though the authors do not elaborate the details too much. By and large the analysis seems to boil down to a search for examples of the phenomenon the researchers were looking for. They describe the analysis as iterative in that they conducted a sequence of close readings of the texts of the selected speeches. The authors focused on elements which they describe as the moral content used by the presidents speaking about terrorism. No mention is made, for example, of the numerous checks and procedures that Potter (2003) proposes to ensure quality in the analysis.

Not surprisingly, the presidents framed terrorist violence as morally reprehensible. But, more unexpectedly, it was framed as apolitical. In other words, there was nothing to justify terrorist violence and it was merely violence and destruction for its own sake. Terrorism is different from other forms of political violence. Terrorists slaughter senselessly innocent, decent citizens. The political objectives of terrorists were not elaborated upon other than the destruction of common moral values such as freedom. What set terrorists aside as a category was that they were a particularly evil and omnipresent threat to the US and the world community in general. The scope and severity of the threat posed by terrorists was presented as having only one rational solution. That is, counterterrorism should match terrorism in terms of its scope and severity. The presumed innocence of the victims of terrorism makes claim for the moral condemnation of this form of harm. The US counterterrorist responses was justified for the US counterterrorist response was justified on the basis that the terrorist is beyond the protection of human decency.

The presumption that targets of terrorist violence are innocent extends to those who, by definition, are not civilians: 'No enemy is more ruthless in Iraq than al-Qaeda. They send suicide bombers into crowded markets; they behead innocent captives and they murder innocent troops' (The White House, Office of the Press Secretary, 2007). Not always but frequently terrorist violence is framed without reference to any political aims or goals. Hatred is the motive and killing a basic desire. Terrorist violence is not a means to an end but constitutes an end in itself. Terrorists send children on suicide bombing missions solely in order to subjugate millions under their violent rule. If any reference is made to political motives then the speeches highlight the destruction of Western values universally in the terrorist creed. President Bush said, for example, in 2008 'The advance of liberty is opposed by terrorists and extremists, evil men who despise freedom, despise America, and aim to subject millions to their violent rule' (Miller Center, 2013a, quoted in Pilecki et al.). There were differences between the two presidents but the underlying rhetoric remained similar:

> [bin Laden] was a mass murderer who offered a message of hate – an insistence that Muslims had to take up arms against the West, and that violence against men, women and children was the only path to change. He rejected democracy and individual rights for Muslims in favor of violence extremism; his agenda focused on what he could destroy-not what he could build. (The White House, Office of the Press Secretary, 2011)

President Obama juxtaposes the community of free nations with the violent terrorist threat. The stress is on the post-9/11 terrorist as being new throughout the presidential speeches which is used to justify the need for new counterterrorism strategies:

> After 9/11, we knew we entered a new era – the enemies who did not abide by any law of war presented new challenges to our application of the law; that our government would need new tools to protect the

American people, and that these tools would have to allow us to prevent attacks instead of simply prosecuting those who carry them out. (The White House, Office of the Press Secretary, 2009)

The implication is, of course, that the old counterterrorism regime prior to 9/11 was inadequate in that it allowed 9/11 to happen. The strategy became proactive in preventing terrorist attacks in the future rather than merely allowing the law to impose punishments on wrong-doers.

The presidential speeches and the phrase 'the war on terrorism' place discourse about counterterrorism into one of war and military discourse. Bush held that enhanced interrogation methods had provided information which saved the lives of innocent parties and prevented new attacks. Terrorists are not referred to as suspects but as detainees or unlawful combatants. 'America will never seek a permission slip to defend the security of our country' (Miller Center, 2013b, quoted in Pilecki et al.) said Bush in 2004.

We might ask ourselves just how effective a discourse analytic study this is. There is no doubt that the study is situated by the authors within the realms of discourse analytic work. It uses the right terminology and refers to some of the most important publications in discourse analysis such as those by Billig, Edwards, Potter and Wetherell. So, at least superficially, the paper has the trappings of a discourse analytic study. Yet all of the expectations of the research are embedded in the introduction which draws quite widely on the literature on terrorism and the war on terrorism. Not all or not much of this is discourse analytic in nature and the authors seem to hint at this when they argue that discourse analysis could bring something new. So the analysis was pre-empted by the introduction. The speeches were read and re-read to identify sections relevant to the war on terrorism. The way in which terrorism and counterterrorism are framed largely becomes the analysis. From the introduction it is clear that the authors expect the speeches to involve moral exclusion. There is no evidence that deviant cases formed part of the analysis. Did the presidents ever speak differently of terrorism? There may be no such examples but it would help matters if the authors confirmed that they looked for them. Just what does it mean when terrorists are framed as apolitical? After all, the imposition of alien values (e.g. anti-freedom) on other countries would seem to be a political act of enormous proportions. What seems to be happening is that the presidents are avoiding any implication that terrorists have legitimate political aims. There is an inconsistency in the framing of 'terrorist' which moves between illegitimate political intentions which violate Western values enormously to their being killers for killing's own sake. Denial of legitimacy or delegitimisation might be an alternative way of construing the framing.

Evaluation of social constructionist discourse analysis

Among the achievements of discourse analysis is that it has brought to psychology theoretically coherent approaches to working with detailed textual material including in-depth interviews and recordings of conversation. Its limitation is its particular perspectives on how that textual material should be understood and interpreted. Unless one is prepared to buy into this body of theory then the end product will not be recognisably discourse analysis. For example, for researchers who want to see in their data a way of accessing the realities of their participants' lives, discourse analysis lends little or no support – the reverse is more accurate as discourse analysis is not about glimpses of reality but about how reality is constructed. Language is not seen as representational in discourse analysis. No matter how acceptable the basic principles of discourse analysis may be, it is a perspective on the nature of language in social interaction not a way of using interviews, focus groups and other textual material to extract the realities of the individual's life. Other qualitative methods may provide better ways of dealing with people's experiences in life and the narratives they tell. This is an issue which discourse analysis not only critiques other types of research over, but it is a problem for discourse analysis itself in that it begins to marginalise the interview and focus group data that were once at its centre. The search for natural language to analyse limits the topics which discourse analysis can address – we can only interview victims of sexual abuse about their childhoods, for example. We cannot hope to obtain more naturalistic data. To suggest that we have alternative methods of analysis which are more amenable to a realist perspective on the data merely leaves the problem of how discourse analysis can inform us about reality, if at all.

Langdridge makes an important point in this respect which basically boils down to the issue, 'Is what is appropriate in philosophical debates always good for psychology?':

> Although I have considerable sympathy for the arguments from discursive psychology, simply because there has been a turn to language – or, more accurately, text – in a great deal of continental philosophy does not mean that the equivalent step must necessarily follow in psychology, as if all developments in continental philosophy represent progress (an enlightenment idea itself). Philosophy is a discipline of contestation and, furthermore, if we are to take the claims of the postmodernists seriously, then newer will not always be better or – perhaps more pertinently – what is fashionable will not always be superior to that which is not fashionable. I think that it is ironic indeed that some of the most relativist of psychologists apparently seek to impose a methodological hegemony on the discipline through their unquestioning acceptance of a select group of continental philosophers (and it is a very select group). (Langdridge, 2007, p. 160)

In examination discourse: 'Discuss'! Of course, Langdridge's point is a fundamental one which reflects a number of themes which arise at various points in this book. But of particular importance is the question of the future direction of qualitative psychology. Just how much freedom do or should psychologists have to develop a distinctly psychological version of qualitative research? To what extent should they be constrained by the philosophical roots of other disciplines? The attention that qualitative psychologists give to philosophy is substantially greater, it would appear, than that which quantitative psychologists devote to the philosophical roots of the quantitative approach. Why is this? How far should quantitative psychologists stray from the philosophical underpinnings of their endeavours?

It is an unfair criticism of discourse analysis to suggest it is an 'anything goes' or subjective approach to research. It is not a means of 'putting words into the mouths' of participants. There is always a risk of this but this can only happen when the 'built-in' checks which should be part of the analytic procedures are rendered ineffective for some reason. Not only is there a substantial variety of ways in which the quality of qualitative research may be assessed (see Chapter 16) but there are inbuilt checking mechanisms which are part-and-parcel of the method as was indicated in the earlier section on 'How to do discourse analysis' (pp. 233–40). Where there is a problem, possibly, it could be the consequence of the limited space available in research publications for the qualitative researcher to provide full support for their analysis. So the reader may not always be in a position to evaluate the analytic claims against the data. Book-length investigations are the most thoroughly presented and argued studies.

Perhaps it is unnecessary to point out that some discourse analytic studies are better than others. Like all areas of research, you will find dismal examples purporting to be discourse analysis. It is not wise to judge the entire field on the basis of the worst examples. Related to this is the warning that the term 'discourse analysis' is not *Appellation d'origine contrôlée* so studies of dubious worth are labelled by their authors as 'discourse analysis' despite their lacking any semblance to what we have discussed in this chapter.

The two versions of discourse analysis – social constructionist and Foucauldian – do not make for entirely amicable bedfellows. From outside, the arguments seem slightly overblown no matter their validity. Nevertheless, what Foucauldian discourse analysts have to say about social constructionist discourse analysis can be informative about its limitations. One of Parker's (2012) arguments is that social constructionist discourse analysis adopts a relativist position that there is no reality. Such a viewpoint implies that morality and political stances have no bedrock. If everything is relative then, the argument goes, there is no basis to argue for one political position rather than another. That is, a moral position is not possible. At the same time some have criticised social constructionist discourse analysis especially in its affiliation with conversation analysis as being positivist. Parker (1990a, b) also has no taste for the ethnomethodological minutiae of social constructionist discourse analysis. While it might be possible to regard Potter and Wetherell's notion of interpretative repertoires as having similarities to the idea of discourses as discussed in Parker's work on Foucauldian discourse analysis, the two approaches slipped apart. Both interpretative repertoires and discourses are abstracted or synthesised from texts but there was to be no reconciliation. For one thing, Potter and Wetherell gradually moved away from interpretative repertoires in the move towards a more conversation analysis-based approach. Indeed, the notion of interpretative repertoires was not an important feature of Edwards and Potter's book *Discursive psychology* of 1992. Beyond that, Parker sees the term interpretative repertoire as being uncomfortably similar to behaviourism's notion of behavioural repertoire. Parker (2007) added:

> Discursive psychology . . . wipes away historical analysis and even the social context for the bits of text it analyses. What people say about something is pedantically repeated, and the functions of the talk spelt out to the reader; often the exercise is as pointless as it is mind-numbingly unilluminating. (p. 137)

This affirms mainly that social constructionist discourse analysis is not about a broad historical sweep to one's data or even the broader social context in which text can be understood. It does not attempt to deal with these things. Some may find an analysis devoid of these things less than riveting. However, research is about choices and every researcher has the choice of doing things differently if they can demonstrate the benefits of doing so.

In their turn Potter and Wetherell (Potter, Wetherell, Gill, & Edwards, 1990) thought that Parker's approach was inadequate because it reified the notion of discourse. That is, discourses were imparted with the ability to do things and change things – Parker imbues discourse with agency. One can treat the two forms of discourse analysis as resources available to be used when and how the researcher sees fit (Bozatzis, 2014). But one could say this of any qualitative analytic methods. It avoids decisions about precisely where different approaches win and lose. It also avoids questions of superiority. Potter and Wetherell and Parker tend to caricature each other's preferred approach as one might expect. Skirmishes of this sort in academic life are, of course, common and tend to be a handicap rather than a substantial contribution. But this reconciliation is not too helpful when one is seeking to understand the nature of the two different approaches. The debate will continue when we turn to Foucauldian discourse analysis (Chapter 11).

CONCLUSION

Discourse analysis (and qualitative analysis more generally) is a relative newcomer to psychology despite being based on ideas which emerged at about the middle of the twentieth century. Even so, it is more than a quarter of a century since the first psychological discourse analysis studies were published. For comparative purposes, if we take the field of forensic psychology we find that its development as a substantial field of psychology is of much the same vintage. It is probably time, then, that psychology in general came to appreciate that discourse analysis is primarily a way of conceptualising a field of research rather than a method in the sense of operations and procedures leading inexorably to an analytic outcome. For that reason, in this chapter the major features of the theoretical foundations of discourse analysis are emphasised as much as the closely focused procedures which some psychologists would prefer discourse analysis to be.

The discourse analysis literature tends to mystify the analytic processes involved a little. Indeed to talk about discourse analysis as a craft or a skill perhaps indicates that it needs to be learnt 'at the feet' of some Master of Discourse Analysis – an apprenticeship if one prefers. But, as we have seen, there is a lot to be learnt simply by reading and putting what one reads into practice. Take time to learn the basic theory, read some classics in the field and publications closer to your own specific interests, and work with your data in light of all of this. Although perfection is not guaranteed, you should emerge with a passable analysis.

KEY POINTS

- Discourse analysis is based on early work carried out by linguists and philosophers of language, especially during the 1950s and 1960s, which theorised language to be a working set of resources that gets things done rather than considering language merely to be representational of something. This approach uses larger units of speech and text other than words or sentences. Theory is a major component of discourse analysis and the analytic procedures are not valuable unless combined with an understanding of the accompanying central theory. So discourse analysis is a method in the fullest sense of the word rather than a technique.

- In general, the procedures employed by discourse analysts show more than a passing resemblance to what is done in qualitative psychological research in general. However, there are distinct preferences in terms of the sorts of data used in discourse analysis. Increasingly, in discourse analysis the use of recordings of naturally occurring speech is seen to have advantages over research interviews in most circumstances. The central theme of discourse analysis is the idea of speech as doing things – such as constructing and construing meaning – and this guides the analysis as well as the sorts of data which are appropriate.

- Social constructionist discourse analysis has proven to be one of the more influential of the modern qualitative data analysis methods. Its analytic procedures basically involve the search for discursive devices and similar language features in various sorts of text. Some of the stimulus to research has been the consequence of a fairly close allegiance with conversation analysis. Since conversation analysis has a 50+ year history of research and theory, it can provide additional ideas about everyday language use over and above those identified in Potter and Wetherell's original project.

ADDITIONAL RESOURCES

Arribas-Ayllon, M., & Walkerdine, V. (2008). Foucauldian discourse analysis. In C. Willig & W. Stainton-Rogers (Eds.), *The SAGE handbook of qualitative psychology* (pp. 91–108). Los Angeles, CA: Sage.

Coyle, A. (2007). Discourse analysis. In E. Lyons & A. Coyle (Eds.), *Analysing qualitative data in psychology* (pp. 98–116). London: Sage.

DAOL, Sheffield Hallam University. Discourse analysis online. extra.shu.ac.uk/daol/resources/#departments (accessed 6 March 2015).

Potter, J. (2003). Discourse analysis and discursive psychology. In P. M. Camic, J. E. Rhodes & L. Yardley (Eds.), *Qualitative research in psychology: Expanding perspectives in methodology and design* (pp. 73–94). Washington, DC: American Psychological Association.

Slembrouck, S. (2006). What is meant by 'discourse analysis'? www.english.ugent.be/da (accessed 6 March 2015).

Walton, C. (2007). Doing discourse analysis. In E. Lyons & A. Coyle (Eds.), *Analysing qualitative data in psychology* (pp. 117–130). London: Sage.

Wiggins, S., & Potter, J. (2008). Discursive psychology. In C. Willig & W. Stainton-Rogers (Eds.), *The SAGE handbook of qualitative psychology* (pp. 73–90). Los Angeles, CA: Sage.

Willig, C. (2008). Discourse analysis. In J. A. Smith (Ed.), *Qualitative psychology: A practical guide to research methods* (2nd ed., pp. 160–185) London: Sage.

Both major types of discourse analysis are covered.

YouTube. Discursive Psychology: Loughborough diaries 3 Derek Edwards. https://www.youtube.com/watch?v=We8rDiimFmY&feature=fvwrel (accessed 6 March 2015).

YouTube. Loughborough Diaries 2: Jonathan Potter. https://www.youtube.com/watch?v=I4wJyFumjn8 (accessed 6 March 2015).

CHAPTER 10

Conversation analysis

Overview

- Conversation analysis is built on the assumption that the sequence and structure of a conversation are rule-bound and meaningful to participants in the conversation. The object of research is to identify the nature of these rules.

- There is a sense in which conversation analysis can be regarded as behaviourist since its analytic practices are based on what can be seen in the transcript of the conversation and are, thus, observable. In other words, a basic methodological principle of conversation analysis is that the analyst concentrates solely on what can be seen to be happening in conversation.

- Conversation analysts focus on natural conversation in the form of recordings of things such as meetings, therapy sessions, telephone calls and the like.

- Conversation analysis was developed in the 1960s by the late Harvey Sacks and Emanuel Schegloff. Jefferson transcription is essential to conversation analysis and was contributed by the late Gail Jefferson.

- A major influence on conversation analysis was ethnomethodology (originated by Harold Garfinkel) with which it shares many characteristics.

- Among the topics studied by conversation analysis are turn-taking in conversation, the structure of conversational openings and the ways in which mistakes in conversation are corrected (repaired) by the participants in the conversation.

- Conversation analysis requires a close and highly detailed focus of the minute detail of conversation and nothing is ruled out as being irrelevant in a conversation to the analysis of that conversation. So, interruptions, pauses and so on are essential information in understanding the conversation from the perspective of the participants.

- Conversation analysis does not draw on psychological explanatory concepts such as motives and feelings. If the members of the conversation refer to them then they are part of the analysis, otherwise they are regarded as unknowable and irrelevant.

What is conversation analysis?

In conversation analysis the conversations of people, irrespective of context, are regarded as being full of both precisely organised and coherent talk. Each word, partial word, utterance and detail about pronunciation has the potential to be meaningful in conversation and consequently has the potential to be analysed. These things are not necessarily planned but if they can be heard in conversation then they may be treated as significant by participants in the conversation (Edwards, 1995). To enter the world of conversation analysis is to enter a world in which detail is regarded as the key to understanding. Conversation analysis was developed by Harvey Sacks and Emanuel Schegloff in the 1960s and its influence began to spread increasingly widely in successive decades. Although conceived as a sociological perspective on language, it has influenced linguists, psychologists and others. Despite Sacks's greater status as the founder of conversation analysis, the first published research paper on conversation analysis was the work of Emanuel Schegloff. Ten Have (1999) suggests that the ethos of conversation analysis has always been 'an unconventional but intense, and at the same time respectful, intellectual interest in the details of the actual practices of people in interaction' (p. 6).

According to Loos, Anderson, Day, Jordan and Wingate (2009):

Conversation analysis is an approach to the study of natural conversation, especially with a view to determining the following:

- Participants' methods of
  - turn-taking
  - constructing sequences of utterances across turns
  - identifying and repairing problems, and
  - employing gaze and movement
- How conversation works in different conventional settings.

This definition is not simply about what conversation analysts do but it is also loaded with indications about the way in which they do it. For example, it involves natural conversation, it is about how participants in a conversation do certain things within a conversation, and it is comparative across different settings for conversation. The definition also indicates that conversation analysis is not simply the study of conversation, but that it is the study of conversation carried out in a particular way. Conversation analysis has a special interest in such matters as how participants produce or achieve turn-taking in conversations, how utterances within a given turn in the conversation are constructed, and how difficulties in a conversation flow are identified and rectified. The interpretations of the situation as revealed in the conversation are more salient to conversation analysis than arbitrary, theory-led speculations suggested by previous research (Wooffitt, 2001). So hypothesis testing based on cumulative and all-encompassing theory is not involved.

Another way of looking at conversation analysis is to examine its theoretical assumptions. A number of them seem to be all-important according to Wilkinson and Kitzinger (2008). These fundamental assumptions are as follows (see also Figure 10.1):

- *Talk is conceived of as a type of action* This tells the researcher to concentrate on what is done by people in conversation rather than concentrating on what they say. Thus, conversation analysts study inviting, disagreeing and much more. The study extends into more formal or organisational settings so the talk between therapists and patients may be subject to analysis.
- *Talk/action is organised structurally* This leads to the question of just how talk is structured and organised – exactly what the rules are governing structure in conversations. The rules both constrain and enable social interaction.

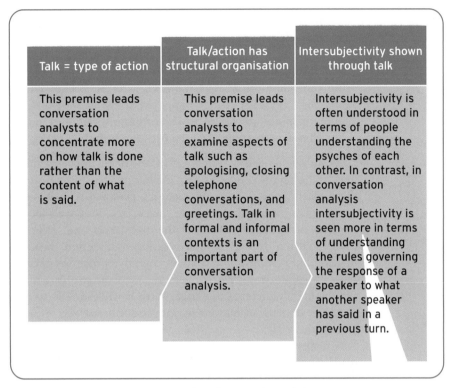

Talk = type of action	Talk/action has structural organisation	Intersubjectivity shown through talk
This premise leads conversation analysts to concentrate more on how talk is done rather than the content of what is said.	This premise leads conversation analysts to examine aspects of talk such as apologising, closing telephone conversations, and greetings. Talk in formal and informal contexts is an important part of conversation analysis.	Intersubjectivity is often understood in terms of people understanding the psyches of each other. In contrast, in conversation analysis intersubjectivity is seen more in terms of understanding the rules governing the response of a speaker to what another speaker has said in a previous turn.

FIGURE 10.1 The basic theoretical assumptions of conversation analysis

- *Talk is a key feature of intersubjectivity and integral to it* This, in conversation analysis, is not some sort of deep psychological process. It is displayed in the way in which one individual responds to the turn of another individual in conversation according to the rules of who then will be able to respond within the rules of the structure of talk appropriately as both share the rules. There is no consideration of the personality or characteristics of the individual speaker as such in this demonstration of intersubjectivity. Wilkinson and Kitzinger give the example of the person who recognises that the other is telling a joke and laughs appropriately at the punchline of the joke.

Conversation analysis has a close ally in discourse analysis of the sort developed by Potter and Wetherell (1987). Indeed, they share a lot in common at the level of conversational detail. So the previous three theoretical fundamentals do not define conversation analysis as they are shared by discourse analysts. However, Foucauldian discourse analysts (Chapter 11) are not, in general, wedded to the ideas involved in conversation analysis.

One of the most difficult but most basic characteristics of conversation analysis is its aversion to considering anything other than that which can be observed directly in conversation. In our everyday lives, we are used to joking about Freudian slips whenever we hear a slip-of-the-tongue or we try to find other motivations for what people say. Conversation analysis has no truck with such psychologising (or grand sociologising for that matter). So motivations, attitudes and other psychological notions are out but so too are sociological notions such as culture, social structure, power and gender. What the participants in a conversation see and hear are the basic building blocks of conversation analysis (CA). Antaki makes the point in this way:

Perhaps the defining mark of CA is its commitment to working with what it sees and hears. Or rather, with what the participants in the scene see and hear. It is wary of explaining what's going on in a scene by appeal to things that are hidden from the participants. . . The most obvious reason why CA doesn't like to appeal to things like a person's inner feelings or motivation is that we usually can't know what those are – and, arguably, it doesn't matter . . . If you and I meet, we work out our business together knowing nothing about our respective inner lives. What we do know about is what each other's *outer* life is like: that is to say, what we say and do. Sometimes we display 'inner' emotions or thoughts; sometimes not; sometimes those displays are meant to be accurate; sometimes not. Nobody hears *pleased to see you* as necessarily accurate (or inaccurate). (Antaki, 2009b)

So, in conversation analysis, the researcher eschews the idea that there are internal psychological processes that explain what is going on in conversation. These are things such as motives, temperaments, personality traits and so forth. Of course, the participants in the conversation, themselves, may well incorporate such psychologising into their understanding of the interaction and, more importantly, mention this psychologising during the conversation. Interaction through talk is not regarded as the external manifestation of inner cognitive processes in conversation analysis. In this sense, whether or not participants in conversations have motives, interests, intentions, personality characteristics and so forth is irrelevant in terms of the researcher's analysis. The domain of interest in conversation analysis is the structure of conversation (Wooffitt, 2001).

A mainstream quantitative psychologist is likely to experience 'culture shock' when reading conversation analysis-based studies for the first time (Howitt & Cramer, 2011). The conversation analysis report often looks like a stripped-down version of the more conventional research report. Of course, conversation analysts from a psychological background accommodate more to psychological traditions in their writings especially where they appear in psychological journals. Nevertheless, often conversation analysis studies have few references to the published literature – that is, the literature review may be sparse. Details of sampling might be just a list or table of the general details of the small number of people that took part in the study. Often there is relatively little detail about the broader social context in which the conversations took place. To expect more is to miss the point of conversation analysis. The intellectual thrust of conversation analysis lies in the belief that the conversation itself and no more is sufficient to understand the principles of what happens when people converse. Consideration of factors beyond the conversation's transcript diverts attention from the important analytic tasks.

Silverman (1998) describes several methodological rules for conversation analysis based on Sacks' writings. The following are some of these basic principles:

- *Methodological rule 1: Gather observational data* Conversation analysis is driven by the data rather than armchair or other forms of grand theory. For Sacks, the data are probably not research interviews.

- *Methodological rule 2: Make a recording* There is no way of remembering the pauses, hesitations, inflexions, intakes of breath and so forth which are embedded in and informative about conversations.

- *Methodological rule 3: Concentrate on the conversation as behaviour* This is to emphasise that conversation analysis is not about what is going on in the heads of those involved in the conversation. Group members see what the other people are doing in terms of language – for example, they may be lying, they may be arguing, they may be reporting, and so forth. To understand conversation one needs to concentrate on the conversation.

As we have seen, conversation analysis had its origins in Harvey Sacks's and Emanuel Schegloff's ideas about how a science of conversation could be developed (see

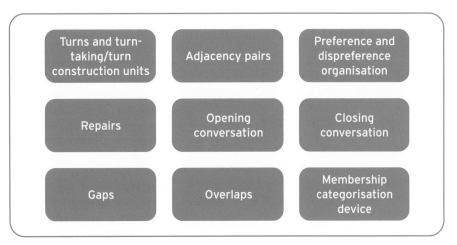

FIGURE 10.2 Key areas of theory in conversation analysis

also the next section). This means that conversation analysis is 50 or so years old. Not surprisingly, substantial quantities of theory have accumulated along with numerous research studies since the 1960s. As a consequence, the would-be conversation analyst needs to familiarise themselves with this general theory otherwise they risk constantly re-inventing the wheel. Much the same is true for discourse analysis – but it is not true for thematic analysis and grounded theory where the task is to learn the method and not the findings and theory which emerged out of the application of the method. That is, thematic analysis and grounded theory do not refer to any particular sort of content – conversation analysis, on the other hand, focuses on conversation. Thus one cannot regard conversation analysis as a method such as experimental design is – a psychologist learns about experimental design almost as if it is a general resource that can be applied irrespective of circumstance. To use the principles of good experimental design does not involve learning a load of theory derived from experiments. So there is a lot of theory to be learnt on the way to being a good conversation analyst. Fortunately, there are a lot of summaries of conversation analysis theory to help speed up the process (see the recommendations at the end of this chapter). Figure 10.2 brings together some of the main theoretical areas in conversation analysis. Box 10.1 provides a short introduction to some key conversation analysis concepts.

Box 10.1

KEY CONCEPT

A short guide to conversation analysis concepts

The following covers some of the major areas of conversation analysis shown in Figure 10.2. It is important to remember that all of the topics dealt with in this box have each been subject to many lengthy studies in books and journal publications. What is presented here is just the beginning of the vast amount of relevant theory. In other words, the following is to whet your appetite for conversation analysis and not to satisfy it.

Turns, turn-taking and turn construction units (TCUs)

Conversation, in conversation analysis, consists of turns. A turn is essentially 'a turn to speak' or a turn-at-talk. That is, a turn is a person's conversation before a different person takes over the conversation. So a turn can be several hundred words or something much shorter – even just a grunt. Thus the turn is essentially the major unit of analysis for content analysis. The primary focus of conversation analysis is on adjacent turns in order to understand how the second turn is 'designed' to fit with the previous turn. The researcher also examines the nature of the subsequent turns in the conversation. So the strategy is to understand how turns cohere together in patterns. Essentially the researcher is working with the same building blocks of conversation as the participants in the conversation in their task of giving coherence to the conversation. Turns are a creation of the interaction rather than entirely pre-specified. So, for instance, a speaker can signal another speaker that it is a particular second speaker's turn to speak. A speaker who has taken over in the conversation has both the right and obligation to include a 'turn construction unit' (which is basically a complete speaker turn) which includes a 'transition relevance space' at which the next speaker may begin to speak – though it does not have to be the case that the potential next speaker speaks at that point. One question is just how these turns to speak get distributed among those party to the conversation. This can happen in very straightforward ways, as in the following. You might wish to check out the Jefferson transcription system in Chapter 6 if you have problems with the following:

```
1          (3.2)
2 Mom:     (C'n) we have the blessi-ih-buh-Wesley
3          would you ask the blessi[ng¿ please¿
4 Wes:                             [Ahright.
5          (0.2)
6 Wes:     Heavenly fahther give us thankful hearts
7          (fuh) these an' all the blessings °ahmen.
8          (.)
9 Vir:     >°Ahmen.<
```
(Schegloff, 2007, p. 6)

Mom fails to signal the next turn properly in line 2 since the request for the blessing is originally directed generally. She corrects this at the end of line 2 and in line 3 by directly addressing Wesley. The transition relevance space, then, is clear. There is another turn relevance space in line 7, not mentioned by Schegloff, in the 'ahmen' at line 7.

Concerns that turn-taking does not occur in all languages in this way are a potential limitation on conversation analysis theory but also potentially a stimulus to theoretical refinement. 'Italian conversation' or contrapuntal conversation generally is the way of referring to this problem. The basic problem that attention is being drawn to here is that in some cultures speakers may, at times, speak together without this being a mistake or conversational problem. In other words, sometimes in conversation Italians show 'a parallelism of turns or moves by the conversationalist' (Prevignano & Thibault, 2003, p. 166) which means that accounts of conversation based on turn-taking may be inadequate.

Adjacency pairs

This builds on the idea that many turns are essentially pairs – the two turns are by different speakers, they come next to each other in their basic form, and the two turns belong to the same type. Examples of adjacency pairs include question–answer, greeting–greeting, summons–answer and telling–accept (Liddicoat, 2007, p. 107). An example of a summons–answer adjacency pair is:

```
1 Mom:    hey Becky,
2 Becky:  in a minute
```

Adjacency pairs may seem simple, but they have considerable impact within a conversation because the adjacency pair organises the later turns by setting up expectations about the later interaction. In the above example, the summons–answer adjacency pair signals that Mom has something important or urgent to say. If, instead, she merely talks about something decidedly non-urgent then this expectation is not met by her later turns.

Preference and dispreference organisation

Turn-taking in conversation characteristically suggests that there is a preference for some first turns to be followed by a particular kind of second turn. These are conversational preferences and not psychological ones. The preference is part of the mechanism of conversation or turn-taking. Thus a question like 'are you feeling any better now?' is more likely to be followed by the answer 'yes' rather than a 'no'. Preferred following turns tend to be rather short. Dispreferred second turns tend to be more elaborate and tend to provide an account of why it has been chosen. Preferences in turn-taking are illustrated in the study described in Box 10.3 later in the chapter.

Repairs

A key objective in conversation analysis is to find evidence of repeated patterns which arise out of the participants' joint endeavour to produce conversation. An example of such patterns lies in the conversation analysis notion of 'repair'. Things go wrong in conversation and all sorts of problems can occur. Repair describes the process by which the participants in a conversation go about correcting these errors. It is argued that the pattern is for members of a conversation to prefer the repair to be done by the person who made the error in the first place – that is, the preference is for repairs to be self-corrected rather than corrected by another member. There might be a very short gap before the next person to speak actually begins. This gap may be used by the person who caused the problem to correct or repair it. This would be classified as a transition space repair since it essentially took place in the area of transition between the two exchanges. However, it is clear from conversation analysis that 'repair' is a complex matter. For example, simply in terms of where the repair takes place there are several possibilities apart from the transition space repair. So the repair could also

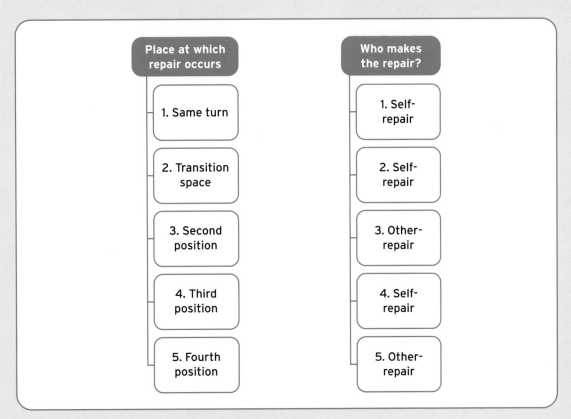

FIGURE 10.3 Positions for self- and other-initiated repairs

be effected (a) in the turn where it occurred (same turn repair), (b) in the turn after it occurred (second position repair), (c) in the turn after the turn in which it occurred (third position repair), and so forth. What this means is that the person making the repair varies with the point in the conversation exchange. This is shown in Figure 10.3.

A simple repair can be seen in the example above – the key turn is this:

1	(3.2)
2 Mom:	(C'n) we have the blessi-ih-buh-Wesley
3	would you ask the blessi[ng¿ please¿

This is a simple self-repair. Mom initially made an open request which meant that anyone around her table could have responded. She quickly repairs this error by specifically addressing Wesley. Things get much more complex if we distinguish who initiates the repair from who makes the repair.

. . . one second pause	
Police:	Hello
Other:	American Red Cross
Police:	Hello, this is Police Headquarters . . . er, Officer Stratton . . .
(Schegloff, 1968, p. 1079).	

Opening conversation

The topic of Schegloff's (1968) paper – the first published conversation analysis paper – was 'Sequencing in conversational openings'. This study was based on 500 or so openings taken from telephone calls involving a disaster centre. In this paper, Schegloff formulated the first rule of telephone conversation (the distribution rule for first utterances). This rule states that whoever answers the call speaks first. Deviant cases in which this rule is broken are used in order to develop the analysis of conversational openings further. So, for example, in the following telephone conversation the police have called the American Red Cross but there is a one second gap at the start of the conversation at which point the rule suggests that the American Red Cross should say something like 'hello'. However, this does not happen and so it is the Police who try to sort out the conversational problem. The following excerpt illustrates this happening in a conversation:

Closing conversation

Conversation does not end, it closes. Speakers use a variety of practices to close conversations (Liddicoat, 2007). These are sequences in the conversation which do not necessarily end in closure but are points at which closure may be chosen. Closing sequences are familiar in telephone conversations:

Don:	okay?
Phil:	okay
Don:	bye
Phil:	bye

In conversation analysis, the exchange of 'bye' in the above is the closing sequence. The 'okay?' and 'okay' are described as pre-closing sequences. The pre-closing sequence in this case is intended to verify the appropriateness of bringing the conversation to an end. It is fairly

self-evident that Don's 'okay?' potentially could lead to the end of the conversation. However, this is not necessarily so, as in the following illustration:

Don:	okay?
Phil:	just one last thing . . .

Of course, there is a problem with this. Don could say okay at many stages in the conversation without it signalling the verification of the end of a conversation. The concept of 'Closing implicative environments' is used to describe the series of actions in a conversation where the ending of the conversation is a possibility. These can take the form, among others, of announcing closure ('I've gotta go now'), making arrangements ('Let's meet outside the lecture on Thursday'), formulating summaries ('So we won't invite Jacqui'), appreciations ('I'm really grateful that you cared enough to call') and back references ('You've got a note of the arrangements for next week?').

Gaps

There are places in a conversation where it is possible that another speaker will take over – this is not a certainty. Such places are known as transition relevance spaces. Usually if there is a transition from one speaker to another it occurs smoothly without either a gap or an overlap of speakers. But, of course, problems do arise. Liddicoat writes:

> The normal value for the transition space, a beat of silence, indicates that nothing special is being done in the transition between speakers. However, it is possible that the transition space may be longer than normal, for example as a gap, or shorter than normal, as in the case of overlap. Both of these possibilities have an interactional importance above and beyond speaker change itself. (Liddicoat, 2007, p. 79)

Some gaps in conversation are attributable to a particular person in the conversation but for others no such responsibility exists. Usually these are distinguished in Jefferson transcription – if the gap is a 'collective responsibility' then it is placed on a separate line but if it is identifiable as 'belonging' to another speaker then it is placed appropriately as part of their turn. However, when in doubt the fallback position is 'attribute the gap collectively' and there is a degree of variability in this aspect of transcription. Gaps can be repaired as in the following, though, in this case, the conversation remains problematic because the gap of 0.6 seconds is followed later by a long one of 2.5 seconds:

D:	.hh 'cause that's no fun, is it?
	(0.6)
D:	when you are having to struggle like that.
M:	huhm
	(2.5)

(simplified from ten Have, 1999, p. 121)

Overlaps

Places where there is no gap between the turns of speakers and no overlap of speaker's words is where *latching* occurs. This is signalled in Jefferson transcription with an = sign. Overlapping is produced by any of the speakers in the conversation. The speaker who is speaking up to the point at which the overlap occurs may be responsible because they signalled the end of their turn but carried on speaking or, on the other hand, the second speaker simply comes into the conversation too soon. Overlaps where a speaker comes into the conversation slightly early can indicate that the second speaker in the turn has understood 'the trajectory' (Liddicoat, 2007, p. 85). Instances of this would include when a student asks a lecturer a question which the lecturer answers or reformulates before the student has completed the question.

Overlaps can be problematic such as when two speakers self-select to take the next turn.

Membership categorisation device

Language is full of numerous membership categories – dad, doctor, student and so forth. The information brought into a conversation by the introduction of a membership category can be highly significant in the conversation. For example, to explain that Gill is Andrea's mother is to introduce a membership category which is laden with information relevant to the contents and structure of communication. Of course, some membership categories tend to go together, such as mother, daughter, son, father, family and so forth. Such a collection of member categories which go together is known as a membership categorisation device. One problem with membership classification analysis is that it is heavily reliant on what the researcher says a particular category brings to the conversation. That is, the information is partly extrinsic to the data being analysed which is not typically the case in conversation analysis.

Membership categorisation is a feature of conversation analysis. Membership categorisation analysis is derived from this but is to some degree established independent of conversation analysis (Butler, 2008). See Box 10.2 later in the chapter for more on membership categorisation.

The development of conversation analysis

Conversation analysis is generally accepted to have originated in the work of the American sociologist Harvey Sacks (1935–75). However, equally influential on its long-term development was the work of Sacks's friend from postgraduate days, Emanuel Schegloff

(1937–), who carried out a great deal of the formative work in the field and Gail Jefferson (1938–2008) who brought the detailed transcription of conversation to the level of a fine art (see Chapter 6). Sacks had published relatively little when he was killed in a car accident and so it was down to Schegloff and Jefferson to take the crucial steps of gathering together Sacks's lectures which had been recorded and then transcribing and organising them into a book.

Sacks had trained as a lawyer which partly stimulated his interest in language and may have encouraged his concern with what, to others, might appear the minutest detail. Probably more important are the direct influences on Sacks in terms of how social scientific research should be done. Two strands of sociological thinking are usually cited as being key to understanding Sacks's work and, consequently, constitute the intellectual roots of conversation analysis. These were social interactionism, especially as it appeared in the work of the sociologist Erving Goffman, and the ethnomethodology of Harold Garfinkel.

Erving Goffman (1922–1982) was a Canadian-born sociologist. His major contribution was his dramaturgical account of social interaction (e.g. Goffman, 1959). For Goffman, social interaction should be thought of as a social institution which has its own organisation in terms of norms and moral obligations. This is not reducible to the psychology of any individual involved in the interaction – an assumption of conversation analysis too. Goffman's work involved naturally occurring behaviours in all of their complexity:

> Like Goffman, Sacks had no interest in building data-free grand theories or in research methods, like laboratory studies or even interviews, which abstracted people from everyday contexts. Above all, both men marveled at the everyday skills through which particular appearances are maintained. (Silverman, 1998, p. 33)

> Goffman insisted that social interaction is to be conceived as a social institution in its own right, with its own normative organization and moral obligations, which, in turn, are linked to other aspects of the social world through face, role and identity. (Heritage, 2003, p. 3)

Sacks wanted Goffman to be his PhD supervisor but Goffman withdrew. Basically, Goffman did not like conversation analysis's (relative) neglect of the non-conversational aspects of social interaction (Silverman, 1998).

The other major influence on Sacks's thinking lay in the 1960s ethnomethodology developed by the American sociologist Harold Garfinkel (1917–2011). Garfinkel's key concern was to understand the way in which social interaction in real, everyday life is conducted. A particular focus of ethnomethodology was the ordinary conversation. The word 'ethnomethodology' indicates Garfinkel's method of studying the common-sense 'methodology' used by people (ordinary conversationalists) to conduct their social interactions. Interactions between people consist of largely unproblematic sequences and Garfinkel wanted to know how interaction is managed and constructed to be largely problem free.

A key Garfinkelian notion was his belief that interactions between people involve the search for meaning. This is not to suggest at all that everyday interaction is meaningful in itself – the suggestion is that members of a social interaction see it as meaningful and try to understand what is happening as meaningful. Garfinkel relied on a sort of 'experimental' research to demonstrate this. In McHugh (1968), students attended 'counselling' sessions in a university's psychiatric section. This was a set-up since the student did not interact directly with the counsellor and the only feedback from the counsellor was a random reply of 'yes' or 'no'. Thus this was a totally incoherent, chaotic and meaningless social situation. The students, however, did not see the situation in this way and imposed meaningful, organised views. Garfinkel's task was with the fine detail of the sense-making/meaning-finding processes in social interaction. This focus influenced Harvey Sacks.

There was a further type of and more direct influence on the development of conversation analysis. In the 1960s, Sacks became interested in occupational practices of employees working at the Los Angeles Suicide Prevention Center (Heritage, 1984). (Sacks had gone to work alongside Garfinkel at the Center for the Study of Suicide at the University of California, Los Angeles.) The Suicide Prevention Center received telephone calls from suicidal people or people who were involved in some way with a suicidal person. These conversations were routinely recorded and transcribed by a secretary, though fairly clumsily and inadequately (Cmerjrkova & Prevignano, 2003). These transcripts allowed the telephone calls to be examined in a new way by Sacks. The staff at the Center were preoccupied with getting the name of the caller because this allowed the unit to document its credentials as an organisation deserving public financial support. According to Schegloff in an interview, Sacks married their problem with:

> a particular call to the suicide center in which someone 'didn't hear' what the answerer at the Suicide Prevention Center had said and by the time the 'repair' was accomplished (we weren't calling it repair at the time, of course; it was just an observation), somehow the caller had managed to avoid identifying himself. (Cmerjrkova & Prevignano, 2003, p. 23)

It appeared to Sacks and Emanuel Schegloff that something interesting was happening. That is, if the person answering the telephone at the Suicide Prevention Center could not get the caller's name at the beginning of the call then they would not get their name at all during the course of the conversation. The usual process in the 'successful' calls was that the Centee would answer the phone by saying something like 'Hello, I'm Alan Davies, can I help you?' and the caller would reply something like 'Hello, I'm Sue Collins'. However, if the caller replied saying something like 'Sorry – I did not hear your name' and the Center repeated 'This is Alan Davies' but the caller did not then give their name then there was a problem – the Center never got the caller's name. Schegloff (Cmerjrkova & Prevignano, 2003) identifies this realisation as the moment conversation analysis began. Following this, Sacks began to work in earnest with the data from these telephone calls and, also, with recordings that he managed to acquire from a number of group therapy sessions with adolescents conducted by a psychologist affiliated with the Center. Telephone conversations and psychotherapy sessions have had a rich tradition in conversation analysis since then.

One last notable feature of conversation analysis needs to be mentioned: the contribution of Gail Jefferson to conversation analysis. Her major development was the system of conversation transcription which is virtually, nowadays, universal in conversation analysis work. This is discussed in much greater depth in Chapter 6 on transcription.

How to do conversation analysis

There are three important stages in conversation analysis:

- *Obtaining/making a recording* This may be audio alone but it increasingly might be a video. Video is a little more tricky than it sounds because of the preference for/ insistence of conversation analysts that their data should be natural conversation. The precise parameters of what sort of talk is acceptable as conversation are unclear – perhaps talk produced in overtly research settings is the main source of contention.

Also, conversation analysis would not generally be considered as a way of studying plays and books because they do not contain real-life conversation. It should be noted, then, that the birth of conversation analysis was out of recordings and transcriptions of real-life telephone conversations and psychotherapy sessions. There is no question that these are real-life conversations of sorts. The advent of video recording has brought to conversation analysis the possibility of incorporating visual aspects of conversation – such as gaze which is indicative of whether a participant is paying attention. The use of video brings its problems, though, including that of the participants being identifiable. According to Heath and Luff (1993) offering a final veto to the participant is often enough to sway them towards agreeing to being videoed.

- *Transcription* In conversation analysis, the recordings are always transcribed, nowadays, using the Jefferson transcription system (Chapter 6).

- *Analysis* This involves the identification of notable features of the transcription (or recording) and then developing ideas about the nature of the conversational devices involved in these significant features. Conversation analysis does not start with theoretical notions to be tested against the conversational data. Instead, the analysis seeks to understand the nature of the rules used by people in everyday life while making conversation. The participant's interpretations of the interaction as revealed by the conversation are the basis of conversation analysis.

The fundamental strategy of the conversation analyst is to work through their fragments of conversation making notes where anything strikes them as being of interest or significant. The number of observations that can be written down as a part of the analysis is unlimited, though the analyst must confine their analysis to what can be observed in the data. So they do not personally speculate about the motives of the speaker or whether the speaker was trying to achieve some unrevealed outcome in the conversation. The mindset of the conversation analyst is on what can be seen in the transcript in possibly what seems at first trivial, irrelevant detail. The transcripts used by conversation analysts are messy in the sense that they contain symbols and notation representing non-linguistic features of the conversational exchanges. The transcript tries to show fidelity to the original recording and so includes false starts to words, gaps between words and gaps between participants' turns, for example. Although sometimes one sees simplified transcripts which are light on symbols, this may not always be seen as good practice since it removes something that the reader might consider important if only it had been included.

According to Drew (1995), the following are the major methodological matters which underlie carrying out a conversation analysis:

- Conversation analysis aims to identify the sequential organisation and patterns of conversation.

- A particular contribution by a participant (i.e. a turn) is regarded as consequent on the sequence of turns which come before it in a conversation. It is an assumption of conversation that each turn should fit appropriately and coherently with the previous turn. In other words, adjacent turns should fit together effectively and meaningfully. Of course, this does not always happen in reality in which case there may be ensuing difficulties in the conversation. But the basic assumption of both the analyst and the participants in the conversation is that turns succeed each other meaningfully.

- Conversation analysts study the design of each turn or the machinery of conversation. That is, how is it possible to understand the activity that the turn is designed to perform in terms of the detail of the verbal construction of the turn?

- Participants are active participants in conversation and develop analyses of the verbal behaviours of others in the conversation. However, the conversation analyst unravels the nature of these analyses from the detail of each participant's utterances. Contributors to a conversation interpret one another's intentions and attribute intention and meaning to each other's turns through their talk. (The researcher finds out about these intentions and meanings through examination of the transcript. The researcher does not provide them and does not seek other evidence of what they might be, e.g. by interviewing participants in the conversation later.)

● The researcher seeks to show the recurrence and systematic nature of patterns in conversation. The patterns are demonstrated and tested by the analyst. This involves referring to collections of instances of the feature of conversation which is being studied. If the researcher is studying how lecturers bring tutorials to an end then the collection would be of transcriptions of the ends of tutorials.

● Conversation analysis presents the evidence in such a way that other researchers can confirm or challenge the ones made by the original researcher. This involves making entire transcripts available to other researchers or the provision of excerpts from the data which demonstrate particular features of the analysis (i.e. they are not selected simply because they support what the researcher claims). The extent to which such data exchange occurs appears not to have been documented as yet.

● The researcher can then move on by attempting to apply their analysis to other domains of conversation. This may involve data gathered from new and different research locations which allows their analysis to be generalised (or otherwise) in new circumstances.

While it is common to read that conversation analysis has no set way of proceeding, there are some fairly strict parameters within which conversation analysis operates. Understanding these should help keep the novice conversation analyst on the 'straight and narrow'. Ten Have (2007) suggested a seven-step model of the research practices involved in a conversation analysis. Ten Have's steps are probably best regarded as an idealised account of the research process. It is unlikely that they precisely describe the procedures of any particular conversation analyst. The steps are summarised in Figure 10.4.

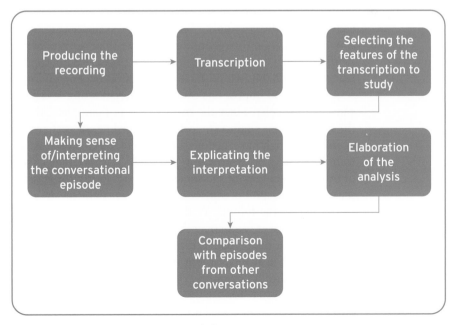

FIGURE 10.4 Steps in doing conversation analysis

Step 1   **Producing the recording (i.e. the materials to be analysed)** The recording is vital in conversation analysis. Indeed, the analyst may prefer not to 'collect data' in the sense of making a recording of conversation themselves. Instead, it is part of the tradition of conversation analysis that the researcher uses extant recordings in the form, say, of telephone conversations routinely recorded by organisations. In terms of data, conversation analysis is less attracted to recordings of conversations that the researcher makes happen such as qualitative interviews and focus groups. Thus the ethos in conversation analysis encourages the choice of naturalistic or naturally occurring conversations whenever it is available. Of course, what is natural conversation is a problematic issue, in itself. The conversation analyst does not need to be present at the conversation, say, making notes and the analyst would see no point in doing so. Of course, the recordings are done by a machine but humans decide what is to be recorded and when it is to be recorded. Apart from this, a recording is basically unselective and what is recorded is not the product of the conversation analyst's questions and it has not undergone a tidying-up process. This original recording remains a point of reference throughout the analysis and later. In this way it can be used for checking purposes (Drew, 1995) but it can also be subjected to a completely new analysis in a way which mostly is not possible in psychology because of the problems of accessing data.

This is, perhaps, a slightly traditional or idealised view of the data for conversation analysis in that it stresses the importance of non-interventionist data collection – that is, the secondary use of recordings already made for non-research purposes. However, there is no embargo on the use of other data and you will find good examples of the use of researcher-initiated data (e.g. focus groups) being used for conversation analysis.

As in most aspects of research, there are choices to be made and, so long as the choices are consistent with what the researcher wishes to achieve, the details of the data are a factor in the analysis and not a stumbling block.

Step 2   **Transcription** Transcription is dealt with at some length in Chapter 6. Conversation analysis needs detailed transcriptions of conversation. Although some of the transcriptions that are used in this chapter are light on symbols indicating additional features of speech beyond the word itself, it has to be remembered that we have used examples from different periods in the development of conversation analysis – so modern standards do not always apply. Transcription systems cannot, by definition, completely capture what is on the recording any more than the recording is an exact reproduction of the original conversation. Indeed, a transcription capturing every nuance of the recording probably would have no advantages over the original recording. The transcription system imposes its own characteristics on the data which, for most purposes, cause no difficulty. Since the transcript is not complete, the analyst may need to check the transcription against the original recording or, perhaps, check parts of the analysis against the original recording where there may be doubts. Even within these limits, a transcriber may produce a transcript which is different in some way from the product of other transcribers of the same recording. Partly for this reason, the tradition is that the researcher should transcribe their own data in conversation analysis. This may help generate the familiarity that the analyst needs with their data but it also means that the analyst is familiar with what can be heard on the recording – that is, there is more information available to the analyst than can be found in the transcript. Having the transcript in front of them to work from, nevertheless, means that the researcher is encouraged to focus on the rich but minute detail of conversation.

It is not unusual for a conversation analysis study to be based on just a few minutes of conversation especially where this raises special issues (as in the examples in Boxes 10.3 and 10.4 later in the chapter). One consequence of this is that the research reports can contain all of the transcribed data on which the analysis is based. In other words, the data are completely available to other researchers to 'validate' (see Chapter 16 on quality in qualitative research). This is unusual in most forms of qualitative and quantitative research.

Step 3

Selecting the features of the transcription to study Ten Have (2007) recommends that the researcher concentrates on a feature of the conversation selected for analysis. That is, it is not analytically useful to try to deal with the entirety of the conversation and, consequently, it is necessary to select a feature (or possibly features) to form the starting point for the analysis. Of course, what can be expected from an application of conversation analysis methods depends very much on the level of sophistication of the researcher. A student exploring the basic procedures is obviously operating at a different level from the advanced researcher who is working on an important and novel theoretical issue. The novice conversation analyst does not need to choose an area of research which is startlingly original. Indeed, it is still a useful learning experience for a student to replicate someone else's work. This could take the form of selecting a well-established concept which is pertinent to a particular piece of conversation that the student has selected or, at a more advanced level, essentially replicating someone else's published work in a different conversational context. The examples in Boxes 10.2 and 10.4 are obvious candidates for this but there are many others.

Harvey Sacks is presented in the conversation analysis literature as being rapaciously interested in the conversation that surrounded his everyday life. Of course, such a general interest, in itself, is not the certain path towards the development of any field of research. Many people are fascinated by conversations but have no contribution to make in terms of conversation analysis. The preference for ordinary, mundane conversation expressed by Sacks does not instantly help in identifying topics for research. Indeed it is a little daunting to read how out of mundane data can emerge interesting research findings – it sets the bar a little too high, if anything. Of course, there are some principles which can be applied to a conversation in order to identify features for research:

- Parts of the conversation which seem not to be going well are a likely area of focus. These can, in part, be identified from the words but also from where repairs occur.
- Once some basic understanding of conversation analysis theory has been achieved, then this may suggest issues for consideration. For example, it is often suggested in conversation analysis that there is a preference to allow self-repair of errors rather than repairs by others in the group. This may be so but is it the case in all conversations – what about where friends are having a drink together? Is this a situation in which the mistake is repaired or is it one where it is highlighted, say, in the form of a humorous comment or laughter?
- There may be parts of the conversation which the researcher simply does not understand. It is unclear what conversational processes are involved. Such excerpts pose an analytic challenge.

Although conversation analysis tends to rely on features intrinsic in the data to suggest areas for development by the researcher, it can underplay factors extrinsic to the data itself as stimuli for research ideas. For example, the applied relevance or applicability of research findings is a common justification for research. Sacks himself was somewhat dismissive about the possible applications of conversation analysis. Nevertheless, both the highlighted examples of conversation analysis in this chapter (Boxes 10.3 and 10.4) use extrinsic arguments as justification for their choice of data. For Toerien and Kitzinger (2007) this is achieved by drawing in the concept of emotional work from outside conversation analysis and for Antaki, Finlay and Walton (2007) the external stimulus is the rights of people with learning difficulties.

While as part of a training exercise in conversation analysis it may be appropriate to simply pick out a 'noteworthy' feature of a conversation or several conversations to pursue, this is difficult to maintain as a strategy at more advanced stages. In a sense, it is a common issue in research just how to identify a topic to research. Howitt and Cramer (2011) discuss this in some detail. The short answer is that the sophisticated level of asking conversation analysis research questions requires a sophisticated level of knowledge of the research literature. Now this is fairly typical of most of the qualitative data analysis methods described in this book and reinforces the need to appreciate that qualitative methods should be regarded as areas of research more than as research design, data collection and data analysis techniques. There are few short cuts to achieving this other than careful and detailed reading of research publications. Probably many a time-pressured student studying for their first degree in psychology will wince somewhat at this suggestion. Reading does not guarantee, of course, good ideas but without reading in one's chosen academic field then there is virtually no chance that they will emerge. It is likely that any researcher's early work will be strongly derivative of the work of others but gradually a distinctive approach and style can develop. To be sure, fortune favours any researcher who finds a golden nugget of previously unnoticed detail in conversation but that, in general, is not how developments in the field are likely to unfurl. Of course, gaining access to recordings of a particular sort of conversation might, in itself, provide just the stimulus that the researcher needs. One never knows – out of a researcher's non-research activities may arise an interest in and opportunities for them to investigate a particular sort of natural conversation.

Of course, social change may bring changes relevant to the study of conversation analysis. For example, mobile telephones and regular telephones with caller identification make Sacks's original observations and notions about the initial turns in conversation defunct. Modern telephones including mobiles and some landlines tell their user who is calling – or at least whose phone is calling. So what are the new rules of telephone conversation? Or are the old rules applied and problems created as a consequence? Conversation changes – so why not conversation analysis?

No matter how tentatively, it should be possible to wrestle from conversation an issue that conversation analysis can help answer. Take heart, for example, from the following comment by a student:

> I decided to take the Conversation Analysis course in my third year, which was a much more technical introduction to the basic mechanisms of ordinary conversation. Within a few weeks of starting that course, CA became a passion. I found myself listening to people's conversations in a new way in my everyday life. Then in one class [the lecturer] briefly mentioned CA research on people with communication disorders and mental health problems, and I knew right away what I wanted to do for my final year project. I've known a lot of families which include people with Alzheimer's and I worked in a residential home which included Alzheimer's patients for nearly a year. I wanted to work on ordinary conversations with people with Alzheimer's in the hope that Alzheimer's could become less frightening to people. So that's what I did . . . (cited in Kitzinger, 2007, p. 137)

Step 4   Making sense of/interpreting the conversational episode Researchers are part of the culture that produced the conversational episode. Hence, they can use their own common-sense knowledge of language to make sense of the episode. This is appropriate since it is essentially what participants in the interaction do when producing and responding in the conversation (in adjacent turns, for example). Typically the analyst may ask what aspects of the conversation do or achieve during such exchanges. The relations between different aspects of conversation can then be assessed. Of course, the process of interpretation will be built on the following and more:

- A detailed reading and re-reading of the conversation to familiarise oneself with what is going on in the conversation.
- An attempt to use the content of the conversation to access how the members of the conversation are making sense of each of the turns and other elements of the conversation.
- The researcher's personal understanding of conversational exchanges as a person generally involved in conversations.
- The researcher's general knowledge of research and theory in conversation analysis.

Step 5   Explicating the interpretation The conversation analyst is a member of the broad community whose conversations they study. Consequently, as we have seen, the researcher's native or common-sense understanding of what happens in an episode from a conversation is an important resource. Nevertheless, this is insufficient as an explication without bringing the links between this resource and the detail of the conversational episode together. That is, the analyst may feel they know what is happening in the conversation but they need to demonstrate how their understanding links to the detail of the conversation. The analyst needs to be sensitive to the fit of their analysis to the data but prepared for instances where the analysis and the data simply do not work together. It may also involve revising the explication.

Step 6   Elaboration of the analysis Once a particular episode has been analysed, it has to be set in the context of the rest of the conversation transcription. This may allow a fuller understanding on the episode in question, though, equally, the entire transcription may raise questions about the adequacy of the analysis so far. Later sequences in the conversation may in some way, directly or indirectly, relate back to the analyst's chosen and key conversational episode. This referral back may help the analyst appreciate how the people in the conversation made sense of the original episode. The consequence of this may be a need to reformulate the analysis or replace it entirely with a new, better fitting analysis.

Step 7   Comparison with episodes from other conversations A conversation analysis need not end with a particular conversation and the researcher's analysis of it. There is the question of whether other instances of conversation, seemingly similar, support or detract from the analysis. This stage is extremely important because individual conversational episodes are not considered in conversation analysis to be unique. The mechanisms and ways in which a conversational episode is both produced by conversationalists and understood by other conversationalists are expected to re-occur across different conversational episodes. Some conversation analysis studies collect together different 'samples' of conversation so that comparisons may be made to find similarities and dissimilarities which may help refine the analysis.

Distinguishing between Steps 4 to 7 above is not so easy in practice as it is in theory. But they can be usefully seen as part of a schematic way of looking at the processes involved in conversation analysis. It is not being suggested that these different steps constitute a necessary and invariant sequence through which every conversation analysis will necessarily progress. It is important to remember that it is only the short-term aim of conversation analysis to interpret a particular episode taken from a conversation. The real aim of conversation analysis is the basic ethnomethodological objective of understanding the methods and structure of everyday social activity.

When to use conversation analysis

Conversation analysis is a particular approach to understanding language in action, so it cannot be regarded as a general approach to qualitative data analysis in the way that, say, thematic analysis and grounded theory are. It is a method of research in a full sense of the term 'method' rather than the modern usage which fails to distinguish techniques for collecting and analysing data from a systematic view of how knowledge should be developed in a particular field. Conversation analysis is a fully fledged approach to how we should study conversation. Understanding what this is depends on understanding the intellectual roots of conversation analysis especially in ethnomethodology. It is hard to write more than a few sentences about conversation analysis's stance on data collection – the substance of the appropriate data is little more or less than that recordings of naturally occurring conversations should be used. This is clear and not very demanding to implement in the sense that data-collecting skills are not at a premium. It is how conversation analysis deals with conversation which distinguishes it. We should not forget that conversation in groups has been studied in various ways by psychologists. For example, group decision making, jury decision making, some attitude and opinion research, and so forth each fundamentally involve conversation. However, none of these approach conversation in a way which would satisfy the principles of conversation analysis. It seems easier to say what conversation analysis is by providing an 'agenda' of the sorts of things that conversation analysts investigate. For example, Butler explains:

> The focus [of conversation analysis] is on investigating the sequential organization of talk-in-interaction, and examines various conversational practices, including the organization of turns-at-talk, actions such as asking, telling, agreeing and assessing, and how things such as coherence, 'trouble', and word selection are relevant and consequential for the production and understanding of conversation, or, talk-in-interaction. (Butler, 2008, p. 19)

So the circumstances in which a researcher should consider conversation analysis are (a) where the data are in the form of conversation but (b) where the analysis of conversation is in terms of how conversation is done, how it is sequenced, and how the participants in the conversation understand what is happening. Quite clearly, conversation analysis should not be used when you have data in the form of conversation but the research questions are of a different order. For example, one would not use conversation analysis to answer questions like 'Do men use more instrumental talk?', 'Does conversation in groups lead to more group cohesion?' and 'Are juries biased against young witnesses?' These are all valid questions to ask about conversation. However, they are not the sorts of question that conversation analysis would answer.

Examples of conversation analysis studies

The illustrative research studies for this chapter are to be found in Boxes 10.2 to 10.4. In order to illustrate some of the variety of conversation analysis studies, three different studies are described:

- The first example (Box 10.2) introduces the concept of membership categorisation devices. These are simply the ways that in speech we begin to create or refer to categories of (usually) people. It is an important area of conversation analysis and is well worth reading to understand this aspect of conversation analysis research and theory better.

- The second example (Box 9.3) uses theory from emotional labour research. This is merely the extra 'strokes' which tea ladies, hairdressers, salespersons and so forth deliver when they are carrying out the normal duties. It is worthwhile noting this use of theory since it begs the question of what other theory is appropriate to conversation analysis? Are there theories in psychology which could be used?

- The third example (Box 9.4) involves conversation analysis with groups of people including those who have learning difficulties. This study is interesting also because it relates to a social policy issue. The original paper is worth reading because it is a skilfully crafted report.

Box 10.2

ILLUSTRATIVE RESEARCH STUDY

How membership categorisation devices work

Initially it is not easy to grasp how conversation analysts go about understanding language in its social context. It is worthwhile, then, to contrast how conversation analysis can tackle a problem in a way which is different from what would be done in other fields of psychology. A good example of this is to take the example from forensic psychology (and criminology) of the various mechanisms which perpetrators of crimes attempt to justify or from which they try to exonerate themselves. The tactics that they employ include denial, blaming the victim and minimisation. These are commonly referred to outside of conversation analysis, so how would conversation analysis deal with similar issues?

Stokoe (2010) provides a good example of the use of the conversation analysis concept of membership categorisation device. She used available police interviews with men suspected of assaulting women. A large body of British police interrogations of violence suspects was used. In each of her examples, the man in question denied assaulting the woman. Stokoe used conversation analysis to further understand how, when and where these denials take place during the interviews and the responses they engender from the interviewing police officers. The police interviews (she calls them interrogations) were anonymised and then transcribed using the Jefferson transcription system as is standard practice for conversation analysis studies. The article is exemplary in the quantity and quality of the methodological detail it provides and can be recommended as a model for qualitative writing. She refers to 'category based

denials' in which the basic idea is that men of their sort or men in general simply do not hit women. Such denials routinely follow direct questioning about assaults but, more importantly, the denials are part of lengthy narratives which do not focus on or involve violence. In these high-stakes settings of the police interview the suspect constructs two membership categories – maybe the sort of men who do hit women and the sort of men who do not hit women or the sort of people men hit (other men) and the sort of people men do not hit (women). This was combined with the sequential analysis procedure to be found in Sacks' (1992) and various researchers' ideas about membership categorisation deriving from this. Stokoe writes

> I identified numerous instances of the phrase 'I wouldn't' or 'I don't hit women' and its variants, which are the focus of the current article. For each instance, I examined its location in the ongoing interaction, the design of the turn in which it appeared, and the action(s) being done in that turn. I also examined the design and action-orientation of police officers' responses, and whether they topicalized the categorial phrase itself or responded to the 'primary action' (Robinson, 2004) of the turn. (p. 62)

In the police interviews, the category 'man' and 'hitting women' were used as if they belonged together or were tied together in the suspect's thinking. There is no linguistic or logical reason why this should be the case. The way in which categories are used can be described as fluid and to some extent creative. It is not predictable just how categories are going to be used in a particular instance as there are many different possibilities. These possibilities are informed by a range of categorisation devices. The suspect's denials were related to language categorisation devices but not entirely determined by them. However, similar sorts of language categorisation devices were found to be embedded in similar action-orientated aspects of the interviews. This is partly because the police interviews all had much the same structure, etc. That is, they are to a degree predictable.

To clarify this, we can take an example from Stokoe's writings. The background is that the suspect was under arrest for an offence of causing bodily harm to both his neighbours – a male and female couple. He had spotted the couple photographing him through his living room window at night where he was sitting naked in full view of passers-by. They claimed to be collecting evidence of this indecent exposure whereas the suspect 'excused' himself by claiming that a skin condition made wearing clothes uncomfortable. The suspect accepted that he had assaulted the man but denied any assault on the woman, as can be seen in the extract. The female neighbour had made a statement in which she claimed that he had kicked her down. Here is part of that interview – P indicates the police officer and S indicates the suspect:

Extract 3: PN-61

1 P1: .hhhh D'you remember <u>k</u>ickin' 'er:=

2 S: =No. <u>N</u>ot <u>h</u>e:r.

3   (0.9)

4 <u>S</u>: I do the <u>m</u>an but not 'er no.

5   (1.7)

6 P1: .pt so you've <u>n</u>ot kicked <u>h</u>er at all.

7   (0.9)

8 S: °No.°

9   (2.2)

10 S: <u>Swung</u> 'er about, kept 'er <u>o</u>ff me that's all.

11   (2.4)

12 P1: D'y'<u>m</u>ember 'er falling down to the gro:und.

13 S:.hhhhhhhh

14   (0.3)

15 S: ↑M:ye:ah.ˊSee I wer-‹I was pullin' 'er u- (0.2) ar- ar

16   pullin' 'er arm t'kee- keep 'er awa:y from me like.‹an'

17   I swung 'er <u>a</u>:rm like that.=Don't forget I'm still this

18   ra:ge, an- (0.4) an: uh she fell t- fell t- fell to the

19   la:wn.

20.   (1.1)

21 S:→   But the way's not to kick a ↑wo↓man as you

22 might say.

23   (.)

24 S:→   I wouldn't <u>d</u>:o that..shih

25   (0.8)

26 S: →   Wouldn't be ri:ght (0.2) tuh- f'me to <u>do</u> ↓ that.

```
27          ((papers rustl[ing))
28 P2: →    [But [you'd kick a bloke] in the 'ead three=
29 S [()]
30 P2 =ti:mes.
31          (0.3)
32 S:.hhhhhhh HHH well, hhhh he was my main concern of what
33          was: (0.5) my main upset at the time was the bloke
34          that- wh- he was the one with the camera.
```

Stokoe suggests that the following are the key features of an analysis of this extract:

- The suspect denies kicking the woman to the ground at line 2 – this is not responded to by the police officer verbally, though his silences are quite long. The suspect takes another turn at line 4 where he is essentially repeating what he had said at line 2.

- There is still no response from the police officer after line 4 and the suspect repeats his earlier admission that he assaulted the man.

- At line 6 the interviewing police officer 'formulates' or summarises what the suspect has said when he says 'so you've not kicked her at all'. This formulation the suspect deals with as if it is the same as the original question and claims not to have kicked at line 8.

- There is then a long gap in the interview (line 9) which the suspect interrupts by admitting to a 'downgraded' act of swinging the woman about apparently to stop her attacking him. This covers two separate turn construction units.

- The interview officer moves on to ask the suspect whether he remembers the woman falling to the ground without implying the agency which led to the falling.

- The suspect acknowledges this and elaborates on what he had claimed happened in line 10. He claims to 'pull' the woman's arm as a way of keeping her off of him. It was during the course of this that she fell onto the 'lawn' he says (line 18) Of course, a lawn would be softer than ground; in general, therefore, he is again downgrading the level of seriousness of what he had done.

- At line 21, the suspect accounts further for what he had said at line 15 by saying: 'But the way's not to kick a ↑wo↓man as you might say. (.) I wouldn't d:o

th:at' (lines 21–24). In this the account moves from what is a general statement about what people (men) do to a specific statement about what the suspect's actions would be (not to kick women). This sort of move is a common feature of claims (Edwards, 1994). The suspect also moves the issue from the female neighbour to women in general in this statement.

- The suspect then repeats that he had not kicked the woman when he says 'Wouldn't be ri:ght (0.2) tuh-f'me to do ↓that'.

- During his follow-up question to this, the police officer 'invokes' this denial by stating 'But you'd kick a bloke in the 'ead three ti:mes' (lines 28–30). Again you can see the use of generalised statements referring to 'a bloke' rather than the specific man in question. Stokoe points out that this is to use generalised gender categories. Blokes versus women is the generalised gender category here. Thus exactly the same membership categorisation device is being used by the police officer as by the suspect.

- In lines 32–34 the suspect admits the assault on the other 'man' but denies assaulting a woman. In this way, the suspect identified his own gender category thereby making it relevant to what he has to say.

Overall, the extract shows, according to Stokoe, how by creating membership of equivalent categories (equivalence in this case being in terms of physical strength and levels of vulnerablility) somehow the act of assault is portrayed as more acceptable or justifiable. In other contexts, young people may well deny assaulting older people to similar effect. Of course, other membership categorisation devices might have been used – for example 'neighbours' but this probably would not be helpful to the suspect in this example given that he admitted one assault on the male but not the other on the female neighbour.

Box 10.3

ILLUSTRATIVE RESEARCH STUDY

Conversation analysis: feeling good and emotional labour in the beauty salon

Emotional labour is relational work that people do as part of their paid job. It is a concept which makes apparent aspects of work which are often unacknowledged such as masking one's own personal feelings in favour of a positive company persona, mending colleagues' egos, intervening to prevent arguments and so forth. There is an idea that such emotional labour is unrewarded which puts women, in particular, at a disadvantage since it is not regarded as a skill or talent – merely something that women do naturally. 'In the highly gendered, low-paid world of beauty therapy' (Toerien & Kitzinger, 2007, p. 163) not only do the workers provide the services formally charged for but they have to do the work of emotionally pampering as well as physically pampering their clients in order to ensure that they will be repeat customers. This involves making the client believe that she is being treated individually and not as part of some production line. Toerien and Kitzinger point out that research has discussed emotional labour generally but that studies of the mechanics of how emotional labour is done had not previously been carried out:

> emotional labour is dependent on subtle interactional competences that beauty therapists must practise routinely; they cannot just turn them on for special, emotionally charged situations, like dealing with an enraged or grieving client. (pp. 163–164)

Emotional labour is not a concept from conversation analysis but more broadly from sociology.

The data are a six and a half minute recording of interaction in a beauty salon in which the apparent task is removal of hair from the customer's eyebrows. Usually this would involve discussion of what method of hair removal would be employed – waxing or plucking. But this episode is different – a negative case – as waxing is clearly the method to be employed. Although the recording generated 110 lines of Jefferson transcription, only 22 lines were discussed in the analysis.

01 Cli	>>Thing is<<um (.) I nor:mally: (0.4) get
02	them just plu:ck:ed. = 'Cause sometimes when
03	I get 'em wa:xed they sta:y <u>redfora:ges?</u>
04	Like not just a day but (0.4) a
05	[<u>few da:ys?</u>]
06 BTh	[(Are) you quite se:n]sitive
07	[with it.]
08 Cli	[<u>Re:</u>ally sensi]tive skin.
09	(.)
10	And I got a [Date tonight so] uhha ha ha ha
11 Bth	[we'll see how]

12	I'll see how yuh- ‹I mean.hh it's <u>not</u> really
13	really <u>hot</u> the wax so you should be o:ka:y
14	with it. Hhh [but] we- I'll do one little=
15 Cli	[Yeah?]
16 BTh	bit and if it fee:ls like it *is* fa:r too hot
17	then we'll lea:ve it ‹'cause if you're
18	[going out] you don't=
19 Cli	[(°and/can just°)]
20 BTh	[want (to be red#eyes] do: you#.
21 Cli	[eheh heh heh heh.hh]
22 Cli	Yea:hh. Can just pluck 'em (.) °or something.°

We learn nothing about the setting of the interview other than it is somewhere in small-town UK, nothing about the beauty therapist (BTh) and nothing about the client (Cli).

If we ignore conversation analysis for a moment, we can see the emotional labour involved in this excerpt. The customer has some concerns about having the wax treatment which she fears might leave a red mark and she has a date that night. The beauty therapist offers a trial with the wax which she tells the customer is not really hot. So here she is doing emotional work dealing with the woman's concerns and also with them in relation to her date that night. But how is all of this to be seen in conversation analysis terms?

The client's turn in lines 1, 2 and 3 is constructed as a statement indicating what she normally has done – her eyebrows are simply plucked. Waxing is presented as potentially problematic and she essentially offers a reason for not using waxing without telling the beauty therapist not to wax but to pluck. Reading on through the transcript to the beauty therapist's turn starting at line 12 and going through to line 17 we can see a repair at line 12 when the beauty therapist corrects herself ('‹I mean.hh') from what appears to be indicating that she is going to go ahead with the waxing ('I'll see how yuh') to being rather more reassuring (caring of the client's emotions) by raising the possibility of the trial. But the way that this turn is constructed seems to indicate that everything is ready for the wax treatment and that plucking has not been planned for as an alternative. According to Toerien and Kitzinger,

the crucial thing in the beauty therapist's turn between lines 12 to 17 is:

> she tailors all aspects of her response to the client's concerns; her response is hearably 'non rote'. Her immediately responsive turn (lines 6–7) is a good example of this. Note how she avoids leaping to an immediate decision, but instead displays herself to be working toward one that is fitted to the individual client . . . This turn is not only built to show that she is taking into account the client's concern about her skin's reaction to waxing, but also that she recognizes that not all clients are the same – that certain skin types may be more prone to redness than others. (p. 166)

In this report, Toerien and Kitzinger succeed in demonstrating some of the ways in which emotional work (largely to do with making the client feel special by treating her as an individual) is constructed conversationally on this occasion in the beauty salon. It is not intended as a general perspective on emotional work and talk but a demonstration of the utility of conversation analysis in this context. Despite the lack of situational detail not being usual in psychology research reports, the focus of conversation analysis on the participants' utterances is highlighted by their omission. In actuality, it is difficult to imagine what more detail could have added in terms of the analysis. That is not to say that such detail would be irrelevant to other forms of analysis, merely that it does not particularly help conversation analysis. By the way, in line 20 where it reads '[want (to be red#eyes] do: you#' the# sign means that the words in between are spoken in a shaky voice.

Box 10.4
ILLUSTRATIVE RESEARCH STUDY
Conversation analysis: learning disabilities and categories

Antaki, Finlay and Walton (2007) take a common theme in conversation analysis – identity in conversation – which they investigate in relation to institutional talk between care staff and residents (people with learning difficulties). They argue that, conversationally, disempowerment may be on the agenda despite the stated purpose of the conversation being to solicit the views of the residents. Antaki et al. are not arguing that this disempowerment is a regular feature of life in this sort of care institution but that the potential for it is there – despite requirements on staff to recognise that their clients have the ordinary rights of any other citizen. Antaki et al. suggest that disempowerment is shown most obviously:

> simply in the process of interaction, in the ways in which turns are taken, troubles signalled and so on. What we see is that the staff direct the interaction towards certain statements, signal when a resident's utterance is a source of trouble and lead the residents to producing particular types of statements . . . In doing so, the identities of the residents as incompetent and dependent,

and the identities of the staff as knowledgeable and as in charge are acted out in the moment-by-moment details of the interaction . . . (p. 12)

However, Antaki et al. suggest that there is a more subtle and analytically interesting way in which identity is dealt with conversationally. In the conversation studied, the staff involved in the discussion session conversationally linked care workers into a set of categories which included friends and family members. In this way, the residents were coached about who they should regard as friends, i.e. friends, family members and care workers. Antaki et al. point out that coaching someone about something implies that they need coaching:

> In effect, the staff treated the residents as having an identity impaired in its powers of basic social discrimination. They are treated as being unable to tell who their friends are, and being in need of having to count care staff among them. (p. 13)

The data on which this conclusion is based include the following:

119		Mel	<u>what</u> kind of relationship do you have with her dear
120			(1.9)
121		Nat	<u>alright</u>
122			(1.0)
123		Mel	umm
124			(.3)
125		Tim	(coughs)=
126	→	Nat	= (is) she (.) she's <u>a</u>lright
127			(.2)
128		Mel	she's <u>a</u>lright =
129		Nat	= yeah =
130	→	=Ann	=<u>so</u> she's a <u>friend</u>=

(Antaki et al., 2007, p. 10)

Line 130 is an instance of what is referred to as a formulation which is an example of the more general category of adjacency pair. The formulation may summarise some of what has gone before or, as in this case, it can draw out the implication of what has gone before. The formulation has a preferred response – agreement. In other words, line 130 is constructed in a way that the likely (conversationally preferred response) is agreement. According to Antaki et al., such formulations are substantially commoner in institutional talk and ordinary conversation is characteristically egalitarian. The formulation is full of interpretation and does not have to be totally consonant with what has gone before. After all, 'alright' in British vernacular language does not signal that something is good, merely that there is no particular problem or issue. So Nat has not indicated a good relationship which might be equated with friendship – a tendentious interpretation by Ann. The conversation went on as follows and Ann's tendentious interpretation is confirmed by Mel:

131	Nat	= yeah (.) °she's a [friend°
132	Ann	[yeah
133		(.5)
134	Nat	Stacey's a friend
135		(.2)
136	Mel	right (.6) so er (.3)...

(Antaki et al., 2007, p. 10)

Of course, some might suggest that a single sample of conversation, no matter how interesting, does not replace evidence of the frequency of such conversational disempowerment of people with learning disability. Antaki et al. are well aware that their data can only answer questions about how this disempowerment is achieved. Conversation analysts do not refer to personality traits and attitudes as ways of explanation, of course, but some might well describe Ann and Mel as patronising in their interaction with those who live in the care home. Is there no point at which such characteristically patronising aspects of conversation warrant becoming explanatory in their own right? Furthermore, if other workers do not show this pattern then how can we explain conversation solely in terms of conversational structures rather than aspects of personality? Has the learning impairment got nothing to do with the structure of the conversation? Would, say, a university student be so ready to categorise a lecturer as their friend simply because another student interprets their comment that lecturer X is 'alright' to mean that lecturer X is the student's friend?

Evaluation of conversation analysis

It is difficult to evaluate conversation analysis as a general method for the qualitative psychologist's toolbox. It was never developed to be a general approach to the analysis of verbal data – instead it is a theoretically embedded approach to understanding the structuring and sequencing of conversation. However, this in no way detracts from the power of the conversation analysis approach when applied to conversational data. The growing interest in conversation analysis over the past 40 or 50 years is testament to the power of its perspective. What is more surprising, perhaps, is the general fidelity of much recent conversation analysis work to Sacks's original vision of conversation analysis. Can this survive conversation analysis's adoption by psychologists? Many essential conversation analysis ideas have made their way into psychology through the often closely related approach of discourse analysis discussed earlier (in Chapter 9). One question, then, is the extent to

Box 10.5
CONTROVERSY
Is conversation analysis political?

To what extent can researchers use conversation analysis in research with a political thrust? This issue is a developing one between qualitative psychologists in general and some proponents of conversation analysis. The fundamental question is just what can the politically engaged researcher gain from employing conversation analysis. One view is that the scope of conversation analysis is too restrictive to allow engagement with political matters. The focus of conversation analysis is on the minutiae of the conversation usually with little or no reference to the broader social context of the conversation. The assumption is that what needs to be known is to be found within the conversation. In addition, since characteristics of speakers such as their social role, class and so forth have not been the focus of conversation analysis, then relationships between the powerful and powerless are not dealt with. Critics such as Billig (1999), Buckoltz (2003) and Wetherell (1998) can be identified among those claiming that this is a weakness of conversation analysis. And, at least superficially, they would seem to have a point. There are no basic concepts in conversation analysis which deal with the political or power relationships. In mainstream psychology, researchers willingly speak of dominance and power but this is not the case, traditionally, in conversation analysis. The argument is not that power-related concepts be incorporated, merely that their absence says something about the nature of conversation analysis and broadly would support the critics. Only the grossest of references to gender relationships during the course of conversation or the employment of gender as a topic in conversation seem to be the exceptions from the absence of 'power' in conversation analysis.

In contrast to this, we can consider the feminist researchers who use conversation analysis in their work. Feminists are clearly a group of researchers for which power – especially in relation to gender – is a central and essential concept. Important feminist conversation analyses are available. Wilkinson and Kitzinger (2008) suggest that examples of this include Goodwin (1990), Speer (2005), Stokoe and Weatherall (2002), West (1979) and Zimmerman and West (1975). Underlying this debate is an important problem of the extent to which any research method including conversation analysis should be confined by the strictures of its originators. Just how far should conversation analysis be willing to incorporate ideas from outside its basic ambit? To be sure, conversation analysis has great appeal because of its radical approach and what it has achieved based on this. However, the question is to what extent can it be adapted and still retain its vitality and rigour. We have seen that conversation analysis tends to ignore speaker characteristics but, at the same time, researchers have readily extended it to conversations in more formal settings such as therapy. If it is all right to study both informal and formal conversation which imply different power relations, then why is it not all right to include power directly as a consideration in research? Then the question becomes one of why is it acceptable to incorporate one structural aspect (power) into conversation analysis if it is not acceptable to incorporate other structural aspects such as gender and other speaker characteristics? The implication of all of this is that future conversation analyses may not always keep strictly to its purest form. It would seem a distinct possibility that psychologists will adapt the method to their own needs which may, in its turn, result in psychological conversation analysis being recognisably different from, say, the sociological version.

which conversation analysis will begin to absorb psychological ideas and the extent to which the original anti-psychology stance of conversation analysis will, or will need to, change in psychological conversation analysis (see Box 10.5 also). Remember that conversation analysis sets itself expressly against internal psychological mechanisms as explanations of everyday conversation. Now quite a lot of these psychological mechanisms seem relevant to what goes on in some conversations. The long-standing idea of suggestibility is a good example of this. Suggestibility is a sort of generalised tendency to be influenced by attempts at verbal coercion – so, for example, some people are more susceptible to falsely confess during police interviews than others. Just why should a psychologist not be prepared to include such factors in explanations of conversation other than that Sacks says that this sort of thing is inappropriate? Why is it any more reasonable to import a sociological concept such as 'emotional labour' (see Box 10.3) into conversation analysis than a psychological concept of suggestibility? In this context, then, it is worth noting the following comment about the work of Emanuel Schegloff, one of the founders of conversation analysis:

> [Emanuel Schegloff] on the other hand, often takes his analyses that extra small step into speculating about conversational participants' motives or intentions (e.g., Phyllis found the topic boring; Shane's stance on etiquette was ironic), but only after a detailed examination of the conversational moves and as it is warranted by the empirical evidence. (Lapadat & Lindsay, 1999, p. 72)

In many ways, conversation analysis is alien to the ways in which much psychological research is carried out. As Silverman suggests:

> Sacks's work presents something of a paradox. On the one hand, it deals with everyday events, like a telephone conversation or a newspaper story, with which we are all familiar. On the other, Sacks's analysis of these events derives from a highly complex way of reasoning, leaning to a level of detail which even his peers can find challenging. (Silverman, 1998, p. 1)

Most qualitative data analysis techniques involve an attention to detail which is different from that involved in quantitative data analysis. Conversation analysis, nevertheless, is somewhat out on a limb when it comes to the extent of the detail that it addresses. In many ways this is stimulating but it can also be frustrating when the analysis is somewhat dull or uninspired. Nevertheless, conversation analysis brings a new perspective which is different and consequently refreshing to qualitative data analysis methods. At its best, conversation analysis is an invigorating discipline.

A useful summary of some of the general features of conversation analysis can be found in ten Have (2007). Among these are the following issues:

- The competence at conversation which is assumed by conversation analysis seems to be a sort of generalised conversational competence rather than a relatively specific one. This is fine when the conversation under study is fairly run-of-the-mill and everyday. In this case, the analyst can employ their own personal everyday conversational competence to help in the analysis of conversations. But what does this say about the conversations which occur in organisations which are highly specialised? What competency can the analyst employ in such contexts? For example, imagine the conversation was between senior managers at an investment bank. What analyst is competent to analyse this?

- There seem to be problems associated with the difference between interpretation and analysis. Interpretation tends to be to do with understanding an individual episode whereas analysis is a term for a broader activity in which mechanisms and procedures are proposed which apply more generally. Some conversation analysis, as a consequence, may be described as interpretation rather than analysis.

CONCLUSION

In psychology, conversation analysis is beginning to provide a new focus or a new set of analytic tools which may benefit and invigorate a range of applied fields of research together with a relatively new (to psychology) perspective on language. Nevertheless, conversation analysis draws on intellectual traditions which have not gained much ground in psychology since their introduction into sociology in the 1950s and afterwards. Ethnomethodology is the most important influence on the development of conversation analysis but has not been adopted at the core of psychological research. Furthermore, conversation analysis reverses many of the principles which have guided mainstream psychology's research methods. For example, the focus on conversation with little attention to the context of the conversation or the details of those taking part in the conversation seems to overturn good practice in many areas of psychology.

KEY POINTS

- Conversation analysis emerged in the 1960s in the context of developments in sociological theory. Ethnomethodology was developed by Garfinkel and reverses the approaches of the grand-scale sociological theories of that time. Ethnomethodology concerned itself with everyday understandings of ordinary events constructed by ordinary people.

- Conversation analysis is a logically tight and consistent approach to understanding how conversation works. As such, it is best seen as a theory of language rather than a research method. Of course, conversation analysis does have its own specific way of working but this is entirely within the agenda laid down by Sacks and his colleagues. As such, if you wish to buy into the method then you are also buying into the theory. One corollary of this is that theory and method go hand-in-hand. Thus it is not possible to carry out the method without understanding the theory.

- Conversation analysis requires a detailed analysis and comparison of the minutiae of conversation as a process. Little is drawn into the analysis from outside the conversation. So conversation analysis has no interest in many psychological ideas such as personality, attitudes and so forth. In that sense, it is an alternative way of doing research from these familiar psychological approaches.

- Close analysis of the data is an essential characteristic of conversation analysis. In particular, the Jefferson conversation transcription system encourages the researcher to examine the close detail rather than the broad thrust of conversational data. The transcription is interpreted, reinterpreted, checked and compared within itself but also with other transcriptions of similar material in the belief that there is something 'there' for the analyst to find.

ADDITIONAL RESOURCES

Antaki, C. (n.d.) *An introductory tutorial on conversation analysis* (plus other related tutorials): homepages.lboro.ac.uk/~ssca1/sitemenu.htm, homepages.lboro.ac.uk/~ssca1/tthome.htm, homepages.lboro.ac.uk/~ssca1/home.htm (accessed 24 April 2015).

Burr, V. (2015). *Social constructionism* (3rd ed.). London: Routledge.

Drew, P. (2008). Conversation analysis. In J. A. Smith (Ed.), *Qualitative psychology: A practical guide to research methods* (2nd ed., pp. 133–159). London: Sage.

Liddicoat, A. J. (2007). *An introduction to conversation analysis*. London: Continuum.

Stokoe, E. The science of analyzing conversations, second by second. https://www.youtube.com/watch?v=MtOG5PK8xDA

ten Have, P. (2007). *Doing conversation analysis: A practical guide*. London: Sage.

Wilkinson, S., & Kitzinger, C. (2008). Conversation analysis. In C. Willig & W. Stainton-Rogers (Eds.), *The SAGE handbook of qualitative psychology* (pp. 54–72). Los Angeles, CA: Sage.

YouTube. Conversation Analysis Loughborough Diaries 1. Charles Antaki. https://www.youtube.com/watch?v=fxTkOF-xcr8 (accessed 24 April 2015).

YouTube. Conversation Analysis: Respecifying Milgram's obedience studies: Matthew Hollander. https://www.youtube.com/watch?v=UqL67ZtTxk4 (accessed 9 September 2015).

YouTube. Conversation Analysis: Doing a thesis – research questions and lit reviews. https://www.youtube.com/watch?v=wV3aTdauH9c (accessed 24 April 2015).

CHAPTER 11

Foucauldian discourse analysis

Overview

- Foucauldian discourse analysis has its roots in the seminal writings of the French philosopher, sociologist and psychologist Michel Foucault. Foucault's works are extensive and, not unexpectedly, his ideas developed and sometimes changed during his lifetime. His interest in mental hospitals, medicine and prison are perhaps the most significant aspects of his work – the discourses associated with major institutions of the state.

- The concept of discourse in Foucauldian discourse analysis shares with other forms of discourse analysis the idea that language does or achieves things – more than mere communication. But in Foucauldian discourse analysis the focus is not on the minutiae of conversation and text. Instead, a far more broad or macro-level analysis is engaged with. Indeed, discourse in Foucauldian discourse analysis is closer to systems of expert knowledge and ideologies. In comparison, to the Foucauldian approach, social constructionist discourse analysis (Chapter 9) is somewhat fine-grained and microscopic in its approach.

- Historical is probably the quickest description of Foucault's work. This term hardly applies to any mainstream psychology other than histories of psychology. Nevertheless Foucauldian ideas have been brought to psychology in a number of ways. The best known advocate of Foucauldian discourse analysis in psychology (and its formulator) is Ian Parker. Over the years he has offered a relatively systematic and organised approach to discourse analysis, perhaps learning the importance of this from Potter and Wetherell's (1987) example.

- Put simply, Foucauldian discourse analysis involves reading relevant documents or texts in order to identify the discourses which they manifest or partially manifest. Objects or things of a material or social nature are mentioned in these texts in relation to discourses. These objects or things can be just about anything so we shall not attempt to specify them. That is, the objects or things are nouns in the text. Objects or things which think are referred to as subjects in relation to discourses. So subjects are basically people but, for example, they could be thinking animals or talking trees in some circumstances. Objects and subjects are positioned or located by the contents of the discourse – subjects and objects will, in a way, be defined as having a particular sort of position in society and in relation to each other by the discourse. In a sense, then, the discourse tells the subject of the discourse what they are. Since the discourse situates people (subjects) in terms of power relationships, the discourse can then amount to a way of controlling people. That is, the discourse tells them what their place is.

- In psychology, Foucauldian discourse analysis has tended to be associated with a radical movement known as critical psychology. Foucauldian ideas can be used in critical psychology but they are not quite the same thing. Nevertheless, Ian Parker, especially, has critiqued psychology in ways which hardly differ from Foucault's critique of other social institutions.

- Critical psychology is essendtially a collection of critiques of mainstream psychology and its links with various aspects of social power. It is not psychology applied in a critical way outside of the discipline in the usual formulation.

- To some, writings on Foucauldian discourse analysis tend to read as being overtly political in a way which most mainstream psychology is not. (Which does not imply that psychology is not political.) So power, empowerment and resistance appear repeatedly as emblematic concepts.

What is Foucauldian discourse analysis?

Postmodern/poststructuralist thinking assumes that knowledge is contingent on both cultural and historical matters. In other words, knowledge (especially social knowledge) has to be understood with reference to both its historical development and the social/cultural context in which knowledge emerges. The work of Michel Foucault (1926–1984) embodies this as well as the work of a single individual can. Foucauldian discourse analysis in psychology may be regarded as a structured if not formularised adaptation of Foucault's ideas. Out of a wide body of ideas produced by Foucault, Foucauldian discourse analysis tends to dwell on his ideas about social institutions, discourse and power. Foucauldian discourse analysis differs strikingly from social constructionist discourse analysis (Chapter 9) in terms of its political informed and radical elements (Bozatsis, 2014). It is often presented as a means of tearing down the edifice of mainstream psychology. To be sure, most qualitative methods aim to replace mainstream psychology with something better (though they might disagree what this better thing is). To a greater extent, though, Foucauldian discourse analysis sees itself in actively political terms. Foucauldian discourse analysis repeatedly refers to concepts such as oppression, resistance and inequality – evidencing the political nature of this form of analysis. It has to be stressed that Foucault himself operated primarily at a historical rather than a psychological level and we can only guess whether or not he would be entirely happy with psychological Foucauldian discourse analysis. Foucault is tremendously important throughout the social sciences and beyond. Research based on his work is common in a wide range of other disciplines in the social sciences and the humanities. However, whether these are close to psychological Foucauldian discourse analysis is not so clear. We will save the term for the approach formulated from within psychology. Sometimes Foucauldian discourse analysis is referred to as Foucaultian discourse analysis and you will also find it without the letter l in Foucauldian. It is possible that the Foucaultian version is American spelling, though there is no consensus why there is this disagreement. Of course, the Potter and Wetherell version of discourse analysis (Chapter 9) also seeks to be similarly radical in that it has fundamental disagreements with much of mainstream social psychology but it is less political in conventional terms.

According to Parker et al. (1995):

> Foucault's work has been invaluable in drawing attention to the way language is organized around different systems of meaning which offer positions of power to certain categories of people and disempower others. These systems of meaning are discourses. In recent debates inside psychology, critical writers studying structures of power in discourse have been taking seriously what oppressed people have long known, that the way we talk is bound up with privilege and, sometimes, resistance . . . (p. 10)

These words may seem to be a million miles away from the usual things one reads about in books on research methods – reliability, validity, triangulation and the like. They are not typical of much writing in qualitative research methods either for that matter. The usual stuff of psychology, in general, is not to bring issues of power to the forefront. This means that Foucauldian discourse analysis is possibly the most diffi-cult of the qualitative analysis methods to reconcile with other forms of psychological perspective. But the point of Foucauldian discourse analysis is that it takes the often benign understandings of phenomena associated with social institutions and reformu-lates them in terms of power and dominance. This can apply as much to the activities of psychologists and psychiatrists, for example, as other more patently powerful social institutions. Critical psychologists, however, mainly critique psychology rather than other social institutions in their writings.

Fadyl and Nicholls (2013) use the term 'history of the present' to describe the work of Michel Foucault. He was interested in systems of thought (psychiatric knowledge, scientific knowledge and similar expert/elite knowledge). In his writings, he challenges us by undermining or even turning upside down the self-evident nature of some of the truths which are currently valued. What is self-evident is revealed as being not-self-evident, in other words. The knowledge of the world which is held dear is actually unstable and contingent. Foucault wanted to know what the social conditions and circumstantial problems were which may have resulted in a particular way of think-ing about the world. Discourses have a developmental trajectory such that the way in which we see the present is the consequence of past discourses. That is, discourses concerning the present represent an unfolding or iteration of this historical change in the discourse. How the present is made possible entails understanding the historical processes which led to the emergence of the discourse in the first place and contribute to its continuation in the second. Discourses connect up historically and they achieve things – determine what we believe the world is like and what we are in relation to it. The purpose of history in discourse analysis is to 'make visible' (Fady and Nicholls, 2013) just how a particular feature of life came to adopt its current form.

Power in Foucauldian terms is regarded as productive – i.e. productive power is a more descriptive term and perhaps should be used in preference. It is not really con-ceived as an entity in its own right. Instead productive power emerges or comes into existence in interactions. That is, productive power is a function of social interactions. Power in immediate or day-to-day life categorises the individual, fixes the individual to their own identity, and imposes 'truth' on the individual which they and others have to recognise in that individual. In other words, this is a particular kind of power which makes the person a subject – the subject of the discourse (Foucault, 1977). Or perhaps considering that the individual is subjected or subjugated to the discourse may make it a little clearer. The implication is that discourse does things.

As we have already indicated, Ian Parker (1956–) is probably the most familiar name associated with Foucauldian discourse analysis but there are others such as Valerie Walkerdine. Parker co-founded the Discourse Unit at Manchester Metropolitan

University with Erica Burman in 1991. Although it is not entirely possible to typify Parker's output in one book title alone, *Revolution in psychology: Alienation to emancipation* (Parker, 2007) gives something of the flavour. Unlike Potter and Wetherell, neither Parker nor Burman is a social psychologist, so their work only touches on social psychology. Parker's background in psychology includes being a practising psychoanalyst and Burman can be described as a feminist developmental psychologist and group analyst. Within Foucauldian discourse analysis one will not find the level of detailed analysis of conversation, for example, which characterises social constructionist discourse analysis. Nor will one find painstakingly transcribed Jefferson-based transcriptions that are also characteristic of Potter and Wetherell's approach. These would be seen as largely irrelevant if not counterproductive to the agenda that Foucauldian discourse analysis sets itself. Parker operates with a wider brushstroke than this – conversational detail is too microscopic to challenge the macro social vision. Nevertheless, Parker (1992, 1994) and Willig (2013) have offered relatively simple step-by-step instructions indicating how Foucauldian discourse analysis should be carried out. In that respect, they emulate the educative/instructional approach which Potter and Wetherell (1987) adopted for *Discourse and social psychology*. The political aspect of Foucauldian discourse analysis is partially a reading of Foucault's work but also an importation or imposition from other sources including varieties of Marxism. Characteristically, then, Foucauldian discourse analysts report many influences on the approach besides Foucault; in particular, the revisionist Marxist writer Louis Pierre Althusser (1918–90). The concept of power is central to both Foucault and Althusser but rather different versions of the idea. It is productive power for Foucault and oppression for Marxism.

So, underlying psychological Foucauldian discourse analysis is the demand that qualitative psychologists face up to mainstream psychology critically and without compromise. This is not really in the sense of seeking alternative ways of doing psychology but in order to tackle the harm that psychology is seen to be doing. In other words, a Foucauldian discourse analysis will show how power works within the immediate topic as well as the broad institution of psychology according to Parker. Critique is the fundamental objective.

Is the meaning of discourse the same in Foucauldian as social constructionist discourse analysis? Well not quite or not really according to one's perspective. In both cases, discourses are to be found in texts of all sorts – conversation, media output, historical documents, interviews or whatever you like which consists of words (or even symbols). In social constructionist discourse analysis, text is considered to be so replete with discursive features that it is difficult to maintain a distinction between the two. The text is doing all sorts of things discursively – arguing, persuading, creating identity, creating status and so forth. Although discourse can do 'big' things, discursive processes may be seen to be at work within the smallest scrap of text. So in that sense, social constructionist discourse analysis is fulsome in its recognition of a multitude of discursive processes in rather ordinary text and beyond. Partly for this reason, social constructionist discourse analyses uses finely tuned, some would say microscopic, levels of analysis. In social constructionist discourse analysis, the discourse can be made fully apparent from the text. However, discourse in Foucauldian discourse analysis is a broader thing, much more abstract, and something the analyst has to unravel or unveil from the text from a broader perspective. In Foucauldian discourse analysis, discourses are looked for in texts of various sorts (historical records, conversation, interviews, advertisements, media output and so forth). There may be only fragments of the discourse within any piece of text. So the task of the Foucauldian discourse analyst is to specify what the nature of the wider discourse is. In other words, Foucauldian discourse analysts need to be able to recognise a discourse in the text. But we need to get a bit closer to the nitty-gritty of what a discourse is in Foucauldian discourse analysis. We can start with Foucault, of course. For him discourses are:

> groups of signs, verbal performances, acts of formulation, and a series of sentences or propositions . . . a group of statements that belong to a single system of formation (Foucault, 1969/1972, 107–8).

In keeping with this, for Parker (1990a, p. 191) discourse is: 'a system of statements which constructs an object.' So what discourses do is part of Parker's definition. Examples of discourses are clinical discourses, economic discourses, natural history discourses and psychiatric discourses. That is, discourses are associated with elite or specialist knowledge systems. Indeed, you can read some textbooks on Foucault's work in which the term discourse is not to be found. Of course, discourse should be pluralised as discourses given that things (objects) can be constructed differently by different discourses. Psychiatric and economic discourses could both apply to a thing like unemployment, for example, though differently. Since discourses do things in the world then the purpose of discourse analysis is to systematise ways of talking about and writing about things. Ultimately, these should lead us to understand better just what the discourse is about and what it does.

Different discourses do not necessarily articulate well with each other and part of Foucauldian discourse analysis is to identify the different tensions between the different discourses. Discourses can reproduce the world and/or they can change (transform) the world. There is no great mystery involved in understanding this. Topics that we are all familiar with such as illegal immigration and welfare scrounging illustrate this perfectly. The idea of a war against drugs is another example of a discourse. It is a dominant way of looking at drugs in recent times but it brings with it ways of thinking and doing. The discourse forms a sort of vehicle for social action. It legitimises harsh treatments of those involved with illegal drugs, for example. It also positions the subjects of the discourse such as ordinary people and drug pushers in particular ways – and in relation to one another. There is nothing that can be meaningfully described as natural about the idea of a war on drugs – it is a notion constructed socially and has powerful consequences. There are other ways of talking about drugs such as personal choice which positions the drugs user away from criminals. Many drug users manage their involvement with drugs relatively unproblematically and lead relatively untroubled and socially untroubling lives according to this viewpoint. History has important things to say too. At the end of Victorian times opium was regarded as little more than a medicament such as for soothing babies. No matter how outrageous this appears nowadays, it was possible to buy small cheap packages of opium from a pharmacy without prescription (Howitt, 1991). A discourse concerning opium as a medicament quite clearly is at tension with the discourse of the war on drugs. The historicity of discourse is one feature which is highlighted in a discourse analysis. Unfortunately, this sort of analysis is beyond the scope of most newcomers to qualitative psychology. Nevertheless, many researchers outside the field of psychology have carried out important historical analyses of various discourses. These can be refreshing reading. (e.g. Nye, 2003).

In a sense, discourse categorises the social world – that is, it creates categories. By doing so, the thing to which it refers becomes more apparent to members of the culture. Discourses about the environment make the environment an object of attention irrespective of the subject position of the individual in respect to this discourse. They make the environment apparent in circumstances where historically they may not have been – such as booking an air ticket somewhere. A discourse about immigration can frame immigration as a threat whereas a competing discourse may frame immigration as an economic boon. Discourses can be interlinked – so immigration discourses and economic discourses may be closely related. Once a discourse has become established, even things which are not truly realities will be regarded as real. The Foucauldian discourse analyst's work, therefore, is not simply (or even) based on conversation or other text. There is intellectual work which precedes the practicalities of discourse analysis. It is the task of the analyst to identify the discourses in any form of text. Just how does one know when one has identified a discourse in a piece of text? Parker (1992) listed important features of discourses which will help the analyst recognise one when there is one in the text being dealt with. Here are some of the most important features:

- *Discourses are to be found realised in texts* In itself, the text does not systematically indicate what the discourse is. For one reason, the realisation of the discourse in the text is usually only fragmentary. It is the analyst's task to interpret connotations of the discourse and its implications in the text. Think of the medical style of discourse that you would experience in a hospital. We all know something of medical knowledge which one could consider a medical discourse. We will not experience the full extent of medical discourse on a trip, say, to accident and emergency, but we will definitely experience fragments of that discourse.

- *Discourses systematically configure the things (objects) which they are about* The analyst needs to understand this Foucauldian idea (Foucault, 1972) as they carry out their analysis. They need to critically investigate the things that a text refers to as well as describe them. Again, in medical discourse the things referred to include patients and medical staff – they are some of the subjects (thinking objects) of medical discourse. But there may be other things such as medical science referred to in the discourse or even holistic medicine. Objects and subjects of discourse will be given positions or locations within the medical system by the discourse. Of course, medical discourse is a big thing to describe and identify.

- *What kinds of person are 'spoken of' in the discourse* We can bear down a little more on the nature of the subjects of a discourse, that is, who are the subjects contained in the discourse? Discourse enables a particular kind of self to be enmeshed by it. Parker uses the Althusserian concept 'ideological interpellation' to support his argument that a discourse 'speaks' to people (none of us can avoid medical discourse) and positions us within the institutional system. The simple example of the subject position of being a patient, as an instance, tells us a lot about who we are and what we should do within a medical institution such as a hospital. The analyst's task is to make clear the sorts of person the discourse involves. Given that the discourse in text is incomplete and fragmentary, the analyst needs to formulate the discourse intelligibly.

- *Discourse should be approached as a coherent system of meanings* A discourse represents an object through the use of metaphors, analogies and mental pictures. The analyst turns these into statements which are understandable in terms of how the culture understands the object of the discourse. In other words, a discourse may appear in a range of guises in a text and the discourse analyst needs to construct a description of the discourse such that it is understandable and meaningful. A discourse is not a hodgepodge of meaningless and incoherent aspects.

- *The same object may be constituted very differently by different discourses* A discourse often will imply or even presuppose other discourses. Again, taking medical discourse as an example, it is obvious that the medical discourse implies a health discourse as well as an illness discourse. We can also add in discourse about alternative medicines. The interrelationships between these discourses are complex without question. And they are often difficult to resolve and deal with simply. For example, medical discourse may well hold that formal medicine is scientific – but then so might discourse concerning claims that acupuncture is scientific. So the discourse analyst may well need to identify the ways in which different objects are portrayed by different discourses in order to find ways in which these are similar and different.

● *Discourses will refer to past discourses about the same object* Historical changes bring about the new way in which the object is constituted or conceived. The same object will have been constituted by different discourses in the past. What is the change and why did it happen or why was it necessary? The task of the analyst is to consider just how and when the discourse in question emerged. The analyst needs to identify the historical changes which led to this. For example, medicine changed immeasurably when the medical profession emerged in Victorian times. Of course there were doctors before professionalisation but things changed markedly with professionalisation.

The analyst also has to consider the issue of the relationship between the uncovered discourses and the broader ideological framework. What are the implications of the discourses for ideology and vice versa? Of course, ideology is an abstraction and does not appear immediately in the discourses, let alone the text. Power relationships may be apparent or implied in the discourses. Discourses allow and partake in the reproduction of power. The power of the medical profession allowed it to have a big say and role in relation to issues like sexuality, drunkenness, and so forth (Howitt, 1992). Finally, in Foucault's work discourses relate to institutions in the sense that the work of social institutions is partly achieved through discourses. Furthermore, there are idiosyncratic discourses which can be found in texts originating in institutions which would not be found in more mundane, everyday discourses.

The development of Foucauldian discourse analysis

It is difficult to know where to begin an account of the development of Foucauldian discourse analysis. No intellectual endeavour is without its antecedents. Nevertheless, if we focus on Foucault the man we will get a good idea of why he and his work are so influential on a wide cohort of social scientists and others. Above all, we should remember that Foucault's ideas spread widely throughout a range of intellectual disciplines. We have to take this for granted as our task is to explain the emergence of his work into psychology. The basic biography of Michel Foucault (1926–84) has elements which would attract many a politically orientated, left-wing, radical psychologist among others. It is far from easy to classify Foucault. 'Psychologist' would fit in that he taught psychology for a living for a good few years. His work was most certainly not mainstream psychology of the time. Though his early intellectual work was about the history of psychology, his famous works were a certain sort of history of medical and social sciences. He is more likely to be described as a social theorist, philosopher, historian of ideas and a philologist. But he was also a literary critic. You might also describe him as a poststructuralist and so a postmodernist thinker. But labels like these were not to Foucault's liking. Although there are elements of his being something of an establishment figure, in the latter part of his life he became a political activist, taking direct action in terms of human rights abuses, penal reforms and racial equality. That is, he associated with left-wing movements. His early family life was decidedly upper middle-class. Bourgeois is probably the best description. Marxism and communism had some small part in his early life, though he rapidly rebelled against racist elements in French communism. Most definitely he rejected elements of Marxism – such as the idea of a class struggle or war. His early life was troubled and he was a self-harmer who first attempted suicide in 1948. His father sent him to a psychiatrist at Hôpital Sainte-Anne. The psychiatrist suggested that the suicide attempts may have been related to Foucault's gay lifestyle.

From the point of view of a modern academic, Foucault's academic progress initially seems a little less than focused. Like many distinguished French philosophers he attended l'École Normale Supérieure where his interest in philosophy developed under the tutorship of Louis Althusser and others. In the early 1950s he studied for his doctorate in the philosophy of psychology at the Fondation Thiers. At about the same time he taught psychology at the École Normale Supérieure and the Université Lille Nord de France. Jean Piaget, Karl Jaspers and Sigmund Freud were influential on his studies. But philosophers such as Friedrich Nietzsche (1844–1900) were more influential in the longer term. Foucault's first book was published in 1954: *Mental illness and personality (Maladie mentale et personnalité)*. The underlying argument of *Mental illness and personality* was that illness is culturally relative. Its important discussions referred to Marx, Heidegger, Pavlov, Freud, Emile Durkheim and Margaret Mead. But in his lifetime Foucault would be influenced by playwrights and poets in significant ways too. He wrote for literary journals at various stages. But then he served as a cultural diplomat at Uppsala, Sweden before returning to France. Shortly afterwards his first truly noteworthy book was published – *The history of madness* in 1961. This work influenced the anti-psychiatry movement in Europe and elsewhere during the 1960s. Again in the early 1960s he obtained work at the University of Clermont-Ferrand. There he published two further important works – *The birth of the clinic* (1963) and *The order of things* (1966). Gradually he was evolving a histographical approach which he termed 'archeology'. This involved a painstaking review of the important records of the institution – minutes of committee meetings, publications, memos, letters, submissions to government, and so forth – and any other sources imaginable. Rather dry stuff admittedly but transformed in the hands of Foucault. In 1970 he became a member of the Collège de France. After this came other important works such as *The archeology of knowledge* (1969), *Discipline and punish (*1975) and the three-volume *History of sexuality* (1978–86).

Foucault's work basically linked knowledge and power; not in the sense that knowledge is power but in the opposite sense that power controls and defines what is knowledge. So 'scientific knowledge' is used for social control. A good example of this is the idea of 'madness' which in the eighteenth and nineteenth centuries was used to categorise and stigmatise groups like the poor, homeless and any other group that deviated from the norm. Foucault's interest was the ways by which power is used to 'objectivise subjects' in modern society. Among these ways is how the authority of science has been used to classify knowledge about populations of people. The purported universal scientific truths concerning humanity are no such thing. They merely are expressive of a particular society's moral, ethical and political investments at that time. Followers of Foucault argue that power hierarchies may be exposed through the analysis of discourse. These in their turn may be examined by questioning the areas of knowledge which are used to legitimate these power structures. Hence, Foucault's work relates to forms of critical theory.

Foucault, in a sense, turned knowledge on its head. The history of the idea of mental illness can be construed as the story of the emergence of an enlightened view of madness. Madness is not historically a fixed category but one which was created through discourse which served a social purpose. Discourses change over time. For example, the French physician Phillipe Pinel (1745–1826) is usually credited as being responsible for introducing humanity into the treatment of patients in mental hospitals, replacing the brutal regimes which had previously characterised these institutions. Foucault saw this version of history as being hypocritical. The idea that the mad were medically sick (i.e. mentally ill) and so needing medical treatment was not clearly better, in Foucault's view, than any earlier ideas about madness. Simply put, classifying such people as mad formed the basis of excluding them from society. The mad challenged bourgeois morality essentially because they did not fit in with bourgeois society and so had to be excluded. Mental hospitals, for example, were repositories for paupers in Victorian times.

The route by which Foucault's work entered psychology is basically part of the turn to discourse and qualitative psychology in psychology of the 1980s. Potter and Wetherell (1987) in their version of discourse analysis drew upon Foucault's work in respect to his approach to the self. There is no real emphasis on Foucault otherwise in this sort of discourse analysis. Foucauldian ideas made their first significant inroads into Anglo-American psychology in the 1970s but especially in the book *Changing the subject: Psychology, social regulation, and subjectivity* (1984) by Julian Henriques, Wendy Hollway, Cathy Urwin, Couze Venn and Valerie Walkerdine. In part, the book demonstrated how Foucault's ideas could be applied to a psychological perspective. According to John Shotter (1999): 'it can now be seen as one of the earliest outline expressions of the agenda for the sphere of psychological inquiry now coming to be known as Critical Psychology' (p. 482). This link between Foucauldian ideas and critical psychology should not be taken to indicate that the Potter and Wetherell version of discourse analysis has no stake to claim on the broad concept of critical psychology. It has (e.g. see Hepburn, 2003). Other examples of the influence of Foucauldian ideas on psychology can be found in the work of Ian Parker, particularly in the field of mental health, in the books *Deconstructing psychopathology* (Parker et al., 1995) and *Deconstructing psychotherapy* (Parker, 1999a).The relative impact of the two strands of discourse analysis is difficult to assess. It is notable, though, that the psychological research literature has many more citations for Potter and Wetherell's *Discourse and social psychology* than for Henriques et al.'s *Changing the subject*.

In psychology, Ian Parker has probably the most energetic proponent of Foucauldian discourse analysis and probably did the most to originate it. To some extent, this emulates the pedagogic tradition manifest in Potter and Wetherell's approach which led to the impressive success of social constructionist discourse analysis. From the start, Potter and Wetherell provided clear instructions for discourse analytic procedures which were easy and readily implemented by students and established researchers. It perhaps should be said that Foucauldian discourse analysis is somewhat more challenging than the social constructionist approach in some ways. Foucauldian discourse analysis is naturally difficult to absorb if one has no prior knowledge of Foucault's ideas. This can involve some challenging reading, though, of course, there are numerous textbooks describing Foucault's ideas which speed up the process. Textbooks like Fillingham (1993) and Gutting (2005) may do the trick for you.

Parker tends to pack a lot of different ideas into his writings, which sometimes feels like overload at first. For example, Foucauldian discourse analysis is often discussed alongside a wide range of different varieties of critical psychology. Indeed, distinguishing the boundaries between Foucauldian discourse analysis, critical psychology and other radical ideas is not easy when reading his work. Critical psychology is discussed in Box 11.1. The most important thing that critical psychology has in common with Foucault's work is the broad concept of power. Critical psychology is a rather eclectic set of ideas and theories which do not make particularly easy reading to readers coming from a mainstream psychology background. Perhaps the best way of describing the situation is that critical psychology is an umbrella term which enwraps Foucauldian discourse analysis as well as other aspects of psychology to do with power.

So, to recapitulate, Foucault's attraction to radical, left-wing psychologists is not at all difficult to see. Foucault was radical in many aspects of his work and life. He personified certain issues in his lifestyle and these spilled over into his work. He was also an activist and it is hard to think of psychologists who were so committed to political causes. Yet, all of his life, he would reject what others saw in him as not being him. So, for example, he was a member of the communist party briefly in his early years, though he rapidly rejected the party. He made dismissive comments about communism, such as 'Marxism exists in nineteenth-century thought as a fish exists in water; that is, it ceases to breathe anywhere else' (Foucault, 1994, p. 262). In plainer English, Foucault is in many ways enigmatic and several ideas were pinned on him which he would not accept and dismissed. He changed, of course, during his lifetime and so one needs to carefully specify which version of Foucault one is discussing. Foucauldian discourse analysis in psychology presents a restricted approach to Foucault's work, yet nevertheless a challenge.

Box 11.1
KEY CONCEPT
Critical psychology

The concept of 'critique' from which the word critical comes is a fundamental aspect of German classical philosophy. That this is where the meaning of critical in critical psychology comes from so needs to be understood. For the philosopher Immanuel Kant (1724–1804), it amounted to exploring the limits of theoretical and practical reasoning. It seeks to demarcate or identify these limits precisely. It can be seen as being in contrast to dogmatism which assumes that reason works through knowledge without any identification of the limits to which the reasoning applies. Part of the problem is that of trying to shoe-horn a wide variety of non-mainstream psychologies under a label (critical psychology) which does not always fit too well:

What is critical psychology? We are not entirely sure. It has picked up on some of the 1960s radical psychology and anti-psychiatry critiques . . . It is friendlier than mainstream psychology to feminism, and some qualitative researchers and discourse analysts hang around it sometimes looking for approval from it in odd moments when they think the discipline is not watching them. For sure critical psychology is broad. Broad enough, for example, for us to agree that the 'Status Quo' is bad and the 'Good Society' is good;

and broad enough for us to disagree about what exactly each of those terms mean. (Goodley & Parker, 2000, p. 4)

Or, perhaps more amusingly, something of the problem of pinning down what critical psychology is can be seen in Ian Parker's conversation with the philosopher Slavoj Žižek. Adroitly, the philosopher turns things so that Parker is doing much of the answering and Žižek poses apt questions:

Slavoj Žižek: This critical psychology, this is a code word for Marxist Psychology?
Ian Parker: For some it is a mixture of those things, and I wanted to ask you about the mixture of things that it is
Slavoj Žižek: How does it locate itself in relation to psychoanalysis and cognitivism?
Ian Parker: Again, it depends
Slavoj Žižek: Oh, you don't have a party line, my goodness, this is anarchism. (Parker, 2009, p. 355, speaker identities added)

This captures the somewhat chaotic nature of reading some critical psychology rather well.

However, the lack of clarity about critical psychology does not go away when more serious definitions are considered. For example, Stainton Rogers and Stainton Rogers (1997, p. 44) do their best to define the field and take a big step to the meaning of critical psychology clearer. They explain that critical psychology consists of a: 'salmagundi of critical, perturbing and radical thought to which one can attach such labels as: feminism, French theory, neo-Marxism, post-structuralism, post-phenomenology, postmodernism and the sociology of scientific knowledge'. To save you looking it up – since I had to – a salmagundi is a sort of seventeenth century salad. That is, a hodgepodge.

Critical psychologists have been generous to share their working space with each other even when they find that they have little in common or where at another time or in another place they might be at loggerheads with each other. But a few essentials will help us to understand the basic things which are central when attempting to define something as critical psychology. The fine detail of quite what should go in the box and what should be left out is probably too big a task for a short discussion. Politics and power will summarise it for now.

Just to remind you for clarity's sake, modern psychology became emancipated from its primary home discipline of philosophy during the latter half of the nineteenth century. So in this book we refer to modern psychology as that emerging in the 1870s with the founding of the first teaching and research laboratories for psychology. Wilhelm Wundt's name is forever associated then in the history of psychology as a laboratory-based science. Not that Wundt advocated the laboratory as the place to study all aspects of psychology. In particular, Wundt doubted that the more social aspects of psychology were suitable for the laboratory treatment. He proposed that *Volkerpsychologie* (as he termed the more social aspects of psychology) should employ quite different methodologies, not based on laboratory methods. This aspect of Wundt's work did not gain equal eminence with the laboratory work, though in recent times it is common for psychologists to raise Wundt's dual methodological approach to psychology. The experimental and reductionalist branch of psychology prevailed (see Chapters 1 and 2 if you want more). In this book we refer to this as mainstream psychology given that it has long dominated modern psychology and achieved great power. Schisms of all sorts were built into psychology right from its very beginnings. Disagreements, tensions and conflicts are part and parcel of psychology and usually no more resolved nowadays than in the beginnings of modern psychology. Somewhat ironically, Georges Politzer (1929–74), the French philosopher and psychologist, diagnosed the

problem in the early decades of modern psychology. Psychology was suffering from simply too many critiques. The critiques may have changed but the deluge did not abate. Scientific psychology critiqued old-fashioned psychologies, followers of Wundt critiqued scientific or mainstream psychology, and so forth.

So is critical psychology that part of psychology which criticises or rejects the way that mainstream psychology goes about its business? Up to a point the answer to this is yes. Critical psychology sees mainstream psychology as a political institution rather than a neutral, value-free scientific enterprise conducted by detached personnel. Critical psychology regards mainstream psychology as working politically to privilege some and disadvantage others. Psychology has successfully provided a wide range of services to powerful institutions including those of the state. These services are endemically oppressive in their nature. So mainstream psychology provides oppressive technologies to control the mentally ill who may challenge society's structures, for example. Less is said about precisely what is meant by oppressive psychology and whether all mainstream psychology is oppressive. Fairly common examples are found such as psychology's role in wartime, for example in the recruitment and training of soldiers, and the way psychology was involved in dealing with migrants into the USA at the beginning of the twentieth century. More generally, it is held that psychology contributes to the containment of social misfits which it (and psychiatry) labels as mentally ill or worse. Contesting such an oppressive psychology is regarded as the appropriate strategy. Often the idea that psychology is oppressive is buttressed by the importation of Marxist ideas. In Marxism, capitalist society is oppressive by its very nature with much of the population subjugated to the broader service of the elite. If psychology serves such an elite then it too is oppressive by its very nature. Resistance is another concept used regularly in critical psychological writings. In Marxist theory, the subjugated proletariat may creatively and actively resist their subjugation. Hence to refer to resistance is both a natural choice for critical psychology but it serves as reinforcement of the idea that society is oppressive. It also implies that critical psychology can help mobilise people to resistance.

Critical psychology paints a picture of how psychology's mainstream sees the edifice of psychology. Putatively mainstream psychology regards itself as a well-founded discipline dedicated to the accumulation of concrete knowledge of a specific sort. The enterprise is seen as being scientific, non-partisan, detached and, above all, objective. It is also seen as benign for the most part – there to help people by virtue of the vast quantity of psychological knowledge to be assimilated and applied. Mainstream psychology mainlines quantitative work which is regarded as reflecting fundamental truths by virtue of its foundation in science. Within critical psychology writings, the specific personnel of psychology's mainstream are rarely mentioned by name. In contrast, those who write from a critical perspective populate their writings with a lengthy lineage of named individuals. Thus mainstream psychology is portrayed as an undifferentiated mass. There is little engagement between the mainstream and critical psychologist so it is not absolutely clear that mainstream psychologists actually do think in the ways claimed of them. It seems unlikely that the bulk of mainstream psychologists employ an unmodified positivistic viewpoint in their work.

In the first half of the twentieth century, psychology learnt to make itself increasingly useful, if not indispensable. That is, it began to earn its keep, so to speak. Psychological techniques were offered for sale as solutions to industrial society's problems such as workforce recruitment, the identification of children who were problematic in the education system, improving ways of selling industrial products, and generally helping with society's misfits through therapy and so forth. At the same time, of course, the state encouraged more psychological research in universities through various mechanisms of funding. Not all disciplines were able to match psychology in this respect but economics and criminology were similarly placed. So, mainstream positivistic psychology dominated because it aligned psychology with the arena of social control in various forms. Psychology was used as if it were a tool to be employed by those willing to pay, directly or indirectly. The growth of psychology in America and elsewhere early in the twentieth century was predicated on psychologists serving as functionaries in the more general apparatus of social control. The psychology myth that it is value-neutral can be seen as a way of neutralising the oppressive nature of the mainstream discipline. In order to deal with the way in which particular groups are privileged by psychology and granted access to social and public goods, the theory and practice of psychology needs to be transferred to the advantage of socially excluded and vulnerable groups. Such mobilisation can be seen in terms of action research of the sort that Ian Parker and others advocate (Goodley & Parker, 2000).

The word psy-complex occurs fairly commonly in some parts of the critical psychology literature. Spelt out in full it is the psychological-industrial complex (Rose 1985, 1996). This is simply the idea that psychology is tied to powerful interests. It acts as a factotum to those interests by providing techniques of social control. Psychology's beginnings may have been modest but now it amounts in itself to an entire industry increasingly engaged in evermore aspects of society. Social problems under its influence become psychologised and the individual held responsible.

Just how is it possible for a discipline to see itself as scientific, borrowing its scientific accoutrements from physics, yet be critiqued as partial, oppressive and in the pocket of the powerful? Critical psychology sees the answer to this and similar questions in the socially constructed nature of psychological knowledge. Probably the vast majority of critical psychology is comfortable with or adopts a social constructionist view. While it had been common in other disciplines from the 1960s onwards, it was the work of Kenneth Gergen (Gergen, 1985a, 1991, 1995) and John Shotter (1995b) that facilitated its crossing over disciplinary boundaries into psychology. A powerful aspect of social constructionist thinking is its rejection of the notion that psychologists act as honest brokers in the discovery of knowledge. Knowledge does not lie waiting to be uncovered like diamonds in a mine, knowledge is a social creation. According to social constructionism, the real or material world cannot be represented by people other than from a subjective position of some sort. Knowledge, then, is a reflection of subjective positions – it does not equate to outside reality. Objective and universal truths, a mainstay of mainstream psychology, are simply constructed from these subjective positions. That is, the bedrock of mainstream psychology is nothing other than a particular subjectivity. Social constructionists generally accept that there is an objective world populated by people – the intractable problem is getting the undistorted view of what it is. People's experiences are the consequence of historically and cultural specific discourses. A person begins to articulate a discourse which then develops in the context of their interactions with others in that culture.

In their work *Social construction of reality*, Berger and Luckmann (1966) made arguments which strike at the usual assumptions of mainstream psychology as well as other disciplines. Their basic idea was that theories come first and the reality unveiled by research is constructed in the likeness of those theories. What psychology does then is merely to reaffirm those theories in a sense. One can say that the function of psychology, then, is ideological in that the version of reality that psychology builds actually services certain social needs. A simple example of this might be the instance of behaviourism. Industrial society in the early part of the twentieth century required workers who engaged in only a small part of the production process, to put it in a basic form. Behaviourism conceived of people in such an atomistic way. Behaviourist research reaffirmed itself and in so doing subjectified people within the mechanistic, industrial complex. 'Psychologies produce reality, which in turn serves the base for its reaffirmation' (Berger & Luckman, 1966, p. 326).

Can all qualitative psychology be seen as critical psychology? Probably not, since by now it should be clear that critical psychology tends to refer to a particular agenda of things and that being in some way critical of psychology is not enough. Cognitive psychology, for example, attacked the once mainstream behaviourist psychology of the mid-twentieth century at its roots. But it merely took over the mainstream without change to what some see as the oppressive nature of psychology. And voices within critical psychology are dismissive of some qualitative methods as if they had 'sold out'. Indeed Goodman and Parker (2000) write that 'much 'qualitative' research in psychology now has been press-ganged into mainstream empiricism and positivism' (p. 3). Whether this is criticism or a form of factionalism may be judged in the fullness of time. The political aspects of critical psychology can be seen to have been most effectively and decisively upheld by feminist psychology in particular. Maybe the criteria for membership of the critical psychology club need to be more carefully specified. Subdivisions within critical psychology are endless. There is the idea of critical discourse which is different from social constructionist discourse analysis because of its central focus of social power and social inequality. So the way in which power is constantly reaffirmed through language is crucial in critical discourse analysis:

> critical discourse analysts want to know what structures, strategies or other properties of text, talk, verbal interaction or communicative events play a role in these modes of reproduction. (van Dijk, 2001, p. 300)

Hepburn (2003) suggests that it also includes issues of politics, morality and social change. Dominance involves the exercise of power by elites, institutions and other social groupings (van Dijk, 2001). This exercise of power is associated with a number of different forms of social inequality – racial, ethnic and gender. Of course, language does not work solely in one direction and so it has the potential to serve the interests of disadvantaged peoples such as in the rhetoric of 'Black power'. This, although reflecting on some of the wide issues of critical psychology, moves more to the use of qualitative approaches beyond the politics of psychology to politics more widely. Terminology can be confusing because it can refer to different things. So for example it is common to see references to critical discourse analysis which, on investigation, appear to be little or no different from a Foucauldian discourse analysis – but not necessarily so!

How to do Foucauldian discourse analysis

Basically, the typical Foucauldian (critical) discourse analysis treats interviews and similar texts as part of a 'bigger picture' beyond the immediate context in which the words were said. This bigger picture could include, for example, the entire body of psychological writing on mental health. Discourses 'facilitate and limit, enable and constrain what can be said (by whom, where, when)' (Parker, 1992, p. xiii). Furthermore, discourses also carry descriptions of the object of the discourse. So, if the analysis is of marriage, built into the discourses about marriage are 'descriptions' of the nature of marriage. The discourse also identifies the key subjects of the discourse – in this case they might be husband and wife but it could also include family, for example. Each of the subjects in the discourse will have their own subjective experiences consequent of the discourse – this is generally referred to as subjectivity or subjectivities.

Foucauldian discourse analysis can be described as macro-textual since it seeks to understand discourse at a broad, societal level. It is about how texts of all sorts relate to major aspects of the organisation of society. The other form of discourse analysis described in this book, based on the interpretation by Potter and Wetherell (1987), could be described as micro-textual since the analysis tends to stay firmly at the level of the social interaction which produced the text.

The materials used in Foucauldian discourse analysis are any which carry meanings. So Foucauldian discourse analysis can use interviews and other forms of verbal

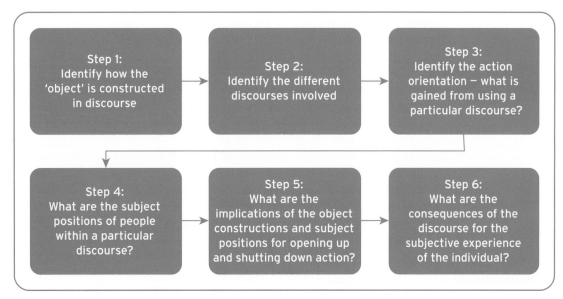

FIGURE 11.1 A summary of Willig's (2008b) steps for Foucauldian discourse analysis

interaction if this meets the purpose of the analysis. However, the method can incorporate books, textbooks, broadcasts, telecasts, films and even pictures. Any of these can be seen as imbued with meanings. Of course, these different types of material can carry very difficult implications and this should be considered as part of the analysis.

The following is a stylised account of how to do Foucauldian discourse analysis (Figure 11.1) (Willig, 2008b):

Step 1 Identify how the 'object' is constructed in discourse The 'object' in Foucauldian discourse analysis is the topic under study, which is primarily dependent on the research question being addressed. So it could be marriage, the army, an aspect of psychology, redundancy or any one of an endless number of topics. The object is treated in the text as having a range of different features and the task of the analyst is to identify the various ways in which the object is construed in the text(s) under consideration. So the analyst needs to identify just where references (direct or indirect) to the object are to be found. There may be circumstances where the object is simply not mentioned by name but it is implied. The object may be referred to euphemistically or in a range of other indirect ways. Simply highlighting them with a highlighter pen may be sufficient to locate such references and associated material relevant to understanding the way in which the object is constructed.

Step 2 Identify the different discourses involved So the sections of the text which are relevant to the object of the discourse have been marked up and identified. What is essentially the same discursive object may be constructed in rather different ways. In Box 9.3, we saw that there were two distinctive constructions of marriage: (a) the romantic repertoire and (b) the realist repertoire. So the analytic task at this stage is to review the material very carefully in order to identify the different discourses that are to be found in the data. While the two marriage repertoires mentioned above may appear to be fairly obvious, this overlooks the fact that there might have been expected other discourses such as a religious discourse for marriage which, in fact, did not appear – possibly because of the age group of those interviewed. It is important to remember that discourses are not a characteristic of individuals and that one individual can employ more than one discourse during the course, say, of an interview.

Step 3   **Identify the action orientation – what is gained from using a particular discourse?** Just what is the consequence of referring to a particular discourse in relation to its object at a particular point in the text? What is the function of this and how is it related to other constructions which appear at about that point in the text? For example, if the text refers to a romantic conception of marriage then this may allow a divorced man to blame his divorce on his wife for not being romantic. If the text referred to a realist repertoire then it might help the man explain his divorce on the basis that he had become unemployed. In Willig's (2008b) words: 'A focus on action orientation allows us to gain a clearer understanding of what the various constructions of the discursive object are capable of achieving within the text' (p. 116).

Step 4   **What are the subject positions of people within a particular discourse?** A subject position refers to where a particular individual is situated within the system of rights, obligations and duties which those who use a particular discourse are buying into. They define 'discursive locations from which to speak and act' (Willig, 2008b, p. 116). Supposing that the discourse is a romantic one, then the locations of both partners are essentially defined by this. The romantic discourse's expectations of women are quite different from those of men. Consequently, although they are not rigid in the way roles are, subject positions indicate a lot about what might be said and done from these different subject positions.

Step 5   **What are the implications of the object constructions and subject positions for opening up and shutting down action?** In other words, what is the role of the object construction and subject position in practice? Keeping with the example of discourses of marriage, a religious discourse might shut-down actions leading to divorce. Just what are the options for action?

Step 6   **What are the consequences of the discourse for the subjective experience of the individual?** What is the relationship between a discourse and subjectivity? Discourses construct social and psychological realities for the individual in terms of (a) seeing the world and (b) being in the world. 'We are now concerned with what can be felt, thought and experienced from within various subject positions' (Willig, 2008b, p. 117). So, for example, it might be the case that in terms of the romantic discourse of marriage, a man may experience great confusion if his wife leaves him because he has lost his job.

To anyone who has read Foucault, this account of discourse analysis seems to ignore much of how he understood power. Hook (2001) takes both versions of discourse analysis to task for locating power in the constructive power of language. Hook explains: 'Foucault's conception of discourse is situated far more closely to knowledge, materiality and power than it is to language' (p. 542). But, of course, power changes historically in the discourse of marriage, for example. In the twenty-first century the institutions surrounding marriage can be seen to be much weaker than they were in the nineteenth century when both church and state exercised more power, in part, through language. So perhaps a Foucauldian account of marriage in the nineteenth century would involve discourses which then were more associated with all forms of institutional power. Perhaps, nowadays, the power of marriage lies more in language than in social institutions.

When to do Foucauldian discourse analysis

Foucauldian discourse analysis is best at providing the big picture of the way that people experience the world. It shares the phrase 'discourse analysis' with other forms of qualitative analysis but, in general, this is where the similarity ends. Foucauldian discourse analysis does not concern itself with the minutiae of speech or conversations. It is not about how Darren convinces Jasper of the rightness of his position or to do something. No the picture is a much bigger one than that and much wider as Foucauldian discourse analysis has its feet firmly planted in a particular approach to history which, in theory, is difficult to avoid. The Foucauldian social world is populated by institutions of one sort or another including state institutions. So, not surprisingly, institutions such as medicine, prison, education, policing, the church, welfare, industries and the like have potential to be addressed by Foucauldian discourse analysis. For the most part, these are not topics familiar to most psychology students on most psychology degrees. Even if they were, the Foucauldian approach to them would be very different from mainstream approaches. Nevertheless, if you are tempted at social analysis at this sort of macro-level then you would be following in the footsteps of many researchers in many disciplines of study who have taken Foucault's ideas and applied them to their field of interest. Of course, Foucauldian discourse analysis is particularly attractive to researchers whose work lies within any of these institutions. For example, nursing studies and clinical psychology are obvious contenders. Of course, some psychologists work in this sort of setting and so some research questions that arise out of these settings may well deserve a Foucauldian treatment. Some areas of psychology, too, like clinical psychology, psychotherapy, educational psychology, business psychology and the like, in terms of practice are firmly entrenched in medical, educational and other institutions which were the prime targets for Foucauldian discourse analysis. Not surprisingly they have been critiqued in similar terms.

Having decided that the macro-ballpark of Foucauldian discourse analysis is for you, a further consideration is whose version? Although one might expect that psychological Foucauldian discourse analysis was quintessentially the same as any other version, this is not quite the case. Foucault was not responsible for the step-by-step approaches of Parker or Willig. These concentrate mainly on the process of identifying discourses in any suitable text. They do not elaborate in much detail the sort of wider analysis which is needed. For example, they do not provide step-by-step instructions for carrying out the historical analysis which is the bedrock of Foucault's analytic work. It would seem that this is provided by secondary sources much of the time. Of course, there are excellent secondary sources which may help with the historical aspects of the Foucault approach. Scholars in many fields have been influenced by him and have carried out this sort of analysis. These need to be tracked down as part of your research process. Whether or not you should or would be able to carry out a fully fledged Foucauldian historical analysis is to push ambition a little bit further. One might suggest that you should immerse yourself in the wider literature on any of the institutions which may be in your purview. This is not narrow psychological research but a broader exploration which stretches through the social sciences into the humanities. Of course, in research you are rarely alone and others may well have already gone down this pathway, starting from a base in psychology. What this boils down to is the question of whether it would be appropriate to base your Foucauldian discourse analysis firmly in the writings of Foucault rather than the sort of syntheses of the approach provided by others including this chapter. The answer to this may lie in a reading of some of Foucault's works or books about Foucault. If these maintain your interest then this may be the appropriate way forward for you. But some would think that this is putting one's toe in the bathwater too soon and that a gentler process of being led by the hand would be more appropriate. In this case the Parker or Willig step-by-step methods may well be suitable. It would be advisable, in this case, to refer back to Foucault from time to time, as difficult concepts may well need to be checked against the original. That is, you could use a hybrid approach drawing on both sources.

One thing that will become patently obvious is the range of radical ideas which Parker's version of discourse analysis draws on. Even more patently obvious is the strong political thrust throughout Parker's work. Now the pretext of this is that Foucauldian discourse analysis readily elides with critical psychology especially in Parker's writings. To a novice researcher, some of this text is particularly difficult as it would require a wide knowledge base of critical psychology to clarify some of it. Furthermore, there is a tendency to generalise substantially beyond the immediate discussion to broad matters of the politics of oppression, subjugation, resistance and the like. The agenda is broadly left wing. It is difficult to know the extent to which such blatant politics would be well received in most psychology departments let alone qualitative psychologists in general. This sliding from Foucauldian discourse analysis, to critical psychology and finally to a political stance would have to be done very well in order for it to be seen as acceptable. This may be a tall order for most students.

There is also a risk of feeling tied to too many masters in this sort of analysis. That is to say, can the analysis go beyond Foucauldian discourse analysis yet still remain a Foucauldian discourse analysis? To be critical of Foucault's approach would eventually result in something that is not Foucauldian at all – though it could just be better. This is not a serious prospect, of course, for student work and is hardly an issue. However, the achievable outcome is probably showing one's understanding of the approach by demonstrating that one can apply Foucauldian ideas in a relatively novel setting. If one is impressed by Foucault's ideas then this is likely to include settings which are of particular interest to you. Where such an analysis begins to fail the researcher is the likely point at which cogent criticisms of Foucault may be made – or you may need to add your own ideas into the analysis in order to make it work. There are any number of publications using Foucault's ideas which show the way.

Examples of Foucauldian discourse analysis

A variety of Foucauldian discourse analysis studies are summarised in Boxes 11.2, 11.3. and 11.4:

- The first example (Box 11.2) is a study of the medicalisation of a common sexually transmitted disease. Although the authors do not claim it to be Foucauldian discourse analysis in the psychological sense, it is a good, straightforward example of the style of work which can be carried out in Foucault's broad style.

- The second example is by Ian Parker who chose to analyse the text on a children's toothpaste box to show the wide applicability of Foucauldian discourse analysis (Box 11.3).

- The third example is of the application of Foucauldian discourse analysis to the issue of the environmental tourist (perhaps in itself an oxymoron). Of particular note is that the researcher returns to Foucault's writings when faced with an analytical concerning to about agency (Box 11.4).

Box 11.2

ILLUSTRATIVE RESEARCH STUDY

Foucauldian discourse analysis: the medicalisation of sexuality

Polzer and Knabe (2012) researched Canadian news media texts, magazines and public service publications dealing with vaccination against Human Papilloma Virus (HPV). HPV is a sexually transmitted infection which can be linked to later cervical cancer. It may be the world's commonest sexually transmitted infection. There is something like one hundred different HPV viruses. Polzer and Knabe's methodological approach is best summed up as feminist critical discourse analysis but very Foucauldian in character. The first approved HPV vaccine offered protection against just four of the many HPV viruses but, importantly, two of these are associated with around 70 per cent of cases of cervical cancer, the other two being associated with 90 per cent of cases of genital warts. The condition became a public health issue in the USA and Canada of substantial proportions. In Canada, for example, there is a free voluntary, school-based three-dose vaccination programme for girls aged between 9 and 13 years. It is well established from research that vaccination before the onset of sexual relations is the most effective.

Few members of the public would have heard of HPV a few years ago but growth of information was fast and at a staggering rate, according to Polzer and Knabe. Public awareness of HPV is now high and references to it are to be found throughout popular culture. This may, in part, be due to the aggressive marketing of the vaccines by their makers which are heavily promoted as a medical breakthrough. Others in the media would caution against the vaccine's use. But, overall, encouragement to accept the vaccine was common in the media. Popular representations treated HPV as a single disease despite the large number of different viruses involved. Furthermore, they discuss HPV infection and cervical cancer as if they were the same thing, which they are clearly not. This sort of conflation tends to deflect attention from the routine facts about HPV. Polzer and Knabe summarise these as:

- HPV can be carried by both genders.
- Transmission between sexual partners is easy.

- Most instances of HPV are short term and clear spontaneously.
- Long-term, persistent, undetected and untreated infections are associated with cervical cancer.

Marketing, nevertheless, has been in terms of the prevention of cervical cancer and not as a means of control of sexually transmitted infections. Furthermore, newspapers would refer to the vaccines as preventing cervical cancer. For comparative purposes, cervical cancer is about the 20th most deadly cancer in women and amounts to about 1 per cent of deaths from cancer. Lung cancer is 25 times more likely to be involved in a cancer death and breast cancer is about 15 times more likely.

HPV illustrates how women's bodies and lives have become medicalised. This is a modern use of the term medicalisation which in the past generally referred to the way in which social problems such as alcoholism and non-marital sex were reconceived as medical problems. This led to their being dealt with by medics as if they were diseases or illnesses in some form to be treated with medical procedures. Sex was regarded as a social problem. Grave health warnings and medical treatments for masturbation illustrate this medicalised approach (Howitt, 1991). The more recent use of the term medicalisation (Nye, 2003) involves a dynamic process which involves different stakeholders treating matters as if they were medical in nature. So, female sexual dysfunctions can involve stakeholders such as government departments and agencies, pharmaceutical manufacturers, research funding bodies, university researchers, urologists, and so forth, as well as the media. The term biomedicalisation has been employed to describe the way in which technology has become integral to our conceptions of health and health care. A closely related idea is that health can be achieved by identifying and surveillance of the health risks in individuals and populations (Clarke, Mamo, Fosket, Fishman, & Shim, 2010). Neomedicalization (Batt & Lippman, 2010) refers to the way in which pharmaceutical companies and other corporations use the risk of future disease to create and develop new markets. A rather benign example of this would be the sales of blood pressure monitors to the general public. All of this means that health is being turned into a commodity to be marketed. By promoting new products as choices then ideas of empowerment and autonomy central to feminism are subverted in an easily accepted or unnoticed way. Public health priorities increasingly place emphasis on the responsibilities of individuals. Members of the public are expected to reduce risks to their health through the use of medical and self-surveillance. Drugs and other devices may be seen as purchases commensurate with this requirement. Being at-risk of a disease state becomes a disease state in itself which the individual is given the responsibility for making sure that it does not happen. One might consider the idea that obese people should be denied health treatment as a version of this. Medicalisation in its various forms neutralises the political reasons for ill health since the focus narrows to be on individuals and their biological characteristics. Polzer and Knabe write:

> the possibility that HPV may lead to cervical cancer, and the possibility of foreclosing this risk through vaccination, has the effect of pathologizing nascent female sexuality. (p. 346)

So Polzer and Knabe argue that HPV effectively pathologises nascent female sexuality. This is not achieved by claiming a sexual abnormality or dysfunction. Instead what is normal is pathologised. In other words a typical life experience (in this case sexual relations) is linked to the possibility of contracting HPV and, consequently, the possibility of developing a cancer in the future.

Their critical discourse analysis involved Canadian newspaper, magazine and brochure material concerning HPV vaccination written in the English language. The sample involved 180 newspaper and 48 articles from magazines. Readership levels and diversity were among the selection criteria. Both gender neutral and gender specific magazines were used. The search term for the material was HPV. This term first appeared in 1986, though the majority of the material studied was published during 2006–2007. Discourses do not merely reflect reality; they also involve ways of thinking and speaking about something which impose boundaries about what is considered and accepted to be the truth or facts – in other words, legitimate knowledge. Some ways of thinking are enabled by discourses but others are constrained by discourses. That is, they both construct and frame knowledge. Some responses come to appear to be reasonable, justifiable and natural. Other responses come to appear illogical or illegitimate.

The analysis procedure involved multiple close readings of the texts typical of qualitative analysis. The elucidation of meanings and the nature of the framing were the objectives. These would be conveyed through various rhetorical and linguistic strategies including metaphors and images. Although they give little by way of detail, the authors explain that they developed a coding template based on an initial subset of the textual material. This template was then applied to new data and further refined as necessary. They describe the process as an iterative one which led, eventually, to the identification of two main themes which broadly summarised the media content:

The construction of nascent female sexuality which they describe as being privileged in

- HPV vaccination discourse.
- The parental responses evoked by this construction.

The risk presented by HPV is posed as a productive tension which involves the destigmatisation of the condition by portraying it as being extremely common (which it is) while at the same time being amplified in terms of the risks, etc. that it poses. The virus is seen as being ubiquitous – analogous to other conditions such as the common cold. Statistics provide another source of evidence of its ubiquity. Indications that it is easy to catch HPV further destigmatise the condition. Sexual penetration is unnecessary to catch it and skin contact may be enough. In this way, once regarded as fairly innocent, sexual explorations become framed instead as risky activities. At the same time, the possible dangerous outcomes of HPV are emphasised in the media coverage. The epidemiological relationship between HPV and cervical cancer frames it as a serious matter and a sexually transmitted infection which warrants public attention. Cervical cancer is framed as a killer disease and statistical evidence in support of this presented. For example, the media would claim that about 1400 women annually contract cervical cancer in Canada, of which 400 die. In contrast, they fail to acknowledge much of the time that the incidence statistics for cervical cancer are declining and the recovery rate improving. Worldwide statistics for cervical cancer are worse than the Canadian figures but worldwide statistics are quoted without any attempt to put this in context. The disease is not entirely preventable through the use of condoms, which leads to the view being expressed that there is no such thing as safe sex. Young people are presented as knowing little about sexually transmitted infections and do not engage in preventative health practices. In other words, teenagers are unreliable risk managers.

The second thrust emerging in the analysis concerned parental responsibilities. Since virtually any form of sexual contact exposes a young girl to HPV then vaccination is offered as a reasonable and responsible act which allows the parents to protect their daughters. This duty to protect appears directly in newspapers:

'Every nine- to 13-year-old girl in the country should be vaccinated against the sexually transmitted virus that causes cervical cancer'. (Kirkey, 2007, p. A1)

Testimonials by parents concerning their adoption of vaccination for their daughters are presented unproblematically given the link between the infection and cancer. Who wouldn't want to protect their daughters in this way? It is presented as the right decision in the media extracts. Other examples include the following from a cervical cancer survivor:

'I would never, ever want anyone to go through what I did because of a stupid little virus. We should do whatever we can to protect people, including vaccination' she said. 'If anybody is against this, I'll take them for a visit to the cancer ward.' (Picard, 2007, p. A11).

The authors' conclusion is that a particular discourse is privileged in HPV vaccination texts. This is the view that nascent female sexuality is risky. Parents have a responsibility of managing the risk by the HPV vaccination strategy and by communicating health risk information to their daughters. The emergence of sexuality is the point at which pathogenisation occurs. The authors pose certain questions which can be construed as a critical argument in this context. For example, how do pharmaceutical interests shape the way in which sexual health and sexual health education are construed using the concept of risk? How will this shaping by the pharmaceutical industry affect young women's first sexual experiences and the ways in which they imagine them? In what ways does framing parent–daughter communications in terms of HPV vaccination and risk interfere with truly open communications between parent and daughter?

Box 11.3

ILLUSTRATIVE RESEARCH STUDY

Foucauldian discourse analysis: the case of the toothpaste packet

Perhaps in an attempt to show how discourse may appear in the most unlikely of places, Parker (1999b) carried out a discourse analytic reading of text printed on a toothpaste box. This may be thought of as a trivial basis for an analysis but this triviality illustrates the levels to which discourse permeates. Although he refers to 20 analytic steps in the process, we will concentrate on outlining the important basic steps as they appear in Parker's journal article. A number of discourses are illustrated especially what may be described as the therapeutic discourse. This presents the reader (subject) as feeling in a relationship with the author of the text in order to allow the text to do its work discursively. There is research literature on the therapeutic relationship between psychotherapists and counsellors which cannot be discussed here

for lack of space. The Foucauldian idea of the 'conditions of possibility' is drawn upon. These allow the therapeutic relationship to work. In order to carry out the analysis, Parker explains how the researcher must 'systematically tease apart the text, identifying objects and subjects, networks of relationships, and the contradictions between different images of the world' (p. 578). In other words, identify the nature of the discourses found which, in this case, included the therapeutic discourse. How is reality constructed by this discourse?

The brand of toothpaste in question ('Natural Toothpaste for Children') is aimed at a specialised market. It is a US product and is to be found for sale in wholefood shops. The front of the box is laid out as follows textwise (Parker, 1999b, p. 578–579):

**Tom's of Maine
Natural Toothpaste for Children
With Fluoride
SACCARIN FREE
Silly Strawberry**

The back of the box contains a list of ingredients, their purpose and source, and the following paragraph and other material:

WHAT MAKES THIS NATURAL? All major brands of toothpaste for children contain saccharin, artificial color, and taste supersweet. We take a simple approach – use natural ingredients to make it taste good and work well. Compare our natural ingredients with any other brand and make your choice.

Children under six years of age should be supervised in the use of toothpaste.

A message for parents in the form of a letter appears on one side panel of the toothpaste box:

The Story Of Our Children's Natural Toothpaste

Dear Parent,

We think the time is right to make a natural toothpaste just for children. For over 20 years we have committed ourselves to natural oral and body care products. Many adults have come to trust our natural toothpastes made without saccharin or synthetic flavors, preservatives, dyes or animal ingredients. We now offer a delicious and effective natural toothpaste with sensible ingredients and natural fruit flavors created with your child's taste in mind. It contains none of the stripes and "sparkles", neon colors and sweet bubble gum flavors you see in other brands. Our gentle formulation is low in abrasivity and contains fluoride to help prevent dental decay.

Try it and let us know what you and your child think.

Your friends,

Kate & Tom Chappell

A message for children appears on the other box side panel in a child-like scrawl:

JUST FOR KIDS by Luke Chappell (age 8¾)

About Animals – Do you like animals? At home we have a dog Hershey, a bird Eli, and a hamster named Carol. At Tom's of Maine my Mom and Dad make sure our products are safe without testing them on animals. If you have a favorite animal, draw a picture and send it to me.

About Recycling – At home we recycle cans, bottles, newspaper and plastic. Tom's of Maine gave our town greenbins so each family can separate and store their recycled things until a special truck picks them up every week. If you do recycling at home, let me know. I'm trying to get recycling news from all the states.

Parker points out that the messages are already in the form of words but non-word material could be used in the analysis if available. So pictorial material would need to be turned into words and then the cultural connotations of these words listed for analysis. Among Parker's first thoughts about the text was that the reader is addressed in a personal way. The naturalness of the toothpaste appears to be connected in some way to the simplicity of the form of communication between the authors of the text and the reader. Just what are the objects referred to in the toothpaste text? These are not simply material objects like toothpaste but social objects too. Your list may be different from Parker's but he suggests that the main ones are as follows:

- *The natural*: this is used as an adjective in relation to toothpaste and toothpaste for children, ingredients, oral and body care products, and fruit flavours. It is also likened to 'simple' and 'sensible'.
- *Taste*: things which taste supersweet and things which taste good are presented as being in opposition.
- *Gentle formulation*: this combines the absence of abrasivity with the presence of fluoride.
- *Commitment*: as indicated by the statement that they had committed themselves to natural products for over 20 years.
- *Trust*: as in the manufacturer's commitment to natural toothpaste.
- *Synthetic flavours*: which Parker describes as being metonymically linked to artificial flavours, stripes, animal ingredients, sparkles, supersweetness and preservatives among other things.
- There are other objects too such as family, child and special truck.

The researcher needs to identify interconnections between objects and begin to highlight any patterns which seem to be present. What is important is the object as it is constructed by the text. There may be other constructions which rely on the researcher's knowledge beyond the text in question. It is too easy to lose sight of what the text is doing if outside matters are introduced. These are not part of the analysis and need to be excluded. So outside knowledge about, say, what issues are posed by the use of preservatives is not part of Parker's analysis. Animal is constructed in the text as something unnatural as a component of toothpaste rather than, say, something to be respected or protected.

Objects which read, speak, write and listen are the subjects in the text and Parker recommends noting their occurrence. The subjects therefore include:

• Tom (who appears variously as Tom Chappell, Dad to Luke, provider of greenbins and a special truck, and Tom of Maine);

• children (who are targets for natural toothpaste, as needing supervision below the age of six, who are owned by parents as when referred to as your child, they personalise animals, etc.);

• Hershey, who is identified as a dog;

• Silly Strawberry, which is marked as a fruit with human attributes;

• and there are other obvious examples on the toothpaste box.

A subsequent task is to choose a descriptive label for the discourses which have been identified. Although a discourse may appear to be lying hidden within a text this is not the best view of what is happening analytically. Reading text involves active interpretative processes. We construct patterns on the basis of what we know about the surrounding culture and on the basis of how we experience discourses outside the text. The way we reconstruct discourses and the position from which we read the text are to be seen in the way in which we identify the discourses. Other researchers may not see our labels as appropriate, of course. Parker suggests that there are six discourses identifiable from the text on the box of toothpaste. He describes these as follows:

• *Child centred*: the message from another child to the child user and the invitation to consult the child about the product are markers of this.

• *Childcare*: involved in warnings about the confectionary nature of other toothpastes, the note about supervising children under six using the toothpaste, and the inclusion of a letter addressed to parents.

• *Confectionary*: major brands of toothpaste are likened to sweets with neon colours and sweet bubble gum flavours.

• *Ecological:* this is shown in natural ingredients, the material on recycling, and the special *recycling* truck and the green bins.

• *Familial*: the letter addressed to the parent guardian and the Chappell family image in the text.

• *Health*: concern about the health effects of saccharine and synthetic flavours together with fluoride's role in the prevention of dental decay.

A further discourse is recurrent in the text, Parker argues, one which joins the child-centred, the ecological and the familial. This is found at the point at which the parent has engaged with the text sufficiently to make comparisons between this and other brands and makes their choice. According to Parker this is accompanied by changes in the childcare discourse which moves from traditional child training ideas to ones involving autonomous self-driven growth. The health discourse changes from a fairly standard medical discourse to one more in the area of mental health and therapy. So we can add in another discourse to the above six:

• *Therapeutic*: Parker sees the manifestation of this in things like the comment that the time is right, the notion of trust, the gentle formulation and the invitation to respond to the manufacturer positioning itself as friends. This is possibly the most difficult of the discourses to appreciate in Parker's account of his analysis and it is not particularly extensively described in the report. It seems a little incomplete and possibly needs returning to in order to establish more more precisely what is meant.

Having identified the discourses in a text, the next analytic step is to trace the historical emergence of each of these discourses. This may help to show how a discourse functions to position subjects 'as the text circulates through culture' (p. 584). Such a more general reflection about the discourses includes the way in which they tell the story of their own origins. By doing so, the historical nature of discourses becomes apparent. So discourse about mental illness, say, includes an account of what things were like in the past. But this obscures the historical continuities underlying the discourse at the same time. Of course, such an analysis requires that the researcher has or can obtain such a historical perspective on each discourse. This may prove difficult especially in relatively new areas of research. Such historical analyses are far from easy and require different skills from those taught in the average psychology methods class. Take, for example, Parker's confectionary discourse. What is our historical knowledge of such a discourse? One might suggest that it is more likely to be found as an account of discourse about food and health than a specific one about sweets. It is known that what is regarded as a healthy diet has changed radically over the years and it may be possible to link this idea of a confectionery discourse with that. Health discourse of the sort identified in his analysis is another discourse which has been subject to historical analysis. The simple example that Parker gives of this is that health has historically been subject to a somewhat contradictory blend of medical and mystical notions. These exist in contradiction with one another. Parker argues that this battle is to be seen in the toothpaste box text. Perhaps the antithesis between natural and medical health remedies is what he is thinking of. The toothpaste is presented very much as a natural thing and its value as lying in this.

The final steps in this Foucauldian discourse analysis were to enquire what institutions are reinforced and what institutions are undermined by this discourse. Let's take the health discourse in the text on the toothpaste box. The discourse challenges medical institutions with their scientific basis since the text concerns natural products represented as being healthy. These are presented in opposition to manufactured products which contain all sorts of undesirable things including meat products. At the same time the discourse, of course,

reinforces natural health notions and the companies which profit from the sale of natural products. These are, as you will have realised, big companies as well as small enterprises which also make money from sales of 'natural' products. Parker also suggests that each of the discourses reflects the complicated ways in which domination and resistance can be identified in discourse (Foucault, 1980). The contradictions within discourses offer possibilities for them to be debated and challenged. Thus there is a challenge in health to science-based medical institutions and for childcare there is a challenge to traditional obedience-based family structures.

Box 11.4
ILLUSTRATIVE RESEARCH STUDY
Foucauldian discourse analysis: The case of ethical subjects

Hanna (2014) describes aspects of his qualitative research into sustainable tourism. This is not a topic which has drawn much or any attention from qualitative psychology though there is relevant quantitative research. Tourism, during much of the twentieth century, was seen as a somewhat benign industry which brought benefits to developing economies while not having the adverse environmental impact that manufacturing might bring. This point of view was no longer sustainable in the 1990s. The World Tourism Organization and the World Travel and Trade Council (WTTC) issued Agenda 21 about then. This was critical of the impact of the travel industry. Ideas changed and now it is generally and increasingly believed that things like worldwide pollution, the depletion of natural resources, global warming, and the exploitation of wildlife, environments and cultures can partly be blamed on tourism. Sustainable tourism is a fairly new idea which constitutes an attempt to alleviate if not put right the negative aspects of traditional tourism. Mainstream psychology has researched things like the psychological profile of the sustainable tourist and the

sorts of individuals who manifest ethical and altruistic attitudes. According to Hanna, these studies say little if anything of the experience of sustainable tourists. The ethical tourist is viewed as a fixed identity which from the qualitative perspective may be questioned. They are also construed as rational decision makers weighing up the pros and cons of their actions. Hanna describes his analysis as drawing on poststructuralist principles in order to identify the dominant discourses which enable and reproduce some of these ideas about sustainable tourism. His aim was to study 'how, through language, participants in my research constructed and understood their identities, self, and practices as ethical or sustainable' (p. 144). In order to help provide a reflexive account, Hannah refers to himself in the first person as 'I'. In this way he suggests that his impact on the research would be highlighted.

Hanna's research focuses on the socially constructed and negotiated truths about sustainable tourism. Furthermore, just how do people as individuals deal with these truths to create identities? Hanna characterises his study as two-stage research. Data were firstly collected from the Internet to help understand how sustainable tourism is dealt with in the public domain. Holidays are commonly booked through the Internet and the Internet can be seen as a good source of understanding how things are constructed socially. The second stage involved a series of semi-structured interviews. Self-defined sustainable tourists were used to avoid the imposition of researcher preconceptions. Hanna explains that he sought an appropriate method of analysis for both types of data by reading and re-reading the texts employing a range of different analytic lenses. They included content analysis, critical grounded theory and Billig's approach to ideology (1991, 2001) among others. Each of these different readings was of some value, Hanna suggests, in understanding the broad social constructions in the data. However, none of them were particularly helpful in relation to what Hannah describes as 'the more intricate negotiations and positions inherent within the interview data' (p. 145).

Foucauldian discourse analysis was closer to what Hanna required analytically, he gradually realised. Subject positions, subjectivities and ways of being are achieved through the nexus of power and knowledge. It appeared to Hanna that Foucauldian discourse analysis would enable ways of addressing issues directly relevant to his research question. The availability of step-by-step approaches to such an analysis were attractive and helpful. Hanna chose to use Willig's six-step process which is described in detail in this chapter (pages 293–294) rather than the 20-step approach of Parker (1992) which is used in Box 11.3. Willig's approach was preferred as being simpler while not compromising the analysis in any way.

Stage one of the analysis was the identification of means by which discursive objects such as responsibility, ethics and holiday were constructed. All references to these objects were identified and subtleties of construction sought. For example, was ethics referred to directly or through less direct metaphors and practices in the interviews? The second stage was to see how these objects were constructed in multiple ways. For example, was the object irresponsibility always constructed as the binary opposite of responsibility. At this stage it begins to be possible to see different discourses being employed in the interviews. Stage three involved the examination of the action orientation which establishes how objects relate to one another. It helps establish what is gained through the use of a particular discourse. Stage four is to enquire into the subject positions afforded by these broader discourses. Just how are the tourist, the holiday company, the host company and the environment positioned in the data? The fifth stage is about the actions which are opened up or shut down by the discourse. So,

for example, what practices and behaviours are legitimate within the discourse which would be available to the sustainable tourist, the sustainable tour operator and so forth? Finally, stage six is the question of the implications of the discourses for the subjective experiences of the individual. Thus it could be asked what the consequences are for a tourist being positioned within a discourse of responsibility. What, for example, might their feelings towards product consumption be as a consequence?

At this point, Hanna began to feel that Foucauldian discourse analysis provided an understanding of the subject as being produced by discourse which he was 'uneasy' about. He felt that the approach worked well with the Internet material but not so well with the interview material. Foucauldian discourse analysis resulted in an analysis which was overly critical but also decidedly deterministic when it came to the interviews. He quotes Brown and Stenner (2009, p. 158) who wrote of a 'relentless and repetitive auto-critique'. Poor analysis in brief for the interviews. Hanna decided that he wanted to give voice to the people he had engaged with in the research interviews. There is no acknowledgement of the reality of existence in Foucauldian discourse analysis, he argues, since what is real is always dependent on discourses and their wider cultural frame of reference. Foucauldian discourse analysis fails to enlist the consistency within a person just as mainstream psychology had failed to capture inconsistencies within a person. Just why do some individuals consistently construct their experiences, their ideas about their self, and carry out practices in one way whereas others do not? One way of putting this is that no place has been found for human agency in Foucauldian discourse analysis. People have their thoughts and actions scripted by the discourses which are the agents of powerful institutions. Hanna asks if it is ethical to construe people as the products of a discursive economy:

Realising a FDA [Foucauldian discourse analysis] approach to my data would offer little more than a critical engagement with the way in which the participants are positioned and constrained through their own language use led me to search for a more ethical approach to the data. Rather than being overly critical of my participants, I wanted to acknowledge that they had actually engaged with something that they saw as ethical or sustainable and that there was more to this than stake management (Edwards & Potter 1992), middle class distinction (Bourdieu 1984), a new form of colonialism (Hanna 2009), or similar – the participants were trying to do something however much myself and other academics can critique the industry or its promotion. (p. 147)

Although this may appear to be a criticism of Foucault at first sight, it is no such thing in the sense that Hanna engages in a further reading of Foucault in an attempt to find what Foucault may have had to say that is pertinent to this issue. It does illustrate how by concentrating on secondary sources we get only rudiments of the original. Hanna finds a great deal in Foucault's writing which addresses the issue that Hanna was concerned about. Volumes 2 and 3 of Foucault's *History of sexuality* was one such valuable source (Foucault, 1985, 1986). Foucault found that there was a need for a notion such as agency to describe the process by which people begin to transform themselves. This is something which is a feature of modern life rather than historically when people could be seen as being subjected in a variety of ways.

So, for example, in writings by Foucault there is referred to what is known as the ethical substance. This refers to the part of the self which a person identifies as being in need of attention. For example, Hanna highlights a segment from one of his interviews which he regards as particularly illustrative. Hannah had asked the question of what made an interviewee, Jayne, interested in engaging in sustainable tourism. Her reply included the following:

> um well I suppose trying to trying to trying to not be to not have too much umm kind of dissonance between what I do at home and what I do when I go abroad really and umm yeah because I suppose I go around kind of . . . you know going for organic stuff or going for fair trade stuff and that kind of thing and so endeavouring to try and keep that keep that going when you know you are actually going to some of the countries where stuff comes from so to be mindful of that really. (p. 148)

One might say that the discursive subject of the above quotation is an ethical attitude and that Jayne is subjectified through this. The discourse might be identified as what it is to be ethical in modern Western society. Thus the dominant discourse is reproduced by Jayne. But this does not seem to capture every aspect of the quotation. In particular, Jayne identifies what she is trying to do in terms of reducing the disparity between what she does in everyday life at home and what happens when she is on holiday. At home she does Fair Trade shopping, buys organic food and the like. As such she positions herself as an ethical consumer. So the question she poses herself is just how to maintain this sort of lifestyle when she is abroad. Normal ways of understanding holidays in the West, such as that one deserves a break, are not necessarily compatible with the idea of the ethical lifestyle being extended into her holidays.

In Hanna's original report, Foucauldian ideas relevant to this are greatly elaborated but this is a short account and not every aspect of the original can be incorporated. Reading the original would help you further. What seems to be especially important in Hanna's analysis is the way that his dissatisfaction with simply applying standard notions from Foucauldian discourse analysis is dealt with. They are not allowed to interfere with the process of reframing the analysis. To be sure this involves additional reading of Foucault but surely this would be essential to any research carrying out a Foucauldian discourse analysis. Hannah's account of the development of his analysis is informative. He explains how he returned to Foucault's writings searching for ideas to develop the data analysis. In these writings were ideas of which Hannah was previously unaware. These allowed Hannah to expand his own thinking about an issue in his initial analysis. The lesson of the study is presumably that people are agentic within a discourse. Or, more generally, that a researcher's responsibility is to push forward in the process of doing research and not simply worship at the feet of even Foucault without trying to do better!

Evaluation of Foucauldian discourse analysis

All psychologists would benefit from reading about Foucault's ideas. Most psychologists work in some sort of institution and are seen to possess elite knowledge, after all. This is Foucauldian territory and many of his best writings are about hospital and similar social institutions. The work of Michel Foucault is too big, too important and too influential to be evaluated effectively in a short section of a textbook on qualitative methods in psychology. There are plenty of books describing at some length Foucault's ideas and putting them under critical scrutiny (e.g. Deleuze, 2006). However, we have a much more limited objective which is to evaluate the psychological approach to Foucauldian discourse analysis – a far more manageable project to handle especially as the primary focus is not on Foucault but the way in which his ideas have been adapted to psychology. Put bluntly, is Foucauldian discourse analysis merely a pale shadow of the man's ideas? If we take the writings of Parker (1994) and Willig (2008b) as being indicative of the nature of Foucauldian discourse analysis in psychology then this just about covers the material in this chapter. So are these psychological approaches up to the task of bringing Foucault's ideas to psychology effectively? Are they up to initiating the neonate researcher into Foucault's method? The answer is probably 'up to a point' but we should not pretend that psychological Foucauldian discourse analysis is a complete approach to doing Foucauldian analysis in psychology. They are helpful in providing a means to identify discourse in texts, for example, but the researcher will probably want to systematically study Foucauldian ideas before a substantial study in this style.

Whether or not we can call psychological Foucauldian discourse analysis a student orientated version of Foucault's method perhaps would make an interesting discussion point. But we are talking about a learning process, so easy access to relevant theory and analytic details in accessible form is important. And there is plenty of such discussions available as we have indicated. When it comes to discussing Foucauldian discourse analysis, the relative absence of crystal clear examples in psychology is noteworthy. Foucauldian discourse analysis has not impacted research to the same extent as Potter and Wetherell's social constructionist discourse analysis. Actually, there is a good case for psychologists to cross over disciplinary boundaries as there are many more Foucauldian analyses of high quality in a wide range of disciplines. Often these are abstracted in PsycInfo and other databases so they may well turn up in one of your literature searches anyway. Foucauldian discourse analysis in psychology does need a much bigger corpus of research in order to make its potential fully clear. Simple references to Foucault do not amount to a Foucauldian analysis in that sense. Moving to concepts such as empowerment, resistance and subjugation can read more like purple prose than thorough analysis. Despite their not really competing for the same space in research, the two sorts of discourse analysis (social constructionist and Foucauldian) occasionally have intellectual spats over one issue or another. There are some major epistemological differences between the two which one needs to be clear about without doubt. The social constructionist discourse analysts, Potter, Edwards and Ashmore (2002), commented as follows about Foucauldian discourse analysis and, particularly, the writings of Parker:

> Parker recruits the tortured, oppressed and murdered people of the world to his philosophical position (critical realism), as if their suffering and death bore testimony to his vision, and sided with his (ambivalent and occasioned) dislike of non-Foucauldian discourse analysis, conversation analysis, ethnomethodology . . .
> (p. 77)

This is a fine piece of rhetoric. Critical realism is a target because Parker (1992) insisted that a realist position is essential if one is to take a political/moral stance on matters. The absence of such a view was responsible for the apolitical/amoral characteristics of social constructionist discourse analysis, he suggested. What Potter, Edwards and Ashmore say above is a caricature, of course, but very recognisable nonetheless. Basically Parker is prone to mix together at least three different agendas into the one enterprise in his writings. To him they are highly related, of course, but from the outside his writings may seem unswervingly programmatic. The three agendas are Foucauldian analysis, critical psychology and a particular sort of politics. Each on its own is a big bite in research terms and together difficult to digest.

Foucauldian analysis should be the bedrock of the approach but politics often arrives early to curtail the Foucauldian discussion. The flow can be from Foucauldian research to numerous critical psychology approaches, a Marxism-based political ethic, a plea to destroy mainstream psychology, and a description of how liberational psychology somewhere in Central or South America is seeking to help the poor and disadvantaged. Of course, there is nothing intrinsically wrong in this – it merely makes a difficult read for newcomers.

Although Potter and Wetherell's social constructionist discourse analysis can appear rather like a toolkit of analytical procedures, this is simply not true of Foucauldian discourse analysis. Apart from the words 'discourse analysis' the two do not really have a great deal in common. They both involve the analysis of texts of one sort or another but they are at the opposite ends of the spectrum in terms of the levels of the analysis. One is about the minutiae of language in social interaction, the other is about the broad sweeping idea of 'a discourse' at a macro level. It should be next to impossible to confuse one with the other. If your wish is to study everyday language and conversation in order to understand what language is doing and how it is doing it, the closed grained work of social constructionist discourse analysis is almost certainly the preferable approach. (Conversation analysis provides an even more microscopic view of what goes on in everyday conversations, telephone calls, professional consultations and the like.) Foucauldian discourse analysis adopts a much wider picture of what is important to analyse in text. The researcher's task is to identify the discourses contained or partially contained within texts. Specifying in detail the nature of the discourse within the text is the next priority. The evidence for discourses is to be found in texts of all sorts, though not necessarily in a complete form. The analyst's task is to piece together as full a picture as possible of what the discourse is from the fragments – specify its characteristics if one likes. Then the question is just what does the discourse do in the world. Discourses are not things, however, and they are created and recreated, produced and reproduced in interactions between people. It hardly needs to be said that such a discourse positions people in general in relation to the discourse. People were subjected to the discourse, if one likes, and dominated by the institutions through discourse.

CONCLUSION

Foucauldian discourse analysis, it should be apparent, will be a challenge to most students who come across it for the first time. This is not surprising because Foucauldian discourse analysis challenges mainstream psychology itself. Critical psychology does much the same. So students may find themselves in the position of studying mainstream topics in psychology as part of their education while, at the same time, being exposed to analyses which challenge the existence of psychology as an institution. Furthermore, the approaches discussed in this chapter question the value of what is being taught on the mainstream modules. That students are taught to critique the discipline that they are studying is, of course, an expectation of any educational process. As such, the critiques of psychology should be welcome. Of course, it goes a little deeper than that. Both Foucauldian discourse analysis and critical psychology are critical of society more generally. Nevertheless, Foucauldian discourse analysis should also be seen as a method of getting to understand social institutions and their role in the social world better. It is, of course, an approach circumscribed by the interests of Michel Foucault. So a Foucauldian discourse analysis will never be psychological in the sense of focusing on the individual. That was not Foucault's approach. Foucauldian discourse analysis may help us to be critical in many of the situations in which psychologists do their work. This list is increasingly long – marketing, education, relationships, health, the community, police work, military, and so forth. This is the sort of level of analysis which most mainstream training in psychology does little to prepare students for. Dissenting voices can make interesting reading and research.

KEY POINTS

- Foucauldian discourse analysis is probably best seen as an attempt to make the ideas and work of Michel Foucault into a workable method in psychology. That is, it offers a reasonably straightforward route to doing a basic Foucauldian analysis on a wide variety of texts of one sort or another. Of course, Foucault's legacy is deep and complex and requires careful and detailed study to achieve any real mastery. This clearly cannot be achieved with a few analytic steps.

- Basic to Foucault's ideas is the way in which institutions (medicine, psychiatry, prisons, etc.) exercise control over people through the way in which knowledge is constructed. Discourses are coherent systems of ideas which effectively position people as subjects within the discourse. The discourse then indicates or even controls how they should conduct themselves. Discourses are not tangible things and are reproduced in social interaction. Discourses have a history, they may superficially change, but ultimately they continue to control.

- Foucauldian discourse analysis tends to be associated with radical and somewhat anti-psychology movements within the discipline, though the method can be applied much more widely than that. These movements can broadly be formulated by the phrase critical psychology. Again, although it does not have to, critical psychology tends to focus on mainstream psychology which is seen as a powerful, harmful institution which contributes technologies, etc. to control people. It tends to use a left-wing political language and draws widely and freely from a range of radical philosophical and other viewpoints. Critical psychology, itself, tends to be poorly defined.

ADDITIONAL RESOURCES

Fillingham, L. A. (1993). *Foucault for beginners*. Danbury, CT: For Beginners.

Gutting, G. ((2005). *Foucault: A very short introduction*. Oxford: Oxford University Press.

Hook, D. (2001). Discourse, knowledge, materiality, history: Foucault and discourse analysis. *Theory and Psychology, 11* (4), 521–547.

Parker, I. (Ed.) (2015). *Handbook of critical psychology*. London: Routledge.

YouTube. Professor Fernando González Rey interviews Professor Ian Parker (Psychologist/England). https://www.youtube.com/watch?v=fEOK_rSkK7M (accessed 12 June 2015).

CHAPTER 12

Phenomenology

Overview

- Phenomenology was a major philosophical movement beginning in the early part of the twentieth century. Phenomenological psychology adapts the principles of phenomenology to the psychological study of significant life experiences.

- Phenomenology's key idea is that the only reliable knowledge that we have of the world is the experience of the world we have in our consciousness. In this sense, phenomenology is built on the idea common in qualitative methods that the 'real world is unknowable directly'.

- The main role of phenomenological psychology is to provide a description of how a particular phenomenon is generally experienced. It should not be primarily about the experiences of an individual, although it can be. Phenomenological psychology highlights exceptions in experiences of phenomena as well as commonalities.

- Modern phenomenological psychology stresses describing the experience of phenomena but also attempts to provide meaning and understanding to what is experienced.

- Phenomenology had its first inroads into psychology through the work of Amedeo Giorgi who provided systematic ways of carrying out phenomenological studies beginning in the 1960s. His vision of phenomenology is very descriptive.

- The founder of phenomenology, Edmund Husserl, advocated that in understanding the phenomena all else should be suspended so that it could be known, described and seen in its purest form unsullied by our prior beliefs and other thoughts. This is known as bracketing. Few phenomenological psychologists believe that complete bracketing is a possibility although it may be seen as a theoretical ideal towards which to aim.

- Although we talk about our experiences using language, the experience of the phenomenon is part of our consciousness and so not dependent on language.

- There are a number of different phenomenological approaches in psychology. Interpretative phenomenological analysis (IPA) is an increasingly popular method especially in health psychology and similar fields. It is discussed in detail in Chapter 13. Narrative psychology has strong associations with phenomenology and so should be considered alongside phenomenological psychology.

- Phenomenological psychology is a broad church and no particular requirements about method dominate. This chapter provides details of how phenomenological research in psychology can be carried out.

- Phenomenological psychology provides a broad framework for studying people's descriptions of their experiences and the strictures of phenomenology itself can inform it in significant ways.

What is phenomenology?

This book contains two chapters dealing directly with phenomenology. This chapter will deal with phenomenology in its more classical forms whereas Chapter 13 concentrates on a relatively modern derivative known as interpretative phenomenological analysis (IPA). Both have things in common but IPA is emerging as a significant qualitative method in its own right and warrants detailed attention. Study the chapters in whatever order suits you as each is intended to be self-contained.

Phenomenological psychology is the application, appropriately adapted, of ideas from phenomenological philosophy. Although some argue that the discipline should be termed phenomenologically-based psychology because it is not what was originally meant by the term, this is usually ignored in favour of the familiar phenomenological psychology. Phenomenology can be seen as something that people naturally engage in since ordinary people, poets, writers, artists and actors routinely pay attention to everyday life and their experiences of it. Phenomenological psychologists do much the same but in far greater detail and much more systematically. Nevertheless, it is important to understand phenomenology as an intellectual idea before making too many assumptions about what is and what is not phenomenology. Phenomenology is one of the oldest qualitative research methods and one with very deep philosophical roots. In phenomenological analysis, the role of the researcher is to:

- Assist the participant to describe the world of their experiences as effectively as they can and as far as possible free from their thoughts and reflections on their experiences. In this way, they are describing the experience as it was experienced, not their experience as they reflect on it.

- Formulate explanations of or understand the meanings of the dimensions of the world as they experience it. In order to do this, the researcher must suspend or disregard their own assumptions and understandings. They need to be open minded so that they can understand the experiences of the other person in new ways, unfettered by prior knowledge and assumptions.

The practical usefulness of phenomenological psychology – actual or potential – can be summarised in the three following suggestions (Polkinghorne, 1989):

- Phenomenological psychology can offer an in-depth understanding of various types of experience (for example, depression or chronic back pain). Knowing just how these are experienced may help practitioners in the field of health or psychology in their work. It helps provide them with empathic understanding of their patients and clients.

- Phenomenology explores human consciousness and experience, which means that it contributes to our richer understanding of humanity. This, for example, may help researchers understand better the findings from more mainstream research. Usually mainstream research presents its findings in terms of correlations and patterns. Whatever the value of this research, it is difficult to make complete sense of such decontextualised findings. Phenomenology can offer ways of grasping their meaning.

- Phenomenological research can inform public policy. Social interventions are unlikely to be successful unless built on real understanding and insight of people and communities. How does one help problem drug users without knowing about their lives from their perspective?

Not surprisingly, one finds many examples of the use of phenomenology in the health and mental health fields. Finlay (2009) suggests that phenomenology addresses the basic questions to be found in Figure 12.1.

It will come as no surprise to find that phenomenology and the word phenomenon are linked. The word phenomenon is common in psychology but its origins are in philosophy where it means the thing as it appears. It is from the Greek for 'appearance' or 'to put into the light of the day'. It refers to any observable occurrence so its use to describe how things appear in our consciousness or conscious experience is understandable. A phenomenon is not the thing in 'the real world' but the thing as it appears in our subjective world – to our consciousness. In phenomenological psychology, then, people's experiences (of the phenomenon in question) are the data. The primary concern is therefore the nature of these experiences – the task of phenomenology is to describe how the phenomenon appears to people. In phenomenology the term *lifeworld* is used to refer to the world that a person experiences through their consciousness and how this is experienced and reflected upon is the focus of phenomenological psychology. Modern phenomenological psychologists regard a person as a conscious participant constructing meaning for their experiences. Not everything is available to our consciousness, of course. There are things which are not accessible but may nevertheless be psychologically important. We can only have access to our conscious experiences and some of these may be beyond expression in verbal terms. These, though, are experiences and may be communicated sometimes by non-verbal means. Things experienced through our consciousness are not to be regarded as linguistic or verbal in nature though usually in research they are expressed in language perhaps in an interview or perhaps in some written statement. Conscious experience, then, is not regarded as a matter of language though language is the medium for communicating about experience.

Phenomenology is a branch of philosophy based primarily on the work of Edmund Husserl (1859–1938) from which phenomenological methods such as phenomenological psychology developed. His basic position can be put simply: the only thing that we humans can reliably know is our conscious experiences. This appears easy enough and it is – deceptively so – but it was not only highly influential in philosophy but, clearly,

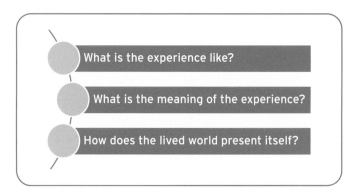

FIGURE 12.1 The basic phenomenology questions according to Finlay (2009)

forms the basis of phenomenological psychology. The central point of phenome-nological research is straightforward and readily understood. A phenomenological researcher studies phenomena and their nature and meaning. The prime focus is on just how phenomena appear to us experientially or in our consciousness. The major strategy is to obtain rich data which are detailed and provide the texture of our expe-riences. Husserl wanted to return to the phenomenon, which is another way of saying that he wanted to know the world as experienced by the individual in their day-to-day lives. He was not so concerned about the things which many modern psychologists have dwelt on – that is, how people think about their experiences. Our attitudes, val-ues and beliefs concerning the things we experience are simply not the experience but our thoughts about our experiences.

Phenomenological psychology seeks to obtain descriptions that their participants give about their experiences. Through these, the phenomenological psychologist attempts to make apparent to themselves the nature of the phenomenon, initially, in the sort of terms or using the sort of language that the participant uses. The hope is to get close to the lived experience of their participant. But there are obstacles to knowing the experiences of other people. One aspect of this is that our understanding of their experience will be affected by things in our own heads – our beliefs, biases, assump-tions, presuppositions, attitudes, opinions and so forth – call them what you will, there are things in our own minds which make it difficult to understand the experiences of others. This stuff needs to be separated out as fully as possible in order to know as purely as possible of the experiences of others. Setting aside these things is not easy and it is unlikely that a full separation can ever be achieved. The researcher wants to understand the experience in its manner of appearing to the participant rather than in its manner of appearing through the eyes of the researcher. This issue was important to Husserl, for obvious reasons, and he suggested the process of bracketing as the way of suspending the influence of our thoughts, etc. so that our understanding of our participant's experiences gets back to the experience as they experienced it – not their experience as we see it from our point of view. The state of being in perfect touch with another person's experiences as they experienced them is known as epoché and is closely connected to bracketing. Husserl proposed methods of reaching this state but, as might be expected, many have cast doubt on the feasibility of achieving epoché. This includes important philosophers who were influenced by Husserl and who helped develop phenomenology but also most phenomenological psychologists.

Husserl's philosophy was holistic in nature and not about the breaking down of the experience into minute component parts – not that in his terms there are such things. This is probably best illustrated by a recollection of Dorion Cairns, one of Husserl's disciples who brought phenomenology to North America. In his writings published after his death, Cairns (2010) recalls vividly one discussion with Husserl:

> I recall particularly one argument about visual perception. I had been defending the doctrine that only perspective appearances are strictly seen. At last Husserl looked down at a box of matches in his hand, turned it this way and that, then, looking me squarely in the eye, reported loudly and distinctly: ' . . . I see the matchbox . . . ' (Cairns, 2010, p. 3)

Cairns wrote that he was startled by this into a recognition of the obvious.

It should be clear from all of this that phenomenology is not about some deep psy-chological, perhaps hidden, rumblings of the psyche – a private world which is not easily shared by others or researchers. This would be a total misconception since it implies psychological phenomena which are removed from the objective world or the real world or the world of reality. So phenomenology is not some obscure variant of psychoanalysis where the interplay of psychological forces needs to be understood in order to make sense of the individual. Husserl's conception, one could say, is far more superficial than that. Consciousness and the experience of phenomena are out there in the world but the subjective experience *is* what can be known and it is not just part of what can be known. Consciousness is about the world in a social, interpersonal and interactive sense. It is this sense of the social in phenomenology which makes it very like most of the other qualitative psychology methods in this book – the emphasis is on what is social rather than the psychology of the inner psychology of an individual. Built into phenomenology are many of the fundamentals of qualitative research in general. Especially important is its rejection of the 'real world' as something which can be known and studied. The real world is not denied in itself; what is denied is that the real world is knowable. What there is to be known is the subjective world as found in the consciousness's experience of phenomena. It is assumed that there is no limit to the number of ways in which ostensibly the same phenomena will be experienced.

One perhaps could describe epoché as the ideal state towards which to aim, but nowadays it is seen as unrealisable in its perfect form. The research will almost certainly have an imperfect knowledge of the person's experiences. It is not possible to slough off one's 'natural attitude' completely for the purposes of research. A view from nowhere (that is to say a positionless point of view) is impossible. This suggests that it is important for the phenomenological psychologist to adopt a self-reflexive point of view in order to understand what it is, which ideally, should be bracketed away from the knowledge of their participants' experiences.

Not all the central ideas in phenomenological psychology come from Edmund Husserl. He had important 'followers' who not only argued vociferously over some of his ideas but, more importantly, had innovative ideas of their own to offer. In particular it was Martin Heidegger (1889–1976) whose reworking of phenomenology was to have a huge impact. His focus was the phenomenological one of understanding 'the things in their appearance'. But his emphasis was more on the nature of existence and what it is to be human. Perhaps this could be described as a philosophy of human nature. Husserl had set about the different task of radically changing the nature of philosophy. Heidegger's new focus was on the context of the person experiencing the world and how they see the world that they experience. This, in a phrase, involved a new emphasis on and concern with the lifeworld. This concept of lifeworld (sometimes called lived world) appeared in Husserl's later writing. However, for those whose focus was existence in the world (i.e. the existentialists) it was even more important as it provided a way of describing the world as experienced by individuals. It is different from the world seen as distinct or separate from the people experiencing it. Rather than seeking to know pure experience, Heidegger and others argued that experience has to be understood as involving embodied and contextualised (situated) persons. For Heidegger it was important to develop methods for interpreting and not merely describing experience. This turn towards interpretation has influenced modern phenomenological psychologists – especially in the form of interpretative phenomenological psychology, which is discussed in detail in the next chapter.

Given the primary focus of phenomenological psychology, it is not surprising to find that methods and procedures have not been standardised in general. Neither is it the case that all forms of phenomenological psychology have exactly the same objectives. There is a sort of continuum of emphasis from that of Husserl, which concentrates on describing the lived experiences in rich detail, to that of Heidegger, which includes an emphasis on trying to understand the meaning underlying the experiences. It is not really possible to have a phenomenological study which is not at some level descriptive. Generally speaking, phenomenological research in psychology adopts the same range of data collection methods as qualitative research in general. The dominant forms of data are probably the qualitative interview and written descriptions of experiences. But any form of data which provides rich information about a person's experiences may be adopted. Furthermore, some, but by no means all, phenomenological researchers might include artistic products such as poems and literature. It also should be added that there are studies which claim to be phenomenological which draw on, for example, modern versions of psychoanalytic concepts. Some might question their status within phenomenology since important theory from outside hardly is in the spirit of the idea of epoché. The major ideas of Husserl's phenomenology are summarised in Box 12.1.

Box 12.1

KEY CONCEPT

The main ideas in Husserl's phenomenology

There are a number of key concepts in Husserl's philosophy, some of which are discussed in the main text of this chapter. It is worthwhile understanding a little more of what Husserl had to say as his ideas occur frequently in phenomenological psychology publications. The most important ideas are probably the following:

- **Reliable knowledge of the world** Fundamental to understanding Husserl's philosophy is the idea that the only knowledge of the world on which we can rely is our conscious experiences. This is in a sense a fundamental principle of qualitative research – that is, there is no knowable real world. This idea of Husserl's that experience is all that can be known clearly contrasts with the more traditional philosophical idea that the mind and the body are distinct. So *it* stands in opposition to the earlier philosophical approach which separated the mind from the outside world but then fell foul of the problem of just how could the mind interact with this outside world? Phenomenological psychology rests on this assumption that experiences are valid knowledge. Mainstream psychologists would refute this on the basis that such experiences are subjective – but that is the point, not a meaningful criticism.

- **Consciousness** This is the stream of experience of phenomena which is purely experience and needs to be separated from other forms of thought. Thus it is pre-reflexive in that it is not a thought-about, considered process. We think about our pure experiences of the phenomenon but these thoughts are not our experience of the phenomena. In Husserl's phenomenology it is important to get back to the experience

as experienced which should not be confused with the experience as thought about, evaluated, embellished and so forth. Bracketing is the process of shedding the influence of thought from the experience of phenomena.

- **Phenomenon** This is from the Greek for 'appearance', 'to show itself', 'to bring into the light of the day', or 'to put into the light', although 'experiences' is also informative in terms of meaning. It really refers to any observable occurrence. As such, it has been used commonly in mainstream psychology but not in the sense in which Husserl meant. Mainstream psychologists would dismiss Husserl's meaning as the experience was in the head of the person experiencing the phenomenon. One can understand it better in the context of phenomenology if we track back to its origins in philosophy. Immanuel Kant (influenced by Leibniz) is credited with introducing the term to philosophy in his *Critique of pure reason* where it was held in apposition to the noumenon. People cannot know the thing in question directly but only through their experiences of it. A noumenon is the thing in question that is to be found in the real world, which, of course, is not really accessible directly as such. The phenomenon is the noumenon as it is experienced by individuals.

- **Intentionality** This is the defining feature of Husserl's consciousness. It refers to consciousness's constant feature of attending to something. That is, consciousness is always of something – it always has an object. If we are not conscious of something then we are not conscious. This something could be a bus, a big bass drum, a person, a thought, etc. Perhaps a better term for intentionality would have been attentionality since this would suggest that consciousness is always attending to something which is a prerequisite of consciousness. Langdridge (2008) explains that the phenomenologist does not conceive of a mind residing inside a body. It is more as if consciousness is turning its light on the world. What the consciousness experiences is what there is to know.

• **The lived world/lifeworld** This is one of Husserl's key concepts though in some senses it is more important to reformists such as Heidegger. It is also a central concept used by phenomenological psychologists. The lifeworld (in German, *Lebenswelt*) is the world that is lived and experienced – the lived world. Experiences within this world are the basis of a phenomenological analysis. Finlay (2009) argues that this lived and experienced world consists of two main things:

  • the world of objects which surround us as they are perceived by us;

  • our experiences of our self, our body and the relationships that we have.

  The lifeworld allows our meaningful existence together in the world. It is the place where interaction between the self and the perceptual world happens. This is not a world of language unlike the focus of many qualitative methods but a world of pure experience. To be sure we think about this experienced

world and articulate it in language but the lived world exists prior to language. In other words, it is a pre-reflective world. The lifeworld indicates that our day-to-day world in which we live is full of meanings. Our actions and interactions in our day-to-day lives are underlain with these meanings. It has to be stressed that the lifeworld is not some totally personal private inner existence accessible only through introspection. The concept of lifeworld should suggest to the researcher the need to pay attention to the lived situation of the person and their social world. Hence, when reading phenomenological writings you will read words to the effect that there is no inner person. People are inevitably part of the social world and can only know themselves on the basis of this outer dimension.

• **Bracketing** This is the process by which the individual or researcher suspends the influence of preconceptions and presuppositions in order to experience the phenomenon in its immediate, direct form without the clouding that theories, beliefs, attitudes and all manner of other influences would bring (see Figure 12.2). Husserl (1913/1931) suggested that bracketing refers to several different things – the following are Finlay's (2009) suggestions about the ones which apply to research:

  • The epoché of the natural sciences – in this the research 'abandons' theories and explanations and knowledge and returns to an unreflective apprehension of the everyday lived world. Epoché is from the Greek for 'stay away' or 'abstinence'.

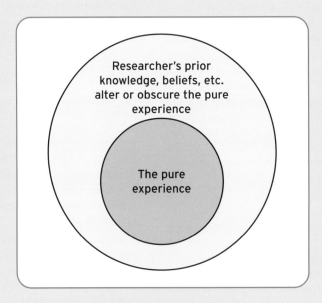

FIGURE 12.2 The problem of separating out pure experience

- In phenomenological psychology reduction where belief in the reality of objects is replaced by a subjectivity of appreciation of meanings and experiences.
- Husserl's transcendental phenomenological reduction – a more radical version of epoché in which a 'God's-eye view' is attempted – though modern researchers see this as unrealistic.

This having been said, one of the consequences is that it is a basic assumption of most phenomenological psychologists that it is not possible to detach a researcher from the presuppositions that they hold. It is wrong to pretend otherwise. Nevertheless, the implication is that the researcher should be continually aware of the issue in their work.

- *Epoché* This is essentially the state of freedom from presuppositions. That is, the condition when the researcher will be best able to get close to the individual's experience of the phenomenon. The phenomenological attitude is to return to 'the things in their appearing'. This involves the researcher doing the following, according to Langdridge (2008):

- Keeping the basic task of the research to capture a description of the phenomenon, rather than seeking to explain. Rushing into explanations including causal explanations or using prior theory is inappropriate and to be avoided.
- Horizontalising experience, by which he means treating all its features as equally important until the analysis has progressed substantially.

The development of phenomenology

The development of phenomenology is a substantial aspect of the development of Western philosophy over the last 250 years or so. More so than any other qualitative method, phenomenological psychology has its roots in that history and cannot be understood without understanding these philosophical origins. Phenomenology has something to say about how we know about the world and it could be described as the science or study of the pure phenomenon. The meaning of this is not, in itself, transparent, and needs some explication to be clear. A starting point is the French philosopher Descartes' dualism of the body. René Descartes (1596–1650) was perhaps the major figure in developing the discipline of philosophy. His idea was that the body could be considered to be a machine – that it is matter with material properties and thus followed the laws of nature which science was there to fathom out. In contrast, there is the soul (or mind) which is not matter and so does not follow the laws of nature. An animal, he asserted, does not have a mind (soul), which is an exclusively human characteristic. Descartes felt that the point at which the body and mind interact was the pineal gland in the brain. His reason for this was that, at the time, the pineal gland was thought to be a unitary or homogeneous structure and he also regarded the soul or mind as a homogeneous structure. Mainly the soul controls the body but there are circumstances where the body influences the mind. When we act emotionally then this is the body influencing the mind. In short, Descartes' view was that objects exist independently of the mind – that there is a mind and there is a physical world. The search to understand the material world is the domain of science and so Descartes' philosophy could be said to be a bedrock of support for scientific endeavour.

Put another way, Descartes can be seen as postulating that the mind can know the real/material/external world – the function of the senses is to reveal to the mind what is in the outside world. And here, of course, is the problem. How do we know that the mind can tap into the material world in this way? It is a supposition, an assumption, which is impossible to confirm. Just how can a material part of the brain (such as the pineal gland) interact with a non-material mind or soul? That, in a nutshell, is the focus of the body–mind problem but, more generally, the dilemma is knowing how the mind (soul) which is non-material gain access the material world – how can the material and non-material interact. Mental phenomena, it could be argued, seem to be qualitatively different from the material body on which they depend. So how can this interaction happen? Descartes' separation of the body and mind is often referred to as Cartesian dualism (see Figure 12.3) – Cartesian being a reference to Descartes. Of course, Descartes' view of the mind and the material world is denied by most qualitative researchers, who argue that there are many viewpoints on the real world. There are ways around this dilemma, of course, such as regarding both as being aspects of the mind or regarding both as aspects of the material world. Such monist (as opposed to dualist) approaches are familiar in mainstream psychology and science in general such as where the mind is equated with a machine-like computer. But neither of these alternative ideas impacted on philosophy in the way that Husserl's phenomenology did. To be clear, Descartes identified the problem in its modern form which is still with us today. In his later work (*Meditations on first philosophy*) Descartes cast doubt on all of his original ideas. He wanted to know just what he could reliably know for certain. For example, he might be dreaming his material existence but his mind or soul could not be dreamt as it is the essence of his self.

Among others who cast doubt on mind–body dualism and in so doing influenced the future development of phenomenology are the German philosophers Immanuel Kant (1724–1804) and Georg Wilhelm Friedrich Hegel (1770–1831). Neither saw value in the idea of an objective physical world about which we could know. Equally important in the development of phenomenology was Franz Brentano (1838–1917). He provided some of the basic ideas of phenomenology including the key argument that consciousness was intentional – put in practical terms this means that consciousness was always consciousness of something. Brentano's important student was Edmund Husserl whose concern was with what we could know reliably about 'the material world'. His answer was that what could be experienced through consciousness is certain knowledge. Consciousness was the seat of reliable knowledge and so reliable knowledge comes from knowing what consciousness experiences. What we could know about through our consciousness was what we could know about. Consciousness is just one aspect of people's mental processes – it is easier for you to know what is meant by it than it is to define exactly what Husserl meant. We can think and cogitate about our experiences but conscious experiences are more basic than that and lack the cognitive involvement that most forms of thinking do. Consciousness is not a language-based concept as such in phenomenology.

There are seemingly fanciful explanations for the development of phenomenology but they can be traced back to Husserl in his Vienna lectures. This is that Europe

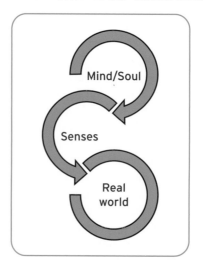

FIGURE 12.3 Cartesian dualism illustrated

was ruined and in turmoil following the First World War as were the ideological and cultural constraints which had previously given a sense of order. Science was increasingly questioned for its 'sterile' positivism which rejoiced in cataloguing facts while philosophy was dominated by the same positivism together with a subjectivism which led nowhere (Eagleton, 1983). Husserl said:

> How does it happen that no scientific medicine has ever developed in this sphere, a medicine for nations and supranational communities? . . . The European nations are sick; Europe itself, it is said, is in crisis. (Husserl, 1954/1970, p. 270).

Against this backdrop, Husserl's ideas could be seen as an attempt to represent certainty amid this endless disintegration of what had been stability before. Husserl was against the idea that we can have reliable information about things in the world. That is, objects in the external world exist independently of the subjective world. What we can be certain about, however, is the way we experience objects in our consciousness. This is the basis of phenomenology and the fundamental point when considering Husserl's philosophy. However, this brings a big problem with it. In order to know with certainty about experiences, things outside of immediate experience have to be kept out – that is they have to be ignored or excluded. In other words, if we let our thought confound our experiences then we have not got back to the pure experience. Husserl's phenomenology has a very concrete objective – to know the phenomenon as experienced by consciousness. The only 'reality' that we can know is the 'pure' phenomenon. Consciousness or intentional experience, it is said, is always of something. Consciousness cannot be of nothing. So intentional experience is always of something.

It was Husserl's famous student Martin Heidegger who provided another key idea in phenomenology. This was the concept of *'Dasein'*. Translated, the meaning of this is 'Being there'. So both men, Husserl and Heidegger, explored the lived world or lifeworld (*Lebenswelt*) which is a person's experience in the ordinary world. For Heidegger, hermeneutics or the study of meaning was a vital prerequisite of phenomenology (Shinebourne, 2011). There are meanings to what is experienced which are hidden or concealed by the manner in which the phenomenon appears in consciousness. This links phenomenology clearly to hermeneutics which is about uncovering meanings in texts. (There is more on this in Chapter 13 on IPA.) So for Heidegger phenomenology was only partly about the manner in which a phenomenon appears in consciousness – it is also about the meaning underlying this manner of appearing. Thus phenomenology must reveal what is hidden by the appearance of the phenomenon. Merleau-Ponty (1968) maintained that what appears in experience has a layer of the invisible – that is the reality of experience. So the process of making manifest what is hidden can be thought of as a matter of interpretation: hence the emphasis of some IPA theorists on interpretation. For Heidegger:

> That which can be articulated in interpretation and thus even more primordially in discourse is what we have called 'meaning' . . . The way in which discourse gets expressed is language (Heidegger, 1962, pp. 203–4)

But meaning is a basic human capacity so what can be revealed is a consequence of the person already being in the world. Previous experience will have its influence on experiences. Interpretation then depends on or is grounded in something that we already have in advance of the experience. So interpretation is based on what has gone before – terms such as fore-having, fore-sight and fore-conception are used for this in the phenomenological psychology literature. Thus experience is in some way involved with our understanding of the world. From understanding this involvement we begin to interpret the meaning of the phenomenon.

Heidegger's style of philosophy was existential in nature and became the background of the existential philosophy of Jean-Paul Sartre (1905–80) as well as the work of Maurice Merleau-Ponty (1908–61). To a degree, phenomenology was a flourishing discipline in the work of these two men for about a quarter of a century after the Second World War. Nevertheless, by about 1970 it was difficult to assess the impact of phenomenology on psychological research. The traditional natural sciences approach still dominated.

There is little doubt that most modern phenomenological psychologists pay allegiance to Husserl and Heidegger. This begs the question of how phenomenology became part of psychology. This is a difficult question to answer. One can search for the origins of the term phenomenology in psychology. In which case the answer would be that phenomenology was a term used as far back as the nineteenth century. But this pre-dates Husserl's work. Another issue in relation to this is whether the work has any similarities to the work of Husserl and the degree of similarity that would be involved. Giorgi (2010), an important figure in phenomenological psychology himself, gives a detailed history of phenomenology in psychology but one conclusion is clear from his review: phenomenology is a temporary if not ephemeral specialism in university departments of psychology. That is to say, Giorgi noted that where phenomenology was taught and researched this usually lasted just a generation of academic staff before it was replaced by something else. So phenomenology had difficulty establishing itself as part of the academic life. Mostly, phenomenological psychologists, however, mention the work of Amedeo P. Giorgi (1931–), himself, as being the first major inroad of Husserl's phenomenology into academic psychology. It should be made clear, however, that other psychologists had adopted phenomenology before this time (see Chapters 1 and 2).

Giorgi began his career, inevitably, in mainstream psychology about which he became increasingly critical. In the 1960s he became a professor in the psychology department of Duquesne University which already had established a strong interest in phenomenology as had the philosophy department there too. He read extensively, searching for alternatives to mainstream psychology, including the works of Husserl, Heidegger and Merleau-Ponty. Giorgi's achievement, more than anything else, was to develop a praxis of phenomenology which could be used by psychologists – that is, he developed a system of workable methods for doing phenomenological psychology. In doing so he showed the psychologists just how to do Husserlian phenomenological psychology rather than merely write about it. (See Box 12.2 for more details about Giorgi's method.)

Box 12.2
KEY CONCEPT
Giorgi's method of phenomenological psychology

Amedeo Giorgi's method of doing phenomenological analysis is thoroughly wedded to the ideas of Husserl. Giorgi intended to create a rigorous descriptive empirical phenomenology. The source of the ideas was Husserl's method of studying the essential structures or the essences of the phenomena as they appear in consciousness (Giorgi, 1985a, 1994). Consequently it is frequently remarked that his is a catalogue-like 'descriptive' approach to phenomenology. In this, as with Husserl, the researcher's main aim is to provide a very detailed description of the phenomenon itself (Giorgi, 1971). The process is one of first of all describing the phenomenon as experienced by the individual with as much fidelity as possible to the original experience. These descriptions are collected from a number of individuals and combined in order to describe the phenomenon itself as fully as possible. He also was committed to avoiding pre-suppositions and the like which were to be bracketed-out in Husserl's terms. Giorgi's focus was on the perspective of those who experience social and psychological phenomena. So his primary source of data are the descriptions that others provide rather than the researcher's own experiences.

The essential essence involves the identification, descriptively, of the invariant characteristics of a phenomenon and its meanings. Giorgi (1985a, 1994) drew on Husserl's idea of studying essential structures/essences of the phenomenon as it was experienced through consciousness. The essential essence is known also as the eidetic reduction. It is a description of what the phenomenologist has identified as the invariant characteristics of the phenomenon as experienced, together with the meanings of these experiences. The starting point is a concrete example of the phenomenon that is being investigated. The researcher takes this and systematically varies it in their imagination in a number of ways. By doing so, the researcher hopes to identify what are the essential features of the phenomenon and what are particular to individuals, accidental or incidental. This is the process of imaginative variation.

Giorgi's method can use any written text but the use of interviews to obtain data is common. Poetry and literature, in contrast, are rare. In Giorgi's style of phenomenology, participants are asked to give concrete descriptions or examples of their experiences. This clearly makes the approach empirical as it yields a description of the essential structures of lived experience. However, this is not an idiographic approach as the researcher may begin with the idiographic but this then helps them develop a general structure of the phenomenon or the essence of the phenomenon. This is based on a number of participants, not just one individual as in idiography. So the end point is an explication of the phenomenon as a whole and the concern is not with the individuals who contributed to this. The idiographic is only a means to the end of achieving an understanding as a whole of the phenomenon involved. The method also uses reduction or the suspension of one's beliefs so that the researcher can get close to the experience of the phenomena themselves. Giorgi (1985b) provides four key steps for the analysis using his method (see Figure 12.4). These are:

• Read the entire description of the experiences. Try to obtain a full or complete impression of the content or, in other words, a sense of what the description contained.

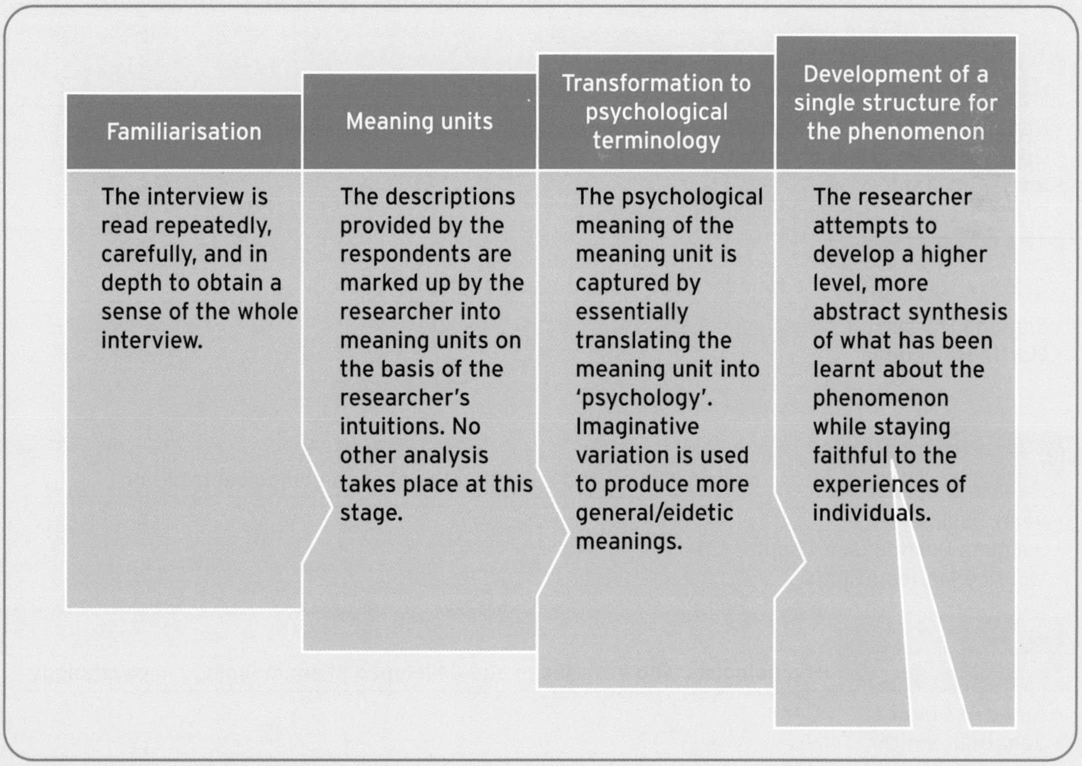

FIGURE 12.4 Giorgi's analytic stages

- Using a broadly psychological perspective, identify the units of meaning contained within the description.

- Translate or transform the everyday language used by the participant in making the description into more psychological terms.

- The meaning units arrived at in the previous stage are transformed themselves into a statement of the nature of the structure of the phenomenon – the dimensions of experience if you will. This is initially

done for individuals but then the analysis seeks to integrate the experiences of all participants. So the analysis proceeds to seek common themes across the individual structural statements. The general statement based on these is essentially the meaning of the phenomenon.

Box 12.3 later in the chapter gives a detailed research example of the use of Giorgi's phenomenological psychology method.

Phenomenology can be said to have taken a hold in psychology although it is just a niche. Perhaps the most important development since Giorgi's innovations has been IPA. This is the focus of Chapter 13, which should be consulted for more of the story of phenomenology in psychology. It is not that IPA is the only recent approach to phenomenology but it is one which has attracted a number of adherents in a number of fields of psychology – health, social psychology, community psychology and the like as well as other fields such as nursing. The number of publications is impressive. But phenomenology is open to change and innovation given its basic and central aim – to document human experience. The extent to which different styles of modern

---

Progenitors   These had an important influence on later key figures.

- René Descartes (Husserl's work was fundamentally opposed to Cartesian ideas)
- Georg Wilhelm Friedrich Hegel
- Immanuel Kant
- Franz Brentano (Husserl's academic mentor)

Key figures   The founders of the main ideas of phenomenology

- Edmund Husserl
- Martin Heidegger

Those influenced   Those who continued and extended the phenomenological tradition

- Jean-Paul Sartre
- Jacques Derrida (see Chapter 13)
- Maurice Merleau-Ponty

Key psychologists   Psychologists who introduced and developed phenomenology in psychology

- Amedeo Giorgi
- Jonathan Smith

FIGURE 12.5 The line of phenomenology's influence into modern psychology

phenomenological psychology rest firmly on the shoulders of Husserl and Heidegger might be questioned. Nevertheless, in the writings of phenomenologists there are numerous echoes back to these philosophers. Knowing something of the history of phenomenology will help you to recognise them when they occur. Phrases such as 'things in their appearing', 'it is of experience that language speaks' and 'there is no inner man, man is in the world, and only in the world does he know himself' litter the phenomenological psychology literature and hark back to the words of Husserl, Heidegger, Merleau-Ponty and others. Figure 12.5 provides a summary of the important influences on and of phenomenology.

How to do phenomenological research

A research epistemology is the theory of knowledge employed by the researcher. It determines how something will be studied by a researcher. Phenomenological psychology is strong on epistemology – Husserl made sure of that – but less clear about just how a phenomenological psychology study should proceed. How does one impose research techniques on a phenomenon? To impose techniques is to impose a particular definition or characteristic on the phenomenon. This may be inappropriate and may explain the willingness of phenomenological psychologists to be very open in terms of appropriate methods for doing phenomenological research. Although it is perhaps something which in general is a positive feature, it is also the very thing which a newcomer to phenomenological research does not want to hear – they would much prefer, probably, to find that there was a single, well-defined method for doing phenomenology. But this is to misunderstand phenomenological research which is defined by its subject-matter and not particular research techniques. One does not need to delve too deeply into psychological phenomenological research to realise that the phenomenological method is largely the questions asked and the broad method of addressing them rather than particular ways of obtaining data and analysing it. So you will find a number of different ways of collecting data employed by phenomenological psychologists. It appears to be the case that every type of data collection technique available to qualitative psychologists in general can have a place in phenomenological research. Interviews and written descriptions are possibly the most frequently used in phenomenological psychology.

Some phenomenological psychologists carry out a phenomenological study on themselves. This, historically, was a common practice in phenomenology. However, frequently these self-studies are used as a sort of trial study in order to begin to understand the phenomenon better prior to a study proper on a sample of research participants. This has a number of advantages, including helping the researcher develop appropriate language with which to communicate about the phenomenon. It may also encourage a more empathic understanding of what the participants experience. These may be sufficient reason for you to undertake such a self-study before engaging in phenomenological psychology of a more formal nature. Another possibility is that it will help you make yourself aware of your own presuppositions which need to be bracketed-out of your understanding of what your participants have to say. But there is no requirement in phenomenological psychology that such a pre-study should take place. Furthermore, there are questions to be asked about whether such self-studies provide too much by way of idiosyncratic ideas about the phenomenon or whether they help the process of bracketing-out prior beliefs, suppositions and other thoughts. It is unlikely, however, that the phenomenological psychologist will not go on to study other people in their research.

There are some procedures which are peculiarly phenomenological in nature and not routinely applied in other qualitative methods. Bracketing, just mentioned, is probably the most characteristic phenomenological procedure. This is true whether or not the researcher is completely committed to Husserl's idea that through bracketing and epoché it is possible to achieve a 'God's-eye view' of another person's experiences. Other qualitative researchers do not use the term bracketing but employ other methods in order to avoid the influence of their presuppositions on their analysis. When the grounded theorist processes their data repeatedly then this is intended to avoid jumping to easy and obvious conclusions. Another method, again discussed earlier, which can be said to be characteristically phenomenological is that of imaginative variation in which the researcher systematically and variedly pushes their understanding of a phenomenon in order to understand the limits of the phenomenon. Simple examples of this from geometry would be to ask when is a circle not a circle? Maybe if the figure contained a straight edge then this would stop it being a circle. Or it could be when the height is not the same as the width. Applied to other concepts such as love, the point of imaginative variation becomes clearer. If the relationship involves violence then is it love?

It is worthwhile repeating here that, in general, phenomenological psychology is not ideographic in character. The purpose of phenomenology is not primarily to understand the individual's experiences of the world – that would be regarded as subjective. The task of phenomenology is to understand the structure of the phenomenon itself. As such, the phenomenologist is not observing a single individual. There is a slight problem in that in its initial stages a phenomenological study may seem to be ideographic since the experiences of a single individual are studied and the structure of their experiences analysed. But this is generally only an intermediary step since several people will be studied in this way in all probability. The final stage is putting these various structures together to present a general view of how the phenomenon in question is experienced. This quite simply is an end point which is not idiographic in intention or effect – it is a study of the phenomenon in itself. It should be added here, though, that such a view depends on adherence to Husserlian notions and so you will find so-called phenomenological studies which are idiographic in that they concentrate on the experiences of one individual. Phenomenology is a broad church, so 'rules' for what is and what is not appropriate in a phenomenological study are hard to find. It is important to realise that under the umbrella of phenomenology are many types of study which differ markedly in terms of their adherence to the views of luminaries such as Husserl and Heidegger.

What is being aimed at in a good phenomenological study is knowledge of the lived experience of individuals which then leads to an understanding of the structure of the phenomenon itself. It is this focus on how things are experienced which sets phenomenology aside from other qualitative methods. So phenomenology is a qualitative methodology with a particular subject matter for its focus – it is not a broad strategy for doing qualitative analysis as thematic analysis or grounded theory are. Perhaps the closest approach to it is narrative analysis (Chapter 14) which some phenomenological psychologists classify as a form of phenomenological analysis. The major difference is that narrative is about the storied nature of people's lives whereas phenomenological psychology is about their experiences as they appear. People's experiences expressed in a narrative form provide a somewhat processed version of the experiences – somewhat removed from Husserl's ideas. Other qualitative analysis methods might be useful in making sense of the experiences of participants as described to the researcher. Indeed, a version of thematic analysis is an essential component of IPA (Chapter 13).

Our description of how to do a phenomenological study uses a framework offered by Groenewald (2004), adapted wherever necessary. Groenewald offered his suggestions as just that and he had no intention to dictate or prescribe a fixed way of doing phenomenological research. The steps based on Groenewald's framework are as follows.

Step 1 — Ensure that you have a broad understanding of the nature of phenomenological research The phenomenological method is only appropriate when your intention is to study how things in the world are experienced. If you are planning a biographical study of an individual, for example, and their lives then phenomenology may not be appropriate. Such a study might focus on the way the individual thinks about their situation and their interpretations of what is happening to them. This is not a phenomenological study but might pass as one among psychologists who know nothing of Husserl and Heidegger's ideas.

Step 2 — The phenomenological researcher does not usually formulate their research question in great detail To do so risks structuring what emerges in their research too much and so interfering with the task of knowing the participants 'in the manner of their appearing'. Indeed, having expectations about the nature of the phenomenon experienced is not part of the Husserlian fundamentals of phenomenology.

Step 3 — The nature of the phenomenon being considered in the research determines which participants should be sought for the study The availability of a certain sort of individual, however, should not be allowed to determine which phenomenon will be studied, according to Groenewald. Probability sampling will almost certainly be inappropriate whereas some form of purposive sampling is likely. The researcher, then, needs to seek out individuals who have experienced the phenomenon in question. Snowball sampling might supplement this as it is a way of getting participants to nominate people they know who also have had experience of the phenomenon. Purposive sampling allows the researcher to try things such as telephone enquiries and Internet searches to help locate more participants. For example, if the researcher was interested in partner abuse then support groups for such individuals might be approached for help. Groenewald argues that something between two and ten participants may be sufficient to reach 'saturation' (see Chapter 8). Saturation is when nothing new of interest is emerging in the later interviews compared to earlier ones. So do not regard a sample of ten as the upper limit since more may be needed in particular studies. The interviews, however, are likely to be long as there is a great deal of detail to be extracted from the participants. The sample may consist of two or more subgroups which differ in important respects that might result in different findings. Groenewald sees this as a form of triangulation: if the *structure* of the phenomenon is the same in each of these groups then this can be seen as a form of validation for a phenomenological study.

Step 4 — Some form of unstructured phenomenological interview is likely to be the preferred mode of data collection The most likely alternative to the interview would be extended written accounts provided by participants of their experiences of the phenomenon. Either way, it is essential that the questions posed encourage the rich detailed descriptions of the phenomena which phenomenology requires. In other words, a great deal of preparation will go into ensuring that the participant talks in detail at length or writes copiously. Although the focus of the data collected will be on the phenomenon as experienced, data collection usually stretches wider than this. That is, anything which may be helpful in understanding the experiences may be part of the data collected. You may wish to introduce the interview with a brief explanation of what it is you want to know about. This, of course, will stress that the primary thing you are interested in is the individual's experience of the phenomenon in question. Some aspects which might be explored are given in Figure 12.6.

Normally the detailed descriptions of the individual's experiences of the phenomenon are obtained first – only later should the researcher allow the more reflexive aspects to be introduced by the participants. So start with a direct question about the experience (e.g. How did/do you experience redundancy?). Concrete examples of experiences should be requested frequently during the course of the interview. Broad impressions and generalisations are *not* the sort of level of detail required in a phenomenological study. Hence, specific, detailed examples should feature strongly in the data. Phenomenological interviews are quite lengthy as a consequence of these requirements. Of course, the interviews are recorded. Essentially the phenomenological

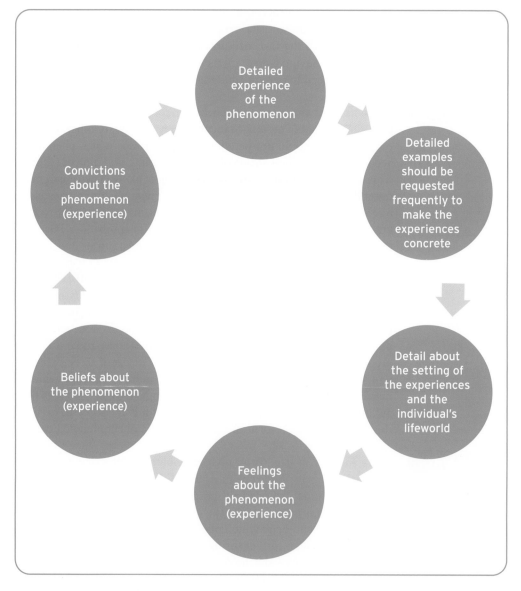

FIGURE 12.6 Some aspects of the phenomenon which may be included in a phenomenological interview

interview can take the form of an informal dialogue – it is reciprocal in nature so simply reading out a list of questions is not what the researcher does. At the same time, the researcher must be aware that they play a role in the construction of the dialogue. As a consequence, the researcher should feel under an obligation to understand what their constructive role is in any particular interview. One approach to the phenomenological interview is the intentional-expressive approach of Anderberg (Anderberg, 2000; Sin, 2010). This technique is useful for obtaining meanings of concepts used by the participant and confirming that the researcher has properly understood them. Basically the interview starts with questions concerning the phenomenon under study. Follow-up questions are used to help the interviewee reflect on the conceptual meaning of terms and phrases that they have employed. So the researcher may interrupt and ask the meaning of any concept that the participant uses – the researcher does not assume that they share the meaning of concepts with the interviewee. In their joint exploration in the phenomenological interview, the topic is explored together by the researcher and the participant. The influence of the researcher is minimised using a number of techniques (Sin, 2010). Key aspects of the intentional-expressive approach to phenomenological interview are to be found in Figure 12.7.

Step 5   It is an appropriate strategy to encourage the participants to try to separate out the pure experience from the more interpretative and evaluative thoughts that are likely to fill their heads. That is, the participants are encouraged to bracket-out all perspectives but the immediate one of their experience of the phenomenon. This means that the participant needs to use language as devoid of intellectual and social ideas as possible.

Rule 1
- The meanings of the expressions and concepts used by the participant are not taken for granted and the researcher avoids making assumptions about these meanings. The temptation is, of course, to assume that certain meanings are simply obvious. Instead the researcher asks follow-up questions in order to extract what the intended meaning was.

Rule 2
- The researcher should not introduce new terms into the conversation. At the same time, should the participant use what the researcher believes is the wrong terminology then the researcher must not correct what the participant said by suggesting a more accurate expression as the researcher sees it.

Rule 3
- The researcher's manner should be attentive and empathic. Once they have posed a question, the researcher must give time to the the participant for them to reflect on the matter and talk about it. This giving of space applies to both reflection and talk. The researcher must also deliberately refrain from facial expressions of agreement or disagreement with the participant's response.

Rule 4
- Leading questions by the researcher are to be avoided. Direct questions suggesting a particular answer or line of thought are inappropriate. Instead the researcher should ask directly about the phenomenon – what is depression like? rather than, is depression different from sadness? The researcher should also avoid asking leading questions. For instance, interviewees were not asked whether they think actual accounting work is different from what they learn at university. Questions can be asked in more than one way in order to encourage rich data containing elaborate descriptions.

FIGURE 12.7 Summary of the intentional-expressive approach to phenomenological interviewing

Step 6   It is important to remember that in phenomenological research the task of the researcher is to know the individual's experiences of the phenomenon and, additionally, reveal what meaning there is in those human experiences. This meets both Husserl's and Heidegger's requirements. What should appear in the analysis is a description of a particular person's experiences as they experienced it and so the researcher must encourage the interviewee to let the essence of the person's experiences emerge. Groenewald recommends using the qualitative procedure of memoing, as is common in other forms of qualitative research, especially grounded theory. The memo is the researcher's field notes concerning what they saw, heard, experienced and thought in the process of data collection. The memo should include both descriptive notes and more reflexive impressions, hunches, ideas and feelings according to Groenewald. The researcher needs to maintain an open stance towards their data throughout the research process.

Step 7   Although this is not absolutely necessary in phenomenological analysis where repeated listening to and processing the original recording may suffice, the data normally should be transcribed using whatever transcription method seems appropriate. Jefferson transcription would normally be avoided but there is no strong reason why it should not be used other than it is time consuming and may add nothing over secretarial-style transcription in this context. The focus, of course, in phenomenology is on the content of the interview, not on the manner of communication. The transcript can be checked together with the participant at any subsequent attempts at analysis.

Data analysis

Groenewald suggests that instead of the term 'data analysis', a better description would be 'explication of the data'. His reason for this is that this latter phrase lacks the implication of breaking the data into parts. Breaking into parts might result in a loss of the integrity or wholeness of the experience of the phenomenon. Groenewald recommends a five part process based on the approach of Hycner (1999). This is illustrated in Figure 12.8 and detailed below.

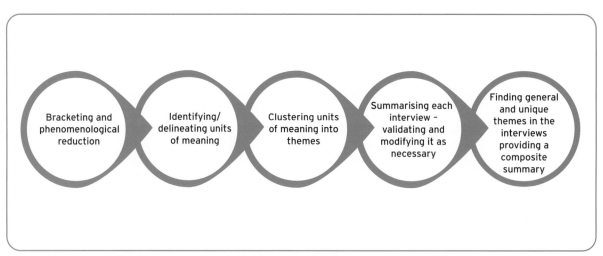

FIGURE 12.8 Steps in phenomenological analysis or explication

| Step 1 | **Bracketing and phenomenological reduction** As explained in the earlier sections of this chapter, phenomenological reduction is the way in which the researcher can be open to the phenomenon itself which in itself has meaning. It is the idea that the phenomenon is viewed from no position – from nobody's point of view. The researcher's own presuppositions are entirely suspended and the researcher's meanings, presuppositions and theoretical concepts are not allowed to impinge on their view of the special experiences of the participant. This is not the same as bracketing employed with the participant during the interview. It is recommended that the researcher should listen repeatedly to the interview recording until they become familiar with the words of the participant. In this way a holistic feeling for the experiences of the participant can be achieved. The 'here and now' aspect of the participant's experiences give them a sense of existential immediacy according to Groenwald. |

| Step 2 | **Delineating units of meaning** This involves making a list of statements or descriptions provided by the participant which seem to best characterise and illuminate their experiences of the phenomenon under study. They can be copied from the transcript of the interview or simply written down if the researcher has decided not to transcribe. Isolating the units of meaning from the interview clearly involves judgement on the part of the researcher. This has to be made at the same time as the researcher is suspending their own presuppositions, otherwise the judgements may be subjective in a Husserlian sense. This list of units of meaning extracted from each of the interviews is then rescrutinised. Any clearly redundant units are discarded. In order to eliminate redundant units the literal content of each unit of meaning must be reviewed together with the frequency that a particular unit of meaning was mentioned. In addition, how the unit of meaning was presented in the interview in terms of non-verbal cues and paralinguistic cues is also taken into account in judging the similarity between units of meaning. It may be found that two superficially similar units of meaning may be actually very different in terms of the weight they are given in the interview or in terms of the sequence of events described by the participant. |

| Step 3 | **Clustering of units of meaning into themes** At this stage the researcher has a list of units of meaning from which redundant ones have been eliminated. In the full holistic context of what the researcher knows from the participant, the researcher attempts to come up with the essential features of the meaning units before them. This is a stage which cannot be delineated in detail as it involves insight. Developing an awareness of the essential features of the list of meaning units is once again a matter of judgement but it is also something that the experienced researcher will find easier than the novice. The units of meaning will be grouped together into clusters much as in some other forms of qualitative research. So there should be a frequent and strenuous process of going backwards and forwards between the clusters that are being built up and the data in the form of tape recording (or the transcript). From these clusters, the researcher can proceed to identify particularly important or significant themes. These are known as units of significance. The clusters do not need to be entirely distinct from each other and there may well be a degree of overlap between different clusters. The nature of the various clusters allows central themes to be suggested to express what is essential about the clusters. |

Some researchers find it useful to adopt Ashworth's (2003) approach to analysis which suggests that the lifeworld consists of a number of essential aspects known as fractions. Quite simply, the researcher needs to consider each fraction in turn when considering the data. The fractions are given in Figure 12.9.

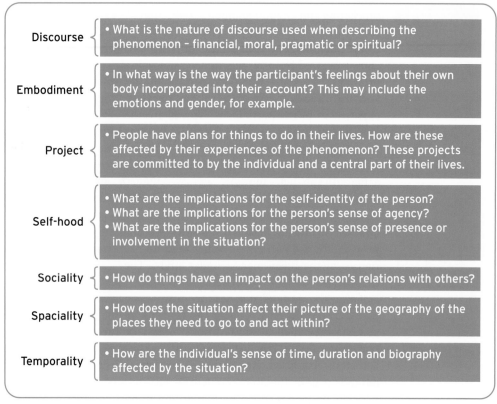

FIGURE 12.9 The seven fractions of the lifeworld according to Ashworth (2003)

Step 4   Summarise each interview, validate and modify The themes which emerge in each interview should be summarised in terms of the holistic context provided by the participant about their lived experiences. It is the world of the participant's experience which needs to be captured in the summary. But remember that phenomenology is not an idiographic discipline and so it is necessary to reconstruct these worlds of experience in relation to each other. Each individual may have a different way of experiencing time, space and material things but each of these should be understood in more general terms in order to capture the essence of the phenomenon. At this stage, a 'validity check' is carried out. Basically the participant is consulted in order to see if the interview's essence has been effectively captured. Modifications may have to be made.

Step 5   General and unique themes for all the interviews and composite summary The final stage is for the researcher to identify the themes which are universal or very common in the individual interviews. At the same time, the ways in which individuals depart from these common themes also should be identified. Avoid suggesting common themes if significant differences better characterise the data. So minority voices should also be brought out as they may effectively counterpoint what in general has emerged. Ultimately, the researcher must bring all of this together by writing a composite summary, emphasising and reflecting the context of the themes identified. At this point, the researcher transforms the language of the participant into a mode of expression which is appropriate for an academic presentation. Speculative exploration beyond the confines of the data may be appropriate.

Box 12.4 later in the chapter describes another approach to phenomenological psychological analysis.

When to use phenomenology

Unlike the methods discussed in earlier chapters, phenomenology is defined in terms of the study of a particular sort of content – a characteristic which it shares with IPA (Chapter 13) and narrative analysis (Chapter 14). It is the study of content and not of the way language is used in relation to this content. Since phenomenology is essentially the study of people's experiences in their lifeworld, then phenomenology should be considered as a possible approach whenever we wish to study people's experiences. There is a slight problem with this: shouldn't such a psychology be called existential psychology rather than phenomenology? The clue is, perhaps, in the name. Phenomenological psychology has its roots in the writings of Husserl, especially when taken together with Heidegger and others. So if you are planning to use phenomenology then you are taking on board some of their theoretical baggage which may sit uncomfortably with a study which dwells on people's evaluations of things rather than detailed descriptions of their experiences. To be sure, there are studies which claim to be phenomenological but which seem not to have been touched at all by Husserl's ideas. We can't do much about them but we can do something about the integrity of the research that we do.

What is the point of adopting a Husserlian approach to research? Well, for one thing research which is informed by theory usually has more than just an edge over research of purely empirical intent. So often the framework of a theory provides support to research which is not merely interesting but makes issues clearer. More than anything, phenomenology rejoices in being a descriptive methodology. This in the context of the broader context of psychology can be regarded as a virtue. Too often has psychology sought to explain things without knowing what those things are. This is impossible from within the phenomenological framework. Furthermore, phenomenology adds a discipline to research which focuses on the role of the researcher. The researcher is posed the dilemma of just how to know the experiences of the participant through that person's eyes – that is, without adopting the viewpoint of the researcher. This is bound to encourage a reflexive attitude to their research in anyone who takes the strictures of phenomenology seriously.

There are alternatives to phenomenology, especially narrative psychology but this has taken a lot from phenomenology. The contrast is simple – the lived life of experiences or the storied life of the narrative. They are different – or to Husserl they would be very different. Of course, other types of qualitative research would have their own perspective on the data collected in a phenomenological study – discourse analysis and conversation analysis would be sceptical of the interviews as providing content and would ask questions about how people talk about experience.

This aside, for anyone interested in people's lived experiences, phenomenology provides a challenging framework on which to build research into some fascinating topics.

Examples of phenomenological analysis

Boxes 12.3 and 12.4 present different ways of using phenomenology. They are as follows:

- The first example (Box 12.3) is simply an example of Giorgi's approach to phenomenology. It concerns the experiences associated with heart bypass surgery.
- The second example (Box 12.4) is a phenomenology-based study of plagiarism. You may recognise some of the comments as being similar to your own or those of your friends.

Box 12.3

ILLUSTRATIVE RESEARCH STUDY

Giorgi's method applied to couples experiencing heart bypass surgery

Whitsitt's (2009) study is a good and typical example of phenomenological psychology which adheres closely to the methodology of Giorgi (2000). This is known as the descriptive phenomenological psychological method. So you should expect a very Husserlian type of analysis which focuses on describing the joint experience of couples, one member of which was in the process of undergoing a serious heart operation. Giorgi's methods focus, as would Husserl, on obtaining data on the experience of the phenomenon in question in great detail. The analysis follows the procedure given in Figure 12.9. With an analysis based on Giorgi's methods one can expect very substantial quantities of descriptive material to be given together with an account of the general structure of the phenomenon under study.

As is common knowledge, a diagnosis of coronary heart disease is frequent in the Western world where it is a major killer. One of the standard medical procedures for coronary heart disease is known as coronary artery bypass graft surgery (CABG), though we will refer to it as bypass surgery. Quantitative research is plentiful on the topic but qualitative research is much less common. Among the findings is that heart surgery patients suffer increased levels of emotional stress both prior to the surgery and after. Their marital relationships tend to suffer because of issues to do with ambivalence, anger, dependency, depression and resentment. Following surgery stress is common and the result of a number of factors including financial burdens following illness, problems of adapting to new roles after the surgery such as those of patient and caregiver, the well-partner is likely to increase their vigilance of the patient, and the couple's sex lives tend also to suffer.

The author suggests that his approach was discovery-orientated. The time-frame of the study was from the time the couple were informed of the need for surgery to several months or years after that surgery. The research focused on the shared meaning of the couples – not the

meanings specific to either the patient or spouse. By shared meanings is meant the congruent beliefs that a couple share about their joint coronary bypass surgery experience. It is a key dynamic in their relationship which helps determine how the couple respond to the trauma of bypass surgery. Shared meanings was first used in this sort of context by Radley and Green (1986).

Whitsitt's (2009) study was based on just three couples, which is not an unusually small sample by phenomenological research standards. The study's purpose was the exploration of the lived experiences of couples with one partner who had gone through bypass surgery. The couples involved were married and living together as a couple. Bypass surgery had been carried out on one of the partners during the previous two years and the researcher chose couples who had not shown excessively high levels of stress concerning the surgery itself. The study was based on face-to-face joint interviews with each of the couples. Joint interviews are unusual in phenomenological research but the phenomenon that Whitsitt intended to explore was the couple's joint experience of bypass surgery. Two separate interviews lasting about one hour were carried out with each couple. The first had the function of obtaining the descriptions from the couples of their experiences. The interview protocol that Whitsitt used involved three broad major questions. Whitsitt (2009) identifies the questions as:

• What was it like for you to go through CABG as a couple?

• What are the primary ways in which you coped together?

• What significance do you attribute to your experiences together?

The researcher then reflected on the recordings of these initial interviews in order to identify matters to be explored more deeply. The second interview provided the opportunity for more detailed interviewing along these lines.

Whitsitt claims to have 'developed a single structure of the invariant meanings of the interview data by synthesising the transformed meaning units' across all of the interviewees' descriptions. What this means is that he first of all identified the meaning units. This can be done simply by marking each meaning unit on the transcription. Then these meaning units (which are of course expressed in ordinary language) are translated into more psychological or academic terms. Imaginative variation is used in this process which basically means that the researcher tries to push the boundaries of the meaning units in order to understand more fully just what each unit is about. In many ways this is little different from the usual procedures in qualitative analysis of working and reworking one's codings. The transformed terminology forms the basis of the rest of the analysis. Eventually, and there are no rules about this, a synthesis of the transformed meaning units into a more generalised set of themes or structure will begin to emerge. One can describe this structure as a higher-level description of the general experience of the phenomenon which captured the nature of how jointly the partners in each couple experienced bypass surgery. The components of this structure take the rich detail to be found in the phenomenological interview and reduce them to their essence. The structure is then a generalised model dealing with the important psychological factors which constitute the structure of the experience of the phenomenon (Giorgi, 2003). The structure does not describe the common experience of the couples necessarily but indicates the important point of variation between couples in terms of their experiences.

The study concludes that the phenomenon of the joint experience of heart bypass surgery has seven inter-related parts:

- Anxiety, emotional upset and surprise in varying quantities characterised the initial experience.

- The couples were told that one member of the couple required bypass surgery.

- The health crisis within the couple was responded to by each partner in terms of long-standing patterns of relating between them and the level of marital satisfaction experienced.

- The crisis tended to make more apparent the aggravating behaviours and habits of the partner as well as their particular strengths.

- The health crisis was permeated by the fear of death but differentially between individuals.

- Tensions within the marital relationship were formed about issues of independence and health.

- In couples where higher levels of marital satisfaction were to be found, more alignment, insight and learning was experienced.

In a sense this is the end point of the analysis but too little detail of the experiences of the couples is to be found in this structure. Much of Whitsitt's research paper is taken up by a detailed explication of, especially, the variation experienced by the couples. This is very long but a small excerpt will perhaps give the flavour. Here is a passage from Whitsitt's discussion of the fourth component of the structure of the phenomenon – aggravating behaviours and attitudes – and strengths. P1 is the patient and S1 their spouse:

Bypass surgery acted as a catalyst for highlighting strengths and weaknesses for both partners in the marital relationship. The crisis magnified each partner's behaviors and attitudes, placing them in bold relief for the other person to see – and not always with positive results. For example, P1 ignored his initial cardiac symptoms as he was 'pretty much in denial,' and only when he could not continue working did he go to the hospital. Even then, P1 did not call S1 until the next day because nothing was going to happen, and he did not want to alarm her prematurely. This irritated S1 and only increased her fears and anxieties about P1's health. P1 also showed an unhealthy compulsion for overextending himself with disastrous results. Prior to his first CABG, he was working out of town, struggling to make sufficient money, dealing with rebellious children, and trying to complete a graduate degree. P1 was 'worn to a frazzle' and experiencing cardiac symptoms, but kept going; in fact he claimed that 'complete willpower' and antidepressants helped him finish his graduate program. P1's drive to push himself beyond what was healthy was an ongoing concern for S1. She referred to him as a lousy patient because 'he's always pushing the limits of everything'; at the same time, she acknowledged that 'P1's drive for independence was a positive aspect in that it aided his recovery.' (p. 155)

It has to be emphasised that this is just one paragraph in many of the description. Psychologists not fully understanding phenomenological psychology's aims may find such extended description somewhat rambling and lacking in a precise focus. That is as may be and simply may reflect the extent to which mainstream psychology favours cause and effect over fundamental description of phenomena.

Box 12.4

ILLUSTRATIVE RESEARCH STUDY

Plagiarism – a scary experience

This example of a phenomenological psychology study has much less allegiance to Giorgi's methods than that in Box 12.3. Instead it uses Ashworth's (2003) method of employing the seven fragments of the lifeworld. Although they do not discuss it as such, the authors are essentially structuring their understanding of the lifeworld – the structure of experience – in terms of the dimensions of these seven fragments. In Giorgi's method the structure emerges out of the analysis and is not, in that sense, imposed by the researcher on their research.

Ashworth, Freewood and MacDonald (2003) studied plagiarism from a phenomenological perspective. The issue of plagiarism is a substantial concern currently in universities. Research suggests that it is escalating in higher education in Western countries. Changes in methods of assessment may be partly responsible since the use of invigilated examinations in favour of course-work assessment has declined. The Internet has increasingly provided students with the opportunity to use cut-and-paste methods of essay-writing. Furthermore, group-based learning may encourage plagiarism of the work of other students rather than the work of experts in the field.

Ashworth et al. suggest that plagiarism is a phenomenon which is specific to a particular culture and historical epoch. This is important because it stresses that phenomenology is about what is out there in the social world rather than the deepest recesses of the psyche. There was a time when the writings of authors were not regarded proprietorially. The Stationer's Company of London introduced copyright as a way of restricting competition between its members. A reference to plagiarism can be found in the records of this company in 1701. It was not until the middle of the eighteenth century that copyright was extended to protect the rights of authors rather than the rights of companies. It is frequently noted that Chinese students can find it strange not to be allowed to use the words of a wise expert. These historical and cultural fragments reinforce the idea that plagiarism is a concept of a particular culture and a particular historical epoch. Plagiarism can therefore be seen historically and culturally.

Ashworth et al. argue that plagiarism is likely to be understood differently by different individuals so care is needed when addressing the Husserlian question 'What is plagiarism in its appearing?' The viewpoint of university academics will be different from that of students, who may vary amongst themselves. According to Ashworth et al., their research located students' perceptions and opinions about plagiarism within their lifeworlds – a fundamental phenomenological concept. The researchers obtained a number of sets of descriptions based on interviews with 12 students, of which just 3 are presented in the journal article. Like much phenomenological research, this study starts with the idiographic analysis of individuals before synthesising these together to give a broader and more general picture of how the phenomenon is experienced. Each of the students discussed in detail experienced plagiarism in very different ways, which suggests that universities cannot assume that there is an unequivocal meaning for the term plagiarism. Students need to go through a process of acculturation in order to share the understanding that universities as institutions have. This is an academic ideal of a creative, original individual who is autonomous and presents their work publicly in their own name.

In this study, the interviewing method did not follow strict phenomenological procedures as the interviews were collected for a rather different purpose. Nevertheless, the interviews did contain much material which was suitable for phenomenological analysis.

The authors discuss the importance of bracketing-out their academic perspective from the data collection and analysis. This is Husserl's technique and, for this study, involved suspending the particularly moral perspective on plagiarism held by many academics. Other presuppositions which had to be set aside include the following: (a) issues of the validity or accuracy of the student's understanding of plagiarism and (b) the assumption that there is a common view of plagiarism among students. Only by doing so can the researcher get close to the lifeworld of the student. Ashworth et al. sought to describe plagiarism in terms which could be described as superficial since there was no attempt to seek an underlying reality beyond that experienced by the experiencer – the student. The phenomenon of plagiarism has to be described in detail in terms of both how things appear to consciousness (called the noema in Husserlian terms) and the manner in which the phenomenon is grasped by the consciousness (the noesis). Although the lifeworld does have essential features and is a universal of humanity, plagiarism is not a fact of human existence.

The interviews with the 12 students were transcribed and subjected to an individual analysis in each case. The researchers describe the process in the following terms 'The analysis entailed a reading of the transcript in terms of its discriminable units of meaning. This having been rigorously done, the meanings are treated in terms of the fragments of the lifeworld . . .' You will recognise the terminology 'units of meaning' and 'fragments of the lifeworld' from the description of how to do phenomenological analysis (see Figure 12.8). This is a way of structuring and focusing the analysis but it is not required in phenomenological research although some researchers recommend it.

A substantial part of the report consists of idiographic analyses of the interviews with the students. Just three are presented by Ashworth et al. These in themselves, it should be stressed, do not constitute a phenomenological analysis, which concerns more general experiences of the phenomenon in question. However, the interview summaries are important steps towards the reader beginning to appreciate the lifeworlds of students around plagiarism. The interviews with the three students selected for inclusion in the report can be summarised as follows:

- Student A: Anxiety that he would be shamed publicly were he to be accused of plagiarism in his work swathed this student's experiences. He described that he would be horrified when he imagined how he would feel if accused of presenting material as his own which was not. There would not be any intention on his part to intentionally fail to reference the source of the ideas he used. He diligently followed the proper processes of referencing his sources without exception and it simply was not in him to reproduce substantial sections of material from a textbook. The prospect of plagiarism simply frightened him and he was surprised that other students seemed not to share this fear and seemed unconcerned if caught plagiarising. This student used a moral discourse when talking about plagiarism. His discourse also involved the idea of academic skills and he spoke of the hard-won skill of referencing

properly. According to the authors, this student saw plagiarism as involving the inclusion of substantial amount of text directly from a published source and then passing it off as if it were one's own. Despite his fear, he was very uncertain about what plagiarism is and deeply worried that any lack of skill in referencing on his part could lead to an accusation of plagiarism against him. He was aware that plagiarism can also involve copying from other students but this was not central to his own perceptions of the phenomenon.

- Student B: She saw academic development as a process of gradual but increasing independence from the work of respected authors. The novice student she saw as near-plagiaristic whereas the more experienced student will show substantial autonomy in their work. In terms of self, she said that students internalise from texts a perspective and so plagiarism is built into being a student. She counted herself in when she said 'We all plagiarise in some way don't we, because we all in our everyday life use phrases that are used by other people. I hold my hands up to that and say yeah I do that.' Although most students are young and just out of school, this student is mature and well travelled. Non-plagiaristic work is what a student grows into and it is not something that is taught to them as such. The young student lacking experience of the world uses the work of others as a method of learning. This student would rather fail because of lack of ability than employ illegitimate tactics. To her, inner values matter such as responsibility and personal pride and these were integral to the way she studied. She saw that self-reliance (as implied by this) will be a feature of post-university life.

- Student C: His degree involved painting and art history. In the former, employing elements of the work of others is not a problem whereas in art history the usual academic expectation that sources of ideas should be cited apply. The artistic and academic parts of his degree were seen as being very different by him in regard to plagiarism. In painting he saw himself as an originator of ideas but in his essay-writing he was more concerned about good work rather than creativity and so he may have used published work in order to structure his essays. The work of others was used for this, though technically this may not be plagiarism since the source is cited. Nevertheless, in a real sense the work was not entirely his own work. The objective of this strategy was to write a better essay. In terms of his discourse, he acknowledged that this can be seen as a matter of morality but his view was that this is mistaken. One's own viewpoint is developed by drawing on the viewpoints of others. Failing to acknowledge the contribution of the authors used as sources is the problem. In painting and other creative arts, the work in the studio is basically collaborative. The student may be encouraged to copy the styles of other artists in their painting, for example. So the process involves the student feeding off the work of others in the creative environment. This means that talk of plagiarism can be seen as inappropriate since it is part of the learning process. Downright blatant copying is plagiarism – that is the direct theft of an idea.

The researchers analyse each of these interviews in terms of the lived-world fragments of discourse, project, selfhood, sociality, spatiality and temporality (they do not discuss embodiment in this respect). However, these analyses are an intermediate stage in a phenomenological analysis. Although there is value in the analysis of the individual interviews, the purpose of phenomenology is not to describe the individual experiences of participants but to provide a description of the phenomenon itself. The next stage is a synthesis of the individual analyses to provide a general description of the phenomenon itself. Ashworth et al. do this using the self-same fragments of the lived world provided by Ashworth (2003) though embodiment is not featured in this case. This aspect of the analysis completes the phenomenological analysis and is discussed in some detail below:

- **Discourse** There was a conspicuous lack of certain discourses such as that of intellectual honesty. Other relevant discourses which were poorly represented include that concerning the integrity of assessment systems in universities and also the scientific discourse in which plagiarism is avoided because science should build an accurate citation of the work of others.

- **Project** In the three examples given above, it is clear that there is a relationship between their experience of plagiarism and their own personal agenda in life.

- **Selfhood** Identity is clearly involved with how plagiarism is experienced. So there was the involvement of their identity as subject specialists. The artist had a distinctive experience for example. One of the students (student A) seemed to lack the 'presence, agency' and 'voice' that are aspects of selfhood. The apparent assurance of the other two students is also reflected in the ways they experience plagiarism.

- **Sociality** Over the 12 interviews, the fragment of sociality is important although it was not a feature of the main three interviews. Sociality may be involved in terms of fairness which is an interpersonal matter, feelings for the plights of fellow students which allow one to let other students use one's own work, shame and embarrassment which are interpersonal, and so forth. Students also sometimes feel angry at academic staff who seem to fail to spot blatant cases of plagiarism.

- **Spatiality** Because plagiarism is a matter experienced in only certain locations (universities), it involves the lifeworld fragment of spatiality. Plagiarism is not a matter experienced in all situations.

- **Temporality** There is a chronological or time dimension to plagiarism. So being short of time to finish an essay may be a pressure involved with plagiarism. But also plagiarism was seen as being involved with the stage of study that the student is at. The new student is more likely to plagiarise than the more mature student.

Evaluation of phenomenology

To the mainstream psychologist, phenomenology may appear to be hopelessly subjective. But this is to fail to understand the issue of what is reliable knowledge. Although it is a question that has troubled philosophy for centuries, too often psychologists fail to understand or even study the philosophical underpinnings of their discipline. If they did, then the importance of Husserl's arguments would be much more apparent to them. His basic position that our experiences are the only reliable knowledge of the world speaks a great deal to mainstream psychology which tends to ignore such issues. Phenomenology focuses on the description of the experiences of people in their lived world. Too much psychological research has bypassed description in a search for cause and effect relationships without understanding the meaning of the things which constitute their causes and their effects. Phenomenology is expressly not about the subjective – the subjective it attempts to exclude in favour of the one certain source of knowledge which is our experiences through our consciousness. For mainstream quantitative psychologists, this is likely to remain an unfathomable conundrum.

Phenomenology has tended not to be accessible to mainstream psychologists perhaps because of the belief that the basics of phenomenology are difficult to understand. Considerable effort would be required, some suggest, to understand what phenomenology involves – that is understand it at a meaningful level. This is as may be, what seems clear is that phenomenology has had only a very limited impact on mainstream psychology (Giorgi, 1998). Mainstream psychologists might also be reluctant to study phenomenology because of the likely unsettling effect such study would have on their ideas about psychology as a science. Taken-for-granted ideas may seem to be no longer tenable.

The value of phenomenological psychology lies in the way it opens up the experiences of people in their lived world from their perspective to the research community. Take the well-researched topic in mainstream psychology of depression – the research literature has traditionally failed to include the voice of the depressed person rather than those of researchers and mental health practitioners. Halling (2002) draws attention to the work of Carter (1988) – an investigation of unipolar depression in women – as a good example of phenomenologically-based research. He focused on how depressed women approach life and on the role of loss in depression. Carter's data came from six women who wrote about their childhood recollections, the events which preceded a spell of depression, and their experiences of depression. One of the findings which emerged was that depression did not occur after the experience of an actual loss in life but instead when the person experienced a loss of hope of a future in which she could feel secure that she was a worthwhile person in the eyes of another. Depression grows out of the childhood insecurity that she is worthy of love. Depression was the consequence of her failure to win the approval of someone she regards as being important to her sense of self-worth. For Carter, depression is not a biological state that simply occurs for biological reasons. There may be biological factors but depression also has to be understood in the context of personal history and personal actions.

Phenomenology does not have a sophisticated conception of language unlike some other qualitative methods such as discourse analysis and conversation analysis. As such, phenomenology can be accused of disregarding the insights of those other methods. These would particularly have a bearing on interviews conducted by phenomenologists. Now the focus of phenomenology on content is clearly very different from that of discourse analysis and conversation analysis which, in general, has some difficulty dealing with content in its own right. Phenomenological psychologists seem to readily take on board the idea that language has experience-shaping functions (in a sense, that is what bracketing tries to deal with in part) and the role of discursive practices, but their conception of language is very different. King et al. (2008) point to Merleau-Ponty's (1945/1962) assertion that 'it is of experience that language speaks'. For instance, sometimes phenomenological psychologists have to stretch the meaning of words or invent new ones simply to be able to describe the nuances of experience. That is, like consciousness, experience is beyond language. King et al. write

> researchers find that, when research participants begin to struggle for words, multiply examples, or begin to lose clarity, it is precisely at this point that discoveries concerning the meaning of a phenomenon for them are near. (p. 82)

Consciousness is not a verbal phenomenon – data collection is, and that is where phenomenology does have some vulnerabilities. Phenomenology and discourse analysis have very different philosophical routes. Discourse analysis makes bold statements about what language is and what it is not. This is very important but there is a danger of overstatement. Langdridge (2008) puts it rather strongly suggesting that Potter and Hepburn's (2005a) argument in particular (see Box 9.1):

> readily makes a category error concerning the question that underpins the research enterprise – the distinction between a focus on content (i.e., the focus of phenomenology) and function (i.e., the focus of discursive psychology) and furthermore overstates the importance of the micro-analytic aspects of conversation. (pp. 1135–6)

Some good-natured trading of punches between phenomenological psychologists and discourse analysts would probably be helpful to both. The phenomenologists need to incorporate issues to do with language and the discourse analysts need to set clearer limits to their claims about the primacy of language – and explain better how the content of language should be regarded. Does language ever communicate unproblematically about experience?

Phenomenological psychology has quite a history but it is in the last 20 years or so that there has appeared a new generation of phenomenological researchers who are having a wider impact than their forebears on psychology. While Smith's IPA (see Chapter 13) has probably gained the ascendency among these, it is interesting that it is more friendly towards mainstream psychology than many other forms of qualitative research. That is to say, the researcher does not have to totally abandon what lessons mainstream psychology has to offer to employ the method. The same might be the case for phenomenological psychology in general where understanding experiences would be an important addition to the objectives of research.

CONCLUSION

Phenomenology and phenomenological psychology emerged somewhat earlier in psychology than other qualitative methods such as discourse analysis, conversation analysis, grounded theory and so forth. However, until the emergence of interpretative phenomenological analysis in the 1990s, growth was tentative and slow within the field of psychology. There are probably a number of reasons for this but, most importantly, phenomenological ideas are rather alien to mainstream psychology and difficult to understand from other perspectives. Other qualitative methods may have emerged later but they tend to be about the use of language rather than the content of experience. All of this is not helped by the somewhat resolutely descriptive approach to

phenomenological psychology that has tended to be the most prominent in the field. Whatever the reason for the relatively slow development of phenomenology in psychology, it is only when their research is about the experience of phenomena in the lifeworld that psychologists need to turn to phenomenology.

Phenomenological psychology has great potential to provide an alternative understanding of many psychological topics. Psychology has traditionally sought to provide causal explanations of the relationships between carefully measured and standardised variables without expending too much effort on the nature of the variables and how they relate to people's experiences. So it could be argued that mainstream psychology would benefit from having more involvement with phenomeno-logical approaches as a way of relating mainstream findings to the experiences of individuals. There are many practitioner fields of psychology where there is a great need for practice to be informed by a better understanding of life as experienced by

clients. Phenomenology is capable of doing that. But it does require accommodation on the part of mainstream psychologists in ways which promote experience as an important aspect of psychology at least on parity with the testing of theories and the search for causal relationships.

KEY POINTS

● Phenomenology is a product of philosophy during the first half of the twentieth century. Its basic concern is with understanding human experience as it is experienced. The radical assumption of Husserl's phenom-enology is the idea that the only reliable knowledge that we have is our pure conscious experience of the phenomena in our lived world. This does not mean that phenomenology is about reductionist analysis of the elements of such experiences and, instead, it is a holistic approach which understands our experiences to be part of the social world that we entered and which we experienced. So experience in phenomenology is a social rather than a purely perceptual thing.

● The major methodological contribution of phenomenology is its insistence that in order to know a person's experience as experienced through the consciousness it is essential to jettison as much as possible of our cognitions which influence the way in which we tend to interpret, evaluate and describe experiences as possible. This is an ideal in phenomenological psychology rather than a state which most phenomenological psychologists believe achievable.

● In a sense, phenomenology's subject matter – experience – is an aspect of living ignored by much of main-stream psychology. From the mainstream perspective phenomenology is erroneously regarded as being subjective whereas from the perspective of phenomenology its subject matter is the most objective that humanity can achieve. The focus of phenomenology (and hence phenomenological psychology) is on describ-ing the phenomenon itself rather than individual experiences of the phenomenon. The study of the individu-al's experience is just the way in which this is achieved. Nevertheless, one finds numerous phenomenological studies which leave the analysis at the level of the individual person.

● Phenomenology is the starting point for any psychological research which has as its objective knowledge of life experiences as experiences. Phenomenological psychology is practised in a range of different ways and their allegiance to Husserl's original ideas cannot always be seen to be close. Nevertheless, phenomenology provides a theoretical and practical context for such studies.

ADDITIONAL RESOURCES

Center for Advanced Research in Phenomenology. Resources. phenomenology-carp.org (accessed 24 April 2015).

Dodson, E. Husserl and the Adventure of Phenomenology – In Twelve Minutes. https://www.youtube.com/watch?v=PjknxljepKA

Giorgi, A. (2009). *Descriptive phenomenological method in psychology: A modified Husserlian approach.* Pittsburgh, PA: Duquesne University Press.

Langdridge, D. (2008). *Phenomenological psychology: Theory, research and method.* Harlow: Pearson Education.

van Manen, M. (2011). Phenomenology Online: A Resource for Phenomenological Inquiry. www.phenomenologyonline.com/ (accessed 24 April 2015).

van Manen, M. (n.d.). Empowering People: Phenomenological Psychology Links. www.empoweringpeople.net/PPlinks.html (accessed 24 April 2015).

www.empoweringpeople.net/PPlinks.html (accessed 24 April 2015)

YouTube. Edmund Husserl's Phenomenology in His Own Words – Rey Ty. https://www.youtube.com/watch?v=L4cxVEAR1JY&feature=fvsr (accessed 24 April 2015).

YouTube. Merleau-Ponty – The World of Perception and the World of Science (English subtitles). https://www.youtube.com/watch?v=uf9TtYdxy3A&feature=related (accessed 24 April 2015).

YouTube. Phenomenological Psychology – Critical Social Psychology (12/30). https://www.youtube.com/watch?v=ozQ8t82RSbA&feature=list_related&playnext=1&list=SP528A6A714B6796B6 (accessed 24 April 2015)

Interpretative phenomenological analysis (IPA)

Overview

- Interpretative phenomenological analysis (IPA) was primarily developed within health psychology in the 1990s as a way of understanding the experience of health issues such as pain. It has also grown in social psychology and clinical psychology.

- The primary concern of IPA is with how individuals experience phenomena and the psychological interpretations of these experiences.

- Like social interactionism and other perspectives, IPA assumes that people attempt to make sense of (give meaning to) their experiences.

- IPA has its roots in phenomenology together with hermeneutics and symbolic interactionism. Furthermore, it emphasises the ideographic as well as the nomothetic. Case studies or small samples characterise the IPA approach.

- Semi-structured interviews tend to be the preferred data for IPA analyses. In these interviews, people are encouraged to freely recall their experiences. The questioning style is designed to encourage richly detailed descriptions of experiences of phenomena. Alternative sources of data may be used if they meet the method's requirements.

- The recording of the interview is usually transcribed using a literal, verbatim approach.

- The account of one participant is usually analysed in depth before the researcher moves on to compare this with accounts from other participants. Themes developed in the initial analysis may be used or added to for the later analyses. Similarities and differences between accounts are important aspects of the analysis.

- Following a period of data familiarisation, the researcher notes impressions and ideas in the left-hand margin of the transcript.

- The researcher looks for themes in the account. Themes should be clearly related to what was said in the interview though they are normally expressed somewhat more abstractly or theoretically than would characterise the words of the participant. Each theme is usually given a short descriptive title. The themes are identified, wherever they occur, by this name in the right-hand margin of the transcription.

- Once the themes have been identified, the analyst groups or clusters them together into broader, more encompassing superordinate themes. These superordinate themes and sub-themes may be listed in a table in order of their assumed importance, starting with the most important. Short verbatim quotations are usually selected to illustrate the theme and the line number from the transcript given as a means of locating the original.

- The major themes are discussed partly in relation to the wide psychological literature on that topic.

- IPA deals with internal psychological processes such as cognition. It is, thus, one of the most clearly psychology-based approaches to qualitative research.

- There is considerable variation in procedures used in IPA.

- Template analysis is different in that it starts with pre-existing psychological concepts, ideas and theory in order to suggest possible themes. These may then be modified or added to in light of the interviews.

What is interpretative phenomenological analysis?

According to Smith, Flowers and Larkin (2009, p. 1) interpretative phenomenological analysis (IPA) is 'committed to the examination of how people make sense of their major life experiences'. More than most of the qualitative research methods described in this book, IPA has its origins in psychology. It was first described by Jonathan Smith (Smith, 1996) and it has grown in popularity since then. Essentially, IPA is about the experiences of individuals working from the basic assumption that the individual who experiences something is the expert about their experiences. The meanings which the individual uses to understand their own experiences and the insights that they supply are central to this approach. Much of the early work on IPA was broadly in the area of health psychology but clinical psychology and social psychology also featured. Reid, Flowers and Larkin (2005) suggest that the following topics are among those where IPA has made an impact: palliative care; people's reproductive decision making, e.g. abortion and adoption; mental health, drugs and addiction, and eating disorders; quality of life assessment following serious illness; new genetics – such as when patients need support following genetic tests; chronic illness such as long-term back pain; and dementia and other degenerative diseases. Examples of titles include:

- 'Becoming "whole" again: A qualitative study of women's views of recovering from anorexia nervosa' (Jenkins & Ogden, 2012).

- 'An exploration of the experience of mothers whose children sustain traumatic brain injury (TBI) and their families' (Clark, Stedmon, & Margison, 2008).

- 'Biographical disruption and the experience of loss following a spinal cord injury: An interpretative phenomenological analysis' (Dickson, Allan & O'Carroll, 2008).

Nevertheless, other areas of research away from the field of health psychology are being researched using IPA especially clinical psychology and social psychology. Examples of non-medical topics include:

- 'Exploring criminogenic need through victim apology letters II: An IPA analysis of post-treatment accounts of offending against children' (Duff, 2011).
- 'The presentation of masculinity in everyday life: Contextual variations in the masculine behavior of young Irish men' (Johnston & Morrison, 2007).
- '"Getting into trouble": A qualitative analysis of the onset of offending in the accounts of men with learning disabilities' (Isherwood, Burns, Naylor, & Read, 2007).

All of these titles reflect fairly open and general research questions. IPA is not about testing hypotheses but about understanding personal experiences of the world. Furthermore, since IPA tends to deal with life-changing events for the most part, it is not the most obvious candidate for casual research on fellow students, for example.

Basically, IPA can be used wherever a person's psychological experiences are being studied through the person's own perspective. The data collection method of preference for IPA researchers is in-depth qualitative interviews, though it is possible that other data might be used – if it deals with an individual's experiences in their own words. However, the surest guarantee that the data will be appropriate for IPA analysis is a carefully constructed, in-depth qualitative interview. As the name IPA implies, the method's primary concern is in the provision and analysis of detailed descriptions and interpretations of conscious experiences (phenomena) in the personal accounts of individuals or a small number of individuals. (Throughout this chapter we use the word phenomenon in this sense which is derived from phenomenology.) Richardson, Ong and Sim (2006) provide a good example of an IPA investigation into chronic pain. Eight people with chronic, widespread pain were interviewed along with a small number of family members. Small samples are typical of interpersonal phenomenological studies because of the amount of labour involved in their analysis. The researchers found, for example, that the experiences of participants could be classified as (a) optimistic about the future, (b) pessimistic about the future and (c) overwhelmed with uncertainty concerning the future. The last category was the dominant one. This provides an example of the basic assumption of IPA that people try to make sense of their experiences and amongst the aims of IPA is for the researcher to understand the meaning given to these experiences. Hence, in an IPA study, it is important that the researcher:

- provides an accurate and effective description of people's experiences;
- tries to make sense of these experiences.

Put another way, the researcher is trying to interpret the interpretations of the people studied in the research. In IPA it is recognised that ultimately it is the researcher's own conceptions of the phenomenological world which form the basis of how the phenomena are understood. This acknowledges that the researcher can never completely know another person's phenomenological world though they can perhaps get usefully close to accessing it.

IPA has links with other forms of qualitative analysis, in particular thematic analysis, and it has similarities to narrative analysis. Figure 13.1 indicates some of the key features of IPA including those identified by Reid et al. (2005). Clearly, with its emphasis on the phenomenological interpretation of experiences, IPA has its own particular focus which is not shared by other qualitative research methods. Similarly, because it does not regard participants in the research as mere providers of text or conversation to be interpreted as conversation, IPA incorporates more elements of the person

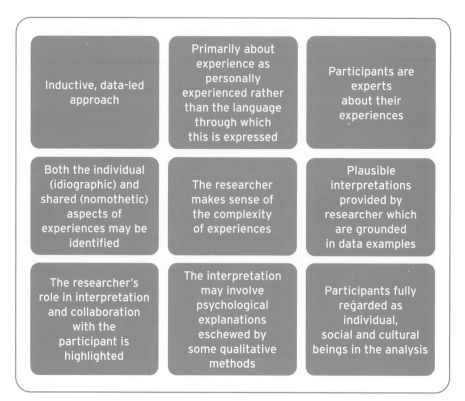

FIGURE 13.1 The key elements of interpretative phenomenological analysis

into the analysis than is typical of, say, conversation analysis and discourse analysis. The focus on how things (phenomena) are experienced is probably the clearest defining characteristic of IPA. Box 13.2 later in the chapter presents an IPA analysis which very much illustrates the general style of the method.

The development of interpretative phenomenological analysis

Very much the same figures who have been influential in phenomenology are claimed as being important in IPA – Heidegger, Merleau-Ponty and Sartre are among the notables whose names dominate Chapter 12 too. What these have in common is that they share a view of humankind as being embodied persons who exist in the world but one which is bound by a given cultural/historical/social context. But these thinkers did not invent IPA. The origins of IPA are seen as lying in the work of Jonathan Smith (1956–) who published in 1996 the seminal paper 'Beyond the divide between cognition and discourse: Using interpretative phenomenological analysis in health psychology'. Writing later, Smith argued the case for:

> an approach to psychology which was able to capture the experiential and qualitative, and which could still dialogue with mainstream psychology. (Smith et al., 2009, p. 4)

IPA researchers make very clear claims that the method has deep philosophical roots:

> One important theoretical touchstone for IPA is phenomenology, which originated with Husserl's attempts to construct a philosophical science of consciousness. A second important theoretical current for IPA is hermeneutics – the theory of interpretation.

A third significant influence is symbolic-interactionism . . . which emerged in the 1930's as an explicit rejection of the positivist paradigm beginning to take hold in the social sciences. For symbolic-interactionism, the meanings which individuals ascribe to events are of central concern, but those meanings are only obtained through a process of social engagement and a process of interpretation. (Taylor, 2008)

So, Smith (1996) proposed his qualitative approach, IPA, as a means of capturing the qualitative and experiential dimension while specifically maintaining a dialogue with mainstream psychology. This allegiance to mainstream psychology is unusual in recent qualitative psychological research.

It should be self-evident that every research method has its own set of theoretical assumptions built into it. This is clearly the case with quantitative data analysis but equally so for qualitative data analysis methods in general. Quantitative psychology (as we saw in Chapter 1) reflects to a good measure the assumptions of positivism and hypothesis testing. Qualitative data analysis methods, including IPA, grow from philosophical and theoretical roots which need to be understood in order to appreciate the nature of the method in full. The particular mix of influences on IPA is different in some respects from the general influences on qualitative research. This is particularly evident in the way in which IPA accepts the role of mainstream psychological theory in interpreting the experiences of people. This is hardly surprising given that IPA emerged out of the discipline of psychology and stills centres on that discipline despite gradually establishing a wider base in other research fields. Consequently, expect to find many more references to general psychological research and theory throughout IPA than one would expect to find in, say, a discourse analytic study. The latter is more likely to be highly critical of psychological explanations and unlikely to use them constructively in the interpretation of data. It is also far less about understanding language than some other forms of qualitative analysis such as discourse analysis and conversation analysis.

Figure 13.2 puts together the claims about the influence of philosophical traditions on IPA. Four influences are identified. For example, Chapman and Smith (2002) are among the researchers who claim that IPA has its roots in phenomenology and

Philosophical influences on interpretative phenomenological analysis (IPA)

Phenomenology (Husserl): the study of conscious experience

Symbolic interactionism (Mead): the mind emerges out of social interaction

Hermeneutics (Heidegger): how we study and understand 'text'

Idiography (Allport): the study of the individual instance in depth and detail as opposed to developing laws based on the general

FIGURE 13.2 Some influences on interpretative phenomenological analysis

symbolic interactionism; Smith (n.d.) refers to hermeneutics as being fundamental to the method; and Shinebourne (2011) has identified the idiographic approach as an important philosophical underpinning of IPA. (Idiography, as we shall see, is the approach to knowledge which concentrates on the individual instance in fine detail as opposed to the nomothetic approach which, briefly, is concerned with developing general laws based on numerous cases.)

Phenomenology

Phenomenology is the systematic study of conscious experiences. It is a general philosophical movement. The Greek word *phainomenon* means 'that which appears' or 'how things appear'. The founder of phenomenology is claimed to be the Austrian/German philosopher Edmund Husserl (1889–1938). Although some of the basic ideas of phenomenology appear in his *Logische Untersuchungen* (1891), the term phenomenology was first included in *Ideen zu einer reinen Phänomenolgie und phänomenologischen Philosophie* (1913). Whether Husserl should be described as a philosopher or a psychologist is difficult since when he was writing the distinction between philosophy and psychology was not as absolute as it is now. Whatever – Husserl was certainly influenced by major psychologists of the period such as Franz Brentano (1838–1917). Among the basic ideas of phenomenology is that there is no clear independence between human experience and reality. That is, reality is made up from things and events but as perceived within the realm of conscious experience. Thus, it can be suggested that phenomenology, alongside much of qualitative psychology, rejects the idea of an objective reality for experiences. In Husserl's thinking, there is a distinction to be made between what is experienced (which is called the noema) and the nature or manner of the experiencing (noesis). So it is possible to experience something in imagination – such as the day you graduate from university – but this is associated with a complex experience such as the outfit that you have on, what you feel, who is there and so forth. Another important concept in phenomenological research is epoché (or bracketing) which is the way in which the phenomenological researcher tries to avoid preconceptions and presuppositions which play a part in how we understand experiences so that the experiences are experienced as they appear for the very first time.

IPA and other phenomenological approaches are ways of understanding conscious experience from the viewpoint of the person having the experience. Familiar and unfamiliar psychological concepts such as thought, memory, social action, desire and volition are studied in IPA. Experience involves conscious intentionality – particular ideas and images which help constitute the meaning of a particular experience. Phenomenology in a variety of manifestations was a major influence on twentieth-century academic thinking the existentialism of Jean-Paul Sartre (1905–80) and others who were influenced by Husserl. But, in addition. American sociology incorporated a version of phenomenology in the form of ethnomethodology (see Chapter 2, pp. 62–64).

Hermeneutics

Taken literally, albeit in ancient Greek, hermeneutics means the analysis of messages. However, it is more clearly seen as the ways in which we go about studying and understanding texts. Text is not to be seen as merely something that is written down. Following the ideas of the Algerian/French philosopher Jacques Derrida (1930–2004), a text should be regarded as including anything that people interpret during the course of their day-to-day lives. Of course, this definition would include the sort of experiences that IPA focuses on. Meaning is a social and a cultural product in hermeneutics and much of qualitative research. Although hermeneutics was originally applied to biblical texts, it should be clear that the approach can be applied to a multitude of aspects of human activity. In hermeneutic traditions, the meaning and importance of human activity are studied primarily from a first-person perspective. The parts of the text are studied in relation to the entirety in a backwards and forwards, looping process. Such processes are familiar in various forms of qualitative data analysis.

Perhaps the following should be added, though it is a slight detour. The term 'deconstruction' has its origins in hermeneutics. The German philosopher Martin Heidegger (1889–1976) introduced the idea, though the emphasis was not the same as the term's modern usage. Heidegger realised that the interpretation of text was influenced by the person doing the interpretation. That is to say, it differs from the text's original meaning. These interpretations have to be deconstructed in order to reveal the contribution of the interpreter to the text's meaning. Such constructions, and hence the necessity of deconstruction, are evident with some religious texts where interpreters essentially alter the original meaning of the texts. So Islam, for example, has various interpretations or constructions despite the original text on which they are based being the same.

For Heidegger, hermeneutics is a prerequisite of phenomenology. Hermeneutics deals with the unravelling of the meaning of texts. At the heart of phenomenology is the process of uncovering meanings which are not apparent in the way in which the phenomenon appears in the consciousness. The meaning is essentially hidden and the researcher needs to engage in a process of making what is hidden manifest. What is disclosed by the participant to the phenomenological researcher is not a virgin idea but something which has been immersed in the world – it is part of the individual's being-in-the-world. In other words, there is a prior historical, cultural and social context to the experienced phenomenon. So interpretation is built on what there is in advance of the experience.

For Heidegger, when a phenomenon is encountered in our lived world, it already has an involvement in our world which can be seen in our understanding of the world. Interpretation lays out what this involvement is. Another way of putting this is that our experiences of the world are linked backwards to our knowledge of the world that we learn as a consequence of being part of the world. The person experiencing the phenomenon engages in interpretation but so does the researcher whose task is to make sense of the experiences described to him or her. Hence the term 'double hermeneutics' is used by Smith (2004) to describe the process by which the researcher tries to make sense of the attempts of the participant to make sense of the personal and social world. One may regard what has gone before as fore-conceptions. The researcher attempts to understand the participant's descriptions of their experiences in relation to a critical and reflexive evaluation of these fore-conceptions. But, of course, the fore-conceptions are not necessarily clear and obvious at the start of the analytic process but may become clear only during the process of interpretation. What the fore-conceptions are may be revised constantly by the researcher when developing their interpretation. There is a risk of misunderstanding here because the 'fore-conception' is not to be found in what the researcher knows but it is to be found in what the participant has to say about their experiences. The role of the researcher is to build on the words said by the participant in order to achieve a more abstract and conception version of what emerged in the phenomenological interview. The researcher's first 'reading' is very empathic to the words of the participant – it is only later that it begins to reflect the speculation and conjecture of the researcher such as the inclusion of psychological theory and findings from past experience so long as these can be related to the participant's account of their own experience.

Under Derrida's influence, deconstruction has come to mean a form of criticism of the interpreter's influence on a text's meaning, whereas it originally meant merely the identification of the different traditions of understanding text. Hepburn provides a summary of how deconstructionism is normally presented in psychological writings:

> Deconstruction is often positioned as the opposite of construction: it is taken simply to refer to 'breaking things down' – the unravelling of a text's assumptions and the overturning of hierarchies. (Hepburn, 1999, p. 651)

In order to gain a more sophisticated understanding of Derrida's concept of deconstruction in psychology, Hepburn (1999) will make a good starting point. But we are beginning to get a long way from IPA with this family tree of philosophy.

Symbolic interactionism

In symbolic interactionism the idea that the mind and self emerge out of social interactions involving significant communications is central. It is a sociological approach to small-scale social phenomena rather than the major structures of society. It has in the past been influential on social psychological thinking, especially what is sometimes termed sociological social psychology. The story of symbolic interactionism begins in the work of the German sociologist Max Weber (1864–1920) and the work of the American psychologist and philosopher George Herbert Mead (1863–1931). Both of these men brought the issues of subjective meaning and social interaction to the forefront. Although Mead is regarded as one of the most important figures in symbolic interactionism, the term is that of Herbert Blumer (1900–87) whose account of symbolic interactionism tends to dominate over other variants (Blumer, 1969).

Despite symbolic interactionism being essentially a sociological theory, it is based on a conception of what people are rather than a conception of what the structures of society might be. Unlike the dominant perspective of psychology, for interactionists people are not the passive recipients of socialisation influences. Instead, people are 'out there' in a social world making their own understandings of that world in relation to their understanding of other people and themselves and the interaction between the two. In symbolic interactionism, a person is continually adjusting what they do in response to the actions of other people. This is dependent on the human ability to interpret the actions of others in relation to their own actions. Or, to put it another way, we can treat the actions of others symbolically and treat these actors as symbolic objects. In our imaginations, we are capable of formulating and rehearsing alternative patterns of action in advance of responding. Furthermore, we have the capacity to regard ourselves and the things we do also as being symbolic objects. In the interactionist perspective, humans construct their social world actively and creatively. Significant symbols occur in circumstances where the sender of the communication has the same understanding of the communication as the receiver of the communication. Language consists of communication involving the use of such significant communications. The ordinary, day-to-day interactions between people (and not social structures) are what society is. This means that society is dynamic and changing in response to the (temporary) outcomes of these interactions.

Just how do these processes work? What does it mean to suggest that mind and conceptions of self develop in the social interactions between people? One has to remember that social processes and communications exist prior to the birth of an individual. The child comes into a world in which people are already formed socially and have interacted with each other to create their understandings of the world. The newborn enters this world and, even from a very early stage, can engage in a conversation based on gestures. That is, they are communicating through gestures before they can communicate through language. The early gestures are communication without a conscious intention to communicate but nevertheless have that effect. Communication is not an individual act but one involving two people at a minimum. Communication is the basic social mechanism through which meaning is learnt and established – meaning is dependent on interactions between individuals. The process is one in which there is a sender, a receiver and a consequence of the communication. In this way, the mind and understanding of self arise. Of course, there develops an intentionality in communication because the individual learns to anticipate the responses of other individuals to the communication and can use this to achieve the desired response of others. So the self is purposive. It is in the context of communication or social interaction that meanings come about in the social world.

An excellent example of symbolic interactionist thought can be found in the dramaturgical approach of Erving Goffman (1922–82), in which human social interaction is regarded as 'scripted'. It is a small step from seeing the importance of interpersonal interaction in the creation of the nature of society and studying the roles which individuals play in interaction. Role-taking is a key mechanism by which we can learn and understand the perspective of others. *Asylums* (1961) is one of Goffman's most influential books. It examines the process of institutionalisation which can be conceived as the inmate's reaction to the structures of such total institutions and the interactions therein. In his book *Frame analysis*, Goffman (1974) claims the intellectual influence of phenomenology on his thinking. Ethnomethodology is also steeped in symbolic interactionism.

The roots of interpretative phenomenological analysis in the idiographic approach

IPA is, fundamentally, an *idiographic* approach focused on the individual (as in any case study) as the unit to be understood. IPA researchers see value in the individual case study which is different from Husserl's approach to phenomenology. Of course, many researchers will begin their analysis with the idiographic study of a particular case but then incorporate similar studies of other individuals. Thus several idiographic studies may be compared and contrasted in order to make more general statements based on a group of individuals. This reflects the classic distinction between idiographic and nomothetic approaches to knowledge which was introduced into psychology by Gordon Allport (1897–1967) in the 1930s although the German philosopher Wilhelm Windelband (1848–1915) was the originator of the distinction:

- Idiographic understanding concerns the individual as an individual in his or her own right. It is about unique cases, things, or events more broadly.

- Nomothetic understanding is concerned with the study of groups of individuals. This group is considered to represent all individuals in that class of people. As a result, in nomothetic approaches it is appropriate to formulate abstract laws or generalisations about people.

The way in which the idiographic or case study is valued in IPA demarks it somewhat from the Husserlian version of phenomenology. It is indicative of the extent to which IPA has travelled away from its roots in his work. As we saw in Chapter 12, the Husserlian approach is best exemplified in phenomenological psychology in terms of the work of Amedeo Giorgi (1985a, 1997). Research is based on individuals but the aim is to explicate the general nature of the phenomenon rather than the experiences of the individual. The idiographic detail may be mentioned but this is more as a way of delineating the phenomenon than valuing the idiographic in itself. One way of putting the difference is to suggest that currently IPA operates at an early stage in Husserl's programme of phenomenology (Smith et al., 2009). This results in a contrast between the third party voice to be found in a Giorgi (Husserl) style study which speaks of the phenomenon itself as a generalisation and the IPA study in which 'an IPA analysis usually takes the form of a more idiographic interpretative commentary, interwoven with extracts from the participants' accounts' (pp. 200–1).

So you will find individual case studies among IPA research reports. According to Smith (2004) the detail provided in the study of an individual helps the researcher appreciate important aspects of the humanity that we all share. This is true also where a study involves several individuals since the analysis starts with the detailed analysis of each individual but then moves on to look at the similarities and differences between individuals which illuminate experiences that they share (e.g. the experience of back pain). Smith et al. (2009) suggest that idiographic research sheds light on what is known from nomothetic research.

How to do interpretative phenomenological analysis

Analysts using IPA do not base their interpretation solely on what the individual in question has to say about their experiences. The analyst adds more to the interpretation. Consequently, IPA involves what Smith and Osborn (2003) call 'a questioning hermeneutics'. They suggest that this involves asking questions of what the participants in their research say such as:

> What is the person trying to achieve here? Is something leaking out here that wasn't intended? Do I have a sense of something going on here that maybe the participants themselves are less aware of? (Smith & Osborn, 2003, p. 51)

Hence, IPA is 'interpretative' and not merely descriptive. The interpretation is not taken literally from the participant's words but is part of a systematic analysis of what is said. One might describe this, then, as a process of critical deconstruction.

Detailed accounts of how to carry out IPA have been provided by Smith and his colleagues (e.g. Smith & Eatough, 2006; Smith et al., 2009; Smith & Osborn, 2003). These accounts of the IPA procedures include acknowledgement of the fact that flexibility is possible and that a researcher may choose to adapt and vary the methods in order to meet the requirements of their own particular study. In other words, IPA methodology is not too prescriptive about how a study should proceed. There are two major aspects of IPA:

- data collection
- data analysis.

These are dealt with separately in the following sections. Figure 13.3 gives a summary of the main aspects of the analysis.

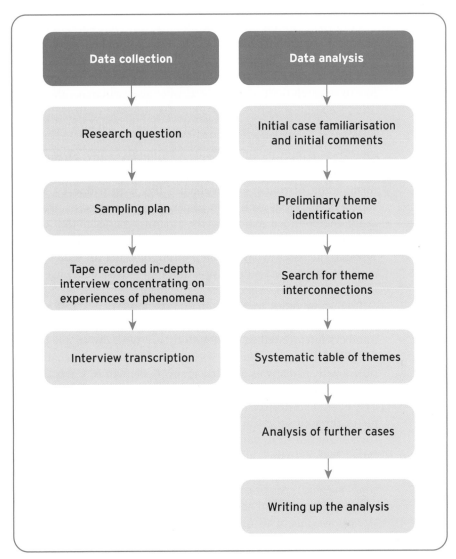

FIGURE 13.3 Stages in an interpretative phenomenological analysis

Larkin, Watts and Clifton (2006) make the point that there are misconceptions about the nature of phenomenology. In particular, assuming that phenomenology is a purely descriptive endeavour is a misconception. However, it is a misconception which makes IPA attractive to some students, especially as it appears to be accessible, flexible and applicable. None of this should be taken to imply a lack of rigour on the part of phenomenological approaches. They suggest that IPA is the 'insider's perspective' – a view which Smith promoted strongly in the early days of IPA. This may have resulted in IPA studies focusing too much on description as a form of analysis than developing the interpretation or conceptual aspects of the method. The step-by-step methods published are rather 'unremarkable' compared with those for other qualitative methods and there seems to be a lot of variability and flexibility. It is recognised that IPA can never produce a truly first person account of experiences as the data are produced by the researcher and participant together. The attempt, though, is to get as close to the first person account as possible. But interpretation in IPA means that a more overtly conceptual account is demanded.

Prior to attempting your first IPA, it is common sense to read at least a few examples of studies which have used IPA. There are a number of studies which can be drawn on and new ones are being produced all of the time. Examples are provided in Boxes 13.2 and 13.3 later in the chapter. Obviously, some will be on topics closer to what you would like to research than others. These, of course, will make the best models to follow.

Data collection: the semi-structured interview

Of course, data collection is dependent, in any study, on the way in which the research question is formulated. This is equally true for IPA. A detailed discussion about the formulation of research questions in IPA is provided by Smith and Osborn (2003). Research questions in IPA do not lead to hypotheses since IPA's approach is exploratory and confined mainly by the area of experience that the researcher is concerned with in any particular study. However, it is possible to formulate a general IPA research question: what are the perceptions that an individual (or group of individuals) have concerning a given situation they experience (phenomenon) and how do they make sense of this experience?

Like some other forms of qualitative data analysis, IPA requires a lot of time for data collection, data transcription and data analysis. As a consequence of this, the numbers interviewed in an IPA study are typically small. Just by way of illustration, there are IPA (case) studies with a single participant (Eatough & Smith, 2006) but others with as many as 64 participants (Coleman & Cater, 2005). Sample size depends very much on (a) the aims of the research and (b) the resources of the researcher. In the case of student projects, time and other resources may, perhaps, allow only for a sample of three to six participants (Howitt & Cramer, 2011). Smith and Osborn (2003) suggest that an IPA sample should consist of relatively similar (homogeneous) cases rather than extremely different examples. One implication of this is that it is better to carry out a study on a specific group such as those with chronic back pain rather than study various types of pain in one study. It is useful to include a table (e.g. Table 13.1) summarising some of the characteristics of each individual participant if the sample size allows this. This enables the reader to contextualise the discussion. Of course, what to include depends very much on the nature and the purpose of the research. It is a useful strategy to adopt where any qualitative study is based on a small number of participants.

Detailed accounts about people's experiences are the foundation of IPA. The quality of the analysis is dependent on the quality of these accounts leads to the description and understanding that IPA applies. Whatever the textual material used for IPA,

TABLE 13.1 Example of summary of participants' table

Participant	Gender	Age	Type of pain	Years since onset
Debbie	F	48	Traffic accident	10
Chris	M	27	Traffic accident	14
Elle	F	22	Work related	3
Karen	F	39	Medical condition	25
Jay	M	33	Work related	12
Martin	M	27	Medical condition	5

it must provide extremely detailed accounts of the experiences. Probably, the level of detail required would be rare, say, in everyday conversations about pain, for example. That is, a great deal of textual material would be ruled out on this basis. The preferred data in IPA, then, is the sort of rich textual material which often can be obtained in open-ended interviewing of the sort discussed in Chapter 3. Of course, the interviewer needs to ensure that the appropriate sorts of description emerge in the interview by using carefully thought-out and relevant questioning. The IPA interview involves a series of open-ended questions intended to help the participant to produce a lengthy and detailed description in their own words. Such interviews will require careful piloting if they are to be maximally effective. So the IPA researcher will normally explore their interview questions and techniques on a small number of people – if the result is that the participants answer freely and extensively then the researcher will probably feel confident that they can move on to the study proper. It should be stressed that other kinds of personal accounts of experiences such as diaries or other autobiographic material could be used subject to the appropriateness of their contents for the purposes of the research.

Nevertheless, to date, researchers in IPA have used semi-structured interviews almost exclusively. IPA interviewing techniques are intended to be applied flexibly. So, the questions that have been planned are not read to the participant in a fixed sequence. The interviewer, instead, needs to be free to explore (probe) things of interest as and when they occur during the course of the interview. It is most important that the interview is led by the participant's issues rather than an agenda imposed by the interviewer. Notwithstanding this, a considerable amount of pre-planning is involved. For example, alongside the questions planned it is also possible to pre-plan at least some of the probes which will be needed in addition in order to ensure that fully detailed information is provided. These probes can be included in the interview schedule. But, of course, the interviewer is free to add new questions and probes where necessary during the course of the interview.

Smith and Osborn (2003) make various suggestions about how the interview questions should be written (pp. 61–2). While these are fairly typical of the advice given about in-depth interviewing in general (see Chapter 3), they warrant mentioning here:

- Questions should be neutral rather than value-laden or leading.
- Avoid jargon or assumptions of technical proficiency.
- Use open, not closed, questions.

The style of interview is described by Smith and Osborn (2003) as having the following general features (p. 63):

- Since it takes time for trust and rapport to build up in an interview, it is important to move slowly towards the main areas of interest. The topics studied in IPA tend to be highly personal and sensitive and so they cannot be rushed into.
- There is a distinction to be made between the effective use of probes and using them excessively to the detriment of the quality of the data. The over-use of probes can detract from the quality of the interview by disrupting the participant's account and they can introduce unhelpful diversions.
- It is important to ask one question at a time and provide sufficient time to ensure a proper and full answer. The participant may need to think and it is quite wrong to interrupt this with another question.
- The interviewer needs to be sensitive to the effect that the interview is having. The interviewer may need to change the way in which a particular interviewee is

interviewed if there appear to be problems or difficulties. There are many different ways in which these may be coped with according to circumstances. A short break or a new style of questioning would be among the possibilities.

It would hamper the interview if the researcher seems unfamiliar with the questions that are to be answered and so spends much of the time checking the questionnaire. Consequently, it is far better if the researcher commits the interview schedule to memory so as to allow a more natural and smooth flow to the interview. (Of course, it is reasonable to take a short break while you check the interview schedule to see if you omitted anything. The interviewee will understand the need for this. It should be done in their presence.) There is every reason to vary the sequence of the interview in light of what the participant says during the course of the interview. As a rule of thumb, it is best to let the interviewee say what they want to say at the point at which they choose to say it. So if the interviewee provides information on something which comes later in the interview's agenda then collect the information at that time and try to remember not to ask the participant for the information again. For example, if the participant is asked a general question about pain but, during the course of their answer, they go into detail about when the pain started then the later question about how the pain started should mentally be deleted from the list.

Furthermore, remember that the interview is guided by what the participant has to say. It is impossible for the researcher to anticipate everything that might be of relevance for inclusion in the list of questions. There will be circumstances, especially at the start of a research study, when the interviewee may raise issues which seem of interest and relevant to the topic in question but this material does not fit neatly into the list of topics included in the interview schedule. Whenever these circumstances arise, the interviewer should seek to question the participant about these new matters. Of course, this means that the interviewer needs to have the flexibility to develop the questions 'off the cuff'. The next step, of course, is to consider whether to include questions about this matter in future interviews in the series. In other words, researchers should be sensitive to the material that participants provide and should not necessarily be precisely bound by their interview schedule. This, of course, does not mean that any sections of the interview may be dropped on a whim.

It would be normal in any semi-structured interview to start with the wider picture and then focus on the detail. Thus semi-structured interviews in IPA would normally start with the general question which would be followed by specific questions and probes. For example, if the research is about pain then it would be usual to talk with the interviewee about pain before asking about details such as when the pain is worse or the effects that it has on everyday activities.

A sound recording is made of the interview so that a full record of what has been said is available to the researcher. The sound recording has the advantage that the researcher is free to pay close attention to what the interviewee is saying rather than trying to make notes. Video recording is not common though might be considered. However, the advantages of video recording might not outweigh its disadvantages.

In IPA the sound recordings are transcribed prior to data analysis. It is far more convenient to read and check a transcript than it is to move backwards and forwards through different parts of a recording of an interview. Of course, you may need to go back to the original tape for clarification, etc. A transcript also facilitates the ability of the researcher to see relationships between the data and the analysis being carried out on that data. With IPA, transcription is usually a version of the literal, secretarial-style (playscript) transcription in which the words said and by whom are the only things recorded normally. Generally, the Jefferson-style transcription in which extra-linguistic features such as voice inflexions, pauses and other aspects are included will have no place in IPA (see Chapter 6 for a discussion of transcription). Nevertheless, there is no embargo on transcribing such additional features as the expression of emotion. Normally, wide margins are left on each side of the transcribed interview to allow comments to be made about any such relevant features. At the time that the transcription is done, the researcher is free to makes notes about any thoughts or impressions they have, since they may, otherwise, be forgotten. These notes may be made on the left-hand margin and the right-hand margin reserved for noting themes which emerge in the analysis stage. Transcription might take eight times the length of the interview. Furthermore, it is desirable not to take short cuts when transcribing the data.

Data analysis

The IPA method, as presented in the literature, may be seen as consisting of four to six main steps. The precise number depends somewhat on the number of interviews carried out and, to a lesser extent, on the duration of the interviews. A single case may be appropriate. Not surprisingly, many of these steps can be seen to be highly reminiscent of the steps in other forms of qualitative analysis.

Step 1

Initial case familiarisation and initial comments As in any qualitative research, the researcher needs to have a high level of familiarity with their data. This is achieved in part by collecting the data oneself, if possible, but also through doing the transcription and eventually reading and re-reading through those transcripts a number of times. The transcription has two margins on each side and the researcher may use the left-hand margin to make a note of anything which might occur to them as being of interest in the data. This is a little like memos in grounded theory. There are no particular rules about how this is achieved. For example, there is no reason to break the transcription down into units of any particular size and there is no requirement that comments are provided for all sections of the transcription. The analyst may include attempts to summarise or interpret what was said in the interview. At a later stage, the comments may seek to confirm, change or point out inconsistencies between what is said and the attempts to summarise or interpret what is in the transcript.

Step 2

Preliminary theme identification Following further familiarisation with the data, the researcher begins to make notes of the major themes that can be identified in what is said in the transcript. The themes are summarised in a few words which constitute a brief phrase or title for the theme. As many words as do the job is the limit to this. The themes are written down in the right-hand margin against the text to which they refer. Basically, there should be a relationship between the theme and what it says in the text but the theme should be expressed in more theoretical or abstract terms. Anyone struggling with this stage might look at grounded theory (Chapter 8) for ideas about how to proceed.

Step 3

Search for theme interconnections Of course, many of the themes that are identified may group together to form broader or superordinate themes. That is, the researcher examines their list of themes and looks for connections between them. These interconnections lead to ideas about what these superordinate themes might be. So a superordinate theme is a cluster of similar but partially distinct themes. Themes which seem to be similar may be listed together and given a more inclusive title. The development of superordinate themes may be carried out in the following ways:

- Electronically by 'copying and pasting' the names of the themes into a word processor document and then moving them around to form closely related clusters.
- The analysis could be carried out using a qualitative analysis computer program such as NVivo.
- Write the names of the themes on index cards or slips of paper. They can then be moved around on the large flat surface of a desk or table. The spatial connections between the themes can then be explored.

The researcher needs to ensure that the themes developed truly relate to what has been said in the interviews. So it is important to compare the theme titles with the data which ostensibly belongs with the theme. So short excerpts (including the page and line number where they appear) of what the participant said which led to the themes should be compared with the superordinate theme title. Some themes may be dropped if they do not fit into any of the superordinate theme clusters – or because it turns out that there is generally little in the data which serves as evidence of the worth of the theme.

It is at this stage that a student researcher may become stuck in the analysis and may need to be helped to move their analysis forwards by thinking rather more conceptually than had previously been necessary to identify themes. Categories and themes need to be replaced by more abstract and superordinate levels of analysis – this is the interpretative stage. According to Biggerstaff and Thompson:

> Moving away from a purely descriptive level of analysis often poses a difficulty, probably because . . . students have a prior grounding in positivist approaches . . . and consequently may feel a sense of discomfort in making interpretations . . . Yet this is where some of the challenges faced by students encountering qualitative methodologies (including IPA) have arisen. In our experience, this fear, though still encountered in some students, is groundless at both theoretical and practical levels. (Biggerstaff & Thompson, 2008, p. 220)

Box 13.1 discusses Smith's (2011) account of the influence of particular significant textual 'gems' on the analysis.

Box 13.1

KEY CONCEPT

The 'gem' in qualitative analysis

One of the difficulties facing any researcher new to qualitative methods is understanding just how a qualitative analysis is done. It is all very well learning important analytical concepts such as 'axial coding', 'turns' and 'epoché' but these are not that much help when first faced with, say, an interview transcript to analyse. Quite what is one looking for? How does one decide what are the important things going on in the interview? Much

of the insecurity involved in carrying out a qualitative analysis disappears with experience but it is never the most straightforward of processes. Smith (2011) discusses an aspect of IPA analysis which may be relevant to other qualitative analyses. He suggests that a particular extract, perhaps just a few brief words of text, may have a 'significance completely disproportionate to its size' (p. 6). These gems may strike the researcher at the very start of the analytic process when the text is being read through to achieve familiarity and engages the researcher's analytic effort at that time. But that is not the only possibility. A particular passage may intrigue or bemuse the researcher who goes back to that passage on a number of occasions during the analysis. Of course, gems are few and far between compared with the more routine text that takes up, say, the bulk of the interview.

Smith quotes the following as an example of a 'gem' from his own work:

> 'I need to be careful about people and I am a bit worried about what's going to happen to me. Are we all going to get rounded up and taken to a camp somewhere?' (p. 7).

These are the words of Kevin during an interview about chronic benign lower-back pain. Smith was very uneasy when he first read Kevin's words and thought that the text signified something but what that was he regarded as 'elliptical' and 'elusive'. Just what sort of camp is Kevin envisaging and why does he mention this in the interview? The words in themselves are very difficult indeed to make sense of and the meaning only begins to emerge out of the entire body of the data including that from other participants and not just the snippet that is the 'gem' which provides analytic focus.

What emerged from the interviews is that many participants in the study in question represent their situation as a battle between their positive self which is threatened by another much more negative self. They experience shame and are self-denigrating in the interviews. Their physical experiences basically dragged down the positive self that they would like to be. Their words imply a sort of alien takeover of their bodies which was taking over their selves. Another participant, Tony, used the following words: 'I'm some waster, they should have someone who is impressive [for a father], to look up to but how can they look up to me with what I do all bad tempered and crippled, dossing about, lying down every 10 minutes. All they see is a bit of a man' (p. 8). So in Kevin's statement 'Are we all going to get rounded up and taken to a camp somewhere?' Smith sees the fear of retribution by those who suffer as a consequence of the back-pain sufferer's 'bad' self.

Not all gems are as attention catching as the above. Smith argues that there is a sort of spectrum of gems from the 'shining' example, the 'suggestive' example, to the 'secret'. These vary in the extent to which the research and the participant can readily 'see' the meaning of the text identified as worthy of special attention. Figure 13.4 illustrates the different varieties involved.

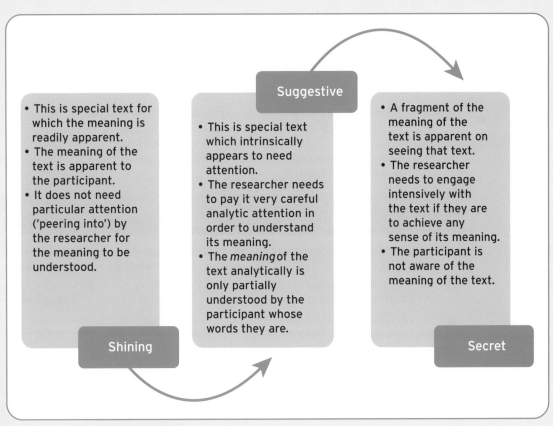

FIGURE 13.4 The varieties of textual 'gems'

Step 4

Systematic table of themes This is a visual way of presenting the structure of superordinate and subordinate themes which have been developed out of the analysis. They are ordered in terms of their overall importance to what the participant was seen to have said, starting off with the most important superordinate theme. The table may include a short phrase from a participant's account to illustrate the theme. It should be noted where the information from the transcript is located. A generic table illustrating this is provided in Table 13.2.

Step 5

Analysis of further cases Where the study is not a single case study, the analysis proceeds to the other cases in much the same way. Themes from the first case may be used for the ensuing cases but, alternatively, each of the new cases can be examined anew. Given the idiographic–nomothetic distinction used in IPA, the researcher needs to consider where the themes are similar between different participants and where they are different and exclusive to a particular individual. This gives an indication of the nature of the variation across different cases. Once all of the transcripts have been analysed, it is appropriate to produce the final table containing the thematic structure unravelled in the analysis. It will take a similar structure to that in Table 13.2.

Step 6

Writing up the analysis The write-up – a project report, a dissertation, a journal article – is best conceived as the final stage of the analysis. This is a common assumption in qualitative research. The report needs to include all of the themes which seemed important in the analysis. Each needs to be carefully described and illustrated with exact quotes from the interview transcripts. Each example should be clear and sufficient to illustrate the theme. The report is where the researcher interprets or makes sense of what participants have said. It is important to make it clear what is interpretation and the basis on which the interpretation has been built. There are two ways of presenting the results in a report. One way is to divide the report into a separate 'Results' and 'Discussion' section. This 'Results' section should describe and illustrate the themes but the 'Discussion' section should show the relationship between the themes identified and the existing literature on the research topic in question. The other way is to have a single 'Results and Discussion' section where the presentation of each theme is followed by a discussion of the literature that is

TABLE 13.2 The structure of the illustrative quotations table for the superordinate Theme A: The phenomenon of paranoia

Superordinate Theme A: The phenomenon of paranoia	Superordinate Theme B	Superordinate Theme C
(a) *Perception of harm: 'People would sit around talking about me, I thought'* Victor 1	(a) Sub-category 1: Illustrative quote	(a) Sub-category 1: Illustrative quote
(b) *Type of harm: 'It felt like people I hardly knew were backstabbing me'.* Janet 1	(b) Sub-category 2: Illustrative quote	(b) Sub-category 2: Illustrative quote
(c) *Intention of harm: 'It felt like I was being deliberately persecuted.'* Norman 2	(c) Sub-category 3: Illustrative quote	
(d) *Acceptability of the belief: 'It was MIS that was behind all of the plotting and telephone tapping.'* Mary 1		

In their work, Campbell and Morrison (2007) refer to the broadest themes as superordinate themes and the sub-categories (e.g. Perception of harm) as master themes.
Based on Campbell and Morrison (2007) and Howitt and Cramer (2011).

relevant to that theme. Either is acceptable. (See Chapter 15 for a fuller discussion of qualitative report writing.)

Box 13.3 later in the chapter illustrates the use of IPA in the context of a case study approach.

When to use interpretative phenomenological analysis

IPA is about people's experiences. So if the research is about how people have personally experienced significant phenomena such as pain or serious illness then IPA is a consideration in terms of methodology. IPA is not a general tool to tackle any form of qualitative data in the way that thematic analysis and grounded theory can be. Furthermore, IPA is not a finely tuned analysis of how people talk about their experiences. It is a 'what they say' rather than 'how they say it' method. King et al. (2008) make the distinction more eloquently:

> There is no question that, as a qualitative methodology, phenomenological psychology contrasts with psychologies of the 'discursive turn.' The work of phenomenologists often rests on language, of course. The interviewee 'expresses' her experience; the researcher reads this expression in terms of socially available constructs. Nothing is clearer. The words and the experience – there is a great distinction here between phenomenological and discursive approaches. For, though there is no resistance at all among phenomenologists to the fundamental experience-shaping function of language and discursive practices, the strongly held position of phenomenology is that it is *of experience that language speaks* . . . (King et al., 2008, p. 82)

Of course, the potential research topics which centre around the theme of 'experience' is enormous. Indeed, it is hard to think of many areas of human activity for which how they are 'experienced' is irrelevant.

Examples of interpretative phenomenological analysis

Boxes 13.2 and 13.3 involve three different aspects of IPA analysis. Brief comments on each of them follow:

- The first example, Box 13.2, concerns the experience of traumatic brain injury. It involves the struggle from the old identity to a new identity as a permanently injured person.
- The second example, Box 13.3, is a case study of an alcoholic woman. Actually, it is really a $N = 1$ study since the analysis is developed from the data. A case study, in terms of its original meaning, is the analysis of a case in terms of current knowledge, which is not quite the same thing.

It is obvious that most of the topics that IPA researchers have addressed are ones which require great sensitivity from the researcher which the student may feel unable to match. So care needs to be exercised before jumping into IPA research lest you step painfully on the sensibilities of your research participants. This is not to suggest that IPA should be out of bounds to student researchers, merely that it may stretch their interpersonal skills and may need careful handling.

Box 13.2

ILLUSTRATIVE RESEARCH STUDY

Phenomenological analysis: the experience
following brain injury

Traumatic brain injury may leave the individual with profound distress. Major changes occur in their circumstances due to the physical and intellectual disabilities which can follow. Depression, anxiety, obsessive-compulsive disorder and post-traumatic stress disorder are some of the outcomes which researchers have noted. Roundhill, Williams and Hughes (2007) discuss the relevance of the concept of 'loss' (as in bereavement) to understanding survival from traumatic brain injury. Bereavement, on the face of things, may be a good way of describing what happens in traumatic brain injury. A growing research literature has developed which has concentrated on questionnaire methods of assessment of bereavement although a small number of studies have explored the experience of such bereavement processes qualitatively. Of course, the experience of bereavement is the sort of phenomenon that phenomenological research would have an interest in. The dual process model of grief suggests that it is an 'oscillating' process between (a) 'loss orientation' and (b) 'recovery orientation'. The study that we will consider (Roundhill et al., 2007) attempts to understand the experience of bereavement over a substantial two-year period following survival. The criteria for inclusion were (a) surviving severe traumatic brain injury that had occurred at least two years before, (b) having insight, memory, verbal skills and so forth so that they could actively participate in the research, and (c) the person had experienced no important bereavements during that period of time.

The participants in this research were recruited with the help of a charity dealing with survivors of traumatic brain injury. A pilot study was employed which involved a victim who had written and given talks about his experiences. He was also part of the discussion with the researchers about what to include in the interview. The participants in the research were six survivors of road traffic accidents and one survivor of an assault. The report includes an informative table summarising the participants' characteristics, i.e. their fictitious names,

their gender, their age, the type of trauma they had experienced, and the number of years since the injury.

The interview itself was the typical semi-structured kind used in IPA and covered the areas of 'loss, coping, awareness, and current self-identity' (Roundhill et al., 2007, p. 244). All of the interviews were recorded and transcribed, though no description is given of the transcription method. According to the authors, they analysed the data using the procedures for IPA (Smith, Jarman, & Osborn, 1999). They also suggest that the analysis took a 'reflexive stance' in which the analyst's role in the interpretation and construction of themes was attended to. The 'reflexive stance' involved keeping a 'reflective journal' during the data collection and analysis stages. This is rather like memo-writing in grounded theory. In this, the analyst 'endeavored to maintain an awareness of the application of the DPM [Dual Process Model] while remaining open to the development of new themes that were not necessarily congruent with the grief theory' (Roundhill et al., 2007, p. 244).

So, it is very clear that the analysis was in part led by pre-existing theory although the research was open to ideas emerging from the interviews. The researchers identified four superordinate themes in their analysis but no subordinate themes. The lack of subordinate themes in the analysis is surprising though it may be a consequence of the very limited number of data sources involved in the study. The structure of their analysis is presented in diagrammatic form in Table 13.3.

Traditional views of bereavement have tended to describe it as a number of stages which have to be 'worked through'. However, this is very different from recent research as encapsulated into the dual process model of bereavement. According to Roundhill et al.:

The DPM posits that individuals need to 'dose' their exposure to the pain of loss, suggesting the need for relief from active mourning and to attend to other demands. The model also enables the consideration of the benefits of a degree of denial in the process of adjusting to loss. This orientation away from grief

TABLE 13.3 The theme structure from interviews about traumatic brain injury

Superordinate theme: emotion focus	Superordinate theme: progress focus	Superordinate theme: issues of control	Superordinate theme: post-injury growth
• **Example:** 'The brain is obviously trying to protect the body, the person inside of it … it would just be too much to take in. It wouldn't be well enough to handle it.' Martin • No sub-themes provided	• **Example:** 'Well first of all I try to address any particular problem that comes along myself. I always try to do it, as I said to you about helping myself with memory and things like that … And "try" is a very wide – although it's three letters it can be very, very long.' Mark • No sub-themes provided	• **Example:** 'If you don't do it, nobody else can do it for you. You've got to do it for yourself. You've got to give yourself something for a goal.' Don • No sub-themes provided	• **Example:** 'I'm completely different, because in my younger days I was a bit of a tearaway. I've quietened down. It's definitely positive, because I would have probably ended up in prison, for a long time, or dead.' Ken • No sub-themes provided

Quotations from Roundhill et al. (2007)

work serves not only as a protective function against overwhelming feelings but also enables other stressors, such as altered role, identity, and the demands of new tasks, to be confronted. The parallel with adjustment following severe TBI [traumatic brain injury] seems clear here, with the individual being required to acknowledge and adjust to circumstances which are often significantly different. (p. 250)

Roundhill et al. suggest that the evidence of the sort of oscillation process between 'loss orientation' and 'recovery orientation' in the dual process model was poorly supported by the interviews. That is, grief does not drip away, allowing the individual to accommodate to their new situation. Despite what the dual process model suggests, it would seem that the survivors of traumatic brain injury initially swing heavily to dealing with the loss and then move on to the recovery process. These different processes, they say, are in a state of dynamic equilibrium and are not a sequence of stages to be worked through and thus dealt with. The

process, according to Roundhill et al.'s participants, may be described in terms of stages as shown in Figure 13.5.

It is not the purpose here to evaluate Roundhill et al.'s contribution to theory. Much more important in this context is how using IPA can lead to theory development. By conceptualising the processes involved in traumatic brain injury survival in terms of bereavement, the researchers offer a way of thinking which makes intuitive sense. However, the dual process model has assumptions which fail to be demonstrated in the experiences of the traumatic brain injury victim. Hence, this is potentially an important theoretical contribution. Not all IPA analyses demonstrate such an impact on theory. But, as an illustration of IPA, Roundhill et al.'s paper has a lot to offer, especially for those who suggest that qualitative research merely confirms the obvious. Like many qualitative research reports, there is only limited discussion of the analysis stages and some expansion of these would benefit newcomers to IPA research.

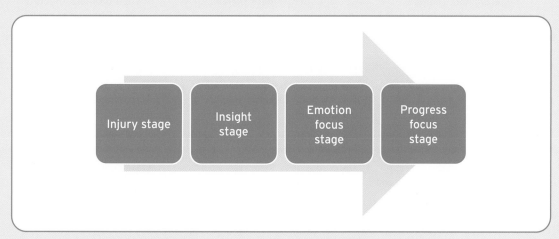

FIGURE 13.5 Stages in the bereavement process in traumatic brain injury survivors

Box 13.3

ILLUSTRATIVE RESEARCH STUDY

Interpretative phenomenological analysis: the alcoholic woman and self and identity

Shinebourne and Smith (2009) describe a case study using IPA of an alcoholic woman's experience of addiction and its impact on her sense of self and identity. Adopting a case study approach involving a single individual is an accepted procedure with IPA. So this research represents the nomothetic orientation of some IPA research. IPA researchers argue that where a person's descriptions of their experiences are exceptionally rich or where the case in question is particularly compelling for other reasons, the case study approach becomes particularly appropriate. There are copious amounts of quantitative research available on alcoholism and alcohol use. Although qualitative research is not so common there is a belief that qualitative methods make available to the researcher the lives of alcoholics as they are actually lived. Radley and Chamberlain (2001) make an argument for the unique power of the case study which renders the research impossible to reduce to a few variables.

The 31-year-old single woman in the study is given the name Alison. She was an attendee at a women's day centre concerned with problematic alcohol use. Although the researchers interviewed four women in total, Alison's interview material was exceptionally rich and detailed. The researchers had a prepared interview schedule which they applied flexibly. Three separate interviews were conducted with Alison, producing about three hours' worth of recordings which were transcribed verbatim for the purposes of the analysis. The first interview was carefully reviewed and issues for further discussion were noted and raised at the second interview. Some of the original questions were returned to in each of the three interviews. This interview structure is an interesting one and may have advantages for relatively inexperienced researchers.

The analysis process followed the initial stages which are outlined in the present chapter. Of course, it was a case study so some of the later stages were not included. Radley and Chamberlain's analysis reports not just the superordinate themes but sub-themes too. In addition, very short illustrative quotations were selected for each theme and the line numbers on the transcript from which they were taken also noted. The theme structure is illustrated in Table 13.4 although the original paper simply

TABLE 13.4 Shinebourne and Smith's (2009) summary of themes with illustrative quotes and page numbers

Superordinate Theme 1: The experience of the self as drunk	Superordinate Theme 2: I created such a character for myself	Superordinate Theme 3: Perception of the self
Metaphoric expressions of the experience of being drunk. 'Big wave' 449	The self changing through drinking. 'Having to drink so much in order to get to this person' 44–5	Metaphors expressing perception of self. 'Mixture of water and fire' 809
Escalating drinking. 'It would just spiral and spiral' 25	The process of becoming the other self. 'My body was taking over a character' 40	Positive appraisals of self. 'Quiet and contemplative' 66
The harmful experience of being drunk. 'Having blackouts, memory loss' 15	Feeling the other self. 'Feeling totally in my body' 1052	Negative appraisals of self. 'I can't really assert myself' 1015
The high and the low of the drinking experience. 'Creative and energetic and interesting' 498	The porous body. 'When you are drunk you are open to spirits visiting your body' 475	Moral judgements of self. 'Guilt and anxiety you have done something wrong' 504–505
Ambivalence and dilemmas. 'If only I could get to that without so much alcohol' 488	The self as a process of becoming. 'From one day to the next I really do change' 1110	

reports the superordinate and sub-themes as a list. This table of themes is the outcome of the sort of back-and-forth process between stages of the analysis which is a feature of most qualitative data analysis methods – if not all of them.

According to the researchers, the first theme illustrates how Alison sees the experience of drunkenness as one of 'flux, oscillation and instability' (p. 155), the second theme presents the transformation of Alison into another personality when drunk, and the third theme illustrates how Alison sees herself as many different parts and her ambivalence about drinking. Each of these superordinate themes is discussed at some considerable length in Shinebourne and Smith. It is interesting to note how in the original paper, the

authors related this final theme of different parts to the general psychological literature on dissociative experiences. In particular, they draw on the work of Seligman and Kirmayer (2008) who:

> maintain that the association between dissociative experiences and trauma is predominantly a Euro-American conception as understood in the psychiatric perspective. In contrast, dissociative experiences in many socio-cultural contexts 'seem to be associated with the expression of alternative selves or identities that were not created in the context of trauma'. (Shinebourne & Smith, 2009, p. 41)

This, of course, provides a refreshingly different perspective on Alison's experiences.

Evaluation of interpretative phenomenological analysis

The good news about IPA for many psychologists is that it is an approach to qualitative analysis which grows out of the traditions of psychology. So when one studies an IPA-based paper the very strong impression emerges that it is rooted firmly in psychology. This is so for both qualitative research and quantitative research in psychology. IPA is not at 'war' with mainstream psychology in the way some other qualitative methods present themselves on occasion. So, for example, it is difficult to find in IPA studies the antipathy to cognitive psychology that can be found in discourse analysis.

At the same time, IPA as a method is nowhere near so highly developed as some other qualitative analysis methods. This may be responsible for the lack of fierce methodological debates in IPA compared with other data analysis methods. Perhaps it is early days for IPA procedures and that schisms have simply not had time to develop. IPA is a broad approach to data collection and analysis which is about the development of a specific area of research – people's experiences of significant life events. As such, IPA does not seem to be as concerned to develop a coherent body of phenomenological theory in the way that other qualitative methods delve deeply into developing their theoretical infrastructure. According to Shinebourne (2011) there is a commonly held view that IPA lacks a sound theoretical basis. She suggests that students believe that IPA is easy to do because the lack of a philosophical background is no encumbrance (see also Willig, 2008b). This may be an unfair claim but Giorgi (2010) argues that IPA has not shown just how its methods relate to philosophical phenomenology and Sousa (2008) even suggests that the underlying theory of IPA is presented in just two pages! There may have been an element of truth in this but this has been substantially rectified in the writings of Smith et al. (2009). In addition, Shinebourne (2011) refutes these claims and argues that the theoretical underpinnings of IPA are both in line with the existential phenomenological paradigm but, more importantly, can link phenomenological research with the wider research endeavour of psychology.

Any researcher new to qualitative research and IPA probably will be less perplexed by its data collection methods than by the process of analysis. Just how does a researcher go about the process of interpreting what is said in an interview in a way which moves beyond the literal meaning of the words to their psychological implications? No matter how close a description is to a full account of the analytic process, there is a stubborn void when it comes to explaining just how to go about an interpretation. Of course, previous theory may be a starting point but it is not a necessary starting point in IPA. Smith discusses this very problem in relation to hermeneutic analysis in general, irrespective of discipline:

> I am left feeling there is still a gap, however: When I try to make sense of this person saying this thing, what is actually happening? Interpretation is a mystery, invokes a sense of wonder and I'm not sure the hermeneutic theory has got near to explaining or saying all there is to say about that mysterious process. Partly because the type of encounter envisaged by hermeneutics was different, when it comes to explaining what is happening when one person tries to make sense of what another person is saying, I would suggest there is still a great deal that remains unknown. (Smith, 2007, p. 11)

Perhaps it is not comforting to know that even the experts have the very problems faced by the rest of us. But at least it is a shared frustration. Again, the more one reads publications on any method the sooner one not only appreciates the difficulties but experiences the various types of analytic solutions that researchers have put forward.

You will find a discussion of template analysis in Box 13.4. This has many similarities to IPA but may be more varied in the ways in which themes are identified. Meier, Boivin and Meier (2008) discuss a procedure called theme-analysis which has many of the characteristics of thematic analysis discussed in Chapter 7. However, like IPA, theme-analysis is built solidly on phenomenological approaches to psychology. They present a detailed account of their method, which has both qualitative and quantitative components. Specifically, it is an approach to the changes which occur during psychotherapy.

Box 13.4

KEY CONCEPT

Template analysis

IPA is not the only way of analysing qualitative data in a way which generates themes. The point of template analysis is to generate a coding scheme (template) which identifies the themes in the data as developed in the researcher's analysis and organises them in a way which is both meaningful and productive. In template analysis the themes are arranged in a hierarchical manner with the broadest categories at the top of the hierarchy and the narrowest themes at the bottom of the hierarchy. The themes, in part, may be developed *a priori* (in advance) of the data analysis. The sources of ideas may well be pre-existing theories, though, equally, they may be the insight of the researcher or dependent on directly examining the data. No matter the source of the themes, they must be established as worthwhile against the actual data. Themes essentially capture the perceptions and experiences of the participants.

Unlike, say, grounded theory, coding in template analysis merely consists of checking the template themes against the data to indicate places in the data where a particular theme can be identified and placing a label or code next to it. Once an apparently satisfactory template is developed on part of the data, it is applied and evaluated against all of the data and, perhaps, modified in light of this.

See King (1998) and Crabtree and Miller (1999) for discussions of templates.

CONCLUSION

Compared with discourse analysis (Chapter 9), for example, IPA seems to be much more content orientated. That is, the domain of IPA is phenomena as experienced by the individual – albeit interpreted through the analysis of the researcher. Although its origins are in the fields of social and health psychology, human experience is an important aspect of many fields of psychology. Thus, IPA eventually may have a niche throughout much of the discipline. Since IPA is built on theories of human experience (especially phenomenology and hermeneutics), one would not expect it to compete with qualitative methods primarily concerned with the theory of language (e.g. conversation analysis and discourse analysis). While the potential is there for a researcher to explore the role of language in action in IPA, this is not too easy a task since IPA accepts that at the core of what people say is something of substance which warrants interpretation and analysis in its own right – not quite the subjectivist/relativist position of other qualitative methods.

Cognitive psychology is often very critically addressed by exponents of discourse analysis – perhaps a better phrase is that cognitive psychology is rejected in discourse analysis. This is most certainly not the case with IPA which accommodates to theory about internal psychological states and cognition. IPA is about a psychological phenomenon which theories of language as action simply do not attempt to incorporate – experience. Probably there could be an extensive debate about the extent to which experience is mediated through language but the bottom line is that IPA theorists do not need to take a strong position on this. They simply need appropriate ways of developing theory about experience.

In short, IPA has radically different historical origins from many of the other methods of qualitative data analysis in this book. Its openness to traditional psychological approaches while insisting on the importance of human experience makes it more amenable to researchers firmly committed to mainstream psychology. One does not have to abandon a belief that mainstream psychology has made substantial progress in terms of understanding the person to be attracted to IPA.

KEY POINTS

- Interpretative phenomenological analysis developed out of the work of health psychologists in the 1990s. Its historical roots are primarily in the philosophies of phenomenology and hermeneutics though the influence of sociology (especially symbolic interactionism) and psychology, in general, are also readily apparent.

- IPA, regarded as a derivative of the phenomenological tradition in psychology and philosophy, is clearly distinguishable from traditional phenomenology in that the researcher is not the person whose experiences are studied. Instead people having undergone significant types of life experience provide descriptions of their experiences. The researcher both describes and interprets these experiences using a variety of psychological concepts and theories.

- IPA shares many techniques with other qualitative methods. In particular, the primary aim of the analysis is to identify themes in what participants have to say about their experiences. The main processes of analysis involve the literal transcription of pertinent interview data which is then processed by suggesting themes which draw together aspects of the data. Further to this, the researcher may seek to identify superordinate (or master) themes which embrace a number of themes identified during the analysis process.

- IPA theory tends to be rather more inclusive of general psychological theory of many different sorts than, say, grounded theory which proponents claim is incompatible with certain kinds of psychological theorising. In many ways, IPA is situated relatively close to thematic analysis – its methods are similar. Nevertheless, thematic analysis lacks the content specificity and theoretical underpinnings which characterise IPA.

ADDITIONAL RESOURCES

Birkbeck College, University of London (2009). Interpretative Phenomenological Analysis. www.ipa.bbk.ac.uk/references (accessed 24 April 2015).

Eatough, V., & Smith, J. A. (2008). Interpretative phenomenological analysis. In C. Willig and W. Stainton-Rogers (Eds.), *The SAGE handbook of qualitative psychology* (pp. 179–195) Los Angeles: Sage.

Larkin, M. (n.d.). Interpretative Phenomenological Analysis: This is a place to find, post and discuss materials and resources for the support of IPA learning and research. ipacommunity.tumblr.com/ (accessed 24 April 2015).

School of Human & Health Sciences, University of Huddersfield (2011). Template Analysis. www.hud.ac.uk/hhs/research/template-analysis/ (accessed 24 April 2015).

Smith, J. A., & Eatough, V. (2006). Interpretative phenomenological analysis. In G. M. Breakwell, S. Hammond, C. Fife-Shaw & J. A. Smith (Eds.), *Research methods in psychology* (3rd ed., pp. 322–341). London: Sage.

Smith, J. A., & Osborn, M. (2008). Interpretative phenomenological analysis. In J. A. Smith (Ed.), *Qualitative psychology: A practical guide to research methods* (2nd ed. pp. 53–80). London: Sage.

Smith, J. A., Larkin, M., & Flowers, P. (2009). *Interpretative phenomenological analysis: Theory, method and research.* London: Sage.

Storey, L. (2007). Doing interpretative phenomenological analysis. In E. Lyons & A. Coyle (Eds.), *Analysing qualitative data in psychology* (pp. 51–64). London: Sage.

CHAPTER 14

Narrative analysis

Overview

- Narrative is a story linking events in a chronological fashion. It involves an interpretation of what we and others do and is produced during social interaction. Narratives are overwritten with moral, evaluative and other themes which are important in understanding how the individual relates to the events.

- Narrative psychology has grown since the 1980s to study the 'storied' self of people. This, basically, is the idea that people think, perceive, imagine and act morally according to narrative structures. Narrative psychology is concerned with the content, structure and function of the stories which we create to account for what is happening to us.

- Narrative analysis is a form of qualitative analysis which is dependent on the ideas developed in narrative psychology. This stresses how narrative is a metaphor for personality. Narrative can be analysed using a wide range of qualitative methods. However, the phrase "narrative analysis" is best reserved for analyses based on the theory underlying narrative psychology, rather than, say, discursive psychology.

- In a narrative, there are changes that occur over a period of time which involve a number of different characters and some form of action. The term 'emplotment' is used to describe how the narrative is put together, including plots and subplots.

- Narrative may be understood using virtually any qualitative research method. For example, social constructionist approaches to narrative concentrate on the ways in which narrative is produced in social interaction. However, this constructionist point of view is not the focus of narrative analysis based on narrative psychology. This sometimes offers a 'realist' interpretation of narratives which assumes that narrative can help the researcher understand how an individual thinks and feels about substantial and ongoing aspects of their life.

- The roots of narrative psychology can be seen in the writings of Wilhelm Wundt, Sigmund Freud, John Dollard, Charlotte Buhler and Gordon Allport. In particular, the interest of some of these in researching people's life stories or life history was fundamental to the emergence of narrative psychology. However, the work of Theodore Sarbin and Jerome Bruner in the late twentieth century was the immediate stimulus to its development.

- The narrative interview can take a number of forms. Perhaps the most systematic is that of McAdams, which helps the interviewee generate a narrative-based account of important events in their life. These interviews are the commonest material on which narrative analysis is carried out.

● Narrative analysis proceeds in a number of different ways. This chapter discusses Crossley's approach in the main.

What is narrative analysis?

The term 'storied self' appears in discussions of narrative. This refers to the way in which we create our 'self' using narratives and stories to account for what has happened or what is happening to us:

> Narrative psychology is concerned with the structure, content, and function of the stories that we tell each other and ourselves in social interaction. It accepts that we live in a storied world and that we interpret the actions of others and ourselves through the stories we exchange. Through narratives we not only shape the world and ourselves but they are shaped for us through narrative. (Murray, 2003, p. 95)

People who have undergone some sort of trauma provide instances of how they often try to make sense of the events that they are going through by creating stories or narratives. A narrative is essentially a written or spoken account of connected events with an underlying time dimension. It is a story and takes the form of a story. This definition, however, fails to indicate just how much our narratives have to do with social interaction and matters such as identity. A narrative is closer to being a substantial chunk of one's life (a life history) than it is about what happened, say, when we went out last night. To tell a friend on the telephone that you went to the movies last night and had an ice cream does not amount to a meaningful narrative for the purposes of narrative analysis. According to Sarbin:

> The story has a beginning, middle and an ending. The story is held together by recognizable patterns of events called plots. Central to the plot structure are human predicaments and attempted resolutions. (Sarbin, 1986, p. 3)

In this chapter, we will regard narrative analysis as a system of analysing narratives using the basic concepts of narrative psychology. However, researchers from other disciplines (and sometimes within psychology) would have a very different view of what narrative analysis is. We will see something of this range during the course of this chapter. The construction of narrative seems to be a human propensity which helps people deal with a confused and disorderly world by bringing a state of orderliness. Narrative in relation to illness is common since illness brings about this very sort of disorder by disrupting the orderliness of regular everyday life. There are many narratives concerning illness to be found – so much so that some see it as evidence of the need to construct narratives or tell stories about their illness. Anatole Broyard (1992), who died of cancer, wrote that 'story telling seems to be a natural reaction to illness. People bleed stories . . . ' However, narratives do not flow unchangingly like blood according to Murray (2000) but are shaped, structured and given form according to circumstances. The task of the narrative researcher is to understand the nature of this.

The difficulty of locating narrative analysis as a field of research

Narrative analysis is a very widely used term which is not always used exclusively for qualitative research (Garson, 2013). Leaving the quantitative approaches aside, there are several different approaches to understanding narrative, some of which have their origin in linguistics and sociology but the origins of others are the work of psychologists. While it is difficult to draw the boundaries for the topic of narrative since it spreads through several disciplines, one can meaningfully identify the start of narrative psychology as being, in the 1970s and especially the 1980s, under the influence of psychologists such as Jerome Bruner, Theodore Sarbin, and Kenneth and Mary Gergen. Given this wide disciplinary interest in narrative, it is not surprising to find that the various approaches do not boil down to a single central method. Figure 14.1 gives a brief glimpse of some influences of other disciplines on narrative, important events in the history of narrative psychology, and aspects of narrative analysis. There are also forms of therapy based on narrative (e.g. White & Epston, 1990). Of course, a person's identity which can be studied through narrative is of therapeutic importance. The important thing here is that narrative analysis is just part of the research field 'narrative' and that other disciplines have their own approaches to the topic. Narrative analysis is a multitude of different things, as we shall see, and it is difficult to specify just what its boundaries are. Narrative analysis is probably too young a field in psychology for a complete consensus to have emerged about exactly what it is and how it is done.

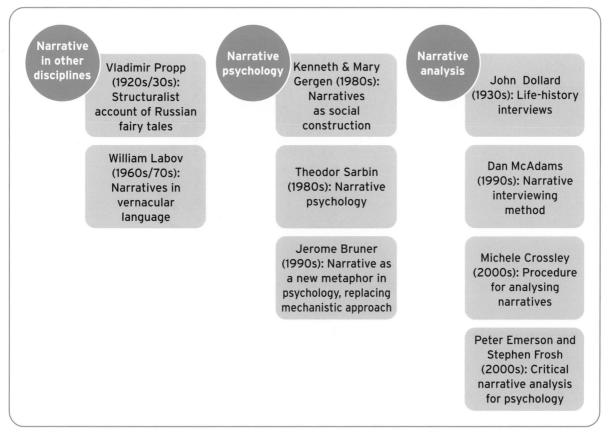

FIGURE 14.1 Some different aspects of narrative

Narrative analysis does not usually involve the fine-grained, line-by-line analyses which characterise, say, some discourse analysis and all conversation analysis (Chapters 9 and 10). Of course, if the researcher wishes to study just how a person constructs versions of their self, for example, through language and conversation in the form of narrative then discourse analysis and conversation analysis may be the appropriate choice. Such an essentially social constructionist (see Box 1.2 in Chapter 1) position on narrative is advocated by Kenneth and Mary Gergen as a way of understanding narratives. More usually, however, narrative analysis as discussed in this chapter accepts that people construct their selves, their identities, their attitudes and so forth in ways which differ according to the social context of the construction. Nevertheless, it also takes the view that narratives communicate things which are the reality of people's lives as they live them. In other words, one point of view is to treat narratives as the person saying something about the real experiences of their lives (e.g. Crossley, 2000).

'Narrative analysis' is a title used to refer to a wide variety of different styles of work. So it may be seen as a sort of umbrella term rather than one which identifies a particular style of research with pinpoint accuracy. The newcomer to narrative analysis may sometimes get confused about what is and what is not narrative analysis. More experienced researchers might simply be used to the portmanteau nature of its use. Horton-Salway (2001) argues that there are three broad types of analysis of narrative – namely the realist, cognitivist and interactionist approaches. These are presented in more detail in Figure 14.2. These stretch from what a quantitative researcher might assume (realism) to the discourse analytic position (interactivism). Each of these is a 'valid' way of exploring narrative but some require skills in other qualitative methods. Murray (2000) extends the discussion of this problem by suggesting that there are different levels of analysis of narrative. His specific focus is on health psychology but his points have wider applicability than that. According to Murray, there are at

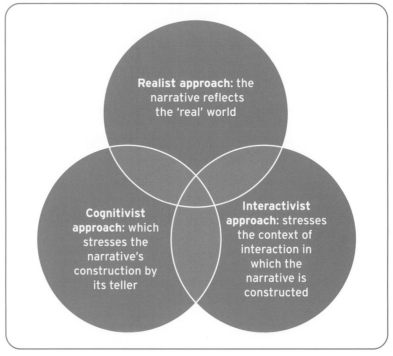

FIGURE 14.2 Horton-Salway's three types of analysis of narrative

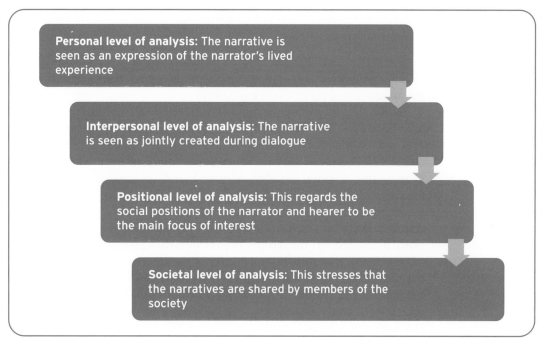

FIGURE 14.3 Different levels of analysis for discourse

least four different levels of the analysis referred to as narrative analysis as illustrated in Figure 14.3. His different levels are not entirely different from Horton-Salway's suggestion, of course. These, it should be stressed, are levels of analysis and not different types of reality.

What is a narrative?

According to Murray (2003), narrative functions to provide order where there is disorder. In other words, the narrator is attempting to bring organisation to something which is essentially disorganised and, consequently, lacking meaning. Disruptions to life due to personal, financial, health or other problems provide challenges to everyday routine and narratives help to restore order and meaning. Consequently, narrative psychology has adherents in the fields of clinical and health psychology where such stressors are commonplace among clients. McAdams (2008) suggests that there are six agreed principles which can be drawn from narrative psychology concerning personal narratives (as opposed to, say, the narratives in books). Personal narratives are sometimes referred to as self-narratives in the narrative psychology literature. The putative agreed principles are:

- Principle 1: The self is storied.
- Principle 2: Narratives integrate lives and provide a coherent account of the individual 'scenes' in the narrative.
- Principle 3: Narratives are told in social relationships.
- Principle 4: Narratives change over time.
- Principle 5: Narratives are cultural texts and reflect the culture and the culture's ways of talking narratively.

- Principle 6: Some narratives are better than others in that narratives are intrinsically intertwined with morality and that some personal narratives reflect psychologically more healthy selves.

These principles are largely self-evident, of course, represent in terms of an alternative to aspects of mainstream psychology.

Broadly, narrative psychology is concerned with the stories which we produce to tell about ourselves and the implications of these stories for understanding our lives. This is a natural part of interaction and people speak narratively even when they have not been asked to do so. Narratives have a point to them which may be in the form of some sort of moral message. Narrative analysis is the application of concepts from narrative psychology to understanding the narratives produced by individuals. In narrative analysis the researcher concentrates on specific instances of narrative to understand the ways in which stories are made by people and how these stories are used in order to understand the world. The perspective of narrative analysis is primarily that of the teller of the story, not the hearer of the story. The hearer (the researcher) carries out the analysis and interpretation but the focus is the person supplying the narrative. It is part of the task of the researcher to elicit suitable data for analysis and there are special techniques of qualitative interviewing which encourage the production of suitable narrative information.

Narratives, then, are part of the way in which people represent their self and the social world both publicly to others and privately to themselves. The main characteristics of a narrative are as follows:

- A narrative involves some sort of transformation which occurs over time.
- There is some sort of action.
- There are various characters.

The word 'emplotment' is sometimes used to describe the ways in which the various parts of a narrative are put together to make a story which would include major plots, some subplots, and diversions and digressions from the main story. The plot gives a narrative structure and connects the story's beginning with the story's end. But, more than that, the plot links different episodes in order to tie the story together.

It should be very clear that the following is *not* a narrative account of someone's life:

I left school when I was sixteen and worked at various jobs for a while. Nevertheless, when I was twenty I went to university. During my time there I became engaged to Chris and we got married three years later. We have three children. I work as a lawyer and my partner is an accountant.

It is not simply that the story is short. The problem is it is little more than a few 'beads on a string' (Dollard, 1935, p. 3). What is clearly lacking is any truly personal information and any use of information in a way which reflects the culture in which the life is lived. Look at the following and the richer narrative style quickly becomes apparent.

My father died when I was eleven and there wasn't a lot of money in the family though we were well cared for. So I left school when I was sixteen to get some cash. I remember that at one stage I had three jobs at one time and helped Mum in a small way financially. Nevertheless, when I was twenty I went to university because mother had remarried and didn't need me so much. I didn't have much of a sense of direction in my life until I met Chris, my partner since then. When things were more secure, we got married three years later when Emma, our first child, was on the way. I was offered a job by her father in his law firm. She felt it important to have the security of a career and she has worked as an accountant ever since the children got a bit older.

Of course, it is part of the task of the researcher to carry out their research in ways which are conducive to the production of rich narrative. Otherwise it might not happen. Of course, qualitative interviewing is one way of getting rich data but geared to the needs of the research. So, qualitative interviews are typical of the data used in narrative analysis.

Narratives have a range of functions in the context of social interaction including the following:

- Holding the attention of others in conversation – once a story is being told then the chances of being interrupted by another is reduced.

- Narratives can be used to provide a way of looking at problems faced by the individual. The narrative can be used to blame others or life's circumstances for the individual's problems.

- Narratives can be used to evidence things that the individual claims. For example, rather than simply express a dislike or prejudice against a neighbour, putting things in the form of a story from one's own experiences tends to be more accepted and successful.

Social constructionism and narrative

Of course, the way in which a narrative is structured depends on factors such as who is the narrator, who is the audience and what is the social context. But it can also be treated as something more real – something representing the substance of people's lives. Thus narrative is slightly problematic within qualitative psychology since it can be regarded as a form of social product in the context of social constructionism. The consequence of this is that the narrative should be regarded as emerging out of the situation of its production and that it will vary accordingly. This is very evidently the basis of the narrative theory of Gergen and Gergen (1983). In contrast, many narrative theorists tend to view a narrative more as if it were some form of *ethnographic* testimony. William Labov (1927–), a linguist who studied vernacular narratives, regarded narratives as essentially real (Labov, 1972). One of the key characteristics of postmodern, qualitative psychology is the rejection of the idea that there is a 'self' or 'identity' which can be studied as if they were some physical object, unchanging and immutable. Social constructionist views of the self hold that self and identity are intimately and inseparably linked to language and language practices which are part of our everyday lives and social interaction. As a consequence, the postmodernist view is that there is no archetypal self which can be understood in isolation from the practices of social interaction and interpretation. According to Crossley (2007), 'If there is no "one" essential nature or self to describe, then the concept of "a" self, of "having" or "possessing" a self, must be abandoned' (p. 132).

Typically, social constructionist approaches to psychology have a difficulty. This boils down to the question of what is happening when people are using language – just what is going on inside of the person when they produce conversation, etc. of the sort that discourse analysts and conversation analysts focus upon? Surely people can be reflexive in the production of language, for example, so just how does this work?

By concentrating on what can be observed in language and conversation, discourse analysis and conversation analysis simply side-step important psychological issues, the argument goes. This is sometimes referred to as the *loss of the subject*. If narrative psychology is to avoid the social constructionist's loss of the subject then the idea that narratives allow the construction of a variety of subjective positions none of which is the 'real' position has to be replaced. Narrative psychology provides an approach to analysis offering opportunities to include this missing subjective element. The subjective element is regarded as 'essentially personal, coherent and "real"?' (Crossley, 2007, p. 131). The way in which a person thinks and feels about what is happening to them is a psychological reality. This is not to deny that people can be contradictory, fragmentary, varied and changeable in terms of how they construct matters in different contexts. It is merely to argue that within this range of possibilities it is usually possible to identify a coherence or relationship between what people say and their experience of self.

So, according to Crossley, narrative psychology adopts what she describes as an underlying realist epistemology (though not all narrative psychologists would agree with this, as we have seen). The idea is that there are facts about a person's conscious experiences of self, etc. which are there to be found out and known by the researcher and it is the task of narrative psychology to seek out and know these 'facts'. None of this is to reject the relativist argument but to imply that somewhere there is a usable degree of consistency – that there is 'something' there. In contrast, the constructionist discourse analysis would regard this as a fundamental (and fatal) problem and reject the use of language to study an individual's experience of a single self. Instead, the discourse analyst would look at the various ways in which self is constructed in the narrative or the narrative interview. Crossley is essentially putting forward the critical realism viewpoint although she does not identify this as such.

A narrative is usually longer than the 'accounts' which are a feature of discourse analysis. The discourse analyst's task can be achieved with relatively short pieces of text but not so narrative analysis. If we take for granted that psychological narrative analysis has the core task of exploring self and identity, then substantive narratives are needed in order to carry out this work. Furthermore, narrative psychologists concentrate on the actual contents of the narrative rather than its discursive features. The narrative will concern some significant event or trauma in the person's life. These events are the reason why the narrative has been produced in the first place. Examples of topics which could be effectively studied using narrative analysis are the experience of childbirth, pregnancy, stillbirth and abortion. Of course, these are the very sorts of topic which interpretative phenomenological analysis (Chapter 13) could also research.

The development of narrative analysis

Some psychologists in the early twentieth century were adherents of the life history, which is essentially narrative, as a means of studying important aspects of people's real lives. According to Murray (2003) we can trace the study of narratives in psychology at least back to Wilhelm Wundt (1832–1920) who in his *Volkerpsychologie* would stress the importance of myths in human life. Others have suggested that Sigmund Freud (1856–1939) developed his psycho-analytic theories by listening to the narratives of his patients in therapy. The names of John Dollard (1900–80) (discussed in Chapter 2), and Charlotte Bühler (1893–1974), a German-born psychologist who helped develop humanistic psychology and was interested in development over the lifespan (Bühler, 1933), should also be mentioned. She carried out studies, for example, exploring the diaries of adolescents. John Dollard's work was varied and included the famous frustration–aggression hypothesis. When he did his research in 'Southerntown' in the 1930s (Chapter 2), he initially was planning an interview study of the personality of Black people. Dollard explored life-history interviews to try to understand and define their qualities. His definition was:

> We will propose an initial common sense definition of the life history as a deliberate attempt to define the growth of a person in a cultural milieu and to make theoretical sense of it. It might include both biographical and autobiographical documents. It is not just an account of a life with events separately identified like beads on a string . . . ; if this were true, every man would be a psychologist, because every person can give us data of this type. The material must, in addition, be worked up and mastered from some systematic viewpoint. (Dollard, 1935, p. 3)

Although this is not quite the same as narrative (for one thing it is a broader approach), his definition can be seen as close to narrative since it includes a person in a cultural milieu and involved oral narratives among other things. In his book on the *Criteria for the life history* he included other matters such as the role of the family in cultural transmission, the importance of specifying the social situation, and the importance of treating the individual as part of a culture.

Gordon Allport (1897–1967) is also frequently mentioned in the development of narrative psychology. His lifelong interest was in personality research where he developed a trait-theory to account for the ways in which people differ. However, his early work included a life-history study of refugees from Nazi Germany (Allport, Bruner, & Jandorf, 1941). It is notable that Jerome Bruner, one of the authors of this report, was to write some highly influential material on narrative psychology nearly half a century later (e.g. Bruner, 1986).

Linguistic work in the 1920s had also begun to lay down the principles of narrative. Vladimir Propp (1895–1970) was born in Russia and worked in the field of folklore. His famous work was *Morphology of the folktale* which gained circulation in the West only in the second part of the twentieth century although it was published in Russia in 1928. He broke the folk tales into small narrative units which are referred to as 'narratemes' which essentially constitute the underlying structure of these folk tales. He identified 31 in all. These included (a) absentation, which involves a family member leaving the secure home environment, producing tension in the story; (b) interdiction in which the hero is warned not to do something; (c) violation of interdiction, which basically leads to the entry of the villain in the story, and so forth. Quite simply, Propp was suggesting structural elements that went into the various stories.

The study of written language, however, as important as it is, is not the only sort of language of interest to researchers including psychologists. During the 1960s, Labov championed the movement away from written language to studying the actual language spoken by people as members of communities. He also made clear the point that Dollard had been concerned with. That is, that narrative is something social but which is nevertheless accessed through individuals:

> We study individuals because they give us the data to describe the community, but the individual is not really a linguistic unit. Many of the people in sociolinguistics disagree with me on this point, and they think that reality lies in the individual speaker, and I take the position that's just the reverse. There are no individuals from a linguistic point of view. (Quoted in Gordon, 2006, p. 341)

Labov established in the 1960s/1970s that the characteristics of conversation in real-life settings can be very different from what emerges in settings where people are being studied by the researcher. One exception to this is where the speaker uses narrative in research settings since this narrative seems to be very similar to the narrative of ordinary everyday conversation:

> The effort to observe how speakers talked when they were not being observed created the Observer's Paradox. Among the partial solutions to that paradox within the face-to-face interview, the elicitation of narratives of personal experience proved to be the most effective. (Labov, 1997, p. 395)

For Labov, a narrative structure is based on there being a temporal structure between a minimum of two clauses. If reversing the two clauses changes the interpretation of the order then these become narrative clauses. One of the principal things which Labov did (Labov, 1972; Labov & Waletzky, 1967) was to provide linguists and narrative psychologists with a general structure by which oral narrative can be understood as a sequential process. The structure of an oral narrative consists of:

- an orientation section (e.g. 'I was walking down the street with Sally who had just split up with her boyfriend');
- an optional summary or abstract in Labov's terms (e.g. 'Her ex caused a big row in public');
- a sequence of narrative clauses (e.g. 'We saw him on the other side of the street and tried not to let him know we had seen him');
- a complicating action which makes the events out of the ordinary (e.g. 'He walked over and began threatening me');
- a resolution (e.g. 'I told her to get away down the street and I was left to deal with him but he backed-off quickly');
- an optional coda/closing section (e.g. 'He's got a reputation for being a trouble maker and losing it at the drop of a hat');
- an evaluation where the view of the narrator is made clear, though it can occur anywhere in the narrative and at more than one point (e.g. 'I suppose I was asking for trouble talking to Sally').

In personality theory, the influence of the narrative perspective was beginning to be felt in the 1970s and 1980s. In particular, Silvan Tomkins (1911–91) began writing about script theory in personality. In this the individual creates a script of their emotional life, featuring salient scenes from their life. It is these different scripts and emotional scenes which constitute the important individual differences between people since these are unique to them (Tomkins, 1979). McAdams (1985) developed a life-story model of identity in which he contended that:

> people begin, in late adolescence and young adulthood, to construe their lives as evolving stories that integrate the reconstructed past and the imagined future in order to provide life with some semblance of unity and purpose . . . The most important individual differences between people are thematic differences in the stories that comprise their narrative identities . . . apparent in the story's settings, plots, characters, scenes, images, and themes. (McAdams, 2006, p. 13)

The point of narrative theory in personality is that the narrative is internally generated and shows how a person's behaviour and experiences may be influenced by this as much as by the 'vagaries of external situations' (McAdams, 2006, p. 13).

However, it is the work of Theodore Sarbin and Jerome Bruner which tends to be identified as the foundation of modern narrative psychology. Theodore Sarbin (1911–2005) proposed that the tradition of mechanistic metaphor which underlies psychology should be replaced with narrative as the basic (or root) metaphor of the discipline. In dominant psychology, many of the characteristics of behaviourism can be seen still in the way humans are conceived. That is, they are treated as if they were mechanisms in which, for example, a stimulus resulted in a response. Thus, the basic metaphor of psychology is that of a machine. Sarbin proposed what he calls the narrator principle:

> human beings think, perceive, imagine, and make moral choices according to narrative structures. Present two or three pictures, or descriptive phrases, to a person and he or she will connect them to form a story, an account that relates the pictures or the meaning of the phrases in some patterned way. On reflection, we discover that the pictures or meanings are held together by the implicit or explicit use of plot. (Sarbin, 1986, p. 8)

Of course, the shift in the underlying metaphor of psychology from that of a machine to that of a story is a radical and decisive shift. It is one which has important implications for how personality is studied. The change from the concentration on personality traits to personal stories is both a change from the nomothetic to the idiographic and a change to an understanding of the person over time rather than at the moment.

The work of Jerome Bruner (1915–) on narrative is to be found in his books *Actual minds, possible worlds* (Bruner, 1986) and *Acts of meaning* (Bruner, 1990). Bruner differentiates between two forms of thinking: (a) the paradigmatic mode – essentially the scientific method which involves classification and categorisation and (b) the narrative approach which concerns how we form everyday interpretations of our world which are expressed in the form of stories. For Bruner, the most clearly defining characteristics of narrative are as follows:

- It deals with people as if they were characters or actors in a unique story of things that happen and describes their mental states.
- The narrative need not be 'real' and so it can be imaginary.
- Narratives involve relationships between the exceptional events of the story and what is ordinary. The former can only be understood as extraordinary in terms of the latter.

In social psychology, Kenneth Gergen (1935–) and Mary Gergen (1938–) argued for a view of narrative which is firmly embedded in social constructionist thinking (Gergen & Gergen, 1983, 1986). This was rather different from, say, the conceptualisations of Propp concerning fairy tales and those of Labov concerning vernacular story-telling which assume that there is something 'real' to be known from the study of narrative. It is inevitable that personal (or self) narratives are involved with the teller's identity. Gergen and Gergen argue that identity is socially constructed but, additionally, the social construction of self takes place through narrative. Gergen puts it this way:

> It is largely through discourse that we achieve the sense of individuated selves with particular attributes and self referential capacities. To be sure, there is 'something' beyond discourse, but what there is makes its way into the practices of cultural life largely through linguistic interpretation. With the discursive construction of identity foregrounded, there are significant ways in which identity is importantly fashioned through narrative. (Gergen, 1998, p. 10)

We have already indicated that a social constructionist version of the nature of narrative leaves the researcher in a difficult position when questions of reality are raised. In social constructionist thinking there is an assumption that narrative is the product of interaction and context. It can also change, and another interaction or another context will produce a different narrative. For that reason, a partial social constructionist view prevails in narrative analysis which accepts the basic argument but counters with the assertion that despite everything, there remains something of substance – something real – which can be learnt about the individual from narrative. In this respect, the Gergen and Gergen approach is something of a sideline in the field.

How to do narrative analysis

Any data which contains personal narratives might be suitable for analysis. Hiles and Čermák (2008) list the following among types of narrative:

- oral versus written narratives;
- fictional versus historical/personal narratives;
- life-story narratives versus isolated event narratives;
- crafted versus spontaneous narratives;
- public versus private narratives.

Murray (2003) suggests that in the research context, the interview is the most likely way of collecting narrative data. He suggests that the two main forms of interview are life-history interviews and episodic interviews. The life-history interview (biographical interview) might begin with a request that the participant tells the interviewer the story of their life starting as early in life as they wish right up to the present time. Probes may be interspersed as appropriate to facilitate the narrative process. The episodic interview is much more focused on particular topics of the life history and seeks to get an extended account of these. The potential range of topics is substantial, of course, and could include things such as one's first week at university, the death of a close relative, being in hospital and so forth.

Michele Crossley's approach to narrative analysis (Crossley, 2000, 2007) typically uses interview data but is not necessarily confined to this. The interviews that she uses are based on McAdams's (1993) procedure when interviewing for narrative analysis. Although much of what appears in Chapter 3 deals with the basics of qualitative interviewing, McAdams's approach is substantially different and has specific rather than generic applications so will be dealt with separately here. Figure 14.4 provides a schematic overview of the stages in Crossley's approach to narrative analysis, including extra considerations about the preliminary data collection phases.

Although a narrative analysis can be carried out on narratives not obtained using McAdams's protocol, *if* you are intending to collect fresh data for a narrative analysis then it may be wise to use McAdams's approach. The important point is that you want your participant's narrative so aim for lengthy contributions from them and relatively short contributions from you. There are other forms of narrative collection (e.g. Mishler, 1986) but, for a novice, the McAdams method is accessible. If you wish to follow McAdams's protocol, you should cover the following areas or use his exact questions (see Figure 14.5):

- *Section 1: Life chapters* The interviewee should think of their life as a book containing a number of different chapters (up to about eight) and identify two or three

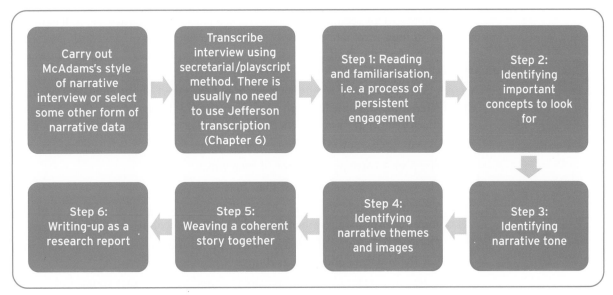

FIGURE 14.4 Crossley's (2007) analytic method for narrative analysis

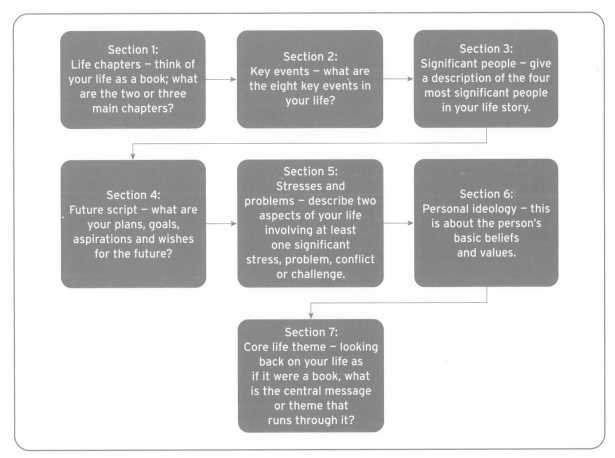

FIGURE 14.5 McAdams's (1993) semi-structured narrative interview protocol

main chapters. This section of the interview has the potential for being lengthy so it is wise to limit it to half an hour or so. The interviewee is (a) asked to name each chapter, (b) describe the broad contents of the chapter and (c) explain how one chapter is followed by the next chapter.

- *Section 2: Key events* The interviewee should be asked about eight key events – which McAdams calls nuclear episodes. These could involve a specific occurrence, a critical incident, a peak experience, a low experience, a turning point or an early memory. The eight key events are:

  (a) The peak experience/highspot of their life.

  (b) The worst or lowest point of their life.

  (c) A turning point in their life – this can be one that they only saw as a turning point retrospectively rather than when it happened.

  (d) The earliest memory they have in their life with details such as who was present, the situation and feelings/thoughts.

  (e) A very important childhood memory – good or bad – that stands out.

  (f) An important memory from their adolescence – good or bad.

  (g) An important memory from adulthood – after the age of 21 years – which may be good or bad.

  (h) One other important memory from any stage of life.

- *Section 3: Significant people* The interviewee is asked to give the name, relationship with themselves, and impact on their lives of *four* people. The list is limitless and ranges from parents through lovers to teachers, etc.

- *Section 4: Future script* Up to this point, the interviewee will have talked about their past and their present. They are then asked about their plans and dreams for the future. Just how will the plan help them be creative in the future and contribute to the lives of others?

- *Section 5: Stresses and problems* We all have stresses and problems at some stage in our life histories. The interviewee is asked to describe two areas of life where such conflicts, stresses and problems have affected them.

- *Section 6: Personal ideology* This section of the interview considers the interviewee's basic beliefs and values by questioning them about their religious and political beliefs. The following areas are covered:

  (a) The participant is asked whether they believe in some sort of god or deity or a reigning force.

  (b) The participant is asked for a nutshell account of their religious beliefs.

  (c) The participant is asked to explain how their beliefs are different from those of most people they know, if they have any.

  (d) The participant is asked to describe how their religious beliefs changed during their life. Have they ever changed rapidly?

  (e) The participant is asked to describe their political orientation.

  (f) The participant is asked to explain their most important value in life.

  (g) The participant is asked to mention anything else that the interviewee could tell the researcher which would help the researcher understand the interviewee's basic beliefs and values about life and the world.

- *Section 7: Core life theme* At the end of the interview, the interviewee reflects back on their life story and identifies the core life theme that runs through the narrative of their life.

According to Crossley (2000), interviews for narrative analysis should be sound-recorded to allow the interviewer the freedom to concentrate on what the interviewee is saying. Transcription should generally be the playscript/secretarial type for reasons of speed of transcription and keeping the transcription easy to read without the clutter of unnecessary detail. Of course, if for some reason the research question requires the sort of detail that goes into Jefferson transcription (Chapter 6) then it is appropriate to use it. Crossley suggests that such a basic transcript takes about four hours for every hour of interview. The transcript should have each line numbered and there should be wide margins on each side of the text much as with interpretative phenomenological analysis, for example. It is worth noting, however, that Hiles and Čermák (2008) recommend that the text is broken down into meaningful segments rather than arbitrary lines as in most transcription methods. In this approach, the segments would be numbered rather than the lines.

Step 1

Reading and familiarisation As with many qualitative data analysis methods, the first stage of the analysis is to read carefully through the transcript of the interview (or other narrative materials) repeatedly to achieve familiarity but also to think about the themes that appear to describe the data. Crossley (2007) suggests that six such readings is about the right number.

Step 2

Identifying important concepts to look for This involves trying to grasp the main elements of the narrative that need to be identified. Based on McAdams (1993), there are three areas to explore and get a feeling for in the transcript:

- *Narrative tone* Broadly speaking the tone of the narrative can be assessed from both the content of the individual's story and the way or form in which it is told. For example, an optimistic story can have that narrative tone because good things happen in the story. Alternatively, there can be an optimistic narrative tone despite the bad things that happen but simply because the outcome is positive.
- *Imagery* Each person uses a unique form of imagery in story-telling which is characteristic of them. Just what sort of imagery does the individual use when describing the 'chapters' for their life narrative and the key events of their life? This may indicate 'personally meaningful images, symbols and metaphors' (Crossley, 2007, p. 140). The next question to ask is where do these images, symbols and metaphors come from? Family background or time in the armed forces may have big influences on these, for example. Equally, the source may be a wider one from within the culture.
- *Themes* What themes dominate in the narrative?

Step 3

Identifying narrative tone Narrative tone should be assessed in terms of (a) the contents of the narrative and (b) the manner and style of reporting the experiences. This is more detailed than in Step 2. This is essentially a matter of judgement though it is not intrinsically difficult.

Step 4

Identifying narrative themes and images Crossley (2007) argues that the researcher should look for both the narrative themes and the images at the same time. This is because there may be considerable overlap in terms of the themes and images. At this stage, you might wish to look at Box 14.1 which discusses six different interpretative perspectives which might be applied to the narrative.

Step 5   Weaving all of this together into a coherent story The images and themes have now been identified but need to be put into a new story form – the story form of a report of a qualitative analysis.

Step 6   Writing-up as a research report Analysis and writing-up are difficult to separate in qualitative research. Separating the two is somewhat arbitrary. This is a common comment on qualitative research practice. See Chapter 15 for details about writing-up qualitative research.

Box 14.2 later in this chapter describes the narrative analysis of the writings of a cancer sufferer.

Box 14.1
PRACTICAL ADVICE
Six interpretative perspectives that might be applied to the narrative analysis

Hiles and Čermák (2008) provide a model for what they call narrative orientated inquiry (NOI) though most of the steps in their approach are similar to those of Crossley (2000, 2007). What is helpful in their approach is that they suggest six different interpretative approaches for narrative analysis (Figure 14.6). It is these that we will concentrate on here.

- *Analytic perspective 1: Sjuzet-fabula* This refers to the distinction between (a) the fabula which is the events which are being recounted in the narrative and (b) the sjuzet which is the way in which the events are being told in the narrative or the 'spin' of the narrator. The convention is that in the transcript of the data the sjuzet is underlined. The sjuzet is not essential to the narrative but it is essential to how the narrative is being told. So the analyst would go through the transcript underlining words, phrases or even entire segments which involve things such as 'emphasis, reflection, asides, interruptions, remarks, and various expressions representing the sequence/causality/significance of the events being related in the story' (Hiles & Čermák, 2008, p. 156). The separation of sjuzet from fabula is not without its problems, of course. Sometimes it will not be clear which of these two categories parts of the narrative belong to. To help deal with this, try reading the story

but miss out the underlined material. What is read out ought to be passable as a story, though perhaps lacking much expressiveness. The underlined material (the sjuzet) is about how the narrator positions themselves in relation to the events.

- *Analytic perspective 2: The holistic-content perspective* This is primarily about the events recounted in the narrative but not exclusively so. It involves searching for patterns within the story which link the narrative's key aspects with the total picture presented (i.e. the best way of describing the narrative overall). In other words, what are the major parts of the narrative and how do they relate to the entirety of the narrative? By repeatedly reading the narrative, different themes will become apparent, some of which recur at different points. These reoccurring themes are the important ones. At the same time, during the analysis the researcher needs to identify the core narrative – the one which is meaningful, stands out in terms of importance and which goes all the way through the narrative. How do the themes relate this major narrative?

- *Analytic perspective 3: The holistic-form perspective* This concentrates on the narrative's form as opposed to its content. What is the plot of the narrative? Hiles and Čermák mention the four major categories of

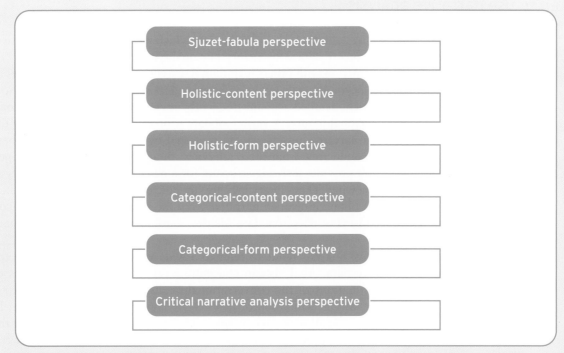

FIGURE 14.6 The main interpretative perspectives in psychological narrative analysis

narrative: (a) romance, which means the affirmation of the social order rather than something to do with love; (b) comedy, which involves breaking then restoring the social order; (c) tragedy, which involves the loss of social order; and (d) satire, which involves a 'cynical challenge to the social order' (p. 157). Do any of these effectively describe the totality of the plot?

- *Analytic perspective 4: The categorical-content perspective* This amounts to a sort of content analysis. The researcher, informed by their research question, identifies the themes which run through the narrative. These themes, in a qualitative analysis, are closely grounded in the data rather than imposed by the researcher.

- *Analytic perspective 5: The categorical-form perspective* This involves choosing some aspect of the narrative which is a particular feature. For example, crying might recur during the narrative. How does this relate to the general form of the narrative? Any feature could be chosen so long as it is about the form of the narrative rather than its content.

- *Analytic perspective 6: The critical narrative analysis perspective* This is the approach to narrative analysis presented in Emerson and Frosh's (2004) *Critical narrative analysis in psychology*. In many ways this approach can be seen as clearly social constructionist since it concentrates on how viewpoints are built up,

meanings created, and similar constructionist themes. Furthermore, the proposed methodology is based on a very close reading of the data of the sort which would not be uncommon in discourse analysis and which is a regular feature of conversation analysis. They refer to research on sexually abusive boys which was based on interview material. They suggest that this method provided them with narrative accounts which:

a) makes more available the kinds of textual material that can contribute to understanding in their own words and from their own points of view how they make sense of themselves and their behaviour, and b) illustrate the social discourses, beliefs and assumption that may be organizing and sustaining these accounts. Thus, it is argued, personal narrative can offer a critical window on processes of social construction of gendered identity that, in relation to sexual abuse, have two apparently contradictory functions. On the one hand, they sustain the 'male monopoly' of abusiveness; but on the other hand, they may also show signs of, or resources for, resistance or alternatives to a boy's apprenticeship to discourses of abusive masculinity. (Emerson & Frosh, 2004, p. 17)

The reference to 'critical' is hinted at in this since what Emerson and Frosh are dealing with is male power, part of the agenda of any critical psychology.

When to use narrative analysis

Narrative analysis, by definition, is applied to data which meet the criteria of narrative. Essentially this means any data with a story-like quality, and may be produced by an individual or in interaction with others including researchers. It will describe a series of life-events but goes beyond merely giving a chronological account of those events. So a narrative will be a rich, detailed account frequently interspersed with a range of comments of a more personal nature. A variety of data sources meet these criteria but the data obtained from narrative interviews are preferred by many psychologists. There are many ways of conducting a narrative interview, though the procedure developed by McAdams (1993) provides a strong structure for a newcomer to narrative analysis and in-depth interviewing. These interviews are not conversational in style since their main objective is to obtain a detailed narrative from the participant. However, if you wish to use other forms of narrative data (diaries, autobiographies, etc.) then that is appropriate too.

The term narrative analysis tends to refer to a wide variety of approaches to the analysis of narrative data. Analysis can concentrate on the structural properties of the narrative, investigations of the conversational or discursive properties of narrative, through to the way in which self or identity are constructed using narrative. In this book, by narrative analysis we mean approaches to analysing data based on the principles of narrative psychology. In other words, a distinction is made between narrative analysis (grounded in narrative psychology) and the analysis of narrative – a more generic phrase which covers several different approaches. There are alternative approaches in the analysis of narrative and quite what options are available depend to some extent on the nature of the narrative and the interests of the researcher. Most forms of narrative could be analysed using thematic analysis (Chapter 7), grounded theory (Chapter 8) and discourse analysis (Chapter 9). If the narrative is conversational in origins then conversation analysis (Chapter 10) could be appropriate. Furthermore, it is possible that the data could be analysed using interpretative phenomenological analysis (IPA) (Chapter 13) since people's descriptions of significant experiences may have many of the features of narrative. There are many similarities between narrative analysis and IPA. However, even though narrative analysis is to some extent phenomenological in approach, it is sufficiently different from IPA to require separate consideration. Narrative analysis refers to concepts such as self and identity primarily in relation to the narrative. IPA would concentrate much more on how the events in the narrative are experienced rather than what the narrative has to say about identity.

Remember, though, that all of these are ways of analysing narratives, and whether it is helpful to refer to all of them as narrative analysis is questionable. Put another way, the analysis of a narrative is best not confused with narrative analysis. In this book, the term "narrative analysis" is used for a form of analysis which depends on concepts from narrative psychology. The potential for confusion is probably self-evident by now. Figure 14.7 details some of the various ways in which narrative may be analysed qualitatively.

The methods of narrative analysis described in detail in this chapter are orientated primarily to understanding personality in a rich and full form, including matters such as self and identity. This does not preclude structural approaches to narrative that investigate the narrative structure and its functions, for example.

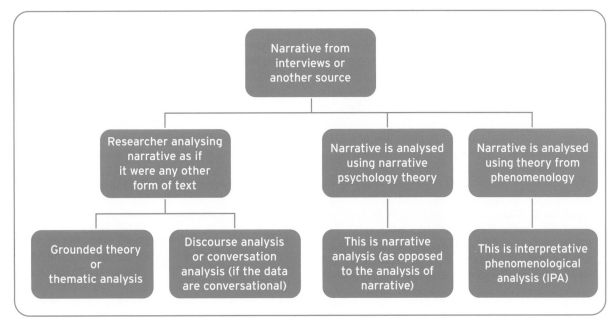

FIGURE 14.7 The analysis of narrative versus narrative analysis

Examples of narrative analysis

For this chapter there is only one example. It is a fascinating one to say the least. It is hard to find narrative analyses which are easily summarised. Others may find it easier than I do. Furthermore, there is no clear body of work which separates narrative analysis from other forms of qualitative analysis. So Box 14.2 is our single research study to present in depth.

Box 14.2

ILLUSTRATIVE RESEARCH STUDY

Narrative analysis: Therapeutic emplotment in a famous cancer sufferer

Crossley (2003) took what she describes as a case study approach to a narrative analysis of the writings of the journalist John Diamond concerning the oral cancer that led to his death in 2001. Oral cancer is treatable if detected early but often it is not and about a quarter of sufferers die. John Diamond was the husband of the famous television cook Nigella Lawson and wrote a regular newspaper diary in which his experiences during the time of his illness were recorded. These were eventually published as a book, together with another autobiographical account in a separate book. The diary entries were the basis of Crossley's analysis. According to Crossley, one of the most fundamental consequences of serious illness is the way in which it shatters our perceptions of our life's development and change over time. People see their lives as projecting into the future. Serious illness drastically changes this lived time since projections of life into the future are in some doubt; the start of a serious illness brings a 'halt' to life. Researchers have found that the major problem for people in such circumstances is to find a new or revised meaning to one's life. Narrative and storytelling are an important way of reattaching meaning to life. The term emplotment describes the process of making sense of life through narrative. Of course, other people impinge on these narratives – family, friends and the medical profession. Del Vecchio Good, Munakata, Kobayashi, Mattingly and Good (1994) describe what they call 'therapeutic emplotment' to refer to the interpretative activity which takes place within clinical interviews. In this, the medic and the patient 'create and negotiate a plot structure within clinical time, one which places therapeutic actions within the larger therapeutic story' (Del Vecchio Good et al., 1994, p. 855). Crossley saw in John Diamond's diary entries illustrations of this 'therapeutic emplotment'.

The diaries cover the period 1996–2001. There are six main stages which underlie John Diamond's diaries, according to Crossley. These are illustrated in Figure 14.8. The approximate duration of each stage is given since the slowness of the passage of time is a key feature of the diaries. Crossley explains that these stages come from a position of hindsight (knowing the outcome) and 'provide a fuller and more coherent picture' of the process than can be found in the original diaries. The following discuss some of the main ideas that Crossley mentions at each stage:

• **Pre-cancer: touch wood phase** At this stage Diamond had thought that he had cancer but then believed this to be incorrect. So he describes how he played with the idea of imagining that he was someone who had just been diagnosed with cancer. He writes about practising the words 'I have cancer' in his head and asks about just how he should say them. Crossley suggests that it is almost as if saying the words and writing them down will, as in a superstition, make them untrue. He believed a 'definitive test' had shown that the lump in his neck was just an unusual sort of cyst. Distressingly, a little later John Diamond's doctor rang to say that he did have cancer. Of course this left him with a dilemma about whether he should deal with this in his column.

• **Learning to live in 'therapeutic emplotment'** In Crossley's paper, this is the longest section. During this period of time, John Diamond's diaries are dominated by descriptions of the various treatments and their effects. Rarely does the horizon of his future rise beyond the treatments; his focus is on the outcome of recovery. It seems that the diary column is being used as a way of coping with the illness and involves attempting to convince himself and his readers that things will turn out alright. He manufactures a sense of optimism in what he writes. Those around him tell him that he will be 'ok', though they probably don't believe what they are saying, he suggests, and the doctor presents the news of his cancer as if it would involve two months of misery followed by something akin to bad sunburn due to the radiotherapy. The 'word' from everyone is of a positive prognosis and he goes along with this. He suggests that protracted illness lacks much by way of a plot and there is a sense of tedium about it. The person that he sees in the mirror is not him.

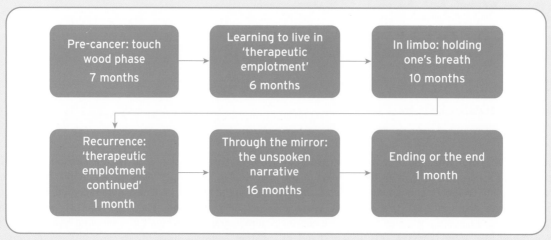

FIGURE 14.8 The stages of John Diamond's diaries

- *In limbo: holding one's breath* John Diamond's surgery and radiotherapy are complete. The 'therapeutic emplotment' had stressed the speed of the treatment process but ending with some sort of 'certainty'. Nevertheless, after all of this John Diamond did not know whether he was cured and he would not know this for weeks or even years. This uncertainty is hard to live with. According to Crossley, others in a similar position have documented this state of affairs.

- *Recurrence: 'therapeutic emplotment continued'* Nearly a year after his treatment had stopped, the cancer is back or, according to Diamond, it had never gone away. It is like 'back to business as usual' as he faces more surgery to restore his tongue. He summons more hope and finds some sort of comfort in the fact that this was the old cancer and not a new one emerging. He hopes to be able to speak better and still writes of there being a chance of a cure.

- *Through the mirror: the unspoken narrative* During this phase Diamond's belief in modern medicine is beginning to erode. He even suggests that part of himself thinks that he has become the victim of a medical confidence trick and his faith in the words of surgeons has failed. During a nine-month period he writes about the experience of chemotherapy which he calls a 'stale hell' and he cannot sleep or eat. Diamond has become resigned as he enters a doctor's office to be told just how much longer he has to live. He has heard bad news 20 or more times before during the course of his cancer. However, he is told that he is in remission and that chemotherapy seems to have worked. Though he is in a sceptic phase, a few months later there is a swelling in his neck and the cancer has spread to his lungs.

- *Ending or the end* About four years after the first appearance of his cancer, he begins to write about how the novelty of cancer has worn off and what he regarded as 'big news'. His cancer has become 'mundane' since cancer goes and comes back – that, for him at that stage, was the nature of cancer. During this phase the doctor tells John Diamond that they would have to start treatment again. His newspaper diary writes jokingly about chemotherapy and how he will have to wear one of those 'jokey' baseball caps like child leukaemia patients. But a week or so later, Diamond is rushed to hospital. The next day he is dead.

The concept of therapeutic emplotment allows one to see how cancer doctors provide a plot structure to patients for their lives in which the treatments are couched within a story of 'hope' – a belief that the patient will be cured. The experience is portrayed as one of immediacy and things being for the moment rather than involving distant horizons. Endings to the therapeutic emplotment are not often made explicit in therapeutic encounters. The focus is the treatment. According to Crossley (2003), John Diamond's diaries illustrate this therapeutic emplotment well in the stage of *Learning to live in 'therapeutic emplotment'*. Of course, there are other narratives which co-exist with that of therapeutic emplotment such as uncertainty and fear which will sometimes surface and, in John Diamond's case, were clearly evident in the stage of *'Through the mirror: The unspoken narrative'*.

In Crossley's (2003) paper, some of the elements of her more general methodology can be seen, although some are naturally missing given the nature of the diary data with which she was working. Stripped of the methodology for collecting narratives through narrative interviews and the need to transcribe the interview, the paper is working with the bare bones of her suggested methodology. However, we can see all of the steps of the method described in this chapter in Crossley's paper (see Figure 14.4). Quite clearly, data familiarisation has to be thorough before any substantial analysis can begin. It is the second stage, *Learning to live in 'therapeutic emplotment'*, which is perhaps not quite what one is expecting from Crossley's (2000, 2007) account of her analytic procedures. It would seem that, in Step 2, an additional factor should be mentioned. That is, sometimes the important ideas for an analysis do not come out of the data but from a knowledge of the research literature and its reflection in the data. The concept of 'therapeutic emplotment' is not an idea that Crossley formulated herself. Instead it was something that she was aware of from the research literature. Of course, some forms of qualitative analysis encourage the view that concepts emerge out of the data. This may be true but it is simply not always the case. One could, of course, suggest that Crossley's (2003) paper is best regarded as an illustrative case study rather than an analysis. When one reads her original paper carefully, although it contains many interesting points, it relies very much on the work of Del Vecchio Good et al. (1994).

Crossley's (2003) paper employs data somewhat unlike those which might emerge from a narrative interview with a cancer sufferer. In particular, it has quite a long timespan and it is not based on data collected at a particular point in time. Thus, it demonstrates quite clearly how the dominant narrative can change markedly during the course of an illness. This sort of data is not normally available to researchers. The study does provide understanding based on compelling data about the lived experience of being a cancer patient. Although this is not normally the stuff of psychology, it is invaluable for those with a clinical or counselling interest in health and illness.

Evaluation of narrative analysis

Narrative analysis, as referred to in this book, is based on theory about the role of narrative in the lives of individuals. The metaphor of narrative has been strongly advocated as an alternative to other metaphors which have been used in psychology. So it is proposed as an alternative to the mechanical metaphor which has people regarded as if they were machines. Positivist psychology, especially where it breaks behaviour down into stimulus–response units, is a good example of the machine metaphor. Other metaphors have been provided by psychologists – for example, Kelly's personal construct theory uses the metaphor of people as scientists. With the narrative metaphor, individuals are seen as complex and interpreters of a series of life events. In other words, the narrative metaphor has people who try to understand themselves and their lives in a social and cultural context. There is a sense of unfolding plot in narratives and they do more than simply account for the past. Narratives inevitably portray the individual as a moral being since narrative and morality are intertwined.

It is inevitable, then, that the evaluation of narrative analysis has to involve an evaluation of narrative psychology in general. Unfortunately, and this may appear a little harsh, narrative psychology is relatively recent, disparate in approaches taken, and lacks a strong synthesis as yet. In other words, it appears to the newcomer to be a somewhat chaotic set of ideas. There are clearly some tangible achievements in narrative psychology – there are narrative-based approaches to therapy, for example Morgan, 2000. However, the impression as yet is of a field which is clearly expanding but one which is not yet fully focused – that is, it is waiting to find its focus. This impression seems to apply to narrative analysis too. Attempts to describe the process of narrative analysis are not so well developed as for other qualitative methods. Furthermore, narrative analysis is relatively infrequent compared with other methods of qualitative analysis. There may be a number of reasons for this. One is, of course, that narrative psychology is too young as a field of research to have reached a stage where its methods are fully established. Another is that narrative psychology has not, as yet, developed a body of theory analogous to that which underlies, say, discourse analysis and conversation analysis. In this context, it is noteworthy that some of the proponents of narrative psychology waited until late in their careers to address the topic formally. This is unusual in research where one would normally expect innovations to come from younger people, eager to build their careers.

So, anyone who attempts a narrative analysis will probably feel a little out on a limb compared with users of most of the other qualitative data analysis methods described in previous chapters. Models are harder to come by, theory more difficult to clarify. But, in the end, anyone interested in narrative analysis is interested in interpreting the stories we tell about our lives in our everyday lives. This is much more about self and identity than any of the other approaches in this book although some of the other methods address topics such as identity regularly. Narrative analysis, certainly as described in this chapter, is much more closely associated with the study of personality than it is, say, with the study of language. It all boils down to the question of what you, as the researcher, are interested in. Among the attractions of narrative psychology is that it is non-reductionist in the sense of seeking to look at the individual as a person in a social environment in totality.

CONCLUSION

By doing narrative analysis you are stepping into the world of narrative psychology which is different from the other approaches in this book while retaining a broadly qualitative ethos. This means, for example, that the researcher familiar with the methods of discourse analysis has quite a lot to learn when it comes to carrying out a narrative analysis. They are not totally compatible approaches. They may not share the same epistemological assumptions in every, or even most, respects. But it is not surprising that psychologists who have a highly developed understanding of the study of language (i.e. discourse analysts) will have some difficulty with an approach which is more an approach to personality than it is to the theory of language. This applies to some of the other qualitative methods in this book but the contrast seems more real in terms of narrative analysis.

Of course, the usual rule of academic study applies here – the more reading on a topic that one does, the more sophisticated one's ideas become. This is inescapable and it is a point that has been made several times in this book. Of course, some sources of information are better than others and some are better at certain times in one's studies than others. So broad overviews, such as the one in this chapter, are very useful at the start of one's studies whereas looking at how other researchers have carried out their research and reported their findings will be more important when you are a little more actively involved in research.

Finally, the problem of where to locate narrative analysis perhaps needs revisiting. Narrative is not really the province of any particular epistemology of research. We have seen that researchers from a wide range of different epistemological positions can claim some sort of interest in the topic of narrative. However, this begs the question of whether any analysis of narrative can or should be narrative analysis. We can take the example of the views of Benwell and Stokoe (2006) who argue that there are 'many different versions of narrative analysis' (p. 143). This, of course, depends somewhat on what the cake is seen as being and how the slicing is to be done.

They include in their list of different 'sources' of narrative analysis the following:

- The structuralist approach (including Labov) which links things such as ethnicity, class and gender to 'different structures and ways of telling directly and unproblematically' (p. 143).

- The phenomenological realm of 'real' experience. They describe Crossley's (2003) approach as a 'strange hybrid of constructionist *and* referential understandings of language, in which language is a window on the mind/experience *and* the site of identity construction' (p. 143). Whether this is or is not fair comment on her writings, Crossley's position in terms of practice appears to be largely one of acknowledging the social constructionist position while advocating narrative realism (Schwandt, 2001).

- The psychodynamic realm of the unconscious.

- A social constructionist approach to the data from narrative interviews as being co-constructed by the interviewer and the narrator.

- The interview is regarded as social interaction purely and simply with the stories told and the process of identity construction within the interview being the consequence of the production of the narrative.

- Conversation analysts and discourse analysts regard narrative as being of interest because it is part of their declared aim of analysing everyday language.

This reinforces the earlier point that there are many different ways of analysing narrative. But there are many different ways of analysing conversation and many different ways of analysing discourse but conversation analysis and discourse analysis are not the best ways to describe all of these. Terminology loses its meaning if allowed to drift too widely. For that reason, it is suggested that narrative analysis is a term best reserved for the analysis of narrative using narrative psychology ideas and concepts.

KEY POINTS

- Narrative psychology is a form of psychology which uses the metaphor of 'narrative' in order to understand personality. As such, it is a developing field in psychology and different from other forms of qualitative research because it is embedded in this general approach to personality. Narrative analysis is a term best reserved for analysis of narrative which is founded on the precepts of narrative psychology rather than those of discursive psychology or phenomenology for example. Narrative psychology has self and identity as central themes. Time will tell if this or some other specific meaning will prevail.

- Narrative analysis is typically based on some form of narrative interview. This is any approach to semi-structured interviewing which seeks to maximise the narrative content of the data. Narrative refers to the stories that we tell about our lives which join together events in the context of evaluative material, commentary and so forth which are informative about the development of our lives as we describe them in the story.

- Narrative analysis is the least standardised approach to qualitative data analysis included in this book. There are relatively few accounts of how to carry out a narrative analysis compared to other forms of qualitative analysis such as grounded theory for which there is voluminous 'how-to-do-it' literature.

ADDITIONAL RESOURCES

Crossley, M. (2000). *Introducing narrative psychology: Self-trauma and the construction of meaning*. Buckingham: Open University Press.

Garson, G. D. (2013). *Narrative analysis*. Statistical Associates Blue Book Series 42, Kindle edition.

Hiles, D., & Čermák, I. (2008). Narrative psychology. In C. Willig & W. Stainton-Rogers (Eds.), *The SAGE handbook of qualitative research in psychology* (pp. 147–164). London: Sage.

Holstein, J. A., & Gubrium, J. F. (2012). *Varieties of narrative analysis*. Los Angeles: Sage.

Mishler, E. G. (1986). The analysis of interview-narratives. In T. R. Sarbin (Ed.), *Narrative psychology: The storied nature of human conduct* (pp. 233–255). New York: Praeger.

Murray, M. (2008). Narrative psychology. In J. A. Smith (Ed.), *Qualitative psychology: A practical guide to research methods* (2nd ed., pp. 111–132). London: Sage.

PART 4

Planning and writing up qualitative research

The final part of this book is concerned with the practical issues facing anyone planning and writing up qualitative research. So chapters on qualitative report writing, assessing quality in qualitative research and research ethics follow. Each of these aspects needs to be considered from the moment that you first begin planning your research. Although this may seem impossible – and it is – keeping the final product in mind at every stage of your research makes a lot of sense. In a curious way, the write-up of a study is a sort of blueprint for the study. So it is something of a pity, then, that the report is the last thing to be done! Nevertheless, always bear in mind that the end point of research is the report – that is what you are working towards. Drafting parts of your report as you progress through your study is not a bad idea. It makes you think about your research in a systematic way and is tangible evidence of how your ideas are progressing. The final report is what you will be assessed on, whoever you are – student or expert. It does not matter, say, how good your interviewing skills are if the report of your research is fragmentary or incoherent. Having an image of the final product in mind will help you address questions such as 'How big does my literature review have to be?', 'How much time can I devote to fieldwork?' and 'Have I got enough data for my analysis?' Keeping one's mind on the big picture helps pre-empt problems.

Chapter 15 deals with writing a qualitative research report. Qualitative research reports tend not to follow the standard structure of a quantitative research report precisely. No single structure for qualitative reports suits every study. Generally a version of the structure of the quantitative research report is used and modified wherever necessary. This has the big advantage of being familiar to all psychologists irrespective of their chosen style of research. They feel comfortable reading reports which utilise this standard quantitative protocol. One advantage is that the reader will know just what to expect in the report (abstract, method, analysis, for instance) and, perhaps more importantly, where to find it. It is a reminder of the high standards of clarity, accuracy and argument that psychology, as a discipline, expects. Some may think that the qualitative research report in psychology should have its own distinctive structure and characteristics. As yet, there are no contenders for what this distinctive qualitative psychology structure should be. This does not mean that a research report in qualitative research will be much the same as the traditional quantitative report. The content will obviously be radically different and reflect the qualitative ethos despite the broad structure being much the same. The radical position of 'separate development' of qualitative and quantitative psychology is not reflected in the copious advice about how to write up qualitative psychology research. Perhaps this is to be welcomed if qualitative methods are to become a resource available to all psychologists.

Chapter 16 is about quality in qualitative research. This is an area which can be subject to fierce debate not only between qualitative and quantitative psychologists but between different factions of qualitative psychologists. Along with a large chunk of statistics and practical classes, all psychology students have the concepts of reliability and validity drummed into them. Reliability and validity do not address all of the quality issues in quantitative psychology by any means. Additionally, they can be decidely inappropriate for qualitative research which generally dismisses the idea that there is a single viewpoint on the world. The arguments are complex but understanding quality criteria is as important for qualitative as for quantitative studies. There is quite a lot for all psychologists to learn in Chapter 16 which will take them well beyond reliability and validity issues. Actually the chapter goes far beyond what is found in general psychology methods textbooks in trying to establish criteria which can be used to evaluate research. The chapter tries to operate at several levels by giving some of the basic criteria which can be used by students new to qualitative research as well as a thorough account of what is expected of qualitative research at the professional level. Chapter 16 should convince even the most sceptical quantitative researcher that qualitative research is not methodologically unsophisticated – and perhaps leave them resting a little less easily in their qualitative bed. It is a fundamental misunderstanding of qualitative research to equate it with a lack of rigour. The typical qualitative psychologist probably worries more about issues of research methodology than the typical quantitative researcher. Of course, qualitative and quantitative research vary in quality – not every study is good.

Chapter 17 deals with ethics and data management in qualitative psychology. It is virtually impossible to carry out any research in psychology without formal ethical approval. It is argued that qualitative research is an ethically problematic endeavour. It is not correct to suggest that the typical piece of qualitative research is in some way 'morally' superior to quantitative research. Qualitative researchers have a very different relationship with the participants who take part in their research from the typical quantitative researcher. Some qualitative researchers seem to involve themselves more in the lives of those who take part in their research than do quantitative researchers. Cooperative research activity between researcher and researched characterises qualitative research and much of the data produced in qualitative research is clearly co-constructed. Chapter 17 takes us through the underlying ethical principles which underpin all psychological research. Some of this is nowadays quite routine – informed consent, freedom to withdraw from the research and confidentiality. But this is only the beginning of ethical considerations in relation to qualitative research. The chapter describes some of the ethical problems which can develop in qualitative research as a consequence, sometimes, of the relationships between researcher and researched but also because data in qualitative research are more transparent. A good example of this is the question of how to deal with data collected from a group of people who are known to each other. A researcher who carries out in-depth interviewing with both partners in a relationship potentially walks in an ethical minefield.

The final chapter of the book is intended to help the newcomer to qualitative research understand a little better what is required when writing-up a qualitative report. Although a qualitative report in psychology generally takes the more-or-less standard structure that is used for quantitative reports, it is sometimes the case that this standard structure needs a degree of modification to make it work effectively for a particular qualitative study. So, most readers will be familiar with the basics of the psychology report when it comes to writing-up their qualitative studies. This structure is discussed in depth in Chapter 15. Unfortunately the shared structure is irrelevant to differences in content between a qualitative and a quantitative report. Furthermore, there are a good number of different types of qualitative study which also need to be taken into account. Each qualitative method usually shares much of the general qualitative ethos but, at the same time, it also has characteristics and assumptions which are peculiar to itself. So, writing a qualitative report needs sensitivity to the epistemological differences between the different qualitative methods and the differences between the qualitative methods and quantitative methods. In order to help sensitise the reader to what is required in a qualitative report, Chapter 18 not only gives general advice about writing up qualitative reports but also contains examples of three reports based on different qualitative methods. Although inspired by published papers, the reports describe studies which are variations from the originals in many respects. Although the originals are usually exemplary write-ups, the ones in Chapter 18 are less than perfect. Read through each of them carefully and identify issues which you think arise that need addressing. The problems (and exemplary things) can be just about anywhere in the write-up. Some of the issues have been identified and they are discussed immediately following the paper. Numbers in superscript indicate roughly where these are in the write-up so this may be a clue to the reader. But look too for other things which have not been identified – you will find some, no doubt.

CHAPTER 15

Writing a qualitative report

Overview

- Writing a qualitative practical report, like any other psychological report, is not easy and it needs time and experience to become good at it.

- It is always useful to follow the model of a published report which is as close as possible in terms of style and content to the research that you have carried out and want to write up. This provides a sound framework for your work and makes the checking of the details of report writing easier.

- Many characteristics of a good practical report are shared by both quantitative and qualitative approaches. In particular, evidence of creativity, diligence and care, and a questioning approach to what is written are universally expected.

- Qualitative research is based on full and rich data often collected by open-ended methods. The analysis which the researcher presents should also be full, rich and transparent in that the researcher carefully and thoroughly considers both congruent and non-congruent aspects of the analysis and tries to resolve any problems rather than ignore them.

- Although there can be a lot of variation in the structures of qualitative reports, it is probably best to adapt the structure of the quantitative research report familiar in psychology. Although it can be changed substantially if appropriate, the structure of the standard psychology report is recommended as a starting point for the qualitative write-up.

- Most disparity with the conventional structure probably arises in connection with the reporting of methodological matters in qualitative research. In particular, it is important to devote substantial amounts of space to the method of analysis employed. This is sometimes overlooked in qualitative report writing but not to do so is a fundamental mistake.

- Considerable care is needed to select appropriate data (text) to support the qualitative analysis. Systematic presentations such as tables and even simple statistics, where appropriate, can make a great deal of difference.

- Care and attention to citations and reference lists are as important for the qualitative report as for the quantitative report.

Is a qualitative research report different?

It hardly needs to be said that the purpose of writing is to communicate your research activities to other people. But this is to imply that report writing is merely a matter of communication. What it overlooks is that during the course of writing a research report, a great deal is learnt concerning whatever one is writing about. It is possible to develop one's ideas through the writing process which thinking alone cannot equal. So it is important to consider report writing as not just communicating one's thoughts but as a way of having one's thoughts. This explains why writing research reports is so difficult – it is hard to communicate clearly and think at the same time. Writing a good research report is a complicated if not downright exasperating task. It involves the skill of juggling lots of different elements into the right order but also conundrums about what to include and how much. Not surprisingly, for many students, initially report writing is outside their comfort zone. Good essay-writing skills help but there is a lot to learn in addition about style, content and structure. Things do get easier with time and experience but report writing never becomes a cinch because the quality bar gets higher as you advance through your studies towards professional level research.

Like many things in life, following the example of others can make things more straightforward. So you will almost certainly find it helpful to follow the examples of how 'experts' write about their research. The more you read published research reports the clearer what is expected becomes. Of course, one has to be a little selective about which publications to use – some are more accessible to beginners than others. University and college libraries (and my office for that matter) were once packed with shelf after shelf of psychology journals with titles along the lines of *The Journal of Space Psychology* or *The Journal of Applied Cognition and Cognitive Therapy* or *Applied Behavioural Studies*. Electronic versions of journals have generally replaced hard copy versions for all but the most popular journals – more or less. Much more convenient are the electronic versions of some of these same journals which most university libraries will subscribe to. Journal articles can be downloaded directly to a computer and printed out, which makes life easier, if not exactly fun.

There is so much to remember when writing a research report that it is a good idea to have a copy of a relevant journal article on your desk in front of you to serve as a model for your own writing. This will help you with relatively simple matters such as the structure that the research report should have and what headings and subheadings are appropriate. Additionally, they can help with the complex and all-important matter of style. Any old journal article will not do – you need one which deals with similar things to your research, especially where a similar methodological and theoretical perspective is employed. There is, naturally, a risk of picking a poor or unhelpful or impossibly difficult article but, generally speaking, the benefits are enormous:

- You have before you a guide to an appropriate structure for your report.
- You can see just how things such as citations and references are done and how they should look.
- The acceptable and effective styles of communication will become more apparent.
- You will form an impression of the appropriate level of detail to include in your report.
- You might even learn some psychology.

In the end, there is no sure-fire formula guaranteed to produce brilliant research reports; nevertheless emulating good models gives you better than a standing start in the race.

Although journal articles do, of course, vary in quality, the good news is that most journals employ several levels of quality control. The most important of these is what is known as 'peer review'. This means that articles submitted to the journal's editor for possible publication will be read and commented upon by experts in the field in question. Rarely would a journal article be accepted for publication without further work being required. The article will probably need to be revised, corrected or improved in some way. While the system is not infallible and poor work can slip through the net, generally it ensures that published articles meet an acceptable standard of quality in terms of content but also conform to the accepted structure. Some journals are more prestigious than others so one can expect to find higher standards throughout in these. Usually, journals produced by psychologists' professional bodies such as the British Psychological Society and the American Psychological Association demonstrate suitably high standards.

Journal articles tend to be better guides to report writing than books. Although qualitative (and quantitative) research is frequently published in book form or as chapters in books, these often are less formal than the style adopted in journals and so are less useful as models for your own writing. Furthermore, books are produced to the 'house style' of their publishers. So, for example, the referencing system used in some books may differ from the style used by, say, the American Psychological Association in its journals.

Remember that the reports which students write at different stages of their studies serve different functions from journal articles – their purpose is educational development and assessment. This has some relevance to things such as word limits but, less obviously, the contents of the reports. Relatively brief reports are expected from students as part of practical classes in psychology. Often these are as short as 1000–2000 words. Final year dissertations are much more substantial and may vary between 5000 and 20 000 words. For postgraduate work such as doctoral (PhD) dissertations the word length increases markedly and may be 80 000 words or even more in the United Kingdom. The important thing to bear in mind is that the 'rules' about word length vary from institution to institution so it is not possible to be definitive about word limits here. So always check this locally.

As a rule of thumb, it is likely that a qualitative research report requires more words than a quantitative one. Among the reasons for this are:

- Many qualitative research reports quote substantial amounts of illustrative text to illustrate features of the analysis.
- Other qualitative reports may include transcriptions of recordings such as interviews or telephone conversations, for example.
- Qualitative research seeks a richer descriptive style in its data which inevitably eats up more space. This is often referred to as 'thick description'.

Obviously these features of the qualitative report are hard to squeeze into conventional word lengths for research reports. So it is especially important to check whether extra allowances or dispensations are given for the word limits in qualitative reports. One approach is to disregard examples and quotations from the material being analysed when totting up word counts for a qualitative report. Generally you should expect no extra allowance for things such as the abstract (summary) or the introduction but it is best to obtain clarity from your lecturer or supervisor if they have not laid down 'the rules' sufficiently clearly already.

Where to aim: the overall characteristics of a good qualitative report

Any research report needs to aim for a high academic standard in all respects – some of which are more important in qualitative reports than in quantitative ones. Qualitative and quantitative research reports actually share features which should be made clear before we move on to the differences. Choudhuri, Glauser and Peregoy (2004) suggest that a high standard research report needs to meet the following criteria:

- It should contain a clear statement of the purpose of the research.
- The research questions employed should be justified logically in the report.
- The data collection methods should be clearly specified and justified.
- The data analysis methods should be clearly specified and justified.
- The report should contain conclusions which are logically related to the data and its analysis.

Although it is hard to define precisely what the ingredients of the perfect qualitative research report are, they include the following:

- The overall structure of the report is consistent throughout and is logically coherent from beginning to end.
- The report demonstrates that the researcher fully understands the nature and assumptions of their chosen methodology and recognises that each methodology has its particular distinctive characteristics not necessarily shared by other methodologies.
- The reader of the report should have sufficient detail at all stages so that they can evaluate for themselves how satisfactory the research is.
- Ideally, the report should demonstrate evidence that its author has been creative (such as in relation to the development of the research ideas or in the analysis). This is not simply being different for its own sake, but it is evidence that the work is moving research in the field forward in important directions.
- At the same time, the report should demonstrate that its author has been diligent and exacting in their preparations for the research (e.g. the literature review), the data analysis and in all aspects of writing the report.
- It should be evident that key concepts and the research findings are fully and properly understood by the report's writer. Always use concepts appropriately and with care.
- Reports can have different target readerships and should be geared to communicating well to this readership. A report solely for the academic community will be written differently from one for, say, a government department.
- The aim is clarity and openness in all stages of the report. There should be no attempt to disguise problems or uncertainties by writing vaguely or opaquely. Obfuscation is inappropriate.
- There is probably more variety in the structures of qualitative reports than there is in quantitative reports. Nevertheless, whatever the final structure it should render the report both coherent and comprehensible. Although this is far less evident among psychological qualitative researchers, those from other disciplines where qualitative research has been more entrenched for longer use a wide variety of approaches to research dissemination. A good account of this can be found in Keen and Todres (2007). There are various creative deviations from the norm of the conventional written report and conference paper. Qualitative researchers are more

amenable to 'creative' deviations from the norm. Keen and Todres set about finding ways in which qualitative research findings are disseminated beyond journals and conferences. This variety helps qualitative researchers in other disciplines deal with both the concerns of research and its dissemination. Keen and Todres explain that dissemination may be through dance, poetry, drama, video, evocative writing and the use of websites. The use of dramatic productions is dealt with in detail in the article. It probably does not need explaining why such communicative methods can help in the dissemination of research findings based on the analysis of rich text and the thick description involved in its analysis.

- The qualitative report should resonate with the qualitative research ethos. So the report should be informed by and reflect the qualitative approach in terms of things such as the researcher's perspective, subjectivity, the historical and cultural context of the topic of the research, and the richness of the data.

- Self-questioning of one's own ideas, arguments and data is an important and necessary characteristic of academic work. Similar but balanced questioning of the work of other researchers should be combined with this.

- Attention to detail in terms of general presentation such as basics like grammar, spelling, paragraphing and the like is part of the overall impression created by any report. While word processors such as Microsoft Word can help enormously with spelling especially, paragraphing is down to the individual. The importance of good writing style is greater in qualitative research than quantitative research. This is possibly because of the origins of qualitative research in more literary socio-cultural traditions than the hard science which gave birth to quantitative psychology. Poor technical use of grammar, spelling and the like are likely to undermine the impact of a report.

The qualitative ethos

The term 'qualitative methods' covers a vast range of different approaches, not all of which are in perfect harmony with each other. There are strong debates between qualitative researchers just as there are between quantitative researchers. Nevertheless, most qualitative researchers share a 'qualitative' culture which ensures that they have more in common with each other academically than they have with quantitative researchers. An understanding of the distinctive characteristics of qualitative research methodology is essential preparation for writing a qualitative research report. Although these characteristics are discussed at various stages throughout this book, some common features of qualitative research can be summarised as follows. It should not be assumed that all qualitative researchers subscribe to each in equal measure:

- Data collection methods are open-ended rather than constrained by highly structured questions that allow little flexibility in terms of responses.

- Data analysis is similarly open-ended in that the analytic task is to fully understand/ account for the data rather than use the data to answer very specific research questions or hypotheses.

- Data collection aims at obtaining very full, rich data usually of a verbal/textual nature.

- The researcher should 'situate' their research sample. A comprehensive picture of the sample studied needs to be provided (Elliott, Fischer, & Rennie, 1999).

This includes characteristics which are important in relation to the research topic. Conventionally the researcher might describe the demographic characteristics of the sample. But this may not be enough for a qualitative study as demographic characteristics may overlook psychological and other factors which may also be relevant to understanding the research. Such descriptions of characteristics are important in that they offer clues as to whether the research findings might be relevant to other groups of people or in a different social context.

- Data analysis aims to engage with the richness of the data.
- Data analysis is generally exploratory rather than confirmatory.
- Data description and data analysis each have an important role and need to be balanced. Data description without analysis is regarded as unsatisfactory.
- Coherence refers to the extent to which the report presents the analytical findings in an integrated way by means of an understandable framework. So, for example, merely giving a list of themes found in the analysis and then describing them is not good enough and fails to provide the necessary coherence. In addition, the researcher should show just what the relationships between themes might be. These relationships may be illustrated visually in a diagram; alternatively the themes might be presented as a story or narrative which describes a process through which a person might pass in terms of these themes.
- There is a close linking of theory with method. Many qualitative methods are notable for their extensive and distinctive theoretical and epistemological underpinnings.
- The analysis should be transparent, which means that it is clear how the analysis is linked to the total body of data through the use of quotes illustrating the range of data as well as the analytic interpretation. The qualitative researcher provides informative examples which illustrate (a) the analytic processes involved and (b) the findings offered. Sufficient detail of the analytic process should be provided to allow the reader to understand the logic underlying the process of analysis. The choice of examples provided by the researcher helps to illustrate, say, how the themes established through the analysis are organised in relation to each other and the extent to which the themes are saturated (i.e. how complete the themes are in terms of the data).
- The analysis needs to be characterised by plausibility, credibility and meaningfulness to both the researcher and the reader.
- The qualitative researcher incorporates their own personal perspective into their research reports, possibly by providing a reflexive (see Box 15.1) account of the study in which the possibilities for subjectivity and bias are acknowledged and incorporated. It is common for qualitative researchers to give some insight into their own personal perspective or frame of reference with regard to the subject matter of the report (Elliott et al., 1999). For example, the researcher may describe their own personal theoretical orientation to research. Alternatively, the researcher may explain their personal involvement or investment in the topic of the study – exactly what are the researcher's values, expectations and experience in relation to the research topic?
- Qualitative research should acknowledge the context in which the data are collected and its implications for the data analysis.
- The target audience for the report should find a personal connection with its contents. Elliott et al. (1999) refer to this as 'resonance with the reader'. The reader should readily appreciate the relevance of the study: it should have some impact on them.

Box 15.1

KEY CONCEPT

What is reflexivity?

The concept of reflexivity has a range of meanings in the social sciences, and though it is not particularly important in mainstream psychology writing, it is commonly mentioned in some forms of qualitative research. It was a concept introduced in sociology by Talcott Parsons (1902–79) to refer to the capacity of people in modern society to be conscious, and to give accounts of, their actions. If you consider that mainstream psychology was dominated by the behaviourist analysis of behaviour as the product of a stimulus and systems of rewards, the importance of Parsons' concept of reflexivity is self-evident. Similar conceptions can be found in more recent sociology such as in the work of the British sociologist Anthony Giddens (e.g. O'Brien, 1999). But these are not the current ways in which the term reflexivity is used in qualitative psychology. Broadly speaking, reflexivity refers in qualitative psychology to the ways in which the researcher has a variety of influences on the research data and research findings. Reflexivity, although it applies in quantitative research, has tended to be dismissed by quantitative researchers as something of a nuisance which if it can be eliminated results in better research. There are numerous ways in which reflexivity has been squeezed out of quantitative research. For example, the common advice to students writing up a quantitative research study is not to write in the first person (I, me, my, etc.). This is tantamount to suggesting that the researcher's experience of the research is irrelevant to the research. This is essentially a nonsense but one which psychologists have gone along with for decades in droves. One does not have to read too deeply in the field of qualitative psychology to appreciate that such personal references are common. According to Nightingale and Cromby, reflexivity involves:

> an awareness of the researcher's contribution to the construction of meanings throughout the research process, and an acknowledgment of the impossibility of remaining 'outside of' one's subject matter while conducting research. Reflexivity then, urges us 'to explore the ways in which a researcher's involvement with a particular study influences, acts upon and informs such research.' (Nightingale & Cromby, 1999, p. 228)

In other words, reflexivity pushes psychologists towards a radical re-think of how they present their role in research.

There are two major types of reflexivity which are involved in qualitative research according to Willig (2008b):

- **Personal reflexivity** This involves considering how we as the researcher influence and guide research. A whole range of factors can be involved, including our life experiences, our politics, and our biases, attitudes and beliefs. What role have these played in shaping the research which we carry out? Not only does it involve the influence that our characteristics have on our research but it also includes the influence that our research has on us.

- **Epistemological reflexivity** This involves the researcher reflecting on the assumptions underlying the research which contributed to the way that the researcher thinks about their research and their research findings. The sorts of questions raised might include the research question and its impact on what emerged in the research and just how did the research method employed influence the findings of the research.

Burr also finds two meanings of reflexivity but they do not entirely or significantly equate to those above of Willig. Thus Burr suggests the following as the first of two meanings of reflexivity:

> it is used to draw attention to the fact that, when someone gives an account of an event, that account is simultaneously a description of the event *and* part of the event because of the constitutive nature of talk. (Burr, 2003, p. 156)

In other words, the status of the researcher as the expert – the authoritative voice – in quantitative research cannot be sustained in qualitative research because it allows a multiplicity of voices and hence no definitive account. Thus, qualitative research is open to debates about power and authority within research. In practice, qualitative researchers are more open to referring the research process back to the participants than is typical in quantitative research. (Of course, this may be to describe bad practice in quantitative research since the stage of 'debriefing' is supposed to accompany all research with human participants. In this, the voice of the participant is supposed to be heard.) Burr's second meaning of reflexivity is:

> reflexivity refers to the fact that constructionism itself is not exempt from the critical stance it brings to bear on other theories. Social constructionism, as a body of theory and practice, therefore must recognize itself as just as much a social construction as other ways of accounting. (Burr, 2003, p. 157)

Actually Burr is giving a particular version of a more general reflexivity thesis – the application of theory to the theory itself and the researcher.

Ultimately, these versions of reflexivity boil down to something quite important – that qualitative research reports can differ quite radically in terms of the style of content from those of the typical quantitative report. So a qualitative report may include more references to the actions, thoughts and opinions of the researcher. The trick, of course, is getting this balance right. The student researcher might feel that it is appropriate to keep such contributions on the light side as they can appear frivolous unless carefully thought out. The traditions of report writing in psychology are strong and it is best to keep broadly within the usual parameters though an intelligent reflexive perspective can make a welcome addition to any qualitative report – and quantitative report for that matter.

The writing style of the report is important in all of this and so the writing should be fluid and lucid. In addition, the author must give the detail and evidence which will convince the reader of the credibility of the research findings and the interpretations provided by the researcher. However, it is worth noting that there are many other characteristics of a good qualitative study which are mentioned by some authors, though there is no universal agreement (see Figure 15.1).

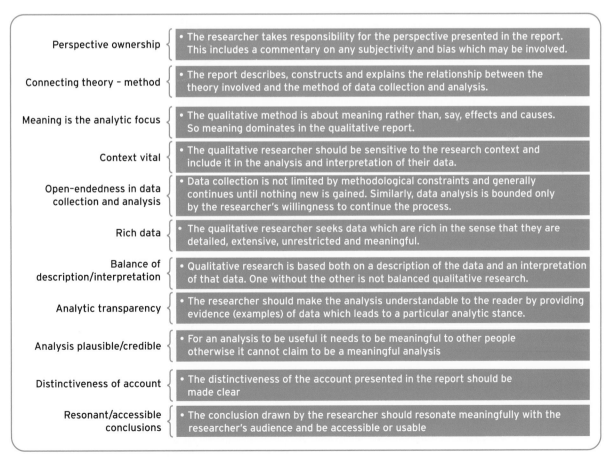

FIGURE 15.1 A summary of some quality criteria for a qualitative report

Of course, many of these characteristics are generally not shared with mainstream psychological research where issues such as hypothesis testing, reliability and validity tend to be pre-eminent. These general characteristics of qualitative research can help guide the researcher and suggest strongly the features of qualitative research reports. Nevertheless, you will need to familiarise yourself with the variety of approaches which can be found in qualitative analysis. Each has its own fairly specific characteristics and expectations as well as features of the general qualitative approach.

Although these criteria for qualitative research broadly constitute the underlying requirements of qualitative research, there can be problems in meeting the criteria:

- Sometimes the data collected fail to meet the requirement of 'richness' of content. The main reason for this is that a novice researcher may not have the interviewing skills to elicit extensive and detailed responses from their participants. Clumsily asked or confusing questions, poor rapport and being uncomfortable with silences are interviewer characteristics which may impact the richness of the data negatively and substantially. Without some experience of in-depth interview methods, it is risky to initiate certain sorts of data collection in circumstances in which time is at a premium. In these circumstances, it might be safer to employ, for example, focus group methodologies for data collection which are a little less demanding on the skills of the researcher – but only if this is appropriate. But the important lesson is that qualitative data collection demands a high level of interviewing skills and similar skills which need training and experience. They are not natural gifts bestowed on qualitative researchers.

- A thorough qualitative analysis requires a substantial investment of time and energy. Inevitably, if these are skimped the analytic work is unlikely to extend much beyond being a mundane commentary. A typical example of this is where the putative 'analysis' consists of little other than a few interesting quotations taken from the data, which are then strung together with a commentary which does nothing more than point out that different people mentioned different things. This might be described as the 'he-said-this-whereas-she-said-that-but-then-they-said-the-other' approach. This does not constitute a quantitative analysis any more than it is good enough in quantitative data analysis to merely provide a table of the data with no further discussion.

The qualitative approach can encourage the inclusion of things which are rare or even unacceptable in quantitative reports. For example, because the general perspective of the researcher and the impact of this on the analysis are important in qualitative research, qualitative reports frequently include material from a personal and reflexive perspective. In contrast, in quantitative research this is almost unheard of because subjectivity runs counter to the quantitative method's search for infallible objectivity. It is perfectly acceptable to refer to 'I' and 'we' in a qualitative report, though not simply to report 'I did this and then we did that' which is somewhat clumsy anyway and misses the point. In qualitative research reports, the researcher becomes the subject of the discussion when issues of perspective, bias, subjectivity and so forth come to the fore.

The structure of a qualitative report

The conventional approach to research report writing in mainstream psychology involves several components as illustrated in Table 15.1. This is well tested and works well for much quantitative research. It is a neat and orderly sequence which deals with the major

TABLE 15.1 The basic headings of a qualitative report based on traditional psychology report structure

A conventional quantitative report	A qualitative report
Title	Title
Abstract	Abstract
Introduction	Introduction
Method	Method
Results	Results and Discussion (alternatively
Discussion	Findings or Analysis and Discussion)
Conclusions (optional or sometimes merged with the Discussion as Discussion and Conclusions)	Conclusions (optional)
List of references	List of references
Appendix	Appendix

features of quantitative research well but not always perfectly. It is especially well suited to reporting laboratory experiments. The reason is that laboratory experiments are built on a number of assumptions. The most important is that research proceeds through an orderly process of theory building and hypothesis testing. Thus it is essential to understand what research has previously been carried out and what theories have been developed to account for the empirically observable data. From this background, new hypotheses are derived to test the theory, so a relatively straightforward hypothesis can be tested by the researcher in some way. This leads to a situation in which the 'results' of the research are separated from the 'discussion' of the research. Producing this is usually quite easy because the results section simply describes the outcome of the test of the hypothesis. The interpretation of the results then follows in the 'discussion' section. In some circumstances, this structure can cause problems even for those committed to quantitative methods. For example, those who conduct surveys involving numerous different questions or measures may find the rigid distinction between results and the interpretation of the results leads to fairly stilted and, consequently, unsatisfactory reports. The structure can cause more profound problems for qualitative researchers.

The difficulty is that the conventional structure is based on the very particular view of how psychological research proceeds. It involves assumptions about how progress is achieved in research which are not shared by qualitative researchers. In qualitative research, the analysis of the data and the interpretation of this analysis are intimately related. For example, the 'themes' which are derived in a thematic analysis are not pre-ordained but are developed as the researcher processes the data repeatedly. The argument for the themes, the themes themselves and the meaning of the themes cannot clearly be differentiated as separate sequential stages. Hence, the conventional structure of quantitative reports, for some, profoundly misrepresents the nature of qualitative research.

Similarly, and more particularly, it should be noted that even the idea of a literature review prior to collecting data imposes a particular view on how an investigation should proceed – that is, the literature review is there partly to structure what is thought about, what the relevant data are, and how they can be interpreted. What if the researcher shunned this and really wanted the analysis to be led by the data? If this is the assumption, then a literature review prior to data analysis may be seen as undesirable. Pure versions of grounded theory and conversation analysis, for example, would eschew the pre-analysis literature review. In other words, the structure of the conventional research report carries its own baggage concerning the nature of research.

Despite this, it is commonly recommended that the structure of qualitative research reports should adopt a modified version of the conventional laboratory report structure. The change is only modest since it usually involves little more than amalgamating the results and discussions sections together. Sometimes it is suggested that this is called 'Findings' rather than 'Results and Discussion'. There are some obvious advantages to this:

- The skills that have been applied to producing quantitative reports can easily be transferred to writing qualitative reports.
- It is a familiar structure which all psychologists are well used to.
- By using much the same report structure, the differences between qualitative and quantitative report writing are levelled.

While these are advantages, there is a big disadvantage – that is, it makes it too easy to forget that a qualitative report needs to be substantially different in certain aspects of its content. Thus, very different things need to be included in the various sections of a qualitative research report. We can adopt the conventional structure but we need to constantly adapt it to the requirements of qualitative research.

This is illustrated clearly in Table 15.2 which provides more detail about what may go under each heading in a qualitative report. These subsections include ones which would simply be seen as inappropriate in a quantitative report. Even where they appear to be the same they can be very different. So it is not unusual to include tables

TABLE 15.2 A detailed structure for a qualitative report

The major components of a qualitative report	Some appropriate subsections – including possible sub-headings	Common faults
Title	This should be informative about the general content of the report. Often a title and subtitle are used.	Not sufficiently informative about the contents of the report.
Abstract	(a) Brief summary of reason for the research. (b) Brief summary of method of the research (c) Brief summary of findings of the research. (d) Brief summary of conclusions.	Failure to summarise *all* major components of the report. Especially common not to summarise findings and conclusions in qualitative reports.
Introduction	(a) Orientating paragraph. (b) Justification and clear statement of the aims of the research. (c) Literature review as appropriate. (d) What has emerged from the literature review which impinges on the research that you carried out? (e) Explanation of why a particular qualitative method was selected as being appropriate. Avoid writing a general justification for choosing qualitative and not quantitative methods. There are many qualitative approaches. (f) Statement of the specific research question you wish to address in your study. Hypotheses are largely inappropriate in qualitative methodology.	Material not sufficiently focused towards the study carried out – that is, too general and wasteful of reader's time. Material does not have a coherent structure especially the literature review. The use of sub-headings may help considerably. Material vague and insufficiently detailed because original sources have not been read.

TABLE 15.2 *(continued)*

The major components of a qualitative report	Some appropriate subsections – including possible sub-headings	Common faults
Method	(a) Rationale for the methodological approach (if not more appropriately placed in the Introduction). (b) Design of the study including interviews/focus groups, etc. (c) Procedures, interviews and other data collection methods used. (d) General information about participants in the research. (e) Ethical considerations. (f) Transcription of data. (g) Strategy for the data analysis. (h) Procedures for assessing the reliability and validity of the analysis.	Failure to present detail of data collection methods used (e.g. focus groups or in-depth interviews) which may be very pertinent to the interpretation of the data. Very common to gloss over the details of the qualitative research analysis, leaving considerable doubt about what was done – or even whether it was truly a qualitative analysis.
Results and Discussion (Findings)	(a) The analysis of the textual material. (b) Quotes illustrating aspects of the analysis or for detailed discussion. (c) Possibly simple quantification to indicate the incidence of different features of the analysis. (d) Tables (e.g. several quotes illustrating a theme or perhaps contrasting the quotes from one sample with those of another). (e) Reflections on methodology and analysis. (f) The major features of the analysis. (g) How the research findings relate to those from other studies in this area of research. (h) Describe attempts to validate the analysis such as discussing it with the original participants. (i) Any methodological issues which place limitations on the research findings. (j) Further implications of the research in terms of possible fruitful lines of inquiry.	Failure to carry out a thorough, systematic analysis. Instead, a few themes are identified and illustrated with quotes without any attempt to embrace all of the data or develop better-fitting themes or categories. This amounts to a failure to recognise the rigour of qualitative methods. Inconsistencies in the analysis.
Conclusions (optional)	In modern practice, a conclusions section is relatively uncommon in many fields of research. Where they appear, the conclusions are often incorporated with the Discussion section and do not appear as a separate sub-heading. Qualitative research studies, because of their nature, may not be conducive to being summarised by a few conclusions.	A common fault is for a conclusion to be stated which does not follow from what has been written previously in the report.
List of references	Follow prescribed method. This may be the standards set by the American Psychological Association publications manual, the department in which you are studying, or some other authority. Consistency is probably the most important requirement.	There are numerous errors that can be made. These are largely avoided by being clear what set of rules you are following and using an appropriate model. Failure to do so will result in inconsistency.
Appendices	Transcripts. Any other materials.	The use of appendices is significantly affected by the type of report that you are writing. Where space is at a premium, the use of appendices has to be sparing. In other reports (e.g. the PhD thesis), accuracy and completeness are more important than amount of space used so the use of appendices may be much more generous.

in a qualitative report but these are more likely to be tables of themes or quotes than they are to be quantitative in any way. For example, in qualitative research a table may list the participants and describe some of their characteristics. In this way, details about individual members of the group of participants are presented. In quantitative research, such features are more likely to be presented in terms of sample means and standard deviations.

The qualitative report in detail

Without doubt one of the best ways to learn how to write up a qualitative research report is to study the writings of researchers in the field which is of interest to you. Of these, you will find journal articles the best source of good models to emulate. This is because journal articles are required to adhere to particular standards of content which chapters in books, for example, are not. Do not forget, either, that lecturers have the journal article as an 'ideal' in their heads by virtue of their training in psychology. So adopting the style of a psychology journal which publishes qualitative research (e.g. *Qualitative Research in Psychology*) is probably the best strategy. As you get further into your studies, the more you are likely to read such articles as preparation for your research, e.g. as part of the literature review. As already mentioned, having a relevant article in front of you as a model is a really good idea as few of us can memorise every last intricate detail of how to write a journal article. Qualitative researchers are probably more likely to go beyond the field of psychology in their literature review so be warned that the standards of report writing are different in disciplines other than psychology. Also be aware that for some qualitative researchers, the aim is to reject all aspects of the quantitative research project so substantial departures from the quantitative writing style sometimes happen. This is most likely in journals of lower status.

Importantly, the qualitative ethos more readily accepts the role of the researcher in the production of knowledge than does the ethos of quantitative research which can be caricatured as the objective quest for extracting knowledge from reality – in contrast, qualitative research can be caricatured as the subjective construction of knowledge. These are caricatures but, nevertheless, they capture something of the difference between the two approaches. One consequence of these differences, as already explained, is that qualitative research reports tend to include more discussion of the researcher's subjective impressions throughout. In other words, writing about how the researcher experienced carrying out the interviews, how the researcher's previous experiences contributed to the research, how the researcher's attitudes and beliefs were impinged by the research findings, and so forth may be included, though omitting the mundane.

The following sections take you through each of the sections of a qualitative research report. We would highlight the importance of *all* aspects of the report and especially what appear to be simple or even trivial matters such as the title and the abstract. These are the initial point of entry for readers into what your research is about. The clearer these are and the more informative, the better the initial impression that the reader will have. They are there to give the reader a good idea about what the report has to say and, as such, structure the reading of the main body of the text. Similarly, although details such as citing sources correctly and listing your references seem more like chores than contributions to the quality of your report, students who do these properly will find that their work is regarded as better quality than those who are slipshod or haphazard about these.

Writing a good title

Research reports are not a diary or chronology of the things that the researcher does. Rather, they tell a story in a relatively structured and comprehensible fashion. Usually, the reader becomes interested in a report because of its title, first, and its abstract, second. These constitute the information about a research report's contents recorded on publications' databases such as PsycINFO and, as such, influence greatly whether a report will be read or ignored (along with search terms that the author supplies to index the article). Consequently the title of a research report needs to be a compact statement of what the report is about. Titles are short (usually about 20 words is the limit) which means that words should not be wasted. Redundant phrases such as 'a study into . . . ', 'an investigation into . . . ' and 'an experiment on . . . ' are seldom seen as a consequence. Furthermore, fanciful or smart plays on words are generally avoided because they communicate little about the content of the report directly. While the titles of novels may indicate little about the book's content and still be effective, this is not the case with research reports. Here are some titles drawn from the PsycINFO database using the search terms conversation analysis (CA), discourse analysis (DA), grounded theory (GT), interpretative phenomenological analysis (IPA), narrative analysis (NA), phenomenology (Ph) and thematic analysis (TA):

- Discovering communicative competencies in a nonspeaking child with autism (Stiegler, 2007) CA
- When May calls home: The opening moments of family telephone conversations with an Alzheimer's patient (Kitzinger & Jones, 2007) CA
- Interacting via SMS: Practices of social closeness and reciprocation (Spagnolli & Gamberini, 2007) CA
- Constructing identities in cyberspace: The case of eating disorders (Giles, 2006) DA
- 'I haven't even phoned my doctor yet.' The advice-giving role of the pharmacist during consultations for medication review with patients aged 80 or more (Salter, Holland, Harvey, & Henwood, 2007) DA
- Constructions of racism in the Australian parliamentary debates on asylum seekers (Every & Augoustinos, 2007) DA
- Never-ending making sense: Towards a substantive theory of the information-seeking behaviour of newly diagnosed cancer patients (McCaughan & McKenna, 2007) GT
- Interpretive subgroup analysis extends modified grounded theory research findings in oncologic music therapy (O'Callaghan & Hiscock, 2007) GT
- Peer devaluation in British secondary schools: Young people's comparisons of group-based and individual-based bullying (O'Brien, 2007) GT
- Women's reflections upon their past abortions: An exploration of how and why emotional reactions change over time (Goodwin & Ogden, 2007) IPA
- Investigating the ways that older people cope with dementia: A qualitative study (Preston, Marshall, & Bucks, 2007) IPA
- Resilience and well-being in palliative care staff: A qualitative study of hospice nurses' experience of work (Ablett & Jones, 2007) IPA
- Cracking the code of genocide: The moral psychology of rescuers, bystanders, and Nazis during the Holocaust (Monroe, 2008) NA
- Exploring young women's understandings of the development of difficulties: A narrative biographical analysis (Brooks & Dallos, 2009) NA

- 'Do you know what I mean?': The use of pluralistic narrative analysis approach in the interpretation of an interview (Frost, 2009) NA
- Narrative, identity, and recovery from serious mental illness: A life history of a runner (Carless, 2008) NA
- A phenomenological analysis of the experience of pivotal moments in therapy as defined by clients (Giorgi, 2011) Ph
- Living with incurable oesophageal cancer. A phenomenological hermeneutical interpretation of patient stories (Missel & Birkelund, 2011) Ph
- Toward caring for oneself in a life of intense ups and downs: A reflexive-collaborative exploration of recovery in bipolar disorder (Veseth, Binder, Borg, & Davidson, 2012) Ph
- Vicarious growth in wives of Vietnam veterans: A phenomenological investigation into decades of 'lived' experience (McCormack, Hagger, & Joseph, 2011) Ph
- Patient perceptions of factors influencing adherence to medication following kidney transplant (Orr, Orr, Willis, Holmes, & Britton, 2007) TA
- 'Why can't they do anything for a simple back problem?': A qualitative examination of expectations for low back pain treatment and outcome (Campbell & Guy, 2007) TA
- Barriers and facilitators of evidence-based practice perceived by behavioral science health professions (Pagoto et al., 2007) TA

All of these have been accepted for publication in professional journals so meet acceptable standards. It is evident from reading them that each tells us quite a bit about the nature of the research being reported though some do so better than others. Nevertheless, some of the titles include eye-catching elements such as 'Why can't they do anything for a simple back problem?' and 'I haven't even phoned the doctor yet' which may not always seem to be very informative in themselves and might be omitted without much or any loss in the information conveyed. There is a tradition of embedding the everyday language of participants in the title in some fields of qualitative research. Thus some participants' voices are 'honoured' with a particular significance to the research and they may be particularly poignant. In our instances of this, the eye-catching elements work because they are associated with very lengthy titles – in one case 25 words long, which exceeds the conventional maximum length of 12 words for a title. They probably should only be used where they add something of significance to an already very clear title. They should not simply be obscure. Just how typical this selection of titles is of qualitative research papers in general is unknown. Nevertheless, it seems common to use a two-part 'title: subtitle' structure consisting of a title followed by a colon followed by a subtitle. This is also not uncommon in quantitative research reports.

Interestingly, the title alone often also gives enough information for the reader to have a good idea of what sort of qualitative analysis the report employs. This is especially the case with the CA and the IPA examples. Of course, the impression created by the title can be confirmed by checking the associated abstract.

What goes into the Abstract?

The abstract is a short precis or summary of the research report. Word limits for the abstract are generally very tight and typically journals will limit them to 100 or 150 words. A student's report might have a slightly longer abstract but wordiness is not the intention in this aspect of report writing. The task is to cover as much as possible of the report's contents in that space. This provides the reader with an opportunity to judge whether the

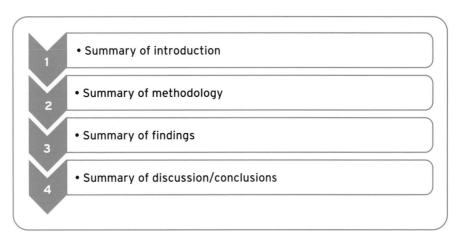

FIGURE 15.2 What goes in the Abstract?

report is relevant to them or, in the case of a student report, it helps the lecturer understand what is coming next in the main body of the report and gives some preliminary indications of how good that report is likely to be. Of course, writing the perfect abstract is no easy task and no two researchers would write an identical abstract for the same report. In other words, there is an element of judgement in terms of what to include and what to leave out.

The key to writing a satisfactory abstract is to ensure that all of the major sections of the report are summarised. These are (1) Introduction, (2) Methodology, (3) Findings and (4) Discussion/Conclusions sections (Figure 15.2). It is unsatisfactory (though a common failing) to leave any out. Probably the commonest error is to concentrate on summarising just the Introduction and Methodology sections, leaving little or no opportunity to summarise the Findings and Conclusions. This is notable in quite a few qualitative reports.

Some journals, but by no means a majority, require a structured abstract in which sub-headings corresponding to the major sections of a research report are included. This disciplines the author into dealing with the entirety of the report. It is a useful tip to write your abstract using the sub-headings of the sections of the report given in Figure 15.2. These may be subsequently deleted if necessary since in this context their purpose is merely to provide a structure to ensure that all necessary sections are covered.

What goes into the Introduction?

The Introduction is the place to set out the purpose, justification and background to the research to be reported later. In other words, it is the rationale for the research that is about to be described. There are certain essential elements, which can be supplemented by others according to circumstances if so desired (see Figure 15.3).

Initial orientating material

This introduces the reader to the broad area of your research using a few brief sentences or paragraphs. The initial paragraph or two of orientating material is extremely important since this begins the process of introducing the background to and the reasons for all that follows. If these paragraphs do not do their job clearly then the reader may fail to appreciate what comes later – they even get a misleading impression of what is to come. The temptation, especially for novices, is to begin with one or two extremely

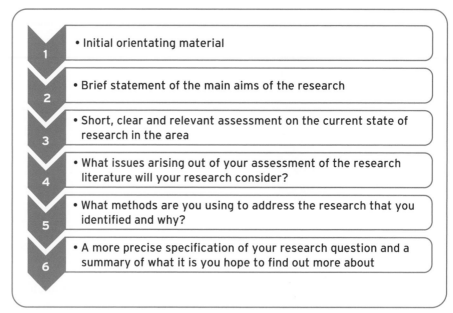

FIGURE 15.3 What goes in the Introduction?

general paragraphs which, in themselves, contribute little or nothing to the substance of the report – which is that defined by the title and abstract. The key to the introductory paragraph(s) is that they should focus the reader's attention immediately on the research to be described. There are any number of ways, of course, for starting a report so it is difficult to give rules about what to do – the important thing is to start with a strong and pertinent statement.

Brief statement of the main aims of the research

What is it that the research attempts to achieve? Research is portrayed as a purposeful activity which is directed to achieving some sort of goal. Of course, it is necessary to tailor your research goals to the research in question and it is not possible to provide a simple statement of research aims which can be adapted for all types of qualitative research. Some of the possibilities might include the following but there are many more:

- The aim of the research was to identify the major themes emerging in focus group discussions of the experience of living with cancer.
- The aim of the study was to explore how text messages are used to maintain friendships after people have moved away from home to a university.
- The major focus of the research was to examine how conversational errors are repaired between friends compared with strangers.

Make a short, clear and relevant assessment on the current state of research in the area

In short research reports, you should not attempt to review all of the literature in the field, though in a long report (PhD dissertations, for example) you may spread more widely. How specific the research review which you describe is will depend partly on how extensive the relevant research literature is. The less extensive, the more widely drawn will be the material from the literature. For conversation analysis and grounded theory, especially, remember that one view is that the analysis is ideally 'unsullied' by past research findings so you may wish not to review previous conversation analyses or grounded theory analyses since this may lead your own analysis inappropriately. Nevertheless, it may be appropriate to discuss other aspects of the research literature pertinent to your general theme. Also, a retrospective literature review will allow the researcher to compare their new analysis with those of others.

Mixed qualitative/quantitative literature reviews

Literature reviews in qualitative reports are often a mixture of qualitative and quantitative studies. Because of the relative infancy of qualitative research in psychology, it may be difficult or impossible to find relevant qualitative research for some, if not many, research topics. This puts an onus on the writer of the report to clearly identify the nature of the research reports they refer to – are they qualitative or are they quantitative? Of course, stylistically this should be done in a manner which does not interfere too much with the flow of the report. This is especially important where research conclusions are discussed without any detail about the research methodology employed. There is nothing wrong or improper about using both qualitative and quantitative sources (though perhaps not everyone will agree with this) but where they do this, many qualitative researchers will be anxious to point out the inadequacies or limitations of their quantitative resources.

What issues arising out of your assessment of the research literature will your research consider?

When trying to understand report writing in psychology, it is important to remember that research is regarded as a process which goes through a number of steps before the research 'yields its findings'. One of the steps in this is the literature review. Now the literature review that is included in the research report is not intended to be all-inclusive or exhaustive and it is not intended to consist of everything that the researcher has read. The literature review is an account of the research literature insofar as it helped the researcher to identify some important issues arising out of previous research. Examples of such important issues might be:

- Thus it is clear that research on doctor–patient interaction has failed to explore how the initial greeting by the doctor influences the later interaction with the patient.

- It is apparent, on the basis of this literature review, that the topic of how neighbours end disputes has not been extensively addressed by researchers to date. Therefore, there is a need for studies of the processes involved.

- It seems that public concern about the levels of knife crime among some young people has created a need for research which elucidates the nature of these concerns.

What methods are you using to address the research that you identified and why?

In qualitative research, the major methods are not entirely familiar to many psychologists, in general, as they are for quantitative methods. Partly as a consequence, qualitative research reports tend to include relatively extended discussions of the analytic methods and techniques used. In particular, extended accounts of the theoretical and conceptual background to the analytic method employed are frequently presented. Of course, how much to include of such material is a difficult matter to decide upon since there are so many different factors involved. If the word length you have is particularly short then clearly there is little space to be devoted to this. Check word lengths as a matter of course and make sure that you keep to them – and don't write anything substantially shorter. As a student, it is desirable to give some background to the type of qualitative analysis you have carried out which can put some pressure on word limits.

A more precise specification of your research question and a summary of what it is you hope to find out more about

Most qualitative research by its nature is exploratory of things such as turn-taking in conversation, people's life histories, themes in how people talk about being victimised by crime and so forth. Specific research hypotheses are rarely tested in qualitative research and, to many qualitative researchers, such attempts seem alien.

What goes into the Method section?

The following components ought to be considered for inclusion in the Method section of your report. It is unlikely that all of them will be appropriate for every qualitative report but it is always helpful to consider their inclusion (Figure 15.4).

Rationale for research method and general approach employed

In the Method section, it is appropriate to provide a more detailed rationale and broad description of the research methods used. To some extent the Introduction will have provided some information but the precise techniques employed need some explanation. For example, you may decide to use a focus group methodology rather than interviews or you

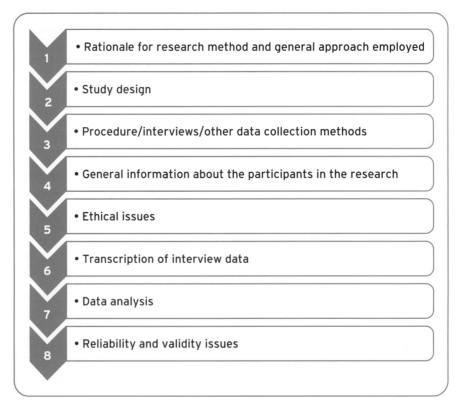

1 • Rationale for research method and general approach employed

2 • Study design

3 • Procedure/interviews/other data collection methods

4 • General information about the participants in the research

5 • Ethical issues

6 • Transcription of interview data

7 • Data analysis

8 • Reliability and validity issues

FIGURE 15.4 What goes in the Method section?

may get the participants to write a life history rather than use in-depth interviews. So it is important that you explain your choices. Of course, there is rarely a clear best single data collection method so you are explaining what led to your decision and, where appropriate, the drawbacks of this choice.

Study design

You need to explain something about your choice of participants (or available textual material) in your research and why they are appropriate for your research. There may be special reasons why it is appropriate to use a qualitative approach with this particular group of participants or reasons why it might be preferable to use one data collection method rather than another. Furthermore, you may choose, perhaps, to carry out an unstructured interview rather than the more usual open-ended questioning. What were the reasons for doing this? In other words, in the study design section you can provide details of your selected approach for obtaining your participants and obtaining data from them. Often, your choices are less obvious than at first appears and by justifying them everyone will come to understand your research better.

Procedure/interviews/other data collection methods

To indicate, for example, that you used open-ended questioning tells the reader only a limited amount about the style of interview that was conducted. It says nothing about the context (physical, etc.) and nothing about the nature of the interaction between the interviewer and interviewee. For example, what steps were taken to ensure that the interviewee was relaxed and communicative with the interviewer (i.e. rapport)? What is the framework for the interview questioning? None of these things is obvious from a simple statement like 'An open-ended approach to interviewing was employed'. Furthermore, it says nothing about the characteristics, experience or competence of the interviewer, all of which may have a bearing on the way in which the interview proceeds. So there is a range of helpful detail about the data collection methods that could be included. This, of course, is not restricted to interviews and is as relevant to other data collection methods. So, for example, if archival materials were to be used there is a great deal to be explained about how this was done – how materials were obtained, selected, prepared and so forth.

General information about the participants in the research

This section provides the necessary information for the reader to understand the nature and extent of your 'sampling'. In quantitative research the participants are usually described in quantitative terms such as the distribution of age, sex and other salient features to the research. Obviously one has to be selective in how much information is summarised in qualitative research. Basic demographic information of the sort just mentioned would possibly be appropriate. How were the participants recruited? What organisations, for example, were they drawn from?

In a quantitative report the following would be the minimum sort of information that should be provided and there is no reason why many qualitative studies should not emulate this level of detail and beyond:

- The total number of participants.
- The numbers of participants in different categories – for example, the number of counsellors involved and the number of clients involved in a study of counselling.
- The gender characteristics of the participants.

- Some indication of the typical participants in the research and possibly an indication of the spread of their ages.
- Major characteristics of the participants or groups of participants. Often this will be university students but other research may have different participant characteristics, e.g. pre-school children, visitors to a health farm. These may also be presented in numerical form as frequencies.
- Make sure that you make reference to any characteristics of the participants which may have implications for the data analysis.
- It is good practice, but not common, to give some indication of refusal rates and drop-out rates for the participants. Refusal rates are the numbers who are asked to take part in the research but say no. Drop-out rates are the numbers who initially take part in the research but for some reason fail to complete all of the stages. Sometimes this is known alarmingly as 'the mortality rate' or the 'experimental mortality'.
- Any inducements or rewards given to participants to take part in the study. So, for example, being given monetary rewards or course credits would be mentioned.

In qualitative research, it is possible to say more about the personal backgrounds of the participants than would be usual in quantitative research reports. Remember that where participants are not numerous in qualitative research, it is possible to supply a table summarising some of the characteristics of each participant. In this way, the reader gets a picture of each participant and not average scores for a group of participants as is usual in quantitative research. As an alternative, there are circumstances in which it might be desirable to provide a sort of potted biography of all or some key participants in the research. While this may not be appropriate, say, in the case of a discourse analysis or a conversation analysis where such material may be seen as superfluous, biographical material may flesh out our understanding of what is being said in some forms of qualitative analysis.

Ethical issues (see also Chapter 17)

In this section you should (a) briefly describe the formal institutional arrangements covering the work, (b) describe the ethical arrangements as you have presented them to your participants as part of the recruitment to your research, and (c) identify any particularly interesting or problematic ethical matters related to your research.

Most, if not all, universities have an Ethics Committee governing research with human participants. So it is probable that you have had to apply for ethical approval in some way or otherwise demonstrated that your work meets the required ethical standards. There may, of course, be arrangements for general ethical approval for research which is of a particular style or there may be a fast track method of obtaining ethical approval for research which lacks potentially problematic aspects.

Whatever the general arrangements, there will be some form of 'contractual' ethical arrangement between you and the participants in your research. Sometimes researchers provide a written statement of the ethical procedures that they will employ which is signed by the participant to acknowledge their understanding of these arrangements. Typical arrangements of this sort might include informed consent (where the participant knows in some detail the nature of the research and the procedures that are to be used), an understanding that the participant may withdraw themselves and their data at any stage, that anonymity and confidentiality will be respected, and so forth.

There may be specific ethical issues related to the research in question which would not be entirely covered by the typical, general ethical arrangements employed by psychological researchers. For example, the writing up of case studies may be particularly problematic as it is easy for individuals to be identified in some circumstances – for example, when they work in a particular position in an organisation and nobody else has an identical role.

Chapter 17 deals with general ethical issues in qualitative research.

Transcription of interview data

The transcription process is an important stage when dealing with qualitative data. There are several different approaches to transcription (see Chapter 6), each of which serves its own special purposes for different styles of research. Simple literal transcription of the interview or focus group needs no expertise on the part of the transcriber other than listening and word processing skills. Jefferson coding includes much more information about the social interaction between the participants in the focus group or between the interviewer and the interviewee. It is a much more skilled task, requiring good understanding of the underlying strategy of this sort of transcription. You should describe the transcription method employed in some detail, deviations from the standard method of doing things, and who did the transcription. In qualitative analysis, the process of transcription is usually regarded as an important part of the analysis of the data as the researcher becomes familiarised with the contents of the interviews, etc. as a result. Each transcription can take several hours. During this stage, preliminary ideas about the analysis of the data may emerge. So it is helpful to the reader, for example, to know that the researcher transcribed their own data or if the task was delegated to an assistant.

Data analysis

The process by which the researcher analyses qualitative data is often missing from qualitative research reports. This is not a good thing as the process involved is a critical aspect of qualitative report writing. There is a great deal actually to be said about a qualitative analysis which the reader ought to know over and above understanding what the broad analytic framework is. Here are some of the things to include:

- What was the process of familiarising oneself with the data? For example, did the analyst transcribe the data/carry out the interviews, etc. themselves?
- What broad methods were used to organise the data analysis? For example, were computers involved in some way and, in this case, what programs were utilised? Some comments on what the program does may be appropriate as this may not be common knowledge. Of course, it is possible to tackle the organisation of the data analysis in other ways. For example, what was done with the transcripts? Were they separated into sections and put on index cards for comparative purposes, for example?
- What data-coding strategies did the researcher use? Was a diary/notebook used to jot down ideas? At what level did the initial coding proceed? For example, was the initial coding on a line-by-line basis? What methods were used to integrate the many initial codings into broader categories? What procedures were used to check the fit of the codings to the data? Thus, potentially, there is a lot of information to be provided. Given that a good qualitative research project devotes copious time to this process, failing to include such information risks the suspicion that the appropriate stages have not been employed or, at the very least, leaves the reader very much in the dark about the care and effort that went into the data analysis.

- It is especially important to indicate any points at which the data analysis method employed departs substantially from the typical approach used by researchers using the same broad method.

Reliability and validity

It should be understood by now that qualitative research takes a wide variety of different forms. Consequently, the objectives of different sorts of qualitative methods should be taken into account when deciding precisely what sort of assessment of 'reliability' and 'validity' is appropriate. To what extent do different researchers involved in the analysis agree on the codings for data categories? There is no necessary assumption in qualitative research that different researchers analysing similar material will necessarily come up with the same qualitative analysis as each other. This is, of course, true of quantitative research where it would not be expected, in general, that every quantitative analyst would generate exactly the same analysis for complex data. The complex issue of reliability and validity in qualitative research together with general issues of quality in qualitative research are dealt with later (in Chapter 16).

What goes in the Results and Discussion/Findings section?

Typically, in qualitative research, it is not possible to make the rigid distinction between the results of the data analysis and the discussion of the data analysis that applies to quantitative research. Consequently, it is best to combine these two sections into one – either calling it 'Results and Discussion' or 'Findings'. This is because in qualitative research it is often impossible to distinguish between the findings of the analysis and the researcher's interpretation of the data. Just what should go into the 'Findings' section? There are two main components (Figure 15.5):

- The findings from your analysis.
- The data to support your analysis – that is usually quotations from the data which can help the reader both understand your analysis and, to a degree, assess the adequacy of your analysis.

The overriding rule should be that these should be presented as objectively and carefully as possible within the broad parameters of the academic approach.

The findings from the analysis

The findings of your qualitative research should be presented as transparently as possible. Details of how you developed your findings should be presented as far as you can. It is also appropriate to discuss ideas that you have rejected. There is nothing wrong with expressing reservations that you have about any aspect of your report.

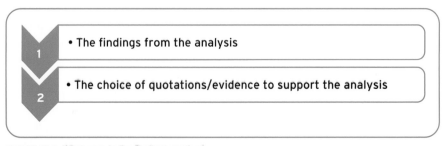

1 • The findings from the analysis

2 • The choice of quotations/evidence to support the analysis

FIGURE 15.5 What goes in the Findings section?

The choice of quotations/evidence to support the analysis

Qualitative research at its best adheres to the highest possible academic standards. That is, one's arguments are carefully assessed against criteria such as logical consistency and empirical data wherever possible. For this reason, the selection of quotes to illustrate the analysis needs to be carefully done. The idea is *not* simply to pick quotes from the data which seem to illustrate the analysis particularly well but to also indicate the extent to which the analysis actually fits the data. In other words, simply selecting supporting quotes because they neatly fit in with your analysis is not good enough because it disguises problems in your analysis. A number of issues are pertinent to the presentation of quotes:

- At a very basic level, the qualitative researcher should ensure that the quotes employed in their reports truly do illustrate or represent what they are claiming in their analysis. Though this is basic, experience suggests that students do not always use quotes which seem to be particularly relevant to the point that is being made in their analysis. There can be any number of reasons for this. The most likely is that they have not formulated what it is they are trying to say in their analysis clearly enough to be able to identify exemplars. The second likely reason is that their analysis was inadequately based on their data in the first place.

- How representative are the quotes? The reader, if given just one quote in support of the analysis, simply cannot assess how well other potential quotes would have fitted the data. This is made more difficult in circumstances in which the reader does not have access to the full transcription of the data. There are ways around this, of course. One is simply to put as many quotes which illustrate a particular aspect of the data as you can into a table or box which the reader can then critically consider (as is recommended in IPA in Chapter 13). This is particularly useful for small studies and most convincing when all relevant quotations can be included. An alternative is for the researcher to discuss the range of material which is relevant to a particular aspect of the analysis and to highlight potentially problematic aspects of the data. So, for example, if the analysis identifies particular themes in the data, the researcher may choose to mention any data which are problematic in relation to that theme. A further advantage of tables and boxes to present quotes is that it is possible to set up a comparison of different groups of participants. Differences between the sexes could be drawn out using a suitable table – that is, a table in which there are two columns of quotations, one for female participants and the other for male participants. Furthermore, the use of tables and boxes can alleviate some of the pressure on space.

- There is a case for quantifying aspects of a qualitative analysis. It is somewhat disconcerting in a qualitative report to read comments such as 'Most interviewees mentioned "grieving"' since there is nothing wrong with stating the precise percentage. Words such as 'most' can imply just about anything from a small majority to nearly all. Using some simple but precise quantitative statements such as '90 per cent of the emails we studied included the theme "friendly greetings"' is not simply more informative but also indicates the extent to which the researcher has been thorough in checking his or her analytical categories against the actual data.

- There have been arguments made about just how distinct quotations should be from the main body of the analysis. Typically, quotes may be typed in italics for emphasis or indented and started on a new line. While this seems quite reasonable, it has been suggested that by making the quotes distinctive, the reader is tempted to skip reading them and so fail to appreciate the nuances of the analysis and monitor the quality of the argument being made by the researcher. There is probably little that can be done about this in many cases. For example, it is impossible to camouflage an extract of Jefferson-transcribed text as it is so characteristically different from most text and exchanges in interviews between interview and interviewee also readily stand out.

- Although some qualitative methods value exact precision in the transcripts of data extremely highly, there are qualitative studies in which this degree of precision is not particularly helpful. This raises the question of what is a useful quote for inclusion. For example, how useful is a quote which is full of local regional dialect and language? Similar problems may occur when the speaker is poor at English because it is their second language, for example. Should such a quote be supplemented by indications of the meaning of the dialect words and constructions? This clearly loses fidelity with the original quote but, perhaps, helps the reader get something out of it which otherwise they might not. Similarly, what does one do about quotes which are translated from another language into English prior to the qualitative analysis? Is this appropriate for the purposes of the study? Even if it is, what can be done to assess whether the translation is accurate? One technique which could be used is back-translation in which the translation is further translated back into the original language by a second translator. The two versions could then be compared for similarity. These are important issues but their impact is likely to be different for different theoretical orientations. It seems unlikely that a conversation analyst or a grounded theory methodologist would be willing to analyse translations because these have less than perfect fidelity to the originals and the nuances of the original language may be lost or may even be untranslatable. How could a Jefferson transcription be applied meaningfully to a translation which may well be in a language which is very different in structure, inflexions and so forth from English? On the other hand, a researcher who is interested in the experiences of migrant workers in the United Kingdom may find the translations adequate for the purposes of their study. There are qualitative analyses published which employ translations simply because the paper is written in a different language from that of the participants. Typically what happens is that the original text is reproduced in one line and the translation given in the next. In conversation analysis and some forms of discourse analysis, both versions are given the Jefferson symbols.

- Identification coding of each quote simply means indicating the source of the quote. Although it would be somewhat unethical to refer to the source of the quote by their actual names, fictitious ones could be used. On the other hand, it is probably more useful to use an identification code which provides some information about the participant. For example, F1, etc. could be used for female participants and M1, etc. for male participants. Of course, a more elaborate scheme could be used. Unfortunately, this has to be balanced against the increased risk that the information in the code could reveal the identity of the participant to a reader. This is probably a bigger risk where the sample of participants is small. One of the big advantages of identification coding is that for reports with numerous quotes it is easy to know which quotes come from the same source. If quotes are not numerous and they come from a small number of participants then this might indicate that the researcher has not sampled the data widely for illustrative quotations.

- Most importantly, quotes in qualitative research are not merely there for illustrative purposes. They serve a vital role in the analysis of allowing what might be described as an informal but vital assessment of the 'reliability' and 'validity' of the analysis which some qualitative researchers believe to be important. However, the meaning of these terms in qualitative analysis is not the same as their quantitative analysis meaning (see Chapter 16). They refer to the presentation of adequate evidence for the reader's scrutiny. Without the provision of sufficient exemplars in the form of quotes, the reader cannot realistically and adequately evaluate the value of the analysis for themselves on the basis of the limited excerpts available to them.

- Consider ways in which the entire transcripts can be circulated to whoever has an interest in seeing them. The Internet makes this easy in many cases, though more needs to be done to increase this form of circulation.

What goes in the Conclusions section?

Given the exploratory nature of much qualitative research, it is frequently impossible to draw up a shortlist of conclusions which does not appear clumsy or in some other way awkward. This is true for some areas of quantitative psychology as well and Conclusions sections are sometimes omitted as a separate heading from research reports. They are nevertheless essential to quantitative studies which have tested a small number of hypotheses. This, of course, is not the strategy of most modern qualitative research. So while you may consider the use of a Conclusions section, you may feel that there are no benefits from including one for your qualitative study. Since a qualitative report may be more about developing analytic ideas than confirming them, it may prove difficult to present a list of conclusions from your study without it appearing too terse or too simplistic. Unless obligatory, include such a section only after considerable thought and then be prepared to abandon it if it appears to undermine or detract from the quality of your report.

Of course, none of this means that you should end your report abruptly. The 'Results and Discussion' (or 'Findings') should end with an effective concluding statement which rounds off the report.

References

The reference list is a major feature of all reports written by academics. Usually the reference list is begun on a separate page at the end of the report (but before any appendices). If space is at a premium, then the reference list may follow immediately after the final section of the main body of the report (e.g. the 'Conclusions' if there is such a section). The reference list is crucial for documenting the source of the evidence used in support of all aspects of the argument that you have made in your report. The references provide the starting point for others to check out your claims if they so wish. So, in order for the reader of your report to be able to check the accuracy and detail of your claims, you must indicate to them the sources of information that you have used. Simply suggesting that 'researchers have discovered that' or 'it is obvious that' is poor scholarship. Identify as precisely as you can the source of your claims. Doing this involves two main components:

- The citation: You cite your sources in the text as, say, '(Donovan & Jenkins, 2003)'. 'Donovan & Jenkins' gives the name of the authors and '2003' is the date of publication (dissemination) of the work. There are many systems in use for giving citations, but in psychology it is virtually universal to use this author–date system. It is known as the Harvard system but there are variants of this and we will use the American Psychological Association's version, which is the basis of those employed throughout the world by other psychological associations.
- You provide an alphabetical list of references by the surname of the first author. There is a standard format for the references, though this varies according to whether it is a book, a journal article, an Internet source and so forth. The reference contains sufficient information for a reader to track down and, in most cases, obtain a copy of the original document.

It is not uncommon, in our experience, for references actually not to contain the support for the argument that they might be expected to. This is clearly bad form and should be avoided.

The citation

While citations in the text of your report may seem straightforward enough, a few things need to be remembered:

- The citation should be placed adjacent to the idea which it supports. Sometimes confusion can be caused because the citation is placed at the end of a sentence which contains more than one idea. Thus, think carefully about exactly where you place the citation – there is nothing wrong with having it part way through a sentence if this is the clearest thing to do.

- Cite your actual source of information and not someone else's whose book or report you are using. So if you read the information in Arrowsmith (2009) then you should cite this as the source. Arrowsmith (2009) may be a secondary source containing material about phenomenology which you think is important. Students are short of time and resources to read only original publications from which to draw information no matter how desirable this is seen to be. So although this would not be at all common in professional report writing, student research reports will often contain citations such as (Dominic, 1999, cited in Arrowsmith, 2009). In this way the ultimate source of the idea is acknowledged but the actual source that you used is also given. To attribute to Arrowsmith ideas which the reader might recognise as those of Dominic would cause great confusion and is fundamentally misleading anyway. In your reference list you would list Arrowsmith (2009) and also Dominic (1999). See also Box 15.2.

Box 15.2

PRACTICAL ADVICE

Dealing with secondary sources

The rules for making citations are that they should refer to work that you have actually read and not things that you have only read about. So you incorporate the author and date of the publication that you have read (Madonna, 2007) into the text and give the citation in full in the reference list. Unfortunately, this causes special problems for students who may only have read about Madonna (2007) in a secondary source such as a textbook. So what should you include by way of a citation in this case? If you simply cite the textbook from which you got the material then there is a problem since the textbook writer (Donague, 2010) appears to be the originator of the idea, which is not the case. Three different solutions are available

to students which are probably more or less equally acceptable:

- In the main body of the text give the original source first followed by 'cited in' then the secondary source (Madonna, 2007, cited in Donague 2010). Then in the reference list simply list Donague (2010) in full in the usual way. This has the advantage of keeping the reference list short.

- In the main body of the text give the original source (Madonna, 2007) but in the reference list insert:

    Madonna, S. (2007). Reflexivity in pop lyrics. *Journal of Psychological Music Research, 5* (3),

361–72. Cited in Donague, M. (2010). *Introduction to modern psychology.* Hereford: Quickbuck Press.

This method allows one to note the full source of both the primary information and the secondary information.

- In the main body of the text give the original source (Madonna, 2007). Then in the reference list insert:

Madonna, S. (2007). Cited in Donahue, M. (2010). *Introduction to modern psychology.* Hereford: Quickbuck Press.

The last two versions are similar except that the first includes details of both the original and the secondary source. Different lecturers may prefer different versions, so check this just in case. No matter what, choose one method and do not mix it with others in your report.

- According to APA guidelines, citations with two authors are cited as, for example, Abbottsbury and Pilkington (2007) and as (Abbottsbury & Pilkington, 2007) when in brackets. Citations with several authors involve more complexity. If there are between three and five authors then their names should all be listed the first time the citation appears but subsequently the reference is given as Brownlow et al. (2010), for example (with the 'et al.' followed by a full stop to indicate an abbreviation). If there are six or more authors then this is given as Brownlow et al. (2010) for the first and subsequent citations.

- Stylistically it is very easy to fall into the trap of presenting the literature review as a list rather than a summary. The main problem is illustrated in the following fictitious example:

> Thomson (2004) was the first to point out that turn-taking in young children does not follow the same 'rules' as that in adults. Berelson (2005) extended this to include turn-taking in adolescents. Abbottsbury and Pilkington (2007) then found that children's turn-taking when conversing with adults was very different from when they are in conversation with other children . . .

This has a fairly monotonous structure in which every sentence begins with a citation. It tends to give the impression that the person mentioned is more important than the idea or research that they contributed. The sooner that you drop this habit, the more smooth and professional your writing will appear. It works far better if your writing concentrates primarily on the ideas and research and the citation is treated as secondary as in the following rewriting:

> Early research on conversational turn-taking suggested that children (Thomson, 2004) and adolescents (Berelson, 2005) do not follow the same rules as adults. It also appears that children adopt different turn-taking strategies when conversing with other children than with adults (Abbottsbury and Pilkington, 2007).

This is better because it focuses on the argument rather than the authorities in the field. The argument will be clearer if it is given prominence.

- When you cite several sources at the same time (Brownlow, 2015; Perkins & Ottaway, 2016; Singh, 2014, 2016) do so in alphabetical order (and then date order if necessary).

- When an author has published several relevant articles in a single year then you need to take special steps to distinguish them. So if Kerry Brownlow published two papers in 2015, they should be identified by the addition of a letter at the end of the date. So Brownlow (2015a) and Brownlow (2015b) are clearly different publications.

They should also be given the extra identifying letter in the reference list. Since the reference list is in alphabetical order, then it is this order which determines which is 'a' and which is 'b'. If both are being cited then to condense things one would put something like (Brownlow, 2015a, b). It is advantageous to distinguish papers by the same author (authors) from each other as soon as possible in your personal documentation/notes since this saves a lot of time later re-reading the articles to identify what is in each of them.

- Try to be honest when listing your citations. There is a preference, of course, for up-to-date citations and thus a temptation to cite sources that you have not used. Avoid this as your lecturers are unlikely to be fooled by citations which, though up to date, are difficult to obtain, for example. Box 15.2 explains how to be honest in making citations. It is important to demonstrate that you have read up-to-date material.

Using a referencing and citation computer program such as *Endnote* or *RefWorks* will pay dividends in the long term although learning to use one takes some time. Your usual word-processing program will be used for your report writing. All of the programs work by allowing you to enter references into a standard template (or several standard templates) and then select them for inclusion in your work in the form of citations and a reference list. You would input details such as the authors, the title of the publication, and so forth into the referencing/citation program. The style of the output can vary greatly according to the user's choice so that the common styles used by academic publications are all covered. These programs are costly, though bona fide students sometimes get heavily discounted purchase prices for the whole program or a student version. But before spending any money it is worth checking whether your university or college has a site licence to use bibliographic software of this sort. Students intending to do a PhD or work in academia should seriously consider the use of these programs. One needs to balance the pros and cons since the time consumed in learning the program may not be offset by the advantages. For more introductory work than a doctoral programme, referencing tends not to be a repetitive process since student essays, etc. are mostly on different topics and so use very different sources. Thus these programs may not be too useful until later stages when references may be used many different times for different reports and publications.

Reference list

References are given under a main heading at the end of your report. Do not confuse a reference list with a bibliography and make sure you use the term bibliography only if that is what you have given. A reference list contains only the sources which you have mentioned in the main body of your report. In contrast, a bibliography is a list containing everything that you have read in the preparation of your report. This may be much longer than the reference list as a consequence because it includes things that you have not cited in the text. Generally a list of references is preferred in academic work. Items in reference lists are *not* numbered in the Harvard system, they are merely given in alphabetical order by surname of the author.

One problem with reference lists is that the structure of individual items varies depending on what sort of source it is. The structure for books is different from the structure for journal articles, for example. Both are different from the structure for Internet sources. Unpublished sources have yet another structure. In the world of professional researchers, this results in the publication of massive style guides for citing and referencing. Fortunately, there are just a few standard patterns. Remember that the house styles of publishers may differ in some respects from other standards. It is a good idea to obtain examples of reference lists from journal articles which correspond to the approved style. They constitute a compact style guide.

Style conventions change with time and you need to be vigilant. Once journal names and book titles were underlined and the typesetter would turn these into italics. Now in the APA system you should use italics rather than the underline in your work. This has the advantage of being less cluttered and has positive advantage for readers with dyslexia as underlining often makes the text harder to read.

The following is indicative of the style that you should adopt for different sorts of source:

- **Books** The structure of the book reference is as follows: Author family name – author initials each followed by a stop/period – (date of publication in brackets) stop/period – title of book with capitals as in example, stop/period – place of publication, colon, publisher name.

  > Silverman, D. (2001). *Interpreting qualitative data: Methods for analysing talk, text and interaction.* London: Sage.

  > Glaser, B., & Strauss, A. L. (1967). *The discovery of grounded theory: Strategies for qualitative research.* Chicago: Aldine.

- **An edited book** Author family name – author initials each followed by a stop/ period – (Eds. or Ed.) stop/period (date of publication in brackets) stop/period – title of book with capitals as in example, stop/period – place of publication, colon, publisher name.

  > Willig, C., & Stainton-Rogers, W. (Eds.). (2008). *The Sage handbook of qualitative research in psychology.* London: Sage.

- **Chapters in books** Author family name – author initials each followed by a stop/ period – (date of publication in brackets) stop/period – title of book chapter with capitals as in example stop/period – initials of editor each followed by stop/period – editor family name – (Ed.) – title of book with capitals as in example (pp. pages of the chapter) stop/period – place of publication, colon, publisher name stop.

  > Charmaz, K. (2008). Grounded theory. In J. A. Smith (Ed.), *Qualitative psychology: A practical guide to research methods* (pp. 81–110). London: Sage.

- **Journal articles** Author family name – author initials – (date of publication in brackets) stop/period – journal article title in lower case except for first word – stop/ period – title of journal in italics or underlined, with capitals on first letter of first word – comma – volume number of journal in italics – comma – pages of journal.

  > Potter, J. (2005). Making psychology relevant. *Discourse & Society, 16,* 739–747.

- **Web sources** For any sort of publication on the Web more or less simply follow the appropriate style such as given above and then the http address from which the source was downloaded. So for an article in an online journal the reference would follow this broad style:

  > Burman, E. (2004). Discourse analysis means analysing discourse: some comments on Antaki, Billig, Edwards and Potter's 'Discourse analysis means doing analysis: a critique of six analytic shortcomings.' *Discourse Analysis Online,* 1. doi:10.1136/bmjopen-2012-602515.

- **For an Internet article** based on a website the style is:

  > Garson, D. (n.d.). *Narrative analysis.* Retrieved 20 August 2009, from North Carolina State University. Website: http://faculty.chass.ncsu.edu/garson/PA765/narrativ.htm.

There are other types of reference but the above cover most of the circumstances. See recommendations at the end of this chapter for sources of more information. Generally, the easiest thing is to get a reference list from a recent APA journal and follow this as an example.

Appendices

Appendices do not feature strongly in journal articles for the simple reason that space is at a premium. However, for student work, the situation is a little different and appendices can serve various useful functions. In the context of qualitative research the appendix may contain transcripts of interviews and detailed samples of, say, the coding process. This helps to establish the nature of the analysis which you carried out. Of course, for some studies, only an illustrative sample of transcripts and coding can be given – again because of space constraints.

CONCLUSION

It should be obvious by now that successful qualitative report writing is a highly demanding task in which a wide range of skills needs to be employed. Equally clearly, one's initial attempts at report writing can be hampered by this complexity and one's lack of skill and knowledge. By taking a systematic approach to report writing based on a standard writing-protocol such as presented in this chapter, some of the initial difficulties can be overcome. Remember, that as a student, by writing a research report you are presenting your achievements for assessment. This means that your report must communicate effectively, otherwise you will appear to be muddled in your thinking. As we have seen, although it is hard work, many of the basics are straightforward. Reference lists and citations may be mind-crunchingly boring to do but they are governed by simple rules. The sooner one adopts a systematic approach to them the sooner getting them right will be routine in your work.

Other aspects of a report can be seen as crucial to effective communication. The title and the abstract are vital to effective communication. The title is the first information that the reader has about the nature of your study. The more informative it is then the sooner that the reader begins to understand your report. So choose a title that communicates quickly and clearly some key aspects of your study. Similarly, the abstract lays out before the reader a readily absorbed roadmap through the main body of the report. The better that you do the abstract the easier the reader's task is in relation to the main body of the report. If a reader does not have a very clear understanding of your report having read the abstract, then all sorts of misconceptions may be built up and the general impression created of confusion on your part. A good abstract requires a systematic approach to what is covered, as we have seen.

The headings and sub-headings you use in your report provide the structure through which the reader absorbs the material. It is, therefore, important that you as the writer ensure that what appears under each heading and sub-heading is logical and in its proper place. One of the functions of headings and sub-headings is to tell the writer what sorts of things should be placed in those sections. Not being systematic about this can make your writing very difficult for the reader to absorb – which does not make a good impression.

KEY POINTS

- It is helpful if you adapt the quantitative report writing conventions when you write up qualitative research. This provides a structure which is generally familiar to all psychologists. However, it is difficult to separate the results section from the discussion section so they may be combined together as a 'Findings' section or 'Results and Discussion' session. As your skills develop, then it may be appropriate to modify this structure still further.

- Careful attention to every aspect of the report is essential for success. Although using citations correctly can seem like a chore, for example, failure to do so is easily spotted and may undermine what is an otherwise extremely well-presented report. It is in your interest to master these technicalities.

- Do not fail to include significant aspects of the detail of the method that you employed and your process of analysis. It is a common failing in qualitative write-ups not to explain how the analysis was performed in some detail. This is a fundamental error.

ADDITIONAL RESOURCES

American Psychological Association (APA). (2010). *The Publication Manual of the American Psychological Association* (6th ed.). Washington, DC: American Psychological Association.

American Psychological Association. (n.d.). Basics of APA Style Tutorial. flash1r.apa.org/apastyle/basics/index.htm?__utma=185732729. 1241987810.1333572867.1333572867.1333572867.1&__utmb=185732729.8.10.1333572867&__utmc=185732729&__utmx=- (accessed 25 April 2015).

APA Style Resources. (n.d.). www.psychwww.com/resource/apacrib.htm (accessed 25 April 2015).

Bibby, P. (n.d.). How to Write a Laboratory Report. School of Psychology University of Nottingham. www.psychology.nottingham.ac.uk/staff/dmr/c81mpr/HOW%20TO%20WRITE%20A%20LABORATORY%20REPORT.pdf (accessed 25 April 2015).

Centre for Writing Studies. (2008). Writer Workshop: Writer resources. University of Illinois at Urbana-Champaign. http://www.cws.illinois.edu/workshop/writers/citation/apa/ (accessed 25 April 2015).

Dr Paper Software. (n.d.). APA Style Basics. http://www.thewritedirection.net/apaguide.net/apaguide.pdf (accessed 25 April 2015).

University of Sussex. (n.d.). A Quick Guide to Writing a Psychology Lab-Report. www.sussex.ac.uk/Users/grahamh/RM1web/How%20to%20write%20a%20lab%20report.pdf (accessed 25 April 2015).

CHAPTER 16

Ensuring quality in qualitative research

Overview

- Generally accepted criteria for evaluating the quality of qualitative research studies are important for a number of reasons. Novice researchers need to be able to self-monitor their own work as part of their learning process. Professional researchers' research proposals have to be evaluated before their work can be commissioned and before their research papers can be published, for example.

- Appropriate quality criteria are dependent, to a degree, on whether a realist or a relativist position underlies the research. Realists believe that there is a reality which can be tapped by the researcher; relativists assume that there are many windows through which researchers try to view reality, though none captures it. The quality criteria for realists tend to be closest to those familiar from quantitative research.

- Nevertheless, there are some broad quality criteria which are shared by researchers of all types: for example, the originality of the research, the importance of the research question asked, and the extent to which the study is convincing.

- Newcomers to qualitative research ought to consider factors such as the investment of time and effort into data transcription and analysis, why the particular analytic approach that they are taking is relevant to their research, and the thoroughness of the fit of their analysis to the data. Qualitative research requires intense effort and intellectual rigour to achieve satisfactory quality.

- Reliability and validity are treated differently in qualitative research compared with quantitative research. In many instances they are meaningless when applied to qualitative research. Since it assumes a multiplicity of perspectives on the world, reliability is not seen as a crucial feature of much qualitative research. Similarly, validity is treated by qualitative researchers as built-in because of the preference for real-life-based data such as recordings of natural conversations. Respondent validation of the findings of qualitative research is another aspect of validity which rarely occurs in quantitative studies.

- Triangulation is a way of establishing the quality of a qualitative research – usually by employing two or more data-gathering methods. However, the way in which these different sets of data are synthesised or brought together in the analysis is crucial.

- The criteria for evaluating professional qualitative research are complex. One scheme for doing this is described in detail.

How should qualitative research be evaluated?

Researchers need to be able to evaluate their own work's quality while learning to be critically but constructively evaluative of the work of others. Just what is it that makes a qualitative study a good one? What are the best criteria to distinguish the best qualitative studies from the dross and lacklustre? These questions are of particular importance to novice researchers in any field of research in order to develop and improve their research skills. Just how will others judge one's work and by what criteria? As we will see, numerous criteria of quality are available, many of them particularly appropriate for qualitative research, but it is not quite so obvious where and when they should be applied. The difficulty is that some of these quality criteria are inappropriate for certain types of research. Where they should be applied can be controversial. It is important to bear quality criteria in mind when planning research – merely applying them to the 'finished product' will result in missed opportunities.

Of course, the appropriate criteria of excellence when evaluating the work of students writing up their earliest qualitative projects are the least demanding. The criteria should be and are more demanding for the work of professional researchers who have submitted their research findings for publication or who are seeking funding to pay for the research they wish to do. The quality criteria, for example, developed by governments and other bodies which commission and/or fund research are very stringent. They have to be since funding bodies need criteria which both differentiate between research proposals and allow their prioritisation for funding. Furthermore, quality criteria are needed in order, for example, to assess draft reports of completed research in order to guide and substantiate requests for revisions.

Since there are many different styles of qualitative research, quality criteria cannot be universal. Consequently, one needs to understand the epistemological foundations of each qualitative method before quality criteria can be applied appropriately. Newcomers to qualitative research quickly become aware that qualitative research involves a somewhat confusing array of different perspectives. Very little is universally accepted by all qualitative researchers. We saw in Chapters 1 and 2 and throughout this text how qualitative research emerged from a variety of historical, philosophical and empirical traditions. These can only be loosely labelled together as 'qualitative research' because of these disparities and, sometimes, a lack of compatibility. For example, discourse analysis and conversation analysis have relatively little in common with phenomenology, interpretative phenomenological analysis and narrative analysis. Much the same is true for quantitative research. As anyone who has studied psychological research methods knows, laboratory and field research fundamentally conflict. The methodological requirements which excite an experimentalist probably seem unrealistic and unhelpful to other quantitative researchers who prefer the challenges of research in real-life settings. Characteristically, quantitative researchers are accommodating to all forms of qualitative research despite their own particular predilections and preferences. It also seems to be the case that qualitative researchers are much more involved in epistemological issues than quantitative researchers, perhaps because their fields of research are not so well established as mainstream quantitative approaches. Generally healthy but occasionally acrimonious debates can be the outcome.

Inevitably, then, given all of this, evaluative criteria for qualitative research have been a matter of some disagreement and controversy. No general consensus exists on the appropriate criteria (Seale, 1999). Some qualitative researchers have accepted that concepts such as reliability and validity (as used routinely in quantitative studies) may have a place in qualitative research whereas others believe that somewhat distinct criteria should apply. Yet others have questioned the suitability of any quality criteria which have their origins in quantitative research for qualitative research. One worry is that the use of quantitative-based criteria may stifle the vigour of qualitative approaches. That is, only qualitative research acceptable from the quantitative perspective would be regarded as being of value. There are three opposing views about the evaluation of qualitative methods (Mays & Pope, 2000):

- *Extreme relativists* This group rejects all quality criteria for qualitative research on the grounds that the different qualitative methods are unique and present a valid perspective though it is different from that of other methods. Consequently, 'this position means that research cannot derive any unequivocal insights relevant to action' (p. 50).

- *Antirealist position* Adherents to this point of view suggest that qualitative research constitutes a distinctive research paradigm. Thus conventional criteria such as reliability, validity and generalisability simply do not apply. This point of view rejects the realist idea that there is a single social reality and substitutes the idea that there are multiple perspectives on the social world which are constructed as part of the activities of researchers. There are some appropriate criteria of quality in qualitative research (e.g. such as the credibility of the analysis to both readers of the research and the participants who took part in the research) but these are different from conventional approaches.

- *Subtle realist position* This accepts that the process of doing research imposes a subjectivity and that different qualitative methods will produce a different perspective on reality. Nevertheless, the subtle realists fundamentally accept that there is a basic reality that can be studied, albeit problematically. The subtle realist sees the purpose of research as an attempt to represent that reality (rather than precisely identify the truth). Thus, potentially, different sorts of research approaches can be examined comparatively. The subtle realist position allows quality criteria adopted from quantitative research to be used to assess the value of qualitative research.

The outcome of all of this is that qualitative researchers have to negotiate a variety of conflicting positions which put methodology 'in danger of getting a bad name' (Seale, 1999, p. 166)! Seale, who describes himself as a subtle realist, argues that the credibility of qualitative research, sometimes, appears to be a consequence of its adherence to an underlying philosophy:

Philosophy is often presented as underpinning the craft of social research, being an arena where various attempts at providing foundations for judging truth claims have come and gone, yet present day opinion seems nowadays, paradoxically, to conclude on antifoundationalism as itself being a philosophical foundation for social research. I think that it is time for social researchers to exploit this paradox, by breaking free from the obligation to fulfil philosophical schemes through research practice, while remaining aware of the value of philosophical and political reflexivity for their craft. (Seale, 1999, p. 466)

Antifoundationalists, to be clear, have a philosophical position which says that there are no particular principles which underlie all forms of valid investigation or inquiry. Seale's point is that antifoundationalism has itself become the basic principle of qualitative investigation! In that sense it is paradoxical – a bit like the suggestion 'The first rule is that there are no rules'. This is important since it questions the extent to which adherence to the philosophical foundations of a particular qualitative method is paramount in determining the value of the research. After all, quantitative researchers rarely bind themselves to the philosophical foundations of their methods. For example, those quantitative researchers whose work takes place exclusively in the psychology laboratory scarcely acknowledge the influence of the logical positivist school of the philosophy of science when evaluating their research and often shun some of the trappings of positivism in their work. Why should qualitative researchers be different from quantitative researchers in this respect? Nevertheless, the incompatibilities between qualitative methods due to their varying philosophical foundations cannot be ignored entirely – certainly at the present stage of their development.

One good example of this might not appear to be a philosophical problem at all at first glance – but it is. Should a researcher wish to use grounded theory (Chapter 8) procedures in their research then they may find the 'literature review' problematic. A grounded theorist adhering to the original Glaser and Strauss (1967) formulation of grounded theory may initially be intrigued by the argument that there should be no conventional literature review. The reason is that if the analysis is to be closely tied to the data then extraneous influences such as the conclusions of previous research may adversely affect this ideal. That is, an analysis is highly suggested by the previous research in the field. There were good reasons why grounded theory, after all, reversed many of the principles of conventional research in ways that not all qualitative methods do. But what if a researcher employs the methods of grounded theory but also has the temerity to carry out a literature review? Does that invalidate their work? Since numerous grounded theory analyses also involve a literature review then one can only suppose that researchers do not find this too problematic in practice.

Despite the disagreement about how different evaluative criteria for qualitative and quantitative research should be, nevertheless the issues of reliability, validity and replicability dominate in discussions of the topic – and that of generalisability. It seems to be accepted that although these may be useful, it is possible that other quality criteria may be more sensitive to the particular needs of qualitative researchers. That is to say, a qualitative study that is reliable, valid and replicable in conventional terms may fail to meet other important but largely unspoken criteria of quality in quantitative research.

Some quality criteria for quantitative research

Just what quality criteria are applied to quantitative research? Are they useful for assessing qualitative research? A brief list of some of the possibilities follows:

- Is the study original and innovative in any way?
- Does the study address research questions which are theoretically, practically or socially important?
- Does the study convincingly establish the claims that the researcher makes?

- Does the study contribute new perspectives on the issues being addressed?
- Does the study resolve important uncertainties that previously dominated the field?

In general, these criteria would seem to be equally applicable to qualitative and quantitative research. It is probably not surprising, then, to find that some researchers have attempted to identify universal quality criteria which apply irrespective of the type of research in question. For example, Denscombe (2002) includes the following criteria, which overlap considerably with the ones just mentioned:

- The contribution of new knowledge.
- The use of precise and valid data.
- The data are collected and used in a justifiable way.
- The production of findings from which generalisations can be made.

Commonsensical as these criteria appear, it is obvious that quality criteria such as these involve interpretation and judgement. For example, just what is the intended meaning of phrases such as 'new knowledge' and 'precise and valid data'? Is not every study a new contribution to knowledge even if that study merely replicates earlier ones? How 'precise and valid' do data have to be to make a study worthwhile and just how do we assess their degree of precision and validity? In the end, this shows that quality criteria are subject to interpretation. You might be wondering at this point just what relevance criteria such as these have to the work of students. Surely it is not the purpose of the research done by students to come up with earth-shatteringly new findings. Box 16.1 gives a brief account of some criteria which students might wish to apply to their own efforts.

Box 16.1

PRACTICAL ADVICE

Quality criteria for new researchers

This chapter contains a great many ideas about evaluating the quality of qualitative research. But most of these apply to the research rather than the researcher. Just what does the novice researcher need to do to ensure that their early attempts at qualitative research are as effective as possible? Many of the criteria to be found in this chapter are not routinely discussed in reports of qualitative research though they are commonly dealt with in general discussions of qualitative methodology. Such discussions often fail to meet the immediate needs of novice qualitative researchers since the basic requirements of qualitative research are not so well established as those for quantitative research where

significance testing, reliability and validity are familiar basic quality indicators.

The following are some ideas which those new to qualitative research might consider as helpful advice and which may help ensure the quality of their qualitative research:

- *What preparation have you done?* Immersing yourself in the qualitative research literature and undergoing specific training in qualitative research would be important steps. It is difficult to understand where you are going with a qualitative research project unless you have a good idea of all of the stages in such research.

- *Are there intellectually valid reasons for deciding to do a qualitative rather than a quantitative analysis?* Negative reasons such as a desire to avoid using statistics are not good enough to justify a qualitative approach. Sometimes what is presented as a qualitative analysis would have been much better had a quantitative approach been adopted.

- *What is the specific qualitative method that you are using and why is it appropriate for your research?* Qualitative research is not a single, generic approach to research but comprises a set of, often, interlinking methods each of which has its own rationale, characteristics and value. So why is it that you intend to carry out a discourse analysis rather than grounded theory?

- *What resources can you bring to your qualitative data collection and analysis?* Because of the nature of qualitative data collection and data analysis methods, considerable personal skills are needed on the part of the researcher. Qualitative research is *not* a matter of distributing questionnaires, tests or other measuring devices but requires skills such as good interviewing techniques, good person management and quickness of thought. In-depth interviewing is a skill, as is facilitating a focus group. The qualitative researcher needs to be in a position to devote considerable amounts of time to activities like transcribing their interviews as well as having some degree of knowledge about their chosen qualitative method. The point is that qualitative research demands both personal and time resources. If either of these is lacking, there will be a constraint on the quality of your qualitative research.

- *How thorough have you been in coding or categorising your data?* It is tempting to be selective in the extent to which you analyse your data. There

may be good reasons for being selective but just what is your justification for being so? If, say, you choose to categorise or code just a small part of your data, you risk failing to optimise the categories that you begin to formulate. It is difficult to know how effective your categories or codings are unless you apply them to all of the data (or a systematic selection). Unfortunately, since the reporting of the analysis process is rarely complete, the reader may assume wrongly that your analysis concentrated on the entire set of data when you chose merely part of the data.

- *Have you gone through a process of refining your codings or categories?* It is an important feature of qualitative research that the initial steps of the analysis process (the codings and categories) are refined by a process of checking and rechecking against the data, etc. The aim of this is to both improve the fit of the codings and categories to the data and to combine and redefine the codings and categories.

- *Which aspects of your data fit the codings or categories that you have developed?* To what extent do the codings or categories apply to participants in your research? Avoid using comments such as 'most participants', 'frequently' and 'rarely' as these fail to indicate with any precision the extent to which your analysis applies throughout your group of research participants. Just say precisely the number of participants that a particular aspect of your analysis applies to.

- *Was your qualitative analysis easy to carry out?* Qualitative analysis is not intended to be easy since a good researcher continually challenges what they have achieved at every stage of the analysis in the hope of producing something more superior. Quality in qualitative research does not come easily.

Evaluating quality in qualitative research

As discussed throughout this book, there is an important distinction between qualitative data collection methods (such as in-depth interviews, participant observation, focus groups and so forth) and qualitative data analysis methods (such as discourse analysis, grounded theory and conversation analysis). Recognising the distinction can remove some confusions which are relevant to the assessment of quality in qualitative research. Quite simply, there are researchers who choose to use qualitative data collection methods, perhaps because the research is exploratory or because the richness of the data is attractive to them, but nevertheless prefer to use quantitative methods in order to analyse the data. Of course, the criteria of quality will be different in these circumstances than if the researcher used the same qualitative data method to collect the data but a qualitative data analysis method in order to analyse the data. 'Rich' data in themselves do not determine the appropriateness of the data analysis method. In other words, judge the value of a qualitative study in relation to what the researcher is trying to achieve and do not simply use the same set of criteria unselectively in all circumstances.

General academic justification and features of the research

There is one school of thought which argues that the criteria for evaluating a qualitative research study are basically the same as those employed generally in academic work of all types. Thus they ought to be applicable to qualitative and quantitative research but, additionally, history, literature, chemistry and so forth. Essentially this view sees intellectual detachment and a questioning stance together with an organised and systematic approach to the issue in question as crucial to quality. This broadly seems to underlie the approach taken by Taylor (2001) to quality in qualitative research. Taylor's criteria are as follows:

- How well is the research located with regard to previous publications on the topic?
- To what extent is the argument employed coherent and intellectually persuasive (rational) as opposed to being based on emotion?
- To what extent does the report contain an analysis based on systematic interpretation of the data rather than leaving the data 'to speak for themselves'?
- How fruitful are the findings of the research?
- How relevant is the research to social issues/political events?
- How useful and applicable are the findings?

Let us look at these criteria a little more carefully.

How well is the research located in regard to previously published research on the topic?

Academic research is conventionally conceived as a cumulative process in which there is a gradual building of research findings, new concepts and new theories. For the individual researcher, this process is often seen as being based on a review of previous research in the research area in question. Not only does the literature review enable the researcher to understand what is known about a field of research but it also allows the researcher to identify aspects which are particularly in need of further consideration and ones which researchers have failed to address. But then the researcher formulates new research, collects new data, analyses that data and attempts to synthesise their analysis in terms of their own research findings and those of other studies. Much qualitative research adopts this model but not all. Some qualitative researchers, as we have seen, eschew the early literature review and begin with the data that they wish to analyse and then proceed to analyse it. They turn to the previous research only after this as a way of assessing the adequacy of their analysis against similar analyses of similar data. Of course, variability in qualitative research is generally regarded more positively than from the quantitative perspective where variability in research outcomes is put down to negative things such as problems in terms of research design and data collection methods. Variability in the qualitative tradition is not only to be expected but is also regarded as a more positive feature. In short, this is not a universal criterion in qualitative research.

To what extent is the argument employed coherent and intellectually persuasive (rational) as opposed to being based on emotion?

Research reports do not simply report research findings. Good research reports involve a well-thought-out and clear argument which leads to a conclusion which follows from the data and the argument. Academic argumentation is a rational and usually cool process dominated by clarity of thought. Academic argument tends to shun arguments which are expressed in terms of emotion rather than rationality. Furthermore, rhetorical argumentation is also avoided. This is not to say that academic writing has to be dispassionate or uninvolved with the topic of the research – but the way in which these are articulated in the research report is important. Much good psychological writing builds from the commitment of the researcher to the outcome of the research. Nevertheless, restraint and balance are the major and overriding expectations of academic arguments. Clearly the data obtained, together with the tightness of the logic of the argument, are crucial in appropriate styles of argumentation. It is important in the academic method that the writer is not seen as merely expressing unfounded personal opinions but is making a case which carries conviction. Thus this criterion could be applied to all qualitative research.

To what extent does the report contain an analysis based on systematic interpretation of the data rather than leaving the data 'to speak for themselves'?

Qualitative data analysis almost invariably involves a great deal of analytic effort if the expectations of researchers are to be fulfilled. There is nothing implicitly in data which equates to analysis. The analysis of data is a complex matter which partly involves the data but goes beyond the data into methodological and theoretical issues. In short, a good qualitative research report includes a significant analysis of the data. The implications of this are difficult to understand in the abstract. Just what does a research report look like if it does not include a significant data analysis? Such a report can happen, for example, when the researcher has in-depth data in the form of interviews but simply selects just a few quotations and strings these together with a linking commentary. This does not amount to a qualitative data analysis. It is the sort of thing that a competent journalist might do but it is not what qualitative research is about. It does not matter how interesting the quotes may be, in themselves they do not provide analysis of the data as a whole. Data analysis is about the synthesis of the material into something representative of but nevertheless different and more abstract than the original data. The analysis gives coherence to the data. It is erroneous to think that data speak for themselves. Stringing large amounts of textual data together may be entertaining but it does nothing to accumulate understanding. After all, novels are entertaining but we do not consider them a qualitative analysis. In qualitative research, researchers develop coding categories which derive from the data and provide, ideally, a close fit with the data in its entirety. In this way the analysis is created or synthesised from the data but it is different from the data itself. The nature of the analysis is partly dependent on the type of qualitative analysis method employed. Data quotations cannot substitute for analysis but they can illustrate and give life to the analysis. So, clearly, an analysis of the data must be regarded as a universal quality criterion for quality research.

How fruitful are the findings of the research?

Fruitful research is productive in terms of new and vigorous ideas, concepts, theories, problems, issues and so forth. It is probably easier to recognise mundane research which is not fruitful than it is to specify just what is fruitful in the best research. Mundane research leaves the reader feeling no wiser and lacking intellectual stimulation because of the lack of new ideas – there is nothing intellectually invigorating to reward the reader. Of course, the fruitfulness of research may be a longer-term matter. For example, crucial studies are those which have a long-term impact by generating and stimulating new investigations and innovative research pathways. The classic studies in any field of research are those that achieve precisely this – this might lead us to the conclusion that fruitfulness is a universal criterion of quality in qualitative research.

How relevant is the research to social issues/political events?

Some qualitative researchers in psychology indicate that they have interests in political and social issues. This is especially the case with those who designate themselves critical psychologists or critical social psychologists. The idea that research should be socially relevant is long established. *The Society for the Psychological Study of Social Issues* was founded in 1936 to help provide 'social and behavioral scientists opportunities to apply their knowledge and insights to the critical problems of today's world' (RadPsyNet, 2009). This society had its origins in psychologists' desire to use their discipline to help solve the social and economic problems of the Great Depression. Interestingly, it was not until 1951 that the similar organisation primarily for sociologists, *The Society for the Study of Social Problems*, was established. Quantitative psychology has contributed a thread of socially relevant research through much of its history which means that social relevance is not a criterion exclusive to qualitative research. It then is notable that some leading qualitative researchers such as Parker (1989) have deplored what they see as the failure of much qualitative research to effectively handle and incorporate social and political concepts – especially the concept of power. On the other hand, there are branches of psychology which are primarily qualitatively orientated to which this criticism cannot be applied. Feminist psychology is primarily qualitative but is built on social and political concepts. Of course, there is also a big difference between research which is based on realistic data (as most qualitative research is) and research with a social and political agenda. Thus, social and political relevance is not a universal criterion of quality in qualitative research and so should be used with caution.

How useful and applicable are the findings?

A purely academic approach to research would stress that the primary function of research is to provide knowledge and understanding of the world. Although some would dismiss this as a sort of 'ivory tower' approach, very little research is designed because of its potential applicability in the short term. For many psychologists, then, understanding the subject matter is the primary objective of research and its application perhaps a bonus rather than a requirement. Historically, in psychology, applied research tended to be dismissed as being of less importance and lacked the esteem granted more purely academic approaches. It was seen as mundane and pedestrian compared with more theory-driven research. But the applied–theoretical dichotomy is a false one and there are excellent examples of applied research which are theoretically fruitful. For example, consider the early research of Harvey Sacks which eventually gave rise to con-versation analysis (see Chapter 10). In this he studied how telephone calls to emergency services can 'go wrong', resulting in vital information not being obtained or the call abruptly terminated. Of course, clinical psychology, educational psychology, forensic psychology and organisational psychology, for example, from mainstream psychology are all fields where the useful and applicable can go hand-in-hand with the highest academic and theoretical standards. In short, usefulness and applicability constitute a criterion of quality which does not apply to all qualitative research nor to qualitative research exclusively.

Overall, it cannot be claimed that Taylor's criteria apply solely to qualitative research since they closely echo criteria which have proven useful in evaluating quantitative research. Furthermore, Taylor's criteria do not amount to a quality-control checklist which can be readily applied to all qualitative research. They do help us clarify which criteria are appropriate to different research methods. In this sense, they provide a starting point for evaluating qualitative research.

Generalisability in qualitative research

The concept of generalisability is well built into quantitative research in a number of different ways. Do the findings of one study generalise to a different sample, a somewhat dissimilar setting, or a different period of history, for example? While the quantitative researcher has always tended to seek the generalisable in the quest to find the universal, not so the qualitative researcher necessarily. It has to be said that qualitative researchers differ in the extent to which they see generalisability as important – some see it as incompatible or inappropriate given the fundamental principles on which qualitative research is based. If there are numerous ways of seeing the world then what does it matter if there are additional ones? Other qualitative researchers may be more inclined towards the idea that their research findings generalise in some way. Yet other qualitative researchers tend to be much more interested in the specific situation of their research so why be concerned whether their research in that given situation generalises? Inevitably, the different types of qualitative research make a single, definitive approach to generalisation seem unlikely. However, discourse analysis and conversation analysis, especially, do seem to develop insights which are applied to more than the research in which they were first developed. This is a form of generalisation. However, crucially, the inapplicability of these insights in another context for whatever reason is rarely seen as a reason to reject the concepts. In truth, quantitative researchers actually live quite comfortably with the inconsistencies of their research findings and do not readily abandon ideas – but this is the practicality not the definitive quantitative methodology. But our primary concern here is qualitative research.

Goodman (2008) provides a very useful discussion of generalisability in relation to discourse analysis. His point is that it is possible to identify findings from discourse analysis studies which appear to more than reflect the findings of other discourse analysis studies. In other words, findings can be identified as generalisable, in his formulation, if it can be shown that a given discursive strategy can bring about much the same 'interactional result' in different settings. In this sense, a particular discursive strategy identified in one study generalises to other studies because what the strategy accomplishes is the same. One such finding is the discursive device of using existing prejudice to justify other prejudices. A good example of this is the way in which people express prejudice against gay and lesbian parents on the basis that they are held responsible for the bullying that their children may experience. Gays and lesbians should not have children because the children will suffer. Goodman gives one example taken from Clarke (2001, pp. 565–6), based on what a specialist in childcare has claimed, to illustrate his point.

> I really have quite strong feelings about the inappropriateness of lesbian and homosexual partners adopting children . . . If you think of a child in school, we know that other children can be cruel and may say to another child, 'There's something different about you, you've got two mummies,' or 'You've got two daddies' . . .

I think we're adding to the complexity of children's situations, and that really concerns me.

The following excerpt taken from Verkuyten (2005) shows the use of prejudice to justify prejudice again:

1. Interviewer: Do foreigners ever get discriminated against, do you think?
2. David: Sure, 'course they do.
3. Interviewer: Well, and why is that?
4. David: Er, well in the way I also get discriminated against, I think discrimination against
5. foreigners is, er, just as normal as me getting discriminated against,
6. 'cos if they tell me I can't have a job, where a woman is being
7. taken on first, I think that's madness, so if I'm being discriminated against, why
8. shouldn't a foreigner get discriminated against? 'Cos let's be honest,
9. foreigners do it far more than we do. 'Cos Turks and Kurds,
10. er, yeah, and Turks and Moroccans. I think them Blacks discriminate against each other
11. even more, yeah, and Antilleans and Surinamese, too. So I think it's way over the
12. top, that they are allowed to discriminate against each other and that if we do it
13. we get, er, punished right away or something like that. I think it's all being blown out of
14. proportion, seeing that the Dutch in general, or Whites, discriminate less bad
15. than the whole lot of 'em do among themselves.

Goodman's point seems well illustrated by his examples. But he goes further and suggests that discursive strategies can be said to be generalisable if:

- a discursive strategy is shown in research to result in a particular rhetorical outcome;
- it can be shown that this particular discursive strategy is used in a much wider variety of conversational settings in order to achieve the same rhetorical outcome or accomplishment;
- if there is evidence that the rhetorical strategy is successful in regularly bringing about a particular rhetorical outcome;
- if a range of speakers use this successful rhetorical strategy in a variety of contexts to achieve the same rhetorical outcome;
- the researcher may begin to recognise how the rhetorical strategy is successfully opposed within the discourse.

Validity in qualitative research

The concept of validity in traditional quantitative research is usually defined in terms such as 'validity is the extent that something measures what it is intended to measure'. This is its usage in relation to traditional psychometric measures such as personality tests, intelligence measures and so forth. Typically this is referred to as construct validity. Quite simply, the issue is to establish how well or the extent to which a psychological measure assesses a theoretical concept (construct) which it is supposed to measure. There are, of course, other forms of validity that quantitative researchers refer to. For example, does the research method validly reflect 'real life'? This is a common issue in relation to the question of the value of traditional laboratory experiments which many have regarded as too artificial to have much, if any, bearing on 'real-life' processes. The term 'ecological validity' has been put forward for this. This refers to the extent to which a study captures 'reality' or 'real life'. There is no statistical way of deciding whether a study is ecologically valid, it is a matter of judgement. Quite clearly many laboratory experiments are so divorced from reality that they lack ecological validity. This tends to overlook the experiments which take place in naturalistic settings. There is a further concept of validity – external validity. This is sometimes confused with ecological validity but is different in that external validity is the extent to which research findings from one research setting can be generalised to other settings.

Just what is the relevance of these traditional types of validity to qualitative research? Ecological validity tends to be assumed tacitly by some qualitative researchers but this really depends on the data collection method involved. Much qualitative research centres on naturally occurring text such as conversations. So, for example, an analysis of emergency telephone conversations, such as that by Sacks (1992), would seem to have built-in ecological validity as it is dealing with an everyday real-world happening. These conversations were routinely recorded by the emergency services for their own purposes – but they constitute data which are appropriate for the purposes of qualitative researchers. Equally, it would be reasonable to assume that a study of news broadcasts based on videos of actual newscasts would also be ecologically valid. But one should not assume the same degree of ecological validity for all qualitative data collection methods. For example, the in-depth psychological research interview may be just as beset with problems of ecological validity as other forms of research. The research interview is not normal everyday real-life conversation by any stretch of the imagination. For example, it is governed by very different rules from everyday conversation (e.g. the interviewee does not have an equal reciprocal right to question the interviewer). Ecological validity can also be a problem in terms of data collected from focus groups or through participant observation when the researcher's true identity is known.

Of course, the conventional concept of validity employed in quantitative research is not without its problems especially when applied to qualitative research. A typical definition of validity is 'the extent to which something measures what it purports to measure', the implication being that there is something out there in the real world which is fixed in its nature and which the researcher is attempting to tap into. So the validity of a measure of intelligence is the extent to which it can be shown to relate to something identifiable as intelligence. The last few sentences, of course, would be alien to many qualitative researchers, particularly those who do not hold to a realist position.

Validity is discussed by qualitative researchers in a number of ways different from its use by quantitative researchers. For example:

- In qualitative research, the issue of validity is usually interpreted as the extent to which the analysis fits the data (usually text). So it is the *validity of the analysis* which is the focus not the objective validity of some scale or measure used. A valid analysis fits the data well.

- There is a tendency to assume that qualitative research is intrinsically more valid than quantitative research. More generally, since the qualitative method is seen as a superior way of obtaining understanding of the social and psychological world, its validity is not really in question. Even if this were to be true of qualitative research in general, it needs to be established for each qualitative study.

- The fidelity of the transcription (e.g. of a conversation) to the original source can be regarded as an indication of the validity of the transcription. Qualitative researchers using transcripts should make stringent efforts to ensure this sort of validity is maximised by checking the transcript against the recording and referring back to the recording whenever appropriate.

The phrase 'justification of analytic claims' is used by Potter (1998) rather than the term validity. This is a useful way of looking at validity in qualitative research since it pinpoints a significant conceptualisation used by qualitative researchers. There is an entire repertoire of ways in which quality in qualitative research can be assessed, according to Potter. Although a little dependent on the type of qualitative research in question, the focus for validity in qualitative research tends to be on the analysis and not the data. Nevertheless, you will find some qualitative researchers who are as concerned with matters such as the validity of the sampling method as much as any quantitative researcher.

Validity in qualitative studies, according to Mays and Pope (2000), involves the following criteria though, as we shall see, other researchers have suggested additional ones:

- *Triangulation* This approach is based on the notion that different methods of data collection should yield comparable results if they are to be considered 'valid'. In qualitative research, triangulation would involve several different sources of data possibly gathered from members of different interest groups, for example. There should be convergence in the results arising from different data sources. A fundamental, but essential, assumption of this is that weaknesses in one source of information should be compensated by the other sources of information. For instance, the researcher might wish to compare interviews with therapists, their clients and partners of the clients. If much the same results emerge from the analysis of each of the three groups, then some would regard this as evidence of validity. Mays and Pope (2000), however, suggest that triangulation is best seen as an approach to making sure that the data collection and analysis is comprehensive – and productive of a greater degree of thought and contemplation about the analysis. (See also Box 16.2 for an extended discussion of triangulation.)

Box 16.2
KEY CONCEPT
Triangulation

Triangulation can be used, for example, when trying to identify the location of an illegal radio station. There are scientific instruments which can indicate the direction from which the radio station is broadcasting by using very directional aerials. However, the radio station could lie anywhere in that direction – it could be 10 kilometres or a thousand kilometres away. By setting up the detection apparatus in a different location, a new direction for the radio station can be found. The two direction lines can be plotted on a map and the intersection of the two found. This intersection precisely pinpoints where the radio station is broadcasting from. Unless the transmitter is moving, the authorities know precisely where to go to close the illegal transmitter down.

The concept of triangulation is used in both qualitative and quantitative research but not in precisely the same way. Essentially in quantitative research triangulation refers to measuring a variable using more than

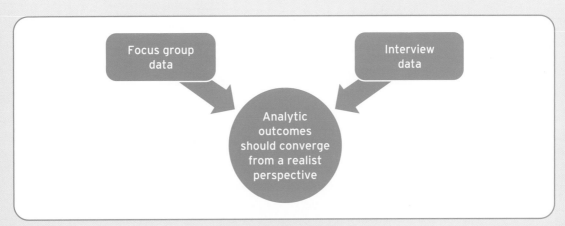

FIGURE 16.1 Triangulation by method

one method, such as using teacher ratings of pupils *and* paper-and-pencil tests to measure intelligence, the assumption being that the two distinct measures of intelligence should correlate if the measures have some validity. This is extended in Campbell and Fiske's (1959) multitrait–multimethod matrix approach to include the measurement of more than one concept. For example, the researcher might research creativity and intelligence using several different measures of intelligence and several different measures of creativity. The measures of intelligence ought to correlate together better than they do with the measures of creativity and vice versa. In this way, the value of the measures can be assessed and also the extent to which the concepts being measured are truly different.

None of this translates precisely to qualitative research where the use of triangulation raises a number of important issues because of the varying epistemological assumptions underlying different sorts of qualitative study. As a simple example, take the researcher who is interested in how employees talk about the ethos of their workplace. One could do this by interviewing a sample of employees of all grades combined. But would it not be better to also carry out focus groups with groups of employees from different grades? Few would dispute this, but when it comes to analysing this 'triangulated' data just what are the researcher's assumptions? One could adopt the realist assumption and compare the outcomes of the interview study with the outcome of the focus group study in the expectation that they will reveal much the same analytic outcomes as shown in Figure 16.1.

But is that what we should expect? Would we expect that a focus group involving employees of different grades would be unaffected by the diversity of job statuses in the group? Would you really say certain things

in front of the boss, for example? You might be happy to say things to a researcher in the anonymous context of an interview that you would not if your boss were present. In other words, the context of data collection can make a big difference to the data and, consequently, to the analysis. This would be expected from any contextualist position such as the anti-realists and the extreme relativists discussed earlier (pp. 36–7). This is illustrated in Figure 16.2. The two sources of data are unlikely to totally converge and they are unlikely to be entirely divergent. It is obvious that these are the extreme possibilities and that in particular cases some position between the extremes of complete convergence and complete divergence will be found.

A distinction must be made between:

- the use of mixed methods; and
- triangulation.

Triangulation does, of necessity, involve mixed methods but the use of mixed methods does not necessarily imply the use of triangulation. Mixed methods refers to the use of more than one research method in a study. Moran-Ellis et al. (2006a) stipulate that these different research methods should be based on different meta-theoretical perspectives. They suggest that this can be a mixture of quantitative and qualitative components or a mixture of very different sorts of qualitative data such as positivistic, interpretative, phenomenological and visual. The use of mixed methods tends to be associated with certain areas of qualitative research especially health and education where the practical policy implications of research are, perhaps, the most evident and where strengthening the research findings by the use of mixed methods has the most obvious advantages. It is less common for theoretical or academically orientated qualitative studies to employ mixed methods – the

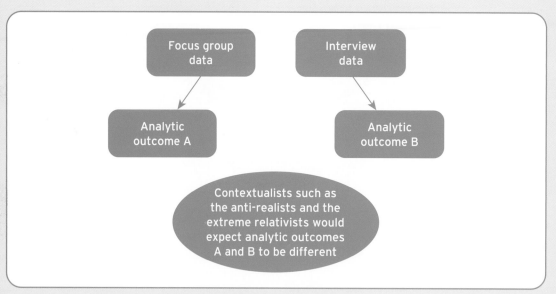

FIGURE 16.2 Triangulated focus group and interview data

point is that the different methods can be employed to research very different things and that the comparison between methods required in triangulation is not part of the research:

> Triangulation is an epistemological claim concerning what more can be known about a phenomenon when the findings from data generated by two or more methods are brought together. (Moran-Ellis et al., 2006a, p. 47)

In other words, triangulation is conceived as a way of increasing our understanding over and above what the methods achieve in isolation.

What has been claimed in this respect?

- **Increased validity model of triangulation** Quantitative researchers, especially, have claimed that the use of two measurement methods enable the researcher to know if something has been accurately measured (Campbell & Fiske, 1959). If two measures do not correlate with each other, then one or both of the measuring instruments is inadequate. Nevertheless, even if they both correlate with each other, then one should not forget the possibility that the two measures share the same flaw – for example, what appears to be a correlation between two different measures of intelligence is actually a consequence of a response set shared by the two measures.

- **Different perspectives – complementarity** This perspective on triangulation takes the view that the use of multiple methods provides the researcher with

multiple perspectives on the phenomenon being studied which is in line with the idea that the phenomenon itself is multi-faceted. While this meaning of triangulation diverges widely from the origins of the concept, it effectively takes a demonstrably qualitative stance on the use of multiple methods.

Just how are the different methods employed in a study combined in the analysis? Triangulation is not always the intention of researchers using multiple methods. Sometimes mixed methods are used in a study for quite different purposes:

- One method can be used to inform the second method – for example, if the researcher carries out a focus group study as a way of generating ideas for a later questionnaire study. In this, one method is seen as subservient to another.

- Mixed methods can be used to increase the depth of the data collected on the phenomenon in question. For example, the researcher may find it helpful to study media reports dealing with a particular issue in conjunction with an interview study – for example, in a study of how the public views immigrants.

- Sometimes a researcher may use mixed methods in a study to economise on data collection. So, for example, it may be that the researcher obtains a variety of different types of information from a single sample of participants but the different aspects of the data are reported entirely separately.

So what should happen when a researcher seeks to integrate different methods of data collection within the same analysis? According to Moran-Ellis et al., the researcher needs to generate a 'tangible relationship' accounting for the different methods, the different data, and the different perspectives involved. Thus merely highlighting differences is not integration. Analytic statements need to be developed which show how the different methods of data collection relate to each other if integration is to be achieved. For example, how do the data from in-depth interviews with managers relate to the data obtained by participant observation?

If the researcher genuinely wishes to integrate mixed qualitative methods then models of how to do this are scarce. One method is called 'following a thread' by Moran-Ellis, Alexander, Cronin, Fielding and Thomas (2006b). This entails the analysis of each different data set separately. Then each of the different data sets is subject to a relevant analysis to identify key themes and analytic questions for subsequent analysis. So an analytic theme is followed from the initial data set through to the other data sets. Thus while the thread is developed inductively in the primary data set it is explored in a more focused manner in the other data sets. Of course, the analysis will start several times in each of the data sets.

- *Respondent validation or member checking* This is simply a check on the extent to which the researcher's account corresponds to those of participants in the research (or new individuals comparable to the participants). The assumption is that if the participants in the research can accept the researcher's analysis then this constitutes evidence of its validity. The difficulty, of course, lies in the assumption that a researcher's perspective should be shared by the participants. So one question is, under what circumstances should such a correspondence be expected? If we remember that substantial parts of qualitative research in psychology owe at least something to ethnomethodology, such a congruence might be regarded as an important criterion. Ethnomethodology seeks to understand the meanings of the social world as seen by ordinary members of that world. An approach which is common in qualitative research of various sorts is to have meetings with research participants in which the researcher presents their research findings. The intention is to promote discussion about the researcher's findings and to allow participants to question the researcher's analysis. Of course, quantitative researchers might regard such 'insider' research as being potentially biased or partisan since it suggests that the researcher is not truly independent but, instead, acts as a conduit for different interest groups.

- *Clear description/explication of the methods of data collection and analysis involved* The procedure for data collection and the processes of data analysis should be crystal clear in a good qualitative report. Information about the way in which the data were collected can have an important bearing on the interpretation of the data. The information can also help address more mundane issues such as the representativeness of the analysis beyond the particular data in question just as it can in quantitative research. Generally speaking, the analytic processes involved in qualitative research are time consuming as well as being meticulous and demanding. This is the only way of producing an analysis which has good fidelity to the data. There is no point in conducting a high-quality study without demonstrating this quality to the reader.

- *Reflexivity* This is a big issue in qualitative research. Essentially it refers to the sensitivity or awareness of the researcher to how they may influence the nature of the data collected and the analysis. For example, the prior assumptions and the biases of the researcher may have an unshakeable impact. Consequently, the expectation is that the researcher should explicate their own experiences, attitudes, values and other potentially 'biasing' factors which may have an impact on the analysis or are pertinent for other reasons. For example, the psychological and social distance between the researcher and the participants can be a crucial aspect of methodology. Qualitative researchers tend to be closer to their participants than quantitative researchers. These relationships are openly discussed in much qualitative research.

- *Attention to negative or deviant instances* The role of negative or deviant cases is very different in qualitative research. In quantitative research, the search for trends in the data includes even the smallest correlation, association or difference – so long as it meets the test of being 'statistically significant'. Perfect relationships are rare in quantitative research. The implication of this is that deviant cases are typical in quantitative data. The smaller the association found in the quantitative study the greater the impact of these deviants, however. This notwithstanding, it would be virtually unknown in quantitative research to give such deviant cases much attention. Instead they are largely ignored because they are conceived as the result of 'randomness' or 'noise', i.e. measurement error. It is almost as if deviant cases are irrelevant. On the other hand, in much qualitative research the deviant case is regarded as an essential part of the analysis. The detail involved in qualitative research often makes it evident that a particular individual or a particular aspect of the data is deviant in the sense that it is incompatible with the overall analysis as it is understood at that time. The researcher is obliged to seek to incorporate deviant cases into the analysis. Deviant cases are not 'swept under the carpet' in qualitative research.

Further criteria are mentioned by Taylor (2001) and Potter (1998). The first two are from Taylor and the final three from Potter:

- *Richness of detail in the data and analysis* The whole point of qualitative analysis is to develop descriptive categories which fit the data well. So, one criterion of the quality of a study is the amount of detail in the treatment of the data and its analysis. Qualitative analysis requires intense processing of the data. Consequently, if the researcher just presents a few broad categories and a few broad indications of what sorts of material fit that category, then this would not appear to be a good quality study. Of course, richness of detail is not readily tallied so it begs the question of how much detail constitutes richness. Should richness of detail be assessed in terms of numbers of words, the range of different sources of text, the verbal complexity of the data, how what? Similar questions apply when it comes to the issue of the richness of detail in the analysis. Just what does this mean? Is this a matter of the complexity of the analysis and why should a complex analysis be regarded as a virtue in its own right? In quantitative research, in contrast, the simplicity of the analysis is regarded as a virtue if it accounts for the detail of the data well. It is the easiest thing in the world to produce coding categories which fit the data well – if one has numerous coding categories then all the data are likely to be fitted into the analysis. Nevertheless, the fact that each of these categories fits only a very small part of the data may imply that the coding scheme is inadequate.

- *Using quantitative techniques where appropriate* Opinions vary greatly on this but some qualitative researchers are willing, in some circumstances, to incorporate quantitative techniques into their, otherwise, qualitative study. For example, qualitative data collected using systematic sampling techniques may be acceptable to some qualitative researchers despite the fact that some very different approaches to sampling have been proposed for qualitative research.

- *Openness to evaluation* In quantitative research reports, the reader is often very distanced from the data. All that is provided, typically, are some summary statistics such as tables, charts, descriptive statistics such as means, and brief indications of the outcomes of inferential statistical analysis such as *t*-tests. In most quantitative reports, the data are not presented for independent examination. In contrast, in qualitative research reports substantial or key textual data are presented to support the analytic interpretation. As a consequence, it could be argued that a qualitative research analysis is more open to evaluation, challenge and questioning by the reader than other forms of research. In fairness, many qualitative reports include a minimal amount of the data used in the study – just a few examples which illustrate the point being made. This is rarely sufficient to question the analysis. Of course, where textual data are provided in full in the form of transcripts the openness of the analysis to challenge is beyond doubt. Potter (1998) points out that a great deal of what the researcher claims has to be taken on trust in qualitative research. This could be remedied by making data files more available, e.g. over the Internet. Of course, there is another issue. Just how can the reader of a qualitative research report who disputes a particular analysis truly challenge the analysis? What does it mean to challenge an analysis? Some online qualitative research journals solve this problem by allowing debate to follow the publication of an article.

- *Coherence with previous studies* Notoriously, in quantitative research, very similar studies can produce very different or, even, inconsistent outcomes. Nevertheless, the coherence of a qualitative study with previous studies has been offered as a criterion of how convincing a study is. Qualitative analyses which are at variance with previous research are more likely to be questioned. This can be regarded as a replicability issue since not only may the coherence of the new study with earlier studies strengthen the new study but, similarly, it may add strength to the older analyses (just as it would for quantitative studies). There are problems with this criterion. For example, if the new qualitative study uses analytic ideas from older studies then, almost inevitably, the analyses will appear to cohere.

- *Participant's own understandings within the data* A rather different aspect of the 'validity' of a qualitative analysis is inherent in the tendency for speakers to interpret what previous speakers have said, for example. In this way, the new speaker's understanding of what went before is incorporated into the data. For example, if the new speaker quickly changes the subject of the conversation then this may give indications of their understanding of what went before. It might be indicative of the belief that the previous speaker has made some sort of *faux pas* which may need to be hidden. In other words, the data have self-checking features for the careful analyst which confirm or disconfirm the analyst's earlier analysis. Box 16.3 describes an advanced scheme for the quality evaluation of, specifically, qualitative research.

Reliability in qualitative research

Reliability and validity have emerged as basic quality control issues in quantitative research. This chapter has discussed the various ways in which validity has been raised in relation to qualitative research. What about reliability in qualitative research? This is much less frequently discussed by qualitative researchers than the concept of validity. There are a number of reasons for this – most importantly is that various qualitative methods have different epistemological positions relevant to the issue of reliability.

Box 16.3

PRACTICAL ADVICE

An advanced quality evaluation scheme for qualitative research

Governments spend large amounts of money on all sorts of social research. Increasingly this involves qualitative research from many different spheres of research – health, welfare, probation and so forth. Inevitably, the question arises of how this research can be systematically evaluated. Clearly consistency in the criteria and the way in which they are applied is important for public organisations if not researchers. Given the lack of agreed standards for quality in qualitative social research, Spencer, Ritchie, Lewis and Dillon (2003) were invited to formulate criteria relevant to the research commissioned by the government. They engaged in a process in which they:

- reviewed the available criteria in the published literature; and
- interviewed key individuals involved in conducting and managing research.

It was important to Spencer et al. that the quality criteria that they developed were appropriate to qualitative research and were not ones which could be applied to research in general. They identified various areas of focus in the quality appraisal (Figure 16.3). For each aspect of the qualitative study under consideration, Spencer et al. provide a minimum of one 'appraisal question' but sometimes as many as five. The appraisal questions are essentially evaluative criteria. A number of quality indicators were suggested for each of these though the scheme allowed for additional criteria to be introduced in specific instances.

The following gives a good indication of the substantial nature of the appraisal questions for each aspect of the research together with illustrative examples of possible quality indicators. The complete assessment document can be downloaded – see Additional Resources at the end of this chapter. It is important to note that their quality criteria conflict with the viewpoints of some qualitative researchers in some instances. Spencer et al.'s evaluation questions are given and illustrative quality indicators for each of these then provided.

FIGURE 16.3 Quality assessment areas for evaluation

(a) Design

Appraisal question 1 'How defensible is the research design?'

Illustrative quality indicators:

1a) How well does the report discuss the relationship between the overall research strategy and the aims of the study?

1b) How effectively does the report discuss the limitations of the research design especially in terms of the value of the evidence used in the study?

(b) Sample

Appraisal question 2 'How well defended is the sample design/target selection of cases/documents?'

Illustrative quality indicators:

2a) Does the study describe carefully the population involved and demonstrate how the sample selected is related to the population? For example, is the sample typical of the population or does it represent diversity in the population?

2b) Does the study explain the rationale for the selection of the sample or the research settings or the documents involved in the analysis?

Appraisal question 3 'Sample composition/case inclusion – how well is the eventual coverage described?'

Illustrative quality indicators:

3a) Does the study provide the reasons why some of those approached to take part in the study did not participate and what sort of cases were not included as a consequence of the procedures adopted? (For example, would people without transport be unable to participate in the study?)

3b) Does the report explain how the sample members could be accessed and the methods by which they were approached? These may affect participation in the research.

(c) Data collection

Appraisal question 4 'How well was the data collection carried out?'

Illustrative quality indicators:

4a) Does the report describe who collected the data, the procedures and materials used to collect data, and supply information about the origins and authorship of documents used?

4b) Does the report describe crucial features of fieldwork such as the conventions used when taking field notes and discuss how the circumstances and methods of fieldwork might have an influence on the data collected?

(d) Ethics

Appraisal question 5 'What evidence is there of attention to ethical issues?'

Illustrative quality indicators:

5a) Does the report describe ethical considerations procedures, the information given participants, the confidentiality and anonymity arrangements for data and the participants' identities, the nature of the information about services available following the study, and the consent procedures?

5b) Does the study contain a discussion of the possible adverse consequences of taking part in the study and how these were avoided?

(e) Analysis

Appraisal question 6 'How well has the approach to, and formulation of, the analysis been conveyed?'

Illustrative quality indicators:

6a) Does the report clearly indicate how analytic categories, etc. have been created and deployed?

6b) Is the form of the raw data described (e.g. transcripts, interview notes, documents)?

Appraisal question 7 'How well has diversity of perspective and content been explored?'

Illustrative quality indicators:

7a) Does the report discuss the relevance of negative cases or unusual cases?

7b) Does the report systematically try to categorise or explain the variation found within the data?

Appraisal question 8 'How well have detail, depth and complexity (i.e. richness) of the data been conveyed?'

Illustrative quality indicators:

8a) Has the report used quotations or observations from the data which contribute to the understanding of the data?

8b) Does the report identify and discuss patterns, linkages and associations in the data?

Appraisal question 9 'Contexts of data sources – how well are they retained and portrayed?'

Illustrative quality indicators:

9a) Does the research describe in detail relevant details of the setting of the study such as the history, background and characteristics of the research setting?

9b) Are the data managed in a way which retains contextual material which is relevant to individual cases?

(f) Findings

Appraisal question 10 'How credible are the findings?'

Illustrative quality indicators:

10a) Do the findings 'make sense' and exhibit a 'coherent logic'?

10b) Do the findings cohere with what is known from other sources?

Appraisal question 11 'How has knowledge/ understanding been extended by the research?'

Illustrative quality indicators:

11a) Does the report clearly and credibly discuss what contribution to knowledge and understanding is made by the research?

11b) Are the aims and design of the study contextualised by what is currently known and understood?

Appraisal question 12 'How well does the evaluation address its original aims and purposes?'

Illustrative quality indicators:

12a) Are there clear relationships between the purposes of the study and the findings as set out?

12b) Does the report explain and discuss the nature of the limitations of the study in terms of the study's aims?

Appraisal question 13 'Scope for drawing wider inference – how well is this explained?'

Illustrative quality indicators:

13a) Does the report include a discussion of the extent to which the findings of the study can be generalised more widely than the sample selected for research?

13b) Does the report contain detailed description of the study's context so that the applicability of the findings to other settings may be assessed?

Appraisal question 14 'How clear is the basis of evaluative appraisal?' (This would apply primarily to qualitative research which is designed to evaluate a social, policy, or institutional initiative.)

Illustrative quality indicators:

14a) Does the report indicate the nature of the source of any evaluative judgements included, such as whose judgement was involved and how the judgement has been reached?

14b) Does the report discuss the unintended consequences of the intervention and what caused them?

(g) Reporting

Appraisal question 15 'How clear are the links between data, interpretation and conclusions, i.e. how well can the route to any conclusions be seen?'

Illustrative quality indicators:

15a) Does the reporting demonstrate links between the analysis and the original data presented which are conceptual in nature and do not merely reiterate the data in similar descriptive terms?

15b) Does the report describe negative instances which do not fit with the analysis because, for example, they lie outside the scope of the analysis? Alternatively, the report attempts to show how negative instances could be brought within the main analytic framework.

Appraisal question 16 'How clear and coherent is the reporting?'

Illustrative quality indicators:

16a) Does the report make clear by highlighting or summarising the key points in a way appropriate for the target audience of the report?

16b) Is the report's structure clear enough to help the reader through the material and does it include signposting such as subheadings to help the reader further?

(h) Auditability

Appraisal question 17 'How adequately has the research process been documented?'

Illustrative quality indicators:

17a) Are the main documents used in the study included in the report? This would include letters to organisations and individuals, questionnaires, instructions for data management, etc.

17b) Are the strengths and otherwise of the methods used and the data sources employed discussed?

(i) Reflexivity and neutrality

Appraisal question 18 'How clear are the assumptions/ theoretical perspectives/values that have shaped the form and output of the evaluation?'

Illustrative quality indicators:

18a) Does the report indicate or discuss the perspectives and values of the researchers which may impact the methodology or substance of the report?

18b) Is there evidence in the report that the researchers are open to revising the conceptualisations, theories and assumptions in light of their experience of the research process?

In quantitative research, the concept of reliability is applied to the measures (of variables) which the researcher is using. There are two main usages of the concept reliability:

- The term test–retest reliability is used to indicate an assessment of how stable or consistent 'scores' on a measure are at different points in time. The belief is that, in general, a measure which correlates with itself over time is a reliable measure – and, hence, a good one. This is the case only to the extent that what is being measured can be expected to be stable over time. So, if we are measuring something which by its very nature is chronologically unstable, good test–retest reliability should not be expected. People's moods are transitory so a good measure of mood might be expected to be unreliable over time. Of course, in quantitative psychology things are usually measured because they are believed to be enduring and unchanging characteristics, such as intelligence, reaction times and so forth.

- The other meaning of reliability in quantitative research is the internal consistency of a measure. In quantitative research, measurements often consist of a set of items (questions, frequently) which are summed in some way to get the measure. These are the ubiquitous scales found in quantitative research. The internal consistency of the scale (the extent to which all of the items are measuring the same thing) is regarded as an indicator of the quality of the measure.

Neither of these has much bearing on most qualitative research. Qualitative researchers eschew the use of scales for various reasons – especially because they violate the requirement of richness of data which underlies most qualitative research. Furthermore, many qualitative researchers would reject the notion that there are fixed, measurable characteristics of individuals. As a consequence, reliability of the sorts just discussed is irrelevant. Qualitative researchers are more likely to regard their data as *situationally bounded*, that is, they do not necessarily expect to find the data they obtain from individuals to be consistent across research situations. For example, they are aware that different researchers may obtain different perspectives from interviewees.

The notion of reliability may be relevant to just a few aspects of qualitative research. For example, the transcription of interviews and other data is regarded as part of the discipline of qualitative research. Consistency of transcriptions between transcribers using the same method would be an ideal. This equates to the reliability of the transcription across different raters. This is rarely, if ever, formally assessed.

CONCLUSION

Very few of the traditional criteria which psychologists use in quantitative research apply to qualitative research directly. Qualitative and quantitative research simply do not have the same intellectual roots and, in various ways, they are in conflict. Indeed, it may well be the case that if traditional evaluative criteria can be applied to qualitative research then that research may well be based on the ethos of positivism. There are a number of criteria for evaluating qualitative research but these largely concentrate on evaluating the quality of the coding or categorisation process (the qualitative analysis). They are best regarded as indicators of quality rather than proof of quality in qualitative research. This contrasts markedly with quantitative and statistical research where there are procedures which may be applied to decide the worth of the research. Significance testing is one obvious example of this when we apply a test of whether the data are likely to have been obtained simply by sampling fluctuations. Internal consistency measures of reliability such as Cronbach's alpha also have such cut-off rules. This leaves it a little uncertain how inexperienced qualitative researchers can best evaluate their research.

In ending, to emphasise how difficult the evaluation and appraisal of qualitative research can be, it is worth mentioning Dixon-Woods et al. (2007) who studied three different ways of assessing qualitative research studies. One was the scheme described in Box 16.3, the second was another systematic system, and the third was expert opinion using no particular scheme. The study design involved having a set of 12 research reports evaluated using the various evaluation methods. Dixon-Woods et al. point out:

Our qualitative and quantitative data suggest that using a structured approach appears to sensitize reviewers to aspects of research practice. However, a structured approach does not appear more likely to produce higher levels of agreement between or within reviewers: in fact, the highest level of agreement is (arguably) achieved without using a structured approach. It could also be argued that the judgements produced using structured approaches are over-elaborated, and biased towards procedural aspects of research practice. (Dixon-Woods et al., 2007, p. 46)

KEY POINTS

- Qualitative research, characteristically, has different goals and assumptions from those of quantitative research. As a consequence, it is important that evaluative criteria which are applied to qualitative research reflect this. It cannot be claimed that there are universal criteria of quality in qualitative research. But this is also true in quantitative research. The criteria for evaluating a survey, for example, are different in many respects from those for evaluating a laboratory experiment.

- Nevertheless, there is a degree of overlap in the applicability of quality criteria across qualitative and quantitative research. That is, some criteria may be of value to evaluating both types of research. Criteria such as the quality, persuasiveness and coherence of the researcher's argument, how well the research is related to previously published research, the potential of the findings for generalisation and so forth would be largely common to both qualitative and quantitative research.

- Other criteria are more exclusively applicable to qualitative research (or quantitative research for that matter). These criteria include in qualitative research such matters as how well the analysis fits with the understandings of the research participants and the richness of detail in the data.

- The criteria for the evaluation of professionally produced qualitative research may be somewhat different and more demanding than what could be expected of newcomers to qualitative research. This is partly because the requirements of a purely academic research exercise may be very different from those for research commissioned at considerable expense by, say, the government. This is not to suggest that newcomers cannot benefit from the more demanding criteria but merely that initially these criteria would be hard to implement fully in terms of the work of novice researchers.

- Qualitative research includes a wide variety of different approaches which may or may not share philosophical and pragmatic assumptions. Thus sensitivity to the differences in perspectives which demand different evaluative criteria is essential. There is no sense in which the evaluative criteria discussed in this chapter fit all qualitative research equally.

ADDITIONAL RESOURCES

Seale, C. (1999). Quality in qualitative research. *Qualitative Inquiry, 5* (4), 465–478.

Spencer, L., Ritchie, J., Lewis, J., & Dillon, L. (2003). Quality in Qualitative Evaluation: A framework for assessing research evidence. A Quality Framework. Cabinet Office: Government Chief Social Researcher's Office, Strategy Unit. www.civilservice.gov.uk/wp-content/uploads/2011/09/a_quality_framework_tcm6-38740.pdf (accessed 24 April 2015).

Willig, C. (2013). *Introducing qualitative research in psychology* (3rd ed., chapter 9). Maidenhead: Open University Press.

Yardley, L. (2008). Demonstrating validity in qualitative psychology. In J. A. Smith (Ed.), *Qualitative psychology: A practical guide to research methods* (2nd ed., pp. 235–251). London: Sage.

CHAPTER 17

Ethics and data management in qualitative research

Overview

- Psychological ethics are the essentially moral principles which have been developed to govern all aspects of psychologists' work including research.

- It should not be assumed that qualitative research is ethically unproblematic. While qualitative research avoids some of the worst ethical violations which have sometimes characterised quantitative research, qualitative research generates its own ethical problems, not all of which are effectively covered by present guidelines. This is partly a consequence of the ways in which qualitative researchers collect data and the rather different relationship that they sometimes have with participants in their research. For example, the chapter examines some of the ethical problems of studies in which a single interviewer interviews couples in an interactive context.

- The historical origins of modern research ethics were in disturbing medical experimentation that took place in Nazi Germany. In addition, concerns about the use of deception in psychological research itself also played their part.

- Psychology's professional bodies (e.g. the American Psychological Association and the British Psychological Society) have published detailed ethical guidelines. Although they are substantially similar, this chapter is based on the more comprehensive American Psychological Association's ethics. So, for example, American Psychological Association ethical principles cover issues to do with the publication of research findings such as plagiarism and fabricating data.

- Deception, informed consent and confidentiality have emerged as being amongst the most important concepts in ethics, though the range of issues is much wider. A researcher needs to be aware of the processes involved in seeking ethical approval from both the organisation they work for and the organisation within which they propose to carry out their study.

- There are legal and ethical requirements about the management of personally identifiable data. Once data have been anonymised then these requirements do not apply. It is recommended that the researcher provides written information to participants about important features of the study and obtains their written agreement to participation.

Does qualitative research need ethics?

Research ethics for qualitative research might be expected to be pretty much the same as those for quantitative research. However, qualitative psychologists often orientate themselves very differently from their subject matter – people. Among the most obvious differences is the way in which participants in research are viewed, construed and treated in qualitative research. Laboratory experimentation, a prime example of quantitative research, ignores everything but a few fairly restricted features of the research participant's behaviour (no rich data collection here). Importantly, the laboratory researcher carefully manipulates the behaviours of those participating in the study. It is no coincidence that these participants were once known as subjects since the term is indicative of the power relationship between researcher and participant – it is that of a powerful person (the researcher) versus a subordinate one (the subject). Participants in this sort of research are effectively disregarded as whole persons – they are instead reduced to just a few variables. In the typical field research, questionnaires are distributed to participants whose function is to tick boxes rather than to express the richness and complexity of their thinking. These may be caricatures of quantitative research but they contain the essence of truth. The result is a somewhat alienated relationship between the quantitative researcher and their research participants. Qualitative researchers, in general, seem more interested in their research participants as people and seek to maintain their human dignity as full participants in the research.

Not surprisingly, because of the different way they relate to their research participants, some qualitative researchers are tempted to regard their qualitative research as ethically or morally superior to that of the quantitative psychologist. As Brinkmann and Kvale (2005, p. 162) put it: 'The qualitative boom has been accompanied by a tendency among qualitative researchers to portray qualitative inquiry as inherently ethical, or at least more ethical than quantitative research.' Closely related to this is the idea of *qualitative ethicism* (Hammersley, 1999). This is the tendency of qualitative researchers to regard their research in primarily ethical terms almost as if achieving ethical goals was the purpose of research. The closer relationship between research participants and researchers in qualitative research may be more rewarding on a human level but this makes certain ethical issues more pertinent and more problematic as we shall see. The relationship between the qualitative researcher and their participants is distinctive perhaps largely as a consequence of the qualitative researcher's search for rich and detailed data. Such data often demand substantial commitment on the part of participants and a closer, cooperative and supportive relationship between researcher and participant. Ethical codes which govern quantitative research are, to some extent, insufficient to deal with the special characteristics and, hence, requirements of qualitative research.

Psychologists, like many other professions, conduct themselves according to moral principles known as 'ethics'. The American Psychological Association probably has the most extensive ethical code but others, such as the British Psychological Society, have their own versions. The ethical issues for qualitative researchers can be very different from those facing the quantitative researcher despite some obvious areas of overlap. While a simplistic perspective on ethics is to regard them as sets or rules or regulations for the activities of psychological practitioners and researchers, this is somewhat inadequate. No system of rules is self-interpreting and so even where we think that we have a good rule then 'we still need to know when and how to apply the rule' (Brinkmann & Kvale, 2005, p. 159). Interpretation regularly faces researchers because the detail of the research setting and the importance of the research topic, for instance, can significantly affect the application of research ethics. Put another way, using an old chestnut, it is a moral principle that one shouldn't kill but what if by killing an extreme dictator one could save many thousands of lives? What then? Does the principle about not killing still apply or does some other principle begin to take precedence? Much the same is true for research ethics – that is, whether an ethical principle should prevail in a particular situation may depend as much on details about the situation as the nature of the ethical principle itself. For example, the confidentiality of information supplied to a researcher by a participant is universal in ethical guidelines. But what if during the course of an interview the participant makes threats to kill a neighbour with whom he has a dispute? Should this information be confidential? And suppose the man goes on to kill his neighbour: is the researcher blameless and beyond reproach because they maintained confidentiality?

Psychological researchers sometimes identify similar dilemmas in their work. Just how should they go about resolving them? Well, the ethical principles of psychologists by and large give the responsibility for monitoring ethical standards to the researcher(s) carrying out the research and the psychological community in general. This might include (a) the researcher(s) seeking the advice and assistance of other psychologists when there are potentially any ethical issues and (b) the entire psychology community monitoring at an informal level the ethical standards employed in the different fields of psychology.

Ethical guidelines sometimes make exceptions where the law or a specific organisation allows certain sorts of research activity which otherwise would seem to be ethically dubious. This clearly is a situation in which there is a conflict between the ethics and the law which some might see as a reason to question the law rather than a reason to disregard the ethics. Ethics are not simply organisational matters but individual matters too. One's personal ethics may mean that one does not do what is otherwise permissible – the researchers who employed deception in their research chose to do so, they did not have to do so. There are areas, of course, where the law is less restrictive than ethical principles. For example, the law generally does not punish psychologists who have sex with their adult clients even though it is against ethical principles.

The ever-widening context in which qualitative psychological research operates demands that researchers are sensitive to a substantial variety of ethical issues. There has been substantial growth in qualitative research in areas such as health psychology, clinical psychology, counselling and psychotherapy, educational psychology, work and organisational psychology, and community psychology (Willig & Stainton-Rogers, 2008). All of these are extremely sensitive areas of research by their very nature. Consequently, qualitative researchers face a complex and demanding ethical environment.

Ethics are important at all stages of qualitative research, as indicated in Figure 17.1. It is a mistake to consider ethics as something to be dealt with solely at the design stage despite the modern requirement to seek ethical approval from universities and other institutions at this stage (I. Shaw, 2008). Ethics in qualitative research, especially, cannot be regarded as a hurdle to be dealt with before data collection begins. The course

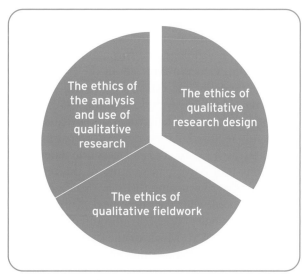

FIGURE 17.1 Shaw's (2008) aspects of ethics for research

of qualitative research is not predictable in many cases, which means that vigilance is continually required in order to deal with the ethical issues which can emerge at any stage in qualitative research.

The development of ethics in psychology

Ethics are an important aspect of modern psychological and social scientific research. Current ethical codes can be traced back to the Nuremberg Code which was developed to govern medical research. Nazi Germany's medical profession had an appalling record of unnecessary and inhumane medical experimentation on human beings. The most notorious medic among them was Dr Josef Mengele. He, for example, gave extremely high voltages of electrical shock to women concentration camp inmates in a study of their endurance levels. At the trial of some of the Nazi doctors in 1947, not only did the judges deliver their verdict but provided principles for the appropriate conduct of medical research. Six of these principles were adopted from elsewhere but four additional ones were contributed by the court. Collectively these are referred to as the Nuremberg Code. Many of these principles will be familiar to anyone with a basic knowledge of psychological ethics. For example:

- Consent to take part in research should be entirely voluntary and given only by people with a legal capacity to give consent. The person should have enough knowledge of the research to give consent in an informed manner.
- The participant in the research has the right to bring the research to an end – but unlike the modern versions of this only if they are mentally or physically unable to continue to the end of the research.

Other aspects of the code do not seem to have exact modern equivalents in ethical codes. For example, the Nuremberg Code indicates that an experiment should provide findings which are for society's good and that unnecessary studies should be avoided.

Following the Nuremberg Code, the American Psychological Association developed its set of ethical principles in 1953 which influenced and guided ethical thinking beyond just psychology and throughout social scientific research (Blodgett, Boyer, & Turk, 2005). Concern grew about the ethics of psychological research from this time onwards and became especially focused on the laboratory experimentation which characterised social psychology in the 1950s to 1970s. While much of this experimentation was of a high intellectual standard and creative and inventive, to be successful it frequently required that participants were misled or misinformed about the true nature of the research (Korn, 1997). Deception dates back to 1897 in psychology when Leon Solomons told participants, some of the time untruthfully, that either one point or two points were touching them in a study of sensory discrimination. What they were told influenced what they perceived. Korn (1997) found that the use of deception in social psychological research substantially increased in the three decades following the Second World War. Much of the classic research of social psychologists used deceit in some form and sometimes the deception was extreme. Deception studies began to attract considerable criticism, especially from the late 1960s onwards – the work of Stanley Milgram (1933–1984) was a particular focus (e.g. Milgram, 1974). In his famous studies he led participants to believe that they were delivering extremely high electric shocks to another person as part of a study of learning. In truth, the research was about the influence of the experimenter in encouraging obedience to the researcher's instructions.

In recent years, considerable ethical scrutiny has been applied to researchers studying humans (and animals for that matter, though this is not an issue for qualitative researchers and hence not covered in this chapter). Institutions such as universities, health services and the prison service have introduced ethical committees to overview research conducted within their ambit. This is usually two-fold:

- institutions monitor research by researchers who work for the institution;
- institutions monitor research in their institutions by researchers from outside of the institutions.

In addition to this are the ethical principles of the researcher's discipline. The complexity of ethical control is illustrated in Figure 17.2. While the aim is to pre-empt possible ethical problems, sanctions can be applied against those who violate ethical requirements. These may be instigated by the researcher's professional body but also by their home institution. Finally, there is the risk that participants may sue researchers and their employers in court when research oversteps the mark.

Ethical guidelines help to protect researchers as well as participants in research. But there is more to it than that. Gross ethical violations by researchers risk bringing psychology as a profession, and not just the offending individuals, into disrepute. The negative consequences of this for all researchers are potentially serious. Organisations and individuals gain autonomy by the application of clear and accepted ethical principles. Self-regulation is generally seen as beneficial given the possible excesses of government legislation concerning the conduct of research. Autonomy is a characteristic of many successful professions such as medicine and the law. They are not entirely free from government legislation but they operate somewhat independently of it. Professions such as medicine emerged as powerful independent bodies during the nineteenth century (Howitt, 1992) and their autonomy meant that they retained control over major aspects of professional activities. Ethics are an important mechanism by which professions regulate themselves and avoid outside (political) control.

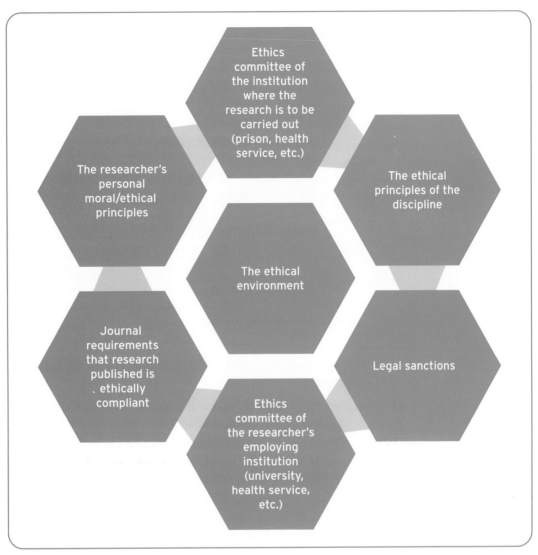

FIGURE 17.2 The ethical environment of qualitative and other research

Qualitative research in psychology is very different from medical research which resulted in the earliest ethical codes. Ethics have become increasingly sophisticated over the years in ways that the judges who framed the Nuremberg Code could not have foreseen. It can be argued that the ethical code of the American Psychological Association is the most sophisticated one directly applicable to psychology. It is adopted in this chapter because of its demanding and comprehensive nature. The most recent version of the American Psychological Association's manual on ethics was first introduced in 2002 and came into effect on 1 June 2003 (American Psychological Association, 2002). The code is conceptually based and so provides an intellectually systematic way of understanding ethical issues. It covers the full range of the professional activities of psychologists, including their roles as educators and practitioners as well as researchers. So, for example, you will find that the code requires that psychology teaching should exhibit fidelity to the current state of knowledge in the discipline.

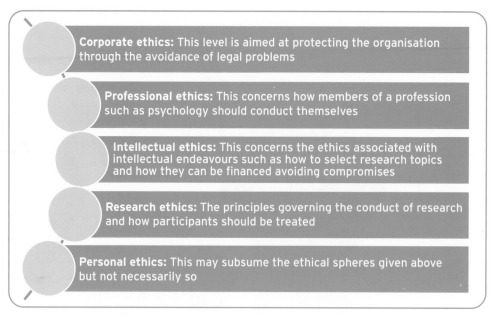

FIGURE 17.3 Johnson and Altheide's (2002) spheres of ethics

There are two important points which should be borne in mind by qualitative and other researchers:

- The American Psychological Association guidelines do not simply apply to professionals in the field of psychology but also students affiliated to the organisation.
- There is an assumption that psychologists should know the relevant ethical standards which apply to their work and the American Psychological Association rejects ignorance of these standards as an excuse.

Researchers often articulate the view that modern research ethics are more to do with the discourse of institutional control than the protection of participants. Bureaucratic procedures serve the function of demonstrating that university managements have control on individual researchers. This perspective is shared by Johnson and Altheide (2002) who argue that there are five different spheres which should be considered when discussing research ethics (see Figure 17.3). These range from the individual researcher's private principles for their conduct to institutional ethics. Although personal ethics overlap with and subsume some of the other ethical spheres, the corporate or institutional level of ethics is primarily to do with legality and the avoidance of legal problems. That is, they serve to defend universities and other providers of research from difficulties and criticism. However, Johnson and Altheide identify the sphere of professional ethics as the one where the most difficulties arise since it grows like a 'bamboo shoot in a rainforest' (p. 65). Professional ethics are particularly relevant to the qualitative researcher because of the rather different and distinctive relationships that qualitative researchers may have with their research participants.

General ethical principles for qualitative research

The American Psychological Association argues that ethics should be based on five different integrating principles (Figure 17.4). These apply just as much to qualitative as to quantitative research.

FIGURE 17.4 The basic principles of APA ethics

Principle A: Beneficence and nonmaleficence

According to this, psychologists should be seen as being to the benefit of people with whom the psychologist engages professionally. That is, psychological work should benefit clients, widely defined. Equally, psychologists should seek to avoid harm to their clients and research participants. This appears to be a reasonable principle but there are circumstances where there may be some doubt about its applicability. For example, what if the research involves interviews with prisoners and they reveal to the researcher that they have committed crimes which are not known to the authorities? Should the principle of beneficence apply and the researcher refuse to pass on such new information to the authorities? What if the prison makes such revelation a requirement for cooperation in the research?

Principle B: Fidelity and responsibility

Essentially the work of a professional psychologist involves relationships of trust with other people. Consequently, they are expected to:

- take responsibility for what they do;
- conduct themselves in accordance with established professional standards;
- make it clear that ethics have a role in all aspects of their professional activities and inform clients and others of this.

They have a responsibility to monitor the ethical conduct of other members of the psychological community including their colleagues.

Principle C: Integrity: accuracy, honesty and truthfulness

Integrity should be manifested throughout every part of a psychologist's professional life. So, for example, it is generally accepted that in some circumstances deception may be appropriate such as when there are clear benefits from the research which substantially outweigh the risks. Nevertheless, even then, the psychologist should correct any harmful consequences.

Principle D: Equity: equal access to psychology's benefits

In their work, psychologists should be aware, for example, of their actual and potential personal biases in order that all people experience fair and just practices from them. For qualitative researchers, this can be regarded as part of a reflexive orientation to the research process. Furthermore, psychologists should neither condone nor engage in unjust practices and should be sensitive to the means by which injustice may be manifest.

Principle E: Respect for people's rights and dignity

It is held that people have the following rights: privacy, confidentiality and self-determination. One consequence of this is that psychologists need to understand why some people may be vulnerable and unable to make autonomous decisions. Children, those who have intellectual limitations and some elderly people are obvious examples of this category. This principle also means that psychologists need to respect (and be able to recognise) differences between groups of people in terms of culture and roles. This means that characteristics such as disability, culture, age, ethnicity, gender, gender identity, language, nationality, race, religion and socio-economic status are all matters for consideration and respect. Psychologists not only must try to avoid biases against such groupings but be critical towards others who fail to reach the expected standard.

Box 17.8 at the end of this chapter indicates some of the complexity of ethics in a characteristic qualitative study.

Ethical procedures in qualitative research

The same basic ethical requirements apply to qualitative psychologists as apply to any other form of psychological research with human participants. There are some special problems for qualitative researchers, as we shall see, as well as idiosyncratic difficulties. However, the following are key matters which may be an issue for researchers.

Institutional clearance

A large proportion of psychological research is carried out within organisations such as schools, hospitals and prisons – and, of course, universities. Many institutions require formal approval to be granted before they allow research to take place within the institution and before they allow members of their staff to carry out research there or elsewhere. Generally, but not always, the responsibility for granting approval lies with an ethical committee. (Sometimes the authority for approving the research may rest with a single individual such as the head of a school.) The procedures can appear to be cumbersome (for example, lengthy forms to complete) though sometimes the committee has a fast-track procedure which can be used where the research is not at all ethically problematic. Qualitative researchers have the same obligations as any other to obtain ethical clearance from the organisation that they work for and any organisation where they wish to conduct their research. For example, a university researcher wishing to carry out research in a prison might need to follow the procedures of both organisations. Although it may appear that qualitative research involves relatively benign methods of data collection, this is something that the qualitative researcher should not take for granted. Some work characteristic of qualitative researchers may not require ethical clearance such as where the study involves archival material and other forms of documentary material (newspapers and magazines, for instance).

However, in almost all other cases it is incumbent on the researcher to obtain the necessary ethical approval.

Any application for ethical approval should be open and honest with no attempt to hide issues. Consequently, the application should:

- exhibit transparency in that it accurately and patently represents the true nature of the research;

- be accurate in terms of the information provided;

- be clear in terms of what it communicates about the proposed research;

- avoid misleading in any way such as through lies, partial truths or by omission;

- act as a template or protocol for the research that is actually carried out – if there are changes then it will probably be necessary to seek further approval.

Most research by students takes place in a university setting. So the ethics vetting procedures of universities are of interest to those planning qualitative research studies. There may be special procedures for student research but not necessarily so. The ethics committee is likely to be a generic committee dealing with *all* research involving human participants irrespective of the disciplinary background of the research. So it would deal with research from disciplines such as sociology, business studies, biology and so forth. One approach involves a two-tiered process of ethics clearance:

- The first stage involves unproblematic research which meets basic ethical standards and raises no ethical difficulties. Such research can be identified using a basic screening questionnaire.

- The second stage is for research which cannot meet these basic standards to be reviewed in detail by the ethics committee. The research may then be approved, approved with provisos or refused ethical clearance, which means that the research cannot take place.

Of course, many types of research are unlikely to be ethically problematic. So there may be provision for the general approval of generic styles of research which have previously met appropriate ethical criteria. Such blanket approval speeds up the ethical clearance process. (It hardly needs to be mentioned here that the work of students can be under severe time and timing pressures.)

Screening questions can be used to identify unproblematic research proposals fairly effectively. The following is a list of the sorts of issue the screening questionnaire might address. Because of their apparent irrelevance to qualitative research, matters to do with invasive physiological or biological techniques have been left out of consideration. If you are planning a research study, decide between true and false for each of the following statements which are based on an ethics screening questionnaire used at one British university. Respond to each of the statements honestly:

- The researcher(s) involved in the study has prior experience of and/or adequate training in the methods to be employed. TRUE/FALSE

- An experienced member of staff will supervise student researchers and junior researchers directly. TRUE/FALSE

- The researcher(s) is not in a position of direct authority over participants in the study (such as when students are recruited by teaching staff at a university to be participants in the research). TRUE/FALSE

- The participants will not be members of vulnerable groups (i.e. children less than 18 years old, elderly people above the age of 65 years, women during pregnancy, individuals with a mental illness, prisoners or otherwise detained people or any other vulnerable group). TRUE/FALSE

- The research procedures are not likely to cause distress of a physical, social, emotional or psychological nature. TRUE/FALSE
- The research procedures are not physically or psychologically demanding on the participants. TRUE/FALSE
- The study does not expose participants to risks or distress greater than the risks and distress of their normal lifestyle. TRUE/FALSE
- If the study includes observations or recording of participants, they will be informed in advance that this will be involved. TRUE/FALSE
- Participants can choose whether to take part free from any pressures and based on informed consent. TRUE/FALSE
- Participants will be fully informed about the study's objectives and details of the procedure before the research commences or at the end if the information would risk invalidating the study. TRUE/FALSE
- Deception is not used in the research either by withholding information from participants or by misleading them in ways which could harm or lead to their exploitation. TRUE/FALSE
- Where the use of deception is proposed, it is unavoidable given the purposes of the study. TRUE/FALSE
- Where deception is used, participants will be debriefed about the true purpose of the study soon after its completion. TRUE/FALSE
- Consideration has been given to how participants will react on being told that information has been withheld or that there has been deliberate deception. TRUE/FALSE
- Participants will be told that they may withdraw from the study at any stage and require that their data (e.g. tapes, notes) are destroyed. TRUE/FALSE
- Information about individual participants in the research will be confidential and not identifiable except with prior agreement. TRUE/FALSE
- Videos and audio recordings will be kept in a secure place and not allowed to be used by third parties. TRUE/FALSE
- Video and audio recordings of participants will be destroyed within six years of the completion of the investigation. TRUE/FALSE
- The researcher has not been offered inducements to do the research by a third party (except for their contractually agreed salaries or for expenses). TRUE/FALSE
- Participants will not be offered inducements other than basic expenses to take part in the study. TRUE/FALSE

How do you decide whether your research is free of ethical problems based on the above? Well unless you answered TRUE to all of the statements which are relevant to your research then there may be ethical problems with your work. This means that you would have to submit a detailed proposal for approval by the committee. Of course, ethical requirements can vary from institution to institution so you need to check what procedures are in place where you are working or studying. Nevertheless, the above should give you a flavour of what might be involved. The following sections provide more information about the ethical basis of these screening items.

As you are probably beginning to realise, obtaining ethical clearance for your research can involve a lot of bureaucracy and a great deal of form filling.

Informed consent in the recruitment of research participants

Informed consent is the principle that participants agree to take part in research freely and in light of the knowledge about what the research is about. This means that participants:

- should not be placed under pressure to participate in the research (e.g. they should not be coerced and they should not be made to fear the consequences of not taking part in the research);
- should understand exactly what participating in the research will involve,

The point is that unless the conditions are met then a person may agree to take part in the research but might have refused had the true nature of the research been clear to them. Informed consent applies to a full range of psychological activities such as assessment, therapy and counselling but its role in research is crucial. Participants should know what they are agreeing to before they can agree to it. Those who lack the capacity to understand what they are being asked to agree to (e.g. children) require special protection. The principle of informed consent means that the researcher should not bamboozle the potential participant into taking part but should explain clearly and in appropriate language just what the research is about. Equally obviously, the way in which things are explained to a university student may need to be different from that given to an elderly person. Informed consent is not absolutely required and sometimes ethical codes permit exceptions. For example, the law might permit studies without informed consent, say, in military contexts. In these circumstances, the researcher's personal ethics may be more important in ensuring that potential participants are fully aware of the nature of the research.

The following provisions would generally suffice to justify the claim of informed consent:

- Potential participants are given accurate information about the purpose, procedures and approximate duration of their commitment.
- Participants understand that they have the right not to take part in the research and that they may withdraw from the research at any stage. It is usually accepted by researchers that this freedom to withdraw includes the withdrawal of any data provided up to this point. Tapes might be given to the participant who withdraws or the transcripts may be shredded and so forth.
- Participants need to know what consequences might ensue from not taking part in the research. Most often there will be no consequences but this is not always the case. For example, I have conducted research in a therapeutic organisation working with sexually abusive men which required, contractually, that the men had to take part in research. Thus a man who refused had failed to fulfil the contract and might be regarded as uncooperative and had further treatment denied.
- Potential research participants should be told about features of the research which might have a bearing on their decision whether or not to participate. So the potential risks, discomforts and negative outcomes should be considered by the researcher and communicated to the participant. One instance of things which might need to be communicated might be the identity of the body funding the research if there is one. Some participants, for example, might be willing to take part in research if it was supported by a charity but not if it were funded by big business.
- If the research has particular potential benefits then the participant may consent to take part in procedures which they otherwise wouldn't. These benefits may be for the community in general, the academic community or for the individual participant. This fuller picture may not be apparent to potential participants unless it is explained to them.

Box 17.1

PRACTICAL ADVICE

Confidentiality problems in qualitative research

Unlike a great deal of quantitative research in which participants are put through the research procedures on an individual basis, as we have seen, sometimes in qualitative research data are collected from a group of individuals. This is particularly the case with focus groups. The researcher cannot guarantee the confidentiality of things said in a focus group as the other group members have access to this information. Where the focus group is made up of strangers then this may reduce the salience of the problem. However, what about circumstances in which members of the focus group know each other? Things which are said in the group may 'leak' out later, perhaps to the embarrassment of the participants. One way of dealing with this would be to warn potential participants of the possibility that they may know other members of the group, thus giving them the opportunity of withdrawing when the problems become clear to them. This sort of problem, of course, may be to the

detriment of the quality of the data if the members find these circumstances inhibiting and, possibly, avoid mentioning certain things.

Another confidentiality issue arises from the detailed information which qualitative researchers obtain as part of their research. The more idiosyncratic the detail in a qualitative report, the greater the possibility that a particular individual can be identified. Of course, the vast majority of readers of a qualitative research report may have no idea of the actual individuals involved but that does not apply universally. Research carried out in a particular organisational setting may not be transparent about identities to the research community but it may be obvious to those in that particular work setting just who is who. For that reason, organisations sometimes require a right of veto on the publication of research carried out in that organisation to prevent what might appear to be critical material becoming public.

- The extent of confidentiality should be explained to the potential participant. Anonymity is usually guaranteed in research. Nevertheless, this cannot be the case for every piece of research. There may be, for example, legal constraints or a contractual agreement between the authorities and the researcher that some sorts of information have to be disclosed such as unknown crimes. Confidentiality issues can be complex in qualitative research as indicated in Box 17.1.

It is important to stress that it may be difficult to meet these requirements in qualitative research. The qualitative researcher only knows with hindsight what will happen during the research and the possible effects of this. The qualitative researcher needs to be responsive and adaptable in their data collecting strategies, which inevitably means that they may touch on matters quite unanticipated when the research was planned – simply because they take their lead from the participant.

Incentives or rewards for taking part in the research need to be made clear to the potential participant prior to the research. Although the general view is that payments or other rewards for participating are best avoided, if they are to be given then this should be made clear in advance. There are several potential reasons for this, including the possibility that the participant may feel offended by a cash payment or some other form of reward. Their motives for participation may be to them much more altruistic and payments may compromise their goodwill.

It would be usual to provide the name and contact details of a third party who may be approached about the bona fides of the researcher as well as further details about the research and their rights as participants. Students doing research would, for example, give details about the person supervising their research. If this person works at a university then this in itself would help confirm that the researcher can probably be trusted.

However, the issue of informed consent may be confounded by the procedures employed by qualitative researchers. The main reason for this lies in the phrase 'the delusion of alliance' (Stacey, 1988). This refers to the 'closer' relationship which may be involved in qualitative research. This can encourage participants to say more and reveal more than they might have in more traditional psychological research. In this, it is much clearer when the researcher is actually collecting data and when they are taking a break from the research task. Because this is relatively poorly demarcated in much qualitative research then the risk of involuntary disclosure of information becomes more serious. I. Shaw (2008) suggests that another way of putting this is to suggest that the researcher has become a covert researcher in this context and such research is highly problematic ethically.

There are additional issues when considering videoing interaction as discussed in Box 17.2.

There are circumstances in which it is not necessary to obtain informed consent. Nevertheless, the requirement that the research is not likely to cause the individual involved stress or harm applies – damage to an individual's reputation is an obvious risk which should be monitored. The main circumstances in which it is permissible to carry out research with no prior consent being sought are as follows:

- The research is based on the use of anonymous questionnaires or observations in natural settings. It is important to maintain confidentiality, nevertheless.

Box 17.2

PRACTICAL ADVICE

Obtaining informed consent for voice recordings and photographic images

Qualitative researchers frequently record interviews and, increasingly, video interactions. So they, especially, need to be aware that such recordings come under the requirement of informed consent. The APA ethical code does, however, allow that there are exceptions in certain circumstances to this requirement.

Recording or photography which occurs in naturalistic public settings does not require informed consent normally. Of course, if the setting is not actually a natural one because, for example, the researcher has dropped a coin to see whether passers-by attempt to return it to its owner or simply keep it for themselves, then this does pose a risk that unsuspecting participants might be identified

personally or even harmed by the recording or photography. Part of the problem is that it is the researcher in these cases who puts the inadvertent participant at risk. In completely natural settings, if the person being filmed or recorded does or says something which is illegal or improper then the researcher has not encouraged this.

The APA code indicates that where research requires deception and this deception is itself ethical, then it is appropriate to obtain consent to use the recording at a debriefing session following the research. In the debriefing session, relevant information should be provided to the participant and questions answered by the researcher.

- The study involves the use of archival materials rather than new data collection. The requirement of confidentiality applies here too.
- The study involves jobs or similar organisational matters but the research puts the participants in no jeopardy related to their employment. Again confidentiality is assumed.
- The research is about 'normal educational practices, curricula or classroom management methods' in an educational establishment.
- If the law or institutional regulations allow research without informed consent then it is ethical to carry out research in these circumstances.

The local ethics committee may nevertheless require ethical clearance in some of the above circumstances and so you need to check.

Several of the circumstances above are particularly pertinent to qualitative research. It should be noted that the above list is based on the American Psychological Association's ethics, which may not be guiding the ethical committee at your university, for example.

It is generally accepted, nowadays, that a researcher will formally obtain the agreement of participants to taking part in the research in light of the information about appropriate detailed knowledge of what the research entails and other information such as the freedom of the participant to withdraw from the study unproblematically. There are a number of advantages to this. The overriding one is, of course, that the researcher has evidence of agreement to participate. Generally speaking, the *consent form* is used to do this but verbal agreement in the course of an interview is an obvious, viable, method in some circumstances. Another important advantage of the consent form is that they generally require the researcher to stipulate details about the ethics-related features of the research which otherwise the researcher may not have considered. Typically a consent form consists of two parts:

- A one page or so description of the study. This is the information sheet or study description.
- A one page form giving details of the 'ethical contract' between the participant and the researcher. This is the consent form itself.

So what should go into each of these? There is no universal consent form, though you can track down a lot of them on the Web easily. However, your particular university or other institutional location may have its own procedure for consent, including a template for the consent form. Your own department may have its own preferred procedure which you should follow. Each consent form, however, has to be tailored to the particular research study in question. Remember that there are circumstances where consent may have to be obtained from a third party, e.g. where the research involves children. Copies of the information sheet and the consent form should be given to each participant for them to retain. Nevertheless, the following should be helpful in general.

The information sheet/study description

The information sheet or study description should be written in everyday language commensurate with the language ability of the participants in the research. Information should be provided detailing the nature of their involvement in the research and any potential risks stemming from participation. The following should be included:

- What the project is about – that is, what the study aims to achieve.
- What the participant is required to do in the study together with details of the time commitments that the research places on its participants.

- What the arrangements for confidentiality of the data are.
- What the arrangements concerning the privacy of personal data are.
- What the arrangements for the security of the data are.
- Who will have access to the data.
- The purposes for which the data shall be used.
- The extent to which participants will be identifiable in publications.
- The voluntary nature of participation in the study.
- The participant has the right to withdraw from the study (including withdrawing their data) without having to give a reason or explanation for this. If appropriate, a statement indicating that withdrawal from the study has no contingent consequences such as the withdrawal of medical services.
- What benefits the research might bring the participant.
- What risks or potential harm the research might pose for participants.
- If you are intending to do further research (e.g. follow-up interviews) at another time or if there is a possibility of doing so, care is needed. You must obtain permission from the participant to contact them in future. Failure to build this in may mean that the participants cannot be contacted again. The Data Protection Act, in the United Kingdom, prevents such unagreed follow-ups. See the later section on the Data Protection Act.
- Contact details for the research team or the supervisor in the case of student research which can be used to obtain further information.
- Contact details for the institution's Ethics Committee in case issues arise which cannot be appropriately dealt with by the researchers or the supervisor.

The consent form

The typical consent form includes various statements about the project and the ethical arrangements which the participant signs to indicate their consent to the study. So the consent form should include things such as the following, suitably modified for the particular research project being planned:

- The title of the research project
- Things that need to be included are
- I (the participant) have been informed about and understand the nature of the study.
- Any questions that I may have had have been answered to my satisfaction.
- I understand that I am free to withdraw myself and my data from the research at any time and that there would be no adverse consequences to me for doing so.
- No information about me will be published in a form which could potentially identify me.
- My data, in an anonymous form, may be used by other researchers.
- I consent to participate in the study as outlined in the information sheet.
- Space for the signature of the participant, their full name, and the date of the agreement.

It is suggested that you use the above to guide yourself when writing your own information sheet and consent form. This is not to make life harder for you unnecessarily but to encourage active consideration of the ethical status of your qualitative research. The different methods used by qualitative researchers to collect data have radically different ethical requirements. For example, it is relatively easy to ensure data confidentiality by using anonymity, etc. when conducting an in-depth interview but highly problematic in relation to focus group data where the researcher simply cannot guarantee privacy and confidentiality given the numbers of participants who cannot be bound effectively by the ethical principles which apply to researchers. Furthermore, if a researcher conducts a participant observation, then many of these considerations may not always apply. So it is generally accepted that observational research in public places may not require the agreement of those observed if they are going about their usual activities in public places. Yet this is a complex area so it is important to check with your local Research Ethics Committee which may have a rather different viewpoint. The point is that a 'one-size-fits-all' approach to obtaining consent is probably inappropriate.

It is important to give consideration about what can be done with the data obtained in qualitative studies. You need the permission of your participants to make it available to other researchers. Not to do so can be a problem because (a) qualitative research has an ethos which stresses the importance of making one's data available to other researchers for verification, etc. but also (b) it may be a requirement of the research's funding body that the data are archived and made available to other researchers. The UK Data Archive (n.d.) has details of the ethical and practical necessities of sharing data.

Legal and ethical management of data

The management of the data collected by the qualitative psychologist is not merely a matter for research ethics committees and may be a matter for data protection legislation. Thus many of the things included on the information sheet and consent form discussed in the previous section are as much about data protection legislation as they are about research ethics. The concept of 'transparency' is used in data protection to refer to the openness of the research to the data givers. Such legislation is common in Western countries but, of course, the detail of the legislation will vary from country to country. In the United Kingdom the relevant legislation is the Data Protection Act (1998). The legislation strikes a balance between the privacy of participants in research and the value of research in modern society, though it applies to all forms of personal data – not just that obtained through research. Universities and other organisations will have institutional and departmental data protection officers. Their job is to ensure that procedures for data handling comply with national legislation. They should be consulted if you are in any doubt as to how the legislation should be implemented for your particular research.

Anyone who carries out research which involves the collection or use of personal information about individuals who can be identified from that data has to comply with the data protection legislation. The sort of data (qualitative or quantitative) and whether or not it is stored in a digital, electronic form or in hard copy, manual form are immaterial. These basic requirements should indicate that the rich, detailed data that qualitative researchers collect fall very firmly and decisively into the domain of data protection legislation. The only exceptions to this are data which already are publicly available such as electoral registers and so forth.

Personal information is more or less any information which can be identified as being about a particular individual. It may come as some relief to know that once any personal identifiers are removed from data then the data protection legislation no longer applies. By employing such procedures as not using participants' real names or those of anyone else mentioned in the research and removing identifying material about locations and so forth the legislation ceases to apply. However, there are arguments that this is, in some cases, an unsatisfactory way of dealing with qualitative material. For example, Nespor (2000) raises issues to do with the anonymisation of identifying features for the place where the research was carried out. If the researcher removes such contextual information then the consequence is that useful features of the data are made unavailable to the reader. It makes a big difference to how data are understood if the full context is provided. Remove this context and something important is lost. Just a final point on this – remember that the digital recording stored on your computer counts as data under the Data Protection Act so you must ensure that the anonymisation procedure has been carried out on this just as much as it applies to any transcriptions of the data. (Some issues in relation to anonymisation are discussed in Boxes 17.3 and 17.4.)

Box 17.3

PRACTICAL ADVICE

Is anonymity really possible for qualitative research?

Qualitative researchers need to consider a wide variety of ethical issues somewhat more carefully than is general in psychology. Ethical standards which generally work unproblematically for quantitative researchers may raise problems for the demands of modern qualitative research. Modern practices in research may impose their own demands on research ethics. Although it has traditionally been the case that academic research involves effective communication with peers, increasingly it has been a requirement on researchers to actively disseminate research much more widely than that. This may have ramifications in terms of the classic ethical principle of anonymity. Tilley and Woodthorpe (2011) discuss the problems of anonymity from their personal perspectives of early-career qualitative researchers wishing to pursue successful careers in academia. They identify, to put it crudely, the ethos of publish-or-perish as problematic in this context. The ethical principle of anonymity, as we have seen, has its origins in biomedical research. A person, for example, with a sexually transmitted disease may not wish the world to know about this and the world has no reason to know that they have the disease. In such contexts, including mainstream psychology, the principle of anonymity works fine, is easy to implement and is routine. Confidentiality is different from anonymity since it is the assumption that information revealed in research will not be communicated to others to the detriment of the person who gives the information. Anonymity may be sometimes a tool to help aid confidentiality but it is not the same thing.

There is an interaction between ethical principles and qualitative research which makes relatively unproblematic and routine ethical expectations apply in a different and more urgent way to qualitative research. For example, Tilley and Woodthorpe ask about the nature of anonymity in circumstances where it is desirable to identify research sites or research participants. This is made more complicated by the fact that sometimes, if not often, research participants actually want their identity to be published. This can occur, for example, when they feel that they have been a victim of some injustice and see in the research a way of rectifying this injustice. A good example of such requests can be found in Howitt (1992) who studied parents who claimed to have been wrongly accused of child abuse. Some of them expressed the wish to be identified. In the end, the parents were anonymised although they may have been identifiable from newspaper reports, for example. However, in this case, the decision to anonymise depended more on legal restrictions concerning reporting court cases involving children than ethics per se. There are circumstances in which the researcher feels that it is important to identify the research site. In the same study by Howitt (1992) he found one family reporting the sexually abusive behaviour of Frank Beck who ran a care home for the local authority. This was before the matter became a national scandal. In these circumstances, would it not have been better to identify the care home and the local authority? Sometimes the research site itself wishes to be identified for some reason – perhaps they are particularly proud of what they do or feel that publicity is in their interest.

Tilley and Woodthorpe accept that there are many circumstances where anonymisation should prevail. They mention specifically research with children, research on highly sensitive topics, and research where obtaining informed consent would be difficult, such as where the participants are people with learning difficulties. Nevertheless, they say, there are circumstances where anonymisation is not desirable. Two examples of this are:

* Research for which knowledge transfer between organisations is important. Other organisations may learn more if the research site is identified. In addition, the researcher may be under an obligation to the funders of the research to be accountable. If a research site appears to be particularly innovative or excellent in some other way then not identifying it may be seen as a detrimental decision.
* Where the aims of the research are thwarted in some way by anonymising the site or the participants. Common examples of this would be where the underlying motive of the research is emancipatory in some way – perhaps it has antidiscriminatory objectives or it is feminist in orientation. Equally the research may feature the participatory involvement of the research team with the community in question.

Not all forms of qualitative research are equally subject to such pressures. For example, the desire not to anonymise may be greater for some ethnographic research studies since a great deal can be lost if the site of the research is disguised. There is a strong case to offer the choice of anonymity or otherwise to the participants where they can be seen as particularly active agents in the research process.

Practicalities often work to undermine the principle of anonymity in qualitative research. The researcher may be required to disseminate their research findings widely to the more general public using, say, newspapers, magazines, radio and television – these are very different media from the academic journals in which most academic research is published. Even where anonymisation has been employed, an Internet search engine may be used to identify the likely research site and, consequently, individuals. The research site may, for example, have mentioned on its web pages that they were helping Professor X with her research. The identity of the research funder may be a strong clue as to the identity of the research site.

At the same time, researchers may be under increasing pressure to employ anonymisation. Academic journal editors may demand anonymity for various reasons. This might be, for example, because the UK Data Protection Act presumes the anonymisation of participants in research. Consequently, the journal may insist on the research site being obscured and individuals presented anonymously.

Box 17.4

PRACTICAL ADVICE

How to anonymise your data

Antaki (2009a) lists ten different guidelines for anonymising data. Although some of them apply mainly to conversation analysis, they do constitute some sound advice about selecting replacement names for the participants in your research. Before doing this you really need to identify every name used in a transcript as well as any contracted names

(e.g. Sam for Samantha). If you don't do this then you will waste time since you may, for example, initially choose a name which has no appropriate shortened version:

* Try to use names which have the same number of syllables as the real name and involve accents placed

in the same place. This will allow them to be fitted into a Jefferson transcription better.

- Keep the new name the same gender as the original name.
- Ensure that the new name has appropriate shortened or diminutive versions if the transcript requires this.
- It is usually best to maintain the ethnicity of a person when choosing a new name in circumstances in which ethnicity is important in the transcript or if it is important to the analysis you are developing.
- Use new names which are similar to the original in terms of its use. For example, John for Peter seems fine but John for Peregrine obviously violates this suggestion.
- Maintain age, class and locality conventions represented in the original name as effectively as possible.
- Usually country names should be left in except in those circumstances in which they will help to identify the person in the transcript.
- Leaving in the actual name of a city is all right if doing so does not identify the person in the transcript. Changing the names can cause all sorts of difficulty as a city such as London cannot be effectively replaced by Bath or Aldershot, for example.

- Town and village names can be replaced by something similar in length, etc. if they risk identifying the participant.
- Institutional names (e.g. names of a particular university) need to be replaced if they risk disclosing a participant's identity.

Wiggins and Potter (2008) make some suggestions about using computer software such as Adobe Audition and Adobe Premier to anonymise participants in a digitally recorded sound recording or a video. For example, Adobe Premier can be used to blur the faces of members of a focus group, etc. and Adobe Audition can distort voices to make the speaker unrecognisable in a sound recording. It is possible to replace identifying names with the name digitally reversed in sound recordings using Adobe Audition. The advantages of this are that the word length and intonation remain unchanged. While this does allow actual recordings and videos to be presented in public, the question remains whether this is sufficient anonymisation – for example, the same program could be used to reverse the name back so that the name would be identifiable. The issue raised by Wiggins and Potter is an important one but the adequacy of their solution needs to be debated.

This brings us to the question of what happens if the data from the research are not turned into an anonymous form and so the Data Protection Act applies. Quite a number of things follow. One is that the Data Protection Act actually requires that the data are only kept as long as they are needed for the purposes explained to those who provided the data. Consequently, the researcher is left to destroy the data at an appropriate stage *if* the data are not anonymised once the research is completed.

If the data come under the data protection legislation then you must also give consideration to their safe keeping. So where are the hard copies to be stored – who has access to the data in this form? Equally, where the data are stored on computer, the question is one of who can gain access to the computer? In other words, procedures have to be decided on to ensure that the personal data are available only to the persons stipulated in the 'contract' with the participant.

When deception may be used

The deception of research participants is regarded as being unacceptable in psychological research in most circumstances. Some psychologists have gone so far as to recommend that deception should be prohibited (e.g. Baumrind, 1985). There are various reasons for this. Systematic research evidence has been summarised as follows:

the available evidence suggests that the direct experience of deception and the suspicion of deception carry with them the potential of provoking significant cognitive-emotional as well as behavioral responses. To the extent that these responses are bound to introduce systematic error variance in the data, they impair, and possibly destroy, experimental control. In light of this danger . . . we conclude that the prohibition of deception is a sensible convention . . . (Ortmann & Hertwig, 2002, p. 125)

This has implications for the work of qualitative researchers. A more trusting relationship needs to be built up in qualitative research between the researcher and participants. Only in this way can the need for rich, in-depth interview data or participant observation data be met. Bowen summed this up in the following way:

> From an ethical standpoint, risks and concerns are greater in qualitative research than in quantitative research. This is mainly because of the close involvement of the researcher with the research process and with the participants. Qualitative researchers often become immersed in the life of respondents. Ethical concerns arise also because qualitative research offers considerable interpretative latitude to the researcher and the data are, on the whole, rife with personal opinions and feelings. (Bowen, 2005, p. 214)

To the extent that it could be reasonably expected that physical pain or emotional distress will be caused then deception should *not* be used. So what are the circumstances in which deception may be legitimate? The ethical guidelines suggest that where the research potentially has 'scientific, educational or applied value' then there is a case for considering the use of deception. What this means is that the researcher should establish the credibility of other ways of carrying out the research. Only where there seems to be no effective alternative to the use of deception should deception be considered. A risk assessment should be carried out to establish the pain and distress the study is likely to produce. But there is more to it than this. It is unlikely that the researcher who proposes a study involving deception can dispassionately evaluate the viability of alternative methods and, perhaps, the amount of pain or distress that the research may arouse. Consequently, it is important to consult with other members of the psychology community about the issue as they may well be in a better position to provide a balanced assessment in this situation.

The use of deception brings its own responsibilities. Most importantly, the researcher has a responsibility to reveal and explain the deception as soon as possible. The recommended stage for doing this is immediately after the data have been collected from the participant. Sometimes there may be a reason to delay the revelation of the deception until the data have been collected from all of the participants. Irrespective of the stage at which the deception is revealed, there should be ample provision for giving the participant the right to withdraw his or her data from the study. In addition, it should be noted that the ethics of the British Psychological Society (2010) make a distinction between deliberate lies and omitting to mention important details about the research's nature. Lying by omission may be as unacceptable as lying by commission. The British Psychological Society indicates that the test of whether omitting information is undesirable may be found in the reaction of participants when they are told that they have been deceived (i.e. at the debriefing). If their response is negative (such as anger, evidence of discomfort) then this clearly indicates that the procedure is unacceptable in this case and consequently should be reviewed. What should happen next is not indicated by the British Psychological Society, though the choices of abandoning or modifying the research are obvious ones.

Research with subordinates and those relatively less powerful

Researchers frequently occupy a relatively powerful position compared with the participants in their research. This may be inevitable since in order to have access to participants, the researcher often has the trust of important members of organisations such as schools, hospitals and charities. Furthermore, one has only to remember the frequent suggestion that psychological research is largely carried out on university students to see that here is a relationship based on power – the university academic researcher over the student research participant. Refusing to participate is more often than not the only power that such potential participants have. Given these power-based relationships which have their basis outside of the research setting, there is the possibility that adverse consequences may follow if they declined to take part in the research. Similarly, they may feel under pressure not to withdraw from a study that they feel unhappy about in these circumstances. Of course, the impact of the superior–subordinate differential can be different when the researcher is also the participant's lecturer and there are inducements to take part in the research or if there are requirements that students take part in a number of research studies as part of their degree programmes. One way around this ethical problem, for example, is to offer other ways for students to obtain course credits which do not involve taking part in the research. Power is an especially important issue in the qualitative interview as discussed in Box 17.5.

Box 17.5

KEY CONCEPT

Power relationships in qualitative interviews

Although these would not be regarded as an ethical issue by most psychologists, there is a sense in which qualitative researchers, especially, should be aware of the power relationships which exist within their interviews. These are relevant to how the qualitative researcher construes their relationship with the participants in the research and are relevant to the way in which the qualitative researcher carries out their research. They undermine the common claims of some qualitative researchers that they have a more democratic or egalitarian relationship with their research participants than is typical of quantitative researchers. The power differentials in qualitative research are a little more subtle, admittedly, but the fact that they are there should make us question the extent to which ethics are effectively dealt with by qualitative researchers.

According to Brinkmann and Kvale (2005), qualitative researchers tend to neglect the following power characteristics of the qualitative interview:

- *Interview power relations are asymmetrical* It is the researcher who defines the nature of the interview by initiating it, by deciding what topics will be covered, by asking the questions and also by terminating the interview process. The researcher is dominant in the relationship.

- *Interviews are largely a one-direction dialogue* Question asking takes place in one direction only – from

the researcher to the participant. Participants don't ask questions and to do so would be disruptive and failing to play the interview by the rules. They are there to answer them.

- *The instrumentality of the interview* While normal conversation is frequently an end in itself with no other purpose or a joint activity, the research interview is there to serve the needs of the researcher. Out of the interview, the qualitative researcher gains text, narratives and so forth which are used by the researcher in fulfilment of their research interests primarily. It is generally less clear what participants in research gain from participation.

- *The manipulative dialogue contained in interviews* According to Brinkmann and Kvale (2005), the researcher follows a largely hidden agenda during the interview. They suggest that the interviewer seeks to obtain information without making it clear to the participant just what it is they are seeking.

- *The researcher monopolises interpretation* Ultimately, it is the researcher who is responsible for the interpretation of the data which the interview provides. The interviewee supplies the material for the analysis or interpretation but contributes nothing else to the process unless the study involves respondent validation.

Inducements to encourage participation

There are a number of ethical considerations which result from offering money or other incentives to potential participants as an inducement to and a reward for becoming a participant in a research study. These include the following:

- Rewards in terms of money or gifts to research participants should be small. Payments can be more than inducements to give up a little time; if they are too large they consequently may be coercive. Large rewards may make it virtually impossible for an impecunious participant to say no. Research guidelines do not stipulate what would be a reasonable reward though some institutions may set limits. One formula for rewarding modestly might be to pay out-of-pocket expenses for items such as bus or train fares to get to the research site plus a small amount of money, paid on an hourly basis, to recompense a little for lost time. Generally, researchers tend to prefer not to pay research participants but sometimes there may be a case for doing so. There is the negative consequence that paying participants might set up an expectation that they always should be paid. Where a researcher cannot afford to pay because they have no relevant funding, this ethos would make for difficulties. Student researchers, of course, probably do not have the financial resources to make any payments to participants in research.

- While this is probably uncommon, from time to time the inducement of professional psychological services are offered as a way of encouraging research participation. Of course, it is assumed that the service provider should be competent to deliver these services. So this would not apply to student researchers because they lack the competence to offer such services. An example of such services offered as an inducement would be counselling. If services are offered, the ethical guidelines advise that the exact nature of the services and the limitations on the provision of these services (e.g. the number of counselling sessions offered) should be given to the potential participants. Furthermore, any risks associated with the psychological service should be clarified.

Box 17.6 discusses some of the practical details associated with the use of inducements in qualitative research.

Box 17.6

PRACTICAL ADVICE

Inducement issues in qualitative research

Although conventionally the issue of inducements in research is put forward as if it were one of the researchers paying to encourage people to participate in their research, there is another aspect which can be overlooked. Participants in research may have expectations of the research in terms of pay-offs for them which were not intended and cannot be met by the researcher. For example, in Howitt (1992) the participants sometimes agreed to be interviewed because of an expectation that the researcher might be able to do something to help them with the false accusations of child abuse that the research was about.

Some participants were under the impression that the researcher was in a position of some power with regard to this. He was not. Of course, it would be wrong to let participants in such research volunteer in the expectation that there would be such a pay-off. A different version of this problem, from his case studies, is exemplified by the parents who clearly admitted sexual abuse of their child but expected, from taking part in the research, some vindication of what they did. Again this is a motive coming from the participant which was not encouraged by the researcher and with which the researcher could not collude.

Debriefing as ethics and methodology

Irrespective of the nature of research, during the final stages debriefing of the participants should take place. Debriefing ideally should involve both the researcher and the research participant in a 'mutual' discussion of the nature of the research, the results of the research, and the conclusions from the research as far as possible. Obviously the debriefing may take place long before any definitive research conclusions are available. One strategy to overcome this is to prepare a summary of the research and its findings for circulation to the participants at a later stage. During the debriefing session itself, the researcher should seek to identify and correct any misconceptions that the participant may have developed about various aspects of the research. There are sometimes good scientific, academic or humane reasons for withholding certain information – or alternatively postponing the main debriefing for a more suitable occasion.

There may be other reasons for a two-stage debriefing process – for example, the research may involve two or more data-gathering stages separated by a considerable period of time. Too much information at the end of the first stage may risk unduly influencing the data which the participant contributes at the later stages of the research.

If one regards debriefing as a method of dealing with ethical issues then this is to ignore its other important functions. Debriefing is the stage at which the researcher learns about the research from the viewpoint of the participant. Properly, the debriefing phase should involve the taking of careful notes since in a sense it is still data – and this is especially so for qualitative research with its emphasis on rich data. The debriefing may enrich the interpretation of the main data in any sort of research and should be considered an essential component of research studies.

Of course, issues may be raised during the debriefing which suggest that there was harm done to the participant in the research as a consequence of deception (or other features of the study for that matter). Reasonable efforts should be made to deal with any such harm which is identified during the course of the debriefing. Researchers, and especially student researchers, do not have the appropriate counselling skills to deal with significant distress. So the researcher should have appropriate courses of action for the participant so that they may contact a relevant professional who should be able to deal with this matter. Helplines and other facilities may be appropriate when the distress is caused by things such as interviewing about intrinsically distressing matters such as abortion, drugs and mental health issues. Similar helpline details are often given by the media when emotive topics are featured on television, for example. There has been research on the effectiveness of debriefing (e.g. Epley & Huff, 1998; Smith & Richardson, 1983) and it seems clear that debriefing may be insufficient to deal with the effects of deception.

The ethics of report writing and publication

The ethical concerns of research do not end with the debriefing of participants following data collection. There are a number of ethical issues which arise in relation to publishing the data which should be noted.

Ethical standards in reporting research

The fabrication of data is ethically wrong and this applies to students as well as professional researchers. There will be circumstances in which a researcher realises that there are errors in the data analysis which they have published journal articles about. This can be achieved by printing corrections or retractions in the journal where the research was first published. Occasionally more malicious circumstances arise. Many years ago, I was part of a team which employed a particular interviewer. Sometime later, a friend of this interviewer told me that some of the interviews had been fabricated. Fortunately, the research team had already identified that this interviewer's data were systematically different from those of the other interviewers and excluded it from the analysis, though, of course, we were not able to show that it had been fabricated. Thus falsification may occur at different stages in the research process.

Plagiarism

Plagiarism occurs when someone takes the work of another person without properly acknowledging its source and gives the impression that it is their own work. Psychologists should not plagiarise and the same should be true of psychology students. Merely citing the source of the material is not sufficient to avoid the charge of plagiarism in circumstances where a large chunk of someone else's work is reproduced. Material that you have quoted directly should be identified using quotation marks and, of course, the pages from which the quotation was taken given in the citation.

In student work, plagiarism may result in firm disciplinary action by their university which, if it is extreme or persistent, may cost a student their degree. Similarly, at the professional level, there may be profound consequences in cases of plagiarism. A famous TV psychiatrist in the UK, Raj Persaud, was suspended by the medical profession for undermining public confidence in his profession through dishonest conduct after he was found guilty of plagiarising the work of others in his publications (MailonLine, 2008).

Making data available for verification

Once your analysis of the data has been published then the data themselves should be available for checking by those competent to do so. This is not for the purpose of giving other people the opportunity to take your data and publish it in some other form. To do this would require your agreement. Making the data available is a way of allowing the claims of the original researcher to be validated. The person wishing to check the data may be required to meet the cost of supplying the data in a verifiable form. Of course, the data should not be made available if by doing so the confidentiality of the source (i.e. their anonymity) might be compromised. Also, and this may happen with funded research, the data may not be made available to other researchers if a third party has proprietorial rights over the data.

It is worth noting that the typical qualitative research paper gives more access to the data than does the typical quantitative research paper which supplies only summary tables and other output. Remember that one should get the signed permission of the participant to distribute the data to the wider research community.

Appropriate credit for authorship of publications

A psychologist should not stake a claim for authorship of a publication to which they have not contributed substantially. The authorship of a publication should start with the individual who has contributed most to the publication and end with the person who has contributed least but nevertheless substantially enough. Senior membership of a research organisation in itself does not warrant inclusion in the list of authors – this is determined by the responsibility that the individual carries for doing the research and writing it up. Those who made a minor contribution may be acknowledged in a footnote. It does not merit a position in the list of authors. Publications which originated out of student dissertations usually ought to give credit to the student as the first (principal) author.

Repeated publication of the same data

It is not proper to publish the same data in several publications. If, for some reason it is done, then the fact that this was originally published elsewhere should be acknowledged in later publications.

The Internet raises special issues which are dealt with in Box 17.7.

Box 17.7

PRACTICAL ADVICE

Ethics and qualitative research on the Internet

Qualitative researchers are attracted to the Internet partly because it is a rich source of text of all sorts in a readily accessible digital form. For example, email not only is a rich source of modern communications but is governed by its own stylistic rules. This interest brings with it ethical issues which are different from those of mainstream research. There are available research ethics for conducting research on the Internet. The British Psychological Society has guidelines for conducting research on the Internet:

www.bps.org.uk/sites/default/files/documents/
conducting_research_on_the_internet-guidelines_
for_ethical_practice_in_psychological_research_
online.pdf

While these are not specific to qualitative research, R. L. Shaw (2008) sees some vital ethical issues in them from the point of view of qualitative researchers.

Verification of participant's identity

There are clearly problems verifying the identity of people on the Internet. For example, chatrooms and discussion forums do not identify contributors other than with what is likely to be an alias. What, for example, if an identity on the Internet appears to be that of a child but, in reality, it is a paedophile pretending to be a child either for purposes of enacting fantasy or to groom a child? What legitimate use could the researcher put the data to? The Internet could be used to contact individuals in order, say, to obtain some demographic information but, of course, that information itself cannot be further verified. Other forms of data collected from the Internet – such as online research questionnaires – may have exactly the same limitations. The culture of masking one's identity on the Internet may increase the likelihood that bogus identities are used even though they may be presented as genuine. This is, naturally, a possibility in other forms of research but face-to-face contact reduces the risk of misleading information. However, as identity is increasingly seen as not a fixed matter but situation specific (e.g. one's identity at work may be very different from one's identity at home) then because a virtual identity is different from a day-to-day identity then there is a sense in which this issue does not matter. There is no reason why a qualitative researcher should not be interested in Internet behaviour in its own right without its reflecting some other aspect of a person's identity although the interplay between the two is of interest.

The Internet: is it a public or a private space?

Although it is clear that in many instances, the Internet is treated as a public space by Internet users and they expect their contributions to be disseminated with few limitations, there may be some circumstances in which the Internet user may believe that their communications are private and will not be published. Shaw argues that such users are few in number as most are well aware of the possibility that their contributions will be distributed. There are a number of questions then that need to be asked including:

* Can all information obtained from the Internet be properly regarded as public information?
* If the researcher participates in a chatroom, just how does the issue of informed consent apply to material obtained in this way?

Confidentiality

There may be limitations on a researcher's ability to keep Internet and email information confidential. One reason for this is that the source website may store information about its members and link this to unsecured email content. Similarly, care is needed not to link material used in research to the person's log-in ID which may then, inadvertently on the researcher's part, allow tracking using search engines, etc.

Informed consent

Shaw points out that it is possible for an Internet researcher to set up a special chatroom for the purposes of research which is password protected and the participants indicate their willingness for their material to be included in the research. They could even ask questions about the research before committing themselves to it as in regular informed consent. Unfortunately, this is not the sort of naturalistic data favoured by most qualitative researchers. So is it acceptable for researchers to use material routinely published on the Internet for their research? For Shaw, this is largely not a problem since she says that such individuals have already given their consent for their contributions to be published. However, would it be correct to suggest that such individuals were happy to have their words subjected to psychological interpretations which then are also published, albeit in a research journal?

Debriefing procedures and the Internet

Of course, debriefing individuals contributing freely to the Internet but essentially anonymously is as difficult as raising issues of their identity with them. However, it is a different matter when a researcher is using an online questionnaire. It can be argued that in these circumstances an automatic debriefing should be incorporated in the researcher's questionnaire design. This debriefing could appear on the screen once the participant has submitted their completed questionnaire and also if they terminate their involvement before the questionnaire has been fully completed. The debriefing information could include standard debriefing information such as how the data may be withdrawn, contact information should this be necessary, an explanation of what will be done with the data, a fuller account of what the research was about, and so forth.

CONCLUSION

Ethical principles should be applied at every stage of a research study. The requirement for fidelity would cover the literature review just as much as the treatment of the data. Ethical principles are broad-brush tools which could never cover every little detail of all types of research. They are principles to be used with care and with sensitivity. Ethics go beyond methodology in the sense that they link with the wider context of research and impose duties on the research community which need to be undertaken seriously, thoroughly and thoughtfully. Research ethics are not for the individual researcher alone – they involve all of the psychological community and colleagues of active researchers, in particular. Except in the simplest of cases, there is every reason to go to colleagues, lecturers and professors for ethical advice. The overwhelming majority of research which is planned by students presents few ethical challenges but that does not mean that problems never arise. Relatively routine issues such as confidentiality and the secure storage of data would be characteristic of the main areas where the student needs to pay careful attention. Their lecturers and supervisors should take an active interest in the ethical aspects of their research. Not all ethical problems are apparent before the start of a research study and some vigilance is required in order to identify any which emerge in the course of the research.

Ethical principles involve an element of judgement in day-to-day research situations. Any student who wants hard-and-fast rules does not fully understand the nature of ethics. Take a situation which may arise quite commonly in qualitative research where participants may answer a wide variety of questions asked by the researcher or may choose to mention things which might not have been mentioned outside the research context. Although causing distress in research is largely to be avoided, according to ethical principles, there will be occasions when participants agree to take part in research knowing the nature of the research but then talk about things which upset them. For example, paedophiles interviewed about their offending behaviour may freely agree to take part in research fully understanding the sorts of issues that the researcher will ask about. The offender may weep because they cannot cope with the nature of their offence. Simply because the offender is upset does not make the research unethical. The offender's distress would be acceptable to most psychologists if the research has potential social benefits or is important for some other reason.

Of course, there are circumstances where factors such as the triviality of the research's purpose would make the creation of similar levels of distress unacceptable. For example, it would be wrong to interview people about their sexual abuse as a child simply as part of a study of the influence of interviewing style on the amount of information generated. The means are not justified by the ends, in this case.

Ethics in relation to qualitative psychological research have yet to be fully charted. The complex relationships between qualitative researchers and their research participants may mean that new ethical issues emerge which are uncharacteristic of those which apply to quantitative studies. Group interviews and group observation methods present ethical challenges for research which have no exact parallels in quantitative work.

KEY POINTS

- Qualitative research differs from quantitative research in its orientation to those who participate in a research study. Qualitative research values the person as an entirety. The ethical problems which arise in qualitative research can, therefore, be very different from those which arise in quantitative research. Some of these issues are not obvious from standard research ethics and require the active vigilance of the researcher.

- The ethical environment in which research takes place is complex and includes bureaucratic elements. It is no longer the case that researchers simply have to be aware of the ethical standards expected from them as members of an academic discipline. Generally, the formal seeking of ethical approval is a key part of any research project. Ethics are not an afterthought but integral to effective planning of research.

- Psychological ethics are based on broad principles rather than prescribed behaviours. As a consequence, the consideration of the ethical aspects of research is an active part of its planning.

- Ethical issues may have to be revisited in light of what happens in the course of the research. Because qualitative methods are extremely variable in nature, the qualitative researcher needs to be extra vigilant and avoid complacency.

Box 17.8

ILLUSTRATIVE RESEARCH STUDY

Micro-ethics in qualitative research:
stuck between research participants

Research ethics tends to dwell on the researcher–participant relationship but the models of research in qualitative research methods can be somewhat more demanding. What about research situations in which a researcher studies both partners in a couple? What problems does this create? Forbat and Henderson (2003) report how one of them interviewed a 'fictionalised' couple, Andy and Bella, about their relationship. Bella has health issues and Andy is her carer. While one partner was being interviewed, the other would keep out of the way and vice versa. This care relationship was undergoing problems and the interviewer feared that violence might be involved. Andy told the interviewer about a particularly 'tense' episode in their relationship. One dilemma for the interviewer was whether to raise this incident with Bella. The ethics of this are somewhat uncertain since just what is the meaning of confidentiality in the context? For example, would it be right to publish Andy's version of the truth alongside Bella's version?

There are a number of ethically-based dilemmas which are inherent in the situation just described:

- **Conflict of interest** Andy and Bella may have different expectations of what the research was about. For Andy it may be to communicate the difficulties of the caring relationship whereas for Bella it may be to communicate the loving nature of their relationship. Similarly, the interest of the researcher in the research might be to fulfil quite a different purpose.

- **Imbalance** The researcher may have a preference for one particular viewpoint in the situation. Given that Bella represents a group of people who have rarely had a 'voice' in society then the researcher might prefer to present things from the point of view of the most disempowered person in the relationship. Forbat and Henderson argue that partiality is likely in these situations and this needs to be acknowledged in the write-up. Not to do so is to engage in the sort of power relationship which characterises a great deal of quantitative research. If qualitative researchers wish to employ more egalitarian approaches in which participants in research are 'partners' with the researcher in the research process then it is important to acknowledge this partiality.

- *Taking sides* The researcher might be expected to take sides in the situation by Andy and Bella. While it is important to avoid doing so, what this means is that information from interviews with one of the partners must not spill over into the interviews with the other partner. Will there be a process of sharing the transcripts, for example? This clearly entails some discussion between the researcher and the couple being interviewed about how this issue is to be managed and contained.

- *Intrusion* Research on two participants can be much more intrusive into their relationship than research involving just one partner. A reasonable policy would be one of 'non-disclosure' but this would have to be agreed by all involved. This might be dealt with simply by one of the partners withdrawing from the study if things got uncomfortable. However, in a relationship

situation this may not be quite so easy as it might at first appear. What was it about the situation which led the other partner to withdraw? Had they something to hide? Just how would it be explained to their partner? So the freedom to withdraw in this case is constrained in these circumstances.

- *Influence* In the dyadic research, the first partner to raise a particular issue is having a disproportionate influence on the way that things proceed. There is a possibility that the particular subject matter was introduced by one of the partners with the expectation that it would be raised with the other partner or even in the hope that the researcher will take sides on the issue. So, there are problems about whether to raise the issue with the other partner.

- *Disseminating results* Ethical problems arise in a number of ways in respect of publication. First of all, confidentiality becomes more problematic when more than one partner is interviewed since there is extra information which may make it easier for the partners to be identified by others. But there is another problem – if quotes are given from both partners in a publication then each partner would find it far easier to identify what the other partner had said during the interview.

ADDITIONAL RESOURCES

Brinkmann, S., & Kvale, S. (2008). Ethics in qualitative psychological research. In C. Willig & W. Stainton-Rogers (Eds.), *The SAGE hand-book of qualitative research in psychology* (pp. 263–279). London: Sage.

Brown, L. S. (1997). Ethics in psychology: cui bono? In D. Fox and I. Prilleltensky (Eds.), *Critical psychology: An introduction* (pp. 51–67). London: Sage.

Economic and Social Research Council. (n.d.). Research Ethics Framework. http://www.esrc.ac.uk/about-esrc/information/framework-for-research-ethics/index.aspx (accessed 12 September 2015).

This contains a number of case studies useful for qualitative researchers as well as an ethical checklist. It may be of greatest interest to PhD students since their work may well be supported by the ESRC.

Mauthner, M., & Birch, M. (2002). *Ethics in qualitative research*. London: Sage.

Roth, W.-M. (2004). Qualitative research and ethics. *Forum: Qualitative Social Research*, 5(2), Article 7. www.qualitative-research.net/index.php/fqs/article/view/614/1331 (accessed 12 September 2015).

This discusses ethical problems stemming from the close relationship between researcher and participants in qualitative research.

CHAPTER 18

Examples of qualitative report writing: learning the good and bad points

Overview

- This chapter presents a number of write-ups of a variety of qualitative research methods as a way of helping improve qualitative report writing.

- The chapter encourages the reader to consider the general ethos of qualitative report writing, to be familiar with the specific epistemology of their chosen methods, to avoid positivistic assumptions except where appropriate, to check the local requirements for the reports such as word length, etc., to take care that illustrative examples actually do make the point intended, and to read and model their work on the style of good and appropriate qualitative reports.

- Three examples of qualitative reports are presented based on the analytic methods of conversation analysis, interpretative phenomenological analysis and thematic analysis.

- The reports contain numbers in superscript form. These refer to the list of critical comments (positive and negative) that is to be found at the end of each chapter.

- There is at least as much to be learnt from the good things identified in the reports as there is through the mistakes and other suboptimal material noted.

Introduction

Since writing is inherently far from easy, everyone needs help in writing a report. This is true for quantitative reports and perhaps a little more so for qualitative write-ups. Partly the problem is the exacting standards required for citations and references. Having to write to a word limit is also not the most straightforward business. What does one include, what does one exclude? Most students will probably have completed assignments using quantitative methods and, as a consequence, should have a reasonable idea about the technicalities involved – what an abstract should be like, how to cite publications which support your argument, how to do a reference list, and what to put in the introduction, method section and discussion for example. The task for your first and subsequent qualitative assignment is to take the skills that you have learnt previously and apply them to the new context. You have been helped in this by the general if not perfect consensus that a qualitative report in psychology follows the structure of the quantitative report as far as possible. It may need slight adaptation but generally very little. This is really important because qualitative reports in other disciplines vary markedly in style from one another and the lack of a standard structure is not helpful to students. Although modifying the standard psychology report structure may be perfectly acceptable, it can feel a little scary departing from guidelines no matter how flexible. One is, after all, moving out of one's comfort zone.

Perhaps more so than quantitative reports, qualitative report writing calls for good quality writing skills. This is partly because many components of qualitative psychology need care and precision when you write about them. Providing interpretations, for example, of what is happening in a conversation can demand adroit descriptions which tax our language skills. Some ideas, after all, are hard to put into words. We also need to be very precise as to what we mean. Not only that, many qualitative writings are challenging to understand on first reading and may use language which is not as clear as it could be. The number of new words and concepts can also be demanding. You should not emulate any of this and you should be as clear as possible. As the report is what you will get graded on primarily, it makes sense to devote a great deal of your available time to writing the report. For many this will involve a repeated process of drafting and redrafting. It is also desirable to allow time for a word-by-word slow reading of your text. It is very easy to get a sentence or even a paragraph out of order which makes your ideas difficult to decipher. It is equally easy to include superfluous sentences which interrupt the reader's flow. In a slow reading, where you take note of what has already been written and make sure that things are not repeated later on, you should pick up most of these problems. In this way you can also make sure that the flow of the argument is sequential.

It is not the intention to summarise all of the advice given elsewhere in this book. Nevertheless we do need to stress that writing up a qualitative report well tends to involve better quality writing skills. This is not surprising as you are dealing with complex ideas and not everyone (if anyone) finds this easy. But practice will make this better. That different people will begin with different levels of writing ability is hardly surprising. So it will take time for some to catch up with the best. It will happen but it does not come easily. Simply being able to write in other words the essence of what your research participants have said to you – that is, present the gist of their comments – is an example of why better writing skills are helpful. Qualitative methods tend to originate in a human science background science background which typically uses more complex writing styles than scientific writing. So the more you practise, rewrite and review your qualitative write-up the better.

The following are some of the important points when preparing a qualitative report:

- You need to remember the general ethos of qualitative research and your specific qualitative method in particular. Qualitative methods are not all the same! Some are closely related but others far apart, so you need to understand the epistemological basis of your chosen analytic method. For example, how acceptable is it to combine your chosen qualitative approach with findings from quantitative research? Researchers using methods such as interpretative phenomenological analysis, thematic analysis and grounded theory are particularly open to contributions from research. Others, such as discourse analysis, narrative analysis and conversation analysis, would exhibit more suspicion about such imports. There are other matters to consider, such as when the literature review is carried out. There are no hard and fast rules but not all methods assume that research ideas are generated by the research review and tested in the research. In grounded theory and conversation analysis, for example, there are researchers who suggest that the literature review should be carried out after the data analysis has been completed. Primarily this guards against the analysis being guided by previous research.

- You will probably need to write more about the basic principles of your chosen qualitative method than one normally would when writing a quantitative report. One reason for this is that some readers may not be fully familiar with your chosen method, so you need to present some background. Just how long into the future this situation will prevail is difficult to say but, for now, you probably need to make space for a description of your methodology. This could include an explanation of why you chose one qualitative methodology rather than another. The other reason is to do with procedural 'oddities' in qualitative methods in the eyes of those who are more quantitatively orientated. For example, sampling really needs careful explanation in qualitative write-ups because sampling can mean something very different from its use in quantitative research. Rarely in qualitative research is 'representative' sampling employed. Sampling is more likely to be about the variety of positions than the mean on some sort of scale. Sampling is more likely to be about the variety of participants than the mean on some sort of measure. It is generally purposive in qualitative research and the purpose of your particular sampling should be explained. Your description of your sample should be as precise as possible and may include anonymised pocket descriptions of each of the individuals taking part in your study. Sample size is also differently applied in qualitative research compared with quantitative. For example the idea of 'theoretical saturation' tells the qualitative researcher when to stop collecting data. This concept, taken from grounded theory, indicates a point at which no new ideas or further clarification relating to the topic under research are being achieved from the data. Sample size, therefore, is not a matter of statistical estimation in qualitative research – which should come as no surprise.

- You would expect, of course, to avoid positivistic assumptions in your qualitative write-up. Make sure to avoid 'inappropriate' language. Writing about independent variables, dependent variables, cause and effect, stimulus and response, intervening variables and the like is to be questioned: these either have no meaning in qualitative research or have such a special meaning that they should be routinely avoided or discussed in a great deal of detail. The literature on qualitative methods does involve some discussion of the use of these concepts and some qualitative methods, such as grounded theory, may involve past quantitative work as part of theory development. However, this is by no means the case with all qualitative methods so the use of such concepts should be carefully examined.

- The use of frequencies, percentages and the like should not be automatically ruled out in your qualitative write-up. However, this should be done, if it is done at all, with caution as, for obvious reasons, quantification is not a primary objective of qualitative research. Things which occur the most frequently in a qualitative analysis may not be the most important aspect of the analysis. Unusual aspects of the data may be analytically more interesting. Things which appear not to fit in with the broad trends in the analysis may have a lot to say to inform theory and conceptual development. It is difficult to see a role for quantification in phenomenological analysis, narrative analysis, conversation analysis and discourse analysis, but quantification may be relevant to thematic analysis and other methods in some circumstances. This is because if the researcher can identify 'themes' then it is not a big step to ask to what extent those themes are to be found in the data. The depth of the analysis is important to consider here. A superficial qualitative analysis is more likely to refer to there being many examples of Theme A, that Theme B is rare, and so forth. However, a more sophisticated analysis is likely to focus on what it theoretically or conceptually interesting. For example, if you carry out a thematic analysis and find that you are writing phrases like 'Most interviews include the fragility theme' or 'Some of the newspaper articles studied mentioned the risk of cancer' then you are implying quantities. What then is wrong with saying more about what that quantity is? If, on the other hand, you are more interested in looking for instances of engaging ideas which emerge out of the research you are much less likely to refer to quantities in any form. Instead these interesting ideas might be unusual features or exceptions to what the analysis in general seems to imply, therefore might be followed up in more depth.

- Check what the local 'rules' are for a qualitative report. These may not always be good news but they do form part of the basis of how your report will be evaluated. One of the rules may concern how qualitative data are counted in your allowed word count. Qualitative data are usually 'wordy' and so if the data you include in your report are counted as part of the word count then the write-up becomes harder. Similarly, appendices can be a way of including extensive qualitative data without affecting the word count. You need to check whether they can be used in this way and if there are any limits. Ask for clarification if issues like this are not clear in local documentation such as that distributed by the professor in charge of the module. Make sure that you understand just what rules apply. Is there a maximum length for the abstract, for instance?

- Very often in qualitative reports, it is not possible to give more than a few indicative samples of the data analysis. This is because the description of the analysis can eat up the word count even if the data are not included in that count. Such illustrative examples are routine in qualitative reports but you need to be very careful to make sure that your illustrative examples are that. It is easy to give, say, an illustration of text which represents a theme in the data according to you which does not appear so to the reader. The reason may be to do with problems with your analysis, of course, but do not compound your problems in your selection of illustrative material. It may be easy to sort out the problem – e.g., you may need to develop the description of the theme better – but nevertheless be very careful.

- Read and model your work on appropriate qualitative reports. You would not expect to direct a Hollywood blockbuster if you had never seen a movie! We all learn from others. Finding published reports along the lines of your qualitative study can be enormously helpful in providing a guide to writing your own study. We are not talking plagiarism here, of course, which will get you in a whole heap of trouble. We are talking about learning from the style, structure and general qualities of published research. Very often such a model can also be used to check how to cite references in the text and present them in the reference list. Basically, this means that you are reading a little more widely than you otherwise would. It cannot be emphasised too much that the basic academic method starts with the work of others. Professional researchers will avidly read pertinent material. It is a priority. There are no shortcuts in the long run and the sooner you start reading beyond what is immediately demanded the more quickly your work will improve.

- You almost certainly will have fewer words available to you than you need when writing your report. Consequently choices will have to be made. Make sure that your stronger material is well to the fore. If you have to cut down on length and cannot achieve this by careful rewriting, give preference to the stronger bits of your argument, etc. and keep any weak, ordinary or mundane text to a minimum.

Examples of qualitative reporting writing

In this chapter you will find several qualitative research reports written in a style more or less appropriate to student work. There is such a range of different qualitative techniques with somewhat different requirements that it is not really possible to give a single, generic example of a qualitative write-up. Instead, several write-ups are provided involving different qualitative methods. The write-ups are not intended to be perfect and from time-to-time rather dubious passages are included as well as more exemplary ones. For example, you might notice a range of typographical and punctuation errors, which tend to be common within student work. The references have been omitted to save space, but should be given at the end of a report. You will see numbers in superscript form in various places in the reports. After each write-up there is a list of good and bad points. Each point is identified with a corresponding numerical superscript. The general strategy has been to present the better reports earlier so that they get progressively worse as you go through the chapter. Each of the reports is fictitious in most respects. Each one is based with varying degrees of closeness on a published study. Probably most of the credit for the good bits goes to the original authors. The deliberate bad bits are my work. You will also find some good and some bad bits which I do not identify. Report writing is not a science but an art or skill involving a lot of points at which judgement has to be employed. Of course, the word length of the report could be varied up or down if necessary.

Example 1: Writing up a thematic analysis

This example is based on Sawkhill, Sparkes and Brown (2012) *A thematic analysis of causes attributed to weight gain: A female slimmer's perspective.* Features of their introduction, method, analysis and discussion have been incorporated in an adapted form together with additional material. Health-related issues are a dominant theme in a lot of qualitative research. Understanding how people perceive weight gain may have implications for the treatment of weight issues in the health sphere. Read through the report critically (looking for both good and bad things) and then compare what you have noted with the criticisms provided at the end. Your thoughts may be equally valid.

ILLUSTRATIVE EXAMPLE OF A QUALITATIVE RESEARCH REPORT

Explanations of personal weight gain: a thematic analysis of semi-structured interviews with slimmers[1]

Annabelle Hopkins

Abstract

As an issue for health psychology, overweightness has links with a variety of theoretically important approaches. Among these are feminism, Foucauldian theory and medicalisation. In modern medical thinking, overweightness defined in terms of obesity is an established risk factor for cancer, heart disease, premature death and so forth. Although obesity in itself is not a disease state in any meaningful sense it is treated as an undesirable risk condition. Their obesity is held to be the individual's responsibility as is the reduction of the risk. Other discourses apply, of course, such as youth and attractiveness. Consumer spending on slimming aids amounted to $33 billion a year and $55 billion a year for weight loss services in 2008 in the USA. Being overweight or obese are lay and medical terms respectively. Obesity is a technical concept defined in medical terms by various measures such as body mass index. Although medical treatments in the form of gastric band surgery are available, more routinely nutrition and exercise are the individual's chosen remedies.

Failure to maintain any successful weight loss is very common in slimming classes. We have little research on how individuals understand weight gain. The available research is almost exclusively quantitative in nature. The present study offers an explorative qualitative approach to perceptions of weight gain to enhance our understanding. Semi-structured interviews were carried out with a total of ten female adult slimming class attendees. A wide range of issues potentially related to weight gain were included.[2]

Introduction

Being underweight has been a major issue in psychological research of all sorts – anorexia nervosa, bulimia nervosa and similar conditions have been extensively researched[3] – less so overweight. Certain conceptualisations of the human body tend to dominate modern thinking. Others tend to be ignored. There is an inclination to regard issues to do with the human body as being medical in nature. Medicalisation is the term for this. However, it is important to note its meaning has changed some-what in modern usage since it was first introduced. Originally the term referred to the way in which ostensibly social problems such as drug and alcohol dependency began to be construed through a medical lens as if they were disease states (Howitt, 1992). Recent usage of the term refers to the general and increasing role of medicine in many aspects of our lives and the more generally medical viewpoint imposed by this (Nye, 2003). Although not a disease in itself, the risk state of obesity becomes to be seen as if it were a disease to be treated. In the modern medical model, the individual has a responsibility to deal with the risk. It is difficult when discussing overweight not to slip into the medical terminology of obesity and the consequent implications of this rather than fatness or plumpness. Obesity we will consider as clinically defined in terms of body mass ratio and refer to overweight in preference wherever appropriate.

Obesity poses not just a risk to the individual but to health services themselves who may not be able to cope. Health statistics suggest that 24 per cent of UK adults met the criteria for obesity (National Health Service Information Centre, 2010). This is dramatised by the view that obesity in children is rising statistically and that obese children become obese adults. Economic consequences of seemingly staggering proportions are attached to obesity, including the costs – economic and otherwise – for the health service (Fullfact, 2011). Obesity is presented as a growing threat to health globally (World Health Organization, 2006). An important consideration in the present research is the extent to which weight gain is viewed from a medicalised perspective.[4]

If we knew more about how people see weight gain then this may feed into the guidance available to weight management services (Butland et al., 2007). Redressing energy imbalance is the focus of most weight management programmes currently available. Such programmes may be jeopardised if there is a clash between their ethos and the individual's belief system. Eating less may not be so easy if the individual was brought up to believe that wasting food is wicked, for example. Illnesses impact on people's lives and they seek to attribute causes when they try to understand and explain these illnesses (Brogan & Levy, 2009). Depending a little on the particular illness in question, as many as 95 per cent of people attribute causes to them.

Even their coping processes are affected by their beliefs and this impacts subsequent behaviour too (Warmsteker et al., 2005). They also have beliefs about how their condition may be cured/treated and there are ties between these and the causes attributed to the condition (Ogden & Flanagan, 2008). This is a fairly complex process and there is no simple mechanical relationship which applies universally – consistency and inconsistency may both be seen. Someone believing in a medical cause of weight gain may link this with a medical solution such as gastric bands. Nevertheless, someone believing themselves to be personally responsible for their weight gain may also see as the solution some form of medical intervention (Ogden, 2007).

Rodin et al. (1977) suggested that attribution for weight gain actually predicts weight loss and its maintenance. A dieter's self-determined weight loss target was related to their perceptions of the origins and causes of weight gain. Warmsteker et al. (2005) showed that someone attributing weight gain to physical causes would lose less weight than the person who attributed weight gain to behavioural causes. Importantly, Ogden (2000) showed that slimmers who managed to maintain their weight loss were not so likely to endorse medical causes for the overweightness. Nevertheless, Brogan and Hevey (2009) indicate that the evidence relates weight gain to behavioural themes. Various passive behaviours such as comfort eating, lower levels of physical activity and over-eating tended to interconnect in their study.[5]

More conjecturally, the research literature suggests a more social or psychological aspect to weight gain than superficially explained by genetics and a simple lack of self-control. Child obesity is increasing at a rapid rate and this ties in with the idea that insecure attachment in childhood relates to eating problems (Ward, Ramsay, & Treasure, 2000) and mood linked overeating in adulthood (Buckroyd & Rother, 2008). There is evidence that some parents use food in a form of behavioural control over their children (Goodspeed-Grant & Boersma, 2005). Other childhood factors that may play a part in obesity are encouragement to overeat, lack of exercise, trauma and rebelling over perceived pressures towards weight control.

Despite the promising findings[6] described above, there is not an extensive corpus of research into perceptions of weight gain. The preponderance of the studies have been quantitative in nature. Qualitative research could contribute a more explorative orientation to research. A number of qualitative methods might be considered suitable for such research including interpretative phenomenological analysis, narrative analysis, social constructionist discourse analysis, and conversation analysis. Each of these would offer different things in terms of scope and emphasis. For example, there is in conversation analysis/discourse analysis a tradition of the study of interaction at family mealtimes which may be relevant (e.g. Wiggins, 2013). However, the present study was more concerned with the various ways in which weight-gain is conceptualised by slimmers. Thematic analysis was regarded as the appropriate strategy as it has no epistemological tensions with the nature of the interview data that were being collected in the research. So the present study set out with the intention of exploring slimmer's attitudes to weight gain as assessed through semi-structured interviewing.[7] The present study was designed to contribute further to our understanding of issues which may have a bearing on the management of weight gain. The research was planned in the hope of developing our understanding of the influences on weight gain. It may have some potential as a basis for future research and practical applications in weight management.

Materials and methods[8]

Participants

Adult females attending a slimming club in the vicinity of the University of Nuneaton constituted the participant group. Slimming club members can be seen as a self-selected group with weight difficulties. A number of organisers of slimming clubs agreed to help in participant recruitment. They made an opportunity to explain the purpose of the research to their members and were supplied with written notes to help them do this.[9] Members of the slimming club were asked to volunteer to take part in the study. Participation was voluntary. Those who expressed interest were provided with written details of the research and asked to telephone the researcher's university telephone number for more information. Those who did were given additional details and their questions answered. Following this, the researcher discussed possible interview arrangements with them. They could

be interviewed either at the university in a private office or at the slimming club premises. Those who agreed to the interview were telephoned up to three times in the two days before the interview to confirm the arrangements. There was a substantial number of no shows for the interview ($N = 9$) despite this. One volunteer withdrew at this stage as she had thought about the matter and felt that the reasons for her weight-gain were too private and personal to be discussed with the interviewer. In total, ten females aged between 31 and 63 years of age participated in the research. Most were in or were retired from professional occupations ($N = 6$) and the rest were in clerical or manual occupations ($N = 4$). There were no participants who were not in paid employment. Recruitment to the study was terminated at the point that theoretical saturation was reached (Glaser & Strauss, 1967). Essentially this refers to the stage at which the researcher finds that nothing new is being achieved conceptually/analytically by the collection of further data. All of the data were conducted by the researcher and so theoretical saturation was relatively easy to identify. Details of the participants are to be found in Table 18.1.

Procedure

All of the interviews were conducted by the author on a one-to-one basis to ensure maximum familiarity with the material throughout the analysis process. Each interview was digitally recorded using a professional quality audio recorder. Two microphones were used for each recording. The locations of the interviews varied and effort was made to ensure that the recordings were of a clear quality and easily transcribed. The length of the interviews varied from 35 to 67 minutes. The participants were encouraged to speak freely at all stages of the research and the researcher conducted the interviews in a friendly and supportive manner, asked points for clarification wherever necessary, and occasionally took brief written notes. The semi-structured interview covered the following areas which were based on the available research literature together with additional ideas developed in discussions between the researcher and her supervisor: daily lifestyle behaviour; the role of fast food chains, media and supermarkets; biological/medical factors; and life experiences in relation to obesity.[11]

TABLE 18.1 Summary of participant details[10]

Participant	Gender	Age	Married/partner	Children	Occupation
Lisa	female	31	Yes	2	manual
Jean	female	42	No	1	clerical
Penny	female	58	No	2	professional
Tracey	female	67	Yes	2	retired professional
Jean	female	35	Yes	0	professional
Pat	female	45	Yes	0	clerical
Nathalie	female	39	No	3	professional
Hilary	female	61	Yes	2	retired professional
Sue	female	46	Yes	2	manual
Norma	female	42	Yes	0	professional

Ethics and data protection

All participants agreed to take part on the basis of informed consent. Before the start of the interview each participant read the written information form which detailed the purpose of and the procedures involved in the study. It was further explained to participants that they were free to end the interview at any stage and would be given the choice of whether or not the data should be destroyed immediately. They were then asked to sign a written consent form. No reference was made to the participant by name during the course of the interview. The recordings were identified using a code number. This made it difficult if not impossible to identify the participant from the interview recording or the transcript. The recordings were stored on CD in a locked filing cabinet. Only the researcher and her supervisor were to have access to these. Transcripts were checked through and any remaining names disguised with pseudonyms. All names given in excerpts are also fictitious. The recordings would be destroyed after the report of the study had been submitted for assessment and assessed.

A debriefing session took place immediately after each interview, giving both the researcher and the participant the opportunity to discuss issues arising from the interview, clarify procedures from that point on, and express thanks and gratitude. This varied from about 5 to 25 minutes in length.

Furthermore, the author and supervisor discussed the ethical and data protection arrangements in light of the ethical guidelines of the British Psychological Society (2010) as well as the more extensive ones of the American Psychological Association (2002) together with the Data Protection Act. This discussion informed the procedures described above. Furthermore, the research was conducted in accordance with the requirements of the Research Ethics Committee of the University of Nuneaton. A pro-forma was completed by the researcher, approved by her supervisor, and submitted to the university ethics committee via the University intranet. Since the research involved no vulnerable group, no particularly sensitive topic, and no physiological or similar procedures and did not involve any deception or withholding of information, the research met the University's ethical requirements.[12]

Analytic procedure

Thematic analysis can be either qualitative and explorative or quantitative using pre-determined, imposed coding categories. The clearest and most formal account of how to do qualitative thematic analysis remains Braun and Clarke (2006) with their inductive thematic analysis. This is informed by elements of other forms of qualitative analysis such as discourse analysis, grounded theory, conversation analysis and so forth. The basic process stresses close familiarisation with the data, the highlighting of notable features and patterns found in the text, the development of categories representative of important aspects of the data, and the repeated checking of the fit of the categories to the data. The process can be described as iterative as it involves repeated approximations until the best thematic categories have been induced by the researcher. The interviews were all transcribed verbatim by the researcher. Given the objectives of thematic analysis, it is not usual to employ any of the more formal speech transcription methods such as that of Jefferson (2004). Nevertheless, important inflexions, such as long pauses, quietly spoken passages and so forth, were noted in the transcription. In the end, these contributed nothing of significance to this particular analysis. In a departure from the Braun and Clarke (2006) procedures, the author made analytic notes as soon as practicable after each interview was completed. In each case, these notes were completed the same day.[13]

Analysis

The analysis provided four themes and these are shown in Figure 18.1.[14] It is important to note that, although each theme has been presented and

expanded upon separately, they are not mutually exclusive and interlink to varying extents. The extracts cited for the purpose of the present study include only a typical example or so of participant quotes.[15]

Theme 1: The role of habits

This refers to habitual or automatic behaviour patterns of various sorts which were held to be causes of weight gain. They were very commonly mentioned in the interviews. Within this broad category were three discrete sub-types of habitual behaviour patterns. Because of their independence and distinctiveness, these were labelled as separate sub-themes of Theme 1. Space only allows for illustrative/typifying examples to be provided.

Sub-theme 1: Factors which trigger a change in habits

Changes in personal circumstances were often perceived as being associated with weight gain. Times when the individual is vulnerable or when personal circumstances have changed are held to be responsible. Feeling not good following a failed marriage, for example, may have been dealt with through

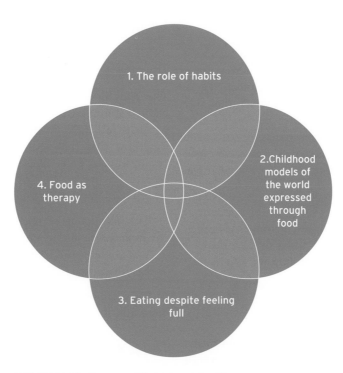

FIGURE 18.1 The themes and their interrelationships

adopting bad eating patterns such as snacking. One participant explained her weight gain in the following way:

'I lost one of my sisters and then ended up at home not able to do much because of a back injury. Eating just became a habit and before too long it occurred to me how much I liked the feeling of a full stomach' (Jean)

Sub-theme 2: Time constraints lead to bad habits

Busy modern lifestyles were seen as obstructing a positive healthy lifestyle. Shortage of time was described as a barrier to good eating and other health-related habits. Diet itself was affected but also how food is used and experienced. Modern life imposes time pressures stopping the formation of positive health habits:

'I drop the kids off at school usually at about eight in the morning and I often eat toast or something while I'm driving as everything is such a rush. Things are much the same at work. My lunch is at my computer and usually I don't stop for a proper lunch break. It's more or less a routine.' (Penny)

Sub-theme 3: Associations between passive eating patterns and behaviour

Participants often would speak of eating watching the television and not at the meal table. This pattern was seen as another weight gain mechanism. There seemed to be a symbolic element in which the table has a connection with food which no longer characterises modern life. However, other aspects of life such as engaging in social activities also encouraged habitual and unhealthy eating patterns. For example:

'It's like when you go to see a movie – you've got to have something. A big soft drink or popcorn or sweets. Someone will suggest getting something. So long as the movie isn't about to start then off somebody goes to get what folk want' (Nathalie)

Theme 2: Childhood models of the world expressed through food

The view was commonly expressed that adult eating behaviours were the result of childhood experiences. Sometimes the interviewees simply made a direct connection between the two. But others saw emotion as in various ways being responsible. For example, the way a family might express love was through food. One participant said:

'Child led feeding is not encouraged. It is mother led. It encourages the idea that eating is a good thing to do and it pleases mummy, you know "one more spoonful for mummy". We over feed our children and they grow up thinking that it is a good thing to eat' (Sue)

Another pointed out:

'There's a bit of a sort of power struggle about food between me and my daughter which you could describe as having something to do with love. After all, when I make a meal I have put loads of love into it so she grows up properly nourished. If she won't eat it then I feel like I've been rejected. So in the end I deal with that by eating the food myself' (Nathalie) [16]

In ways which are seemingly simple, childhood experiences create long-lasting beliefs. For example, eating up everything on the plate before getting up from the table feeds into ideas of what it is to be a good or a bad person even through to adulthood. Clearing the plate might be responded to with 'good girl' whereas not eating up is treated as a wicked waste and, for example, is depriving starving children in far off places of food. Meanings are assigned to food in childhood and they endure into adulthood with negative consequences.

Theme 3: Eating despite feeling full

The body does not simply switch off eating when enough food has been consumed, we also consciously feel full. A number of the participants suggested that they will continue to eat in these circumstances. Sometimes the feeling of fullness was regarded as feeling love or affection or some other emotional hunger that could not be met:

'This may not make much sense to you but my overeating was to feed a hunger through physical things. As a consequence, even when I was full of food I was not satisfied and just kept on eating' (Jean)

There are obvious links between this sort of comment and the final theme.

Theme 4: Food as therapy

Food can be used as a reward and a punishment. It can be a way of dealing with personal issues which are distressing or produce internal conflicts. In this way food is a tool for helping deal with our emotions. It seems to work so well in some cases that it becomes automatic and habituated in our behaviour yet at the same time the process is a destructive one in the longer term as a way of getting rid of unwanted feelings:

> 'We have upsetting thoughts going through our minds always though we don't try to deal with them or ask ourselves why we have these thoughts. Instead we just eat instead of thinking about these issues. Next day, of course, the thoughts and feeling are back and we are in a sort of vicious circle.' (Tracey)

On a more mundane level some participants would self-reward with food after, say, a period of hard work:

> 'I've finished doing the housework so I'll have myself a sit down in front of the television and have a cup of tea and some chocolate. I've done the housework so let's sit down and have a chocolate bar and a cup of tea and watch TV' (Lisa)

Discussion

The primary aim of this research was to better inform weight management research about the ways in which weight gain is explained by ordinary people. This is made more urgent by the increase in obesity rates and the poor success of obesity treatments in the longer term (Ogden & Flanagan, 2008). Four major themes were construed through a thematic analysis of the data. It is notable that these themes reflect largely behavioural causes to explain weight gain. Biological, genetic or medical explanations of weight gain were not apparent in the analysis. That is, there was no evidence of medicalisation in the discourse.[17] One possible explanation of this would be in keeping with the correspondence found between causes and solutions for overweight (Ogden & Flanagan, 2008). On the basis of the consistency idea, it may not be surprising then that those who believe in behavioural explanations of weight gain both attend behaviourally-based weight management programmes and also believe that weight gain is caused by behavioural factors.[18]

Theme 1 reflected a passive lifestyle associated with television watching which was evident in the findings. It also reflects previous research studies. There is a relationship between time watching television and the risk of obesity (Marshall, Biddle, Gorely, Cameron & Murdy, 2004). Energy expenditure may be lowered. Nevertheless, television advertising exposes the viewer to energy rich foods too (Medical Research Council, 2007) and may encourage their consumption. Theme 2 (childhood models of the world expressed through food) also relates to previous research. The mechanisms involved include using food to communicate affection and internalised beliefs about being good or bad developed in relation to food. Theme 3 involved eating beyond satiation. It may imply a reduced sensitivity to satiation cues though this is not clear in the interviews since the women expressed awareness of the satiation cues but nevertheless continued to eat despite this awareness. There are people with lowered sensitivity which is biologically based (Wardle, 2009). So a behavioural account may be needed in addition based on early experiences such as having to clear the plate even when full. Some participants appeared to enjoy the feeling of being full which might be equated with an emotion-related state. Rather than discomfort, feeling full is experienced as emotional comfort. For such people, talk of reduced sensitivity to satiation cues seems incorrect. Theme 4, food as therapy, shows food helping the women cope with daily life's pressures and the difficult circumstances in their lives. Food could be used to reward or punish and effectively was a self-perpetuating process. Emotions were interpreted as if they were hunger in the physical sense. If emotional hunger is starved then dieting may be a failure.

In National Health Service guidelines for obesity treatment are listed healthy eating, physical activity, drug therapy and managing comorbid factors. Causes are put down to a biomedical perspective including hypothyroidism. General Practitioners only refer obese patients for behavioural therapy in 3 per cent of cases and they are six times more likely to refer them to a dietician (18 per cent). All of this implies a medical perspective which did not manifest itself in the present interviews. There was no suggestion that the women were unaware of dietary issues, they had problems in controlling their bad eating habits, etc. There is some evidence that health professionals and members of the general public are not in accord about the causes of and solutions for obesity (Ogden & Flanagan, 2008). More personal examinations of the issues around one's weight gain problems with health professionals may result in a better match between the professional and the member of the public. Several of the women during the debriefing expressed the view that participating in the interview had made them think more about the issue. This sort of self-exploration may have implications for dealing with weight gain.

There are important limitations to the study.[19] There was no independent verification of the themes. Although this is typical of this sort of study, it ought to be asked how much the overall conclusions depend on the specific definition of each category. It might be argued that the important finding of the present study was the behavioural orientation to weight gain that permeated the interviews and consequently the themes. By sampling via slimming clubs the hope had been that participants had given the issue of weight some considerable thought. This was not apparent in all of the interviews. The procedure may have been at fault as it gave no opportunity to the participants to be aware of the interview coverage prior to the interview. That is, they had little prior opportunity to consider their replies. This could be easily corrected by providing the interview schedule earlier in the research process, though this could have other unforeseen consequences. For example, the participant may not attend the interview because the questions are too hard for them to answer, in their opinion. There was no independent evidence of the extent of the women's excess weight or their history of excess weight. Whether or not the women in question would medically be classified as obese currently or at any stage in the past may have some bearing on the value of the research findings. To concentrate on slimming clubs may consequently reflect on the nature of the themes identified. There is clearly a case for replicating the study using a bigger and more diversified group of participants. Medically obese people receiving medical treatments for their condition would be a particularly salient group to include. It would also be of interest to include adults without any weight problem in order to see how far the findings of this study would apply to them. In this way additional or modified themes may emerge. The sensitive nature of talking about weight gain may have featured strongly in the research. In particular, and in addition to the one potential participant who withdrew, there did seem to be some reluctance to take part in the study. To the extent that the personal sensitivity of the issue may have been a more general factor, then this would amount to a substantial design limitation. However, there

was no evidence of this in the debriefing sessions. If anything, the women indicated that they gained positively from the opportunity to think and talk about the issue of weight gain even though some of the issues were potentially emotional.

The broad implication of this study was to highlight the potential need to develop behaviourally-based strategies for weight loss.[20] Solutions to manage weight loss and maintenance may require additional behavioural strategies to support a reduced energy intake and increased energy expenditure model for treatment.[21]

Critical evaluation

[1]The title seems to summarise the basic research and method very succinctly. 'Perceptions' might be just better than 'Explanations'. Alternatively, the title 'A thematic analysis of personal accounts of reasons for weight gain' also seems to summarise things pretty well. A title needs to be as informative as it possibly can be.

[2]Superficially this has all of the appearances of a nicely composed abstract and seems to be a good summary. However, one thing may have struck you. The abstract summarises material which simply does not appear in the main body of the text. For example, feminism and Foucault are mentioned but not discussed in the text, so reference to them in the abstract is a little misleading as to the contents of the report proper. It is possible, of course, that they were in an earlier draft but omitted from the final one. An abstract is a short summary of the report – not the report that you might have written had you had the opportunity. Perhaps there is a little too much statistical detail for the abstract, some of which is not properly given a citation. But there is a bigger problem: the student has not given any information concerning the analytical outcomes of the research. The missing section may have been left out to keep the abstract short. An abstract should cover the main parts of the research report. The missing part might read as follows:

Four major themes were identified, all of which were broadly behavioural in nature: 1) the role of habits, 2) childhood-related models of the world expressed through food, 3) eating despite feeling full, and 4) food as therapy. There was little evidence of medicalised approaches to overweight in the interviews. In contrast, modern lifestyles and changes in personal circumstances typified the perceived reasons for weight gain. The importance of behavioural factors in weight gain should be a future research priority potentially of theoretical and practical significance.

So the abstract with the extra material is now very long at over 500 words. It is usually easy to shorten abstracts. You could try the structured abstract as in Example 3 below as this helps reduce words by reducing the continuity material in the writing. Alternatively, the following is a very much shorter version of the more comprehensive abstract, though it could be even shorter if necessary:

In modern medical thinking overweightness is often defined in terms of obesity. Although obesity in itself is not a disease state in any meaningful sense it is treated as an undesirable risk condition. A person's obesity is held to be their responsibility as is the reduction of the risk. Obesity is a technical concept defined medically in terms of body mass index. Failure to maintain any successful weight loss is very common in slimming classes. Little research is available on how people understand weight gain. The present study offers an explorative qualitative approach to perceptions of weight gain. Semi-structured interviews were carried out with ten female adult slimming class attendees. Four major behavioural themes were developed in the analysis: 1) the role of habits, 2) childhood-related models of the world expressed through food, 3) eating despite feeling full, and 4) food as therapy. There was no evidence of medicalised themes in the interviews. Modern lifestyles and changes in personal circumstances typified the perceived reasons for weight-gain. Behavioural factors in weight gain should be a priority for future research.

The effort you put into an abstract pays off as it creates a good impression and also structures the reading of the full report.

[3]This statement and the next sentence or so would seem to need a citation. Qualitative research neither encourages nor condones sloppiness in relation to the basic report writing skills such as reviewing the literature.

[4]Numerical and other quantitative research has a place in many qualitative reports. You may wish to problematise such data in a critical/evaluative way, but including relevant mainstream research findings can substantially improve the report.

[5]The student has got into a bit of a stylistic fix in this paragraph and the sentences tend to have the same structure – they begin with an author's name and say a bit about their findings. This is somewhat tedious to read. It has the bad effect of stopping the effective telling of the story about the research findings. It reads more like a series of unconnected episodes. Such a structure is very common in student work but it is best avoided. Generally it is easy to rewrite to give a better look to the writing. For example, you should find it easy to move the citations to the end of the sentence and you will find that it reads better. Make sure that you tell the story of the research as clearly as possible. One reason why students adopt this repetitive style is that they rely on very brief snippets of information from secondary sources. They contain far too little information to base one's own writing on. Either use more detailed secondary sources or go back to the originals. You will find the extra information gleaned in this way allows you to adopt a better style and tell the story in a more readable way.

[6]One of the things that you must learn to do in qualitative writing is to avoid terms which have a quantitative ring about them. 'Findings' is a good example of such a term – it implies that the analysis was merely a process of detecting what was in the real world (a quantitative concept) waiting to be found. Qualitative analysis is generally regarded as a more constructed process and needs different language from that used in the usual quantitative study. This does not mean that quantitative research merely uncovers things waiting to be uncovered, it merely means that quantitative researchers are happy to represent their activities in this way. Whether or not 'findings' is appropriate at this point will be left up to the reader. However, watch out for future recurrences where it is undesirable. The final thing that needs mentioning is, of course, that different qualitative methods have different epistemological bases so the above comment may not be universally true.

[7]Oh dear. This has dropped into positivistic language by using the term *attitude*. Furthermore, the research is not about attitudes as conventionally defined in mainstream psychology but about perceptions or experiences of weight gain.

[8]Not so important but would not 'methods' alone do here? This heading reads like it is taken from some old mainstream study.

[9]This sort of thing should go into an appendix or appendices as it is pertinent to the method. The only possible problem with this arises if wordcounts where you are studying include appendices. This is a

general call to use appendices and applies to all of the reports given in this chapter. Mostly they do not do so. Appendices allow you to be far more transparent about all aspects of your research. This may include the data and even the analytic process in detail, but do check the local rules on the use of appendices.

[10]The use of a table of participants and their details is excellent here and nearly always looks good in a qualitative report. Samples in qualitative research can be rather poorly defined otherwise. A table of participants provides the reader with a quick summary of useful details about the people in the study. It can save you word space as a consequence. If the people in the table are linked by a name/code number to the sources of the quotes/comments in the text so much the better. Except on the very rare occasion when such a table would be too large, one should always consider including one. Readers like simple tables as they find them helpful. Do not forget that qualitative research is seen as being person/participant orientated. So such a table may allow you to present your participants as more human than they would in a quantitative study. Of course, large samples may make such a table difficult to include. The reader benefits from consistent participant naming or numbering since it enables the linking of excerpts to a person and helps them understand the sample better. However, more generally it adds a human face to the write-up. Be careful of one thing though: too much detail may make the participants identifiable, so think carefully about the amount of detail to include.

[11]This is a point at which more details of the interview schedule would perhaps be helpful. An appendix giving the questions, etc. would be appropriate. This is a general point for all of the reports. You would expect a quantitative researcher to include full details of this sort and it is equally important in a qualitative report.

[12]Ethical considerations are extremely important in qualitative research. This is a thorough account of ethics for the research and one which touches on data protection, which is an important matter related to ethics. There would not appear to be any particularly difficult ethical issues in this study and the ethics section is largely confirming the stages that the research went through ethically. It might be worthwhile adding something more about the woman who decided not to participate because her reasons for weight gain were too personal for her to discuss. This sort of thing will happen occasionally in research

and is hard to anticipate. The university's ethical committee seems to have either not anticipated the possibility or thought it minor. But as far as we can see, the safeguards of the ethical arrangements had worked given the woman's decision not to take part. This ethics section covers a lot of the necessary bases and can be used as a model for any qualitative report as applicable. It is especially good that the ethical implications of the research were discussed with the student's supervisor. Ethics is not merely a matter of bureaucratic procedures. Always be aware that qualitative research can have special ethical problems which may not have parallels in quantitative studies.

[13]The student does an acceptable job of describing the mechanics of the task of generating the themes. This is presented in a workaday manner as if applying the procedure simply led to the outcome of the analysis. There seem to have been no problems or hiccups in the process. It would be better if the researcher mentioned any difficulties that she had in generating the themes. In particular, it would be good to know if the four themes were exhaustive in terms of the explanations of weight gain provided by the participants. The reader has no way of assessing this unless the student says so in the report. Having the odd one or two reasons which did not fit the analytic scheme would not be much of a problem. Perhaps one might expect one or two participants to mention things which fit none of the identified themes. Explaining that this is the case would not undermine the strengths of the report. Quite the reverse, the ill-fitting material would add to the confidence that the reader has in the analysis. A lack of 'hiccups' may leave the impression that the report has been smoothed out and possibly that the analysis is a little too glib.

[14]The use of the figure is to be applauded and it does make the point that the themes are all interlinked. While Figure 18.1 is in itself useful, maybe it would be more helpful presented somewhat differently. As it stands, the figure merely names the separate main themes and indicates that they overlap in various respects. If instead, Table 18.2 (in Example 3 below) is emulated with modifications then not only can the main themes be given but also subthemes. Furthermore it should be possible to include rather more illustrative quotes from the data but in table form, which usually does not count towards the word count (clever). As the report stands, the illustrative material for the themes is a little bit thin on the ground.

[15]Is this really a case where it is impossible to include all of the relevant text? We are not to know but the suspicion is that there may have been a manageable amount of data to present here. Of course, we are so used to qualitative reports which include just illustrative excerpts that we take this as granted. Nevertheless, it is better to include all of the material on which the categories were built if at all feasible. The more complete the presentation of the data/analysis the more transparent the research process becomes. The creative use of the appendix may be the way forward or perhaps a table of the themes with all of the examples included would work. The latter might be a bit on the large side but they are not unknown in journal articles. The basic point here is that the examples/extracts seem suspiciously few in this particular write-up. At a minimum, it would be good to have the researcher's fuller explanation of why more material could not be provided. She does claim space limitations as the problem but this would assume that qualitative reports are not allowed extra space for the inclusion of data. As it is, there is a possibility that the researcher is omitting the uncomfortable stuff.

[16]There is a possibility of under-analysis here. Theme 2 is about childhood influences on consequent adult eating patterns. However, the second example is split between a reference to this theme but it is not childhood which is used to explain gaining weight. Instead gaining weight is due to *the parent eating up her child's wasted food*. So the question is whether the quote can be offered in support of the theme. There is a possibility of under-analysis and maybe a sub-theme is warranted or an entirely new theme. There should not be a chasm between the presentation of the data and the qualitative analysis. They should both be presented in as much detail as possible in order that the processes involved can be understood. So it is probably in the student's interest to highlight and problematise aspects of their own analysis as this increases the reader's perception that the analysis has been done properly.

[17]Bringing in the subject of medicalisation is a good strategy for this report. Medicalisation is a very good example of social constructionist analysis and works in the context of this study. It is indeed somewhat perplexing that there were no medicalised accounts of becoming overweight in the data collected for this study. The reasons for this may well be just as the author explains. But there may be other reasons. For example, the women in the study may merely be somewhat overweight without approaching obesity. We need to know a lot more about the women to form judgements about matters such as this. Furthermore, there would seem to be a need for a more thorough literature review searching for discussions of personal weight as a medicalised matter. Whether or not the research has been carried out is another question. The literature review feels like it needs a further push to find out if the answers are out there.

[18]This in a student report would be quite impressive as it is a theoretical proposition. Yet it feels like the discussion really has not gone quite far enough. It is as though the study needs a follow up to investigate just when people begin to see weight gain as a medical matter rather than a behavioural one as the research would have it. That is, there may be more than one level of explanation when research begins to ask the right question. If the student suggested such a future study then this would fill out the discussion very effectively – and show the world that here is a student with an understanding of how research works!

[19]One of the things which stands out in the report is the skewed nature of the sample. All of the women were in or had retired from paid occupations. This seems a little unusual and could be a feature of the sample which requires discussion or explanation. Despite good evaluative material in the report, it is curious that this is omitted and may be noted by the reader. The student begins a commendable self-critique of the report. Usually such criticisms should be routinely included in any research report. No research is perfect and it is good that a student can articulate the major (and not so major) imperfections. The problem usually is to avoid banality in these comments. For example, to merely say that the sample size could have been bigger does not indicate how thoughtful a student you are. In quantitative research it might be useful to estimate what size of sample would have yielded significant results in your study given the variance levels you obtained. However, to assume that large sample sizes are automatically better does not show much subtlety. Large sample sizes are very wasteful in time (and finance). In qualitative research merely increasing sample size may have no benefits. Quite often the criterion of theoretical sampling is used (as explained in Chapter 8 on grounded theory). Theoretical saturation is not necessarily the end point of the analysis. It can simply be used as a sign

that the researcher should change their sampling strategy. This change may support or challenge their theoretical/conceptual understanding. That is, the researcher may make their analytic life difficult by choosing a new sample which risks an analytical impasse or some other analytic difficulty which has to be resolved. But in this case, sample size is not mentioned. What is mentioned is the lack of a second analyst to verify the themes. But maybe this requires a little more discussion. The idea relates to the quantitative research concept of reliability but this is a qualitative study. Do the same considerations apply? And if they do then how will the input of the second qualitative analyst be used? Thematic analysis is probably the least qualitative of any of the qualitative analysis methods, but simply taking the quantitative reliability idea without discussion is probably to waste an opportunity. There is a lot of discussion of quality criteria in qualitative analysis to be found in Chapter 16 that would be useful to refer to here.

[20]The student writes about behaviourally-based reasons for weight gain, yet it is far from clear just what is intended by this. Some of the themes can be arguably claimed to be behavioural in nature but this seems a very inadequate way of capturing what is going on in the data. The data include what one can describe as emotionally-based notions but these are generally subsumed under the description of behavioural by the analyst without explanation.

Given that the qualitative research engages in processes which are based on close reading of the data and continual comparisons between the data and the developing categories, it is surprising that this is not at least noted or justified. This reinforces the view that the analysis has not been pushed far enough.

[21]Is this really a fair description of the outcome of the study? After all, the study had asked slimmers their perceptions of the reasons for weight gain. It is of interest that none of the explanations could be described as medical in nature given that obesity is a medical concept. Contrasting the medical with the behavioural is the researcher's chosen interpretation, but use of the word behavioural is a problem given that the analysis found, for example, emotional explanations of weight gain. There is some lack of clarity/inadequacy in the analysis here which ought to be resolved but is not. There might be a better argument in terms of matching strategies for weight loss with perceptions of weight gain than this. But even so, the evidence supporting such a link is not altogether evident from the report. Nevertheless, it is intriguing that none of the participants expressed ideas relevant to the medicalisation of weight problems. Of course this could be an artefact of the sampling but there are other possibilities. This is a good example of an established quantitative research topic requiring extra diligence when a qualitative input is proposed.

Example 2: Writing up a conversation analysis

One of the hardest things is coming up with an idea for research. This is far from being an exclusive problem to students. Good ideas for research can take time. Reading can help, especially if you have some notion of the research that you are interested in doing. In Example 2, the background story is that the student has some experience of working in care homes for the elderly. She thinks that there is research potential in this. She also has an interest in conversation analysis having attended a number of fascinating lectures by her qualitative methods teacher. What can she do to bring these together? She carries out a preliminary literature search using key words such as conversation analysis, care, vulnerable, and the like. This search turns up a research paper by Antaki, Finlay and Walton (2009) concerning the issue of 'choice' in relation to homes for the intellectually impaired. On reading this carefully, she feels that many of Antaki et al.'s ideas could be applied to care homes for the elderly. She finds it difficult to gain research access to replicate Antaki et al.'s study so instead uses interactions between care staff and elderly residents depicted in training videos for care home staff. The write-up which follows is entirely fictional for pedagogic purposes though inspired from time-to-time by Antaki et al.'s writings. Read the report carefully and critically – remember that you are not just looking for bad things. Then compare your critique with the points given after the report.

ILLUSTRATIVE EXAMPLE OF A QUALITATIVE RESEARCH REPORT

The practice of choice for elderly care home residents: A conversation analysis of everyday interactions with carers in training materials[1]

Heidi Nichols

Abstract

The opportunities for self-directed behaviours in institutional settings for the vulnerable can be very constrained. Drawing upon Antaki, Finlay and Walton's (2009) research into 'choice' for people in care with intellectual disabilities, the present study explored how 'choice' was represented in training videos (*At Home in a Home*) for care workers with the elderly. It is common in government level official policy documents to find statements that vulnerable groups in care should be afforded as much independence as possible within the organisational structure. 'Choice' is a common means of expressing this concept though this is not formally defined. Policy documents and institutional mission statements lack working detail of what the concept of choice means in the daily routine. Just what constitutes having a choice and how should choices be offered? Care homes are demanding work environments for members of staff who experience significant time and work-load pressures. Based on her personal experience as a care worker, the researcher has first-hand knowledge of the difficulties of implementing 'choice'. 'Choice' is possible in a number of different ways in the daily routine including bath times, getting up times, bed times, meal times, entertainment preferences, television programmes and so forth. Choices can be resident-initiated or care worker initiated. In day-to-day ethnographic terms, however, 'choice' has to be negotiated through requests, offers and demands interactively. These are conversation-based, of course, and may clash with institutional demands such as staffing levels and so forth. The present study sought to examine how 'choice' is represented in a training video for care workers. A series of training films featuring authentic day-to-day interactions provided the data for the study. The videos deal with different aspects of life in a care home including those such as reception, social activities, mealtimes, bed times and so forth. Interactions involving 'choice' were explicated using conversation analysis. Although there were many indications that members of staff were caring and well-meaning, 'choice' was negotiated in a way which fitted with institutional managerial objectives. That is, day-to-day experiences in care homes failed to implement wider policy implications concerning resident choice in care settings. Furthermore, at the more theoretical level, the analysis raises somewhat awkward questions about the applicability of conversation analysis in this setting.[2]

Introduction

The notion of treating vulnerable people with dignity is common in care work documents including those dealing with intellectual disabilities and the elderly in care. Just what this means in terms of the day-to-day practices of care workers for such groups generally needs explication. One aspect of dignity is self-determination and freedom in choices. Abraham Maslow's (1943) model of human needs is perhaps one of the few psychological theories helpful to our understanding of this. He conceived a hierarchy of human needs with survival/biologically based needs (e.g. the need for food) being at the base of the hierarchy but at the top of the hierarchy is self-actualisation and peak human experiences generally. A person who has their biological needs met becomes free to self-actualise in the most human of ways such as in terms of creativity, religiosity and the more cerebral aspects of human personality. Freedom to fully fulfil the self is presented as a most sublime human achievement. Maslow's work has been subject to a number of criticisms but remains one of the more influential ideas in psychology. This is being offered as a form of yardstick of human dignity in this report. No precise equation between

the two is implied but the self-determination of one's actions gets us somewhere close to what dignity and especially 'choice' would mean in this context. The hierarchy of needs includes biological needs and safety needs, love and belonging, esteem and self-actualisation and the additional level called self-transcendence which Maslow added later.[3]

Antaki, Finlay and Walton's (2009) study provides some of the conceptual groundwork for the present study. They looked at the issues of choice in residential accommodation for people with intellectual difficulties. They point out that at the level of national government, policy is that the mentally defective[4] should have greater control over their lives – with personal choice being important in this. The Department of Health in 2001 issued *Valuing people* which Antaki et al. suggest became something of a manifesto. The principle of giving people with intellectual difficulties a 'say' in their lives was incorporated into law with the *Mental Capacity Act* (2005). The principles underlying this act have filtered down to individual services including care homes. It is Antaki et al.'s conclusion that choice and personal control are to be found enshrined in mission statements in publications at all levels. They appear as 'pervasive' aspirations in brochures for care homes, for example. Yet a lack of clarity seems too endemic in this discussion. For example, Antaki et al. (2009) report that official documents such as *Independence, well-being and choice* (Department of Health, 2005) mentions the term 'choice' over 50 times in 85 pages of text and other documents give a similar impression. The definition of 'choice' in practical day-to-day terms is missing. Antaki et al. write:

> Choice is a notion in the ethnomethodological sense familiar to members of a culture, for whom its use in context is more pressing than its philosophical subtleties. As it applies to these documents, the ordinary sense of 'choice' is so robust that no one will be in any doubt that the agencies involved see that people with ID [intellectual difficulties] lack, or are being denied, an important component of human dignity, and should be given more of it. Thus, official agencies endorse the view that people with ID ought to be given a say in leading a fuller and freer life. (p. 260)

Little in the use of the term 'choice' leads to fine detail about its usage. Antaki et al. write of 'cover-sheet acts' – that is, emblematic statements – as in the following excerpt from *Valuing people* (2001):

> Like other people, people with [intellectual] disabilities want a real say in where they live, what work they should do and who looks after them (p. 31).

While not a clarification as such of the concept of choice, it does imply that the bar is fairly high in official documents. That is, these are not basic choices that in everyday life we would hardly notice (like what to eat, whether to go to a movie tonight). Things like choosing work are far more complex matters than any of these. Yet just how is choice to be implemented and upon exactly whom is it likely to be implemented? In brief, Antaki et al. are posing the question of how 'choice' works in practice. Of course, policy research could address questions of the intent of the policy makers though whether this would explicate things sufficiently cannot be guaranteed. An alternative is the approach which Antaki et al. used. This was to ask just how choice is dealt with in the everyday interactions of care-staff and their clients. This does not imply in itself an assumption that choice is performed in these interactions, merely that the interaction was potentially one of choice. Conversation analysis was used in their study. It is their research model that the present study attempts to build on. It attempts to address Antaki et al.'s fundamental question in a training context.

The researcher has worked in care homes for substantial spells during her adult years. During these times she had a great deal of contact with elderly people in care. This included some who had suffered strokes either before or after they came into care. Apart from age, there are parallels between the elderly and the intellectually impaired as vulnerable groups. Intellectual impairment of some sort is frequently if not always associated with strokes. Having myself worked in the care home environment, Antaki et al.'s work was revealing and novel. They described situations which were highly familiar to me.[5]

The training of care workers, based on personal experience, tends to be fairly minimal. Many care workers receive little or no formal training either before starting work or while working. What training there is takes place in the workplace setting.

Hence a new series of training videos specifically aimed at care workers was of considerable interest. This series (*A Home in a Home*) consists of 12 half-hour videos based on life in a care home. The videos are arranged in terms of broad themes – mealtimes, entertainment, bedtime, relaxation with residents, and relationships with colleagues. The video material appears realistic and the production company confirmed this and explained that filming used remote operated cameras discretely mounted in public areas of the homes involved. There are training manuals to accompany the series of videos and the company (Modern Care Ideas) producing the videos also offers training packages to the care home service industry. I reviewed a set of the videos for instances of 'choice', seeking examples to see whether they promoted the idea of 'choice' or whether Antaki et al.'s conclusion that choice was low level and rare prevailed in this context. The study used conversation analysis just as Antaki et al.'s had.[6]

Method

The purpose of the present research was to assess the nature of 'choice' as represented in the training videos *At Home in a Home*. In light of Antaki et al.'s discussion of 'choice', the video package was carefully reviewed for potential examples of 'choice'. The review was repeated three times because 'choice' seems to operate in very subtle ways in this sort of setting. There were no instances of resident-initiated choice but several in which a resident appeared to be offered a choice. At this stage nine examples had been found which were then edited out of the videos and saved as separate computer files. These files were then reviewed jointly with my supervisor and it was agreed in discussion that seven were clear examples of choice situations. A further requirement should be mentioned. That is, the video excerpts needed to include sections of conversation in full in order that conversation analysis could be applied. All of the seven final examples met this criterion.

The choice of conversation analysis as the analytic method was made partly to follow Antaki et al.'s procedures as closely as possible but also because the data were naturally occurring conversation. Generally speaking, however, the excerpts were short and contained little material which might have prompted the use of another form of qualitative analysis. The conversations were fragmentary and included little or nothing by way of phenomenological or narrative material, for example. Hence content analysis, grounded theory, interpretative phenomenological analysis, narrative analysis and any sort of discourse analysis were inappropriate because of the lack of detailed accounts. Principles from conversation analysis formed the basis of analysing these interactions between care workers and care home residents. The primary references I used in the conversation analysis were the detailed expositions by ten Have (1999) and Hutchby & Wooffitt (1998). Conversation analysis has as its primary focus the way in which an utterance leads to the next utterance. This is an adjacency pair and it helps us to understand just how a certain social action is achieved in the conversation. Some utterance can be seen as expected/unexpected, sufficient/insufficient and tentative/final (Antaki et al., 2009). Its sequential method of analysis makes conversation analysis invaluable for the detailed analysis of everyday conversation.[7]

Data

The data consisted of seven short excerpts from a total of six hours of video. This reflects the relative lack of interaction episodes involving choice in any form. Given that these were training videos, it might be expected that important issues for training would be strongly featured. This was not apparently the case for choice. Some choice situation types did not seem to appear in the videos. For example, resident instigated choices were not featured at all. The examples of choice were almost exclusively ones in which the resident was offered a choice. Some situations would seem to be inherently choice situations such as when care staff were taking afternoon tea around to the residents – the choice here would include what beverage and what sort of sandwich. Dressing could include choice of clothing. Entertainment could include whether or not the resident wanted to play bingo and whether they wanted more than one card to play along with at the same time. Or what sweets, biscuits, etc. they wanted should they win. Specifying a potential choice situation is slightly different from situations where the choice was actually offered. Bearing these things in mind, the selection of excerpt was pragmatic and erred towards over-inclusion of choice situations. It is

not possible to specify the location of the filming of the episodes identified though various locations are listed in the video credits. Similarly, it is not possible to give precise characteristics of the parties in the excerpts. Any information given, such as age, etc. given is estimated from the video and may or may not be accurate. The production company confirmed that none of the video involved staged or acted filming with any care home resident. That is, the exchanges were naturalistic conversation as is *sine qua non* in conversation analysis research.

The selected conversations shown in the video were copied onto separate video files for convenience and to allow precise measurements of intervals of silence. The researcher familiarised herself with the material by repeatedly watching the edited out sequences. In total there were just nine minutes of material prior to transcription. All of the excerpts were coded using the Jefferson system. This is standard practice in conversation analysis. Particularly important in the symbols is the use of timings in brackets (3.0) or (.5) which refer to the time of the silence in seconds or parts of seconds. For very short gaps it is conventional to use the symbol (.) which means a just noticeable gap. Overlapping speech is marked by square brackets next to each other on adjacent lines.[8]

Participants

The participants were care home staff and care home residents featured in the video programmes. Nearly all staff and residents shown were female. There was just one male resident portrayed in any of the selected pieces of interaction. The residents are estimated to range from their early 70s to their mid-90s in terms of age. The care workers were all female and appeared to range from approximately 20 years of age to about 60 years of age. Of course, the sample involved is not a significant issue in this research as the research was conceived as being about choice as portrayed in the training video. It is not directly concerned with choice within care homes in general.[9]

Analysis

In the available space not all of the excerpts can be discussed. So three examples have been chosen to be discussed in detail as they seemed analytically the more important.[10] Antaki et al. (2009) suggest that from their analysis they identified five types of choice offerings which were:

1. choice about matters important to the organisation,

2. choice as a format for a running commentary,

3. choice as reactive to misfires,

4. choice as a format for refusing an expressed preference,

5. choice about abstract, unfamiliar, or underspecified alternatives.

However it was not possible to identify examples of most of these in the present data set. Only the first category seemed to be represented. In terms of the features of this category, Antaki et al. drew attention to matters which were of more importance to the management than to the residents.[11] Toileting is an obvious example of this which occurred in both Antaki et al.'s and the present study as we shall see.

Excerpt 1

The following video excerpt takes place in a resident's lounge where a number of residents are seated. There are three care workers in attendance preparing for the weekly game of bingo. Although care worker 1 addresses the room generally in lines 1 and 2, her attention is largely on Mavis who seems inattentive. Care worker 1 is in her 30s, care worker 2 is in her 50s and Mavis is approximately 85 years of age.

1. c/w1 we're ↑startin' (.) bingo (.) next

2. who wants ter go TOIL::ET? (3.0)

3. yer want TOILET Mavis sweetheart?

4. Mavis (2.0) ((inaudible in general noise))

5. c/w1 ya want the toilet right?

6. Mavis (1.5) ((inaudible))

7. c/w1 'elp me get [Mavis up]

8. c/w2 [yea]

Reading through the excerpt one might take the view that Care worker 1 is putting on a skilled (and probably frequently repeated) conversational performance in difficult conversational circumstances. Adults do not normally ask other adults if they want to go to the toilet. If they do they are unlikely to ask in a public setting with other adults sitting around.

One cannot imagine the chair of a committee asking a specific committee member whether they wanted to go to the toilet before the meeting begins. So we could interpret what Care worker 1 does as a relatively problem-free way of dealing with an otherwise embarrassing situation. First of all everyone is addressed which makes it easier to address a particular individual. Avoiding a debate or argument about toileting could be seen as serving to keep the embarrassment to reasonable proportions.

There are some similarities between this example and Antaki et al.'s example illustrating the first choice category. Both concern toileting. Incontinence is a common problem in care homes. Incontinence episodes are disruptive for the care workers and involve considerable work on the part of the care workers – changing the resident, washing/bathing the resident, cleaning any mess in public areas and so forth. So anticipating toileting needs is in the interest of staff despite its not being in the mind of the residents. The care worker begins by asking the residents generally if any of them wanted the toilet prior to the start of the bingo game (lines 1 and 2). Then Mavis is targeted about this and asked if she wants to go to the toilet (lines 3 and 5). There are lengthy gaps between turns and it is unclear whether Mavis agrees (line 4). What she says is inaudible in the recording and it is likely that the care workers did not hear her reply either because of ambient noise levels. There is no formatting by the care worker in terms of orders or requests. The care worker clearly offers a choice of whether or not to go to the toilet. The formulation 'do you want to' is common format for choices in care homes in my experience. The choices are implicit rather than expressed. The choices include going to the toilet so not to disrupt bingo, going to the toilet during bingo and disrupting the session, or waiting until after bingo. It could be said that this is an empowering choice yet it is not the sort of question that one would, say, ask a child above a certain age. So paradoxically it can be seen as a disempowering question. It positions the elderly resident as dependent and almost treated as a child with limited licence to make a choice. Offering the choice implies that the resident may not consider matters like toileting at the moment or imminently. To the care worker, the question is probably a pre-emptive action to ensure that the bingo session goes reasonably smoothly. Antaki et al. suggest that by presenting the choice in the first place this sort of conversation actually privileges the institution over the resident.

So line 3 is directly addressed to Mavis who has not responded in any way to the care worker's question and line 4 is inaudible. The line takes the form of a question with the implication of choice. It is not known whether Mavis has a history of disrupting the bingo session by wanting to go to the toilet midway. It is possible that attention is directed towards her because she has an incontinence problem. Nevertheless in line 5 Mavis's inaudible speech is taken to be indicative of acceptance. However, the care worker checks that this was Mavis's intention in line 5. Line 6 involves another inaudible response from Mavis. Whatever the response by Mavis, line 7 indicates that that the care worker responds as if it was agreed to by Mavis in line 6. The assistance of another care worker is recruited in line 7. The second care worker quickly responds to this request and appears from the video to have been actively standing by to help take Mavis to the toilet. Quite clearly, the episode involves a choice offer from the first care worker. She puts toileting as a question which clearly could be responded to by yes or no, a choice. The unclarity/inaudibility of Mavis's reply on both occasions does not stop her vocalisations as being interpreted as affirmation that Mavis wants the toilet. It is possible that the care worker heard Mavis's reply more clearly, which was something like a grunt, and took it to indicate that Mavis was not alert enough to reply meaningfully one way or the other. In other words, choice is monitored in light of the considerations not directly evident in the conversation. This reinforces Antaki et al.'s idea that choice can be seen to be subservient to the priorities of the organisation rather than something instigated by the resident.

Where my analysis differs from that of Antaki et al. is over the question of whether choice is actually manifest in this sort of exchange. Constructed as a choice in line 3 it seems to take on a different meaning in light of lines 4 and 6. Imagine that Mavis had clearly signalled 'no' as her reply, then is it feasible that the conversation would have nevertheless flowed in much the same way that it did given the unclarity of Mavis's reply? Our only reason for the assumption that the resident had indicated agreement was that the care worker initiates action to take Mavis to the toilet. The inaudibility of her reply may have furnished an opportunity to make

sure that Mavis went to the toilet at that point. Enlisting the help of another care worker may well have ensured that Mavis was less likely to resist this course of action. This is indeed conjectural but resonates with the analysis of other excerpts discussed later.

There are substantial differences between the setting of Antaki et al.'s study and the training material which formed the basis of my study. Antaki et al. studied groups in a care home setting for people with intellectual disabilities. Physically they are likely to be rather more active than the residents of care homes. Care home residents, especially stroke victims, from my experience, are often very sedentary and many spend considerable periods of time napping during the day. Activity is largely centred around meal times. Television tends to be a fairly constant accompaniment during the day, though not generally paid very much attention. Antaki et al.'s sample is more organised with meetings to discuss matters arising from life in their residential home. This is rare or unknown in care homes for the elderly in my experience. This may in part explain the failure to find closer parallels between the two sets of data.

Excerpt 2

Time pressures can mean in some homes that members of staff have little time to spend individually with residents. There are any number of difficulties which can add to such time pressures. Simple things like deafness, napping, lack of space, overloud television and inattentiveness can make simple tasks like distributing afternoon tea difficult. Furthermore, routine tasks such as afternoon tea are a rare opportunity for staff to interact with residents. Refusals of food are not uncommon in care homes but of course not something that care staff like. They know, for example, that food which is initially refused may be eaten just a little while later. Refusals also would normally be recorded in the daily report from the kitchen which is another pressure. So it is in the interest of staff to make sure that residents take their afternoon food and drink.

Excerpt 2 concerns this very sort of situation where a trolley of food is being wheeled around the lounges for residents to eat from a tray on the small table in front of them. The situation is a care worker offering a resident a choice of soup, sandwiches and a sweet. The setting is again a residents' lounge though quiet, largely because of the absence of television noise. The care workers address each resident in turn. In the example it is the resident Edna's turn. Edna is around 90 years of age and the care worker probably in her 30s:

1. c/w Afternoon Edna. How are you today my sweetheart?

2. I've got slurp heh heh (.5) mushroom or egg sandwich (1.0) ham (.8)

3. nice cheese (1.2) yoghourt and fruit cake today (1) that's it (.2)

4. I like your blouse (1.2) not seen it before (.5)

5. colour suits ya

6. resident (1.5) I'd just like a cuppa tea°

7. c/w (.3) I'm pourin' it for you right now my darling (.)

8. but have a sandwich just for me (2.0)

9. would you like cheese today?

10. resident just half (1.9) I like a good cuppa (1.0) its good tea here

11. c/w so what if I give you half cheese half ham that suit yer?

12. resident you make the best cuppa you do

13. c/w Thank yer my darling. A bit a cake? I'll leave it for you here[12]

Line 6 raises an interesting question about the issue of choice. The resident had been invited to select the food she wanted. One question is whether lines 2 to 5 constitute an invitation in conversation analysis. Usually invitations in conversation need quite a lot of words to turn down compared with when they are accepted. Turning down invitations tend to be difficult. If we regard offering a choice as an invitation to make a choice then we might expect line 6 to be rather complex since the various food items are essentially being rejected. There is a delay at the beginning of line 6 but the rest of line 6 is more or less straightforward. There are indications of a slight softening of the rejection of food with 'I'd just like' but this is nothing like the convoluted ways in which some offers are turned down. So it is hard to decide just what is happening at line 6. Perhaps line 12 is part of the initial decline of food in that it offers a compliment to the care worker

which can be interpreted as dealing with any upset that may have been caused earlier. Edna is treating the conversation as if it were one between friends rather one between individuals with different roles – resident and careworker. The careworker, on the other hand, is merely running through yet another version of a routine institutional exchange in which minor refusals like this are common and unproblematic. Another possibility is that Edna was not being offered a choice between taking food or not taking food. So the care worker's response may actually simply be seen as a way of repairing the conversation in a way which avoids confrontation, for example.

Some of the care worker's conversation is fairly routinised. She portrays a form of warm, caring persona throughout the extract. This can be seen in lines 1, 4 and 5 and to some extent in line 13. The resident responds with a direct compliment in line 12. The list in lines 2 and 3 is structurally complex and somewhat difficult to follow. The joking references to slurp rather than soup at the beginning of line 2 may add to the confusion especially if the resident has hearing problems. The list is not only long it is confusingly presented, then. The famous three part list is certainly not used here (Potter, 1996b). Lines 4 and 5 introduce diversions from the task in hand. Taken together, this may have resulted in the request for a cup of tea in line 6 as opposed to the resident trying to remember what was on offer and making a choice. That is, there are problems in the turn to be found in lines 2 to 5. This is certainly a choice situation in Antaki et al.'s terms as the resident is being asked to make a choice. The resident fails to respond within the appropriate range of alternatives but instead asks for a cup of tea. This could be seen as the resident initiating her own choice or as a way of avoiding the issue of food. The care worker does not deny her this choice (line 7) but applies a little persuasion to get the resident to accept food 'just for me' (line 8). She appears to wait for a reply from Edna (line 8) but gets none before the care worker speaks again. So at this stage a choice would appear to be genuinely being offered. However, when a reply is not forthcoming another offer is made ('would you like cheese today) (line 9). This time Edna does reply, indicating that she would like half a sandwich in line 10. However, Edna's choice is in a sense partly rejected by the care worker who suggests half a cheese sandwich and half a ham sandwich – that is a full sandwich despite Edna's expressed wish. In other words, without any confrontation the care worker has achieved the preferred outcome of the organisation while creating no difficulty with Edna. The conversation actually depends on some of the usual rules of conversation in order to achieve the organisation's desired outcome in this micro situation. Refusing a personal invitation is known to be conversationally more difficult and complex than accepting. The acceptance of an invitation involves just a few words, the rejection of an invitation requires a convoluted explanation by way of excuse.

Excerpt 3

The final example also involves a choice situation on the face of things. However, again based on personal experience, it involves a situation which occurs quite commonly with residents who are profoundly hard of hearing or have suffered severe impairment as a consequence of a stroke. Conversation can be difficult in these circumstances as the normal process of conversational turns is somewhat difficult to accomplish. Nevertheless, a form of conversation does exist which may largely be for the benefit of the care worker rather than the resident. So central is conversation to life that it is difficult to carry out even simple tasks without talking. For example, helping a resident from the armchair, adjusting their positions for comfort, and the like are always accompanied by talking. This is particularly poignant in the case of ill residents in bed and seemingly aware of nothing around them. In care terms, it seems unnatural to physically help a vulnerable resident without talking to them in the process. It is part of the lore of nursing that this sort of thing is important. This, it could be said, would even apply in parent–baby situations where it is common/universal to talk to the baby while, for example, changing it. This is important background to the third example.

Example 3 is as follows:[13]

1. c/w ya can't be comfortable like that

2. ((*lifts resident and rearranges cushions*))

3. did yer son come today?

4. ((*resident shrugs*))

5. don't he usually come at the weekend? with the grandkids

6. ((*resident smiles*))

7. do you want [your water?]

8. resident [its cold]((*pulls shawl around herself*))

9. c/w you've gotta remember to drink your water or you'll get an infection again (.4)

10. yea? ((*care worker lifts the drinking cup to the lips of the resident*))

The talk here seems to be little other than a monologue. In conversation analysis terms there are a number of turn opportunities such as lines 1, 3, 6, 7, 9 and 10. The shrug at line 4 is the only stage at which the resident appears to respond appropriately to the turn opportunity. Even then, it is far from clear that this is based on an understanding/hearing of the question as opposed to, say, being unable to hear/understand what the care worker has said, hence the shrug. This sort of situation is likely to be familiar to any care worker. They will also be aware that vulnerable residents can have good and bad days in terms of lucidity and even hearing. This may explain why the care worker engages in a conversation-like exchange despite the minimal response by the resident. This can only be conjecture since there is just one excerpt involving the resident and the care-worker. This is not a normal, everyday conversation yet some of the rules of conversation nevertheless seem to apply. However, we should be open to the possibility that there are special rules to conversation in the care home setting. That is, irrespective of a response from the elderly person, the care worker would always engage in conversation-like activity when physically engaged with a resident. The lack of a response in everyday conversation would in all probability result in a rapid termination of the conversation if not a response signalling that the speaker had been offended by the lack of reply. Line 7, despite the preceding lines, takes the form of offering the resident a choice – between drinking her water or not. Whether this should be taken as a choice offer is, however, debatable when we consider line 9 ostensibly gives an argument why the elderly resident should drink their water. Another way of looking at the extract is that it consists almost exclusively of self-talk or self-conversation and that it is not geared to or intended to involve a true choice situation.[14] If a choice was really intended the elderly resident is not given the opportunity to express a choice before the care worker takes the matter into her own hands and puts the water to the resident's lips at which point they are almost certain to drink. That is, to refer to choice in these circumstances is curious given that there is a preferred outcome which the care worker will try to achieve whenever possible.[15]

Discussion

This report has provided examples of 'choice' as presented in training videos for care workers. The study was stimulated by Antaki et al.'s research into how 'choice' (an important concept at national policy level) was actually put into effect in homes for the intellectually disabled.[16] The two studies are as one in terms of one major conclusion – that is that choice where it occurred was over relatively trivial matters rather than involving the sort of significant life-style choices that most of us outside of these institutions make regularly. What choices there were tended to be 'managed' to reach the preferred outcome of the management and so they were in no meaningful sense free choices. Beyond this, there was no close correspondence in the details of the outcomes of the two studies. Antaki et al. predicted that in their setting the level of choice intimated by the state level advocacy of choice would not be manifest. This level included choices about marriage, employment and place of residence. What did happen were attempts to introduce choice into day-to-day events through conversation which tended to prefer the management's ideal outcomes. Choices were not something that the residents had brought to the fore and they seemed to have no immediate interest in them. Choices were put into the general agenda of the day such as going to the toilet rather than being directed towards more significant life choices such as where to go shopping. The present study deviated from the conclusions of Antaki et al. as most of the locations/occasions where choice was offered in Antaki et al.'s homes for the intellectually impaired were not replicated in the present data. The reasons for this cannot be clarified any further with the available information.

This may not be surprising as the present study focused on choice in relation to care home training videos. This may have constrained the available type of choice and choice setting considerably. Of course, residents in care homes are possibly more sedentary than Antaki's rather younger sample. Also the ethos of care homes for the elderly tends to be rather less democratic than in the homes which Antaki et al. describe. The conversations which included choice in the present study often contained few features that one might expect in terms of conversation analysis. The concept of turns often did not seem to apply since the talk preceded whether or not the elderly resident had responded meaningfully and appropriately when it came to their turn. The explanation of this in terms conversation analysis theory is somewhat difficult. The contributions of the elderly residents are often extremely minimal which leaves very little for a researcher to work on. The contributions of the care workers appear to be largely predetermined scripts rather than the product of the interaction. This makes it hard to see the excerpts in terms of the detail of the conversation rather than in terms of the context. This is not conversation analytic thinking.

Residents' choice tends to put additional pressure on care workers. It takes time to offer choices, obtain a reply, and act on that choice. With infirm and vulnerable residents the time involved becomes extended. Indeed, it may be impossible to implement choice properly as clearly indicated in the examples discussed above. So it may not be surprising that time-pressured care workers take essentially shortcuts bypassing the time delays of eliciting a clear choice from the somewhat uncommunicative elderly resident. However, this is merely another way of suggesting that government policy insisting on choice is not effectively implemented at the grassroots level. This was much as Antaki et al. found also. Choice implementation in care homes for the elderly has a more precarious meaning than even Antaki et al. found. To be sure, within care homes there are many examples of residents being treated much as any adult would be. However, in our excerpts we saw that some elderly care-home residents were not entirely free to make their own choices. The imperative to achieve the managerial end required within the micro-interactions of daily life in care homes seems to be the priority. Hence, the excerpts involving 'choice' seem to be more about the lack of choice. Choice seemed to be an appropriate thing to offer the elderly resident just as it would be to most other adults and children. Yet any evidence that meaningful choices were being made by the residents and responded to by the care staff did not present itself in these excerpts.

So the training video in this respect failed to effectively promote the idea of choice. To take a balanced view, this was possibly not one of the objectives of the film makers. They were more concerned to provide insight into what life is like in a care home to new staff. To this end, the videos can be regarded as useful. They give useful pointers to good care work. However, the purpose of the present research was not to evaluate this. The videos appear to contain little to support the idea of choice in a meaningful way. Choice functioned more as a tool than a process, The difficulties of doing otherwise should not be underestimated. Antaki et al. put it this way:

> But our results show up some stark differences between, on the one hand, a literal reading of policy recommendations at the level of official mission statements, and on the other, the lived reality of staff who must juggle between the demands of their work schedule (get the residents up, washed, fed, on the bus, and so on) and the 'softer' imperative of asking them to choose. The staff have to first solve the still more fundamental prior puzzle of reimagining the residents' life as, indeed, one in which 'choice' and 'personal control' are realistic aspirations at all. The language of considered choice is not always consistent with the contingencies of residential life . . .[17] (Antaki et al., 2009, p. 264)

Coming from different starting points, the present study and Antaki et al.'s study nevertheless triangulate in their broader conclusions. In contrast, at the theoretical level the implications for conversation analysis theory may differ between the two studies. The present study presents some awkward questions in terms of conversation analysis theory let alone for the implementation of government policy.

There may be reason to ask whether all the excerpts used in this study actually amount to conversation in any conventional conversation analysis sense. According to Gibson (2003) we know two facts for certain about conversation:

> The first is that conversation is rule governed: in the very least, who speaks and what they say are both subject to rules that ensure a basic level of order and intelligibility. Absent such rules, conversation as a recognizable phenomenon would not exist; instead, every encounter would be chaotic,

and chaotic in a distinctive way, as the unmitigated manifestation of the particulars of the people present, their relations with one another, and their physical surroundings. (pp. 1335–6)

The extracts show few manifestations of the rules of turn taking, for example, yet the excerpts proceed on an orderly basis. However, intelligibility between the conversational turns depends at least as much on the introduction of outside contextual ideas as the internal structure of the excerpts. Neither were the encounters chaotic as may be assumed if rules are not followed. For this reason, we are entitled to ask if the excerpts generally were conversations at all. What orderliness there was can be seen to be more in the contributions of the care workers than the inputs of the residents. Perhaps, in this case, the care workers' imposition of a sort of conversational structure cannot be transposed effectively into the principles of conversation analysis.

Gibson goes on to suggest:

> The second thing we know about conversation is that not everyone is dealt the same hand, in terms of opportunities to speak and be addressed, and in terms of what each can hope to say as a speaker and to hear as an addressee. Conversation, in other words, is a site for the differentiation of persons, perhaps, though not necessarily ... along lines established by attributes, personalities, or positions in an encompassing institutional structure. (p. 1336)

It would seem that the excerpts illustrate exactly what Gibson is describing. The excerpts clearly are superficially conversational. Without the orderliness imposed (often unilaterally) by the care workers it is possible that we would be left with a chaotic situation. The orderliness really depends on the role differentiation between the care workers and the residents in these excerpts. These are not conversations between equals although government policy would expect this to be more the case in terms of choice. In fact, where choice is involved the wishes of the individual should pre-empt other considerations. These conclusions are not surprising given the degree of dependency of some of the elderly people involved. The differentiation may be assumed to be the consequence of what Gibson calls 'positions in an encompassing institutional structure'.[18]

Conclusions

In finishing, the conversation analytic work by Gordon, Ellis-Hill and Ashburn (2009) is pertinent. They studied stroke victims in interaction with nurses on a specialist stroke ward. What they noted was that nursing staff controlled conversations. They laid down the topics and controlled the flow of the conversations. That is, the conversations were decidedly asymmetric. The input from the vulnerable residents was minimal – their turns were very short and often barely or not coherent. Also the nurses adopted closed-questioning. Interestingly this was not a notable feature of our excerpts. Little or nothing about the patient's anxieties about their plans for the future, for example, was contained in the conversations. One might suggest, in conclusion, with this in mind that the present study, Antaki et al.'s study, and Gordon et al.'s study begin to converge to highlight an interesting area for future research. There is clearly a need to develop our understanding of these largely 'one sided' conversations. They possibly have implications for our understanding of circumstances in which normal conversation breaks down. To consider them as a version of 'talking to the baby' may be a starting point (though this seems to be a somewhat offensive choice of words). There is an obvious need for further research involving a wider range of vulnerable groups.[19]

Critical evaluation

[1]The title is a good summary of what one is about to read. The two-part structure is common in conversation analysis titles and qualitative titles in general. A possible, eye-catching alternative might be '*Yer want toilet Mavis sweetheart? Choice in a conversation analysis of care home practice*'. This is not quite so informative as the title used but it does quickly get to the heart of research.

[2]The abstract is a generally good summary. One might question the statement 'Although there was every sign that staff were caring and well-meaning' on the basis that the research did not explicitly evaluate these things, this is a small blip in a good summary. But the abstract at over 350 words may be too long to meet with the specific local requirements concerning abstracts. The following is a shortened version of the one used in the report though it is

not truncated as it tries to cover all aspects of the research but it does produce a word count of less than 150 words:

Opportunities for self-directed activity in homes for the vulnerable elderly can be limited – institutional settings for the vulnerable can be very constrained. The present study explored how 'choice' was represented in training videos. Care homes are demanding work environments for staff who experience significant time and work-load pressures. 'Choice' is possible in a number of different ways in the daily routine such as meal choices and bath time. In day-to-day ethnographic terms, however, 'choice' has to be negotiated interactively through requests, offers, and demands. These are conversation based, of course, and may clash with institutional demands such as staffing levels and so forth. Interactions involving 'choice' were explicated using conversation analysis. 'Choice' was negotiated in a way which fitted with institutional managerial objectives and fitted badly with national policy. Furthermore, the findings raise somewhat awkward questions about the applicability of conversation analysis in this setting.

Whether it is appropriate to use the word *findings* in a qualitative report warrants consideration.

[3]The discussion of Maslow's work is a mixed blessing. Showing that one can draw ideas from one's university studies and establish links with other areas is a very good thing. It is also a good thing that the student draws on theory to consider further what a key concept in the study means (choice). However, this is done at a somewhat superficial level. The one citation provided is somewhat elderly and it would have been nice to have some more up-to-date material about Maslow's ideas. For example, what emerges if you do a literature search with the key words 'Maslow' and 'choice'? Do you hit a vein of relevant discussion in this way? The introduction of material of more recent origin would reinforce the impression of a good student who is prepared to dig a little to find informative sources.

[4]People with mental disabilities would be more appropriate language. Qualitative researchers tend to pride themselves on having a more human approach to the people who participate in their

research. Be very, very careful of the language you use as mistakes like this one can cause offence.

[5]The use of personal experience in qualitative reports is generally to be encouraged. Certainly, in this case, the researcher's time working in care homes is pertinent and contributes positively to the interpretation of the data. It provides a form of context which helps understand the excerpts. However, in this case we might ask ourselves whether the researcher goes a little too far in using her personal experience as the 'authority' for various statements in the report. For example, is there no other source to cite which has shown that care workers are under considerable time pressure? In other words, care is needed to make sure that personal experience is used appropriately and does not take the place of good scholarship. Is it not possible to find support for these assertions from the research literature on care homes?

[6]By this stage you may feel that you have read about Antaki et al. (2009) rather a lot. It is also noticeable that the student cites very few papers in total. To be fair, Antaki et al. themselves only cite 11 studies and it is not uncommon for conversation analysis studies to have very short reference lists. However, this is a report for assessment purposes and it would seem that the literature review itself is rather limited or weak. There are various possible reasons for this. The student may simply have not bothered to carry out a literature review. Or there may be very little relevant literature to review. Or the student may have decided that the literature she had found simply was not pertinent. Unfortunately, most people reading the report will have little or no idea of what actually applies. It would be best if the student actually explained the situation. Perhaps she could add somewhere a short paragraph like:

A literature search was carried out using a variety of search terms either individually or in combination. These included the key words choice, care homes, elderly conversation, institutional conversation, requesting, and offering amongst others. Some produced substantial numbers of hits and others none. Combinations were entered where numerous hits needed to be reduced. At a minimum, the abstracts were read for relevance. Very little, if anything, directly relevant to this topic was found. This tends to support the impression

given by Antaki et al. (2009) that this is an emerging research area needing much more research attention.

Of course, if the student had not bothered to do a literature review then she would deserve to be penalised. It should be possible to carry out such a review in a matter of a few days given the modern ease by which publications may be downloaded electronically.

[7]Not all readers will be familiar with conversation analysis procedures especially Jefferson transcription. It might be helpful to include an appendix detailing the main features of Jefferson coding as they apply to the data.

[8]It is good that conversation analysis conventions are described but not at this point where the data are being described. This information would be more appropriately included within an appendix.

[9]There is no discussion of ethics or data protection in this report. As far as one can tell, the data are the sort of archival material (media) to which psychological ethics, university ethics or data protection are usually held not to apply. Despite this, the student might consider including a short comment on the ethics of this sort of research. For example, had the researcher filmed a similar exchange for research purposes, ethical approval and data protection would apply.

[10]If there were seven excerpts available but only three were reported then the researcher should explain why that decision was made. Furthermore, the extra four excerpts might have been helpful to the reader and could be included as part of the analysis to support the claims being made. The transparency of all stages of the qualitative analysis is important, and the inclusion of as much data as possible would enhance this.

[11]The report at this stage seems to be a little oblivious to the needs of the reader. Although an examination of whether Antaki et al.'s (2009) findings apply to the student's study is a reasonable analytic strategy, the reader would have to stop and read Antaki et al.'s paper to begin to understand what is being written here. The student needs to supply the necessary information about Antaki et al.'s analysis and explain why it does not fit the new data. This would need considerably more words. The student probably has to decide whether to omit this part of the analysis. The case for doing so is that this

section of the student's report is not really necessary to the main argument. But this is a difficult choice point and the best tactic is not obvious.

[12]The transcripts need a little bit of attention. In particular, they are not consistent with each other entirely in style and they do not seem to perfectly correspond to Jefferson transcription methods. A little bit of tidying up will make for more professional looking work.

[13]Among the differences between the transcript excerpts appears to be the use of timings such as pauses. The third excerpt has fewer and some would appear to be missing given the flow of the conversation. Of course, there is a lot of discretion in any transcription system and different transcribers would have different styles. However, this is no reason for a transcriber being inconsistent. It is also notable that descriptions of actions are dealt with differently in the different excerpts.

[14]It is interesting that line 8 could be regarded as an appropriate turn to follow the care worker's comment in line 7. The resident could have been referring to the water without this observation. We do not know whether the care worker noticed her pull the shawl around herself. There is nothing in lines 9 and 10 to suggest that she has. So it is possible that Excerpt 3 is more conversational than it appears to the researcher. The non-verbal responses of the resident in lines 4 and 6 may indicate that she does not remember (hence the shrug in line 4) and that she smiles in line 6 may indicate that she heard the mention of grandkids but couldn't think of anything to say as she cannot remember whether their visit had been today.

[15]These excerpts are difficult to analyse with or without the aid of conversation analysis. So it is noteworthy that the student researcher makes no mention of seeking the help of her supervisor or some other person with the analysis. It could be that a little more expertise would help stamp a more definitive reading on the analysis. In light of the potentially controversial nature of the conclusions, seeking help and advice might also seem to be a sensible precaution. In any case, a qualitative researcher is not an artist working dedicatedly but alone in their studio. Research including qualitative research is best regarded as a collective endeavour benefitting from inputs provided by others as well as one's own personal input. The presentation of qualitative findings demands that the researcher's

ideas are clear and clearly articulated. Talking with others about your research at all stages can only make your ability to articulate things better. If the people you discuss it with don't like your analysis then you should take on board their comments in order to further develop your analytic claims.

[16] The language used here is unacceptable in a contemporary piece of writing. Using this type of old-fashioned language should be avoided, particularly if it is likely to cause offence. In qualitative research there is an obligation to treat all research participants with dignity and as persons in their own right. It is useful to ask participants how they like to be referred to. Far from being political correctness this is about treating people as being actively involved in the research rather than as the passive 'subjects' they would have been thought of within mainstream psychology in the past.

[17]When using quotes, make sure that in some way you discuss the quote and make sure that it is absolutely pertinent to what you have to say. In this particular case, I think that the student has led up to the quote and is using Antaki et al. to support her comments somewhat unnecessarily as it adds little but words to her argument. Quoting for its own sake interrupts the flow of a good argument.

[18]Overall, this seems a well-made and fairly strong discussion to end a student report. There are some difficulties – for example, the use of quotes from Gibson does not seem to be well thought through and demonstrates some level of misunderstanding about what constitutes conversation and how it might be identified through conducting a conversation analysis. The student seems to get a little hampered by this in her discussion, making a range of points that lack relevance to the overall report. However, she does recognise that analysis of the very limited conversation of people with intellectual limitations is potentially a challenging but stimulating field for future conversation analysis studies. Drawing on the similarities between several different participant groups (those with intellectual disabilities, the most vulnerable and frail elderly in care, and stroke victims) her lack of expertise in the area prevents her making a rational argument, but does demonstrate her realisation of the difficulties of analysing unbalanced conversations.

[19]The conclusion is in many ways a very good piece of work from a student. It shows that she is prepared to question even the basis of conversation

analysis as well as highlighting a developing research area. Do the conversations in her excerpts actually constitute conversation in conversation analysis terms? That is an interesting question. Furthermore, linking her analysis with the research on nurse–stroke patient conversation makes a striking parallel.

The student clearly demonstrates a capacity to ask questions in keeping with the academic method. That she may have overlooked something such as a relevant paper does not really detract from that and the student is almost certain to be given good credit for her efforts.

Example 3

It should be clear by this point that the expectations of write-ups of different qualitative methodologies are not the same. That is to say, the write-up of a conversation analysis study is not entirely the same as one for, say, an interpretative phenomenological analysis study. Although the broad strategy is the same in terms of the structure of the write-up, there are obvious differences. Conversation analysis reports deal with the detail of text and extensive discussion of the detail of excerpts is usual. Interpretative Phenomenological Analysis reports the analysis process in much more general terms. This is apparent in the following example which is based on the work of Vangeli and West (2012). Although a lot of ideas have been borrowed from Vangeli and West, overall the example is a substantial simplification of their work. There is little or no previous research of a qualitative nature which is pertinent to the study. This is not uncommon in qualitative research naturally. Indeed, the researchers' prior research had been of a quantitative nature. Interpretative phenomenological analysis, in general, is open to quantitative research and research findings. Grounded theory is similarly open to non-qualitative research especially in its original formulation. In an interpretative phenomenological analysis report, findings and theory from mainstream qualitative psychology often intermingle with the interpretation of the qualitative data.

ILLUSTRATIVE EXAMPLE OF A QUALITATIVE RESEARCH REPORT

Identity as the cause of the decision to stop smoking: The effect of adopting a non-smoker identity[1]

Lucinda Poppleton

Abstract

Objective: It is believed that long-term abstinence from smoking requires the formation of a 'non-smoker' identity. The research sought to understand the role of identity in the transition from smoker to non-smoker.

Design: Interpretative phenomenological analysis was employed to study the experience of identity formation and change in a sample of long-term ex-smokers. They were recruits to a university health service's 'quit-smoking' programme. Practical advice and group work was involved.

Method: A total of eight one-year-long quitters were recruited using purposive sampling. All were former attendees at a university health service's quit smoking group. They were interviewed using a semi-structured approach. These recordings were transcribed and subjected to an IPA analysis. In addition, each participant completed a questionnaire about their pre-quitting smoking behaviour and other matters.

Results: A marked sense of personal achievement accompanied a transient identity of 'group stop smoker'. Participants nevertheless retained a degree of attraction to smoking implying an incomplete identity change. Quitters self-defined themselves as non-smokers irrespective of where in the identity transition process they had reached. A totally coherent and untroubled non-smoker identity does not appear necessary in order to achieve long-term abstinence.[2]

Introduction

A smoker's motivation to smoke is usually high because of strong, physiologically-based urges. These urges are partly the consequence of the central nervous system trying to adjust to the absence of nicotine (West, 2009). Dependency on nicotine also has social and psychological aspects. These have been subject to reinforcement by habits and associative learning over the years that a person actively smokes. There remains a great deal more to be understood about the addictive nature of smoking. For example, despite the fact that we know that psychological relapse prevention programmes work for other addictions, there is a lack of evidence to suggest that relapse prevention would work in the treatment of smokers (Hajek, Stead, West, Jarvis, & Lancaster, 2009). It seems important to fill these research and knowledge gaps in order to help people quit smoking more effectively.[3]

Recently research has addressed motivation[4] and identity in respect of smoking behaviour (West, 2006, 2009). One proposal is that identity change is crucial to the process of quitting smoking. The concept of identity and the idea of the self are in various ways linked. They are sometimes difficult to distinguish in terms of the ways in which they are discussed. Characteristics of the self include characteristics of identity. William James' (1890) distinction between the 'I' and the 'me' remains important despite the enormous amount of research on topics like the self and identity in the intervening years. The former ('I') is a self-organising aspect of the individual which is involved with the interpretation of experiences. The 'me', on the other hand, is what we perceive when we self-contemplate. The 'me' is what is generally being referred in theories of identity and it consists of many identities. That is, we all have multiple self-perceived identities. The self changes with our experiences. Stryker & Burke (2000) proposed that we have a different identity for every position or relationship we occupy (e.g. brother, employee). There are certain behaviours which are more or less prescribed for each of the different roles and which we are expected to fulfil by others. Behaving in the manner prescribed by the role not only validates one's role status but is a positive thing in terms of one's self evaluation.[5]

In a not dissimilar way, Tajfel's (1974) Social Identity Theory assumes that a person's self-concept results from the social categories into which they fall and feel they belong. Examples of such social categories would include student, Scottish and so forth.

Stewart-Knox et al. (2005) have discussed such social accounts in connection with the initiation of smoking behaviour. Just how is identity involved in the change from being a smoker to being a non-smoker?

If identity is involved, then theories of identity change would be particularly relevant. Identity Shift Theory (Kearney & O'Sullivan, 2003) applies to addictions and is one such approach to identity change in behaviour change.

Value conflicts develop as a consequence of our behaviours and the distress they cause us. For example, we smoke despite the death of a parent through cancer a few months previously. The feelings of distress lead to behaviour change which can lead to an identity change if they are successful.[6]

In terms of smoking this new identity would be that of a 'non-smoker'. This new identity may help protect the individual from reverting back to smoking.[7] Quantitative studies of identity and smoking cessation in adults have explored the role of the individual's self-concept in smoking and conceptions of a non-smoking self. Both the intentions to quit smoking and the initiation of attempts to quit were predictable from aspects of the self-concept (Moan & Rise, 2005; Van Den Putte, Yzer, Willemsen, & de Bruijn, 2009). The self-concept changes more the longer the period since quitting was initiated (Shadel, Mermelstein, & Borrelli, 1996). Identity change usually has occurred after quitting smoking for six months. Such ex-smokers became more negative towards the typical smoker though having family and friends who were smokers stopped this happening (Gibbons & Eggleston, 1996).[8]

Qualitative studies into the cessation of addictive behaviours are broadly supportive of these findings. They suggest that identity change is involved in recovery from alcohol and opiate addictions. Often dramatic identity changes are observed (e.g. Biernacki, 1983; McIntosh & McKeganey, 2000). Not many qualitative studies of smokers and ex-smokers have been carried out though the picture seems to be rather similar. Hanninen and Koski-Jannes (1999) found a subtle change towards increased self-respect among ex-smokers. Another study found a more positive self-regard for the non-smoking self than the previous smoking self (Brown, 1996).[9]

So there seems to be little doubt that success-ful cessation of smoking is related to a process of identity change. Remaining abstinent seems to cause identity change.[10] However, the research is somewhat patchy and dominated by quantitative approaches. There is a need to understand the pro-cess of identity change in smoking cessation better. For example, is there difference between personal identity change and group identity change. The present study attempts to understand how ex-smok-ers make sense of identity change in the smoking cessation process.[11] The chosen methodology is interpretative phenomenological analysis (IPA) as described by Smith, Flowers, and Larkin (2009). In this, the individual is regarded as a meaning-maker in relation to significant life experiences. It readily addresses issue of change and identity (Dickson, Knussen, & Flowers, 2008; Osborn & Smith, 2006).

Method

Participants

A purposive sample of 8 university staff and stu-dents who had attended the University of Central Aberdeen's health service's quit smoking programme was recruited. A total of 5 females and 3 males par-ticipated. All but one participant was white-Brit-ish. The exception was a black-British male. The university allowed immediate family members of members of staff to enrol onto the programme without charge just as with students. Any person registered as a student with the university or resid-ing at a member of staff's address was eligible. The researcher had been an unsuccessful member of one of the groups and had contact details for others in her group. Other participants were recruited by word of mouth inquiries, posters, the student radio station, and through a posting on the university stu-dent union website. The important selection criteria were that they had to have been abstinent for at least 12 months and that they were still abstinent. The quit smoking programme involved a structured closed-group programme lasting six weeks. The underlying strategy was based on the *Withdrawal Orientated Therapy Approach* of Hajek (1994). It provided advice on the effects of smoking with-drawal and on useful pharmacological aids (e.g. nic-otine patches). The approach includes group work to encourage bonding and mutual support between group members. The research was not conceived in any way as an evaluation study of the quit smoking programme and the programme is incidental to the research as exploring identity change during the quitting process was the sole aim of the research.[12]

Procedure

Those who agreed to take part in the study were interviewed by the researcher. At the start of the meeting, the purpose of the research was explained, the participants were given an information sheet about the research, they gave informed consent to participate following this, and they completed a brief background questionnaire.[13] The interviews were digitally recorded and generally lasted for about 60 minutes. Each participant was assigned a pseudonym which was used to identify the recording and the transcription of the interview. The interviews took place in various, largely makeshift, settings such as refectories, common rooms and tutorial rooms in the Department of Psychology. The interviewer introduced herself as a student conducting research for an assessed project. She explained that very little research had been carried out into the experience of quitting smoking in general and that she was interested in the experiences of successful quitters. Participants were asked to describe in as much detail as possible the process of successfully giving up smoking that they had been through. Each interview was transcribed by the researcher to provide a record of the spoken words. However, no attempt was made to transcribe non-verbal aspects of the interview such as would be done in Jefferson transcription. This is not generally considered necessary for the purposes of interpretative phenomenological analysis which has little interest in how conversation or discourse works. The primary objective is to understand the lived experiences of the research participants. This information does not require transcription beyond the verbal level.

Interview schedule

The semi-structured interviews were organised in a way which allowed the participant to introduce the areas of most concern and salience to themselves. If the researcher's areas of interest had not been spontaneously discussed, they were raised with the participant. These matters included urges to smoke, feelings and beliefs about smoking and its cessation, and identity. This is referred to as funnelling in interpretative phenomenological analysis and elsewhere. Funnelling questioning allows the research to deal with a wide area of the participant's experiences while avoiding overly steering the interview (Smith et al., 2009). One question was specifically about identity. It was: compared to how you thought about yourself when you were smoking, do you view yourself any differently now that you are not smoking?[14]

Analysis

The requirements for the analysis of the data were a method which enabled the systematic classification and understanding of people's experiences. Interpretative phenomenological analysis was chosen because of its epistemological roots in phenomenology and symbolic interactionism (Smith et al., 2009).[15] Interpretative phenomenological analysis seeks to capture the lived experiences of an individual within the social world. Not only is the understanding of the individual of his or her experiences important but also the researcher's role is to actively interpret or make sense of the participant's interpretation. That is to say, the process is one of a double hermeneutic. There are other inductive qualitative methods such as thematic analysis and grounded theory but interpretative phenomenological analysis with its double focus on interpretation was closest to the analytic requirements of the research and its epistemological foundations.

The analytic process involved familiarisation with the contents of the interview followed by a careful process of comparison and re-comparison in order to develop themes which account for substantial aspects of the meaning of what the participants had to say in the interviews.[16] The primary focus was on material related to the concept of identity. This is an inductive process which involved copious note making and attempts to formulate themes. Familiarisation was aided by the fact that the interviewer was also the analyst. The transcription was carried out as soon as practicable after each interview. In no case was this more than four days and generally it was the next day. Analysis began formally as soon as the transcription was complete. The transcriptions were also the work of the researcher which also facilitated familiarisation.

Multiple adjustments were made as themes were postulated and developed. The themes were checked against the transcripts on a repeated basis and the themes reformulated. Progress was discussed on a regular basis with the researcher's supervisor who had published a number of interpretative phenomenological analyses in recent years. Feedback from the supervisor was incorporated into the analysis, especially interpretative frameworks for some of the themes. Ideally a few more interviews may have helped to refine the analysis. However, recruiting participants was a slow, time-consuming process and the pressures of deadlines meant that this was not possible. Nevertheless, the analysis that developed was coherent and closely knitted to the interview contents.[17]

Appendix A [omitted for space reasons from this book] gives the transcriptions of each of the interviews in full.[18, 19]

Results

Three themes revealed themselves in the interviews which related to the research interest in identity in relation to smoking cessation.[20] These themes were labelled as: (1) Fostering a temporary identity of 'team stopsmoker', (2) Transition towards a 'nonsmoker' identity, and (3) Residual attraction to smoking. No useful sub-themes were identified in the analysis. Any that were considered were limited to a very small number of interviews and consequently too limited in scope to be included. Table 18.2 summarises the three identity themes in the interviews and gives a number of representative quotations to illustrate something of the scope of the theme. A more general discussion of each theme follows.[21]

Theme 1: Fostering a temporary identity of 'team stopsmoker'

Teamwork notions emerged as an important theme in quitting smoking for this sample. All interviews with one exception included material which fell into this category. Quitting smoking as part of a group seems to enhance a pre-existing identity for those who attended with friends or family members. Those attending the quit smoking sessions alone also seemed to create new identities with others in the group. So stopping smoking was construed in social terms as a collective team enterprise. Attachments to other group members were

TABLE 18.2 The themes and illustrative excerpts

Theme 1: Temporary identity as team stopsmoker	Theme 2: Transition towards non-smoker identity	Theme 3: Residual attraction to smoking
I wouldn't have gone if we weren't all together I wouldn't have done it. I would have given up. I would have gone to the first meeting and thought what a load of rubbish and not bothered going again.	People get irate about smokers and start waving their arms about complaining. As a smoker you look at them thinking leave me alone sort of thing. But when you quit smoking yourself you understand how nasty and unpleasant smoking is. The stink and the health consequences. You (laughing) become an arm waver.	Smoking is a nice relaxing feeling. I can definitely still remember the feeling even now. If you get the urge then you just have to do something to distract yourself and get it out of your mind.
As I said, I just couldn't bear letting my brother down. He was quitting for my benefit. So I had to stick at it and support him in the end.	Interviewer: Do you look upon yourself in a different way now that you have quit smoking in comparison to your smoking days? Paul: Well I think so. I've become one of the superior folk who don't smoke. Sort of accepted back into society again. (Laughter)...	After a year I don't think that you're over smoking completely. You could say I am 90% there but there is always the unexpected weak moment or bad situation that could take over. I don't think even now after a year you're completely over it. I'd say I'm 95%. I always think that there's a chance of a weak moment could take over. I really do think though that I have just about made it to being a non-smoker.
Being in the group makes not smoking a bigger thing in a way. You've got yourself not smoking but contributed to other people quitting too. There is a real sense of achievement in that.	Interviewer: Do you miss anything about smoking? John: Difficult to explain. Somebody once said at one of the meetings that giving up is like a bereavement. It's like losing a friend or parent – losing something that has been part of you as long as you can remember.	Seriously I've no wish to go back to smoking but you never know when life will throw you a curved ball. I can't explain it really. Things could happen and suddenly there's a ciggie in your mouth.

or became a strong motivation for quitting. Three interviewees referred to the group as a 'team' which gave rise to the title of the first theme. There were various ways in which the team building occurred. In two instances friends had joined the programme as a mutual bet to see who could give up smoking. This seems to have been friendly competition with the hoped-for outcome that both friends would become successful quitters. Another only joined the quit smoking group because he knew someone else who had signed up to the programme. Another person attended not because she seriously wanted to quit smoking but because she wanted to help a friend quit.[22] But in addition to these pre-existing relationships, the groups in general seemed to manufacture the determination to see it through to the end. Social ties and connections were built up between team members yielding a sort of team spirit. One interviewee explained how members of her group organised non-smoking social evenings in the student union bar. One of the reasons for

the importance of the team is that it encourages feelings that one's own behaviour contributes to the success of the other group members:

> The group therapy thing made it from my point of view made it better because you think if I, you don't want to go next week and say sorry I've had a ciggie. It was the embarrassment you know and feeling like I would have felt that I had let everybody down and it is quite. I felt it would have destroyed other people perhaps.

Theme 2: Transition towards a 'non-smoker' identity

In the interviews, all participants referred to themselves in the past with the self-label of smoker. Mostly they referred to themselves as non-smokers in the present. They spoke as if there were two separate social groups – smokers who were the minority unwelcomed by others and lower in the social hierarchy and non-smokers who were the dominant majority. Smokers were referred to as outcasts, outsiders, outnumbered and banished from everywhere. The image is of the socially excluded smoker. One participant, Marcia, said illuminatingly:

> 'Isn't it awful to say but you know I quite look down on people that smoke [laughs]'.

This ingroup–outgroup pattern was common in the identity change process with the quitters moving from an 'inferior' group to the 'superior' group of non-smokers. Not everyone showed this pattern, which was missing in one case. John experienced strong urges to smoke frequently and for him remaining a quitter was becoming increasingly difficult. He had expected that his sense of identity would change to that of a non-smoker but that was not to be to his disappointment:

> I'd brainwashed myself into thinking that at some point it [wanting to smoke] would all dissolve, it would be gone and that would be that. I'd be a happy non-smoker. But it just doesn't appear to be that way. It's always niggling at ya and to think that I've gone through a year of struggling. It is beyond me, to be honest.

John uses the metaphor of brainwashing to describe his experience and, in a sense, was constantly forcing himself to be a non-smoker. He was aware of his failure and his comments suggest that he futilely hoped that a permanent change would occur. Nevertheless, like most other participants, he still referred to himself as a non-smoker. It would seem that this label did not fully correspond to his sense of identity.

Theme 3: Residual attraction to smoking

None of the participants had totally abandoned any attraction to smoking. Smoking was still seen as desirable especially its perceived calming effect. The first example for Theme 3 in Table 18.2 indicates this. It was common for statements to be made which suggested that relapse was possible. This was variously expressed but Brian's comment is illustrative as are others in Table 18.2:

> I do [feel that I could relapse] very easily, very, very easily but I'm determined not to because I've gone this far but it's a very fine line that I tread. I do know that.

Almost all of the interviews showed this sort of possible vulnerability to returning to smoking though generally they also thought that they would resist. In other words, the attraction to smoking was universal, as was the feeling of vulnerability of returning to smoking, though generally they also did not see themselves as going back to smoking. Ann put it this way:

> I don't think even now after a year you're completely over it. I'd say I'm 95%. I always think that there's a chance of a weak moment could take over. Err but I think I'm there now, I really do.

Discussion

The sense of identity in the interviews was generally a somewhat fluid matter which may change almost on a day-to-day basis.[23] That is, although there was a feeling of fixed identities at the same time there is the suggestion of this fixedness being vulnerable. Of course, the team stop-smoker identity was in a sense transient as well. However, the identity did change from 'smoker' towards 'non-smoker' in most of the participant accounts with the process assisted initially by a transient identity of 'team stop-smoker'. The non-smoker category has a provisional tone. Whether one can regard the residual attraction to smoking as a component of the non-smoker identity, a component of the smoker identity, or a component of the smoker identity which carries over to the non-smoker identity is perhaps a matter of theoretical choice with the present stage of our knowledge of identity processes associated with smoking and its cessation.[24]

The formation of a team stop-smoking identity is an important feature of the present data. However, it may be suggested that such an identity is merely an artefact of the quit smoking strategy. All of the participants had been part of group work for a period of six weeks and bonding between group members was part of the strategy for the programme. It can be regarded as a social identity (Tajfel, 1974) with stopping smoking conceived as the group norm. Stopping smoking with people already known to oneself may serve to enhance the salience that group processes contribute to the effectiveness of stopping smoking since it is less effective to try quitting on one's own (Bauld, Bell, McCullough, Richardson, & Greaves, 2010; McEwen, West, & McRobbie, 2006).[25]

Smoking bans may be responsible for the perception of smokers as a socially less acceptable group than non-smokers. This differential perception was a surprise finding to the research. We are often led to believe that smoking advertising tended to glamorise smoking (at least in the past). Assuming that glamour once typified the social context of smoking, it is difficult to identify precisely what factors brought about the change which is so evident in the interviews with these smoking quitters. There is also a question of just what these self-concepts reflect.[26] It might be suggested that there are at least two different levels of identity – the surface level and the deep levels. The surface level is perhaps little more than simply a label reflecting behaviour. The deeper level seems to be much more complex. It involves a whole range of thoughts and feelings about oneself as a non-smoker and elements of the non-smoking identity that the participant is trying to assume.

Vangeli, Stapleton and West (2010) report related findings from a cross-sectional survey of a large sample of ex-smokers. This research suggested that residual attraction to smoking as well as self-labelling as a smoker became less over time. Yet it was still common even for quitters who had maintained their abstinence for more than two years (Vangeli et al., 2010). One possibility is that the non-smoker self and smoker self remain fluid to some extent. The ex-smoker may recognise their vulnerability while at the same time forcefully resisting smoking. How a long-term but failed quitter forms a sense of identity can only remain a matter for future research. It is another question whether different histories of smoking should be dealt with differently in terms of smoking. The 60-year-old with a 45-year history of smoking may find it hard to entirely drop elements of the smoker identity. However, a 20-year-old with a 2-year history of smoking may find an uncompromising non-smoker identity far easier to achieve. Again we do not know and merely place it on the agenda for consideration for research in the future.

Conclusions

Little previous research relevant to the topic of identity and smoking of a qualitative nature is available. So this study takes a step forward in our understanding of the process of identity change in longer-term quitters. Although it seems clear

that group smoking cessation contributes to the ease of quitting, this is not established other than in the interviewees' talk about smoking cessation. Conceptually, some doubt has to be expressed about the idea that smokers move from a smoking to a non-smoking identity over the course of the programme. This seems rather too simplistic. Although participants would talk of smoking and non-smoking identities, this description ignores as much as it reveals. The non-smoking identity seems to include elements which would readily be classifiable as the smoking identity if this were not a group of smoking quitters. Perhaps a better way of understanding the non-smoker identity is to regard it as a successful smoking-quitter identity. We do not have the data to compare this smoking-quitter identity with the non-smoker identity that presumably lifelong non-smokers would describe.[27]

There would be a great deal to be gained from future identity research applied to other types of participant groups. These are several and fairly obvious in light of the analysis of the present research. Failed quitters both taking this sort of group programme or those quitting alone are a clear target group. Just how does failure affect identity formation in such groups? Is there a meaningful failed-quitter identity? Understanding the perspective of the life-long non-smoker may also be of some importance. For example, do they manifest a non-smoker identity in the same way as the successful quitters or do they have a distinctive form of non-smoker identity? It could be, of course, that lifelong non-smokers do not incorporate this centrally into their self-concepts. On the basis of some of the unexpected elements of the present study, it may be best not to make presumptions about how identity works in these circumstances.

Critical evaluation

[1] The title is not really in keeping with a qualitative report. It seems steeped in the quantitative tradition with references to causes. It is also inaccurate as the study was not about the decision to stop smoking but about the role of identity in becoming a non-smoker in the context of the quit smoking group. Perhaps a better title, more in keeping with qualitative work in general, would be 'How the transition to a 'non-smoker' identity is experienced: An interpretative phenomenological analysis of group smoking cessation'.

[2] This abstract summarises the research and its results in under 200 words. The use of the structured abstract is good and helps keep the number of words down. Delete the headings and it remains a good concise summary.

[3] This paragraph is not essential to the argument for the research and could, if space is short, be omitted. No harm is done by including it but violating word limits can attract penalties.

[4] There seems to be no detailed discussion of motivation in this report so mentioning it here only serves to misdirect the reader as to the purpose of the research.

[5] The point of this discussion of identity and self is not clear. What is it intended to add? Is the point that self and identity are overlapping concepts? If so, then how does knowing this contribute to understanding the research? There is a feeling of padding in this discussion. There is a substantial amount of qualitative research on identity which might be more appropriately discussed here. The suggestion that we have many identities is very postmodern in itself and perhaps could be the focus of the discussion.

[6] This and the previous three paragraphs are very short. They are difficult to read with the present paragraphing. They could be joined together to give one more substantial paragraph. As such, they would make a more meaningful chunk of information to read. Short paragraphs are difficult to follow since we read a paragraph as a completed piece of information. There are no easy rules for making paragraphs but check your work for sequences of very short paragraphs or very long paragraphs of, say, more than a third of a printed page. You may want to amalgamate short paragraphs or break up a long paragraph.

[7] There is no evidence given of this.

[8] Is the self-concept the same as identity? The report is about identity which makes the leap to a discussion of self-concept a little odd. If they are the same thing then the researcher should explain this.

[9] These studies, on the face of things, are the few qualitative studies of smoking and identity. As such they probably warrant some more detail and/or discussion. One wonders whether they are underplayed because they anticipate most of the important aspects of the present research. If so, they should really put pressure on the analysis of the current data to develop something new.

[10] The first sentence of this paragraph seems sufficient in itself. The second sentence reads in a strongly positivistic mainstream way. It is difficult to find the evidence for this claim in the introduction. Does it mean that the smoker changes their identity back to that of a smoker and then as a consequence starts smoking? Surely not! So what exactly is intended? This all adds to the general feeling that the student is struggling to shed quantitative thinking which creeps back into a qualitative report from time to time.

[11] So where is this in the report – that is, material on the participants' process of sense-making about the identity change process? There is an element of the author talking the talk but not walking the walk required of a qualitative report using IPA.

[12] The description of the quit smoking class is not really necessary here. It is not part of the procedure of this research, therefore any detail is irrelevant to the method section. It could be included as an appendix if the student felt it necessary to include detail for the reader.

[13] So where are these materials presented?

[14] It is useful to have some details of the interview strategy as presented here.

[15] The methodology should be chosen because of its appropriateness for tackling the research question.

[16] The paragraph begins with a very long sentence which ideally should be broken up.

[17] What does 'closely knitted' mean in this context? Is closely knitted a proper picture of the relationship between the data and the analysis in IPA?

[18] This is desirable if permitted within local rules for reports. First of all it gives the reader the opportunity to check your analytic procedures. Secondly it usually allows the reader to put your quotes in context. Thirdly, it draws attention to the amount of hard work that you did.

[19] Reflecting on the report up to this stage, it is notable that we have no sense of the participants as people. There is no table giving details of individual participants so the fuller picture concerning the quotes is rather difficult to form.

[20] This is a very realist statement to make as it assumes that the themes were in there to be found in the data. It would be better to adopt a more constructivist position and write something like 'three themes emerged in the analysis process' or 'three themes were developed through the analysis'.

[21] Such a table is a good way of economising on words and to give a fuller picture of the analysis – is it practicable to put more excerpts in?

[22] The report gives a clear idea of the numbers of participants involved with the various comments. Although you commonly see this in professional reports, comments like 'some', 'most' and 'a few' are vague and ideally ought to be avoided as they are in this report. One of the reasons why researchers find quantification difficult is that their themes are not very well specified, which makes it difficult to know exactly how many individuals were involved, so they avoid the nitty-gritty by giving vague allusions to quantities. However, they do seem to think that quantification is quite important.

[23] This may be so but it is not clear whereabouts this is demonstrated in the data analysis. It reads like an assertion which needs to be documented.

[24] This is an extremely long sentence – about 40 words plus a lengthy citation. It needs breaking up as it is far longer than the ideal sentence length for readability. Many readers will struggle to follow the sentence. It should be routine that you check the word lengths of your sentences. It is probably best to aim for short sentences of up to about 15 words. Isolated long sentences may not matter too much but if you use too many your work will become very difficult to read. Ok, you may find things on your reading lists which regularly use very long sentence structures – but you probably find these very difficult. You will be blamed for lack of clarity if you follow suit, even if Professor X is be regarded as a guru. It is easy to turn most long sentences into several clearer short ones.

[25] Very long sentence which should ideally be shortened.

[26] Does this mean that identity and self-concept are the same?

[27] This shows signs that the writer is willing to push the analysis to a somewhat more abstract level. This is a desirable feature.

CONCLUSION

One of the problems in developing a good report writing technique is that published reports are of mixed quality. Some are excellent but others have shortcomings. These, of course, are not normally identified in the reports. So a student wishing to improve their skills in writing qualitative reports may be in a quandary when deciding what is good and bad about a journal article that they read for example. In this chapter three different student-style reports are presented and partially evaluated. In other words, the chapter explains some of what is good and bad about the reports. This should be helpful though it needs to be understood that many more comments may have been made appropriately, such as around typographical and grammatical errors, or relating to other aspects of missing content that you might have noticed. So you, as the reader, may have thoughts of your own on matters about which the chapter makes no comment. This is not surprising because there are no rules which would result in everyone reading and evaluating the material in the same way. Different perspectives are not a problem as such and it is always useful to get the views of a number of other people about drafts of any report that you write. One needs to get over any feelings of embarrassment when doing so. So if you found things to comment on which were not identified in the chapter then this is a very good thing. It shows that you are thinking hard. Similarly, you may not agree with the comments which appear in the chapter. This disagreement does not mean that you are wrong but merely that there are different points of view all of which may have some validity. The more effectively you can articulate the basis for your disagreement the better it is for your progress.

KEY POINTS

- A qualitative report should be written in a manner sympathetic to the qualitative research method employed. Unless this is done, the writing will probably seem somewhat naïve. To meet this criterion it is important study the epistemological foundations of the method in question and, ideally, those of other qualitative methods. Although qualitative methods share a great deal in common, this is not necessarily universally so.

- It is doubtful that reading about how to write a research report is sufficient to ensure that your initial attempts are of the highest possible quality. Using the reports of professional researchers as models for your own work is always a good idea. Otherwise, every student would be 'reinventing the wheel' when they tackle their first qualitative report. Ideally, the models should be on research topics related to your own but, failing that, a research report employing the same method will be helpful. Obviously, the idea is not to copy that article but use it for guidance on matters of style, presentation and content.

- The skills that you have previously learnt when writing up quantitative research should be valuable when writing up qualitative work. Psychologists generally use much the same structure for both. Sometimes modifications will need to be made to the structure but usually these are minor.

- This chapter should have encouraged you to take a critical perspective on your own writing. To do this well requires some 'space' between finishing the 'final' draft and revising it for submission. Allowing sufficient time for the write-up is always difficult for students because of the nature of the time pressures on them. It is a good idea to begin your write-up as soon as possible in the research process as this can help maximise the amount of time available for the writing process.

ADDITIONAL RESOURCES

Fox, N. (2013). How to write and structure a qualitative paper. www.academia.edu/3073153/How_to_write_and_structure_a_qualitative_paper_Powerpoint_2013 (accessed 13 September 2015)

Sullivan, C., Gibson, S., & Riley, S. C. E. (2012). *Doing your qualitative psychology project*. London: Sage.

GLOSSARY

This is a glossary both of terms in this book and also a general glossary of key concepts in qualitative research to support general reading in the field.

Abstract: A short summary of the overall contents of a research report.

Account: An attempt to explain, justify or legitimate some action.

Accountability: In conversation analysis, ethnomethodology and some forms of discourse analysis, this refers to the expectation that the actions of individuals are, in principle, to be accounted for.

Action: Differs from behaviour because the latter can be simply reflexive or reactive and there is no requirement that behaviour has to be meaningful. Action then refers to actions which are meaningfully orientated to other people. It is a term largely originating in George Herbert Mead's symbolic interactionism.

Action orientated: In qualitative research, a term used to describe the major characteristic of language viewed from a discourse analysis perspective – that is, the idea that language does things.

Action research: This is a term for research which involves experimentation, etc. in an attempt to address a particular social problem. The social problem guides research, not the interests of the researcher. It involves research studies which investigate a social intervention in order to assess its degree of effectiveness. It was first introduced into psychology by Kurt Lewin.

Adjacency pairs: Two turns in conversation which follow a standard and expected pattern for those involved, e.g. one person says 'good morning' and the other person replies 'good morning'. From conversation analysis.

Advocacy: Combining the normal role of researcher with political action, which attempts to change a situation, etc. in the interest of the group being studied.

Affinity group: A focus group in which the members are already familiar with each other.

Agency: This is a concept somewhat like that of free will but sociological in nature rather than psychological as in the case of free will. Agency or human agency indicates the ability of individuals to plan and assess their own actions, develop hopes and wishes, and reason about their situation. The opposite to agency would be the idea that what people do is determined by matters external to themselves – that is determinism.

Aide-memoire: A list of things, such as questions or issues to cover, used as a memory aid in, for example, qualitative interviewing.

Allo-ethnology: The ethnology of others (other cultural groups).

Analysis of variance: The statistical technique that allows a researcher to analyse complex experimental designs such as two-way and three-way factorial experiments.

Analytic generalisation: The process by which the analysis of a particular case is linked to a more general theory.

Analytic induction: Part of the process of analysing qualitative data. Having become intimately familiar with their research data (usually the transcripts), the researcher attempts to develop working ideas or hypotheses to explain what is going on in the data. The idea is then tested against other instances or parts of the data. It is essentially the opposite of the deductive processes used to generate hypotheses from theory which are then tested as demonstrated in the positivist approaches to research.

Analytic rigour: The stance in analysis which encourages the analyst to check the various stages of the analysis one against the other and apply the quality criteria appropriate to that type of qualitative analysis.

Androcentric: Giving precedent to 'men's' viewpoint and thereby neglecting women's experiences.

Anonymisation: The process of changing names, locations, etc. in recordings, transcriptions and reports which otherwise might prejudice the anonymity of participants in research.

Anti-essentialism: The belief that there is no predetermined or 'natural' nature of the world and people. In particular, there are no predetermined essential characteristics of people.

Antifoundationalism: The philosophical view that there are no principles that underpin all types of valid research investigation or inquiry.

Antinaturalism: This is the view that social phenomena cannot be effectively studied using the methods of the natural sciences. It is associated with the idea that social sciences should attempt to understand rather than seek causal explanations.

Anti-realist: Rejects the realist position that there is a single reality to be studied.

Applied research: Research which focuses on seeking solutions to problems.

Archival research: Research based on archived documents of any sort.

Archive: A collection of any sort of documents.

Artefact: Any sort of material product of cultures including photographs and diaries.

Attribute: A general property of anything which may have more than one category (e.g. gender). Used much as the quantitative concept of variable is.

Attrition: The loss of participants from a research study due to things such as failure to turn up for an interview.

Audit trail: Documentation of the research process and data collection in order that others can verify the researcher's activities and thoughts about their data.

Authenticity: The idea that qualitative research by its very nature and approach creates a genuine understanding of the experiences of those whom it studies.

Autobiographical account: A life-history account in the words of the person in question rather than the researcher.

Autobiography: A lengthy, self-produced account of one's life.

Auto-ethnology: This is the ethnology of ourselves (our culture) either carried out by ourselves or by others. More recently it has come to mean attempts to combine ethnographic together with autobiographical (inwardly looking) approaches.

Axial coding: In grounded theory, it is the process of linking together (relating) the analytic codes and concepts to one another. It is only important in certain variants of grounded theory.

Behaviourism: The school of psychology which regarded what is measurable and observable as the basis of good scientific knowledge. So behaviour was typically broken down in stimulus–response units and the conditions under which a stimulus produces a particular response studied. So it is deterministic in nature and essentially reductionist.

Bias: When research is subject to the pre-existing judgements, etc. of the researcher which affect the outcomes of the research.

Biographic method: This refers to procedures used to both generate an individual's life-stories and also to interpret those life-stories.

Biographic writing: Forms of writing which are biographical in character.

Biography: A lengthy account of someone's life produced by another person.

Body: In the body–mind dichotomy, the body is the physical part which deals with emotions, etc.

Bracketing (in ethnomethodology): This is the setting aside of common-sense assumptions about the world so that the researcher can study how these assumptions are made to work in everyday social interaction.

Bracketing (in phenomenology): This is a term from phenomenology (especially Edmund Husserl) which indicates the stance of the researcher when attempting to suspend normal judgement based on their everyday understanding of the natural world. Consequently, if fully achieved, the phenomenon (phenomenological object) can be perceived more directly without the assumption that the phenomenon refers to something that is 'real' in the 'real' world (i.e. without the assumption of realism). In this way, the phenomenological nature of perceiving and remembering can be studied.

Breaching: A deliberate violation of social conventions for research purposes – especially in ethnomethodology. It allows the study of how individuals cope with and negotiate the new situation and make it meaningful.

Bricolage: Refers to the multiple methodologies used in qualitative research.

Bricoleur: Because of the multiple aspects of the field of qualitative research (bricolage), some use the term bricoleur to describe the qualitative researcher. This is because of the sheer diversity of the tasks involved in qualitative research.

CAQDAS: *See* Computer-aided qualitative data analysis software.

Career: The process of progression through a social setting.

Case: In qualitative research this is a specific instance of the thing chosen for study. In quantitative research, a case refers to an individual participant usually but can be any single instance of the unit of analysis (a family, an organisation, etc.).

Case study: A research investigation based on a single unit of analysis – study of one individual, one factory, one episode of news, etc.

Categories: Classes or divisions of things.

Causation: Where changes in something are responsible for changes in something else.

Chronology: An account of events, etc. in the order in which they happened.

Closed ended question: *See* Closed questions.

Closed questions: A closed question is one which supplies the interviewee or respondent with a limited range of answers from which to choose to answer the question. It is associated with quantitative approaches in psychology. Most psychological scales, tests and measures adopt this approach as it eases quantification and analysis of data.

Code: A named category used to break data down into its components.

Code book: *See* Coding frame.

Coding: This is the procedure of categorising similar aspects of one's data under the same verbal label (e.g. 'anxiety about the future', 'money worries' and 'stress-free period of life' – or whatever is appropriate). Coding is a flexible process and the categories may change in light of the experience with the data. In quantitative research the categories would be pre-specified by the researcher whereas in qualitative research the categories generally are based on the researcher's involvement with the data.

Coding frame: A listing of the codes to be applied in a data analysis setting which defines the codes and provides guidelines for their use.

Coding manual: In quantitative analysis, this is a set of instructions containing all of the categories that can be used to categorise each aspect of the data.

Coding paradigm: In grounded theory it is another term for 'theoretical codes'.

Cognition: Internal processes of thought.

Cognitive psychology: That branch of psychology which studies mental thought processes involved in language, memory, problem solving, etc. Cognitive psychology is largely quantitative in nature and frequently criticised by qualitative psychologists such as those involved in discursive psychology.

Cognitivism: This is the belief in the ability of internal mental states postulated by the researcher to contribute to understanding of psychological phenomena.

Collective narratives: Narratives produced/shared by a number of people.

Computer-aided qualitative data analysis software: Usually referred to as CAQDAS. This refers to computer programs such as NVivo which can help the qualitative researcher organise, code and recode qualitative data. Many researchers do not regard its use as essential since cutting and pasting, etc. on a good word processing program will allow much the same flexibility. Popular with grounded theory analysts.

Concept: This is a general, abstract idea which develops from specific instances.

Confidentiality: The protection of the anonymity of participants in research.

Consensus group: A group (e.g. focus group) in which the members try to reach a consensus or agreement.

Constant comparison: The process of checking an aspect of the data and analysis against all other aspects of these.

Constructive alternativism: This is George Kelly's name for his theory which accepts that there is one true reality but that it is experienced from one of numerous perspectives – called alternative constructions.

Constructivism: The idea that people have a role in creating their knowledge and experiences.

Constructivist grounded theory: An approach to grounded theory identified by Kathy Charmaz but dismissed as qualitative data analysis by Barney Glaser rather than being grounded theory.

Content analysis: A very general term to refer to ways of categorising textual data to allow comparisons to be made between aspects of the data and to describe the contents of the data.

Contextualism: This is the idea that different conversational contexts have different standards to determine what is accepted as knowledge. So different social contexts have different epistemological criteria and standards.

Contrast questions: These help individuals make sense of their social worlds by asking them in what way two things are different or asking them to compare two things.

Convenience sampling: The recruitment of an easily accessible group of people to provide data for a study. For example, university students may choose to study other university students because of the ease of doing so.

Convergent inference: When in mixed qualitative and quantitative research methods the conclusions from the two are consistent.

Conversation analysis: An approach to studying language built on the assumption that conversation is governed by 'rules' which are understood by members of that conversation.

Cooperation: Grice's idea that conversation is a cooperative activity.

Cooperative inquiry: Involves research activity in which researchers work with non-researchers on topics where they share interests.

Core category: From grounded theory, this is an analytic category which is central, occurs frequently, and generates connections readily with other categories in the analysis.

Co-researcher: A term used by some qualitative researchers to describe the participant and involves a different conception of the participant's role.

Counter-discourses: The idea from Michel Foucault that for every political discourse which claims to be the truth there is another discourse which challenges its legitimacy.

Covert research: A form of participant observation or ethnographic research in which the observer is not identified as a researcher to those studied.

Creation myth: Accounts of the creation of a culture which are widely accepted by members of that culture but, nevertheless, are essentially myths. By extension, the idea of creation myths has been used to cover accounts of the origins of academic disciplines, etc.

Crisis: The point at which an earlier paradigm of research becomes untenable in light of the current research findings and a new way of seeing things is likely to develop. Often used by qualitative researchers to suggest that present quantitative methods are failing.

Crisis of legitimation: The authority of the interpretative texts which characterise postmodern psychology is open to question and cannot be addressed using the conventional criteria of positivism such as reliability and validity since these are not accepted in postmodernism. There is, then, the question of how to discriminate between good and bad interpretations. That is, the crisis of legitimation is the problem of who can legitimately claim the best interpretations of text and the criteria on which such legitimacy can be based.

Critical case sampling: Seeking instances or cases which provide a dramatic or especially clear instance of something.

Critical discourse analysis: A form of discourse analysis in which the production, maintenance and removal of social power is a major analytic concern.

Critical narrative analysis: A form of narrative analysis which claims to take a critical social perspective.

Critical psychology: Approaches to psychology which assume that power is an important influence on people and how the discipline contributes to social inequalities.

Critical realism: A doctrine which combines an acceptance of an objective, external world (i.e. the realist perspective) with the view that we can know the world only through the medium of our thought and perception. The central problem then becomes accounting for the relationship between the two.

Cultural anthropology: A branch of anthropology which uses ethnographic, linguistic and other methods and data to study human cultures.

Data triangulation: *See* Triangulation.

Debriefing: Discussing with participants the purposes of one's research and their reactions to that research after their participation in the research is complete.

Deception: Essentially misleading the participants in a study about the real purpose of the study.

Deconstruction: The analysis of text to identify or expose the underlying contradictions and ideological assumptions below the superficial meaning. It is based on the work of Jacques Derrida.

Deductive: A way of conducting research in which hypotheses drawn from theory guide the research. Typical of quantitative research.

Deductive coding: The production of codes on the basis of prior knowledge, theory and assumptions. The codes are not developed in interaction with the data.

Delphi group: A group of experts brought together in a forecasting study. It uses a facilitator to summarise what the experts have said. The experts are encouraged to revise their forecasts on the basis of what the others in the group say in one or more further rounds of forecasting.

Depth interview: An extensive and detailed interview. In this book the term qualitative interview is preferred.

Descriptive: Concentrating on identifying the features and characteristics of things rather than influences or effects or explanations.

Descriptive phenomenology: This is another name for Edmund Husserl's transcendental phenomenology.

Determinism: This is the philosophical idea that everything in human and social life is causally determined by a sequence of things which went before. Hence, behaviourist stimulus–response theory can be seen as deterministic.

Deviant cases: In analysis, cases which do not fit with the thrust of the analysis. In qualitative research, deviant cases are regarded not as a nuisance but as a stimulus towards a more refined analysis.

Dialogical: Taking the form of a dialogue or including dialogue.

Dialogical phenomenology: Interview with the co-researcher which involves that person contributing issues, themes, etc. during the interview. Note that co-researcher has the same meaning as research participant.

Diary: A personal chronicle of events either requested by a researcher or instigated by oneself. It provides appropriate text for some forms of qualitative analysis.

Disconfirming case analysis: *See* Deviant cases.

Discourse: Can simply mean the verbal exchanges between people but can also mean a system of ideas, images, metaphors and so forth which are used to construct things in particular ways. It can be seen as the things we say and think.

Discourse analysis: Various approaches to the study of language which either identify types of discourse within it or the means by which the discourse is constructed.

Discursive construction: The process by which people socially construct phenomena through the use of talk, language and conversation.

Discursive practice: This is the talk/conversational activities of people which involves the way in which meanings are created and understood.

Discursive psychology: A variety of psychology which is based on the principles of social constructionist discourse analysis. It identifies mental and social concepts as being a construction of social interaction. For example, rather than memory being something residing somewhere in the human mind, memory can be socially constructed in interaction such as over a family photograph album.

Discursive resources: Things which can be used in creating discourse such as narrative, rhetoric and so forth.

Discursive turn (also the turn to discourse): The trend especially in social psychology for researchers to study discourse rather than more traditional psychological issues. It is analogous to the 'turn to language'.

Divergent inference: This refers when the implication of the findings for a mixed qualitative–quantitative study are different for the qualitative and quantitative components.

Documentation: Any form of record which belongs to a participant which did not involve the researcher's intervention. So photographs, newspaper cuttings, official documents and so forth may all be useful in some forms of qualitative research (especially ethnography/participant observation).

Double hermeneutic: Used by some interpretative phenomenological analysis researchers to describe the situation in which researchers engage in the process of making sense of a person's own making-sense processes.

Dramaturgical: *See* Dramaturgy.

Dramaturgy: Erving Goffman's sociological view that context, time and the audience are related to the actions of people. It is drama in the sense that one person is presenting themselves to another in a performance which is built on values, expectations and so forth.

Ecological transferability: This is a term used in mixed quantitative and qualitative methods to refer to the generalisability of the findings. It replaces the quantitative term ecological validity and the qualitative term transferability in the mixed method context.

Emergent data: Data which emerge as the data collection proceeds.

Emergent theory: A rather dubious concept which implies that theory is in some sense inherent in the data and emerges under analytic scrutiny.

Emic: An analysis of cultures involving the perspective of members of that culture.

Emic perspective: The perspective of an insider.

Empirical evidence: Evidence based on experience or observation.

Empiricism: The belief that the validity of knowledge comes from it being based on observation.

Emplotment: The process by which a sequence of events is transformed into a chronological narrative or story form with an identifiable plot.

Empowerment: This refers to processes by which personal and community strength can be achieved such as in terms of the development of the self and the social and spiritual. Often refers to the inclusion into decision-making processes of people previously excluded. It is a concept used in feminist psychology and by Foucauldian discourse analysis, for example.

Epiphany: Something which happens in a person's life-story which changed them or provided a significant turning point.

Epistemological assumptions: The particular assumptions underlying a particular epistemological position.

Epistemology: A central area of philosophy which focuses on various aspects of knowledge such as its nature and its sources. So it is possible to speak of qualitative and quantitative psychology having different epistemological foundations or assumptions.

Epoché: *See* Bracketing (in phenomenology).

Essentialism: The idea that things have an essential nature which is capable of being identified.

Ethics: The principles of proper conduct including in research.

Ethnographic: To do with ethnography.

Ethnographic methods: Methods of close study of a natural group such as participant observation, in-depth interviewing and documentary evidence.

Ethnography: Research in which the researcher immerses themselves in a social setting to observe events directly. Ethnography also can refer to the product of ethnographic research.

Ethnology: The branch of research which studies cultures and their social structures. It is the equivalent of social (cultural) anthropology.

Ethnomethodology: A sub-field of sociology which seeks to explain how social order is achieved through interaction.

Etic: The analysis of cultures from the perspective of a non-member of that culture (a stranger).

Etic perspective: The perspective of an outsider – e.g. that of a social researcher.

Existant: Something that exists.

Existential phenomenology: A version of phenomenology based on the writings of the philosopher Martin Heidegger.

Externalisation: In the social construction of reality the stage at which a way of thinking about the world is incorporated into social practices.

Extreme case formulation: The use of extreme case formulations in discourse is to build up or exaggerate things. The outcome can be that the account seems more plausible.

Extreme relativist: One who assumes that different methods of qualitative inquiry provide a unique but valid perspective on the world.

Face: From Erving Goffman, it refers to an image of the self expressed in terms of socially approved attributes.

Facilitator: The person responsible for running a focus group. The facilitator may be an expert in this activity employed by the researchers for that purpose.

Facticity: The belief that there are real objects with real characteristics. In phenomenology, this is replaced by the idea that things have their existence in consciousness.

Feasibility study: A precursor to the main study which attempts to indicate the financial viability or general practicality of the major research.

Feminism: A form of discourse aimed at equality for women. Issues to do with gender differences and women's rights are central.

Feminist research: A form of qualitative research drawing on feminism for its focus and viewpoint.

Field notes: These are the records made by a participant observer or ethnographer of all aspects of what has been observed together with any comments that the researcher has to make on these notes.

Fieldwork: The stage of data collection in the actual research site.

Fit: The degree of match between such things as the categories and data.

Focus group: A form of group interview conducted by a researcher (facilitator or moderator) designed to stimulate group interaction rather than individual comments.

Focused coding: This follows initial coding and it is a process of reviewing the initial codes to possibly combine codes into more general ones or to reject ones which are not useful.

Footing: From Erving Goffman's theory but common in discourse analysis. This refers to the frame that is being using in interaction. A change of footing is a change in that framework.

Formal theory: The analytic outcome at the end point of theory development in grounded theory.

Formulation: In conversation analysis, a summary of the main thrust of what has gone before.

Foucauldian discourse analysis: A form of discourse analysis deriving from the work of Michel Foucault which seeks to identify the discourses within textual material of all sorts.

Frame: From Erving Goffman's theory but occurs in discourse analysis. This refers to mental structures which determine the way that we act, what are good and bad outcomes of our actions, etc. A frame determines the way we see the world. The interpretation of talk is determined by the frame that the listener understands is applicable at the moment.

Funnelling: Structuring question order from the most general question down to the most specific question.

Gatekeeper: Persons who 'open the doors' in a social setting thus enabling the research to be carried out.

Genealogy: Michel Foucault's concept which describes his method of identifying the history of important ideas.

Gestalt psychology: The term *Gestalt* means a shape or figure. It is a theory that holds the mind to operate in a holistic way and that it operates in a manner of self-organisation. Gestalt psychology was influential on social psychology.

Goodness of fit: *See* Fit.

Grand theory: Any sort of theory so long as it involves a very broad and general explanation of a social or psychological phenomenon. Usually used in the context of grounded theory to indicate sociological theory before the 1960s.

Grounded theory: A form of analysis (and to a lesser extent data collection) which includes a multitude of methods to generate theory/analysis which is a close fit to the data.

Group discussion: A procedure for data collection in which a group of participants debate some issue among themselves for the benefit of the researcher. There is no assumption that the discussion will be led by a facilitator as in focus groups.

Hard data: Data based on a natural science approach to research – putatively 'objective' data. Similar to quantitative data.

Hawthorne studies: A major industrial study involving interviews, participant observation and so forth. The Hawthorne effect denotes the tendency for industrial production to improve following research and other interventions irrespective of the nature of that intervention.

Hegemony: The dominance of any group over others.

Hermeneutics: Generally this is the study of the interpretation of texts, though its modern usage extends to anything subject to interpretation.

Holism: The idea that the whole is greater than the combined parts of the whole.

Holistic: The idea that the whole is more than the sum of its parts. So things cannot be effectively studied by breaking them down into their component parts.

Holistic view: The viewpoint of the holistic approach.

Homogeneous sampling: Sampling or recruiting people to ensure that they are relatively similar rather than very different. Some experts on focus groups recommend homogeneous sampling to ensure that participants interact freely together.

Horizonalisation: This is a step in the phenomenological analysis process according to some. It involves identifying all of the significant statements made by the participant relevant to the topic. All of these statements are regarded as being of equal status or value.

Humanism: A general term applied to philosophies, methods and beliefs which have human beings at their centre as opposed to, say, divinity. A very loosely defined idea.

Humanistic psychology: Psychology based on humanism.

Hypothesis: A proposed explanation which may be subject to further tests or something accepted as true for purposes of developing an argument.

Hypothetical realism: A form of realism which assumes that the cognitive abilities of people have evolved through a process of engagement with the external (real) world.

Hypothetico-deductive: The idea in quantitative research that a researcher develops hypotheses from theory and tests these hypotheses empirically as part of the process of theory building. It is the antithesis of the qualitative approach.

Idealism: The philosophical view that accepts only minds and ideas – physical objects only exist in perception.

Identity: Individuality or sense of a personal or social self.

Ideology: A broad set of beliefs which form a relatively coherent perspective on the world and the way things should be. It is a doctrine.

Idiographic: Concentrating on the explanation of the individual (person) rather than the characteristics of groups.

Illocution: What is done by speaking words such as threatening, instructing and demanding.

Imagery: Mental pictures/images.

In vivo coding: Using the words or concepts employed by participants in the research to name the codes developed while analysing data. It is a grounded theory idea.

In-depth interview: A lengthy interview intended to obtain extensive rich and detailed information from an individual. Referred to as qualitative interviewing in this book.

Induction: The development of theory out of data. Deductive is the development of hypotheses to test theory.

Inductive reasoning: A form of reasoning based on the individual circumstance which is then generalised to a range of circumstances.

Information sheet: *See* Participant information sheet.

Informed consent: Where individuals agree to take part in research on the basis of full knowledge of the important features of the data collection process.

Intentionality: Refers to the characteristic of consciousness as a process which actively is directed outwards towards phenomena (or objects).

Inter-coder reliability: The extent to which two coders agree on how to categorise or code each aspect of the data.

Internalisation: In the social construction of reality this occurs when shared conceptions of the world have become incorporated into social practices which are then internalised into the thinking of individuals.

Interpretative phenomenological analysis: A form of qualitative research which concentrates on the experiences of people with health issues and so forth.

Interpretative repertoire: Culturally provided systems of linguistic devices which are used to build accounts. Often difficult to distinguish from ideologies and discourses.

Interpretivism: A view of social research which requires the researcher to understand the subjective meaning of interaction.

Intersubjectivity: Basically this is to do with things which occur between two people or two minds. It is a descriptive term of the nature of the self and human activity. The experiences, meanings, actions and so forth of the individual are created intersubjectively through the interaction of two or more people. They are constructed through these interactions which involve both agreements and disagreements which lead to shared, co-produced states. It is the process by which individuals achieve knowledge of a particular phenomenon through their subjective experiences.

Intertextuality: The way in which features of one text (widely defined) are represented in some way in another text.

Interview: A formal conversation between a minimum of two people. In the research setting, this consists of an interviewer who largely asks the questions and an interviewee who largely answers them.

Interview guide: A list of areas to cover in a semi-structured interview.

Interview schedule: A list of questions to be asked in a structured interview. Similar to an interview guide but more formal and systematic than an interview guide.

Iterative process: A process characterised by repetition and recurrence. Usually, the process leads to a small but worthwhile improvement which can be built on by further reiterations.

Jefferson transcription: This is a way of turning recordings into written text which includes additional, non-lexical, features such as pauses, overlaps, loudness and so forth. It is a requirement for conversation analysis data.

Joint action: Interaction and the outcomes of interaction are regarded as being jointly produced by those who are interacting rather than interaction being seen as a succession of contributions from individuals.

Key informant: Members of the community who are crucial or important in the process of planning and executing participant observation or ethnographic research.

Latent code: Codes which go to a level of analysis deeper than the superficial features of the data.

Life-history interview: A semi-structured interview designed to collect long-term biographical information and description from individuals.

Life-story interview: See Life-history interview.

Linguistic repertoire: Or discursive repertoire. It refers to the clusters of ideas or other things which tend to co-occur when people construct accounts.

Literature review: Usually the written evaluation of the main arguments and research findings in the research literature on a particular topic included in the research report. Often used to refer to the entire process including the literature search.

Literature search: The procedures by which a researcher identifies and locates the pertinent previous publications on a particular research topic. It largely consists of searching databases such as PsycINFO.

Locution: Speaking.

Locutionary act: Performing an act of speech.

Logical positivism: A school of the philosophy of science which holds that the task of science is to develop theory which leads to general laws. This is particularly associated with behaviourist psychology. It is based on logical inferences based on observable facts.

Loss of the subject: The criticism of social constructionist approaches which argues that constructionism, because of its concentration on social interaction, disregards and can say nothing about the individuality of the actors in such exchanges.

Manifest codes: Codes developed in qualitative analysis which are closely related to the superficial content of the data.

Manner: One of Grice's maxims which suggests that brevity, clarity and orderliness characterise appropriate contributions to conversations.

Maximum variation sampling: Choosing participants not to be representative but to provide the greatest variety in relation to the topic of the research.

Meaning making: The process of making something meaningful.

Member checking: This refers to a variety of ways in which feedback from participants in the research is used by the researcher to assess simple matters such as accuracy of the research or more complex matters such as the credibility of the study. Sometimes the term respondent validation is used instead.

Memo: A detailed 'diary' or record of a researcher's thoughts and ideas relevant to the analysis of their research. This has its origins in grounded theory.

Memoing: *See* Memo-writing.

Memo-writing: The process of creating a memo.

Metaphor: The imagery incorporated into speech or any other form of text.

Methodolatry: The idolatry of method – valuing method above knowledge.

Methodology: The study of the rules, procedures and practices by which research in a particular field of research obtains knowledge. Thus, conversation analysis has its own distinct methodology. However, it tends to be used in psychology to refer to the techniques by which data are gathered – questionnaires, focus groups, etc. These should be known as methods.

Methods: This refers to the various techniques which are involved in data collection and its accumulatation. These include ethnology, interviews, questionnaires and the like. Each of these is a different method.

Microanalysis: An analysis concentrating on the smaller detail of the data.

Mixed method: A mixture of qualitative and quantitative approaches to research (or any other broad categories of method).

Mixed methods sampling: This is where sampling has been done using probabilistic procedures but purposive sampling has been used in order that inferences will be clearer.

Moderator: The same as a facilitator.

Modern psychology: Psychology is a very ancient area of intellectual interest. In this book, modern psychology refers to the psychology developing after the 1870s when the first psychology laboratories were set up in Germany and the United States.

Monomethod design: Same as a monostrand design.

Monostrand design: Either a qualitative or a quantitative approach has been taken – they have not been mixed.

Multiple case studies: Using several case studies but keeping them distinct analytically.

Multi-strategy research: Research combining qualitative and quantitative methods.

Naive realism: The unquestioning belief that there is a reality for researchers to identify. Critical realists and others may share this basic belief but accept that research taps a variety of realities or perspectives on reality.

Narrative: This can be used to refer to any spoken or written material. However, it is generally taken to refer to material which takes the form of a story.

Narrative analysis: This can be any form of analysis of narrative although, in psychology, it is probably best reserved for the analysis of narrative based on concepts, etc. from narrative psychology.

Narrative explanation: This is an explanation of events which takes the form of a story about past events. The story gives an account of and an explanation for the events.

Narrative identity: An individual identity as constructed through narrative.

Narrative inquiry: The broad field of interdisciplinary study of narrative.

Narrative psychology: The investigation of the nature of human experience and story-based accounts of these experiences. An approach to psychology which sees in stories and narratives a way of understanding the progression of personality through life.

Narrative realism: This is the idea that personal stories are the lived nature of human existence. It reflects the told character of existence.

Narrative tone: This is a term from McAdams. It refers to the broad tone of the story under study. For example, some narratives are replete with optimism and hope whereas others indicate mistrust or resignation.

Naturalism: Basically the idea that social and human sciences should adopt the scientific (natural science) approach.

Naturalistic: Research taking place in a real-life setting which involves little or no researcher-imposed control.

Naturalistic inquiry: Forms of research which stress the importance of studying social action from the viewpoint of social actors. That is, first-hand accounts from participants in social interaction are the basis of understanding.

Naturalistic paradigm: The assumption that there is no single true interpretation of reality. The focus of research is on how individuals create their own understanding of reality within the context of their social existence.

Negative case: A case or an instance in the data which goes against the hypothesis/ analysis as it has developed up to that point.

Negotiated reality: Reality as created between two or more people interactively.

Noema: This is a concept from Edmund Husserl to describe the phenomenological idea of the object, i.e. the content of a phenomenon such as a thought or perception.

Noesis: The nature or manner of experiencing rather than what is experienced. From phenomenology.

Nominal group: A decision-making group in which group members present a solution to a problem, the different solutions are listed, and finally the group members rank these different solutions in terms of preference.

Nomothetic: Law-like generalisations based on a number of cases. Usually based on measures taken by the researcher.

Normative: Based on generally accepted standards of evaluation.

Null hypothesis testing: The approach in inferential statistics in which the aim of the researcher is to accept or reject the null hypothesis. This is the basic approach to significance testing that all psychology students learn.

NVivo: A common commercial form of computer-aided qualitative data analysis software.

Objective: Unaffected by personal characteristics including motivations and values.

Objectivism: A philosophical viewpoint that social phenomena and their meaning exist independently of social actors. The idea that there is a reality which can be known independently of the person involved in knowing this reality.

Ontology: An aspect of metaphysics in which the nature of being and existence is the focus of study.

Open coding: In grounded theory this is the process of data category development closely based on the data under consideration. It involves assigning codes to the lines of transcript, etc. It is the first analytic stage in coding development which then becomes increasingly conceptual.

Open interview: Another name for unstructured interviews.

Open-ended observation: Observation with no pre-conceived observation categories in mind. The observation categories are generated from the data.

Open-ended question: A question which the interviewee answers freely without the constraints of fixed alternative answers from which to choose.

Open-question: *See* Open-ended question.

Operational definition: When a concept is defined in terms of the procedures used to measure it.

Oral history: Accounts of past life events and reflections on them as expressed in interview and similar forms by the individual(s) living that experience.

Oral history interview: A qualitative or semi-structured interview which involves the participant describing past events, etc. and reflecting on them.

Origin myth: An account of the origins of something (e.g. psychology) which is symbolic rather than factual in nature.

Other: Any other individual apart from the self though it carries the implication of stranger in some contexts.

Overall theme: The major topic in the data.

Overt research: Research in which it is evident to the participants that they are being researched.

Paradigm: A concept from Thomas Kuhn's *Structure of scientific revolutions*. A paradigm is a broad way of conceiving and understanding a particular area of research. Sometimes this can be put into crisis because of its failure to deal with new knowledge from research. This can result in a paradigm shift in which the crisis results in a radically different way of looking at the previous paradigm. However, paradigm is a very loosely used concept and is often used to denote a particular and distinctive way of looking at a branch of study. Qualitative psychology is sometimes referred to as a different paradigm from that of mainstream psychology.

Participant as observer: The situation in which an individual who is primarily a participant in a group or more general social setting provides information about the activities of that group based on their experiences within that group.

Participant feedback: Comments, etc. from a participant in a research study to the researchers on their experience of being in the research or on the analysis of the data formulated by the researcher.

Participant information sheet: Information detailing aspects of the research particularly pertinent to the issue of informed consent. It is usually accompanied by an ethics consent form.

Participant observation: A form of fieldwork in which the researcher is actually in a particular research situation witnessing personally what is happening. It has its origins in cultural anthropology.

Performative: An utterance of language which has a particular social effect.

Perlocution: The consequence of speech on the hearer – that is, the act that the speaker has carried out.

Personal documents: Any form of documentary material written for personal rather than official reasons, e.g. diaries, letters, autobiographies, photographs.

Perspectivism: Essentially the idea that there are different perspectives which guide ideas. Closely related to relativism.

Phenomenological psychology: Forms of psychology built on phenomenological ideas.

Phenomenology: The careful description of everyday conscious experiences as they are experienced. Associated with many different types of philosophy including Edmund Husserl's transcendental phenomenology and the existentialism of Jean-Paul Sartre.

Pilot interview: An interview carried out with the purpose of evaluating critical aspects of an interview in order to deal with unanticipated problems in its implementation.

Pilot study: A preliminary study which is designed to evaluate the feasibility and value of a larger-scale study.

Piloting: The process of trying out a research study or an interview, etc. in order to identify problems or to evaluate a methodology or procedure.

Polysemy: The idea that a word or text can have a number of different meanings.

Positioning: Establishing one's personal position within or in relation to a particular discourse. It is also possible to position another person within a particular discourse.

Positivism: A philosophy attributed primarily to Auguste Comte which holds that valid knowledge is that based on what can be observed through the senses – or empirically to put it another way. More generally it is the use of the methods of natural science to study psychological or social scientific issues.

Postmodern: After the modern period, which was the historical period when science dominated thinking and science was seen as the solution to all problems. The postmodern period is associated with philosophical ideas different from those of positivist science in which ideas of an accessible 'reality' have been replaced by ideas of multiple 'realities'. There is little precise agreement as to the meaning of the term other than it represents a rejection against the 'modern' thinking which followed the Enlightenment.

Postmodernism: The ideas and philosophies associated with the postmodern period. The precise nature of these is difficult to specify but qualitative researchers express a range of postmodern principles.

Poststructuralism: This would be embraced by the term postmodernism but it is not quite the same. It largely refers to the intellectual attack on structuralism that emerged in 1970s France with the work of influential figures such as Michel Foucault, Jacques Derrida, Jean Baudrillard and Roland Barthes. In particular, among the structuralist notions attacked by the poststructuralist, the idea that meanings are stable is rejected in favour of the view that they constantly change and shift. This applies to the categories underlying explanations by academics.

Poststructuralist theory: Theory based within the poststructuralist perspective.

Practice: The everyday activity of practitioners – but is often extended to refer to the everyday activities engaged in by people such as how they go about doing conversation.

Pragmatism: A philosophical position which accepts the value of knowledge solely in terms of its usefulness to humanity's goals and needs. It assumes that knowledge is relative.

Prescriptive coding: Coding which is decided upon prior to examination of the data. It is not an approach to coding which fits readily with the ethos of qualitative research.

Primary data: The data as originally collected.

Primary research: Research for which the data are collected by the researcher who subsequently carries out the analysis. Secondary research can refer to data re-analysed by another researcher later but it can also refer to a subsequent, unanticipated analysis by the researcher who collected the data.

Prompts: Additional questions or queries which an interviewer incorporates into an interview to clarify answers or encourage the elaboration of what has been said.

Psy-complex: This refers to psychology complex which includes psychological institutions, psychology professionals and psychological services to other institutions.

Purposive sampling: The selection of members of a sample with a particular purpose in mind – for example, recruiting participants because they have experienced chronic illness.

Q methodology: This is a method with its antecedents firmly in early research on the statistical technique, factor analysis. It can be used to explore subjective experiences. Q methodology has appeared in recent discussions of qualitative research but has little in common with the approaches used in this book. The Q sort is a method of data collection.

QDAS: Qualitative data analysis software – same as CAQDAS.

QSR NVivo: The full name of NVivo.

Qualitative: To do with the qualities of things rather than quantities.

Qualitative content analysis: The analysis of text using categories which arise out of the data. Very little if at all different from thematic analysis.

Qualitative research: Research which is based on rich textual rather than numerical data.

Quality: One of Grice's maxims which suggests that what is said in conversation should be truthful and sincere.

Quantification: Turning into numbers.

Quantitative research: Research which either collects data in a numerical or quasi numerical form or otherwise seeks to impose quantities on the analysis. Typically mainstream psychology.

Quantity: One of Grice's maxims which suggests that sufficient information should be provided in conversation to make what is said understandable.

Queer theory: This is a form of poststructuralist theory which provides a critique of issues to do with sexual identity and is critical of non-gay ways of thinking and heterosexism. Queer theory is strongly influenced by Michel Foucault.

Radical behaviourism: The behaviourist philosophy formulated by B. F. Skinner. Among its characteristics is the proposal that all behaviour is determined rather than subject to free will. In this way, among many others, radical behaviourism is the antithesis of the assumptions of qualitative psychology.

Reactivity: The tendency of the process of being studied to affect the activities of those being studied.

Reading: A particular perspective on a text.

Realism: The theory that there is an external world which is independent of thought and our perceptions of that world.

Realist epistemology: The assumption that there is a real, physical world which can be directly studied. Often held to be a fundamental of science and positivism.

Received view: A passed-on view of the nature of things or the world which is adopted uncritically by the receiver of that worldview.

Reductionism: The belief that the whole is a sum of its parts. Thus, complex aspects of human activity can best be studied by breaking them down into their component parts. The antithesis of holistic.

Reductionist: To do with reductionism.

Reflexivity: The stance in research in which the researcher considers the implications of the knowledge they create in terms of the procedures of data collection, the biases of the researcher, and their presence in the situations they investigate.

Relation: One of Grice's maxims which suggests that good contributions to conversation should be relevant to the conversation.

Reliability: The idea from quantitative research that measures should exhibit consistency over time and internally over the various sub-sections of the measure.

Repair: Attempts to remedy or otherwise deal with 'embarrassing' errors in conversation.

Research question: In academic research of all sorts, the research question is the question which the research seeks to address.

Respondent validation: This is a fairly common term in qualitative research by which the opinions of the participants in the research (or similar groups of people) are approached about the findings of a research study in which they took part for their comments and evaluation.

Rewrite techniques: *See* Rewriting.

Rewriting: This is an approach to creating general theory in grounded theory analysis. It literally involves rewriting a grounded theory analysis in an attempt to generate a more widely applicable theory; for example, by simply writing a theory in less specific terms as an aid to generalisation.

Rhetoric: The methods by which arguments are made persuasive and convincing.

Rhetorical psychology: The psychological study of rhetoric.

Root metaphor: Different ways of studying a particular discipline adopt different metaphors to suggest the broad nature of that which is being studied. Behaviourism had the root metaphor of people as machines. The term root metaphor then refers to the basic way in which people are conceived in research. The term comes from narrative psychology which has the basic metaphor of people as storytellers.

Sampling: Although this means the process of selecting a representative group of participants to represent the population in quantitative research, it has a very different meaning in qualitative research. The commonest use is in theoretical sampling which means the selection of further cases or instances by selecting those which will contribute most to theory development.

Saturation: When additional participants or data no longer bring new information which encourages the refinement of the analysis. That is, nothing new is being learnt by doing more data collection. It can serve as a means of deciding when no further participants will be recruited but, equally, it can be indicative of when a particular stage of analysis is complete.

Science: Natural sciences such as physics, chemistry and the like.

Scientific method: Usually used as a synonym for positivism.

Scientism: The belief that the natural sciences have primacy and authority compared with other approaches to knowledge, e.g. religious and philosophical knowledge.

Secondary analysis: The analysis of data by researchers who were not involved in the original study of that data. Alternatively, it is the further analysis of data in ways which were not anticipated originally by the researcher.

Selective coding: In grounded theory this is the process by which one of the categories in the analysis is identified to be the core category. All other categories are then related to this. It is a late stage in the building of theory.

Semiology: The discipline involved with the study of signs.

Semiotics: The study of signs and the processes by which they produce meaning. It involves the search for the deeper meaning of documents and other material.

Semi-structured interview: Alternatively in-depth or qualitative interviews in which the interviewee is encouraged to talk in depth and at some length about a topic(s). The interviewee is free to answer in whatever way he or she wishes. The interviewer often has only a skeletal version of the questions they intend to ask. In other words, a semi-structured interview has a loose structure compared with that of a structured interview and a relatively tight structure compared with an unstructured interview which has no prepared structure at all. Semi-structured interviews are generally the choice of qualitative researchers.

Sense making: The process of giving meaning to events.

Sensitivity: See Theoretical sensitivity.

Sign: A term in semiotics referring to the signifier or manifestation of a sign and the signified (the meaning of the sign).

Situationally bounded: The idea that qualities are not fixed in research but change with the situation in which they are assessed.

Social construction: Some aspect of knowledge created by people through interaction or the process of doing this.

Social constructionism: The idea that knowledge is constructed by people during interaction.

Social constructionist: To do with social constructionism.

Social constructionist discourse analysis: The form of discourse analysis particularly associated with Jonathan Potter and Margaret Wetherell. It contrasts with Foucauldian discourse analysis.

Social representation: A concept from Serge Moscovici. It refers to the way that members of a culture collectively share a constructed understanding of the nature of a social object. Once a highly influential theory in social psychology but essentially replaced by not dissimilar ideas from social constructionism.

Sociolinguistics: The study of language in terms of its social and cultural aspects.

Soft data: Data collected not using 'objective' natural science methods. Possibly similar to qualitative.

Software package: Computer program or set of programs such as NVivo in qualitative research.

Speech act theory: The theory of language particularly associated with J. L. Austin which draws to the forefront of analysis how things are done with words or language as social action.

Stake: The assumption of members of a conversation that speakers have a vested interest in the positions they put forward in conversation.

Story: A set of meaningful events presented with a chronological structure.

Structuralism: Ways of theorising about the world which are concerned with the unobservable structures which underlie the world. Since these structures cannot be observed, they have to be inferred. Mental structures are often proposed in psychology. However, structuralism was the first major school of psychology in the modern period. Piaget adopted a form of structuralism in his theories of child development. Most likely, however, in qualitative psychology structuralism refers to sociological thinking immediately prior to the current postmodern (poststructuralist) period.

Structured interviews: Interviews in which all of the questions are standardised in advance of data collection. Almost invariably, this involves offering a limited range of response alternatives for the interviewee to choose from.

Subject position: In discourse analysis, this is the location of the individual within a discourse that they employ. So it is the rights, obligations and duties which, for example, the citizen has in a law-and-order discourse.

Subjectivism: The idea that everything including interpretations, etc. reflect nothing but reports of the views of individuals. Another closely related word for this is relativism. An alternative use of the term indicates that subjectivity is essentially what we refer to as reality. The latter usage comes from phenomenology.

Subjectivities: The idea that different individuals have different lived experiences of the world. Hence, it is the plural of subjectivity.

Subjectivity: Most usually in qualitative psychology this refers to the lived experiences of people such as their experience of self. Alternative meanings are concerned with epistemology and refer to personal viewpoints, unwarranted arguments, or biased accounts. It is, therefore, just the personal view of an individual.

Substantive theory: This, in grounded theory, is the stage of theory which is developed prior to the formal theory which is the outcome of grounded theory.

Subtle realist position: The acceptance that different research methods impose different subjectivities and, consequently, different perspectives on reality. The idea of a basic reality is accepted though it is problematic to study it. The task of researchers is to represent what is possible of that reality.

Superordinate theme: A cluster or group of themes (sub-themes) which are related in some way and given a descriptive label.

Symbolic interactionism: This is a major approach to social psychology originating in the work of George Herbert Mead and Herbert Blumer. Basically it is the idea that a person develops meanings for the world through social interaction with the world. These meanings then determine the individual's interaction with the world.

Talk-in interaction: A phrase used in conversation analysis which essentially describes the nature of conversation as construed in that field.

Template analysis: A form of analysis which pre-specifies many of the categories used in the analysis.

Text: Any data which are imbued with meaning. They do not have to be words or other forms of verbal data but usually are.

Thematic analysis: This is a form of qualitative analysis which seeks to 'work up' or identify the major areas (themes) in the textual data studied.

Theme: A 'topic' identified within some text.

Theoretical coding: In grounded theory, this is a higher level of coding which applies a set of codes which developed out of the data at an earlier stage of the analysis. The researcher has essentially derived a theoretical model which is being applied to the data.

Theoretical sampling: A term originally from grounded theory which describes the process of choosing new cases or even research locations on the basis of their capacity to inform the analysis that has been achieved thus far.

Theoretical sensitivity: In grounded theory this refers to the personal qualities of researchers which equips them to develop good quality grounded theory. It is dependent on factors such as previous experience, reading in the field of interest, the ability to understand data, and insight.

Thick description: There is a lack of clarity about the meaning of this. Although it implies the collection of a lot of detail about something that is being studied, it also involves a degree of initial interpretation in its intentions, meanings, circumstances and so forth.

Three-part list: The idea in conversation analysis that in ordinary conversation the use of lists of three 'items' are common and conversationally effective. For example, I came, I saw, I conquered.

Transcendental phenomenology: This term describes the sort of phenomenology associated with Edmund Husserl. It is the study of what is left when consciousness is stripped of hypotheses about the phenomenon being studied. It is the consciousness following bracketing or epoché.

Transcription: The process of putting into the written word data which are in spoken form such as interviews, conversations, telephone calls and focus group interaction. It almost always involves audio (and sometimes video) recording in modern qualitative research.

Transferability: The equivalent in qualitative research of external validity in quantitative research. That is, the extent to which the findings can be transferred to other situations than the one of the original research.

Transparency: The openness of a researcher's procedures (including analysis) to inspection and criticism.

Triangulation: The use of three (or more) different sources of information to help establish how sound a researcher's inference is. The triangulation may include different data sources, researchers, methods and so forth. Essentially more than one vantage point is being used to assess one's conclusions. Generally, this implies that there should be convergence of the conclusions from, say, different methods which may not be a warranted implication for qualitative methods.

Turn: In conversation analysis the bounded contribution of an individual in a conversation separated by other speakers (or the beginning or end of the conversation).

Turn-taking: The notion from conversation analysis that during conversations individuals take turns in being the speaker.

Unit of analysis: The major unit which is under consideration in a research study. In psychology, this is the individual but the concept could be used to refer to neurons, groups, institutions, cultures and so forth. In qualitative research, the unit of analysis can be a particular aspect of text, for example.

Unstructured interview: An interview which has no pre-planned structure. Sometimes used synonymously with semi-structured interview. However, a semi-structured interview has an interview guide to pre-structure the interview to a degree.

Validity: A quality criterion in the quantitative epistemology. Of dubious value in qualitative research.

Variable: Something that can be named and measured. It is an endemic common term in quantitative psychology but a rarity in qualitative writing.

Verstehen: From German. The word means 'understanding'. It is a difficult concept because of its many related meanings in social sciences. Wilhelm Dilthey, a German philosopher, first used the word in distinguishing the natural sciences from other sciences. The former seeks general laws whereas the human sciences seek to understand meaning. Max Weber used it to mean where a researcher approaches another culture or subculture using the perspective/point of view of that culture or subculture rather than the researcher's own.

Written discourse: Language in its written form.

Written language: Language as it is written down as opposed to spoken.

REFERENCES

Ablett, J. R., & Jones, R. S. (2007). Resilience and well-being in palliative care staff: A qualitative study of hospice nurses' experience of work. *Psycho-Oncology*, *16* (8), 733–740.

Adams, W. A. (2000). Introspectionism reconsidered. Presented at 'Towards a Science of Consciousness'. *Consciousness and Cognition*, *15* (4), 634–654.

Allport, G. W. (1940). The psychologist's frame of reference. *Psychological Bulletin*, *37*, 1–28.

Allport, G. W. (1942). *The use of personal documents in psychological science*. New York, NY: Social Science Research Council.

Allport, G. W., Bruner, J., & Jandorf, E. (1941). Personality under social catastrophe: An analysis of 90 German refugee life histories. *Character and Personality*, *10*, 1–22.

Altheide, D. L. (1996). Qualitative media analysis. *Qualitative Research Methods* Vol. 38. Thousand Oaks, CA: Sage.

American Psychological Association. (2002). Ethical Principles of Psychologists and Code of Conduct. www.apa.org/ethics/code2002.html (accessed 24 April 2012).

American Psychological Association. (2009). PsycINFO: Your Source for Psychological Abstracts. www.apa.org/psycinfo/ (accessed 5 July 2009).

American Psychological Association. (2011). American Psychological Association's PsycINFO® Database Surpasses 3 Million Records. www.apa.org/news/press/releases/2011/01/database.aspx (accessed 11 April 2012).

Anderberg, E. (2000). Word meaning and conceptions. An empirical study of relationships between students' thinking and use of language when reasoning about a problem. *Instructional Science*, *28*, 89–113.

Antaki, C. (2007). Mental-health practitioners' use of idiomatic expressions in summarising clients' accounts. *Journal of Pragmatics*, *39*, 527–541.

Antaki, C. (2009a). Anonymising Data: Ten Guidelines for Changing Names in Transcripts. www-staff.lboro.ac.uk/~ssca1/pseudos2.htm (accessed 24 April 2012).

Antaki, C. (2009b). What Counts as Conversation Analysis – And What Doesn't. www-staff.lboro.ac.uk/~ssca1/analysisintro.htm (accessed 24 April 2012).

Antaki, C., Billig, M., Edwards, D., & Potter, J. (2003). Discourse analysis means doing analysis: A critique of six analytic shortcomings. *Discourse Analysis Online*, *1* (1). www-staff.lboro.ac.uk/~ssca1/DAOLpaper.pdf (accessed 24 April 2012).

Antaki, C., Finlay, W. M. L., & Walton, C. (2007). The staff are your friends: Intellectually disabled identities in official discourse and interactional practice. *British Journal of Social Psychology*, *46*, 1–18.

Ashmore, M., & Reed, D. (2000). Innocence and nostalgia in conversation analysis: The dynamic relations of tape and transcript. *Forum: Qualitative Social Research*, *1*, (3). qualitative-research.net/fqs-texte/3–00/3–00ashmorereed-e.htm (accessed 24 April 2012).

Ashworth, P. (2008). Conceptual foundations of qualitative psychology. In J. A. Smith (Ed.), *Qualitative psychology: A practical guide to research methods* (2nd ed., pp. 4–25). London: Sage.

Ashworth, P., Freewood, M., & MacDonald, R. (2003). The student lifeworld and the meanings of plagiarism. *Journal of Phenomenological Psychology*, *34* (2), 257–278.

Ashworth, P. D. (2003). An approach to phenomenological psychology: The primacy of the lifeworld. *Journal of Phenomenological Psychology, 34* (2), 145–156.

Atkinson, J. M., & Heritage, J. (1984). Transcript notation. In J. M. Atkinson & J. Heritage (Eds.), *Structures of social action: Studies in conversation analysis* (pp. iv–xvi). Cambridge: Cambridge University Press.

Atkinson, M. (2008). Max Atkinson Blog. Gordon Brown's Gaffe Shows what Gail Jefferson Meant by a 'Sound Formed Error'. maxatkinson.blogspot.com/2008/12/gordon-browns-gaffe-shows-what-gail.html (accessed 24 April 2012).

Augoustinos, M., & Tileaga, C. (2012). Twenty five years of discursive psychology. *British Journal of Social Psychology, 51,* 405–412.

Augoustinos, M., Tuffin, K., & Rapley, M. (1999). Genocide or a failure to gel? Racism, history and nationalism in Australian talk. *Discourse & Society, 10,* 351–378.

Austin, J. L. (1962). *How to do things with words: The William James Lectures delivered at Harvard University in 1955.* J. O. Urmson (Ed.). Oxford: Clarendon.

Austin, J. L. (1975). *How to do things with words.* Cambridge, MA: Harvard University Press.

Baars, B. J. (1986). *The cognitive revolution in psychology.* New York: The Guilford Press.

Bailey, L. F. (2014). The origin and success of qualitative research. *International Journal of Market Research, 56* (2), 167–184.

Barbour, R. (2007). *Doing focus groups.* Los Angeles, CA: Sage.

Barker, R. G. (1968). *Ecological psychology.* Stanford, CA: Stanford University Press.

Barker, R., & Wright, H. (1951). *One boy's day. A specimen record of behavior.* New York: Harper and Brothers.

Barlow, D. H., & Hersen, M. (1984). *Single case experimental designs: Strategies for studying behavior change* (2nd ed.). New York: Pergamon Press.

Bartlett, F. (1932). *Remembering.* Cambridge: Cambridge University Press.

Batt, S., & Lippman, A. (2010). Preventing disease: Are pills the answer? In A. Rochon Ford & D. Saibil (Eds.). *The push to prescribe: Women and Canadian drug policy* (pp. 47–66). Toronto: Women's Press.

Baumrind, D. (1985). Research using intentional deception: Ethical issues revisited. *American Psychologist, 40,* 165–174.

Beaugrande, R. de (1996). The story of discourse analysis. In T. van Dijk (Ed.), *Introduction to discourse analysis* (pp. 35–62). London: Sage.

Becker, H. S., & Geer, B. (1982). Participant observation: The analysis of qualitative field data. In R. G. Burgess (Ed.), *Field research: A sourcebook and field manual* (pp. 239–250). London: George Allen and Unwin.

Benneworth, K. (2006). Repertoires of paedophilia: Conflicting descriptions of adult–child sexual relationships in the investigative interview. *The International Journal of Speech, Language and the Law, 13* (2), 190–211.

Benwell, B. M., & Stokoe, E. (2006). *Discourse and identity.* Edinburgh: Edinburgh University Press.

Berelson, B. (1952). *Content analysis in communication research.* Glencoe: Free Press.

Berger, P. L., & Luckmann, T. (1966). *The social construction of reality: A treatise in the sociology of knowledge.* Garden City, NY: Anchor.

Berman, R. C. (2011). Critical reflection on the use of translators/interpreters in a qualitative cross language research project. *International Journal of Qualitative Methods, 10* (2). ejournals.library.ualberta.ca/index.php/IJQM/article/view/8222 (accessed 17 April 2012).

Bevis, J. C. (1949). Interviewing with tape recorders. *Public Opinion Quarterly, 13,* 629–634.

Biggerstaff, D., & Thompson, A. R. (2008). Interpretative phenomenological analysis (IPA): A qualitative methodology of choice in healthcare research. *Qualitative Research in Psychology, 5* (3), 214–224.

Billig, M. (1987). *Arguing and thinking.* Cambridge: Cambridge University Press.

Billig, M. (1991). *Ideology and opinions: Studies in rhetorical psychology.* London: Sage.

Billig, M. (1992). *Talking of the royal family.* London: Routledge.

Billig, M. (1996). *Arguing and thinking: A rhetorical approach to social psychology,* (2nd ed.). Cambridge: Cambridge University Press.

Billig, M. (1997). Rhetorical and discursive analysis: how families talk about the royal family. In N. Hayes (Ed.), *Doing qualitative analysis in psychology* (pp. 39–54). Hove: Psychology Press.

Billig, M. (1999). Whose terms? Whose ordinariness? Rhetoric and ideology in conversation analysis. *Discourse & Society, 10,* 543–558.

Billig, M. (2001). Discursive, rhetorical and ideological messages. In M. Wetherell, S. Taylor & S. J. Yates (Eds.), *Discourse theory and practice: A reader* (pp. 210–221). London: Sage.

Billig, M. (2008). *The hidden roots of critical psychology: Understanding the impact of Locke, Shaftesbury and Reid.* London: Sage.

Billig, M. (2012). Undisciplined beginnings, academic success, and discursive psychology. *British Journal of Social Psychology, 51* (3), 413–424.

Blodgett, L. J., Boyer, W., & Turk, E. (2005). 'No thank you, not today': Supporting ethical and professional relationships in large qualitative studies. *Forum: Qualitative Social Research, 6* (3), www.qualitative-research.net/index.php/fqs/article/viewArticle/31 (accessed 24 April 2012).

Blumer, H. (1969). *Symbolic interactionism: Perspective and method.* Englewood Cliffs, NJ: Prentice Hall.

Bogardus, E. S. (1926). The groups interview. *Journal of Applied Sociology, 10,* 372–382.

Bourdieu, P. (1984). *Distinction: A social critique of the judgement of taste.* London: Routledge.

Bowen, G. A. (2005). Preparing a qualitative research-based dissertation: Lessons learned. *The Qualitative Report, 10* (2), 208–222.

Bozatzis, N. (2014). The discursive turn in social psychology: Four nodal debates. In N. Bozatzis & T. Dragonas (Eds.), *The Discursive turn in social psychology* (pp. 25–50). Chagrin Falls, OH: Taos Institute Publications.

Braun, V., & Clarke, V. (2006). Using thematic analysis in psychology. *Qualitative Research in Psychology, 3,* 77–101.

Brink, E., Karlson, B. W., & Hallberg, L. R.-M. (2002). To be stricken with acute myocardial infarction: A grounded theory study of symptom perception and care-seeking behavior. *Journal of Health Psychology, 7* (5), 533–543.

Brinkmann, S., & Kvale, S. (2005). Confronting the ethics of qualitative research. *Journal of Constructivist Psychology, 18* (2), 157–181.

British Psychological Society. (2010). Ethical Principles for Conducting Research with Human Participants. www.bps.org.uk/sites/default/files/documents/code_of_human_research_ethics.pdf (accessed 24 April 2012).

Brooks, E., & Dallos, R. (2009). Exploring young women's understandings of the development of difficulties: A narrative biographical analysis. *Clinical Child Psychology and Psychiatry, 14* (1), 101–115.

Brower, D. (1949). The problem of quantification in psychological science. *Psychological Review, 56* (6), 325–333.

Brown, S., & Stenner, P. (2009). *Psychology without foundations: History, philosophy and psychosocial theory.* London: Sage.

Broyard, A. (1992). *Intoxicated by my illness.* New York: Random House.

Bruner, J. (1986). *Actual minds, possible worlds.* Cambridge, MA: Harvard University Press.

Bruner, J. (1990). *Acts of meaning.* Cambridge, MA: Harvard University Press.

Bryant, A. (2002). Re-grounding grounded theory. *Journal of Information Technology Theory and Application, 4,* 25–42.

Bryant, A., & Charmaz, K. (2007). *The Sage handbook of grounded theory.* London: Sage.

Bryman, A. (1988). *Quantity and quality in social research.* London: Routledge.

Bryman, A. (2004). *Social research methods* (2nd ed.). Oxford University Press.

Bryman, A., & Bell, E. (2003). *Business research methods.* Oxford: Oxford University Press.

Bucholtz, M. (2000). The politics of transcription. *Journal of Pragmatics, 32,* 1439–1465.

Bucholtz, M. (2003). Theories of discourse as theories of gender. In J. Holmes & M. Meyerhoff (Eds.), *The handbook of language and gender* (pp. 43–68). Oxford, UK: Blackwell.

Bühler, C. (1933). *Der Menschliche Lebenslauf als Psychologisches Problem.* [The Human Course of Life as a Psychological Problem.] Leipzig: Hirzel.

Bulmer, M. (1984). *The Chicago School of Sociology.* Chicago, IL: University of Chicago Press.

Burgess, R. G. (1982). Styles of data analysis: Approaches and implications. In R. G. Burgess (Ed.), *Field research: A sourcebook and field manual* (pp. 235–238). London: George Allen and Unwin.

Burgess, R. G. (1984). *In the field: An introduction to field research.* London: Allen and Unwin.

Burman, E. (2004). Discourse analysis means analysing discourse: Some comments on Antaki, Billig, Edwards and Potter's 'Discourse analysis means doing analysis: A critique of six analytic shortcomings'. *Discourse Analysis Online.* extra.shu.ac.uk/daol/articles/open/2003/003/burman2003003-t.html (accessed 24 April 2012).

Burman, E., & Parker, I. (Eds.) (1993). *Discourse analytic research: Repertoires and readings of texts in action.* London: Routledge.

Burr, V. (2003). *Social constructionism* (2nd ed.). London: Routledge.

Butler, C. W. (2008). *Talk and social interaction in the playground.* Aldershot: Ashgate.

Cairns, D. (2010). Nine fragments on psychological phenomenology. *Journal of Phenomenological Psychology, 41,* 1–27.

Calder, B. (1977). Focus groups and the nature of qualitative marketing research. *Journal of Marketing Research, 14* (3), 353–364.

Campbell, C., & Guy, A. (2007). 'Why can't they do anything for a simple back problem?': A qualitative examination of expectations for low back pain treatment and outcome. *Journal of Health Psychology, 12* (4), 641–652.

Campbell, D. T., & Fiske, D. W. (1959). Convergent and discriminant validation by the multitrait–multimethod matrix. *Psychological Bulletin, 56,* 81–105.

Campbell, M. L. C., & Morrison, A. P. (2007). The subjective experience of paranoia: Comparing the experiences of patients with psychosis and individuals with no psychiatric history. *Clinical Psychology and Psychotherapy, 14* (1), 63–77.

Canter, D. (1983). The potential of facet theory for applied social psychology. *Quality and Quantity, 17,* 35–67.

Carless, D. (2008). Narrative, identity, and recovery from serious mental illness: A life history of a runner. *Qualitative Research in Psychology, 5,* 233–248.

Carter, S. S. (1988). Unipolar clinical depression: An empirical-phenomenological study. Unpublished doctoral dissertation, Duquesne University, Pittsburgh, PA.

Chapman, E., & Smith, J. A. (2002). Interpretative phenomenological analysis and the new genetics. *Journal of Health Psychology, 7* (2), 125–130.

Charmaz, K. (1995). Grounded theory. In J. A. Smith, R. Harré and L. V. Langenhove (Eds.), *Rethinking methods in psychology* (pp. 27–49). London: Sage.

Charmaz, K. (2000). Grounded theory: Objectivist and constructivist methods. In N. K. Denzin and Y. S. E. Lincoln (Eds.), *Handbook of qualitative research* (2nd ed., pp. 503–535). Thousand Oaks, CA: Sage.

Charmaz, K. (2006). *Constructing grounded theory: A practical guide through qualitative analysis.* Thousand Oaks, CA: Sage.

Chomsky, N. (1973). Psychology and ideology. *Cognition, 1,* 11–46.

Choudhuri, D., Glauser, A., & Peregoy, J. (2004). Guidelines for writing a qualitative manuscript for the *Journal of Counseling & Development. Journal of Counseling and Development, 82* (4), 443–446.

Ciclitira, K. (2004). Pornography, women and feminism: Between pleasure and politics. *Sexualities, 7,* 3, 281–301.

Clark, A., Stedmon, J., & Margison, S. (2008). An exploration of the experience of mothers whose children sustain traumatic brain injury (TBI) and their families. *Clinical Child Psychology and Psychiatry, 13* (4), 565–583.

Clarke, A., Mamo, L., Fosket, J., Fishman, J., & Shim, J. (2010). *Biomedicalization: Technoscience, health and illness in the U.S.* Durham, NC: Duke University Press.

Clarke, V. (2001). What about the children? Arguments against lesbian and gay parenting. *Women's Studies International Forum, 24* (5), 555–570.

Clarke, V., Burns, M., & Burgoyne, C. (2008). Who would take whose name? *Journal of Community and Applied Social Psychology, 18* (5), 420–439.

Clay, R. (2005). Too few in quantitative psychology. *APA Monitor on Psychology, 36* (8). www.apa.org/monitor/sep05/quantitative.html (accessed 24 April 2012).

Cloonan, T. F. (1995). The early history of phenomenological psychological research in America. *Journal of Phenomenological Psychology, 26* (1), 46–126.

Cmerjrkova, S., & Prevignano, C. L. (2003). On conversation analysis: An interview with Emanuel Schegloff. In C. L. Prevignano and P. J. Thibault (Eds.), *Discussing conversation analysis: The work of Emanuel Schegloff* (pp. 11–55). Amsterdam: John Benjamins.

Coates, J., & Thornborrow, J. (1999). Myths, lies and audiotapes: Some thoughts on data transcripts. *Discourse and Society, 10* (4), 594–597.

Cohen, D. (1977). On psychology: Noam Chomsky interviewed by David Cohen. Excerpted from *Psychologists on Psychology: Modern Innovators Talk About Their Work,* Taplinger, 1977. www.chomsky.info/interviews/1977--.htm (accessed 24 April 2012).

Coleman, L. M., & Cater, S. M. (2005). A qualitative study of the relationship between alcohol consumption and risky sex in adolescents. *Archives of Sexual Behavior, 34,* 649–661.

Comte, A. (1975). *Auguste Comte and Positivism: The essential writings.* G. Lenzzer (Ed.). Chicago, IL: University of Illinois Press.

Cowles, E. (1888). Insistent and fixed ideas. *American Journal of Psychology, 1* (2), 222–270.

Coyle, A. (2007). Discourse analysis. In E. Lyons and A. Coyle (Eds.), *Analysing qualitative data in psychology* (pp. 98–116). London: Sage.

Crabtree, B. F., & Miller, W. L. (1999). Using codes and code manuals: A template organizing style of interpretation. In B. F. Crabtree & W. L. Miller (Eds.), *Doing qualitative research* (2nd ed., pp. 163–177). Newbury Park, CA: Sage.

Crossley, M. (2000). *Introducing narrative psychology: Self-trauma and the construction of meaning.* Buckingham: Open University Press.

Crossley, M. L. (2003). Let me 'explain': Narrative emplotment and one patient's experience of oral cancer. *Social Science and Medicine, 56,* 439–448.

Crossley, M. L. (2007). Narrative analysis. In E. Lyons and A. Coyle (Eds.), *Analysing qualitative data in psychology* (pp. 131–144). London: Sage.

Danziger, K. (1997). The varieties of social construction. *Theory and Psychology*, 7 (3), 399–416.

Danziger, K., & Dzinas, K. (1997). How psychology got its variables. *Canadian Psychology*, 38, 43–48.

Davidson, J. (1984). Subsequent versions of invitations, offers, requests, and proposals dealing with potential or actual rejection. In J. M. Atkinson & J. Heritage (Eds.), *Structures of social action: Studies in conversation analysis* (pp. 102–128). Cambridge: Cambridge University Press.

Dearborn, G. V. N. (1920). Review of the Lia-speaking peoples of Northern Rhodesia. *Journal of Abnormal Psychology*, 15 (4), 283–288.

Del Vecchio Good, M., Munakata, T., Kobayashi, Y., Mattingly, C., & Good, B. (1994). Oncology and narrative time. *Social Science and Medicine*, 38, 855–862.

Deleuze, G. (2006). *Foucault*. London: Continuum.

Denscombe, M. (2002). *Ground rules for good research: A 10 point guide for social researchers*. Buckingham: Open University Press.

Denzin, N. K., & Lincoln, Y. S. E. (2000). Introduction: The discipline and practice of qualitative research. In N. K. Denzin & Y. S. E. Lincoln (Eds.), *Handbook of qualitative research* (2nd ed., pp. 1–28). Thousand Oaks, CA: Sage.

Dereshiwsky, M. (1999). The Five Dimensions of Participant Observations. jan.ucc.nau .edu/~mid/edr725/class/observation/fivedimensions/reading3-2-1.html (accessed 24 April 2012).

Dickson, A., Allan, D., & O'Carroll, R. (2008). Biographical disruption and the experience of loss following a spinal cord injury: An interpretative phenomenological analysis. *Psychology and Health*, 23 (4), 407–425.

Dixon-Woods, M., Sutton, A., Shaw, R., Miller, T., Smith, J., Young, B., Bonas, S., Booth, A., & Jones, D. (2007). Appraising qualitative research for inclusion in systematic reviews: A quantitative and qualitative comparison of three methods. *Journal of Health Service Research Policy*, 12 (1), 42–47.

Dollard, J. (1935). *Criteria for the life history*. New Haven, CT: Yale University Press.

Dollard, J. (1937). *Caste and class in a southern town*. Garden City, NY: Doubleday.

Drew, P. (1995). Conversation analysis. In J. A. Smith, R. Harré & L. V. Langenhove (Eds.), *Rethinking methods in psychology* (pp. 64–79). London: Sage.

Du Bois, J. W., Schuetze-Coburn, S., Cumming, S., & Paolino, D. (1993). Outline of discourse transcription. In J. A. Edwards & M. D. Lampert (Eds.), *Talking data: Transcription and coding in discourse research* (pp. 45–89). Hillsdale, NJ: Erlbaum.

Du Bois, W. E. B. (1899). *The Philadelphia Negro: A social study*. Philadelphia: University of Pennsylvania.

Duff, S. (2011). Exploring criminogenic need through victim apology letters II: An IPA analysis of post-treatment accounts of offending against children. *Journal of Aggression, Conflict and Peace Research*, 3 (4), 230–242.

Eagleton, T. (1983). *Literary theory: An introduction*. Oxford: Basil Blackwell.

Eatough, V., & Smith, J. A. (2006). 'I feel like a scrambled egg in my head': An idiographic case study of meaning, making and anger using interpretative phenomenological analysis. *Psychology and Psychotherapy: Theory, Research and Practice*, 79, 115–135.

Edley, N. (2001). Analysing masculinity: Interpretative repertoires, ideological dilemmas and subject positions. In M. Wetherell, S. Taylor & S. J. E. Yates (Eds.), *Discourse as data: A guide for analysis* (pp. 189–228). London: Sage.

Edwards, D. (1994). 'Script formulations: A study of event descriptions in conversation'. *Journal of Language and Social Psychology*, 13 (3), 211–247.

Edwards, D. (1995). Sacks and psychology. *Theory and Psychology, 5* (3), 579–597.

Edwards, D. (1997). *Discourse and cognition.* London: Sage.

Edwards, D. (2012). Discursive and scientific psychology. *British Journal of Social Psychology, 51* (3), 425–435.

Edwards, D., & Potter, J. (1992). *Discursive psychology.* London: Sage.

Edwards, D., & Middleton, D. (1988). Conversational remembering and family relationships: How children learn to remember. *Journal of Social and Personal Relationships, 5,* 3–25.

Ehlich, K. (1993). HIAT: A transcription system for discourse data. In J. A. Edwards & M. D. Lampert (Eds.), *Talking data: Transcription and coding in discourse research* (pp. 123–148). Hillsdale, NJ: Erlbaum.

Elliott, R., Fischer, C. T., & Rennie, D. L. (1999). Evolving guidelines for publication of qualitative research studies in psychology and related fields. *British Journal of Clinical Psychology, 38,* 215–229.

Ellis, D., & Cromby, J. (2012). Emotional inhibition: A discourse analysis of disclosure. *Psychology and Health, 27* (5), 515–532.

Emerson, P., & Frosh, S. (2004). *Critical narrative analysis in psychology: A guide to practice.* Basingstoke: Palgrave Macmillan.

Epley, N., & Huff, C. (1998). Suspicion, affective response, and educational benefit as a result of deception in psychology research. *Personality and Social Psychology Bulletin, 24,* 759–768.

Every, D., & Augoustinos, M. (2007). Constructions of racism in the Australian parliamentary debates on asylum seekers. *Discourse and Society, 18* (4), 411–436.

Fadyl, J. K., & Nicholls, D. A. (2013). Foucault, the subject and the research interview: A critique of methods. *Nursing Inquiry, 20* (1), 23–29.

Fairclough, N. (1993). *Discourse and social change.* Cambridge: Polity Press.

Festervand, T. A. (1984–1985). An introduction and application of focus group research to the health care industry. *Health Marketing Quarterly.* Special Issue: Marketing ambulatory care services, *2* (2–3), 199–209.

Festinger, L., Riecken, H. W., & Schachter, S. (1956). *When prophecy fails: A social and psychological study of a modern group that predicted the destruction of the world.* New York: Harper Torchbooks.

Fillingham, L. A. (1993). *Foucault for beginners.* Danbury, CT: For Beginners.

Finkelhor, D., Mitchell, K. J., & Wolak, J. (2000). *Online victimization: A report on the nation's youth.* Alexandria, VA: National Center for Missing and Exploited Children.

Finlay, L. (2009). Debating phenomenological research methods. *Phenomenology & Practice, 3,* 6–25.

Fish, S. (1989). *Doing what comes naturally: Change, rhetoric and the practice of theory in literary and legal studies.* Oxford: Oxford University Press.

Flick, U. (2002). *An introduction to qualitative research* (2nd ed.). London: Sage.

Flyvbjerg, B. (2006). Five misunderstandings about case-study research. *Qualitative Inquiry, 12* (2), 219–245.

Fontana, A., & Frey, J. H. (2000). The interview: from structured questions to negotiated text. In N. K. Denzin & Y. S. Lincoln (Eds.), *Handbook of qualitative research* (2nd ed., pp. 645–672). Thousand Oaks, CA: Sage.

Forbat, L., & Henderson, J. (2003). 'Stuck in the middle with you': The ethics and process of qualitative research with two people in an intimate relationship. *Qualitative Health Research, 13,* 1453–1462.

Foucault, M. (1954/1976). *Mental illness and personality.* New York: Harper and Row.

Foucault, M. (1961/1965). *The history of madness (a history of insanity in the age of reason)*. New York: Random House.

Foucault, M. (1963/1973). *The birth of the clinic*. New York: Pantheon.

Foucault, M. (1966/1970). *The order of things*. New York: Pantheon.

Foucault, M. (1969/1972). *The archeology of knowledge*. New York: Pantheon.

Foucault, M. (1975/1977). *Discipline and punish*. New York: Pantheon.

Foucault M. (1977). *Discipline and punish: The birth of the prison* (trans. A Sheridan). London: Penguin.

Foucault, M. (1978). *The history of sexuality: Volume 1, An introduction: The will to knowledge* (trans. R. Hurley). London: Penguin.

Foucault, M. (1980). *Power/knowledge: Selected interviews and other writings 1972–1977*. Hassocks, Sussex: Harvester Press.

Foucault, M. (1985). *The history of sexuality: Volume 2, The use of pleasure. Volume 2* (trans R. Hurley). New York: Pantheon.

Foucault, M. (1986). *The history of sexuality: Volume 3, The care of the self* (trans. R. Hurley). New York: Pantheon.

Foucault, M. (1994). *The order of things: An archaeology of the human sciences*. New York, NY: Vintage Books.

Freud, S. (1909). *Analysis of a phobia of a five-year-old boy* (Vol. 8 *Case Histories*). London: Pelican Freud Library.

Freud, S. (1918). *Totem and taboo*. Translated by A. A. Brill. New York: Moffat, Yard Co.

Frith, H., & Gleeson, K. (2008). Dressing the body: The role of clothing in sustaining body pride and managing body distress. *Qualitative Research in Psychology*, 5 (4), 249–264.

Frost, N. (2009). 'Do you know what I mean?': The use of a pluralistic narrative analysis approach in the interpretation of an interview. *Qualitative Research*, 9 (1), 9–29.

Fullfact. (2011). How much does obesity cost the NHS? https://fullfact.org/factchecks/NHS_reforms_David_Cameron_speech_obesity_costs_foresight_Department_of_Health-2732 (accessed 11 June 2015).

Garson, G. D. (2013). *Narrative analysis*. Statistical Associates Blue Book Series 42, Kindle edition.

Gee, D., Ward, T., & Eccleston, L. (2003). The function of sexual fantasies for sexual offenders: A preliminary model. *Behaviour Change*, 20, 44–60.

Gergen, K. J. (1973). Social psychology as history. *Journal of Personality and Social Psychology*, 26 (2), 309–320.

Gergen, K. J. (1985a). The social constructionist movement in modern psychology. *American Psychologist*, 40, 266–275.

Gergen, K. J. (1985b). Social constructionist inquiry: Context and implications. In K. J. Gergen & K. E. Davis (Eds.), *The social construction of the person* (pp. 3–18). New York: Springer-Verlag.

Gergen, K. J. (1991). The saturated self: Dilemmas of identity in contemporary life. New York: Basic Books.

Gergen, K. J. (1985). The social constructionist movement in modern psychology. *American Psychologist*, 40 (3), 266–275.

Gergen, K. J. (1998). Narrative, moral identity and historical consciousness: A social constructionist account. Draft copy appearing as 'Erzahlung, moralische Identiat und historisches Bewusstsein. Eine sozialkonstructionistische Darstelung.' In J. Straub (Ed.), *Identitat und historishces Bewusstsein*. Frankfurt: Suhrkamp. www.swarthmore.edu/Documents/faculty/gergen/Narrative_Moral_Identity_and_Historical_Consciousness.pdf (accessed 24 April 2012).

Gergen, K. J. (1999). *An invitation to social construction*. London: Sage.

Gergen, K. J., & Gergen, M. (1983). Narratives of the self. In T. R. Sarbin & K. Scheibe (Eds.), *Studies in social identity* (pp. 54–74). New York: Praeger.

Gergen, K. J., & Gergen, M. M. (1986). Narrative form and the construction of psychological science. In T. R. Sarbin (Ed.), *Narrative psychology: The storied nature of human conduct* (pp. 22–44). New York: Praeger.

Gergen, K. J., and Graumann, C. F. (1996). *Psychological discourse in historical perspective*. New York: Cambridge University Press.

Gergen, M. (2008). Qualitative methods in feminist psychology. In C. Willig & W. Stainton-Rogers (Eds.), *The SAGE handbook of qualitative research in psychology* (pp. 280–295). London: Sage.

Gibbs, A. (1997). Focus groups. *Social Research Update, 19* sru.soc.surrey.ac.uk/SRU19.html (accessed 12 February 2009).

Gibson, S. (2013). Milgram's obedience experiments: A rhetorical analysis. *British Journal of Social Psychology, 52,* 290–309.

Gibson, S. (2014). Discourse, defiance, and rationality: 'Knowledge work' in the 'Obedience' experiments. *Journal of Social Issues, 70* (3), 424–438.

Gilbert, G. N., & Mulkay, M. (1984). *Opening Pandora's Box: A sociological analysis of scientists' discourse.* Cambridge: Cambridge University Press.

Giles, D. (2006). Constructing identities in cyberspace: The case of eating disorders. *British Journal of Social Psychology, 45* (3), 463–477.

Giorgi, A. (1971). A phenomenological approach to the problem of meaning and serial learning. In A. Giorgi, W. Fischer & R. von Eckartsberg (Eds.), *Duquesne Studies in Phenomenological Psychology,* Volume 1 (pp. 88–100). Pittsburgh: Duquesne University Press.

Giorgi, A. (1985a). Sketch of a psychological phenomenological method. In A. Giorgi (Ed.), *Phenomenology and psychological research* (pp. 8–22). Pittsburgh, PA: Duquesne University Press.

Giorgi, A. (Ed.) (1985b). *Phenomenological and psychological research.* Pittsburgh, PA: Duquesne University Press.

Giorgi, A. (1994). A phenomenological perspective on certain qualitative research methods. *Journal of Phenomenological Psychology, 25,* 190–220.

Giorgi, A. (1997). The theory, practice, and evaluation of the phenomenological method as a qualitative research procedure. *Journal of Phenomenological Psychology, 28,* 235–260.

Giorgi, A. (1998). The origins of the *Journal of Phenomenological Psychology* and some difficulties in introducing phenomenology into scientific psychology. *Journal of Phenomenological Psychology, 29* (2), 161–176.

Giorgi, A. (2000). *The descriptive phenomenological method* (Learning Guide, Course RES3130). San Francisco: Saybrook Graduate School and Research Center.

Giorgi, A. (2003). The descriptive phenomenological psychological method. In P. M. Camic, J. E. Rhodes & L. Yardley (Eds.), *Qualitative research in psychology: Expanding perspectives in methodology and design perspectives in methodology and design* (pp. 243–273). Washington, DC: American Psychological Association.

Giorgi, A. (2010). Phenomenological psychology: A brief history and its challenges. *Journal of Phenomenological Psychology, 41,* 145–179.

Giorgi, B. (2011). A phenomenological analysis of the experience of pivotal moments in therapy as defined by clients. *Journal of Phenomenological Psychology, 42* (1), 61–106.

Glaser, B. G. (1978). *Theoretical sensitivity: Advances in the methodology of grounded theory.* Mill Valley, CA: Sociology Press.

Glaser, B. G. (1982). Generating formal theory. In R. G. Burgess (Ed.), *Field research: A sourcebook and field manual* (pp. 225–232). London: George Allen and Unwin.

Glaser, B. G. (1992). *Basics of grounded theory analysis. Emergence vs forcing.* Mill Valley, CA: Sociology Press.

Glaser, B. G. (1998). *Doing grounded theory: Issues and discussions*. Mill Valley, CA: Sociology Press.

Glaser, B. G., & Strauss, A. L. (1965). *Awareness of dying*. Chicago, IL: Aldine.

Glaser, B. G., & Strauss, A. L. (1967). *The discovery of grounded theory: Strategies for qualitative research*. New York: Aldine de Gruyter.

Goffman, E. (1959). *The presentation of self in everyday life*. Garden City, NY: Doubleday.

Goffman, E. (1961). *Asylums: Essays on the social situation of mental patients and other inmates*. Garden City, New York: Anchor.

Goffman, E. (1974). *Frame analysis: An essay on the organization of experience*. London: Harper and Row.

Goodley, D., & Parker, I. (2000). Critical psychology and action research. *Annual Review of Critical Psychology, 2*, 3–16.

Goodman, S. (2008). The generalizability of discursive research. *Qualitative Research in Psychology, 5* (4), 265–275.

Goodwin, M. H. (1990). *He-said-she-said: Talk as social organization among Black children*. Bloomington, IA: Indiana University Press.

Goodwin, P., & Ogden, J. (2007). Women's reflections upon their past abortions: An exploration of how and why emotional reactions change over time. *Psychology and Health, 22* (2), 231–248.

Gordon, M. J. (2006). Interview with William Labov. *Journal of English Linguistics, 34*, 332–351.

Goulding, C. (2002). *Grounded theory: A practical guide for management, business and market researchers*. London: Sage.

Grbich, C. (2007). *Qualitative data analysis*. London: Sage.

Grice, H. P. (1975). Logic and conversation. In P. Cole & J. Morgan (Eds.), *Syntax and semantics 3: Speech acts* (pp. 41–58). New York: Academic Press.

Groenewald, T. (2004). A phenomenological research design illustrated. *International Journal of Qualitative Methods, 3* (1), www.ualberta.ca/~iiqm/backissues/3_1/html/ groenewald.html (accessed 17 April 2012).

Gumperz, J. J., & Berenz, N. (1993). Transcribing conversational exchange. In J. A. Edwards & M. D. Lampert (Eds.), *Talking data: Transcription and coding in discourse research* (pp. 91–122). Hillsdale, NJ: Erlbaum.

Gutting, G. ((2005). *Foucault: A very short introduction*. Oxford: Oxford University Press.

Halling, S. (2002). Making phenomenology accessible to a wider audience. *Journal of Phenomenological Psychology, 33* (1), 19–38.

Hammersley, M. (1996). The relationship between qualitative and quantitative research: Paradigm loyalty versus methodological eclecticism. In J. T. E. Richardson (Ed.), *Handbook of qualitative research methods for psychology and the social sciences* (pp. 159–174). Leicester: BPS Books.

Hammersley, M. (1999). Some reflections on the current state of qualitative research. *Research Intelligence, 70*, 16–18.

Hammersley, M. (2010). Reproducing or constructing? Some questions about transcription in social research. *Qualitative Research, 10*, 553–569.

Hanin, Y. L. (1980). A study of anxiety in sports. In W. F. Straub (Ed.), *Sport psychology: An analysis of athletic behavior*. New York: Movement Publications.

Hanna, P. (2009). Conceptualising sustainable tourism – ethics, inequalities and colonialism. *Enquire, 2*, 1–22.

Hanna, P. (2014). Foucauldian discourse analysis in psychology: Reflecting on a hybrid reading of Foucault when researching 'ethical subjects'. *Qualitative Research in Psychology, 11* (2), 142–159.

Harré, R., & Gillett, G. (1994). *The discursive mind*. London: Sage.

Harris, Z. (1952). Discourse analysis. *Language*, 29 (1), 1–30.

Hayes, N. (2000). *Doing psychological research gathering and analysing data*. Buckingham: OU Press.

Heath, C., & Luff, P. (1993). Explicating face-to-face interaction. In N. Gilbert (Ed.), *Researching social life* (pp. 306–327). London: Sage.

Heidegger, M. (1962). *Being and time* (trans. J. Macquarrie & E. Robinson). New York: Harper & Row.

Henriques, J., Hollway, W., Urwin, C., Venn, C., & Walkerdine, V. (1984). *Changing the subject: Psychology, social regulation and subjectivity*. London: Methuen.

Henwood, K., & Pidgeon, M. (1994). Beyond the qualitative paradigm: A framework for introducing diversity within qualitative psychology. *Journal of Community and Applied Social Psychology*, 4, 225–238.

Hepburn, A. (1999). Derrida and psychology. *Theory and Psychology*, 9 (5), 639–667.

Hepburn, A. (2003). *An introduction to critical social psychology*. London: Sage.

Hepburn, A. (2004). Crying: Notes on description, transcription, and interaction. *Research on Language and Social Interaction*, 3 (3), 251–290.

Heritage, J. (1984). *Garfinkel and ethnomethodology*. London: Polity.

Heritage, J. (2003). Presenting Emanuel A. Schegloff. In C. L. Prevignano & P. J. Thibault (Eds.), *Discussing conversation analysis: The work of Emanuel A. Schegloff* (pp. 1–10). Amsterdam: John Benjamins.

Hiles, D., & Čermák, I. (2008). Narrative psychology. In C. Willig & W. Stainton-Rogers (Eds.), *The SAGE handbook of qualitative research in psychology* (pp. 147–164). London: Sage.

Hollway, W. (2005). Commentary on 'Qualitative interviews in psychology'. *Qualitative Research in Psychology*, 2, 312–314.

Holmberg, R., & Larsson, M. (2006). Fatal attractions on the road to an ethnography of organizing. Presentation at Symposium on Current Developments in Ethnographic Research in the Social and Management Sciences. University of Liverpool, Management School. 13–14 September 2006.

Hook, D. (2001). Discourse, knowledge, materiality, history: Foucault and discourse analysis. *Theory and Psychology*, 11, 521–547.

Horton-Salway, M. (2001). Narrative identities and the management of personal account-ability in talk about M.E.: A discursive approach to illness narrative. *Journal of Health Psychology*, 6 (2), 261–273.

Howitt, D. (1991). *Concerning psychology*. Milton Keynes: Open University Press.

Howitt, D. (1992). *Child abuse errors*. London: Harvester Wheatsheaf.

Howitt, D. (1995). *Paedophiles and sexual offences against children*. Chichester: John Wiley.

Howitt, D. (2012). *Introduction to forensic and criminal psychology* (4th ed.). Harlow: Pearson Education.

Howitt, D., & Cramer, D. (2011). *Introduction to research methods in psychology*. Harlow: Pearson.

Howitt, D., & Cramer, D. (2014). *Introduction to research methods in psychology* (4th ed.). Harlow: Pearson.

Howitt, D., & Cumberbatch, G. (1990). *Pornography: Impacts and influences*. London: Home Office Research Unit.

Howitt, D., & Owusu-Bempah, J. (1994). *The racism of psychology*. London: Harvester Wheatsheaf.

Husserl, E. (1892). *Philosophie der Arithmetik. Psychologische und logische Untersuchungen*. Halle: Pfeffer.

Husserl, E. (1913/1931). *Ideas: General introduction to pure phenomenology [Ideen zu einer reinen Phänomenologie und phänomenologischen Philosophie. Erstes Buch: Allgemeine Einführung in die reine Phänomenologie]* (trans. W. R. Boyce Gibson). London: George, Allen and Unwin.

Husserl, E. (1954/1970). *The crisis of human sciences and transcendental phenomenology.* Trans. by David Carr. Evanston, IL: Northwestern University Press.

Hutchby, I., & Wooffitt, R. (1998). *Conversation analysis: Principles, practices and applications.* Cambridge: Polity Press.

Hutchinson, A., Johnston, L., & Breckon, J. (2011). Grounded theory-based research within exercise psychology: A critical review. *Qualitative Research in Psychology, 8,* 247–272.

Hycner, R. H. (1999). Some guidelines for the phenomenological analysis of interview data. In A. Bryman & R. G. Burgess (Eds.), *Qualitative research 3* (pp. 143–164). London: Sage.

Isherwood, T., Burns, M., Naylor, M., & Read, S. (2007). 'Getting into trouble': A qualitative analysis of the onset of offending in the accounts of men with learning disabilities. *Journal of Forensic Psychiatry and Psychology, 18* (2), 221–234.

Itzin, C. (Ed.). (1993). *Pornography: Women, violence and civil liberties.* Oxford: Oxford University Press.

Jahoda, M., Lazarsfeld, P. F., & Zeisel, H. (1933). *Die Arbeitslosen von Marienthal.* Leipzig: S. Hirzel.

Jahoda, M., Lazarsfeld, P. F., & Zeisel, H. (2002). *Marienthal: The sociography of an unemployed community.* Edison, NJ: Transaction Books.

James, W. (1902/1985). *The varieties of religious experience.* Cambridge, MA: Harvard University Press.

Jefferson, G. (1996). On the poetics of ordinary talk. *Text and Performance Quarterly, 16* (1), 1–61.

Jefferson, G. (2004). Glossary of transcript symbols with an introduction. In G. H. Lerner (Ed.), *Conversation analysis: Studies from the first generation* (pp. 13–23). Philadelphia: John Benjamins.

Jenkins, J., & Ogden, J. (2012). Becoming 'whole' again: A qualitative study of women's views of recovering from anorexia nervosa. *European Eating Disorders Review, 20* (1), 23–31.

Johnson, B. E. (2011). The speed and accuracy of voice recognition software-assisted transcription versus the listen-and-type method: A research note. *Qualitative Research, 11,* 91–97.

Johnson, J., & Altheide, D. L. (2002). Reflections on professional ethics. In W. I. C. van den Hoonaard (Ed.), *Walking the tightrope: Ethical issues for qualitative researchers* (pp. 59–69). Toronto: University of Toronto Press.

Johnston, C. A. B., & Morrison, T. G. (2007). The presentation of masculinity in everyday life: Contextual variations in the masculine behavior of young Irish men. *Sex Roles, 57,* 661–674.

Jones, D., & Elcock, J. (2001). *History and theories of psychology: A critical perspective.* London: Arnold.

Josselson, R. (2014). Editorial: Introduction to qualitative psychology. *Qualitative Psychology, 1* (1), 1–3.

Kant, I. (2007). *Critique of pure reason* (trans. M. Weigelt). London: Penguin.

Keen, S., & Todres, L. (2007). Strategies for disseminating qualitative research findings: Three exemplars. *Forum: Qualitative Social Research, 8* (3), Art 17. nbn-resolving.de/urn:nbn:de:0114-fqs0703174 (accessed 4 April 2012).

Kelly, G. A. (1955a). *The psychology of personal constructs. Volume 1: A theory of personality*. New York: Norton.

Kelly, G. A. (1955b). *The psychology of personal constructs. Volume 2: Clinical diagnosis and psychotherapy*. New York: Norton.

Kidder, L. H., & Fine, M. (1997). Qualitative inquiry in psychology: A radical tradition. In D. Fox & I. Prilleltensky (Eds.), *Critical psychology: An introduction* (pp. 34–50). London: Sage.

King, N. (1998). Template analysis. In G. Symon & C. Cassell (Eds.), *Qualitative methods and analysis in organizational research* (pp. 118–134). London: Sage.

King, N., Finlay, L., Ashworth, P., Smith, J. A., Langdridge, D., & Butt, T. (2008). 'Can't really trust that, so what can I trust?': A polyvocal, qualitative analysis of the psychology of mistrust. *Qualitative Research in Psychology*, 5, 80–102.

Kirkey, S. (2007). Young girls require HPV vaccine, panel says: Virus spread through sex causes cervical cancer. *National Post*, 31 January, A1.

Kitzinger, C. (2007). Editor's Introduction: The promise of conversation analysis for feminist research. *Feminism and Psychology*, 17 (2), 133–148.

Kitzinger, C., & Jones, D. (2007). When May calls home: The opening moments of family telephone conversations with an Alzheimer's patient. *Feminism and Psychology*, 17 (2), 184–202.

Kitzinger, C., & Willmott, J. (2002). 'The thief of womanhood': Women's experience of polycystic ovarian syndrome. *Social Science and Medicine*, 54 (3), 349–361.

Klein, L. (2001). Obituary: Professor Marie Jahoda *The Independent*, 8 May www.independent.co.uk/news/obituaries/professor-marie-jahoda-729096.html [no longer available for access].

Kohlbacher, F. (2006). The use of qualitative content analysis in case study research. *Qualitative Social Research*, 7 (1). www.qualitative-research.net/index.php/fqs/article/view/75/154 (accessed 25 June 2009).

Korn, J. H. (1997). *Illusions of reality: A history of deception in social psychology*. New York: State University of New York Press.

Kracauer, S. (1952). The challenge of qualitative content analysis. *Public Opinion Quarterly*, 16, 631–642.

Krueger, R. A., & Casey, M. A. (2000). *Focus groups. A practical guide for applied research* (3rd ed.). Thousand Oaks, CA: Sage.

Kuhn, T. (1962). *The structure of scientific revolutions*. Chicago, IL: University of Chicago Press.

Kvale, S. (1996). *Interviews*. Thousand Oaks, CA: Sage.

Kvale, S. (2007). *Doing interviews*. Los Angeles, CA: Sage.

Labov, W. (1972). *Sociolinguistic patterns*. Philadelphia: University of Pennsylvania Press.

Labov, W. (1997). Some further steps in narrative analysis. *The Journal of Narrative and Life History*, 7, 395–415.

Labov, W., & Waletzky, J. (1967). Narrative analysis. In J. Helm (Ed.), *Essays on the verbal and visual arts* (pp. 12–44). Seattle: University of Washington Press.

Lambert, S., & O'Halloran, E. (2008). Deductive thematic analysis of a female paedophilia website. *Psychiatry, Psychology and Law*, 15 (2), 284–300.

Langdridge, D. (2007). *Phenomenological psychology: Theory, research and method*. Harlow: Pearson Education.

Langdridge, D. (2008). Phenomenology and critical social psychology: Directions and debates in theory and research. *Social and Personality Psychology Compass*, 2/3, 1126–1142.

Langford, D. (1994). *Analysing talk*. London: Macmillan.

Lapadat, J. C., & Lindsay, A. C. (1999). Transcription in research and practice: From standardization of technique to interpretive positionings. *Qualitative Inquiry*, *5*, 64. qix. sagepub.com/cgi/content/abstract/5/1/64 (accessed 27 August 2009).

Larkin, M., Watts, S., & Clifton, E. (2006). Giving voice and making sense in interpretative phenomenological analysis. *Qualitative Research in Psychology*, *3* (2), 102–120.

Lawes, R. (1999). Marriage: An analysis of discourse. *British Journal of Social Psychology*, *38*, 1–20.

Leary, D. E. (2014). Overcoming blindness: Some historical reflections on qualitative psychology. *Qualitative Psychology*, *1* (1), 17–33.

Lester, J. N. (2014). Negotiating abnormality/normality in therapy talk: A discursive psychology approach to the study of therapeutic interactions and children with autism. *Qualitative Psychology*, *1* (2), 178–192.

Levitt, H. M. (2015). Qualitative psychotherapy research: The journey so far and future directions. *Psychotherapy*, *52* (1), 31–37.

Liddicoat, A. (2007). *Introduction to conversation analysis*. London: Continuum.

Locke, A. (2008). Managing agency for athletic performance: A discursive approach to the zone. *Qualitative Research in Psychology*, *5* (2), 103–126.

Locke, A., & Edwards, D. (2003). Bill and Monica: Memory, emotion and normativity in Clinton's Grand Jury testimony. *British Journal of Social Psychology*, *42* (2), 239–256.

Loos, E. E., Anderson, S., Day, D. H., Jordan, P. C., & Wingate, J. D. (2009). Glossary of Linguistic Terms. www.sil.org/LINGUISTICS/GlossaryOfLinguisticTerms/ WhatIsConversationAnalysis.htm (accessed 25 June 2009).

Lunt, P., & Livingstone, S. (1996). Rethinking the focus group in media and communications research. *Journal of Communication*, *46* (2), 79–98.

Luria, A. R., & Bruner, J. (1987). *The mind of a mnemonist: A little book about a vast memory*. Cambridge, MA: Harvard University Press.

Lynd, R. S., & Lynd, H. M. (1929). *Middletown: A study in contemporary American culture*. New York: Harcourt, Brace, and Company.

Lynd, R. S., & Lynd, H. M. (1937). *Middletown in transition: A study in cultural conflicts*. New York: Harcourt, Brace, and Company.

MacLean, L. M., Meyer, M., & Estable, A. (2004). Improving accuracy of transcripts in qualitative research. *Qualitative Health Research*, *14*, 113–123.

MacMillan, K., & Edwards, D. (1999). Who killed the princess? Description and blame in the British press. *Discourse Studies*, *1* (2), 151–174.

MacWhinney, B. (1995). *The CHILDES Project: Tools for analyzing talk* (2nd ed.). Hillsdale, NJ: Erlbaum.

MailonLine (2008). 'Dishonest' TV psychiatrist Dr Raj Persaud suspended after admitting plagiarism. www.dailymail.co.uk/news/article-1027762/Dishonest-TV-psychiatrist-Dr-Raj-Persaud-suspended-admitting-plagiarism.html (accessed 3 July 2009).

Marchel, C., & Owens, S. (2007). Qualitative research in psychology: Could William James get a job? *History of Psychology*, *10* (4), 301–324.

Marsh, P., Rosser, E., & Harré, R. (1978). *The rules of disorder*. London: Routledge & Kegan Paul.

Marshall, M. N. (1996). Sampling for qualitative research. *Family Practice*, *13*, 522–525.

Matheson, J. L. (2008). The voice transcription technique: Use of voice recognition software to transcribe digital interview data in qualitative research. *The Qualitative Report*, *12* (4), 547–560.

Mayo, E. (1949). *Hawthorne and the Western Electric Company: The social problems of an industrial civilisation*. London: Routledge.

Mays, N., & Pope, C. (2000). Assessing quality in qualitative research. *British Medical Journal, 320,* 50–52.

McAdams, D. P. (1985). *Power, intimacy, and the life story: Personological inquiries into identity.* New York: Guilford Press.

McAdams, D. P. (1993). *The stories we live by: Personal myths and the making of the self.* New York: William C. Morrow and Co.

McAdams, D. P. (2006). The role of narrative in personality psychology today. *Narrative Inquiry, 16* (1), 11–18.

McAdams, D. P. (2008). Personal narratives and the life story. In O. John, R. Robins & L. A. Pervin, *Handbook of personality: Theory and research* (pp. 241–261). New York: Guilford Press.

McArthur, T. (1992). *The Oxford companion to the English language.* Oxford: Oxford University Press.

McBain, W. N. (1956). The use of magnetized tape recording in psychological laboratories. *American Psychologist, 11* (4), 202–203.

McCaughan, E., & McKenna, H. (2007). Never-ending making sense: Towards a substantive theory of the information-seeking behaviour of newly diagnosed cancer patients. *Journal of Clinical Nursing, 16* (11), 2096–2104.

McCormack, L., Hagger, M. S., & Joseph, S. (2011). Vicarious growth in wives of Vietnam veterans: A phenomenological investigation into decades of 'lived' experience. *Journal of Humanistic Psychology, 51* (3), 273–290.

McHugh, P. (1968). *Defining the situation: The organization of meaning.* Evanston, IL: Bobbs-Merrill.

Medical Research Council. (2007). The Healthy Living and Social Marketing Literature. A Review of the Evidence. webarchive.nationalarchives.gov.uk/20080814090217/ dh.gov.uk/en/Publicationsandstatistics/Publications/PublicationsPolicyAndGuidance/ DH_073044

Meier, A., Boivin, M., & Meier, M. (2008). Theme-analysis: Procedures and application for psychotherapy research. *Qualitative Research in Psychology, 5,* 289–310.

Merleau-Ponty, M. (1945/1962). *Phenomenologie de la Perception.* Trans. C. Smith, *Phenomenology of perception.* London: Routledge & Kegan Paul.

Merleau-Ponty, M. (1968). *The visible and the invisible, followed by working notes.* Trans. by A. Lingis. Evanston: Northwestern University Press.

Merton, R. K. (1949). *Social theory and social structure.* New York: Free Press.

Merton, R. K. (1987). The focussed interview and focus groups: Continuities and discontinuities. *Public Opinion Quarterly, 51* (4), 550–566.

Merton, R. K., & Kendall, P. L. (1946). The focused interview. *American Journal of Sociology, 51,* 541–547.

Merton, R. K., Fiske, M., & Kendall, P. L. (1956). *The focused interview: A manual of problems and procedures.* Glencoe, IL: The Free Press.

Michell, J. (2003). The quantitative imperative: Positivism, naïve realism and the place of qualitative methods in psychology. *Theory and Psychology, 13* (1), 5–31.

Milgram, S. (1974). *Obedience to authority: An experimental view.* New York: Harper and Row.

Miller, P. J., Hengst, J. A., & Wang, S-H. (2003). Ethnographic methods: Applications from developmental cultural psychology. In P. M. Camic, J. Rhodes & L. Yardley (Eds.), *Qualitative research in psychology: Expanding perspectives in methodology and design* (pp. 219–242). Washington, DC: American Psychological Association.

Miller Center. (2013a). Farewell Address to the Nation (January 15, 2009) George W. Bush. Charlottesville, VA: University of Virginia. millercenter.org/president/speeches/speech-4454

Miller Center. (2013b). State of the Union Address (January 20, 2004) George W. Bush. Charlottesville, VA: University of Virginia. millercenter.org/president/gwbush/speeches/speech-4542

Mishler, E. G. (1986). The analysis of interview-narratives. In T. R. Sarbin (Ed.), *Narrative psychology: The storied nature of human conduct* (pp. 233–255). New York: Praeger.

Mishler, E. G. (2005). Commentary on 'Qualitative interviews in psychology', *Qualitative Research in Psychology*, 2, 315–318.

Missel, M., & Birkelund, R. (2011). Living with incurable oesophageal cancer: A phenomenological hermeneutical interpretation of patient stories. *European Journal of Oncology Nursing*, 15 (4), 296–301.

Monroe, K. R. (2008). Cracking the code of genocide: The moral psychology of rescuers, bystanders, and Nazis during the Holocaust. *Political Psychology*, 29 (5), 699–736.

Moran-Ellis, J., Alexander, V. D., Cronin, A., Dickinson, M., Fielding, J., Sleny, J., & Thomas, H. (2006a). Triangulation and integration: Process, claims and implications. *Qualitative Research*, 6 (45), 49–55.

Moran-Ellis, J., Alexander, V. D., Cronin, A., Fielding, J., & Thomas, H. (2006b). Analytic integration and multiple qualitative data sets. *Qualitative Researcher*, 2, 2–4.

Morgan, A. (2000). What is Narrative Therapy? www.dulwichcentre.com.au/alicearticle.html (accessed 2 September 2009).

Morrison, D. E. (1998). *The search for a method: Focus groups and the development of mass communication research*. Luton: University of Luton Press.

Muehlenhard, C. L., & Kimes, L. A. (1999). The social construction of violence: The case of sexual and domestic violence. *Personality and Social Psychology Review*, 3, 234–245.

Murray, M. (2000). Levels of narrative analysis in health psychology. *Journal of Health Psychology*, 5, 337–347.

Murray, M. (2003). Narrative psychology. In J. A. Smith (Ed.), *Qualitative psychology: A practical guide to research methods* (pp. 111–131). London: Sage.

Natanson, M. (1973). *Edmund Husserl: Philosopher of infinite tasks*. Evanston, IL: Northwestern University Press.

National Health Service Information Centre. (2010). Statistics on Obesity, Physical Activity and Diet: England 2010. www.ic.nhs/stats (accessed 6 June 2010).

Nespor, J. (2000). Anonymity and place in qualitative inquiry. *Qualitative Inquiry*, 6, 546. qix.sagepub.com/cgi/content/abstract/6/4/546 (accessed 26 August 2009).

Nightingale, D., & Cromby, J. (Eds.). (1999). *Social constructionist psychology*. Buckingham: Open University Press.

Nikander, P. (2008). Working with transcripts and translated data. *Qualitative Research in Psychology*, 5, 225–231.

Norris, S. (2002). The implication of visual research for discourse analysis: Transcription beyond language. *Visual Communication*, 1 (1), 97–121.

Nye, R. A. (2003). The evolution of the concept of medicalization in the late twentieth century. *Journal of History of the Behavioral Sciences*, 39 (2), 115–129.

O'Brien, C. (2007). Peer devaluation in British secondary schools: Young people's comparisons of group-based and individual-based bullying. *Educational Research*, 49, 297–324.

O'Brien, M. (1999). Theorising modernity: Reflexity, environment and identity in Giddens' social theory. In M. O'Brien, S. Penna & C. Hay (Eds.), *Theorising modernity: Reflexity, environment and identity in Giddens' social theory* (pp. 17–38). London: Longman.

O'Callaghan, C., & Hiscock, R. (2007). Interpretive subgroup analysis extends modified grounded theory research findings in oncologic music therapy. *Journal of Music Therapy*, 44 (3), 256–281.

Ochs, E. (1979). Transcription as theory. In E. Ochs & B. B Schiefflin (Eds.), *Developmental pragmatics* (pp. 43–72). New York: Academic.

O'Connell, D. C., & Kowal, S. (1995). Basic principles of transcription. In J. A. Smith, R. Harré & L. Van Langenhove (Eds.), *Rethinking methods in psychology* (pp. 93–105). London: Sage.

O'Connell, D. C., & Kowal, S. (1999). Transcription and the issue of standardization. *Journal of Psycholinguistic Research, 28* (2), 103–120.

Ogden, J. (2000). The correlates of long-term weight loss: A group comparison study of obesity. *International Journal of Obesity and Related Metabolic Disorders, 24,* 1018–1025.

Oliver, D. G., Serovich, J. M., & Mason, T. L. (2005). Constraints and opportunities with interview transcription: Towards reflection in qualitative research. *Social Forces, 84* (2), 1273–1289.

Onions, P. E. W. (n.d.). Grounded Theory Applications in Reviewing Knowledge Management Literature. www.bmu.ac.uk/research/postgradconf/papers/patrick_Onions_paper.pdf (accessed 10 October 2009).

O'Rourke, B. K., & Pitt, M. (2007). Using the technology of the confessional as an analytical resource: Four analytical stances towards research interviews in discourse analysis. *FQS: Forum: Qualitative Social Research, 8* (2), Art. 3, www.qualitative–research.net/index.php/fqs/article/view/224 (accessed 27 June 2012).

Orr, A., Orr, D., Willis, S., Holmes, M., & Britton, P. (2007). Patient perceptions of factors influencing adherence to medication following kidney transplant. *Psychology, Health and Medicine, 12* (4), 509–517.

Ortmann, A., & Hertwig, R. (2002). The costs of deception: Evidence from psychology. *Experimental Economics, 5* (23), 111–131.

Owusu-Bempah, J., & Howitt, D. (2000). *Psychology beyond Western perspectives.* Leicester: BPS Books.

Pagoto, S. L., Spring, B., Coups, E. J., Mulvaney, S., Coutu, M.-F., & Ozakinci, G. (2007). Barriers and facilitators of evidence-based practice perceived by behavioral science health professionals. *Journal of Clinical Psychology, 63* (7), 695–705.

Parker, I. (1989). *The crisis in modern social psychology.* London: Routledge.

Parker, I. (1990a). Discourse: Definitions and contradictions. *Philosophical Psychology, 3* (2), 189–205.

Parker, I. (1990b). Real things: Discourse, context and practice. *Philosophical Psychology, 3* (2), 227–233.

Parker, I. (1992). *Discourse dynamics: Critical analysis for social and individual psychology.* London: Routledge.

Parker, I. (1994). Discourse analysis. In P. Banister, E. Burman, I. Parker, M. Taylor & C. Tindall (Eds.), *Qualitative methods in psychology: A research guide* (pp. 92–107). Milton Keynes: Open University Press.

Parker, I. (Ed.). (1999a). *Deconstructing psychotherapy.* London: Sage.

Parker, I. (1999b). Tracing therapeutic discourse in material culture. *British Journal of Medical Psychology, 72,* 577–587.

Parker, I. (2002). *Critical discursive psychology.* London: Palgrave.

Parker, I. (2005). *Qualitative psychology: Introducing radical research.* Maidenhead: Open University Press.

Parker, I. (2007). *Revolution in psychology: Alienation to emancipation.* London: Pluto.

Parker, I. (2009). Critical psychology: A conversation with Slavoj Žižek. Annual Review of Critical Psychology, 7, pp. 355–373. www.discourseunit.com/arcp/7.htm

Parker, I. (2012). Discursive psychology now. *British Journal of Social Psychology, 51,* 471–477.

Parker, I. (2014). Critical discursive practice in social psychology. In N. Bozatzis & T. Dragonas (Eds.), *The discursive turn in social psychology* (pp. 190–204). Chagrin Falls, OH: Taos Institute Publications.

Parker, I., Georgaca, E., Harper, D., McLaughlin, T., & Stowell-Smith, M. (1995). *Deconstructing psychopathology*. London: Sage.

Passmore, J. (1967). Logical positivism. In P. Edwards (Ed.), *The encyclopedia of philosophy*, Vol. 5 (pp. 52–57). New York: Macmillan.

Patton, M. Q. (1986). *How to use qualitative methods in evaluation*. Newbury Park, CA: Sage.

Picard, A. (2007). Scientific breakthrough or unproven fix? *The Globe and Mail*, 26 March, A11.

Pilecki, A., Muro, J. M., Hammack, P. L., & Clemons, C. M. (2014). Moral exclusion and the justification of U.S. counterterrorism strategy: Bush, Obama, and the terrorist enemy figure. *Peace and Conflict: Journal of Peace Psychology*, 20 (3), 285–299.

Pole, C., & Lampard, R. (2002). *Practical social investigation: Qualitative and quantitative methods in social research*. Harlow: Pearson Education.

Polkinghorne, D. (1989). Phenomenological research methods. In R. Valle & S. Halling (Eds.), *Existential-phenomenological perspectives in psychology* (pp. 41–60). New York: Plenum.

Polzer, J., & Knabe, S. (2012). From desire to disease: Human papillomavirus (HPV) and the medicalization of nascent female sexuality. *Journal of Sex Research*, 49 (4), 344–352.

Potter, J. (1996a). Discourse analysis and constructionist approaches: Theoretical background. In J. E. Richardson (Ed.), *Handbook of qualitative research methods for psychology and the social sciences* (pp. 125–140). Leicester: British Psychological Society.

Potter, J. (1996b). *Representing reality: Discourse, rhetoric and social construction*. London: Sage.

Potter, J. (1997). Discourse analysis as a way of analysing naturally occurring talk. In D. Silverman (Ed.), *Qualitative research: Theory, methods and practice* (pp. 144–160). London: Sage.

Potter, J. (1998). Qualitative and discourse analysis. In A. S. Bellack & M. Hersen (Eds.), *Comprehensive clinical psychology, Vol. 3* (pp. 117–144). Oxford: Pergamon.

Potter, J. (2001). 'Wittgenstein and Austin'. In M. Wetherell, S. Taylor & S. J. Yates (Eds.), *Discourse theory and practice: A reader* (pp. 39–56). London: Sage.

Potter, J. (2002). Two kinds of natural. *Discourse Studies*, 4 (4), 539–542.

Potter, J. (2003). Discourse analysis and discursive psychology. In P. M. Camic, J. E. D. Rhodes & L. Yardley (Eds.), *Qualitative research in psychology: Expanding perspectives in methodology and design* (pp. 73–94). Washington, DC: American Psychological Association.

Potter, J. (2004). Discourse analysis. In M. Hardy & A. Bryman (Eds.), *Handbook of data analysis* (pp. 607–624). London: Sage.

Potter, J. (2012). Re-reading discourse and social psychology: Transforming social psychology. *British Journal of Social Psychology*, 51, 436–455.

Potter, J., & Edwards, D. (1990). Nigel Lawson's tent: Discourse analysis, attribution theory and the social psychology of fact. *European Journal of Social Psychology*, 20, 405–424.

Potter, J., Edwards, D., & Ashmore, M. (2002). Regulating criticism: Some comments on an argumentative complex. In I. Parker (Ed.), *Critical discursive psychology* (pp. 73–81). Basingstoke: Palgrave Macmillan.

Potter, J., & Hepburn, A. (2005a). Qualitative interviews in psychology: Problems and possibilities. *Qualitative Research in Psychology*, 2 (4), 281–307.

Potter, J., & Hepburn, A. (2005b). Action, interaction and interviews: Some responses to Hollway, Mishler and Smith. *Qualitative Research in Psychology*, 2 (4), 319–325.

Potter, J., & Hepburn, A. (2009). Transcription. www-staff.lboro.ac.uk/~ssjap/transcription/transcription.htm (accessed 17 June 2009).

Potter, J., & Wetherell, M. (1987). *Discourse and social psychology: Beyond attitudes and behaviour*. London: Sage.

Potter, J., & Wetherell, M. (1995). Discourse analysis. In J. A. Smith, R. Harré & L. V. Langenhove (Eds.), *Rethinking methods in psychology* (pp. 88–92). London: Sage.

Potter, J., Wetherell, M., Gill, R., & Edwards, D. (1990). Discourse: Noun, verb or social practice? *Philosophical Psychology, 3*, 205–217.

Povee, K., & Roberts, L. D. (2014). Qualitative research in psychology: Attitudes of psychology students and academic staff. *Australian Journal of Psychology, 66*, 28–37.

Preston, L., Marshall, A., & Bucks, R. (2007). Investigating the ways that older people cope with dementia: A qualitative study. *Aging and Mental Health, 11* (2), 131–143.

Prevignano, C. L., & Thibault, E. A. (2003). Continuing the interview with Emanuel Schegloff. In C. L. Prevignano & P. J. Thibault (Eds.), *Discussing conversation analysis: The work of Emanuel Schegloff* (pp. 165–172). Amsterdam: John Benjamins.

Propp, V. (1927/1968). *Morphology of the folktale* (trans. L. Scott, 2nd ed.). Austin, TX: University of Texas Press.

Prus, R. C. (1996). *Symbolic interaction and ethnographic research: Inter-subjecitivity and the study of human lived experience*. Albany, NY: State University of New York Press.

Psathas, G., & Anderson, T. (1990). The 'practices' of transcription in conversation analysis. *Semiotica, 78*, 75–99.

Puchta, C., & Potter., J. (2004). *Focus group practice*. London: Sage.

Radley, A., & Chamberlain, K. (2001). Health psychology and the study of the case: From method to analytic concern. *Social Science and Medicine, 53*, 321–332.

Radley, A., & Green, R. (1986). Bearing illness: Study of couples where the husband awaits coronary graft surgery. *Social Science & Medicine, 23* (6), 577–585.

RadPsyNet (2009). Society for the Psychological Study of Social Issues (SPSSI). www .radpsynet.org/notices/orgs.html#spssi (accessed 8 August 2009).

Rapley, T. J. (2001). The art(fullness) of open-ended interviewing: Some considerations on analyzing interviews. *Qualitative Research, 1* (3), 303–323.

Reeves, C. (2010). A difficult negotiation: Fieldwork relations with gatekeepers. *Qualitative Research, 10* (3), 315–331.

Reid, K., Flowers, P., & Larkin, M. (2005). Exploring lived experience. *The Psychologist, 18* (1), 20–23.

Rennie, D. L., Watson, K. D., & Monteiro, A. M. (2002). The rise of qualitative psychology. *Canadian Psychology, 43*, 179–189.

Richardson, J. C., Ong, B. N., & Sim, J. (2006). Remaking the future: Contemplating a life with chronic widespread pain. *Chronic Illness, 2* (3), 209–218.

Roberts, C. (2007). Qualitative Research Methods and Transcription. www.kcl.ac.uk/ schools/sspp/education/research/projects/dataqual.html (accessed 14 October 2009).

Roberts, J. M. (2014). Critical realism, dialectics, and qualitative research methods. *Journal for the Theory of Social Behaviour, 44* (11), 1–23.

Robinson, J. D. (2004). The sequential organization of 'explicit' apologies in naturally occurring English. *Research on Language and Social Interaction, 37* (3), 291–330.

Rose, N. S. (1985). *The psychological complex: Psychology, politics and society in England*. New York: Cambridge University Press.

Rose, N. S. (1996). *Inventing our selves: Psychology, power, and personhood*. Cambridge: Cambridge University Press.

Roundhill, S. J., Williams, W. H., & Hughes, J. M. (2007). The experience of loss following traumatic brain injury: Applying a bereavement model to the process of adjustment. *Qualitative Research in Psychology, 4*, 241–257.

Sacks, H. (1992). Lecture 1: Rules of conversational sequence. In E. Jefferson (Ed.), *H. Y. Sacks Lectures on Conversation; Vol. 1* (3rd ed.). Oxford: Blackwell.

Sacks, H. (1995). Lectures on conversation Volume ll. In G. Jefferson (Ed.), *Harvey Sacks, Lectures on conversation*, Volumes l & ll (pp. 1–131). Oxford: Basil Blackwell.

Sacks, O. W. (1985). *The man who mistook his wife for a hat*. London: Picador.

Salter, C., Holland, R., Harvey, I., & Henwood, K. (2007). 'I haven't even phoned my doctor yet.' The advice-giving role of the pharmacist during consultations for medication review with patients aged 80 or more: Qualitative discourse analysis. *British Medical Journal*, *334*, 1101.

Sarbin, T. R. (1986). The narrative as a root metaphor for psychology. In T. R. Sarbin (Ed.), *Narrative psychology: The storied nature of human conduct* (pp. 3–21). New York: Praeger.

Sawkhill, S., Sparkes, E., & Brown, B. (2012). A thematic analysis of causes attributed to weight gain: A female slimmer's perspective. *Journal of Human Nutrition and Dietetics*, *26* (1), 78–84.

Schegloff, E. A. (1968). Sequencing in conversational openings. *American Anthropologist*, *70*, 1075–1095.

Schegloff, E. A. (2007). *Sequence organization in interaction: A primer in conversation analysis*, Volume 1. Cambridge: Cambridge University Press.

Schwandt, T. A. (2001). *Dictionary of qualitative inquiry* (2nd ed.). Thousand Oaks, CA: Sage.

Scott, M. M. (2005). A powerful theory and a paradox: Ecological psychologists after Barker. *Environment and Behavior*, *37*, 295–329.

Seale, C. (Ed.) (1998). *Researching society and culture*. London: Sage.

Seale, C. (1999). Quality in qualitative research. *Qualitative Inquiry*, *5* (4), 465–478.

Seligman, R., & Kirmayer, L. (2008). Dissociative experience and cultural neuro-science: Narrative, metaphor and mechanism. *Culture, Medicine and Psychiatry*, *32*, 31–64.

Settles, I. H., Pratt-Hyatt, J. S., & Buchanan, N. T. (2008). Through the lens of race: Black and white women's perceptions of womanhood. *Psychology of Women Quarterly*, *32*, 454–468.

Shaw, I. (2008). Ethics and the practice of qualitative research. *Qualitative Social Work*, *7*, 400–414.

Shaw, R. L. (2008). The Society's Guidelines for Ethical Practice in Psychological Research on the Internet: What do we make of them? *Qualitative Methods in Psychology Newsletter*, *5* May, 7–9.

Sheldon, K., & Howitt, D. (2007). *Sex offenders and the Internet*. Chichester: Wiley.

Shinebourne, P. (2011). The theoretical underpinnings of interpretative phenomenological analysis. *Existential Analysis*, *22* (1), 16–31.

Shinebourne, P., & Smith, J. A. (2009). Alcohol and the self: An interpretative phenomenological analysis of the experience of addiction and its impact on the sense of self and identity. *Addiction Research and Theory*, *17* (2), 152–167.

Shotter, J. (1995a). Dialogical psychology. In J. A. Smith, R. Harré & L. Van Langenhove (Eds.), *Rethinking psychology* (pp. 160–178). London: Sage.

Shotter, J. (1995b). In dialogue social constructionism and radical constructivism. In L. Steffe & J. Gale (Eds.), *Constructivism in education*. Hillsdale, NJ: Lawrence Erlbaum Associates Publishers, pp. 41–56.

Shotter, J. (1999). The social construction of subjectivity: Can it be theorized? Review of Julian Henriques, Wendy Holloway, Cathy Urwin, Couze Venn, and Valerie Walkerdine: Changing the subject: Psychology, social regulation and subjectivity. *Contemporary Psychology*, *44*, 482–483. pubpages.unh.edu/~jds/CP_99.htm (accessed 7 August 2008).

Shye, S., & Elizur, D. (1994). *Introduction to facet theory: Content design and intrinsic data analysis in behavioural research*. Thousand Oaks, CA: Sage.

Silverman, D. (1997). The logics of qualitative research. In G. Miller & R. Dingwall (Eds.), *Context and method in qualitative research* (pp. 12–25). London: Sage.

Silverman, D. (1998). *Harvey Sacks: Social science and conversation analysis*. Cambridge: Polity Press.

Sin, S. (2010). Considerations of quality in phenomenographic research. *International Journal of Qualitative Methods*, 9 (4), 305–319.

Smith, J. A. (1996). Beyond the divide between cognition and discourse: Using interpretative phenomenological analysis in health psychology. *Psychology & Health*, 11 (2), 261–271.

Smith, J. A. (2004). Reflecting on the development of interpretative phenomenological analysis and its contribution to qualitative research in psychology. *Qualitative Research in Psychology*, 1, 39–54.

Smith, J. A. (2005). Advocating pluralism. *Qualitative Research in Psychology*, 2, 309–11.

Smith, J. A. (2007). Hermeneutics, human sciences and health: Linking theory and practice. *International Journal of Qualitative Studies on Health and Well-being*, 2, 3–11.

Smith, J. A. (2008). Introduction. In J. Smith (Ed.) *Qualitative psychology: A practical guide to research methods* (2nd ed., pp. 1–3). London: Sage.

Smith, J. A. (2011). 'We could be diving for pearls': The value of the gem in experiential qualitative psychology. *QMiP Bulletin*, 12, 6–15.

Smith, J. A. (n.d.). Interpretative Phenomenological Analysis (IPA): What is It? www.ccsr.ac.uk/methods/festival/programme/wiwa/smith.doc (accessed 24 April 2012).

Smith, J. A., & Eatough, V. (2006). Interpretative phenomenological analysis. In G. M. Breakwell, S. Hammond, C. Fife-Schaw & J. A. Smith (Eds.), *Research methods in psychology* (3rd ed., pp. 322–341). London: Sage.

Smith, J. A., Flowers, P., & Larkin, M. (2009). *Interpretive phenomenological analysis: Theory, method, and research*. London: Sage.

Smith, J. A., Jarman, M., & Osborn, M. (1999). Doing interpretative phenomenological analysis. In M. Murray & K. Chamberlain (Eds.), *Qualitative health psychology: Theories and methods* (pp. 218–241). London: Sage.

Smith, J. A., & Osborn, M. (2003). Interpretative phenomenological analysis. In J. A. Smith (Ed.), *Qualitative psychology: A practical guide to research methods* (2nd ed., pp. 57–80). London: Sage.

Smith, S. S., & Richardson, D. (1983). Amelioration of deception and harm in psychological research: The important role of debriefing. *Journal of Personality and Social Psychology*, 44, 1075–1082.

Sousa, D. (2008). From Monet's paintings to Margaret's ducks. *Existential Analysis*, 19 (1), 143–155.

Spagnolli, A., & Gamberini, L. (2007). Interacting via SMS: Practices of social closeness and reciprocation. *British Journal of Social Psychology*, 46 (2), 343–364.

Speer, S. A. (2005). *Gender talk: Feminism, discourse and conversation analysis*. London: Routledge.

Spencer, L., Ritchie, J., Lewis, J., & Dillon, L. (2003). *Quality in qualitative evaluation: A framework for assessing research evidence. A quality framework*. Cabinet Office: Government Chief Social Researcher's Office, Strategy Unit. www.civilservice.gov.uk/wp-content/uploads/2011/09/a_quality_framework_tcm6–7314.pdf (accessed 24 April 2012).

Spradley, J. P. (1980). *Participant observation*. New York: Rinehart and Winston.

Ssasz, T. (1986). The case against suicide prevention. *American Psychologist*, 41 (7), 806–812.

St Louis University, Qualitative Research Committee (2009). Qualitative Research Journals. www.slu.edu/organizations/qrc/QRjournals.html (accessed 24 April 2012).

Stacey, J. (1988). Can there be a feminist ethnography? *Women's Studies International Forum, 11* (1), 21–27.

Stainton Rogers, R. and Stainton Rogers, W. (1997). Going critical? In T. Ibáñez and L. Íñiguez (Eds.), *Critical social psychology.* London: Sage.

Stiegler, L. N. (2007). Discovering communicative competencies in a nonspeaking child with autism. *Language, Speech, and Hearing Services in Schools, 38* (4), 400–413.

Stokoe, E. (2010). 'I'm not gonna hit a lady': Conversation analysis, membership categorization and men's denials of violence towards women. *Discourse & Society, 21,* 59–82.

Stokoe, E. H. (2003). Mothers, single women and sluts: Gender, morality and membership categorization in neighbour disputes. *Feminism and Psychology, 13* (3), 317–344.

Stokoe, E., & Weatherall, A. (Eds.) (2002). Gender, language, conversation analysis and feminism. *Discourse & Society* special issue, *13* (6).

Strandmark, M., & Hallberg, L. R-M. (2007). Being rejected and expelled from the workplace: Experiences of bullying in the public service sector. *Qualitative Research in Psychology, 4,* 1–14.

Strauss, A., & Corbin, J. (1990). *Basics of qualitative research: Grounded theory, procedures and techniques.* Newbury Park, CA: Sage.

Strauss, A., & Corbin, J. (1994). Grounded theory methodology: An overview. In N. K. Denzin & Y. Lincoln (Eds.), *Handbook of qualitative research* (pp. 273–285). Thousand Oaks, CA: Sage.

Strauss, A., & Corbin, J. (1998). *Basics of qualitative research: Grounded theory, procedures and techniques* (2nd ed.). Newbury Park, CA: Sage.

Strauss, A., & Corbin, J. (1999). Grounded theory methodology: An overview. In A. Bryman & R. G. Burgess (Eds.), *Qualitative research,* Vol. 3 (pp. 73–93). Thousand Oaks, CA: Sage.

Stubbs, M. (1983). *Discourse analysis: The sociolinguistic analysis of natural language.* Oxford: Blackwell.

Sudddaby, R. (2006). From the Editors: What Grounded Theory is not. *Academy of Management Journal, 49* (4), 633–642.

Taylor, C. (2008). Online QDA. onlineqda.hud.ac.uk/methodologies.php (accessed 24 April 2012).

Taylor, S. (2001). Locating and conducting discourse analytic research. In M. Wetherell, S. Taylor, & S. J. Yates (Eds.), *Discourse as data: A guide for analysis* (pp. 5–48). London: Sage.

ten Have, P. (1999). *Doing conversation analysis: A practical guide.* London: Sage.

ten Have, P. (2007). *Doing conversation analysis: A practical guide* (2nd ed.). London: Sage.

The White House, Office of the Press Secretary. (2007, July 24). Remarks by President Bush on the Global War on Terror. kabul.usembassy.gov/bush_072407.html

The White House, Office of the Press Secretary. (2009). Remarks by the President on national security. www.whitehouse.gov/the-press-office/remarks-president-national-security-5-21-09

The White House, Office of the Press Secretary. (2011). Remarks by the President on the Middle East and North Africa. www.whitehouse.gov/the-press-office/2011/05/19/remarks-president-middle-east-and-north-africa

Thomas, G., & James, D. (2006). Reinventing grounded theory: Some questions about theory, ground and discovery. *British Educational Research Journal, 32* (6), 767–795.

Tileaga, C. (2007). Ideologies of moral exclusion: A critical discourse reframing of depersonalization, delegitimization and dehumanization. *British Journal of Social Psychology*, *46*, 717–737.

Tilley, E., & Woodthorpe, K. (2011). Is it the end for anonymity as we know it? A critical examination of the ethical principle of anonymity in the context of 21st century demands on the qualitative researcher. *Qualitative Research*, *11* (2), 197–212.

Titchener, E. B. (1898). The postulates of a structural psychology. *Philosophical Review*, *7*, 449–465.

Toerien, M., & Kitzinger, C. (2007). Emotional labour in the beauty salon: Turn design of task-directed talk. *Feminism and Psychology*, *17* (2), 162–172.

Tolman, E. C. (1948). Cognitive maps in rats and men. *Psychological Review*, *55* (4), 189–208.

Tomkins, S. S. (1979). Script theory. In H. E. Howe, Jr, & R. A. Doemstbeoer (Eds.), *Nebraska Symposium on Motivation*, Vol. 26 (pp. 201–236). Lincoln, NE: University of Nebraska Press.

Tseliou, E. (2013). A critical methodological review of discourse and conversation analysis studies of family therapy. *Family Process*, *52* (4), 653–672.

UK Data Archive (n.d.). Manage and Share Data: Consent, confidentiality and ethics in data sharing. www.data-archive.ac.uk/sharing/confidential.asp (accessed 26 August 2009).

University of York, Department of Sociology (n.d.). Culture, Interaction and Knowledge: Sociology at York – Past, Present and Future. www.york.ac.uk/sociology/about/news-and-events/department/past-events/culture-interaction/45-years/day-two/ (accessed 24 April 2012).

van Dijk, T. (2001). Principles of critical discourse analysis. In M. Wetherell, S. Taylor & S. J. E. Yates (Eds.), *Discourse theory and practice: A reader* (pp. 300–317). London: Sage.

Vangeli, E., & West, R. (2012). Transition towards a 'non-smoker' identity following smoking cessation: An interpretative phenomenological analysis. *British Journal of Health Psychology*, *17*, 171–184.

Verkuyten, M. (2005). Accounting for ethnic discrimination: A discursive study among minority and majority group members. *Journal of Language and Social Psychology*, *24* (1), 66–92.

Veseth, M., Binder, P.-E. Borg, M., & Davidson, L. (2012). Toward caring for oneself in a life of intense ups and downs: A reflexive-collaborative exploration of recovery in bipolar disorder. *Qualitative Health Research*, *22* (1), 119–133.

Vidich, A. J., & Lyman, S. M. (2000). Qualitative methods: Their history in sociology and anthropology. In N. L. Denzin & Y. S. Lincoln (Eds.), *Handbook of qualitative research* (2nd ed., pp. 37–84). Thousand Oaks, CA: Sage.

Voutilainen, L., Peräkylä, A., & Ruusuvuori, J. (2011). Therapeutic change in interaction: Conversation analysis of a transforming sequence. *Psychotherapy Research*, *21* (3), 348–365.

Wardle, J. (2009). Current issues and new directions in psychology and health: The genetics of obesity – what is the role for health psychology? *Psychology & Health*, *24*, 997–1001.

Watson, J. B. (1913). Psychology as the behaviorist views it. *Psychological Review*, *20*, 158–177.

West, C. (1979). Against our will: Male interruptions of females in cross-sex conversations. *Annals of the New York Academy of Sciences*, *327*, 81–97.

Wertz, F. J. (2014). Qualitative inquiry in the history of psychology. *Qualitative Psychology*, *1* (1), 4–16.

Wetherell, M. (1998). Positioning and interpretative repertoires: Conversation analysis and post-structuralism in dialogue. *Discourse & Society, 9*, 387–412.

Wetherell, M., & Potter, J. (1992). *Mapping the language of racism: Discourse and the legitimation of exploitation.* Hemel Hempstead: Harvester/Wheatsheaf and New York: Columbia University Press.

Wetherell, M., Taylor, S., & Yates, S. J. (Eds.) (2001). *Discourse as data: A guide for analysis.* London: Sage.

White, M., & Epston, D. (1990). *Narrative means to therapeutic ends.* New York: Norton.

Whitsitt, D. R. (2009). A phenomenological exploration of coronary bypass surgery as experienced by three couples. *Journal of Phenomenological Psychology, 40* (2), 140–177.

Whyte, W. F. (1943). *Street corner society. The social structure of an Italian slum.* Chicago, IL: University of Chicago Press.

Whyte, W. F. (1984). *Learning from the field: A guide from experience.* Beverly Hills, CA: Sage.

Wiggins, S. (2013). The social life of 'eugh': Disgust as assessment in family mealtimes *British Journal of Social Psychology, 52*, 489–509.

Wiggins, S., and Potter, J. (2008). Discursive psychology. In C. Willig & W. Stainton-Rogers (Eds.), *The SAGE handbook of qualitative research in psychology* (pp. 73–93). London: Sage.

Wilkinson, S. (1997). Feminist psychology. In D. Fox & I. Prilleltensky (Eds.), *Critical psychology: An introduction* (pp. 247–264). London: Sage.

Wilkinson, S., & Kitzinger, C. (2008). Using conversation analysis in feminist and critical research. *Social and Personality Psychology Compass, 2* (2), 555–573.

Willig, C. (2008a). Discourse analysis. In J. Smith (Ed.), *Qualitative psychology: A practical guide to research methods* (2nd ed., pp. 160–185). London: Sage.

Willig, C. (2008b). *Introducing qualitative research in psychology* (2nd ed.). Maidenhead: Open University Press.

Willig, C. (2013). *Introducing qualitative research in psychology* (3rd ed.). Maidenhead: Open University Press.

Willig, C., & Stainton-Rogers, W. (2008). Introduction. In C. Willig & W. Stainton-Rogers (Eds.), *The SAGE handbook of qualitative research in psychology* (pp. 1–12). London: Sage.

Witcher, C. G. S. (2010). Negotiating transcription as a relative insider: Implications for rigour. *International Journal of Qualitative Methods, 9*, 122–132.

Witzel, A., & Mey, G. (2004). I am NOT opposed to quantification or formalization or modeling, but do not want to pursue quantitative methods that are not commensurate with the research phenomena addressed. *Forum: Qualitative Social Research, 5*(3), Article 41. www.qualitative-research.net/fqs-texte/3–04/04-3-41-e.htm (accessed 24 April 2012).

Wooffitt, R. (2001). Researching psychic practitioners: Conversation analysis. In M. Wetherell, S. Taylor & S. J. Yates (Eds.), *Discourse as data: A guide for analysis* (pp. 49–92). London: Sage.

Woolgar, S. (1996). Psychology, qualitative methods and the ideas of science. In J. T. E. Richardson (Ed.), *Handbook of qualitative research methods for psychology and the social sciences* (pp. 11–24). Leicester: BPS Books.

Wundt, W. (1912). *An introduction to psychology.* Translated by R. Pintner. New York: The MacMillan Company.

Yin, R. K. (2003). *Case study research: Design and methods* (3rd ed.). Thousand Oaks, CA: Sage.

Zimmerman, D. H., & West, C. (1975). Sex roles, interruptions and silences in conversation. In B. Thorne & N. Henley (Eds.), *Language and sex: Difference and dominance* (pp. 105–129). Rowley, MA: Newbury House.

INDEX